The First Moderns

The First Moderns

The Architects of the Eighteenth Century

Joseph Rykwert

The MIT Press
Cambridge, Massachusetts, and London, England

This book was set in VIP Times Roman by Achorn Graphic Services, Inc. and printed and bound by The Murray Printing Company in the United States of America.

Library of Congress Cataloging in Publication Data

Rykwert, Joseph, 1926–
    The first moderns.

    Bibliography: p.
    Includes index.
    1. Neoclassicism (Architecture)   2.   Architecture,
Modern—17th–18th centuries.   I.   Title.
NA600.R94   724'.1   79–22123
ISBN 0-262-18090-1

Anna, tibi . . . .

Contents

Acknowledgments

My greatest debt is to the many scholars who studied this period before me, from Cornelius Gurlitt onwards; many bibliographical entries are an inevitably inadequate return for all I owe them. But, like every teacher, I have also learned a great deal from my students who have done specialized work on the problems with which I have also wrestled: especially Yoshihige Akahoshi, David Leatherbarrow, Solomon Kaufman, Mohsen Mostafavi and Alberto Perez Gomez. While the book was in the making I discussed a number of problems with the late Michael and with Elizabeth Ayrton, Allan Braham, Manlio Brusatin, Italo Calvino, Augusto Cavallari-Murat, Françoise Choay, John Fleming, Boris Ford, Vittorio Gregotti, Antoine Grumbach, Robert Gutman, John and Eileen Harris, Wolfgang Herrmann, Licisco Magagnato, Frank Manuel, Marianne Michel, Christian Norberg-Schulz, Werner Oechslin, Lionello Puppi, Cesare da Seta, Leo Steinberg, Manfredo Tafuri, Georges Teyssot, Franco Venturi, John Wilton-Ely, and André Zavriew. There is a further debt to those friends who have read a part or the whole of the typescript and who made suggestions and correction, as well as some encouragement: Anita Brookner, Robin Middleton, John Summerson, Dalibor Vesely, and Anthony Vidler. Robin Middleton has also allowed me to look at some of his unpublished material and conceded the use of some illustrations he had gathered for his own book. His generous encouragement was always ready when my own spirits were flagging. Paul Breman was always willing to listen to my problems and give me the freedom of his remarkable private library. The bulk of the illustrations from engravings were prepared by Barry Woodcock and Mohsen Mostafavi; my uncle, the late Stefan Goliger, very kindly undertook to find material for me in Paris.

The forebearance of librarians and their patience with a wayward borrower make me the debtor of Dr. William's and the London Library, those of Essex University and Princeton University, and the Royal Academy.

The First Moderns

1

Classic and Neoclassic

The words *classic* and *classical* suggest authority, discrimination, even snobbery—class distinction, in fact. *Neoclassical* is associated with revolution, objectivity, enlightenment, equality. I propose to examine the growth of these associations, particularly as they apply to architecture: since words have a way of offering the unexpected facet, when examined with care.

The birth of what we now call neoclassicism was part of a cataclysmic change in the nature of society and in ways of thinking. Many of the ideas that were forged during this upheaval are still with us. Disguised by their apparently rational and objective formulation, they are sometimes dangerously inhibiting. But ignorance of their true nature may often prevent us from forging them to our own use.

At the height of the period which is usually called neoclassical, the term was as yet uncoined, and even when the period was on the wane, its proponents simply saw it as synonymous with the "right," the "classical" manner. In a conversation recorded on 2 April 1829, Goethe, perhaps the greatest poet of his age, expressed his contempt for the new French poets of the time: "I call 'classic' what is healthy, and 'romantic' what is sick," and he adds, "most of what is new is not romantic just because it is new, but because it is weak, sickly, and diseased, and the old is not 'classic' just because it is old, but because it is strong, fresh, jolly and healthy." [1]

Goethe was using the words *classic* and *romantic,* which constantly escape definition, to express prejudice, a usage still with us.[2] Such prejudice may be romantic-bad and classic-good (Jean Cocteau, say, or Stravinsky) or vice versa (Frank Lloyd Wright, or John Ruskin before him). Although the word *romantic* acquired its implications only a century or so before Goethe used it in the way just quoted, the word *classic* has a much older history. Its modern associations still echo its original meaning. The word refers to an ancient tradition. The sixth king of Rome, Servius Tullius, graded all Roman society into six groups called *classes* according to their income; all were expected to contribute money to the defense of the state, except the lowest, the *proletarii,* who had no money to contribute and therefore could only give their children, their *proles.*[3] Ancient writers derived the word *classicus* from *calare,* "to call" (*classicus* was a contracted form of *calassicus*); the word was even applied to the trumpets with which Roman assemblies were summoned, and this meaning was retained throughout the Middle Ages.[4] By the time of the late republic, however, the word *classicus* was no longer used for the members of any class but the first, the richest.[5] Writing about 160–170 A.D., the grammarian Aulus Gellius makes use of these words as terms of literary criticism, taking them very much for granted. Certain turns of phrase and syntactic quirks, he observes, suffice to show whether the writer is *classicus* and *assiduus* or *proletarius.*[6] Then, in the Middle Ages, the word *classic* was replaced by *canonic,* from the Greek word *kanon* meaning a "rule" (also a "ruler," and even a "T-square" or "set square"), and hence a canon was the law which regulates, which upholds what is best: the word *classic* returned not only to the old meaning of war trumpet but also came to mean a peal of bells, a summoning noise, in the ancient sense. The Italian humanist writers, as may be expected, had restored the word *classicus* to its ancient meaning by the end of the sixteenth century.[7] The French followed, and by the end of the century, an English writer could speak of "classical and canonical" authors, using the medieval and the ancient terms as synonyms.[8]

By the seventeenth century, *classicus* ("classic") meant not only excellent and choice, or first-class, but also antique; the antique had by then assumed the role of an unquestioned and unquestionable model of excellence. Not only writers, painters, and architects but also statesmen and religious reformers based their practice or policy on the emulation of the antique. The antique meant the republican Rome described by Livy or Cicero to some; to others it meant the imperial idea extolled by Virgil and Ovid; yet others wanted a return to the first flowering of the "Peace of the Church" under Constantine which Eusebius had eulogized.

Clearly the word *classic* has a variety of implications in different contexts, even if it is taken in the sense of "ancient and exemplary," which is now commonly given to it. And clearly, too, the implications of authority and distinction are part of the very makeup of the word.

Neoclassicism is more difficult to circumscribe. It arose as a term of abuse at the end of the nineteenth century. "A man must be a scholar before he can make neo-classicism even tolerable in art," writes an anonymous *Times* correspondent in the early 1890s (he is criticizing a mediocre painting).[9] At the same time, however, in France and Britain particularly, neoclassicism was a literary sobriquet. But if you were to take a look at current dictionaries, you would find that the German *Grosser Brockhaus* takes it to refer to the more sober twentieth-century architecture (Auguste Perret, Adolf Loos, Mies van der Rohe, Peter Behrens, Gunnar Asplund), while the French *Grand Larousse Encyclopédique* treats it largely as a musical movement, involving Weber and Schubert but also Mendelssohn's rediscovery of Bach, the early work of Saint-Saëns, and finally Stravinsky.

But the neoclassicism which is the subject of this work is not the matter of these definitions, nor yet is the twentieth-century literary movement that involved T. E. Hulme, Ezra Pound, and T. S. Eliot, nor even the French brand: Stravinsky's later ballets, "Satie and le Six," "Cocteau and the Synthetic Cubists." The term is used in a more conventional way to describe the architecture (though it may be used equally for all the visual arts, and even for literature and music and the minor arts) of the second half of the eighteenth century, and particularly as the eighteenth century passed into the nineteenth. Many years ago Sigfried Giedion pointed out the difficulty of dealing with neoclassicism in the same way that one deals with most styles in the history of art. Taken *en bloc*, it presents such a curious divergence of aims, such a variety of formal vocabularies, that it has none of the subconscious, internal coherence which historians demand of a style. It may even be seen (and Giedion has interpreted it like this) as a movement concerned with surface manifestation only, operating as a wallpaper pasted over an uncomfortable crack in history: that between the baroque and the romantic period.[10]

Whatever the phenomenon was, movement or style, it had a separate and quite different existence from that emulation of antiquity—a neoclassicism by extension—which dominated European thinking since the beginning of the fifteenth century: the literary, figurative, monumental remains of republican, imperial, or early Christian Rome which were not always correctly identified by the men of the Renaissance, whose stylistic criticism did not always go beyond that of their medieval predecessors.

For many centuries, the temporal power of the papacy was justified by a lengthy document, the Donation of Constantine, which was widely accepted for half a millenium as a fourth-century document. Then, as the fifteenth century drew on, various ecclesiastics attempted a stylistic criticism of it, until in 1517, in a frontal attack on the abuse of papal power by a Neapolitan humanist, Laurence Valla, it was roundly declared a forgery.[11] In the same way, the monuments of antiquity which littered many of the older towns, and Rome most conspicuously, were the subject of reappraisal and criticism. The baptistery of Florence Cathedral, for instance, a building erected in part in the fourth century, in part in the earliest medieval period, was held to be a temple built by Julius Caesar until the eighteenth century, in spite of some tentative scepticism.[12]

Other buildings, particularly the more conspicuous ancient ruins, were considered more carefully. The few architectural texts—the treatise of Vitruvius, passages in Pliny the Elder's *Natural History,* the letters of his nephew Pliny the Younger (with their elegiac descriptions of his two villas), the lives of various emperors which recounted their building activities—all were read for evidence about Roman (that is antique) building generally, and matched against the ruins, particularly the more prestigious ones in Rome itself.

Throughout the fifteenth, sixteenth, and even seventeenth centuries the assumption was current that antiquity was unified and homogeneous. Of course, antiquity had evolved from "rude" beginnings; but it had been devised by the Egyptians and perfected by the Greeks until it achieved its apogee in the art of imperial Rome, whose vestiges, such as the triumphal arches and the temples on and around the Roman Forum were taken as evidence not only of the development of Roman but also of Greek and Egyptian architecture.

If one looks at Sebastiano Serlio's illustration of a tragic scene (based on a text of Vitruvius),[13] one will note a street flanked by "antique" palaces leading to a triumphal arch, which is also a city gate—beyond which are pyramids and obelisks. These *regalia res* were to serve as a background for the stories of Greek heroes as told by some of the Greek tragedians and known in translation, but espe-

Sebastiano Serlio, The Tragic Scene, *represents a city in antiquity: colonnaded, stone-built, with pyramids and obelisks outside its walls.*

Sebastiano Serlio, a modern town; mixed Gothic and "antique" architecture, painted plaster finishes, visible wooden construction.

cially for the Latin plays of Seneca. Nor were the pyramids and
obelisks thought irrelevant to the deeds of Theseus or Oedipus.

But ever more accurate observation and the increasing attention
to the details of the ancient texts, which their circulation in printed
form certainly sharpened, inevitably directed attention to certain
discrepancies. Vitruvius' comments and rules did not always tally
with the evidence of the ruins, for these sometimes showed techniques of construction not described by Vitruvius, such as concrete
vaults and domes. But more particularly, the orders measured in the
antique buildings often did not conform to the rules provided by the
Roman writer.[14]

An order is a column-and-beam unit, regulated by a proportional
rule and garnished by a set repertory of ornament and moldings. It
was regarded by the Greeks and the Romans, and later by Renaissance architects, as the touchstone and tonic of architecture, as the
epitome and guarantee of architectural perfection. The repertory
was very limited: Vitruvius described one Etruscan order and three
Greek ones—Doric, Ionic, and Corinthian; Renaissance theorists

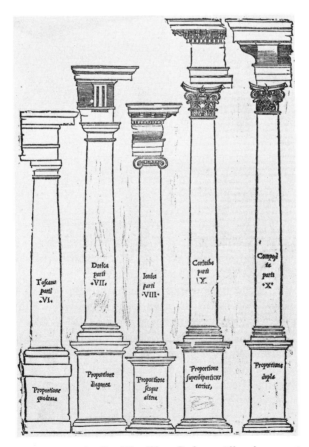

Sebastiano Serlio, The Five Orders. *All subsequent
illustrations of the five orders refer to this first formulation.*

John Shute, the Corinthian order.

(beginning with Serlio in 1537) added the fifth order; the Composite. Although many attempts were made to increase this repertory—by adding "national" orders, for instance—the five orders remained the essential elements of architectural composition from the beginning of the sixteenth to the end of the nineteenth century, and even into the twentieth.

Vitruvius had derived the proportions and the ornaments of the Doric and Ionic orders from a man's and a woman's body respectively, and the Corinthian from that of a young girl.[15] This derivation was given a mystical and hermetic interpretation by some sixteenth- and seventeenth-century writers. But the matter was also familiar to anyone who took an interest in architecture. When a tired and much feted Gianlorenzo Bernini arrived in Paris on 2 June 1665, where he had come—at vast expense to Louis XIV—to design the new Louvre buildings (his design was abandoned, to be replaced by Perrault's), he was met outside the town by Paul Fréart, the Lord of Chantelou. After the preliminary compliments "he [Bernini] said that the beauty of everything in the world, as of architecture, consists in proportion; that you might say that it is a divine particle,

since it is derived from the body of Adam, who was not only made
by God's hand, but who was made in his image and likeness; that the
variety of the orders of architecture proceeded from the difference
between the bodies of man and of woman'' and writes M. de Chantelou nonchalantly in his diary, ''he [Bernini] added several other
things on this matter, which are familiar enough to us.''[16]

This diary, composed by Paul Fréart, one of the principal connoisseurs at the French court and Poussin's patron, was written for the
author's brother Roland Fréart de Chambray, who had published
one of the most popular architectural handbooks of the time some
fifteen years earlier. Roland Fréart's treatise was a pattern book of
the orders. But unlike those of his predecessors, it did not give one
recipe for each order but compared and criticized the various rules
given by Vitruvius and more recent writers with orders found in
ancient buildings and sometimes even with those used in a building
by a ''modern'' architect, even though they had not been described
in a treatise. Fréart de Chambray intended to give the architect

*After Fréart de Chambray, the origin of the Corinthian
order: a literal interpretation of the Vitruvian legend,
though the text suggests that the basket was laid on
top of a monument.*

After Claude Perrault, the Corinthian order and its origin. The plate is derived from Fréart's; but the anecdote is omitted. The pinned sheet shows the capital as described by Vitruvius compared with an actual antique example, the columns of the Pantheon.

interested in proportion a method for discriminating between the various models he might imitate, helping him to choose the most apt, the most "correct." Among these, he also included the curious Corinthian "Profile" of the temple of Solomon, one that perhaps because of its exalted origins was not used very extensively, if indeed at all in any known building. It is the "flower of architecture, and the Order of Orders[17] . . . though I dare not affirm," says Fréart, "[it was] to have been precisely the same Profile with that of Solomon's Temple . . . yet as near as one can approach to that Divine Idea from its description in the Bible and some other famous Histories mentioned in that great work of Villalpanda's . . . I conceive it to be sufficiently conformable."

The work of Villalpanda to which Fréart refers is that Spanish Jesuit's three-volume commentary on the Book of the Prophet Ezekiel, in which the prophet is granted a vision of the rebuilt temple.[18] Villalpanda's vast, literally massive commentary with many engravings was a justification of the divine origin of the orders, not only as tokens of the divine ordering of the human body—in the

*Fréart de Chambray's version of the order in the Sol-
omonic temple reconstructed by J.-B. Villalpanda.*

form Bernini had conversationally and quite casually described to
Chantelou—but in a much more dogmatic sense; they were actually
part of the divine gift of the temple "type," either drawn by the hand
of God itself or drawn by Solomon under direct guidance from God;
the proportions and ornaments of the order, as they were "seen" by
Ezekiel, were identical to those of the temple Solomon built, and the
temple seen and described by Josephus Flavius[19] in all ways was
identical to Solomon's first building. Furthermore, the orders of
architecture, as known from Vitruvius and from ancient buildings,
were derived from the divine model, which united the perfections of
all the orders in one. Classical architecture was therefore the only
true architecture, not only because it conformed with reason—in the
way the ancient authors had set out—but also because it was directly
based on divine revelation.

In the atmosphere of hermetic learning and bigoted piety that
pervaded the Spanish court, Villalpanda's message was comforting:
the "advanced" architecture of Italy was not only a repository of
ancient "gentile" wisdom, being derived ultimately from the exam-

ple of the Egyptians (whose revelations included the prophecy of a savior—hence the recurrence of sibyls in Christian iconography), but the more "correct" it was, the nearer it came to divine revelation.

In spite of much learned objection, Villalpanda's reconstruction of the temple was treated as the type of all splendid building; it was reproduced partially or wholly in buildings and models, in treatises and Bible illustration.[20] For the thinkers and writers of the fifteenth and sixteenth centuries, the imitation of the ancients had been a re-evocation of a pagan past, whose inner secrets, despite contradictory appearances, could be regarded as conforming with divine mysteries because of the natural force of the intellect and the virtues of philosophers (Pythagoras and Plato in particular) to whom equitable Jupiter taught mysteries as valid as those which Jehovah had taught Moses.[21] In the more fervent and much less tolerant Counter-Reformation atmosphere (more fervent and less tolerant in Spain than elsewhere) it became a work of piety for Philip II and his Jesuit protégé. Architecture participated in the general concern with *sacrosancta vetustas* ("most holy antiquity"). The teaching of Vitruvius on proportion was treated throughout the Middle Ages, as well as during the Renaissance, as having the force of a revelation and as a teaching about the microcosm—a teaching which was echoed by Bernini's remarks quoted earlier. These associations allowed little dispute. That which was drawn by the hand of God could not be derived from earthly precedent. Inevitably, other authors argued like Villalpanda, not only those who looked for divine guarantees in matters such as architecture but all those who associated architecture with literature and ideology. Inigo Jones, for instance, some twenty years after the publication of Villalpanda's works, went to measure and reconstruct Stonehenge for King James I (who occupied the British throne with dubious legitimacy). The elaborate genealogies worked out at the time for the House of Stuart traced its descent both from David, the King of Israel, and from the mystical Brutus the Trojan, a reputed grandson or great-grandson of Aeneas, who was, according to Geoffrey of Monmouth, the founder of London and by the antique eponymous method gave his name to Britain.[22] Geoffrey of Monmouth, a twelfth-century chronicler, was the great source for the mythical prehistory of Britain. Most versions of the Arthurian legend depended on his chronicle, and it furnished material for innumerable openings of British histories, as well as for the work of the epic and tragic poets, Shakespeare's *King Lear* and Spenser's *Faerie Queen.*

Reflecting on those antiquarian fantasies, Inigo Jones restored Stonehenge as a hypaethral temple to the god Caelus or Uranus.[23] Not, of course, that Inigo Jones held Stonehenge (or Stone-Heng, as he called it) to be an absolute norm for all architecture. He merely argued that a work of such technical resource and geometrical perfection could not have been produced by a barbarian people—such as the British natives described by Tacitus and Suetonius; it must, therefore, have been a work of classical civilization.

Stonehenge, detail of the standing stones.

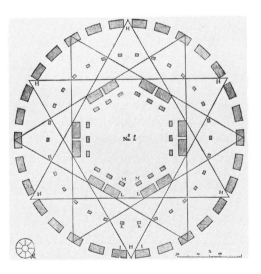

Stonehenge restored as a Roman temple by Inigo Jones, projection.

Stonehenge restored as a Roman temple by Inigo Jones. Plan showing proportional scheme based on four interlaced equilateral triangles, giving a base of twelve sides, based on Vitruvius' plan of a theater stage proportion.

However, although the guarantee of *sacrosancta vetustas* may have seemed adequate to English seventeenth-century antiquarians, later evangelicals required firmer guarantees. John Wood the Elder, following them in his little guide to Stonehenge of 1747, imagined the "British" King Bladud (a legendary founder of Bath, excogitated by the medieval antiquarians, Geoffrey of Monmouth in particular) as identical with the Hyperborean priests of Apollo who appear in the Delphic legend; and Bladud was thought to be privy to the theory of planetary revolution, which he imparted to the Druids who "subsisted until *Augustine* the Monk came into Britain and, by the Order of *Pope Gregory* the *Great,* silenced it for the same reasons that *Galileus* was condemned by the Inquisition of *Rome* in the year 1633."[24]

But this antipapist stab is isolated. Wood took the opposite attitude to Inigo Jones: "the Work would appear to me as a Wonderful production of the *Roman* Art and Power, if *Britain,* in the most early Ages of the World, had not been Famed . . . for the Learning of her Natives."[25] He had already declared his interest and his views on architectural history in an earlier and more substantial book: *The Origin of Building: or the Plagiarism of the Heathens detected.*[26] This plagiarism of the heathen was the presumed derivation of ancient architecture from scriptural patterns: Noah's ark, the Ark of the Covenant in the desert, Solomon's Temple, and the vision of Ezekiel.

The very formula of Pythagoras' theorem is derived by Wood from the measurements of the ark and the age and number of animals which Abraham was ordered to offer: "Jamblichus tells," Wood says, "that Pythagoras was twenty-two years in Egypt learning geometry . . . This was about nine hundred years after the ark was made; and therefore our present researches are intended to find out the emblematical meanings of the several parts of the Tabernacle."[27] The relation is established by a long chain of supposition, as is the relation between the desert tabernacle and the origin of the orders.[28]

Again, like Villalpanda and many of his predecessors, Wood looked in scripture for a justification and a guarantee of the absolute value of mathematical proportions; this presupposition of absolute value is basic to the theories of all "classical" architecture (including the medieval speculations on the fundamental precepts of building)[29] and has its roots in the discovery—attributed since remote antiquity to Pythagoras—that the length of a plucked string (or for that matter of a tube or pot filled with water which is struck to produce a sound) corresponds in quantity to fixed tonal differences. A proportion of $1:2$, for instance, will give an octave difference; $2:3$ will give a fifth; $3:4$ a fourth; $8:9$ a tone, and so on.[30] In classical antiquity this idea was connected with the idea of the microcosm, the proportions which govern the human body being a miniature of universal harmony. Cicero's short essay *On the Dream of Scipio* and the commentary on it by the Latin grammarian, Macrobius, was perhaps the most familiar expression of the idea for many centuries.

It also became familiar through Boethius' and St. Augustine's treatises on music, and it was widely reinterpreted in the Middle Ages.[31] The Platonic renaissance in the fifteenth and sixteenth centuries gave it enormous authority, so that it became a staple part of artists' speculations.[32] In the seventeenth century the idea was given new validity. Bernini, as the quotation above from his conversation with Chantelou indicates, regarded it as a basic principle, and the orders as its most positive incarnation.[33] The teaching of the idea seems to have gone unquestioned by all schools.

In seventeenth-century France the idea was given a more rigorous formulation by an Oratorian priest, René Ouvrard, who had no particular architectural training, but as the master of music at the Sainte Chapelle (he had formerly been a precentor of Rouen cathedral), was a fairly well-known musician. In a book—or rather a pamphlet—*Harmonic Architecture*,[34] he even reproached the ancients for their laxity in the use of musical proportion since "we claim . . . that there is such an analogy between proportions of music and those of architecture that what shocks the ear in one, shocks the eye in the other."[35] This in itself is not remarkable: it is an echo of traditional Neoplatonic teaching, as expressed, for instance, by Leone Ebreo two centuries earlier: "In the objects of all external senses there may be found good, useful mild, and delightful things, but the grace which moves the soul to particular love (which is called beauty) is not found in the objects of the three material senses, which are taste, smell, and touch, but in the objects of the two spiritual senses, sight and hearing."[36] Leone Ebreo, who before his conversion was known as Jehudah Abravanel, speculated on the immortal harmony inherent in material things, perceptible to the "spiritual" senses.[37] Starting from this background, Ouvrard studied the detailed musical implications of the orders and the types of buildings described by Vitruvius, as well as those mentioned in scripture, and their possible applications in building practice. He concluded severely: "These rules are infallible and based on the analogy of our two noble senses, in which our soul desires the same proportion . . . let them—the architects who have not given the matter enough attention—realize that this is the only means which will give their art sure and incontestable principle and that there shall be no true architecture which is not harmonic."[38]

Ouvrard, like so many contemporary writers on architecture, dedicated his pamphlet to Jean Baptiste Colbert, who was at that time (and was to remain until his death in 1683) Louis XIV's superintendent (that is, minister) of building as well as of finances. This position, of course, made Colbert the most powerful patron of the arts (building in particular) in France, perhaps in the world. Although Louis, in spite of a fanatical attention to detail, does not seem to have had a clearly defined taste either in literature or in the visual arts, Colbert did and knew how to impose it discreetly—the king and the minister have been compared to Augustus and Maecenas.[39] The king, and Colbert as well, cared for glory more than for anything else. Glory was a guarantee of immortality; but before that, glory was an instrument of policy. It was therefore essential to enroll the arts in the service of the French crown.

The policy of the monarchy—initiated by Richelieu and developed by Mazarin—demanded the centralizing not only of the fiscal administration under the strictest possible state control to promote economic expansion but also of political life, by concentrating administration as well as fashion first on the Louvre and then on Versailles.

Colbert's method of patronage worked by selective commissioning and also by structuring the artistic life of the country into salary—or gratuity—receiving groups, most of which were called academies. The words *academy* and *academic* were to assume such an enormous importance that it might be worth digressing briefly at this point to consider the development of the notion and the practice with which they were associated.

Academy is another word with a remote ancestry. Its ancestor "Academus" is the mythical hero who owned a garden about a mile from the Dipylon gate in Athens; it became a public garden when Cimon left it to the city. But its fame is due to Plato who held his school there, much as the fame of the Lycaeum, an exercise ground at the other end of town, is due to Aristotle. Academy soon came to mean the whole group of Plato's followers and was certainly used like that by Cicero,[40] by whose time the group had fissured into sects. The word eventually came to be applied to the great library of Alexandria and to bodies like Caesar Bardas' scientific group in ninth-century Constantinople. However, the first "modern" academy was founded by Alcuin of York at Charlemagne's court. The institution was perpetuated throughout the Middle Ages, though sporadically. In the fifteenth century, proliferation acquired momentum; Antonio Beccadelli's Antonian or Pontanian Academy in Naples and Pomponio Leto's Academy in Rome began the trend, although the first official body of this type is Lorenzo de' Medici's Platonic Academy, which formed itself around Marsilio Ficino in the 1440s. Starting as an informal philosophical discussion group, it became a literary institute; it then broke up, and finally, in 1582, transformed itself into the Accademia della Crusca, which produced its great Italian dictionary some thirty years later.

As the century wore on, literary, scientific, and artistic societies of this kind multiplied and spread outside Italy. There was one or more in every town, so that by the middle of the eighteenth century there were seven hundred of them in Italy alone.[41] In the meanwhile, several academies of artists were started in the sixteenth century, perhaps the earliest being Giorgio Vasari's Accademia del Disegno in Florence, which was "incorporated" in 1563.[42] The most influential was the Bolognese academy of the Caracci, which started, rather casually, about half a century later, and where the three elements which were to become the foundation of all "academic" art school teaching—drawing from the life, drawing the antique (in the form of plaster casts), and instruction in the geometry of perspective—were already the essential subjects.

In the meanwhile, academies diversified. Scientific academies became relatively common, and in the 1620s a group of French patricians instituted the regular meetings that were incorporated as the French Academy by Louis XIII (under Richelieu's patronage) in 1635. One of its primary duties was the preparation of a "standard" dictionary of the French language, which, however, took sixty years to bring out. Under the rule of Louis XIV and Colbert, academies continued to proliferate. The French Academy required a subcommittee, the "little academy," whose purpose was to commemorate the great deeds of the King, and it later became the Académie des Inscriptions. The Academy of Architecture, one of the last, was founded on the death of the reigning *premier architecte du Roi,* Louis Le Vau, in 1671, and its director, the engineer-builder François Blondel, became the king's ex-officio advisor.[43]

Artists had, of course, been organized previously, chiefly into guilds which supervised apprenticeship to individual masters in their studios, accepted candidates for licenses, and regulated work conditions. But the guilds had neither the antiquarian nor the theoretical pretensions of the new academies. The Academy of Architecture, moreover, had a new task. Up to that time it was a normal part of the architect's work to undertake, as contractor, the building of what he designed. Certainly Le Vau, old Mansart, Robert Cotte, Pierre Lescot, and the other major architects from Philibert de l'Orme onward, who were also trained as master-masons, regarded building and contracting as part of their duties. Now members of the academy were precluded from this function by their appointment, which marked, in fact, the creation of a proper professional elite. But although it was not the task of this new elite to undertake what was almost manual work, they were obliged to build up a body of theory, even of rules, for the future of architecture. In this context, René Ouvrard's pamphlet assumes a certain importance. The first director of the academy, François Blondel, who was also its professor, was very much impressed with Ouvrard's writing and recommended his book in his lectures.[44]

Blondel was a mathematician by training, somewhat old-fashioned in his cast of mind. Although quite prepared to adopt a critical attitude toward the examples of the ancients, he was not prepared to flout the traditional teaching concerning the unity of the "spiritual" senses and the informing tradition of the harmonious microcosms.[45] In spite of opposition within the academy, Blondel's successor, Philippe La Hire, was an even more stringent purist. The first two directors thus certainly took to heart the academy's task "to strip architecture of its vicious ornaments, to retrench the abuses which the ignorance and the presumption of workmen have introduced into it."[46]

There were plenty of examples of buildings that needed to be stripped and chastened in this way. The most offending, however,

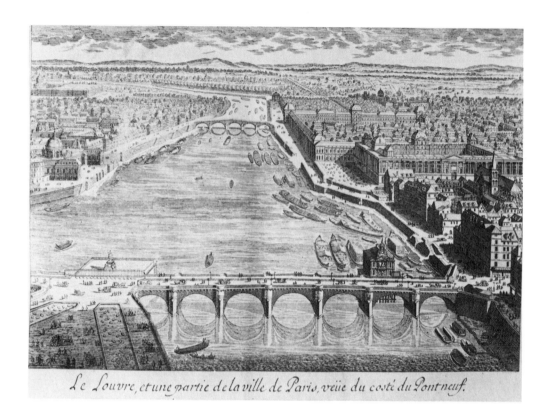

Le Louvre, et une partie de la ville de Paris, veüe du costé du Pontneuf.

The Louvre and Institute, aerial view after Pérelle. The dome of the Assumption church by Charles Errard is visible in the background, on the right. The site of Ste. Anne-la-Royale is on the same bank as the Institute, almost opposite the Tuileries Palace.

was the Order of the Theatine Fathers, which had, at the request of the Queen Mother Anne of Austria, commissioned their celebrated confrère, Guarino Guarini of Modena (who was also a distinguished mathematician), to design for them the most extravagant of Piedmontese Baroque churches, Ste. Anne-la-Royale, provocatively sited on the other side of the river from the main *carré* of the Louvre (now 32 Quai Voltaire). The church, as well as the scandalously opulent and theatrical acts of worship performed in it, exemplified the unwelcome Italian influence which most sections of French society rejected. The church was put up in 1665, finished (to much modified designs) almost half a century later, and totally destroyed in 1823.[47] Guarini, however, left a treatise as well as a considerable corpus of building in Turin (Palazzo Carignano, the Chapel of the Holy Shroud, San Lorenzo), which show him to have been the most outré follower of Borromini.

Bernini, who had no love for his great rival and Roman contemporary, would certainly have disapproved of Guarini's excessive freedom with volume, his borrowings of medieval and even Moslem forms, and the apparent capriciousness of his geometry. Certainly men like the two Fréart brothers, who were not only Bernini's ad-

Paris, Ste.-Anne-la-Royale, by Guarino Guarini, section.

mirers but the friends and patrons of Poussin, would have found Guarini's work very distasteful.

It was, in fact, part of Roland Fréart's purpose to castigate the excesses, both overinventive and overpedantic, of his contemporaries, as well as to provide an academy of architecture in a slim volume. Fréart not only disapproved of "mascaroons, wretched *Cartouches* and the like idle and impertinent *Grotesque* with which they [the slow and reptile souls who never arrive at a full knowledge of the art] have infected all our modern architecture,"[48] but he did not care for the non-Greek orders. His book thus concentrates on the Doric, Ionic, and Corinthian orders, while making concessions to the Latin "inventions," the Tuscan and Composite.

Fréart's argument concerned the wide, *savant* public of his time. Not only architects used his book but sculptors and painters as well.

Nicolas Poussin, The Last Supper *or* The Sacrament of the Eucharist, *from a series of the Seven Sacraments. National Gallery of Scotland. Lent by the Duke of Rutland.*

Poussin received and read it as soon as it was published;[49] his fascination with the *modes* of ancient music prompted him to construct the space of a picture in terms of the orders, to harmonize with the general proportions as well as with its color scheme, so that the event represented might have a total environment. Poussin's passionately antiquarian pictures of the seven sacraments are the most obvious examples of such treatment.[50] His assiduous quest for the exact gesture and setting was inevitably read as another form of hermetic reference. Poussin's art corresponded perfectly to the stoic gallicanism which he shared with the Fréart brothers and with which his most consistent Roman patron, Cassiano del Pozzo, very much sympathized.[51]

Compare Poussin's earnestly archeological *Last Supper*, which takes place in a Tuscan triclinium, with the Upper Room in a *Last Supper* by Philippe de Champaigne, the self-confessed Jansenist who had been a close friend and contemporary of Poussin's.[52] His Upper Room is barely furnished at all: the most prominent object in the picture is the unfolded tablecloth, whose pleats make a gridded, altarlike rectangle in the middle. It is almost as if the action of unfolding the cloth, an action which is everyday, familiar, and domestic was described so graphically that any member of Champaigne's public might identify it with the spreading of the cloths on the altar for the Eucharistic celebration. This commonplace detail has, in Champaigne's admittedly weaker painting, the force of Poussin's hermetic scene-setting.[53] This comparison of the two pictures

Philippe de Champaigne, The Last Supper. *Louvre, Paris. From Port-Royal.*

indicates a shift and a dissension. The sacred precedent for all the antique detail on which Poussin drew for his *Last Supper*—as Inigo Jones did for his reconstruction of Stonehenge—the detail which Villalpanda had revalidated in his great sleight-of-hand by which the orders turned out to be a divine institution, even a divine dictate, all that was anatomized and reduced in the double solvent of Cartesian analysis and the Jansenist conviction that the will, in whose realm taste operated, was irredeemably corrupt. Antiquity therefore was to become a mere repertory of detail. But to Poussin, Blondel, and Jones and to generations before them, antiquity was much more than that: it was the source of a method which was enshrined in the touchstone of the orders through which the harmony of the noble senses, of sight and sound, was guaranteed, as the orders, by Villalpanda's leap of an *interpretatio Christiana* keyed the architects' and artists' practice and speculation into revealed truth. It was timeless teaching which provided a rule but was also validated by the great precedent: golden past. Antique greatness and Holy Writ were its two guarantors, and with their help all significant remains from the past—such as Stonehenge—must be interpreted. It was a teaching, too, whose unchangeable ordonnance allowed the greatest range of sober variety within the hoary tradition.

Notes to Chapter 1

1. J. W. Goethe (1948–1954), XXIV, p. 332 (conversation with J. P. Eckermann), and later, on the way Hugo's great talent was spoiled by 'romanticism', pp. 759 f.

2. On the meaninglessness of the term "romantic," see A. O. Lovejoy (1941), p. 261; see, however, R. Welleck (1963), pp. 128 ff.

3. Livy I. 43. Cf. Ennius, Annals fr. 18 and Aul. Gellius, Noct. Att. XVI, 10. For an early use of *proletarius* to mean "common," "clumsily said," see Plautus, Miles Glor. III, 157.

4. M. T. Varro, *De Lingua Latina,* V, 91; J. du Cange (1937–1943), s.v. *classicus, classicum.*

5. So Aulus Gellius, XVIII, 10, quoting M. Cato.

6. *Classicus assiduusque aliquis scriptor non proletarius*, Aulus Gellius, Noctes Att. XI, 8.

7. Antonio Segni and Orazio Ricasoli Rucellai are usually quoted in this context.

8. Sir E. Sandys (1599); NED s.v. *classic.*

9. *The Times (London)*, 6 May 1893, p. 17, col. 2. The painting *The Sleep of the Gods* by Arthur Hacker (ARA, 1894) was described in the course of a notice of the 1893 Royal Academy show. The term "neoclassical" was also used, interchangeably with neo-Hellenic.

10. S. Giedion (1922), pp. 11 ff.

11. L. Pastor (1891–1953), 1, pp. 18 f.

12. E. W. Anthony, *Early Florentine Architecture and Decoration* (1927), pp. 77 ff.

13. Vitruvius, V, 6, ix.

14. What is more, one order found in ancient buildings, in the Colosseum for instance, and later described as "composite," is not described at all by Vitruvius.

15. Vitruvius, IV, 1; IV, 7.

16. P. Fréart (1930), p. 20.

17. *A Parallel of the Ancient Architecture with the Modern . . . written in French by Roland Fréart, Sieur de Chambray . . . Made English for the Benefit of Builders by John Evelyn, Esq.* (London, 1723), p. 76.

18. Ezekiel 40–44: 3. J. Prado and J. B. Villalpanda (1596–1602).

19. J. Flavius, *Jewish Antiquities*, VIII, 2; XI, 4.

20. R. Taylor, "Architecture and Magic: Considerations on the Idea of the Escorial," pp. 81 ff; W. Hermann, "Unknown Designs for the Temple of Jerusalem by Claude Perrault," pp. 143 ff.; in D. Fraser, H. Hibbard, and M. J. Levine, eds. (1967).

21. E. Panofsky (1960), pp. 178 ff.; cf. E. Cassirer (1935), pp. 12, 117 f.

22. Cf. M. Drayton (1612), Book I, lines 304 ff., and comment on line 312. A very popular versified version of Geoffrey's account is given in Thomas Heywood's *Troia Britannica or Great Britaine's Troy* (London, 1609), the sixteenth canto, pp. 413 ff.

23. *The Most Notable Antiquity of Great Britain, Vulgarly Called Stone-Heng . . . Restored by Inigo Jones, Esq. . . . to Which are Added Chorea Gigantium, or Stone-Heng Restored to the Danes by Dr. Charleton and Mr. Webb's Vindication of Stone-Heng Restored . . .* (London, 1725), pp. 59 ff.

24. *Choirguare, Vulgarly Called Stonehenge . . .* by John Wood, Architect (Oxford, 1747), p. 22.

25. J. Wood (1747), p. 68.

26. By John Wood, Architect (Bath, 1741).

27. J. Wood (1741), p. 71.

28. J. Wood (1741), p. 76.

29. On the medieval speculations, see for instance, O. von Simson (1956), pp. 21 ff, or P. Frankl and E. Panofsky (1945).

30. See collection of texts in R. Wittkower (1952).

31. O. von Simson (1956), pp. 25 ff.

32. Cf. R. Wittkower (1952).

33. R. Wittkower (1952).

34. René Ouvrard, *Architecture Harmonique ou Application de la Doctrine des Proportions de la Musique à l'Architecture* (Paris, 1677).

35. R. Ouvrard (1677), p. 4.

36. Leone Ebreo, *Dialoghi d'Amore*, S. Caramella, ed. (Bari, 1929), p. 226.

37. L. Ebreo (1929), pp. 227, 317 ff.

38. R. Ouvrard (1677), p. 30.

39. A. Adam (1952), II, p. 9.

40. *De Oratore* III, 18 ff. Cf. N. Pevsner (1940), pp. 1 ff.

41. J. Jarkius (1725), passim.

42. N. Pevsner (1940), pp. 95, 296.

43. L. Hautecoeur (1943–1957), II (1), pp. 462 ff; Cf. B. Teyssèdre (1967), pp. 77 ff.

44. F. Blondel (1698), II, p. 756.

45. F. Blondel (1698), II, p. 250; Blondel's opening speech to the Academy, in H. Lemonnier (1911–1929).

46. L. Hautecoeur (1943–1957), II (i), p. 465.

47. J.-F. Blondel (1752–1756); R. Wittkower (1958), p. 269.

48. R. Fréart de Chambray (1723).

49. He wrote to Fréart de Chantelou about it on 29 August 1650; Fréart de Chambray had spoken of Poussin in the most flattering terms in his introductory Epistle.

50. There are two sets; the first painted for Cassiano del Pozzo is now at Belvoir Castle (except for the *Baptism* in the National Gallery of Art, Washington, D. C.). The second, painted some years later for Fréart de Chantelou, is in the National Gallery of Scotland. On the two sets see A. Blunt (1967), I, pp. 186 ff. There is a related painting of the *Institution of the Eucharist*, painted for Louis XIII, to be placed over the high altar at St. Germain, and now in the Louvre: A. Blunt (1967), I, p. 189, n. 48.

51. On Cassiano del Pozzo, see F. Haskell (1963), pp. 98 ff. On Poussin's religious opinions, see A. Blunt (1967), I, pp. 177 ff., and more recently, H. Hibbard, *Poussin: The Holy Family on the Steps* (London, 1974), pp. 43 ff.

52. They had shared a room when they were both young, in Paris. Philippe de Champaigne had been close to Port-Royal long before his daughter, Catherine, became a nun there. He had done a portrait of Cornelius Jansens,

but it was probably a posthumous one, which was engraved by Morin. *The Last Supper* was painted as an altarpiece for Port-Royal and is now in the Louvre.

53. Philippe de Champaigne was very much aware of the contrast, as is apparent from his strictures on Poussin's antiquarian "slavery" in his lecture to the Academy of Painting. *Procés-Verbaux de l'Académie Royale...* ed. Anatole de Montaiglon (Paris, 1875–1909), III, pp. 127 ff. Henri Brémond made an eloquent case against considering Philippe de Champaigne's painting, and particularly the *ex-voto* for the recovery of his daughter (Louvre, Paris, No. 1934) as Jansenist in style (1923–1926, vol. IV, pp. 178 f.). This should be read in conjunction with his general strictures on the very existence of a Jansenist style (1923–1926, vol. I, pp. 1 ff.). Yet, although Brémond rightly points out that Philippe de Champaigne *also* painted for the Jesuits, yet his loyalty was to Port-Royal; and all that remains of it, visually, we owe to Philippe's devoted record. He also painted the main altarpiece of the church, and designed the frontispiece of Antoine Arnauld's most sharply controversial book on frequent communion. Insofar as Port-Royal had a visual embodiment, it was his painting. For the conventional view of the Jansenist style as represented by Philippe see A. Blunt (1953), pp. 173 ff.

2

Positive and Arbitrary

René Ouvrard answers a hypothetical enquiry of contemporary architects on why Vitruvius, who has become the great master of architecture since Claude Perrault had "made him speak French" and had made him comprehensible through his learned remarks, made no mention of these harmonic proportions. Ouvrard explains that although Vitruvius did not call them harmonic proportions, nevertheless "all the proportions which he recommended are harmonic . . . we take here the term 'harmonic proportion' to mean those distances which, when translated into sound, are harmonies or consonances in music."[1]

Perrault's translation of Vitruvius was another enterprise sponsored by Colbert. It was a splendid work, illustrated with a great many plates, dedicated to the king, and made Claude Perrault's architectural reputation. Nearly a century later, it was still quoted as the best edition among several hundred.[2] Curiously enough, Perrault had taken the opposite view to Ouvrard's about the consonance between sight and sound. Indeed, Perrault contradicted him directly. Having, at the beginning of his short treatise on the orders of architecture, listed the varieties of orders in earlier books and in ancient monuments, he goes on: "Now all this proves that you cannot hold proportions in architecture to please the sight for reason unknown (to the observer), or that they exercise their effect of themselves as musical harmonies affect the ear, notwithstanding the ignorance in which the listener may be of the reason for their accord."[3]

In breaking the assumed unity of the "spiritual" senses, Perrault poses a problem: if harmony in architecture does not have that unquestioned rightness which Vitruvius, Scripture, and scholastic as well as neoplatonic philosophy had taken for granted, then how is the architect to go about making buildings harmonious and beautiful? And do these terms of praise continue to point his aim?

The context in which Perrault considered such questions shows them to be crucial to the future of all architectural speculation. The Perraults were a clannish, very clever family, sometimes too clever for their own good. They had come from Touraine and were presumably of merchant stock. But Claude and Charles' mother was Pâquette Leclerc, daughter of a noble Norman family, and their father, Pierre, was an *avocat* counsel of the Paris Parlement and had passed into that office-buying section of the bourgeoisie which was already forming into the *noblesse de robe*. Of seven children, six sons were born: Jean, a lawyer, who died young; Pierre, who became a tax-farmer *(receveur de finances)*; Claude, physician and architect; Nicholas, theologian and doctor of the Sorbonne; Charles, Colbert's assistant and the author of the fairy tales, and his twin François, who died in infancy.[4] The clannishness is demonstrated by the case of Pierre (the son), who was a secondary victim of the change of tax policy at the fall of Fouquet and the takeover of

Colbert in 1664.[5] His fall meant some hardship for the family:[6] capital had been tied up in buying the post, as was the custom of the time. But he does not seem to have suffered glumly, or in isolation. Apparently, the brothers lived together at their country house at Viry in the Limousin as well as in Paris.[7]

In his retreat, Perrault translated the burlesque epic by Alessandro Tassoni, *La Secchia Rapita* ("The Stolen Pail"). By the time *Le Sceau Enlevé* was published in 1678, however,[8] Pierre's brothers were not quite as committed to the burlesque genre as they had been when they were young. In the wake of many elders and betters, the Perraults completed a joke translation of the sixth book of the *Aeneid*, the one which deals with Aeneas' descent into the Underworld. It had been started by Charles and his friend Berain, and they were assisted first by Claude, then by Nicholas.

The poem is almost unreadable nowadays; the parody has lost all relish. It needed the enormous vogue of the epic in the middle of the seventeenth century to give it point. Note that the parody is not directed against Virgil but against those contemporaries of Perrault who insisted in theory and in practice that the close imitation of the ancients was the only proper way for an artist to proceed.[9] This, of course, was the very idea which Tassoni had repeatedly attacked, as he did the critical apparatus which his contemporaries had refurbished from ancient sources to support it. He attacked both in the name of nature and the vivid, immediate experience of it and in the name of progress. Tassoni's gods and heroes, like those of his followers writing in various languages, were therefore deliberately set in everyday, undignified positions and even beset by the more awkward aspects of what are colloquially known as "the calls of nature."[10]

This demotion of the superhuman beings, a demotion the "grand style" could not absorb, was a problem for Milton, for instance (the Archangel Raphael's notorious explanation of angelic sexual life),[11] as it was generally in epic poetry. Tasso and Ariosto had shown the way, and epic poems in the sixteenth century, although still based on antique precedent, dealt with great deeds of Christian heroes. This was another potent reason for preferring modern to ancient: the moderns were Christians. This argument was put forward by various critics, most emphatically by Jean Desmarets de Saint-Sorlin, the author of the epic poems *Clovis* (1657), *Marie Madeleine* (1669), and *Esther* (1670).[12]

Beside such Biblical themes as Saint-Sorlin's the epic material of the struggle between Moslem and Christian had a strong appeal. The Turks were still a great and menacing European power—and were to remain so even after their catastrophic defeat under the walls of Vienna in 1683. However quiescent the menace may have seemed in the France of the 1650s, however attractive the receptions of the Great Porte ambassadors, the struggle with the infidel was a topical theme for epic.[13] But in fact the most influential epic poet, Jean Chapelain, wrote his major work about Joan of Arc. *La Pucelle* appeared in 1656 after a long and public gestation. Its appearance, when Chapelain was sixty, confirmed his official reputation as the great poet of the day.[14] Colbert, with his assistance (even Colbert was not sure of his own taste: when in Mazarin's service he had been very impressed by the cardinal's superiority to him in this matter) then formed a small subcommittee of the French Academy, the *Petite Académie,* which was to guide the minister in all matters concerning the state patronage of the arts. This was to include not only the choice of artists but also such matters as the composing of inscriptions for triumphal arches and for medals to be struck in honor of the king, and by extension the study of numismatics and other antiquities—hence its later title, Académie des Inscriptions, under which it has become one of the most illustrious philological learned societies.[15] Charles Perrault had come to Chapelain's notice with two odes composed for royal occasions; in February 1663 he was also appointed to the "Little Academy" and almost immediately became its secretary, although he was not to take his seat in the Académie Française until several years later, in 1671.[16]

To his contemporaries, his fame was based on government service, and to a lesser extent on his verse, mostly occasional, although his epic on St. Paulinus of Nola (with a letter to those newly converted) gave him a certain standing. But much of his writing was controversial. Of this by far the best known was the lengthy (1,800 pages) conversation on the parallel between the ancients and the moderns.[17] There are three interlocutors: an enlightened *abbé* represents the "moderns" and wins hands down; the "ancients" are represented by a lawyer, a *président;* and the *abbé* is seconded by a temporalizing and rather etiolated literary *chevalier.* The conversation takes place in the gardens of Versailles whose splendors are a refrain on the superiority of modern times. But the book, published in four parts over a period of eight years, was a commentary on a great literary event called not the *parallel* but the *battle*[18] between the ancients and the moderns. The battle may be said to have started in earnest at the foundation of the French Academy and would flare up every now and then, as in the business of the language in which honorific inscriptions were to be composed, which produced François Charpentier's invective on the *Excellence de la Langue Française* of 1683.[19] It became a major issue between Perrault and Boileau and continued well into the eighteenth century.

It was a close battle: the protagonists were all acquaintances and colleagues. Nor was it only a battle about taste. It also concerned the artistic policy of the autocratic French state, a matter which could have radical effects on some protagonists: the brutal closure of the Academy of Architecture and the withdrawal of the royal pension and patronage from its members in 1685 was an episode which—although not directly connected to the immediate issues— illustrates its similarity to the battles between the "modernists" and "proletarian" classicists in the Soviet Union during the late twenties and early thirties of this century.

But beyond this the battle concerned a matter more crucial than the artistic and political issue. It was a dispute about the nature of history and the relation of the past to thinking, to speculation. The earliest skirmishes of the battle had taken place (as I wrote earlier) in Italy; a parody of Homer, on the Italian model, was one of the Abbé Boisrobert's *pièces de résistance.* The Italian Tassoni had "jostled" Homer, a certain disdain for whose roughness was to be a constant theme of polemic and parody, as it became acceptably commonplace in the period to compare Homer's roughness unfavorably to Virgil's elevated tone.

The Abbé Boisrobert, Richelieu's clown and literary stooge, was the cardinal's principal agent in the negotiations which preceded the founding of the French Academy in 1635 (the official incorporation was delayed by the *Parlement,* to Richelieu's extreme annoyance until 1637).[20] Its members had already been meeting privately as the Académie des Beaux Esprits for some time. Whether they were really meant to be, as one author has called them, Richelieu's literary police,[21] they certainly acted as that for instance, when issuing their adverse opinion of Corneille's *Le Cid.* Corneille was on the side of the ancients; Racine was to be even more explicitly so. Against such giants, the "epic" efforts of the moderns, Chapelain's *Pucelle* or Saint-Sorlin's biblical ladies seem to be not much stronger meat than the burlesques of the Perraults. But the burlesque as well as the epic poets were moved by a belief shared by many people at the height of Louis XIV's reign: that things were so good that improvement could only be marginal. It was the matter, of course, of innumerable laudatory dedications addressed to the king. The making of such dedications, already copious, became an industry, since Colbert forbade any to be addressed to himself (Desgodetz's *Ruins* and Perrault's *Ordonnance* as well as the first edition of his Vitruvius had been so dedicated).[22]

The dedications spoke of the age of Louis as having equaled and even surpassed that of Augustus. Even allowing for the panegyrists' hyperbole, there were many who must have felt something of this. In the rhapsodic poem "The Age of Louis the Great," which was read by the Abbé de Lavau at a session of the French Academy on 27 January 1687 (a session which celebrated the king's recovery from an operation for a fistula)[23] the opening couplet announces the theme:

> La Belle Antiquité fut toujours vénérable
> Mais je ne crus jamais qu'elle fut adorable.

And the poem goes on to compare

> . . . sans être injuste
> Le Siècle de Louis au beau Siècle d'Auguste.[24]

The Age of Louis is shown in the end to be even superior: because dominated by "the wisest of men and greatest of kings." The attempt to place the attack on antiquity under firm royal patronage provoked an immediate reaction. In spite of the jubilant tone of the occasion, Boileau walked out of the French Academy during the

Sébastien Leclerc, Louis XIV being shown round the Academy of Science by Colbert. This "fictionalized" representation, the frontispiece of Perrault's Histoire des Animaux, *shows the author's design of the Observatory being built beyond the Academy's garden.*

reading, slamming the door.[25] La Fontaine, Boileau, and Racine ranged themselves against Perrault: the translation of Longinus by Boileau, open letters, prefaces to plays, and finally Perrault's extended book, all became occasions for a skirmish. One of the most brilliant single sallies is Fontenelle's *Digression sur les Anciens et les Modernes*.[26] Sides were taken outside France. Jonathan Swift, a born satirist, had his allegiances clear; writing in the early 1690s, in the *Battle of the Books,* he gave a short account of the campaign in a prose epic. During this battle "Homer . . . took Perrault by mighty force out of his saddle then hurled him at Fontenelle, with the same blow dashing out both their brains."[27]

Since the admirable grandeur of the ancients was not at issue, nor the necessity of learning Greek and Latin[28] for any man of education—with all that this implied about classical culture in the arts, and to some extent in science as well—the difference between "ancients" and "moderns" does not always seem clear nowadays. Not even the necessity of a high moral tone was at issue between Perrault and Boileau; nor was the polemic a simple matter of personal rancor. Profound convictions about the nature of past achievement and the nature of progress were at odds. Nature, so Perrault maintained, had always formed men of genius and was not exhausted; even if the continuity of culture may be broken by such things as long wars. The sciences and arts flow for a while underground like rivers, but as soon as peace is restored, advances will continue, reinvigorated. So, after the hiatus of the Dark Ages progress was resumed in the two succeeding centuries. In another quasi-theological work, this time by a Jesuit, Dominique Bouhours (who was a friend of Boileau, and like all of his society, an enemy of the Jansenists), another and ancillary notion to Perrault's is advanced: that the torch of civilization passes from country to country; as the Romans inherited it from the Greeks, so in their age the French had from the Italians.[29] But Perrault was only marginally concerned with national progress, since the future seems in any case of very limited interest: "I rejoice," he says, "to see our age having arrived, in some way, at the pinnacle of perfection. And if for some years progress has been advancing with a slower step . . . I still rejoice in thinking that in all probability we have not much to envy those who will come after us."[30]

Of course, when he wrote that in 1688, Perrault was at the height of his influence and his output. He had made his way, as had his brothers, in that most competitive of organizations, the court of the Sun King. The events which marked his ascent also involved the rise of his brother Claude, the physician, to whom he pays such generous tributes in the *Mémoires*. Perrault the physician's fame is primarily that of an architect: though he was more of a polymath than any other member of the family. From childhood he had been interested in drawing, Charles the bureaucrat says in the *Mémoires*.[31] He had had no formal architectural training.

His involvement with building, and building on a vast scale, was certainly in part due to his brother's careful management of an awk-

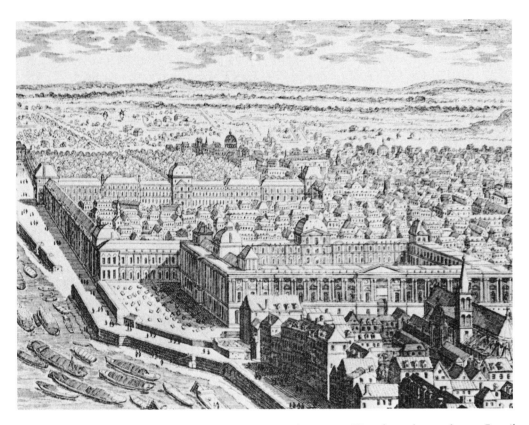

The Louvre and Tuileries at the end of the seventeenth century. View from the southeast. Detail from Pérelle.

ward situation: the king returned to Paris in 1660; Mazarin's death and Fouquet's fall and disgrace gave him full power. Louis XIV, determined to be the enlightened autocrat, decided to have a suitable palace built in Paris; the court had adequate country quarters at Vincennes, but the Louvre and the Tuileries had many gaping holes. In February 1661 there had been a fire in the Louvre, and its effect was to speed the work started in the previous administration. The design of the Eastern facade was Le Vau's, who as *premier architecte du roi* had already done much work and was still to do a great deal in the Tuileries.[32] Indeed, although the project was ready and the foundation started, some walls standing ten feet high, Colbert, who had meanwhile taken charge of royal building and was as determined as the king that the building would do him honor, regarded the scheme with disfavor. Everything had not been done to give the palace "a facade worthy of the prince for whom it was built."[33] With the court settled temporarily in the Tuileries, various Parisian architects were invited to comment on Le Vau's scheme, a rather curious procedure which marked Le Vau's temporary disfavor. Colbert never quite forgave him the work at Vaux-Le-Vicomte for his predecessor, the disgraced tax-farmer Fouquet. Le Vau was soon returned to the king's favor; however, there was a

certain glee in his less fortunate contemporaries' comments, many
of which were in the form of drawings. François Mansart, the celebrated architect of the Val-de-Grâce church and of the Château at
Maisons, produced a number of variants on a Louvre façade; there
were schemes by Claude, the physician, and by other architects, by
Le Vau's brother François, by Pierre Cottard, by Léonor Houdin,
and probably others unknown.[34] Colbert, so Charles tells us, "although he was charmed by my brother's drawing would not be
negligent in a business of this magnitude."[35] He decided to appeal to
the Italians. A form of program was devised by Charles Perrault and
sent—through an Italian ecclesiastic, a former domestic of Cardinal
Mazarin—to Poussin, who seems to have been made responsible,
together with the French ambassador, for conducting a kind of limited competition among Roman architects. The schemes of Pietro da
Cortona, Carlo Rainaldi, and Bernini are known. They—to quote
Perrault again—took no notice of the conditions laid down, and sent
"very bizarre designs, which showed no taste for *belle et sage* architecture."[36] No doubt however (despite Perrault's attribution of
its success to the private influence of the Italian ecclesiastic, Elpidio
Benedetti who also happened to be a friend of Bernini) the most
impressive of the Italian projects was that of Gian Lorenzo Bernini,
then in his late sixties, perhaps the best known artist of his day in
any medium. After some criticism sent by letter, a new project,
much less interesting plastically and less ambitious in scale was sent
to Paris. The king then suggested, in the most flattering terms that
the great man should come to Paris, where the business might be
concluded. His journey was a kind of royal progress.[37] His arrival in
Paris was again triumphant. To Paul Fréart, the royal envoy sent to
meet him and to attend on him, Bernini made the remarks about
proportion quoted earlier.[38] But in spite of the enormous sums of
money paid him, the honors and the compliments, Bernini realized
rightly that he was surrounded by hostility from French architects
and from some officials, and so he worked secretly. Perrault, managing to sneak in, prepared a criticism of the scheme, which he
discussed with Colbert; so that although building started again on
Bernini's scheme when he returned to Rome in the autumn of that
year (having refused to stay in Paris because of the cold), his project
was shelved.

Bernini's presence in Paris left its mark, of course. The project
had stimulated universal curiosity, even expectancy. And yet nothing definite (the famous bust of Louis XIV apart) was accomplished
during the Parisian visit.[39] Some designs for altar pieces at the Val-
de-Grâce and in the Carmelite church are attributed convincingly to
Bernini. They were diversions, and the Louvre project was left in
abeyance for two years. By the spring of 1667, the king was no
longer interested in tearing down the old Louvre to make way for
Bernini's vast rectangle, and his representative, Matteo de'Rossi,
was paid off and returned to Rome. Colbert then appointed a commission made up of Le Vau, the painter-impressario Charles Le
Brun, and Claude Perrault to produce a new scheme; the decision to

build the present colonnade was taken on May 14, and the foundations for Bernini's building destroyed.[40] According to Charles Perrault it was his brother who designed the facade which was finished by 1680 and which has remained almost unaltered. François d'Orbay "invented the calumny"[41] that the facade had been designed by Le Vau; others still have attributed it to d'Orbay himself on the basis of Le Vau's drawing. The issue is not relevant to my argument. In fact in that short period the context of the debate had changed: the king (against Colbert's advice) shifted the focus of his attention to Versailles. But it was Perrault's appointment as architect of the Louvre and not his authorship of the scheme which seems interesting to me.

Claude had been trained as a physician. Like his brother, he had great literary talent and had himself published a burlesque epic, *Les Murs de Troie, ou l'Origine du Burlesque* in 1653. By the time of the Louvre dispute he was already a fairly well known medical practitioner and had become a member of the Académie des Sciences on its foundation in 1666, although appointed primarily as a comparative anatomist. He practiced as a physician only for the benefit of his family and friends, although he seems also to have treated poor persons free. In that sense, Boileau's jibe[42] on the bad physician who turns good architect is not entirely justified, although Boileau did apparently have some cause for complaint. Claude went on studying comparative anatomy until the end of his life: which was brought about in October 1688 by a cut incautiously made while dissecting the cadaver of a camel which had died in the Jardin du Roi. Though of course Perrault was 75 at the time.

He had published a number of books: there was the burlesque epic, already mentioned; a treatise on comparative anatomy (a chameleon, a beaver, a dromedary, a bear, a gazelle);[43] a collection of scientific essays; and a posthumous collection of engineering inventions. The edition of Vitruvius, first published in 1674 and greatly refurbished for the second edition of 1685, must have been in prepa-

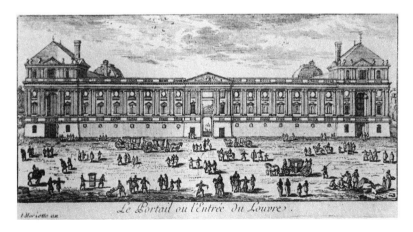

The eastern facade of the Louvre, engraved by J. Mariette for Pérelle. An early modification of the executed scheme with a blind basement under the colonnade and angle pavilions.

François Le Vau, eastern facade of the Louvre, presentation drawing of 1664 (?) on which, presumably, Claude Perrault's project was based. Nationalmuseet, Stockholm.

Gianlorenzo Bernini, project for eastern facade of the Louvre. Presumed competition project. Courtauld Institute of Art.

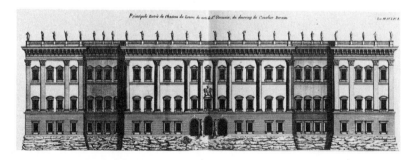

Gianlorenzo Bernini, eastern facade of the Louvre, final project, after Mariette. Courtauld Institute of Art.

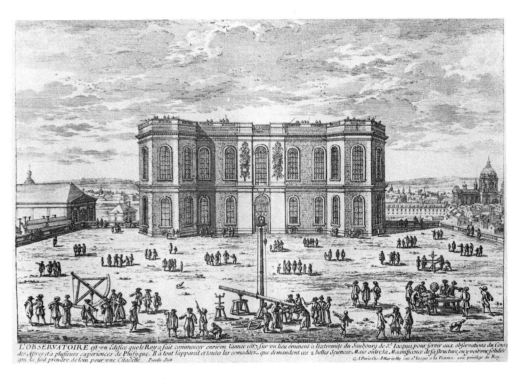

Paris, the Observatory, by Claude Perrault.

ration for several years. The printing privilege (equivalent of
copyright registration) is of March 1673, although payments for illustrations were already being made to engravers in 1668.[44] The assumption has been made that he had already been working for two or
three years on the book, perhaps in connection with his brother's
appointment to the "Little Academy." He also published an
epitome of Vitruvius in 1674 and in 1683 the book I quoted at the
beginning of this chapter, the *Ordonnance de Cinq Espèces de Colonnes*.

The revolutionary nature of Perrault's doctrine is summed up in
the detailed preface to the *Ordonnance*. The point of departure is the
criticism of the traditional, "classical" doctrine. Perrault abandons
explicitly—as I suggested earlier—the immemorial doctrine of an
analogy between pitch and length, between visual and musical harmony; the proportions which an architect must observe "are not
certain and invariable as are those which make for the beauty and
harmony of sounds in music, and which do not depend on us, but
which nature has delimited (*arrestée*) and established with exact precision so they may not be changed without instantly shocking the
least sensitive ears."[45]

No such agreement exists, Perrault goes on, about beauty in architecture. Had such consonance existed, an exact agreement of the
monuments of antiquity between themselves and with the modern
masters might have been expected; but such is not the case. Perrault
examines, using the traditional method of measuring building mem-

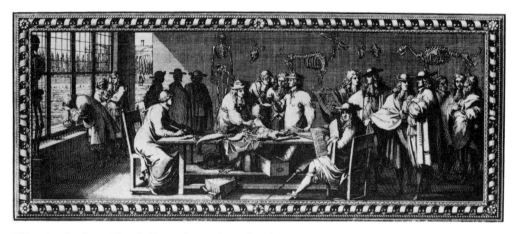

Sébastien Leclerc, Claude Perrault (on the right of the central group, holding the knife) conducts an animal dissection.

bers, by module and minute (that is one-half and one-sixtieth of the diameter; a method already used by Vitruvius) the differences in the projection of the capital of a Doric column. He quotes the Colosseum and the Theatre of Marcellus, Alberti, Scamozzi, Serlio, Palladio, Vignola, and Philibert de l'Orme and finds they differ as from $2\frac{1}{2}$ to 17 minutes. It is difficult to know where he found his measurements: had he used the two most obvious sources, Fréart de Chambray and the newly published collection by another protégé of Colbert's, Antoine Desgodetz,[46] he would have found the differences much smaller (Alberti $7\frac{1}{2}$, the others ranging from 11 to 13, the Colosseum order alone projecting $16\frac{6}{7}$). But although he had—wittingly or otherwise—exaggerated differences between the masters, he had a valid cause: the differences suggested that the traditional argument lacked force.

But Perrault does not abandon it altogether: on the contrary, he sets out to rescue it against apparent contradiction: The ancients [so he begins the book] believed with reason that the rules of proportion which give beauty to buildings were taken from the human body, and that as nature formed solid bodies adapted to labour, and those who should be adroit and agile in a lighter mould, so there are different rules in the art of building . . . those different proportions accompanied by the ornaments which suit them make the different orders of architecture.[47]

The analogy between the different bodies and the orders is the one to which Bernini also alluded in the passage which I quoted earlier. But Perrault goes on to say that the difference between the orders is the only thing which is precise about them. The actual dimensions vary considerably, although within limits. As in a human face, proportions may change (as the face does when crying or laughing), yet the principal measurements must keep a certain relationship for it to remain attractive. So the approximate proportion of the orders is necessary, if only to maintain the analogy to the body. But if the self-evident harmonies of music (about which all are agreed), may no longer be taken as an a priori justification of architectural beauty, it must be found elsewhere. Music pleases for self-evident reasons: there is no disagreement between musicians on the basic principles of harmony analogous to the difference between architects about proportions.

The musical absolutism seems hardly tenable at that time: Perrault the physician was very interested in music and had indeed written a paper on the music of the ancients.[48] It was, in his view, very like oriental monodic music. Like modern orientals, the ancients were unfamiliar with polyphony or counterpoint, yet their notion of pitch was the same as ours: indeed, it was universal.

This sets aside all the discussion on ancient music. But it also rejects, if only by implication, the firm distinction which the most subtle and prolific writer on the problems of acoustics, Marin Mersenne, had made when he distinguished the scientific problems of acoustics from the criticism of music. It was Mersenne who established a correlation between the vibration of the eardrum and of the sound-producing instrument.[49] With all that, Mersenne had a firm belief in the therapeutic value of harmony and in its absolute power, even when he had abandoned his early belief in the accounts which ancient writers gave of cures affected by music: and he came to believe that modern music might reach a power beyond that of the ancient.[50]

It was Mersenne, however, who was to receive Descartes' clearest account of a subjective aesthetic theory. While both maintained the importance of their auditory measurements, the explanation for finding one sound more pleasing than another eluded Mersenne. In a famous sentence, foreshadowing the psychological laboratories which were still three centuries away, Descartes writes to Mersenne that were a dog whipped five to six times to the sound of a violin, he would no doubt howl and run away whenever he heard its music.[51]

In this, Perrault parts company with Descartes as to the quality of auditory perception. But he still follows in establishing the steps of his reasoning. Pitch, whatever else may be changeable, is universal, because its basis is the quantitative relation between the eardrum and the vibration of the instrument. But since the quantity need not be known to the hearer for the mechanical effect to take place, this relationship is at a lower threshold—as Mersenne had already maintained—than the visual one.[52] Our choice of pleasant and unpleasant sound is made according to experience and the recognition of similarities.[53]

This seems to set aside the vast discussion in France and Italy which had been going on for a century or more about this issue.

From this it seemed to Perrault to follow that musical harmonies

> 'make their effect of themselves': if the mind [*l'esprit*] is touched through the mediation of the ear by that which results from the proportion of two strings (without having knowledge of this proportion), it is because

the ear may not give [the mind] *knowledge* of such a
proportion; but the eye, which can give knowledge of
whatever proportion which it makes you like, may not
make the mind feel any effect of this proportion *except
by the very knowledge which it gives of that proportion
from which it follows that what is agreeable to the eye,
is not at all due to the proportion unless the eye does
not [already] know it.*[54] [my italics]

There is one point at which the two beauties are parallel: the harmony resulting from the laws of statics which is produced "naturally
and through itself" is not comparable to what is usually understood
as proportion in architecture, but is parallel to the absolute beauty of
musical harmony.[55]

Because musical harmony is self-evident, it does not require the
support of association; because musical quantity is not itself directly
perceptible, the effect of music must be wholly abstract, wholly
dependent on relationships.[56] It is the way of operating these unchangeable musical harmonies which is changeable and may be
compared to the variations in architectural proportion. Nevertheless, Perrault reflects, one may like proportions "which conform to
the rules of architecture" without knowing why one likes them;
there must therefore be some reason for saying why one does like
them. The "problem is to know if this reason is ever something
positive . . . or if more often it is not founded upon habit . . . like that
which causes a fashionable dress to please by its proportions."[57]

At this point Perrault introduces criteria which have marked the
discussion of architecture ever since. There is positive and convincing beauty, mechanical (as it were) and inevitable; on the other
hand, there is arbitrary beauty, which depends on inclination *(pré-
jugé)*. This inclination is not to be despised; it is "the natural foundation of faith, which only an effect of the inclination to let the knowledge and the good opinion we have of someone who assures us of
something, of which—though we know nothing of it—dispose us not
to doubt it; it is also an inclination which makes us like fashionable
things, and the ways of speaking which fashion has fixed at court."[58]

Fashions change: it therefore follows that they cannot be *positively* good. They imply that following fashion, exercising choice in
this matter, is something which must also have its internal rules. But
these rules are imposed neither by "nature, nor reason, nor common
sense."[59] And yet rules have to be established. In an introductory
letter which Claude Perrault addresses to Colbert he explains that
the *Ordonnance* is a kind of appendix to his edition of *Vitruvius,*
since the master thought that the need for ancient rules was self-
evident, and therefore did not argue their necessity, nor did he explain credibly why the orders are the touchstone of architectural
beauty.[60]

To this end, Perrault sets out which are the positive and which the
arbitrary beauties in architecture. The positive ones must have the
same character as musical harmony. They must be obvious to all,
must please for their own sake, must be singular and affect

everyone. These beauties are richness of the materials; the grandeur, magnificence, and delicacy of the workmanship; and symmetry: that is, the equality and the measured correspondence of the parts of the building between themselves.[61]

Once a balance of these qualities was achieved this good order was esteemed and admired so that it became the rule for other builders. As, when you "passionately love a face, although it may have nothing perfectly lovely about it except the complexion, you never tire of finding the proportions so agreeable that you would not believe that it could be more beautiful if the proportions were changed." [62]

"Good taste is based on the knowledge of one and the other of these beauties; but it is certain that the knowledge of arbitrary beauties is more proper to the formation of what is called taste, and that it is this which alone distinguishes the true architects from those who are not so; since to know most positive beauty, it is enough to have common sense . . . true architects, as has been said, do not approve any (among buildings of differing proportions) but those which are in the middle between the two extremes."[63]

It is these mediocre orders which Perrault presents to his readers. But he is also interested in another problem: the "modern" authors, overawed by the ancients, have unnecessarily complicated the simple matter of their application. By reducing the orders to commensurate *probable* proportions he claims to return to the simple method of the ancients. There is to be a new module (one-third instead of one-half of the diameter) which he subdivides into five sections. He arrives at this number by the lowest common denominator of the good examples of each order so as to arrive at the simplest fractional system possible. By these means he gives "the orders of

St. Martin, Troyes, after Grosley (see note 61).

architecture the precision, the perfection and ease for memorizing which they now lack.''[64]

> The rules of beauty had been too long—art having in the barbarous Middle Ages sought refuge in the cloisters—in the hands of theologians, over-respectful of authority, so that to elucidate a text of Aristotle seemed more important than to discover whether it was true or not.[65] The truth is, there is no other way of explaining the origin and continuity of the orders; common sense will tell you that things for which no explanation may be found are inexplicable[66] . . . and that they have no other origin than chance and the

The five orders, module demonstration plate from Claude Perrault's Ordonnance.

Claude Perrault's "rationalized" Corinthian order from the Ordonnance. *Engraving by C. de Châtillon.*

caprice of a workman who didn't bother to seek for a
reason to determine something whose precision did
not matter.[67]

Perrault apologizes for the seeming paradox: it is necessary to
"demystify" a professional secret, and so return to the arbitrary
origins of the orders, a sort of return to the sources by eliminating
the accretions through the search for the lowest common denominator. Something analogous was attempted in another field,
which Perrault considered as having no positive or natural rules:
the form of letters.

The French crown had long patronized printing, in spite of a lapse
at the time of Francis I. Louis XIII decided to set up a private press
in the Louvre, and Richelieu raised it to the level of a major state
enterprise. Two great purchases of matrices were made: the Gene-
van Greek ones of Francis I and the set of Oriental faces collected by
Savary de Brèves, who had been ambassador to the Sublime Porte;
these were bought in 1632 and made the royal presses perhaps the
richest oriental printer in Europe after the Congregation for the
Propagation of the Faith in Rome. At some point (as yet unverified,

but about 1640) the press was institutionalized. Its major work includes a folio Virgil with a frontispiece by Poussin (who also did other work for the press). After various vicissitudes, as when the twelve-year-old Louis XIV printed with his own hand the first page of the press' edition of Philippe de Commines' *Chronique et Histoire,* a new director was called upon to reorganize the house, and a special type was to be designed for it, after consultation with the Academy of Science. Perrault was of course a member of that academy: but the committee did not include him: there were four other members of the academy, two engravers and Grandjean,[68] the great punch-cutter. They evolved a scheme of modules and subsections: each letter was fitted into a square composed of 2,304 square units, that is, 6×8 units to a side. The most remarkable effect of this innovation was that the serifs, which had hitherto had sharp points, being based on stone-cut antique letters, lost the fiction of reproducing the chiseled form and acquired a more abstract, engraved look, becoming square-toed with a blunt end $\frac{1}{48}$ of their height.[69]

Of course the business of fitting the letter into a square is an old one: Leonardo and Dürer had both drawn alphabets of that kind. And a French printer, Geofroy Tory, had published a treatise on the forms of the Roman letter, in which the letter forms are set in a square subdivided into 100 units. But Geofroy Tory is concerned throughout the book not only to play on the allegorical properties of the letterforms; he is also insistent in relating them (in a system based on the contemporary understanding of Vitruvius) to the microcosm. The human body in the square and the circle is compared to the letters, and more elaborate speculations follow, as, for instance, the relation of various letters to parts of the body, much as the zodiacal signs were related to them in the "astronomical medicine" of the time.[70]

Such speculations were wholly alien to the devisers of the *Romain du Roi.* They submitted a very voluminous report (written by one of their number) which was never printed, although the accompanying engravings (by Louis Simonneau) were. And Grandjean cut the punches, so that by 1702 the first book, an account of the medals struck during the reign of Louis XIV, was ready.[71] Although Grandjean had not followed the committee's recommendations exactly, the font was marked by a little spur, the size of a serif projecting from the lowercase *l.*

But the blunt serif and strong contrast between the thick and thin strokes led Fournier-le-Jeune to consider it a watershed of printing,

Romain du Roy, cut by Philippe Grandjean: specimen capital letters.

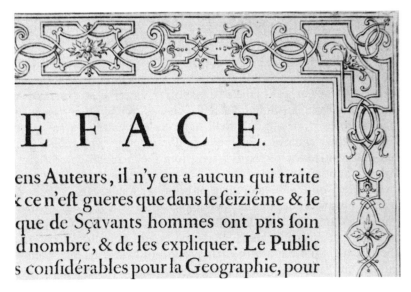

Romain du Roy, cut by Philippe Grandjean. Specimen page of the text of Médailles sur les Principaux Evènements du Règne de Louis le Grand, *Paris, 1702. Note the spur on the lowercase l.*

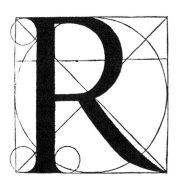 

Capital R *and* M *from alphabet designed for Luca Pacioli's* De Divina Proportione *(1509), attributed to Leonardo da Vinci.*

leading to the "modern" types, such as those of Bodoni in Italy and Didot in France, in contradiction to the "old" or, in French, the *ancien* faces which had been current hitherto.[72]

The wealth of Oriental types in the royal printing works is curious. But while the nomenclature evolved by the printers returns the argument to the Perraults, the association of extreme abstraction, in the name of rationalism, with a consciousness of the Orient suggests other themes with which I shall have to deal later. To return to Perrault: the committee for the scientific printing type reclassified and systematized letterforms away from their calligraphic origins. The resultant effect, nearer engraving than calligraphy, was to have a vast effect on the development of printing. Analogously, Perrault justifies his procedure by the need to provide a probabilistic abstract framework on which the modern worker can deal rationally with seemingly arbitrary forms, such as the orders of architecture. The liberties he takes both with their proportion and their ornamental garnish are justified by this end. The grand, archaic dignity, the mysterious power with which Ouvrard endowed the orders, seemed empty to Perrault. The authority of the ancients, he reasoned, was not based on their inherent greatness or even superiority, but on the need to structure our experience by an appeal to its very continuity. He says this much explicitly in the preface to the great edition of Vitruvius:

> Beauty has no other foundation than the imagination [*la fantaisie*]; which works in such a way, that things are pleasing if they accord with the idea each one of us has of their perfection. Rules are therefore essential to form and to correct this ideal, and it is certain that if nature refuses rules to some particulars, as she has to language, to the characters of the alphabet, to clothes, and to all that depends on chance, on the will and on habit, then human institutions must supply them, and for that a certain authority is necessary which will do duty for positive reasons.[73]

Perrault argued that an authority such as Vitruvius' would have been essential to architecture even if he had never existed; we must acknowledge this authority because of the preoccupations of the time, because of his antiquity and his exalted patrons, but also because the extent of his learning and the dexterity with which he has mastered it. Perrault's argument may seem cynical; I do not think it is really that, even if it has a certain flavor of that high libertinism whose chaplain was Pierre Gassendi and which had evident affinities of method with Descartes. Perrault's affinity with Descartes in particular is clear in his analysis of commonly held opinions and in an attempted synthesis by deduction from the primary intuitions to which the ideas have been stripped; clear too in the matter of *habitus* and its relation to human freedom.[74] But again, he seems nearer—in equating *habitus* with the need to restrain the imagination by rules—to certain *libertins* who regarded institutions, both political

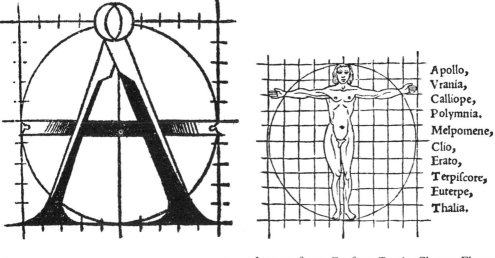

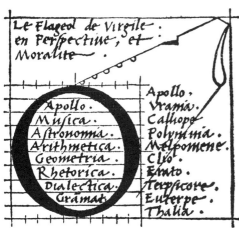

Letters from Geofroy Tory's Champ Fleury *(1526); the letter* A *shows the compasses and rule as the origin of the alphabet; the letter* O *as a meditation on the human body, the muses, and the arts: Virgil's flute.*

and religious, as necessary for the restraining of human brutishness, although based on falsehood.[75] It would be too easy to see in this the confirmation of Boileau's opinion, expressed privately—and not published until after his death[76]—that Descartes "had cut poetry's throat."

The opportunist stance (and I use the word here descriptively, not as a term of abuse) also defers to Port-Royal. The reader may remember Father Nicholas Perrault's connection with Arnauld and Jansenist theology; Charles Perrault claimed to have inspired the first *Provinciales.*[77] And indeed the nature of imagination and the perception of beauty as discussed in Claude Perrault's preface to his Vitruvius, which I quoted earlier, are a kind of brutal development of Pascal's intuition in the *Pensées* that:

> there is a certain model of charm and of beauty which consists in a given relation between our nature, strong or weak, such as it is and the thing which we like.[78]
>
> Everything made according to this pattern is agree-

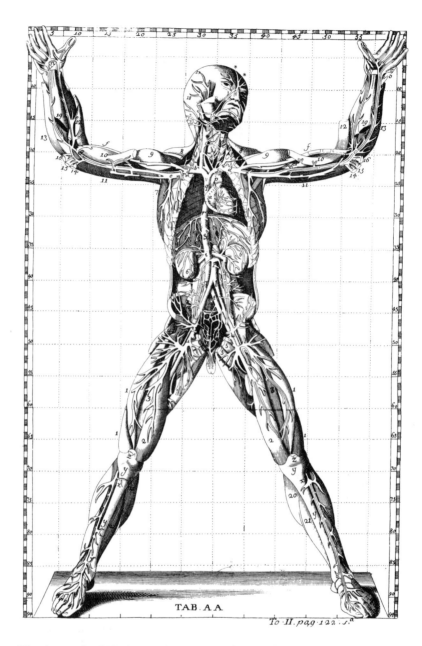

The Anatomized Human Body on a Locational Grid. *From James Winslow.*

able: whether house, song, speech, verse, prose,
woman, birds, rivers, rooms, clothes, etc. Everything
which is not made according to the model displeases
those who have good taste. As there is a perfect relation between a song and a house made according to
this good model, because they resemble that unique
model, although each after its kind; in the same way
there is a perfect relation between things made according to a bad model. Not that this means that there
is one bad model: there is an infinity of them.[78]

As may be expected, Pascal's thought is opaque with implications, whereas Perrault eludes by an uncertainty about his terms:
"the term imagination is much in use, yet I find it difficult to believe," writes Nicolas Malebranche a year after the publication of
Perrault's Vitruvius, "that all those who pronounce it have a distinct
notion of its meaning."[79] Still an "objective" aesthetic had its defen-
dant in Perrault's very circle: Pierre Nicole, the disciple and faithful
companion of the great Arnauld, who accompanied him into exile
while Nicholas Perrault warmed his heels at the fires of Viry, wrote
some years earlier *Treatise on True and False Beauty,* which first
appeared in Latin in 1659 and went through several editions but was
not published in French until 1698. It appeared as an appendix to a
collection of epigrams. This was the only true treatise on the general
theory of art published in the seventeenth century: Racine wrote
enthusiastically to a friend that God had prepared it specially for
him.[80]

In Nicole's theory—which Perrault seems to have followed (he
was probably familiar with the short text, and certainly with the
ideas[81])—there are also two kinds of beauty. But his view of the
matter is much more subtle than Perrault's. All beauty, he says,
belongs to nature. And he uses "nature" almost as if he were referring to the scholastic duality of *naturans* and *naturata;* since beauty
is in the relation between the object, the thing perceived, and the
subject, the perceiver. Many think that beauty may be judged by
sensory pleasure. This, Nicole says, is mistaken: there is no rule
more false, since it is custom and the opinion of others which determine our taste.

True beauty is found only when reason has carried us beyond
impressions. Judgment must accord with the nature of the thing and
the nature of the beholder. Yet not all beholders discriminate by the
right criteria, since there are false natures and warped minds. We
must appeal to a well-formed mind, to a sound nature, to know what
beauty is. And again there is force in aggregate judgment. True
beauty corresponds to the taste of all times. False beauty, if it has its
followers, does not keep them for long, since this kind of beauty is
against nature, which inspires distaste towards that which does not
come from it. Although more subtle and less accommodating than
Perrault's teaching, the similarity is evident. And Nicole too finds
that the artist must come to terms with his public's fallen nature, too
weak to endure being constantly tensed. Hence the same harmony

may not please us all the time. Our ears do not remain content with too excellent harmonies, and therefore musicians have introduced false notes which they call dissonances. Metaphor and hyperbole perform the same function in literature as does dissonance in music.[82] The aesthetic sociology, which Perrault shares with Nicole, also makes him insensitive to the problem of *je ne sais quoi:* a brief reference to the attraction of grace on the first page of the *Ordonnance* and the problem is forgotten. While the lively debate of the critics continued,[83] Perrault set out the rules by which the practitioners of building could reduce the wayward impulses to the dictates of taste, and the unknown factor of attraction, which some of his contemporaries even equated with grace in the theological sense.[84]

Jansenist thinkers may not have had much influence on the aesthetic speculations of the eighteenth century; but through Perrault and through many other disciples, Nicole and his circle had an overwhelming effect on the lower reaches of artistic thinking of that time. I hope to demonstrate particularly that the division between positive beauty, which is accessible through reason (I return to Perrault's coarser coinage), and arbitrary beauty, with which taste and therefore the corrupt part of one's nature are involved, would lead, among other things, to an attempt at creating an architecture which would appeal to reason alone and have no truck with the whims of taste: thus forgetting the more subtle and more instructive lesson of Nicole.

The admission of dissonance as well as of hyperbole and metaphor is a reminder that the *précieux* of a generation earlier were not entirely alien to Port-Royal. They held that "Metaphor was the most ingenious and witty, the most volatile and wonderful, the most jolly and enjoyable, the most fluent and fertile part of the human intellect" and indeed "to speak plainly seems little glory."[85]

The *précieux,* in this context, would have aligned themselves with the "moderns," against whom stood the protagonists of the grand style, which seemed to many *précieux* the very *parlare piano* they so despised; the phrase is Emmanuele Tesauro's. Tesauro, a Piedmontese Jesuit (later a secular priest) was one of the last protagonists of the *précieux* style, and perhaps its most prolific theorist. Nicole's idea that dissonance is essential to sharpen the taste of the listener is already put forward in a treatise on music, the work of Vincenzo Galilei, which was the manifesto of the Florentine Camerata. Galilei (the father of the astronomer) was emphatic about the primacy of the intellect over the senses and therefore of the need for music to concern itself with conveying the meaning of sung words as its principal duty. The main product of the influence of the Camerata was the dramatic opera. But here I am concerned not with opera but with Galilei's idea that he was combatting polyphony by an appeal to the monodic music of antiquity. His book, in the form of a discussion, a dialogue about ancient and modern music, returns forcibly to the theme of the parallel between musical and spatial proportion.[86] In Galilei's book, the ancients inevitably won. A century later Charles

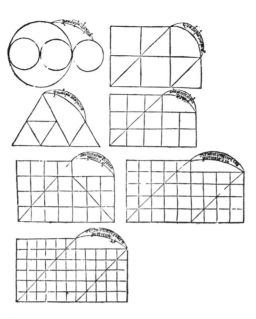

The geometry of sound demonstrated by Vincenzo Galilei in the Dialogo della Musica Antica et della Nuova.

Perrault revenged the moderns in his *Parallèle*.[87] But he, too, believed that the music of the ancients was monodic and that it was in some way preserved in Oriental music. It was not only Oriental music which interested him: he suggested, for instance, that in a royal palace certain rooms or suites of rooms should be decorated in foreign, particularly in exotic "styles," as a compliment to foreign ambassadors and visiting potentates, that these (like the exotic animals in the royal ménagerie at Versailles, the animals his brother dissected) had an educational as well as a diplomatic value. Perrault was heralding a new attitude, which in all Europe was producing a current of expectation about the marvelous Orient. This would light up the dark corners of antiquity, but also dim its luster.

Notes to Chapter 2

1. R. Ouvrard (1677), p. 15 f.

2. G. Poleni (1739), pp. 115 f., 120 ff. On the importance of Perrault's translation, see below.

3. Claude Perrault (1683), p. iv. The *Ordonnance* appeared nine years after the first edition of Vitruvius, as an appendix to it, and about a year before the second edition.

4. There was also a daughter, Marie, who died aged fourteen. Most of the family were buried in one tomb, built at St. Etienne-du-Mont, hard by St. Geneviève at Claude's and Charles' expense, *piis parentum fratrum, sororis manibus bene precantes* in 1674: Pierre the elder and Pâquette; Marie, Nicholas, Pierre the younger. Jean (*Burdigalae jacet, ubi obiit*) was commemorated. Piganiol de la Force (1765), vol. VI, pp. 118 f. M. Soriano (1972), pp. 117 ff., 129 ff.

5. M. Soriano (1968), pp. 269 ff. Pierre Perrault was obviously used by Colbert as an exemplary victim, since he was regarded generally as a partisan of the new dispensation.

6. Charles Perrault (1909).

7. J. Barchillon (1962), pp. 20 ff. Cf. A. Hallays (1920).

8. Tassoni had entered the lists for the "moderns" quite explicitly himself. The tenth chapter of his *Pensieri* (1576) consists of a series of essays demonstrating the equality—and even the superiority of the moderns over the ancients (pp. 297 ff.). On the religious problem, see pp. 301 f. On architecture, see pp. 319 ff. The chapter ends with a comparison of Greek and Roman and a strange, eloquent appeal for honor to the public executioner.

9. See Boisrobert in the preface to Scarron's *Virgile Travesty*.

10. Perrault was not innocent of this kind of thing: the diarrhoea of the sybil, Aeneas' pox and the impotence of Charon are all gleefully described. See M. Soriano (1968), pp. 245 ff., and (1972), pp. 36 ff., on burlesque scatology and its implications.

11. *Paradise Lost,* VIII, 617 ff.

12. On Desmarets' other career—for which he was equally well-known to his contemporaries—of heresy-hunter and persecutor (he was, for instance, principally responsible for the condemnation and burning at the stake of the "illuminatus" Simon Morin), see H. Brémond, 1923–1926, vol. VI, pp. 486 ff. On his mystical work, the *Délices de l'Esprit*, see pp. 447 ff. On Pierre Nicole's dismissal of Desmarets, see vol. IV, pp. 475 ff.

13. A. Adam (1962), II, pp. 54 ff., on the burlesque in the French literature of the time, pp. 78 ff.

14. "Le plus grand poète qui ait jamais été," he is called in the pension accounts of the academy. Cf. H. Kortum (1966), p. 81. On Chapelain's position as a critic, see E. B. O. Borgerhoff (1950), pp. 31 ff. Ironically enough, of all his published works the one still most read is the academy's condemnation of Corneille's *Cid,* of which he confessed himself to be the principal author in spite of his ambiguous feeling about the play and his real admiration of the author. Voltaire, for one, thought that the whole document was written in Chapelain's handwriting (P. Corneille, 1765, vol. I, p. 302) and reported de Scudéry's original attack on Corneille, Corneille's answer, the reference to the academy, and the academy's judgment (vol. I, pp. 245 ff.). Chapelain's admission to Balzac that, in spite of its disobedience of the rules it charmed by an *agrément inexplicable* is rightly stressed by Borgerhoff (pp. 38, 45).

15. Académie des Inscriptions, *Histoire de l'Académie Royale des Inscriptions et Belles-Lettres Depuis son Establissement jusqu'à Présent*, (1717), I, pp. 1 ff., and its transformation, pp. 25 ff. Cf. A. Hallays (1920), pp. 42 ff.

16. Charles Perrault, *Mémoires*, 1878, p. 83 ff. M. Soriano (1972), pp. 117 ff. On his entry into the academy, see pp. 156 ff. A. Hallays (1920), pp. 51 ff.

17. Charles Perrault (1688).

18. A. Hallays (1926), p. 132 f.

19. On this whole episode, see H. Gillot (1914).

20. C. J. Burckardt (1971), III, pp. 373 ff. Cf. Dilke (1888), pp. 17 ff. Boisrobert was very much a literary "modern." See A. Adam (1962), pp. 146 ff.

21. A. Adam (1962), I, pp. 228f. The rather circumspect way in which Boisrobert acted on Richelieu's orders, however, is related by Voltaire in his edition of Corneille's works (1765, I, pp. 109 ff). For a summary of the political aspect of the affair, see C. V. Wedgwood (1974), pp. 102 ff.

22. M. Soriano (1972), p. 123.

23. It was the king's second serious operation, and no one, to the knowledge of his doctors, had performed the operation since antiquity. The king's surgeon, Dr. Felix, reconstructed the operating instruments which "Galen had used for this operation." See E. Degueret (1924), p. 174. In fact the operational technique was known through Celsus (VII, 3) and its place in the history of medicine was discussed by Daniel Le Clerc (1729), pp. 542 f., almost in the same terms as Degueret's. Felix performed the operation several times in various Paris hospitals to perfect his technique and observe the results. By the time he performed it on the king (18 November 1686) he was quite familiar with it. The king endured it with exemplary courage, after which the operation became very fashionable, and many people suffering minor ailments asked to have it performed on them. It was the subject of a special publication: *Récit de la Grande Opération du Roi Louis XIV* by M.-A. le Roi. See also J. B. Wolf (1970), pp. 438 ff. It is notable that the official opening of the quarrel was itself an archeological—or at least a philological—reconstruction of an ancient procedure. The fact that the procedure was a medical one only adds emphasis to the occasion.

24. Charles Perrault reprinted the whole poem at the end of the first volume of his *Parallèle* (1688; 1964, pp. 165 ff.).
    A rough translation (preserving the rhymes) would run as follows:

> Beautiful Antiquity was always revered
> But I never believed she should be adored.
> The ancients I behold without bending my knee
> They were great, it is true—but men such as we;
> And I can, without any fear of seeming unjust
> Compare the age of Louis to that of Octavius the August.

25. The venerable bishop of Avranches tried to calm Boileau in vain; Racine adopted a tone of ironic compliment. See Perrault himself (1909), pp. 135 f. See M. Soriano (1972), pp. 211 f.

26. Bernard le Bovier de Fontenelle (1955).

27. *The Works of Jonathan Swift*, 1758, I, p. 149.

28. Charles Perrault (1688) pp. 254 f.

29. A. Adam (1962), pp. 77 ff.; J. B. Bury (1932), pp. 83 ff.; E. Cassirer (1951), p. 301.

30. Charles Perrault (1688), I. pp. 98 f.

31. Charles Perrault (1909), p. 40. Cf. M. Soriano (1972), pp. 132 ff.

32. L. Hautecoeur (1943), II, 1; pp. 187 ff., 270 ff.

33. Charles Perrault (1909), p. 40.

34. L. Hautecoeur (1943), II, 1, p. 273 ff; B. Teyssèdre (1967), p. 62 ff. See however Albert Laprade (1960), p. 129 ff.

35. Charles Perrault (1909), p. 40 f.

36. Charles Perrault (1909), pp. 46 ff. Benedetti had attempted to induce Bernini to come to Paris for Mazarin, first to work on the cardinal's palace, then on the Château of Vincennes (E. Dilke, 1888, p. 57). Benedetti also acted as the agent of the French crown in Rome at the time of the founding of the academy (H. Lapauze, 1924, vol. I, pp. 19, 73).

37. F. Baldinucci (1948), pp. 48 ff.

38. See chapter 1.

39. Bernini's studio was one of the main curiosities of Paris that year. C. Wren, like many other foreigners, called on him: see chapter 6.

40. L. Hautecoeur (1943), II, 1, p. 441 ff.

41. Charles Perrault (1909), p. 80. Cf. however, A. Laprade (1960) passim; the whole book is in fact devoted to the rescuing of the facade for d'Orbay with the passion of a contemporary. There is a clear, if somewhat sceptical examination of Laprade's detailed argument by M. Soriano (1972), pp. 146 ff. Boileau, too, joined in the dispute on d'Orbay's side in his *Neuf Réflexions Critiques* on Longinus (N. Boileau, 1729, III, pp. 178 ff.), although he only cited him as witness to Le Vau's authorship. But then his witness was anything but disinterested.

42.   "De méchant médecin devient bon architecte
             Son example est pour nous un précepte excellent.
             Soyez plutôt maçon, si c'est votre talent."

Art Poétique, IV, 24 ff. (N. Boileau, 1729, II, p. 86). Boileau unrepentantly maintained that his lampooning of Claude Perrault was a "modest revenge for all the slurs that he put about on me" (1729, III, p. 176), and in mock repentance, epigrammatizes: "vous êtes, je l'avoue, ignorant médecin mais non pas habile architecte." The connections between the two families are so complex that even an expert at untying such knots (M. Soriano, 1972, passim) finds them too much for him. It is probable, at any rate, that Perrault was involved as a consultant in the operation (for stones in the bladder?) which may have left Boileau either incontinent or impotent (M. Soriano, 1972, pp. 260 ff.). At any rate, much of volume 3 of the 1729 edition of Boileau's works is devoted to his acrimonious and sometimes petty exchanges with Perrault. It also includes the letter with which the great Arnauld, from his Belgian exile, makes peace between his two cross followers (IV, pp. 126 ff.) in May 1694; Arnauld found that Perrault had exceeded the bounds of reason and decency. For Perrault's reaction, see M. Soriano (1972), pp. 267 ff.; but see also A. Hallays (1926), pp. 15 f., 129 ff. To be fair to Perrault, Arnauld was prejudiced in Boileau's favor: see H. Brémond (1923–1926), vol. IV, pp. 306, 473.

43. Published in 1671 (with illustrations by Sebastien Le Clerc, who was also to do the Vitruvius and the *Ordonnance*. On Le Clerc as an engraver, see F. Courboin (1923), II, pp. 3 ff. A useful summary of Perrault's scientific career is given by J. Lévy-Valensi (1933), pp. 521 ff.

44. *Comptes des Bâtiments* (1881), I, p. 281. "Pour une traduction de Vitruve," says the entry; it has always been assumed that it was Perrault's. Cf. A. Laprade (1960).

45. Claude Perrault (1683), p. iii. Perrault simplified the uniformity of musical theory for his polemical purposes. He seems deliberately to ignore the vast discussion between the followers of "ancient" music and the innovators, such as Zarlino, a discussion which had been enthusiastically followed in France. On the problem of irrational proportions, which was raised in this discussion (notably of $1:\sqrt{2}$, recommended by many architectural treatises including that of Vitruvius) he says nothing; and even leaves Vitruvius' mention of it (VI,4) without comment.

46. A. Desgodetz (1683). He may have seen the plates before the book was issued: Claude Perrault (1683), p. xxvii.

47. Claude Perrault (1683).

48. "De la Musique des Anciens," in *Œuvres Diverses de Physique et de Mécanique de MM. Claude et Pierre Perrault* (1721), pp. 295–321, II, esp. pp. 301 ff. Perrault remarks also on the parallel between some remarks of Cassiodorus and the description of Iroquois Indian music (p. 304) and has an aside on Chinese lacquer panels "où ils usent d'une propreté et d'une justesse presqu'inimitable mais où il n'y a ni dessein, ni proportion, ni esprit" (p. 315). Cf. Charles Perrault (1688) IV, p. 260 ff.

49. R. Lenoble (1943) pp. 482 f.

50. R. Lenoble (1943) pp. 338 f., 528 f. See M. Mersenne (1634), pp. 267 ff., A. Pirro (1907), pp. 99 ff., on Mersenne's discussion of this problem with Descartes.

51. R. Descartes (1953), p. 925, letter to Mersenne dated 18 March 1630. On the importance of this passage see W. Tatarkiewicz (1976) III, pp. 361 f. And yet in April 1634 he writes to Mersenne again about this problem, quoting the parallel of musical and architectural proportion, setting aside the quibbles about minor variations. To Huygens he recommended the construction of a clavichord whose strings would be divided into the extraordinarily large number of 3,600 fractions! Mersenne also adopted this division. See A. Pirro (1907), pp. 12 ff.

52. Mersenne (1634), pp. 14 ff.

53. This association as a basis for taking pleasure was already implied strongly in the very early musical compendium (paragraph 4), though the scale of measure between the object and the senses, which perceive, is also postulated as a condition in the next section. Both in the *Principes* (1953), pp. 658 f., and in the *Passions de l'Ame*, pp. 735 ff., Descartes returns to the problem of the relation between sight, which he describes as infinitely more subtle than hearing in the *Principes*, and the most important in affecting our attitudes in the *Passions*; yet without relating these matters systematically.

54. Claude Perrault (1683), p. iv.

55. As in fortifications, for instance; Claude Perrault (1683), p. xv.

56. Perrault also argued by induction from his own anatomical researches. The ear, Ouvrard (1677, p. 8) had argued was a subtler organ than the eye and could therefore communicate exact consonances to the brain; in this assumption Blondel followed him. But Perrault, writing as an anatomist could state the exact opposite of the received opinion with complete assur-

ance. The ear is the coarser of the two organs, and that fact is exactly what gives the perception of sound its abstraction, whereas the eye is much more complex—and therefore presumably the better instrument for registering. Yet precisely because of this complexity, the eye can communicate knowledge, and knowledge, being learned, is unlike in its effect to the operation of common sense.

The anatomical distinction gives force to an older debate in French thinking about art, on the distinction between *bon sens* and *jugement:* but on this, see R. Bray (1927), pp. 114 f., 127 ff.

57. Claude Perrault (1683), p. vi.

58. Claude Perrault (1683), p. viii.

59. Claude Perrault (1683), p. x.

60. Claude Perrault (1683), introductory dedication.

61. Claude Perrault (1683), p. xi. At least one curious provincial building, the church of St. Martin-es-Vignes at Troyes, seems an almost literal application of Perrault's theory: the plain lower story representing positive beauty, the upper story, which consists of an octastyle Corinthian portico, linked to the lower walls by the conventional volutes (though they were never executed, since funds ran out). It was the work of a learned local cleric, a Canon Maillet, who is otherwise unknown and is the frontispiece to an existing Gothic church. (L. Hautecoeur, 1948, vol. II, pp. 718, 733). It seems to have been begun soon after 1680. See p. 37.

62. Claude Perrault (1683), p. xii.

63. Claude Perrault (1683), pp. 3 ff. Taste, or rather what is good taste and how it may be formed, was a problem which occupied many critics and philosophers as well as artists. The Royal Academy of Architecture discussed it (soon after its official opening session) on 7 and 14 January 1672; and returned to the subject on 8 August 1681 (*P.V.* I, pp. 3 ff; the subject was raised by Blondel; the later session was in the presence of Colbert and was rather solemn. The terms were, that later time, borrowed entirely from Perrault: *P.V.,* I, p. 321). It became one of the more frequent topics of the Academy's discussion, and went on reappearing in the minutes until its demise (see below). On the role of taste in Perrault's theory, see, variously, W. Herrmann (1973), pp. 63 ff., and W. Kambartel (1972), pp. 79 ff. Perrault had addressed himself to a problem which had concerned French criticism for over a generation: the problem of reconciling rules of art with variety of taste. The notion that taste can differ according to country and climate was first set out by Antoine Godeau (one of the group who called themselves *Illustres Bergers;* R. Bray (1927), pp. 173 ff.). It was very much accentuated by the extension of the public for the arts, an extension which many of the "ancients" resented. They wrote for the *honnêtes gens,* who appreciated by using their judgment, formed not by their *esprit,* but by its familiarity with the rules. That is how, in fact, D. Bouhours (1709), p. 290, defined good taste: a harmony or accord between *esprit* (here in the sense of *wit*) and reason.

64. Claude Perrault (1683), p. xxvi.

65. Claude Perrault (1683), p. xvii. He means, of course, scholastic theologians.

66. The "common sense" is that which Descartes speaks of in the *Discourse on Method,* at the very beginning; he is in turn echoing Montaigne's remarks on the same subject ("On Presumption," book II, ch. 17.)

67. Claude Perrault (1683), p. xiv.

68. Philippe Grandjean de Fauchy, a gentleman from the Mâconnais, was the first royal punch-cutter ever to be appointed.

69. A. Bérard (1868), p. 78 ff.; A. Christian (1905), p. 273 ff. Stanley Morison (1963), p. 28 ff.

70. Geofroy Tory (1526).

71. L'Académie Royale des Inscriptions et Médailles. *Médailles sur les Principaux Evènements du Règne de Louis le Grand, avec des Explications Historiques*, 1702. Cf. D. B. Updike (1937), I, p. 241 ff.

72. S. Morison (1968), p. 28 ff., 39 ff. A. Hutt (1972), pp. 5 ff., 28, 44 ff. Fournier was to become the typographical expert of the *Encyclopédie* much as J. -F. Blondel was its architect; see chapter 10.

73. Claude Perrault (1684), p. i. See also W. Herrmann (1972), pp. 31 ff.

74. Charles Perrault takes a dutiful attitude to Descartes in his *Hommes Illustres*, 1696, but a more critical one in the *Parallèle*, 1688, I, p. 47 f.; IV, pp. 166 ff., 220 ff. He was inevitably an eclectic and seems to owe something to Gassendi of whom he speaks familiarly in the *Parallèle*, II, p. 60. See A. Perez-Gomez (1977), pp. 15 ff.

75. A. Adam (1964), p. 22 ff. Cf. W. Tatarkiewicz (1967), p. 481 ff.

76. Remark reported in a letter of J. -J. Rousseau. Cf. W. Tartarkiewicz (1967), p. 419.

77. Charles Perrault (1909), p. 12 ff.

78. Pensée xxxviii in *Œuvres* (1963), p. 582.

79. "Traité de Morale," in N. Malebranche (1962-), XI, pp. 135 ff.

80. Letter 6, quoted in W. Tatarkiewicz (1974), III, pp. 363.

81. He certainly accepted Arnauld as his mentor: see note 2 of this chapter.

82. W. Tatarkiewicz (1967), p. 420 ff.; A. Adam (1948), II, p. 175 ff.

83. See E. B. O. Borgerhoff (1950), pp. 186 ff.

84. Bossuet, in his *Traité de la Connaissance de Dieu et de Soi-même* (E. B. O. Borgerhoff, 1950, p. 198) is a usefully central point of reference. A somewhat different account of this problem is given by W. Herrmann (1973), pp. 64 ff.

85. E. Tesauro (1655), pp. 164, 146.

86. V. Galilei (1581), p. 135 ff.

87. Charles Perrault (1688), IV, p. 274 ff. In his commentary on Vitruvius V, 4 (1684, pp. 158 ff.), Claude also comments on the return of taste to homophony and on the similarity between ancient diatonic and modern 'just' tempering.

3

The Marvelous and the Distant

In 1670 there appeared, as if by magic, the first building of a new kind in Europe—a palace in the Chinese style. Louis XIV had bought (the limits to his gardening irked him) the little village of Trianon, to the northwest of his palace at Versailles. He had it razed and, with a speed which amazed his contemporaries, built over it a group of pavilions: a long one (divided into five bays) in the middle, and two squarish ones of different sizes on each side. The building was to serve for banquets: the center pavilion was a salon, the two larger side ones were for preparing soups on one side, for the buffet and fruit on the other; the two smaller ones for jams and entremets. Since it was all pulled down in 1687 when Louis XIV found it too small even for intimate parties, it is known only from drawings, engravings, and contemporary descriptions. If you look at the engravings, however, the Pavillon de Porcelaine will not seem Chinese at all. The whole building is single story but crowned with a high mansard roof; the corners have standard rusticated quoins, and there are pediments over the center three bays of the main pavilion; the pediment on the entrance front is supported by four Roman Doric pilasters.

What impressed contemporaries as "Chinese" was the decoration: the court and the exterior are paved and faced—as is the interior—in blue and white, and occasionally willow-pattern tiles. Where the tiles stop there were paintings in faience coloring: blue-and-white with some yellow and violet, and everywhere large quantities of mirror. The roof, apparently the most "Chinese" feature, is elaborately decked out with earthenware, glazed flowerpots and large birds; again the coloring is repeated. In the gardens there were orange trees, Indian chestnuts, and a flower garden of tulips and carnations, flowers which were still thought of as eastern, exotic.[1]

To contemporaries, this Oriental fantasy seemed to contain something of the miraculous. The enviably fecund novelist, the Comte de Préchac, celebrated it in a fairy tale, *Sans-Paragon et la Reine Fée*. The hero of the story (a thinly veiled allegory of Louis XIV) takes a Chinese princess on a water promenade of his palace gardens, Versailles, presumably. The princess is not impressed with its splendors, since as she says, her father, the emperor, preferred simple, proper houses to the most splendid palaces. Whereupon the hero, to finish the promenade, leaps out of the boat, strikes the ground thrice with his magic wand and lo! There is a porcelain palace, all shiny, its parterres flowering with jasmine.[2]

Whether Préchac composed it at the time or later (it was not published until 1698), he was mindful of the vanished exoticism. There is no doubt that the appearance of the Trianon was intended to inspire marvel: "Everybody thought of this palace as an enchantment, as it had only been begun at the end of winter, and was discovered ready in the spring, as if it had sprung from the ground with the flowers of its garden."[3]

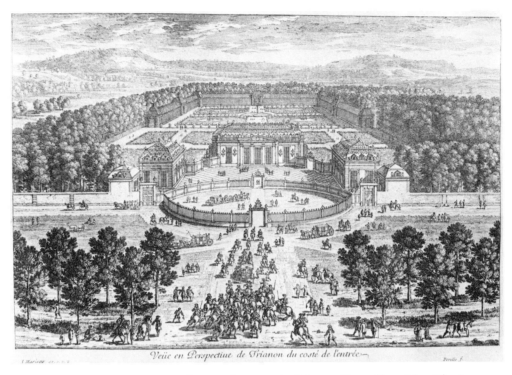

The main entry into the Pavillon de Porcelaine at the Trianon, Versailles. After Pérelle.

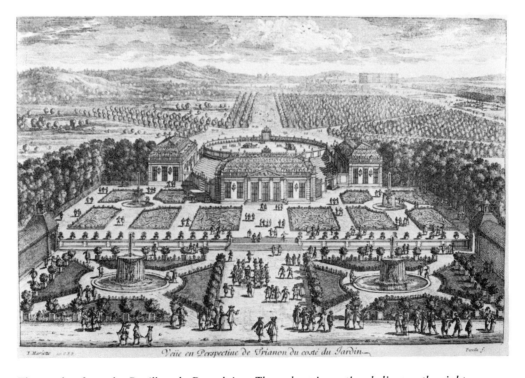

The garden from the Pavillon de Porcelaine. The palace is on the skyline on the right.

The Trianon was sited symmetrically with another exotic and therefore "marvelous" part of the gardens, the *ménagerie* of exotic animals[4] (in which, as I have already pointed out, Claude Perrault performed his lugubrious business of dissection). The marvelous was a genre well known to critics, not just a spontaneous and unqualified ejaculation: Aristotle had recommended the use of the superhuman and marvelous in tragedy—the *deus ex machina*[5]—and the literary teachers of the seventeenth century adopted an interpretation of this adage and subdivided it into classes, which they did with most things. The marvelous could be pagan (as the appearance of gods in the action of a play) or Christian (the appearance of angels or the intervention of vision and miracles in the life of saints) or simply magical. Ariosto was often blamed for overdoing this device;[6] but it was allowed by Christian epic writers—such as Saint-Sorlin—to relieve the monotonously elevated style of the action.

Thus the high tone of Versailles was relieved by the marvels of the Ménagerie and the porcelain Trianon, although this last little resembled its model: the porcelain pagoda of Nanking.

Whether conceived by Mme. de Montespan or the king himself, the dying Le Vau from whom it was commissioned, or François d'Orbay who certainly built it, the Trianon appeared at the height of the Oriental frenzy in France.[7] Even Molière's poor M. Jourdain appeared to his music and fencing teacher in an Indian cotton robe and dreamed of marrying his daughter to a Turkish prince. The counterfeit prince talked joke Turkish, which was in fact Venetian dialect.[8] But people only a little better informed than M. Jourdain would probably not have been taken in. Turkish manners and Turk-

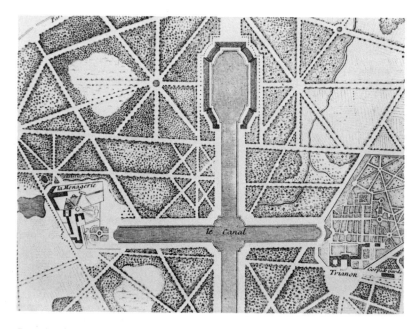

Detail of the plan of the palace gardens at Versailles, showing the Ménagerie and the Trianon on either side of the Canal. After Mariette.

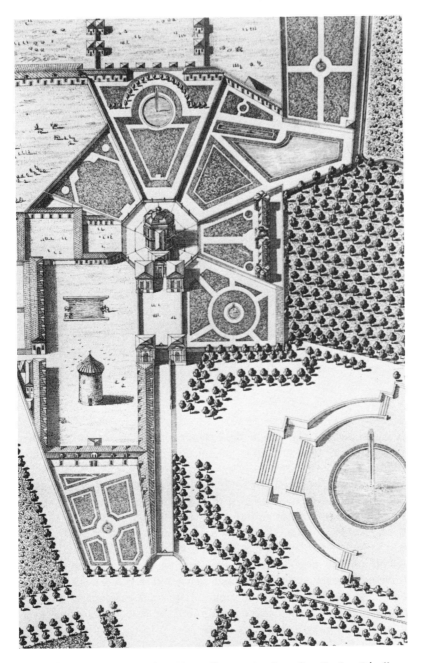

The Ménagerie in the park at Versailles: projection. Detail after Pérelle.

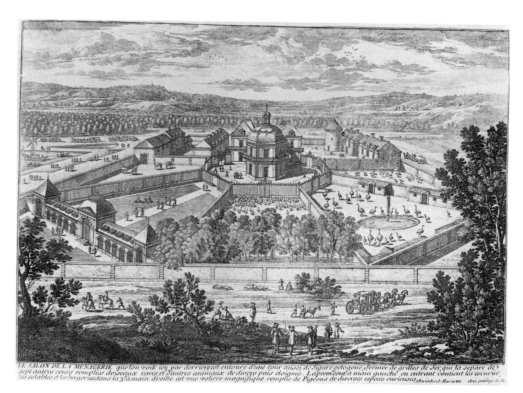

A view of the Ménagerie at Versailles. After Pérelle.

ish customs were known at the French court, and among the richer merchants. France had always kept up relations with Turkey, and the ambassador to the Sublime Porte was equipped with an orchestra and with a staff of scholars. Antoine Galland, who was to become professor of Arabic at the Collège de France, went in the retinue of one of these ambassadors to conduct conversations with the high clergy of the Orthodox church about their faith; his mission was stimulated by a dispute between the great Arnauld and Pierre Nicole on one side, and a Calvinist minister on the other. Galland traveled all over the Middle East; he visited the Greek islands, Cyprus, and the Levant; he spent one Easter in Jerusalem, and on his return he saw Athens, where he admired the Parthenon before Venetian bombs blew it to pieces in 1687.[9]

Galland collected not only antique coins but also Oriental books and antiquities for Colbert at the behest of the French Indies company. But Colbert was not the first of such collectors. Mazarin had gathered some Persian and Turkish pieces; an English ecclesiastic, Archbishop Laud of Canterbury, had collected Raga miniatures.[10] But before the middle of the sixteenth century only a trickle of Oriental objects came into Europe. Silk had been imported since Roman times and had also been imitated. There were occasional pieces of porcelain or ivory: to be treated in the sixteenth century certainly, and even in the seventeenth, as a *lusus naturae* and set in a silver or gilt mount much as large nautilus shells or ostrich eggs had been mounted earlier. But in the seventeenth century Chinese and Japanese lacquer, boxes and decorative panels, came to be imported into Europe. These were not only bought for very high prices but also imitated and even forged, although porcelain continued to elude the forger.

Various half-successful efforts were made, mostly in Italy, to produce imitation porcelain.[11] Ultimately two alchemists, J. F. Böttger and E. W. von Tschirnhausen, were to find a way to make it, at the expense of the porcelain-crazy Augustus the Strong, king of Poland and elector of Saxony, who used to spend a large proportion of his revenues on having porcelain either made or imitated. The Meissen factory was set up in 1710 as a result of this discovery; and the discovery of china clay (kaolin) at Aue in the elector's Saxon territory led to the establishment of Meissen and Dresden as centers of china manufacture, which they have remained.[12]

Throughout the sixteenth century Chinese porcelain arrived in increasing quantities, through normal commercial deals or in the luggage of envoys. Ambassadors usually took scholars and draftsmen with them. But in the case of information about China, the missionaries proved more important, since they gained access to the inner life of the Chinese elite. St. Francis Xavier had died in Macao, still within a foreign enclave, in 1552. But Matteo Ricci, an Italian Jesuit, entered China, settled in Peking, and was recognized as the equivalent of a mandarin—a "graduate preacher"—soon after 1600. He and his successors in the Society of Jesus not only spoke and wrote Chinese but counted familiarity with the Confucian classics as part of their missionary training. In their wake came painters; the most distinguished of them was Giuseppe Castiglione S. J.,[13] known in China as Lang-Shih-Ning. He translated mannerist iconography into silk or paper paintings; but he also adapted Chinese themes into his hybrid style.[14]

There had been previous contacts—Marco Polo, of course, and waves of missionaries. One of them, John of Monte Corvino had even been appointed archbishop of Cambalus, or Pekin, in 1307. Earlier, Kublai had sent two Nestorian monks, Mongol-speaking Chinese perhaps, westward with an idea—which was certainly current in Europe at the time—of concluding an offensive anti-Muslim confederacy. And there had been many others, as there had been caravans which reached the Levant, if not Europe.[15] In the sixteenth century ships were bigger and better built; European traders were more aggressive and expansionist, and their discoveries, as well as those of the missionaries who often preceded them, were widely publicized.

It is hardly surprising therefore that the ever-curious Charles Perrault should have informed himself about Chinese characters: at any rate he had the notion that each character corresponded to a word—which it does for typesetting and punch-cutting purposes—although he only used this particular to show the superiority of the Latin alphabet.[16] Elsewhere in the same book, the fourth volume of the *Parallèle* again, returning to the business of perfect or absolute and arbitrary beauty, he argues for the equality of various national *tastes* in music. Colbert, he says further, who was interested in the national "styles" of music and dance (not the parodies you might find in Molière) had suggested that if the Louvre were ever finished (it was not finished when Perrault wrote this, and Colbert had in the meanwhile died), its interiors should not be restricted to the French style—some apartments or suites might be in the Italian, Spanish, German, even Turkish, Persian, Mongol, and Chinese styles—and that should extend not only to the ornament but also to furniture, as well as to the *commodités* of those distant countries, so that visiting foreigners might be delighted to find themselves, as it were, in their own country; furthermore—and this was perhaps a weightier reason for both Colbert and for Perrault—one might find the whole magnificence of the world enclosed in one building.[17]

Analogous arguments moved, or seemed to move, collectors who assembled stuffed mermaids, fossils and exotic works of art, old masters, drawings, and *lusus naturae*. The "possession" of a world picture and the provision of points of extreme reference were always operative motives. But in the seventeenth-century metropolitan cities the motive was sharpened. The visiting merchant, the returning expatriate, and the novelty-seeking local, all were avid for the new tastes and sensations. How else can one explain the unprecedented spread of new beverages over the western world? Coffee, tea, and chocolate were virtually unknown in the Mediterranean and in northern Europe in 1600; by 1700 they were a common merchandise.[18] Moreover shops providing these two commodities had become new social institutions. The spread of the coffeehouse was particularly rapid. The first known coffee shop is to be found in Mecca at the end of the fifteenth century; in Cairo there was one in 1592, and in Venice about 1640, while Marseilles had one fourteen years later. There was one in Paris by 1680, and a brave soldier who was given the Turkish army's stock after the siege of 1683 was lifted opened the first café in Vienna.

Coffee and tea went on being imported; although people did think of planting them. In 1709 Antoine Galland, whom I mentioned in another context, heard of a coffee plant in Paris which had produced berries. In 1714 Louis XIV was given a coffee tree by the Dutch Estates and had it planted at Marly.[19] But the plant needed a hotter climate and a different soil: it remained, like tea and chocolate, an exotic and an imperial import.

Antoine Galland had himself written a short monograph on coffee, as a commentary on an Arabic manuscript in the royal library.[20] But, of course, Galland is remembered not for such bits of erudition, innumerable though they were, but for his translation of the *Thousand and One Nights,* the first into a European language. Galland had come across the story of Sindbad sometime in the late 1680s or in the 1690s and had translated it; he then realized that it was part of a much larger collection of tales and procured a manuscript from the Levant. The twelve volumes of his translation appeared between 1704 and 1714. He catered to a taste which was already well established. It had grown from the medieval custom of regarding exotica as quasi-natural objects, to be mounted in precious metals, like ostrich eggs or shells, to invade whole walls of rooms, and brought with it a curiosity about the way of life the objects implied: the conflict between the Empire and Turkey, which culminated in the Siege of Vienna in 1683. The lifting of the siege flooded Vienna with exportable orientalia, of which coffee had been a part. Their integration into the European way of life meant more than a passing fashion: it was part of a major and rapid change, paralleled by the domestication of the marvelous.

La Fontaine had raised the fable to a literary genre; although he depended on Aesop and the other ancient fabulists, like them he adopted a definite moral tone, quite different from that of the fairy tales. Both the literary fabulists and the tellers of fairy tales relied on speaking and acting animals, even animate objects, as heroes; but it is one thing to tell a story in which a frog allegorically represents a vice and quite another to have it turning into a Prince Charming. This second kind of tale, which goes back to an immemorial spoken tradition almost everywhere in the world, became highly fashionable as a literary form in the late 1680s; the fashion was quite spent by the beginning of the new century, but it remained part of a written literature for children from that time onwards.

The fashion had been started by Mme. d'Aulnoy and by Charles Perrault. In 1691 "Patiente Griselde" had appeared anonymously in the *Receuil de l'Académie*, and the succeeding years brought a crop of the tales, which were collected as *Histoires du Temps Passé* (Old-time Stories) in 1697. At first anonymous, their authorship was none the less widely known. They had an enormous public success and brought on Perrault the renewed fury of the "ancients."[21]

The fairy tales had a double interest: they recalled a different antiquity, one which was national and French; they did not rely therefore on ancient precept and had no need of the academic rules and categories to which even the *Contes* of La Fontaine seemed subject; being a free genre they allowed the fancy an apparently unlimited range. At the court of Louis XIV they were a wonderfully cathartic diversion, as later the false simplicities, the games of shepherds and shepherdesses, would attract the dangerously artificial court of Louis XVI. The witches and goblins, the farmyard cruelties, and the enchantments were in a sense the progeny of the burlesque epic. Like the coffee trees of Marly, like the calicos of the *Bourgeois Gentilhomme*, this was an attempt to domesticate the *merveilleux;* an attempt that has its curious reflection in the many accounts of imaginary travels—such as Gulliver's—which became very popular about the same time.

The rooms in the styles of different nations were a proposal of the 1690s. The Pavillon de Porcelaine had been done twenty years earlier. But from the time of the Trianon, Chinese rooms and other exotic interiors proliferated. Chinese rooms in particular became *de rigueur* in all European palaces. At a time when all European princes aspired to their own Versailles from which to contemplate a wholly domesticated, tame nature and in which they would be able to pass from room to room admiring their own achievements and the extent of their domains as no one perhaps had been able to since Hadrian in his villa at Tivoli, exotic rooms were incorporated into the plans of palaces or Oriental pavilions built in gardens.

Daniel Marot, one of the French Protestant architects who had left France for Holland after the revocation of the Edict of Nantes, engraved such a room in his pattern-book *Nouvelles Cheminées*[22] and may well have been responsible for the Chinese rooms, composed like the Trianon de Porcelaine of blue-and-white tiles and jars massed into elaborate compositions. Having worked first for the Prince of Orange in Holland, he moved with him to Britain for a short while when the Prince became William III and arranged something after the same manner at Hampton Court.

Such rooms became quickly popular all over Europe: J. F. Eosander von Goethe arranged a large mirror-and-porcelain one at Charlottenburg about 1705; another, similar arrangement was made at Pommersfelden in 1713. Although the demands for authenticity became increasingly stringent, the combination of mirror and *chinoiserie,* of reflection, shimmer, glint seemed irresistible. Mirror, particularly, still retained some of its magic character.[23] Fire-making mirrors, distorting mirrors (called *sorcières* in French) were thought of as remarkable curios. Although the manufacture of plate glass, and therefore of large mirror panels, became increasingly easy and cheap in the second half of the seventeenth century (and was, of course, promoted in France by Colbert), yet the mirror was a marvelous object, and the association of mirror and *chinoiserie* has almost something "natural" about it. The *Spiegelkabinett* of mirror and porcelain retained its popularity, as at Würzburg or Schönbrunn, and even Capodimonte lacquer seems, from the outset, to have required a closer attention to the features of Chinese style. In spite of Perrault's strictures,[24] quoted earlier, it was very popular. Again German, French, and Italian palaces have lacquer rooms: Ludwigsburg in Württemberg (1714–1722), Juvarra's splendid one at the Turin Regia (1734), or the Chinese rooms at the Bayreuth Hermitage (1750)—all these having a more determinedly Chinese character than the more flippant *Spiegelkabinette.*

But the stylistic proliferation was soon tried outside the house—in garden buildings; these exoticisms became even more common than the rooms in different styles had been earlier. The famous ones were built at Sans-Souci (1745–1747) and at Drottningholm (1753–1769), both perhaps like the Trianon de Porcelaine, conceived if not designed by kings, and later the Favorita at Palermo (1799) or the Brighton Pavilion (Moorish on the outside, though the original scheme of 1803 was in the Chinese style, as much of the interior remained) or yet the Swedish-British Pagoda (1763) in Kew Gardens. This remains the most accurately Chinese of all these follies. I will have occasion to discuss it further on, in the context of the Chinese garden (or the *jardin anglo-chinois*) in which so many of such buildings were sited).[25]

Villa Palagonia, Bagheria near Palermo, by Tomaso Napoli and Agatino Daidone, after 1715: the mirror salon, done after 1750, which is reputed also to have had a mirror paving.

Villa Palagonia, detail of the mirror ceiling of the salon. The silvering of the mirrors has entirely tarnished.

Chinese porcelain room, Royal Palace at Portici, now in the Capodimonte Museum, Naples. Foto Alinari.

Charles Perrault had proposed not just Chinese but also Arab, Turkish, Venetian, and other national rooms, and the custom of working in different national "styles" grew increasingly common throughout the eighteenth century. Indeed, Chinese-style furniture, sometimes even incorporating panels of genuine Chinese or Japanese lacquer, became a common pattern of display furniture, Chinese Chippendale being almost a decorative "style" in its own right. Elaborate marquetry pieces, using ivory on figured woods, had been imported from Western India by Portuguese travelers; Goa became a center for an Indian-Portuguese autonomous ornamental school. Later ivory-veneered furniture became popular in Europe, although on a smaller scale and at higher prices than lacquer. European counterfeits of Oriental styles began to appear in the 1650s, and soon a native European manufactured lacquer appeared. Its prime document, the *Treatise of Japanning and Varnishing* by John Stalker and George Parker was published in Oxford in 1688. The East India Company sent European craftsmen and pattern-books out to India to induce workmen there (lacquer was thought to come from India)[26] to produce work suitable for the European market, but these efforts were not very successful. Although porcelain was later to be made in China which incorporated Western heraldic designs—and made to order—as far as lacquer was concerned, the European market could absorb as much of it as ever was exported from the Far East, however alien the designs.[27]

By the middle of the century, there was no sizable European house which did not have its Chinese room, either of wallpaper or lacquer panels, its tiles and Ming porcelain vases. Chinese festivals, Chinese theatrical extravaganzas, and fancy-dress costumes gave the fashion its continuing currency. Moreover, ever more precise and reliable reports, many of them illustrated, were coming out of China.

One of the last Ming princes to claim the throne was baptized Constantine by a Jesuit missionary:[28] nevertheless, the Manchu emperors continued to patronize the Jesuits. A German, Adam Schall von Bell, was appointed president of the Board of Mathematics; the K'ang Hsi emperor continued to use the Jesuits as diplomats, medical advisors, and astronomers. In 1692 Christianity was officially declared one of the state cults, but by this time, the French members of the Society of Jesus had taken an increasing interest in the Chinese mission, and most of the Jesuit Chinese publications were in French.[29]

European nations continued, however, to court the Chinese government in the hope of obtaining trading privileges. On the whole they did rather worse than the missionaries: they would be allowed into the outer courtyard of the imperial palace at Peking, they would kowtow to the empty throne over the gate and then would be led away. They were, however, usually entertained on their way sumptuously at government expense. Sometimes they would carry with them draftsmen or even scholars; the most important of these was Jan Nieuhoff, steward—as he called himself—of the embassy of the Dutch East India Company to Peking. His book, the first authoritative illustrated work on China, appeared in Dutch and Latin in Amsterdam in 1665,[30] and in English in 1669,[31] with—as an appendix—a précis of Athanasius Kircher's *China Monumentis*.[32]

Nieuhoff's book as well as Kircher's were known to any European interested in China; they were certainly published in time to inspire the *Trianon de Porcelaine*.[33] Builders and architects, who knew Chinese architecture only through them, may well have thought that the buildings which they were raising were in the Chinese style, even if they appear to us as remote from it as the Trianon. In any case Nieuhoff's engraver (and Hollar who reengraved the plates for the English edition) was not always faithful to Nieuhoff's drawings and descriptions, and these in turn presented

The Porcelain Pagoda at Nanking. After J. Nieuhoff.

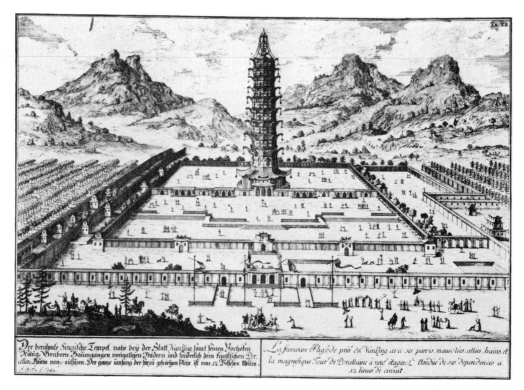

The Porcelain Pagoda at Nanking, Fischer von Erlach's interpretation of Nieuhoff's image and text.

Chinese objects through European eyes. For all that, Nieuhoff's illustrations are definitely more "authentic," more precise than Kircher's, who, in any case, was only marginally concerned with architecture.

Kircher presumably received a copy of Nieuhoff's book, and certainly there would have been one in the Collegio Romano, where Kircher had been professor of mathematics and where he still resided, collecting, magpie fashion, antiquities of all kinds: broken Greek and Etruscan pots, Mexican featherwork, Chinese silks and jades—the Museum Kircherianum was to become the nucleus of the modern Roman Museum of Prehistory and of Ethnology. The Collegio Romano, together with the Congregation for the Propagation of the Faith, must have possessed the finest libraries and collection of Sinica in Europe, and Kircher certainly had access to both. He would have used it in compiling his *Oedipus Aegyptiacus*, a treatise on a universal symbol-language and on the Egyptian and satanic origin of all idolatory, showing parallels between Egyptian, Indian, Chinese and Mexican religions.[34] Kircher also wrote on magnetism, on harmony and dissonance, on the Tower of Babel and many other subjects. He was one of the most extraordinary polymaths of his day. In the informal academy which gathered round the exiled and eccentric Queen Christina of Sweden, he was perhaps the most brilliant. Another distinguished member of the circle was the antiquarian Giovanni Pietro Bellori, who was the Queen's librarian and numismatist, as well as a most influential art critic.[35] Bellori was very much a partisan of antiquity against the "moderns," if these terms may be referred back from the French dispute to the Italian scheme. He was, as is known from a number of sources,[36] very influential on a young German sculptor in bronze and medallist who, in spite of his attachment to Bellori, seems to have worked a little in Bernini's studio in the early 1680s and was introduced to a range of objects and ideas which must have seemed quite astonishing to a young arrival from Vienna.

Johann Bernard Fischer, this young sculptor, is better known by his title acquired much later: J. B. Fischer von Erlach. He had gained a reputation in Rome, and had worked for the viceroy of Naples, for whom he cast a couple of medals of Charles II of Spain. It may well be that these medals brought him the notice of the Austrian court. At any rate he was already a "famous virtuoso" in 1688, when he had barely returned from his Italian apprenticeship.[37] He had been there sixteen years, it seems, and was thirty-two years old. His rise was then meteoric. Tutor in architecture to the king of Hungary (1689), architect for the Imperial Triumph of Joseph II (1690), in 1690 he completed the first project for the imperial palace on the hills of Schönbrunn, a series of town palaces and country houses, another project for Schönbrunn, churches in Vienna and Salzburg and added to his fame the title of nobility and academic honors.

In spite of a wretched private life and an obsessional fear of rivals, Fischer von Erlach was the most successful architect in German lands of his day, the best-known German architect since Elias Holl nearly two centuries earlier. This highly successful practitioner meditated for many years—he seems to have started about 1705—a large book which would be a new kind of treatise on architecture.

The book appeared finally in 1721, a few years before his death, with an elaborately engraved French and German text,[38] as Italian was no longer considered useful or suitable for this purpose. It was reprinted several times, twice with an English translation.[39] It dispensed with the usual section dealing with the orders of architecture: this was a spectacular innovation, if a negative one. There were five books or chapters. The first gave an account of the seven wonders of the world. The idea of the seven wonders had been current since antiquity, and although the number was sometimes altered and the individual "wonders" were not always the same, they had provided a trope since medieval times, when various attempts to "visualize" them were made; the most elaborate iconography had been developed by the Flemish artist Martin van Heemskerck, famous for his sensitive and loving drawings of Rome at the end of the sixteenth century.[40]

Fischer prefaced these seven wonders with the eighth, the wonder of wonders among human works, the temple in Jerusalem, as it had been restored by J. B. Villalpanda, a restoration which I mentioned earlier.[41] He is not deterred by French scepticism about this restoration,[42] and in fact does not take his restoration from Villalpanda's book directly but mediated by the work of two German *trattatisti*, the mathematician Nicolaus Goldmann and his disciple, the architect Christoph Leonhard Sturm, who published an architectural treatise based on his master's work;[43] its fifth part was a meditation on mathematical proportion as revealed in the Villalpandian reconstruction of the temple.[44]

Fischer's seven wonders are the Hanging Gardens of Babylon, the Pyramids, the temple of Zeus at Olympia, the Mausoleum at Halicarnassus, the temple of Diana at Ephesus, the Colossus of Rhodes, and the Pharos at Alexandria; beyond the "classic" seven he also included restoration to the temple at Nineveh and some very fanciful variant pyramids, the Persian Tombs, the Parthenon, the Transformation of Mount Athos into a gigantic statue, which is also a city (derived from *Vitruvius*, preface to book II), the Cretan labyrinth and further assorted Greek and Egyptian antiquities.[45] The second book, called *Of Lesser-Known Roman Buildings*, includes both buildings known from ruins, such as the Aqueduct of Carthage or Diocletian's baths and his palace at Split, and some known from literary sources only: the Golden House of Nero or the Naumachia of Domitian. This book, strangely, includes Stonehenge, which Fischer copies from that book of Inigo Jones's which I mentioned earlier;[46] although following the antiquarian William Camden[47] he considers it a prehistoric tomb and not a Roman temple as Inigo Jones had done. He ends this section with the Borromeo Gardens on Isola Bella, which (he says) were based on unknown Roman works, although it is also clearly the model for Fischer's reconstruction of the Hanging Gardens of Babylon.

The third book is the extraordinary one. Titled *Of Some Arab and Turkish Buildings as Well as about Modern Persian, Siamese, Chinese, and Japanese Architecture,* it contains a number of engravings of baths and mosques, including a detailed one of St. Sophia; the buildings of Mecca and Medina; the great bridge at Isfahan; the palace at Bangkok; and a number of Chinese buildings after the engravings in Nieuhoff's relation: the Imperial Palace at Peking (The Forbidden City); the porcelain pagoda at Nanking, and a number of lesser Chinese examples; two suspension bridges, unfamiliar in Europe; and an artificial mountain for a picturesque Chinese garden,[48] several decades before the passion for the *jardin anglo-chinois* spread throughout Europe.

The fourth book—*Of the Author's Invention and Design*—is devoted to buildings and the fifth is *Vases, Both Ancient (Egyptian, Greek, and Roman) as Well as Modern, Together with Some Inventions by the Author.*

The layout of the book, as I have suggested, is quite without precedent. The treatment of Egypto-Babylono-Greek architecture as one category, and Roman building separately, so as to suggest a continuity of development is new: it continues into the third book which spans the whole of Asia. European medieval architecture, whether Gothic or Romanesque (or even Renaissance and

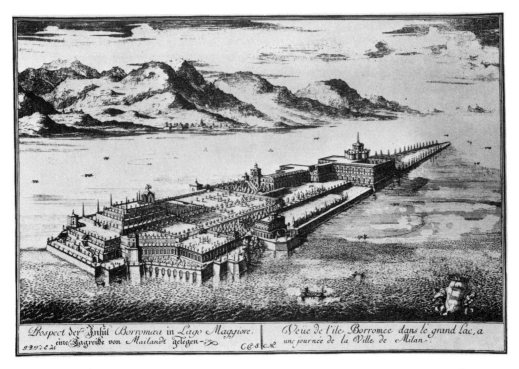

Aerial view of the Borromeo Gardens in the Lago Maggiore. After Fischer von Erlach.

An artificial Chinese garden rock. After Fischer von Erlach.

Mannerist—except for the Borromeo Isola Bella!) is excluded. Antiquity and the Far East are the exemplar, but they no longer appear as unified deposit which might be quarried for detail or precept without any care for their historical context.

The implications of Fischer's approach are best seen in a building which he reproduces as one of his grandest designs, and which was in fact built with minor—though telling—alterations by his son, Joseph Emmanuel, after his death. This church, the Karlskirche, as it is known in Vienna, although now surrounded by the buildings of the Ring, was originally sited in the open country. Nevertheless, it clearly had a frontispiece, a facade. This facade was an elaborate programatic exercise, whose elements are all shown in Fischer's *Entwurff*. It is eclectic in intention, and the assembly of elements is intended for reading as a sort of compositional, fugal counterbalance of heavily charged formal elements.

In the terms in which I propose to discuss it, it is clearly a baroque (i. e. "modern") building, dominated by an elliptical dome; the drum, punctuated by bays of double Corinthian columns which support swags the height of the drum attic, make an unmistakable reference to St. Peter's in Rome. This reference is carried on by the two side pavilions, whose arches, Corinthian pilasters (supporting an attic with a rectangular, framed window), and the composition of two figures supporting a central medallion, all deliberately echo the

Istanbul, St. Sophia. After Fischer von Erlach.

flanking elements of Maderna's facade. The organization of a central dome making a central pyramidal element were exploited in Mansart's church of the Minimes in Paris, and less evidently in buildings which Fischer of course knew, such as the Collège des Quatre Nations by Le Vau, or—less evidently—Santa Maria della Pace by Pietro da Cortona.

But the whole organization of the front with its long straight loggia terminated by pavilions at either end deliberately recalls the benediction loggia of St. Peter's. The resemblance would have been even more striking had Bernini's two proposed western towers been added to the front of St. Peter's.[49] But the central hexastyle portico and its attic curving is a deliberate and different allusion. St. Peter's does have a central temple-front element, but its pediment is carried on four columns, and these are three-quarters attached. Fischer uses this element with deliberately programatic effect, as an ''antique''

Church of St. Charles Borromeo (Karlskirche), Vienna, by Fischer von Erlach. Foto Electa.

reference. In a contemporary description, it is read as an allusion to the Roman temple of Jupiter and Peace, highly appropriate since the church celebrates the peace of Rastatt.[50] As the pavilions and the

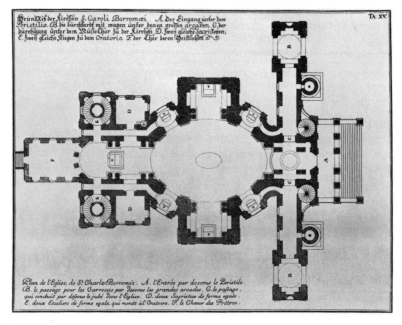

Church of St. Charles Borromeo (Karlskirche), Vienna, plan. After Fischer von Erlach.

Symbol of the Emperor Charles VI, from the dedication to Vermischte Nebenarbeiten, *by Carl Gustav Heraeus, Vienna, 1715.*

dome and the two spiral columns which flank it make a pyramid, so the portico plays a counterpoint to the pyramid.

The antique origin and reference of these elements is evident. The two spiral "historiated" columns of Trajan and of Marcus Aurelius in Rome had both been studied in great detail by one of Fischer's Roman mentors, Giovanni Pietro Bellori.[51] Trajan's forum, in the engraving which appears in the *Entwurff,* is dominated by his column. The two columns are therefore a clear reference to Rome, but they carry a further intention, for the second Rome, Constantinople, had a vast domed church, St. Sophia, preceded by a long narthex, whose minarets appeared on the facade, making (at any rate in the engraving which illustrated the *Entwurff*) a composition which this combination is certainly intended to recall. It is curious that the massing of spiral columns around an elliptical dome is intended as a deliberate reference to a mosque with minarets and that this has the intention of alluding to Rome: the first Rome of antiquity, and the second Rome of Constantine.[52] The composition of twin spiral columns and portico is an invocation of antiquity, that of the columns and dome of Constantine's Christian Rome and that of the side pavilions and dome in the plane behind it of Christian Rome, all referring to the idea that Charles VI's imperial Vienna is the third Rome. The system of allegorical references is carried further. The two columns are a representation of those columns of Hercules through which the fleets of Charles V, the current emperor's ancestor and model, sailed to find the new world and so overcame the old one. But they are also Charles VI's emblem and, as such, appear on his coins. Gustav Heraeus, Charles VI's Swedish antiquary and a friend of Fischer's, explains their meaning as a "not natural, but rather hieroglyphic" device which is "more a moral emblem"[53] for the two columns which signify bravery in war and constancy in peace. They therefore make yet another reference, at yet another level. For the two columns of the temple in Jerusalem were called Jachin and Boaz,[54] which is usually translated as "the firm one" and the "strong one" and which again refer to the two virtues of the emperor's moral emblem: Constance and Fortitude.

In the original program, as is known from the letters exchanged by Heraeus and his friend Gottfried Wilhelm Leibniz, the old philosopher was urging his Viennese friends to crown the two columns with statues of Charles the Great, Charles VI's predecessor in the imperial title, and Charles of Flanders, his predecessor in the heritage of Spain.[55] But the church was a votive one, not only for the peace of Rastatt but for the saving of Vienna from the plague of 1716. The two columns, therefore, carried round the spiral bands the *gesta* of Charles Borromeo (the emperor's patron) during his life and his miracles after his death. The tympanum was crowned with his apotheosis, which was repeated in fresco on the interior of the dome.

The facade is a clear declaration of intent: it is, as Hans Sedlmayr has called it, a *Schauseite*,[56] a display panel almost; but unlike the facade-proscenia of Rome, which often preface buildings apparently quite unrelated to them, it is part of a volumetric progression, as complex as the facade itself.

The pedestrian access is through the portico, and although there are carriage-entrances in the side pavilions, the processional entrance is also the pedestrian one. The volumetry of the interior is announced on the outside by a series of similar lanterns, which crown the main dome, the shallow dome over the sanctuary, the two columns (where the two programatic statues were to stand), and the two spiral staircases at the west end of the church, alluding again to the Jerusalem Temple, which was always known to include priest's dwelling and schools. This reiterates the claim of the Karlskirche to be the new "temple," and Charles VI to show himself a true successor of both Solomon and David (founders of the temple in Jerusalem), of Caesar and Augustus (the temple of Peace was actually founded by Vespasian but the generalized iconographic allusion is nevertheless clear), of Constantine (founder of St. Peter's and first Christian emperor), of Justinian (founder of St. Sophia, the Holy Wisdom in Constantinople whose exclamation "Solomon, I have outdone you" on entering his foundation was the ambition of Charles VI);[57] and this balance of references is achieved by a fugal arrangement of quotations from buildings of an unprecedented geographic and temporal range.

On entering the portico, the "antique" region of this building, the visitor was introduced into a vestibule, a domed space in the narthex. The circular lunette of the narthex is a preface to the vast elliptical "modern" dome of the main volume. Elliptical domes were not altogether a novelty: Michaelangelo had suggested an elliptical chamber in the first project for the tomb of Julius II;[58] Vignola had designed the miniature elliptical "pantheon" S. Andrea in Via about 1550; at the end of the century Ascanio Vitozzi built the vast elliptical pantheon of the Madonna at Mondovi for the House of Savoy. But it was only while the Mondovi church was being built that Kepler formulated the theory of the elliptical orbits of the planets. Nevertheless, the elliptical, sometimes the oval dome, with its cosmic implications, was one of the great baroque innovations. Bernini employed it in the colonnade of St. Peter's, in S. Andrea all'Quirinale, and in the Louvre competition scheme. Borromini less explicitly: in San Carlo alle Quattro Fontane or the dining hall of the Oratory. But after this, in German lands particularly, it became a relatively common form of dome. Both Bernini and Borromini used it in secular buildings, Bernini in the center of his original Louvre project. In Fischer's work it has a programatic power and grandeur which the later projects lack. Even Balthasar Neumann never achieved this grandiloquence, this *gravitas*. Perhaps it was not part of his aim, for by this time the whole intellectual and political atmosphere had suffered a violent shift.

Notes to Chapter 3

1. Tulipomania, which had made and ruined fortunes in Holland, had broken out in 1637.

2. Cited in P. de Nolhac (1901).

3. A. Félibien (1671), in A. Laprade (1960), p. 174.

4. On the building of the *Ménagerie,* see G. Mabille (1974).

5. *Poetics,* XV, 6.

6. It had an analogous part to metaphor and hyperbole or dissonance in music. Cf. René Bray (1927), pp. 232 ff. Cf. also A. Lagarde and Laurent Michard (1970), II, pp. 290 f.

7. Cf. A. Laprade (1960), pp. 173 ff.

8. F.-B. P. Molière, *Le Bourgeois Gentilhomme,* act 4, scene 5; act 5, scene 1.

9. See chapter 7.

10. H. J. Stooke and K. Khandavala (1953), pp. 8f.

11. Charles Perrault (1688), IV, p. 121.

12. Charles Perrault (1688), IV, pp. 273 f.

13. See chapter 6.

14. See M. Sullivan (1973), pp. 213 ff and G. R. Loehr (1940). But he was also the designer of pseudo-European gardens for the Ch'ien Lung Emperor.

15. E. A. Wallis Budge (1928); and G. Pauthier (1859), pp. 25 ff.

16. Charles Perrault, *Parallèle* (1688), IV, p. 121.

17. Charles Perrault (1688), IV, p. 121.

18. However, literature about them began quite early. The first perhaps is a dialogue between a physician, an Indian and a bourgeois by Bartholomé Marandon, 1618. This I know only from a French translation published in *L'Usage du Caphé, du Thé, et du Chocolat* issued anonymously by Jacob Spon (1671) and translated into English (*The Manner of Making Coffee, Tea, and Chocolate . . . with their virtues . . .* by John Chamberlain, FRAS, London, 1685). Spon dedicated his book to a Jesuit, Jean Buissières, who was well acquainted with coffee and knew "que c'est une boisson très-propre pour les personnes studieuses." But the most popular work on chocolate was by Antonio Colmenero de Ledesma (1631), which was translated into several European languages. The Jacob Spon who published the little book on coffee was the same Lyons physician who was shortly to undertake a trip round the Levant and explore Greek antiquities; see chapter 7; and also H. E. Jacob (1936), pp. 31 ff.

19. A. Galland, "Journal Parisien d'Antoine Galland (1708–1715) précedé de son Autobiographie (1646–1715)," in *Mémoires de la Société de l'Histoire de Paris et de l'Ile de France,* XLVI (1919), Paris, 1920, pp. 78, 138.

20. *De l'Origine et du Progrez du Café (Sur un Manuscrit Arabe de la Bibliothèque du Roy).* Caen and Paris, 1699. It ends with this envoy (p. 75):

> Voici une chanson qui a esté mise en musique:
> Ami le sommeil vient au milieu des pots
> Répandre ses pavots
> Et qu'un vin trop fumeux te brouille la cervelle
> Prens du caffé, ce jus divin
> Pour chasser le sommeil et les vapeurs du vin
> Sçaura te redonner une vigeur nouvelle.

21. A. Adam (1948), V, pp. 320 ff. M. Soriano's (1968) study is a psychoanalytical interpretation of the *Contes*. On the problems of authorship and the reception of the books, see M. Soriano (1972), pp. 289 ff. On its context, see G. Cocchiara (1958), pp. 59 ff.

22. D. Marot (1712). See H. Honour (1961), pp. 68, 251; and L. Hautecoeur (1948), II, pp. 680 f.

23. See J. Baltrusaitis (forthcoming).

24. See chapter 2.

25. See chapter 6.

26. H. Honour (1961), p. 37.

27. See chapter 2.

28. The decision was taken by the Ming pretender, Chou Yu-Lang. The empress-dowager was baptized Mary; the empress, Helen; and the crown prince, Constantine, in 1648. But his reign was a long campaign against the Manchus, which ended by his being surrendered to a Manchu general by the Burmese, who at first had given him refuge, in 1661.

The next year, the greatest of all Manchu emperors, the K'ang Hsi, succeeded, aged eight; he ruled until 1722 and is therefore known as the Louis XIV of China. G. Soulié de Morant (1929), pp. 396 ff.; and C. P. Fitzgerald (1954), pp. 487 f., 542 f. The empress' letter to the pope asking for help against the Manchus is reproduced by R. Wilhelm (1929), p. 259.

29. There is a portrait of the K'ang Hsi emperor in Kircher (in J. Nieuhoff, 1669, pp. 68 as well as of Adam Schall von Bell). But see V. Cronin (1955), pp. 276 ff. Cf. R. Dawson (1967), pp. 40 ff. The most important publications at the time, beside the various translations of the Chinese classics, were the Jesuit Fathers' *Lettres Edifiantes et Curieuses*, published irregularly (1707–1773), although, of course, the expulsion and suspension of the French Jesuits in 1764 forced this kind of scholarly publication out of existence: see below, chapter 9.

The presence of the Jesuits sometimes led to the adoption of Latin by Chinese officials for negotiations and Chinese documents. So, for instance, the Russo-Chinese frontier treaty of 1688, though translated into Tartar and Russian, was drawn up in Latin (it was the first treaty of the kind between the Chinese and a European power) by a Jesuit secretary of the Chinese envoys, Jean Gerbillon. Cf. G. Pauthier (1859), pp. 75 ff.

30. *Het Gezantschap der Nederlandtsche Oost-Indische Compagnie aan den grooten Tartarischen Cham*. Other ambassadorial welcomes, their analogies in Egypt and Persia (suggesting that it was a general Asiatic custom), as well as a complete text from the Book of Rites were published by G. Pauthier (1859), pp. 177 ff.

31. *An Embassy from the East India Company of the United Provinces to the Grand Tartar Cham, Emperor of China . . . at his Imperial City of Pekin . . .*, Ingeniously described by John Nieuhoff, steward to the Ambassadors . . . also an appendix of several remarks taken out of Father Athanasius Kircher's Englished by John Ogilby, London, 1669.

32. A. Kircheri SJ, *China Monumentis* (1667).

33. H. Honour (1961), p. 231. The connection he quotes with Jollain *l'Aîné* seems tenuous: he was born in 1697.

34. A. Kircheri SJ *Oedipus Aegyptiacus, Hoc est universalis hieroglyphicae veterum doctrinae temporum iniuria abolitae instauratio . . . ,*

Rome, 1652. The book opens with dedications to the Emperor Ferdinand III printed in Italian, Latin, Greek, Spanish, French, Portuguese, English, German, Turkish, Hungarian, Czech, Illyrian, Croat, Old Slav, Serb, Hebrew, Syrian, Arabic, Aramaic, Armenian, Persian, Samaritan, Coptic, Brahman Hieroglyphs (devised by Kircher himself?), Chinese, and a form of reconstructed Egyptian Hieroglyph. All these—except the calligraphic Syriac inscription, which is engraved, appear to be typeset; although some types must have been cut specially for the occasion. Even then, it is improbable that any typesetter or printer, even Plantin himself, could have boasted of such a choice at that time.

35. On Queen Christina's academy, see below. For a recent estimate of Bellori, see G. Previtali in G. P. Bellori (1976). On Bellori at the court of Queen Christina, see F. Haskell (1963), pp. 158 ff. For his critical work, J. Schlosser (1956), pp. 965 f., 472, 602, 694 f. But see also E. Panofsky (1968).

36. Hans Sedlmayr (1956), pp. 14 ff.

37. Letter of Prince Anton Florian to Prince Maximilian Jakob Moriz von Lichtenstein, 5 September 1688. H. Sedlmayr (1956), p. 273, cf. Sedlmayr (1956), p. 22.

38. *Entwurff einer historischen Architektur* . . . (1721).

39. Full bibliography in G. Kernoth (1956), pp. 17 ff.

40. On the seven wonders, see most recently M. L. Madonna (1976).

41. See chapter 1.

42. Cf. W. Herrmann, "Unknown Designs for the Temple of Jerusalem by Claude Perrault" in D. Fraser, H. Hibbard, and M. J. Lewine (1967).

43. *Der Auserlessneste und nach den Regeln der antiquen Baukunst sowohl als nach dem Antiquen Gusto verneuerte Goldmann* . . . (1721).

44. *Die unentbärliche Regel der Symmetrie* (1720).

45. The original lists (slightly divergent) were formulated by Antipator of Sidon and Philo of Byzantium, but the canon was standardized in the sixteenth century.

46. See ch. 1.

47. Inigo Jones's and William Camden's descriptions are compared by W. Charlton in I. Jones (1725), pp. 6 ff. who also called Stonehenge Chorea Gigantium, as Fischer does; in the same volume, he would have found the reference to Wormius and to the Rollerich Stones which he quotes in his caption.

48. The emblematic intention of these vases is obscure. But vases were given a rather curious place in architectural iconography both because many antique ones were found to be cinerary and because Vitruvius devoted a puzzling passage to the acoustic harmonic properties of metal vases in his description of the theater (V, 5), on which Kircher and others commented. See G. Poleni (1739), pp. 283 ff.

49. In Michaelangelo's scheme, which was well known, the columns were, of course, detached.

50. H. Sedlmayr (1956), pp. 124, 130. The peace of 1714 was one of the three (with Utrecht and Baden) which ended the War of the Spanish succession.

51. 1673, 1679.

52. This oriental character was clearly recognized by Fischer's contemporaries. The French architect Nicolas de Pigage, working for the Elector Palatine Charles-Theodore built a large imitation of the *Karlskirche,* called the mosque, where the two historiated columns reappear as minarets; the building is of the late 1770s. P. du Colombier (1956).

53. G. Heraeus (1721), p. 23.

54. I Kings, 7: 15–22. On the two columns in royal and imperial imagery after Charles V, see F. Yates (1975), passim.

55. Leibniz letter to an unknown person, perhaps to Heraeus of 4 June 1716, in H. Sedlmayr (1956), p. 291; cf. p. 129. Leibniz had been close to the Perraults in Paris and continued to correspond with them after he left, particularly on mathematical problems. Cf. J. Hofman (1974), p. 271, n. 63, and A. Laprade (1960), pp. 307 f.

56. H. Sedlmayr (1956), pp. 123 ff.

57. "So dasz alle Anstalten bey der Streitbarkeit *Davids* und *Caesars* auch mitten im Kriege die Zeiten *Salomonis* und *Augusti* sehen lassen." J. B. Fischer von Erlach, *Entwurff,* 1721, dedication.

58. E. Panofsky (1954).

4

Universal Architecture

Fischer von Erlach's interest in exotic architecture was original, but it was not eccentric. Everywhere in Europe the interest and even the passion for things Chinese was not just a temporary turn of fashion. The encounter of the Christian West with a powerful civilization, which was in some way its equal and in others its superior, had much more of an impact than its meeting with the Mexicans or even the Peruvians. Speculations about the origins of the Chinese, or their connection with the West, with Egypt more particularly, were common. But also interests quite different from the antiquarian ones I have so far mentioned were involved. The Jesuit missionaries presented China to their readers as an ideal society, or nearly so. Confucianism was seen as a moral system based on an archaic, "natural" monotheistic religion. The enormous respect of the Chinese for learning, exemplified by the system of state examinations for government posts, became an ideal of many European reformers.[1] The somewhat flattering account of the K'ang Hsi and Ch'ien Lung emperors contributed to the picture of a well-run society, dominated by a benevolent despot and administered by a meritocracy in which learning and literary talent were the key to promotion. A system of this kind was favored by many *philosophes*. In particular, the system of civil service examinations was often discussed with reference to the Chinese model, in France as well as Britain and Prussia. Nor was the Chinese the only exotic model of social reformers. Throughout the late seventeenth century the intelligent exotic; Turkish, Persian, Tibetan, Chinese, appears in European literature. All these were of course civilized exotics, who criticized Western society from the point of view of a superior, less affected, more "natural" society. Soon, however, a new critic was to appear (even if he was foreshadowed earlier)[2]—the Polynesian, or African, or Amazonian Indian, man uncorrupted by the vices of civilizations, which later eighteenth-century reformers would see in the previously idealized exotic visitors. However, at the time when Fischer established the text of his work, in the first decade of the eighteenth century, the Oriental was still the idealized figure I described. There was therefore an inevitable interest not only in his fashions—which were already familiar and have been described—but in his decoration, his buildings, his way of life. The beverages and some of the foods which the merchants and the state trading companies promoted were a sign of this change. But Oriental buildings were still familiar mostly from the rather cursory descriptions of which I spoke earlier.

Now the eagerness and interest in these matters sharpened the desire for information. Father du Halde's account of China was already a great deal more circumstantial than Nieuhoff's, and his information about Chinese buildings and methods of construction more exact. Some years later Sir William Chambers published a

The Abbey Church of Port-Royal, projected facade with porch, by Antoine Le Pautre.

folio work devoted almost entirely to engravings of Chinese buildings and costume. But, of course, in Fischer's history, Chinese architecture is set beside Siamese, Tibetan, and Indian but also Egyptian, Byzantine, Ancient Greek, and Roman. The implication is that
all of these manners may have something to offer the inquirer—even
if the destroyed temple in Jerusalem is reproposed as the chief
exemplar. In practice this is reflected by a new precision, a new way
of operating with antique elements, evidenced by the Karlskirche.
Grosso modo, the building is still a walled volume. The side pavilions are connected to the center portion by curved walls, the
coupled columns of the dome are more like wrinkles or folds of the
skin on the drum than independent supporting shafts. The building is
articulated in this manner three-dimensionally. On the *Schauseite,*
however, where a clear reference to antiquity is called for by the program, Fischer prefaces the building with six detached columns supporting a pediment, as well as the twin historiated columns which
are set "against" the movement of the facade, of the narthex walls.

   There is nothing unconventional about the pyramidal composition
of this facade, not even about a dome dominated frontally by
two higher elements.[3] The contrast is between a building which depends for its effect on the articulation of the wall by references to
classical ornament, and the orders especially, and the abrupt introduction of a "temple" portico. Which, in any case, is something of a
rarity in the architecture of the seventeenth century. Borromini
never used it; Bernini used it sparingly. The twin churches at the

The Church of the Assumption, Paris, by Charles Errard, elevation. After Mariette.

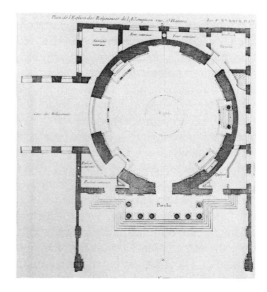

The Church of the Assumption, Paris, by Charles Errard, plan. After Mariette.

The Church of the Assumption, Paris, section. After Mariette.

entrance of the Corso from the Piazza del Popolo (S. Maria di Monte Santo, Santa Maria de' Miracoli) in which he collaborated with Carlo Rainaldi, are exactly this kind of church, a domed space with a temple portico.[4] Bernini of course uses detached columns supporting a straight architrave on a vast scale in the Piazza of St. Peter's; but in that case it was more like the use of the colonnade in a cortile. He also proposed a semicircular colonnade in his unsuccessful competition project for the completion of the apse of Santa Maria Maggiore.[5] But when he built what one might call Pantheon-type churches on his own (Sant'Andrea al Quirinale, the Assunta at Ariccia) the porticoes, though crowned with pediments, are walled, pierced with arches, and ornamented with pilasters.

In France the situation was not different. The most important portico was Jacques Lemercier's side entrance of the Sorbonne church, which had been begun in 1635. In the Val-de-Grâce church nearby, Lemercier and François Mansart did put a tetrastyle carrying a pediment, but it was part of a two-story facade and only had the depth of the columns. Much later Charles Errard, the nephew of the two Fréart brothers, designed a church for the sisters of the Assumption, near the Louvre, on a modified Pantheon-plan: a high domed circular space with a pedimented porch. He sent the design from Rome, where he had become the first director of the newly founded French Academy[6] and on which he presumably worked on his return to Paris during the break in his directorship. Although Errard had complained bitterly about his treatment at the hands of contractors, the building was still much admired in the eighteenth century—if only for its portico.

Occasionally—very rarely in the seventeenth century—a porch is designed without a pediment, and this makes Antoine Le Pautre's porch for Port-Royal, the only building for a real site and client in his book, so remarkable.[7] Since Port-Royal was so very much a building which served as a manifesto for a major religious movement, it is not surprising to find a gallican theologian putting forward the thesis that columnar porches are an essential part of the sacred space of the church, from which all secular concerns and even the sale of objects of piety must be banished.[8]

In France, the proliferation of small, but evident columnar porches after this time is not surprising.[9] But outside France, beside the Karlskirche, a number of similar features appear in various parts of Europe during the second decade of the eighteenth century: the grandest, certainly is Filippo Juvarra's Superga, overlooking Turin; the most familiar, the much smaller SS. Simeone e Giuda in Venice by Gianantonio Scalfurotto, although if Gibbs' original design for St. Martin's-in-the-Fields in London had been carried out, it would certainly have been much more famous,[10] as even this design, in its engraved form, had a good deal of influence: its most spectacular product is Benjamin H. Latrobe's Baltimore Cathedral.[11] About the same time important temple-front porticoes appeared on churches of basilican plan: Andrea Tirali's San Nicola dei Tolentini (of 1718, around the corner from SS. Simone e Giuda) in Venice is a case in point. In any generalized picture of architecture since the fifteenth century, the temple-front portico of free-standing columns seems commonplace. But it was very rare. Palladio, for instance, only used it once on a public building, the little church at Maser, although it does appear in one or two villas (the Malcontenta, the Rotonda). More usually the portico is graphically indicated on facades in the form of pilasters or half-columns. So the eighteenth century ex- amples I have quoted were treated at the time as remarkable.

The force of the innovation goes back again, I suspect, to Perrault. His most important executed building was—as I have already said—the eastern facade of the Louvre. Whatever was the part he played in its conception,[12] there is no doubt that he regarded his connection with pride. It is perhaps the first major colonnade in France in which free-standing columns support a straight trabeation: the only real French precedent being François Mansart's Orléans wing at Blois, which Claude Perrault saw during his trip to Bordeaux in 1669.[13] This colonnade, too, has the contentious coupled columns which were the "modern" feature of the Louvre and which François Blondel attacked at great length in his course at the Academy of Architecture, of which he was president.[14] He attacked it both be- cause it had such scant antique precedent and also because he con-

The Church of SS. Simeone e Giuda, called San Simeone or Simeone Piccolo, in Venice, by G. Scalfurotto.

sidered it unsound mechanically. Perrault, in his turn, defended it at some length in his commentary on Vitruvius.[15] He had not quoted antique precedent for his particular procedure of coupling columns, as Blondel had alleged, but had done so to show that even those, who like Hermogenes, codified ancient practice (he set out the rules for the various kinds of intercolumniation; the quoted passage comes from the commentary on Vitruvius' account of Hermogenes) also made certain definite innovations. Innovation, even in setting out ancient rules, was therefore the practice of the ancients. Perrault goes on:

> But the worst reproach made against our [inter-columniation] is to say that it has something Gothic about it. Well, Gothic architecture may not be the best kind, but it is not to be rejected out of hand. The light in Gothic buildings, the independent articulation of the structure [*dégagement*] which is under discussion, is different in Gothic and ancient architecture. And (here comes the heresy) Gothic is not therefore to be thought the worse for it; on the contrary, the ancients came round to such ways at the end, when they made windows in their temples.

Eastern facade of the Louvre, detailed section and elevation of the colonnade, Claude Perrault. After Pierre Patte.

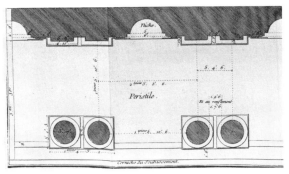

Eastern colonnade of the Louvre, ceiling and carcass plan of one bay. After Pierre Patte.

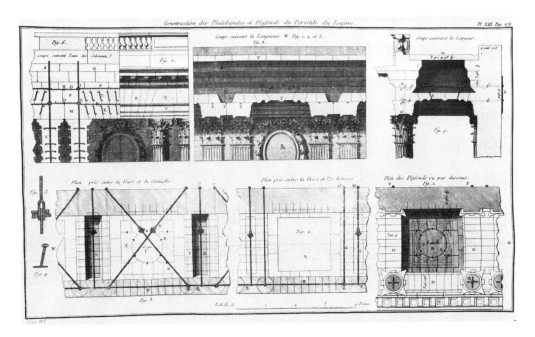

Eastern facade of the Louvre, constructional details showing stone joints and metal reinforcement. After Pierre Patte.

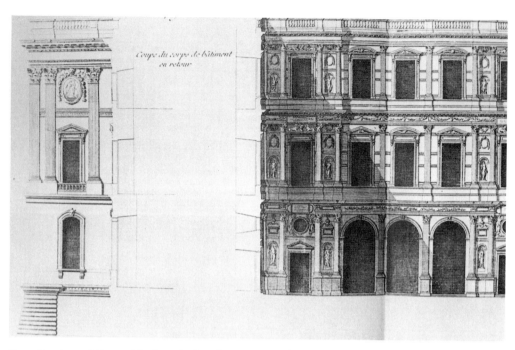

Coordination of Perrault's facade for the exterior of the Louvre with the added eighteenth-century order. After J.-F. Blondel.

Now Perrault returns to the matter of proportion. Of course, the eastern facade of the Louvre, beside the *magnificence* (the word is his) of the double portico, has other classical echoes: most obviously the octastyle pedimented centerpiece, and within it the atrophied triumphal arch set rather curiously into the basement to make the principal entrance of the palace from the east, implying the eastward avenue to the Barrière du Trône, with its triumphal arch—also designed by Perrault, and actually built in lath, cloth, and plaster over a stone plinth.[16]

The innovations which the colonnade provided were evident and provocative, involving the raising of the interior courtyard of the Louvre. As the courtyard which then existed, designed by Pierre Lescot in the sixteenth century,[17] already had a Composite order imposed on a Corinthian one, the crowning story, which would bring the courtyard facade up to the height of the colonnade, could not be in any recognized order: Perrault proposed caryatids. In the end there was a competition for a new "French" order, which Colbert himself won, in a manner of speaking.[18] These formal problems were paralleled by technical ones. The beams carried by the columns of the colonnade were made of two ranges of voussoirs; they were two flat arches, laid on top of each other. This meant that the masonry had to be very elaborately cramped; not that this was particularly new; cramped masonry had been in use since remote antiquity; and medieval masons used metal, even wooden ties quite commonly. What Perrault proposed, however, involved not only very elaborate

Triumphal arch at the Barrière du Trône, by Claude Perrault. This is presumably a view of the full-size "model." After Pérelle.

stone-cutting but cramps and ties in such a complex system that the structure virtually became a reinforced masonry construction, analogous to reinforced concrete.[19]

Perrault's colonnade was admired, emulated, and much discussed throughout the eighteenth century and in the latter part of the century came to be regarded as the principal portent of a new architecture.[20] By contrast, Blondel's arch of St. Denis, the most considerable of his surviving works, did not enjoy such a reputation, although it was treated respectfully enough. Later critics found it too narrow, too heavy; they regretted the absence of columns, disliked the complexity of the imagery.[21] In his *Cours,* Blondel justified not only the proportions in detail, but also the allegorical way in which he devised the ornament which is based on a composition of Trajan's column, the rostral columns in the Forum, Egyptian obelisks, and some other pieces of antiquity. All this is combined in a much more straightforward and modest fashion compared to the extraordinary texture of the Karlskirche and that of earlier, baroque designers. But it is quite alien to the "conventionalized" description of ornament which I have traced in Perrault.

The Louvre facade perfectly embodies this idea; it is *parlare piano* in architecture, however magnificent. The references it carries, for instance, are either quite generalized (triumphal arch, tem-

Triumphal arch at the Barrière du Trône, Claude Perrault's project. After J.-F. Blondel.

Alternative project for the Barrière du Trône triumphal arch by Charles Lebrun. After J.-F. Blondel.

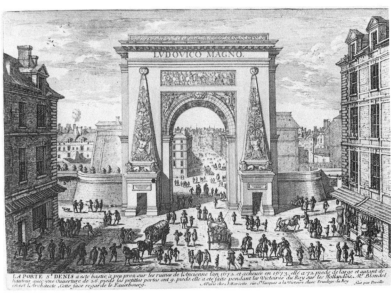

The Porte St. Denis, Paris, by François Blondel, with sculpture by François Girardon and Michel Anguier. The proportions are based on permutations of thirds and fourths dividing a square. The triumphal obelisk-pyramids (replacing columns) were considered a remarkable allegorical device. After Pérelle.

The Porte St. Denis. The defense walls, still visible in the engraving, have been replaced by the Boulevard.

The Porte St. Martin, Paris, by François Blondel and Pierre Bullet.

The Porte St. Martin.

ple front) or else very obvious and literal (variations on L for Louis, trophies of arms, laurel leaves, and so on).

The man of taste, as Perrault had taught and here shows in practice, elevates his building above the merely commonsensical positive beauties by endowing it with its clothing or arbitrary beauty. But these must not fall to the dictates of fancy, of unbridled imagination. They must be regulated by authority and freed from the overtones of metaphor and analogy. This exercise, as much as Blondel's, and the attendant discussions might be interpreted as the fulfillment of the royal command to the Academy of Architecture at its foundation: to discuss the art and the rules of architecture.[22] The realm in which authority would be defied, and strangely enough with Perrault's help, was one in which he was not particularly interested: the proliferation of pattern-books. A flood of these, a new type in the literature of art, was to become a vehicle for a new fashion, of which Perrault would certainly have intensely disapproved, however much he had done to promote it.

1. This is the burden of the last chapter of Voltaire's *Age de Louis XIV* (xxxix) which deals with the quarrel about Chinese rites. See R. Pomeau (1956), pp. 55 ff., 154 ff.

2. Cf. G. Chinard (1970). On American Indians, pp. 193 ff., Montaigne's view. P. Hazard (1961), I, pp. 20 ff.

3. See S. Biagio in Montepulciano, S. Agnese in Piazza Navona in Rome, or even the modified facade of St. Peter's with two tall campanile.

4. R. Wittkower (1975), pp. 44 ff.

5. R. Wittkower (1958), p. 186.

6. H. Lapauze (1924), pp. 9 ff.; L. Hautecoeur (1948), II, pp. 715, 754. J.-F. Blondel's opinion (1771–1777), III, p. 140. It may well be this "Choir of Vestals" for which Frémin displays such contempt (1702), pp. 59 ff.

7. A. Le Pautre (1652), pp. 35 ff.; L. Hautecoeur (1948), II, pp. 146 f. The porch was not, in fact, built.

8. J. B. Thiers (1679). Although most of his arguments are drawn from consiliar canons and church fathers, he does quote Villalpanda in his support—and for that time very daringly backs it up with a quotation from Nicolas Janssens, bishop of Ypres (pp. 199 ff.).

9. L. Hautecoeur (1943-), II, pp. 730 ff.; III, pp. 361 ff.

10. B. Little (1955), pp. 70 ff. Published by Gibbs (1728) himself, pls. 8–15.

11. T. E. Tallmadge (n.d.), pp. 93 f., 110 ff.; and V. Scully (1969), pp. 62 f.

12. See above; cf. L. Hautecoeur (1943), II, 1, pp. 443 ff.; for the extreme view see A. Laprade (1960), pp. 113 ff., 297 ff.

13. Charles Perrault (1909), p. 143. Perrault curiously enough calls it "une plateforme en quart de rond, qui est soutenue par des colonnes isolées, d'ordre ionique [actually, they are Doric] avec des figures au dessus de colonnes." These are no longer there: they were removed at the Revolution, as were the 'plateformes' Perrault mentions. L. Hautecoeur (1943), II, 1, pp. 33 ff.

14. F. Blondel (1698), pp. 228–235. This is the second and complete edition of the *Cours*.

15. Vitruvius (1684), pp. 78 ff.

16. The arch was to commemorate the king's entry into Paris and his plenipotentiary rule in 1660 by the Vincennes road. The assumption that there may have been a competition was made by L. Hautecoeur (1948), II, pp. 455 ff. The best source for the drawings by Sebastien Le Clerc and Le Brun is in A. Laprade (1960), App. 1 and 2. The original scheme was criticized by a jury of architects—the academy had not been instituted. It was nevertheless begun, and Perrault devised a machine for the easy finish of the stones, by a form of *anathyrosis*. Daniel Gittard was named site architect. The project was approved in April and the foundation stone laid on 6 August 1670. Construction had been stopped before Colbert's death, and when Louvois decided to continue, he asked the academy to pronounce (*P.V.*, II, pp. 97 ff.), and there was much talk about triumphal arches all through July 1685. Much of this discussion was devoted to a rather destructive report on Perrault's arch, and recommendations for change on Blondelian lines. See W. Herrmann (1973), pp. 93 ff. Not much more was done, however, and its destruction (bits were falling off the temporary construction) was decided on in 1716. The stone bases (up to a height of ten feet) were sold as building material. For contemporary judgment about this, see

J.-F. Blondel (1771–1777) II, pl. 37. See also Lafont de Saint-Yenne (1752), pp. 34, 151.

17. The material evidence collected by Clarac (1853), pp. 341 ff., 378 ff.

18. On the competition, see G. Wildenstein in *G.B.A.*, May 1964, pp. 257 ff; and A. Blunt (1953), pp. 252, n. 66.

19. Perrault had decided to cover his wrought iron clamps in lead, a fairly common procedure since antiquity. Some of the cramps were buried in the stone, and it seems that the sculptors working on the ornament chipped away so much of it that water actually penetrated through the lead joints, producing rust marks. The ties were free, in a gallery above the soffits of the colonnade, which was formed by the stones behind the cornice and over the screen wall being corbelled towards each other so that much of the ironwork could be inspected. The corbelled gallery was covered by large stone slabs, and all the upper joints were waterproofed with a paste made of urine and metal filings. Perrault had nevertheless to fight scepticism about his structural competence, which indeed greeted his wooden model of the facade. He had an exact structural model made of it in stone and iron, to the scale of 1 inch to 1 foot; presumably only a section of the facade was made up in that way. Nevertheless, although much of it was finished before the king's death, Perrault neglected the Louvre in the later part of his life, and the construction was taken up again by Gabriel and Soufflot (see below, ch. 10) and completed under Napoleon. By the middle of the eighteenth century, there is no evidence that Perrault's constructional model still existed. See P. Patte (1769), pp. 262, 266 ff.; 329 ff.; and J.-F. Blondel (1771), VI, pp. 164 ff.

There had already been other misfortunes on the site: Perrault had insisted on the pediment cornices being made of monoliths and improved or perfected a hauling mechanism for putting them into place. The machine is shown in Perrault's Vitruvius (1684), p. 341. See W. Herrmann (1973), pp. 191 f. But see also A. Laprade (1960), pp. 54 ff., on the display aspect of this operation. It was very much a public occasion, and a special medal was cast to commemorate it. Laprade also quotes Huygens' account of his visits to the quarry and his comments on the transportation of the stones. On the whole of this work, see also L. Hautecoeur (1948), II, pp. 442 ff.

20. See J.-F. Blondel (1771–1777), III, pl. 7. Certain eighteenth-century critics protested that the great opposition of principle between Perrault and Blondel did not lead to an equal difference in their practice; although it seems to me that eighteenth-century critics were remarkably insensitive on this point. See ch. 10.

21. There is no serious treatment of Blondel's achievement in a separate publication. He discusses the arch in his own *Cours* (1698, IV, 12, vi f.). It was not a royal commission, but given by the city council. Blondel also designed the Porte St. Antoine (a rebuilding) and St. Bernard, and with his pupil, Pierre Bullet, the Porte St. Martin. They were part of the general scheme to open the northern borders of Paris. Blondel was insistent on precedent: the walls of his St. Denis arch recall pyramids and obelisks; the Hypnerotomachia Polyphili is quoted as well as Trajan's column. He wanted to add rostral arches and devised an elaborate allegorical scheme for the sculptures.

22. J.-F. Blondel's presidential address at the inauguration of the academy's opening section. H. Lemmonier (1926), I, pp. 2 f. Blondel also reprinted it as the preface to his *Cours*.

5

The Pleasures of Freedom

Architectural pattern-books might be said to go back to Sebastiano
Serlio's *Seven Books of Architecture*, which appeared in installments beginning in 1537 in Venice; it became very popular. Serlio's
"books" were not a treatise, but picture books with captions and
were treated that way all over Europe. Now in other crafts and
arts—in embroidery or topiary gardening, in metal chasing or wood
inlay—pattern-books also appeared with wood engravings. With the
popularizing of metal engraving and etching, they became even more
popular but also more detailed and precise in their suggestions. Insistently, these little books—as most of them are—fill in the empty
spaces, whether in flower beds or counterpanes with serpentine lines,
S or *C* shapes, which contrast with the framework of the page. These
shapes came to be associated with *moresche,* patterns of curved
straps, very popular in France, and perhaps of Moorish origins.
Often these are amalgamated with grotesques, linear patterns of
swags and garlands and cameos. In the fifteenth century the first
Roman archeologists uncovered painted Roman rooms, the most
famous of which was one in the house of Livia on the Palatine. Its
decoration was varied and developed by Raphael and his pupils in
the Vatican Loggie and the Villa Madama, where the first grotesques
appeared, called that after the underground rooms, the *grotte,* in
which they were found.[1]

In the sixteenth century they were taken up by the inventors of
ornament, Polidoro da Caravaggio, for instance, or Pietro da Cortona. They provided a kind of constant undercurrent of ornamental
speculation, within the framework of the decorative schemes of
Louis XIV's reign. In Italy speculations were not fettered in the
same way. Imagination, even fancy, was allowed free reign. Guarino
Guarini, Theatine friar and architect of the church of St. Anne-la-
Royale,[2] was regarded as the chief artificer of unfettered originality
and indiscriminating eclecticism. Later the current would be joined
by the influence of the German ornamentalists, most particularly of
Wendel Dietterlin, whose grotesque and fantastic inventions appeared at the break of the sixteenth and seventeenth centuries.[3]

But however sober the professions which the architects of the
grand style made of their faith, they did not look with disfavor on the
more opulent products of Le Brun's and Hardouin-Mansart's office.
Perrault had himself designed a very elaborately ornate building, the
grotto of Thetis at Versailles. It was the basement of a vast reservoir, which had a capacity of 570 cubic meters of water. It was
destroyed to make way for the enlargements of the 1680s. In any
case the reservoir had been rendered obsolete by the vast
waterworks at Marly, and the iconography of the grotto no longer
applied, since the Thetis of the grotto had been Mme. de Montespan,
long eclipsed. Moreover the site was needed for the vast extension
of the chapel wing. The walls of this *nymphaeum*—the home for
such a humid shrine of nymphs goes back to antiquity and was

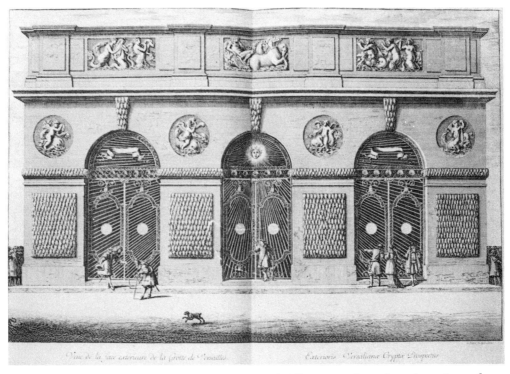

The Grotto of Thetis, Versailles, by Claude Perrault. The gates, shut, show the pattern of rays extending to the three arches. It was one of the first instances, if not the first, of the use of the sun symbol for Louis XIV. After Félibien and Le Pautre.

The Grotto of Thetis with gates open. After Pérelle.

The Grotto of Thetis, sectional perspective, showing the groups of sculpture by François Girardon and Thomas Regnauldin. The central figure shows Apollo washed and anointed by the muses after the fatigues of driving the sun chariot across the sky, while the groups on either side show his horses being watered. The whole grotto faced west. Engraved by Le Pautre.

certainly familiar to the *trattatisti* (to Serlio for instance)—were decorated with elaborate patterns of pebbles, shells, and painted trifles, such as lifelike colored birds. It is this kind of decoration, which was never to be surpassed in France and gave its name to a genre, *rocaille*,[4] from which derives the name of a style, *rococo*.[5] The curved patterns in the grotto of Thetis are, of course, not based on the letters *S* or *C* but on *L*. Even in this buried, relaxed shelter, the formal framework wholly masters the ornament. But the framework of orders and ribs and coffers which kept all such fantasies in check did not survive the turn of the century and the decline of its royal governor.

By 1715 two great dynastic upheavals had brought with them a change in the patronage and the taste of Western Europe. In Britain Queen Anne had died at Kensington Palace in the summer of 1714; it was the end of the Stuart reign; her German successor, the Hanoverian George I, was to be dominated by his entourage of Whig lords, whose Venetian sympathies were to be such a dominant factor in the formation of eighteenth-century taste in Britain and in North America.

Louis XIV died on 1 September 1715, leaving a five-year-old heir, his grandson, protected by the Regency Council. This council, by the laws of inheritance of the French monarchy, was headed by the great king's nephew, whom the king disliked and distrusted for a

Grotto of Thetis, pier surfaced with composition of shells, rocks, and coral, carrying the swagged L perhaps for the first time. One triton blows a conch. After Le Pautre.

Grotto of Thetis, corner piers.

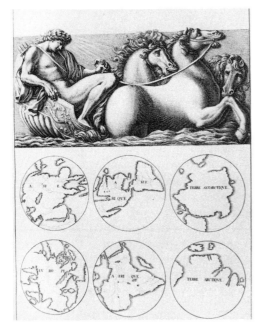

Grotto of Thetis, central panel of the facade showing Apollo's chariot sinking into the sea and roundels of the six continents, including the (as yet undiscovered) Arctic land instead of Australia. After Le Pautre.

Grotto of Thetis, composite shell-faces from the piers. After Le Pautre.

drunk, an atheist, and a libertine: the duc d'Orléans who was in fact a cynical and astute general.

The duc d'Orléans soon broke the old king's testament and the council for the Regency.[6] He ruled France for eight years, until his death. Three years later power passed to Monseigneur Fleury, bishop of Fréjus and the young king's tutor, who was prime minister in all but name (he had, however, become a cardinal on assuming power) and established the most stable and effective government France was to know for some time.

Since the climate of French politics, as well as her fashion, dominated Europe for the century from 1650 to 1750 absolutely, this change is worth noting. It is the duration of the *Régence* and the reign of Fleury that go in the arts by the name of rococo. In a sense, within months of Fleury's death, power passed to the first *maîtresse-en-titre* of Louis XV, Mme. de Pompadour: the style is often associated with her,[7] although her taste, in spite of her association with Boucher, was for more sober kinds of decoration.

Although the manner was passing from fashion in France by 1750, in the rest of Europe, in Germany and Austria especially, it continued to be practiced almost until the end of the century. The exact nature of this manner or movement is difficult to describe and categorize. Many of the nineteenth-century historians who did so

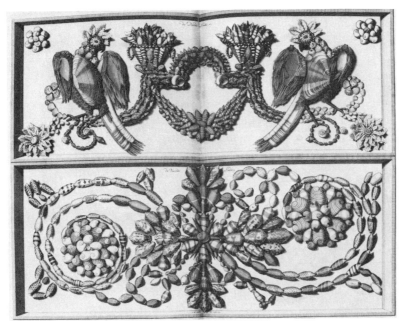

Sample drawers of shells from the vast natural collection of Albert Seba. It is notable that the plates from the collection are illustrated with the sparsest interest in arrangement, except the shell plates, which show the shells arranged into elaborate patterns. It was one of the greatest biological collections formed before the nineteenth century and was bought by Peter the Great. London, British Museum.

François Boucher, La Belle O'Morphi.

treated it as a frivolous ending to a period which they already considered decadent, the baroque.[8] At the time, however, the word *rocaille* meant that category of decoration which Perrault had used with such success in the grotto of Thetis; by transference it was also used for ornament based on such shell-and-pebble work (by further extension also fretwork, monkeys, exotics, and so on). In the background of the manner were, as I have already said, the patternbooks. They were of many kinds. The Italians perfected the invention of the cartouche, a surround for the coat of arms, which at the time when the relation between legitimacy and genealogy had such a powerful revival, were very much in demand. Stefano della Bella, a Florentine disciple of Callot (but familiar with the great compositions of Pietro da Cortona) published such a series in Paris. Naturally, these cartouches had blank centers.[9] He was to be followed by several French designers, who varied, twisted, and distorted his schemes.

The grotesque was elaborated by Daniel Marot and by Jean Berain.[10] Berain's designs were adapted by André Charles Boulle, the mercurial *ébéniste* of Louis XIV, in his famous veneered pieces with ebony, pewter, brass, and tortoiseshell. Boulle already found that the corners of even the courtliest of such veneered pieces needed protection, however great the craftsman's skill. So he developed veneered furniture with gilt brass and copper edgings (*ormolu,* which more properly is the name of an alloy based on copper and zinc also used in this way) which was to be the choice medium of eighteenth-century French and German furniture makers.

There were, besides Berain, several other designers working in

François Boucher, The Painter at Work in his Study. *Paris, Louvre.*

this manner. Best known perhaps were Claude Audran and Claude Gillot, and their toweringly brilliant "junior," Antoine Watteau. Watteau's career (he died in 1721 of consumption, aged thirty-seven) coincided with the Orléans regency. His work is the consummation of the victory of the Rubensists in that other great artistic feud which rent French culture toward the end of Louis XIV's reign, that between the followers of Poussin and of Rubens.[11]

Watteau's might be taken as the epitome of rococo art. The diploma painting which admitted him to the full membership of the French Academy in 1717, *L'Embarquement à Cythère,*[12] shows all his virtues: the liquid paint, sharply, tensely touched line; the exquisite movement of the figures in a stilted dance of sentiment and the promise of pleasure. The stilted sentiment developed by the *Précieux* within the vast framework of the machinery of court life has been delivered of this frame and allied with a sense of the self-sufficiency of pleasure which dominated the literature of the period.

"The idea of pleasure was, from my first coming into the world, the only one which engaged me. The peace which obtained at the time left me with dangerous leisure . . . the little business which people of my rank or my age usually have, the air of falsity, the freedom, example, everything drew me to pleasure; I had impetuous feelings, or to speak more precisely, I had a passionate imagination which was easily impressed"; so one of Crébillon's most popular heroes.[13] The tone, of course, would not be maintained. Feeling freed of structure, pleasure unbridled, has all the dangers to which the rococo novelist alluded. From the individual tragedies of Crébillon's heroines come the novels of passion, the unfortunate des Grieux and his even less fortunate Manon dying consumptively in the exile of the West Indies; finally, after half a century the whole thing was to be purged in the dark work of destruction which Choderlos de Laclos (just such an underemployed soldier as Crébillon describes) imagined in his *Liaisons Dangereuses*.[14] For the time being, however, such ideas or the imaginings of de Sade or Restif de la Bretonne seem rather distant. *Régence* pleasures were still relatively straightforward.

Watteau painted, Crébillon wrote during a radical transformation of the social structure of French life. The regent had not the will, the infant king neither means nor power to continue the vast "ballet" of Versailles. The court could not therefore remain the sole source of fashion or power as it had been even in the last, fustian days of the great king's reign. The impact of all this on architecture is obvious: for a century the development of architecture was tied to the château, to the royal palace in particular. From then on the interesting development would be that of the *hôtel particulier*.

The *hôtel* as a building type had a set topology: a screen wall onto the street with a main gate set in it and the *corps de logis*, the main block of the house, almost always of two or three stories, facing it and connected to the curtain walls by service buildings on either side. Beyond the *corps de logis* there was a garden or park. The invention of the type has been attributed to Mme. de Rambouillet, who held the first *salon*;[15] to Serlio; to Solomon de Brosse; and to others. Like all such types, however, it developed for a number of reasons fairly quickly. The *hôtel* appeared in the first quarter of the seventeenth century. During the reign of Louis XIV its development was thwarted, but as the grip of the Versailles court slackened, the richer bourgeoisie and both nobilities (but particularly that of the robe) developed, rebuilt or even built anew an increasing number of such town houses. In Paris the largest number were grouped in the two faubourgs: St. Honoré and St. Germain.

The old arrangement of rooms *en suite* was found increasingly irksome. The new *commodités* required smaller rooms, greater articulation of the distribution, and complexity of relationships promoted the evolution of the back passage, which provided a loop connection behind the suite of main rooms. With all this, a new barrier appears between the user's body and the bare wall: the *boiserie*.

Paneling had, of course, been familiar since the Middle Ages. But the particular combination of paneling and fabric, or paneling and mirror, which appeared during the first quarter of the eighteenth century is new in several ways. Paneling had early displaced the tapestry at Versailles. The Gobelins tapestry had—it is true—been promoted vigorously by Colbert;[16] but paneling and painting were already usurping their traditional function as absorbents and comforters. The paneling of Louis XIV's preference was a framing of history painting which glorified his reign; or of mirror which reflected the dominion he wielded over nature. This framing would be of gilt, wood or metal, or polished stone, often conceived in terms of the orders and their modénatures. Mirror glass had begun to be manufactured in France, and beyond the court it had become an increasingly cheap commodity in French households.[17] This fashion at least of the court could percolate slowly down the social (or rather the economic) scale. The state patronage which protected the Gobelins factory and indulged Boulle contributed to the buildup of an elaborate system of patronage for the veneer makers and master-joiners who were to create the new manner.[18]

One of its first marks was the muting of the color. In the smaller, smoother rooms of the later seventeenth-century houses the beams were no longer exposed or coffered but covered by a layer of lath-and-plaster, a perfect surface for abstract decoration on a white ground. From such ceilings the patterning was drawn down. In the *agence,* the royal works or office of Jules Hardouin-Mansart, a number of designers were developing the manner. The older Le Pautre, Boffrand, the less directly involved Oppenordt, Mansart's cousin, the older Gabriel, and his brother-in-law, Robert de Cotte, all contributed to it.

The vehicle for it, and the medium for its development, was the pattern-book. Very rarely do these publications, sometimes magnificently printed folios, have any text putting forward a rationale for the *rocaille,* or the *goût nouveau* which they presented. Their ideas appear, usually in allusions, in anecdotes about lives or in the writings of their sometimes eloquent opponents. This is in a sense fair. For the appeal of the *ornamentistes* was not to the past but to nature. They emulated the example of the Torinese masters (Guarini they knew best). It was the courage to break with ancient precedent which they admired in Borromini, as he had in Michelangelo, but they did not appeal directly to such predecessors. Their art, as I have already suggested, had come from the humid garden grottoes, and it appealed directly to nature. Not the exalted, transcendental nature of astronomers or physicists but the nature of the landscape painter. As Watteau had managed to coalesce his style from its Venetian elements (Tintoretto, Veronese) and its Flemish vision in Rubens, so the *ornamentistes* derived their "natural" patterns from such Rubensist heroes as Stefano della Bella, Domenico Feti, or Salvator Rosa or from engravings after the Venetians, or even trivialized details of Rembrandt.[19] All this amalgam was an agreeable background for what occurred in the *petits cabinets* and the *boudoirs* of the *Régence* and the early years of Louis XV. Clearly, with the growth of an urban society independent of the court, the heraldic uses of the *cartouche* became less interesting; it became a decorative device. The Stefanino della Bella or Le Pautre frame was often sliced in two, and two different halves shown on one plate. This device, adopted for reasons of economy, seems to have promoted the desire of the *ornamentistes* to create asymmetrical schemes, or at any rate, asymmetrical devices of all kinds, which were popular with the *goût nouveau,* the *goût pittoresque* of the thirties and forties.[20]

Oriental materials, Oriental themes were, of course, the inevitable extension of the manner. The society of feeling looked to outside critics who might, unfettered by the absurd conventions of Western society, criticize its unnatural ways. Hence, in addition to the novels of sentiment, there developed a genre of social-critical novels, of which the most famous was Montesquieu's *Lettres Persanes.*[21] Hence, perhaps, the tendency not only to represent Orientals in ornamental paintings but also to adapt, as being more "natural," their customs (coffee drinking, the bath, the steam bath in particular) as well as their posture: cross-legged, relaxed, loosely clothed. And of course there followed Oriental pieces of furniture: not the lacquered panels of which I have already spoken, so much as the amply upholstered seats, the ottoman (also called *automane*) the sofa, the pouffe. All these appeared in French and later other European interiors in the second quarter of the eighteenth century, and in a terminology for them in most European languages soon after.

I have tried to put together some evidence for the change of taste from novelists, from poets, and from the practice of the designers, failing any direct avowals by them. But although the designers did not rationalize their intentions, much incidental information is provided by the quarrel of the Rubensists and the Poussinists (which is analogous, though not exactly parallel, to the quarrel of the ancients and the moderns) who showed amply how nature supplemented the precepts of authority. And nature loved the serpentine line. Rubens especially was read at the time as the painter of the serpentine line.[22]

It is curious that however extravagant the efforts of the *ornamentistes,* they very rarely affected much of the exterior of the buildings. Boffrand's most extravagant decorations, the oval interiors of the Hôtel Soubise, were done within a sober two-storied palace in the grand style (coupled columns and all) which he took over from Alexis Delamaire, an older architect. His own executed exteriors are not far removed from the *grand goût.* Even the most daring, the Hôtel Amelot, with its oval *cour d'honneur,* is dominated by an order of giant Corinthian pilasters.

The artist who went furthest in defying any devotion to the *ordonnances,* Juste-Aurèle Meissonier, was something of an exception. He was born in Turin, of French parents in 1693 (1695?).[23] He was certainly familiar with Guarini's work, which was rising in the center of Turin at the time, and through him with Borromini. At any rate by 1724 he had a royal appointment (as designer of silverware) to Louis XV and further promotion two years later. Although he seems to

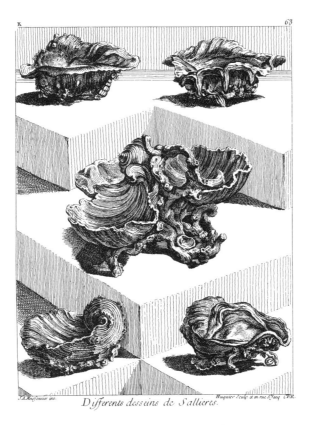

Differents desseins de Sallieres.

*Designs for different shapes of saltcellars, all com-
bining twigs and shells, by J. A. Meissonier.*

have had much work as a designer in metals and later of interiors in
France as well as in Poland and in Russia, he seems never to have
executed a building. In 1726 he presented a project for the facade
and the refacing of the church of St. Sulpice in Paris to its vicar.[24] At
the time work there was under the direction of the Dutch *ornamentiste* Oppenordt and very little is known about the circumstances in
which it was done: whether commissioned or freely done of his
own accord. It does not seem to have any connection with the competition of 1731–1732 (of which more later). Meissonier's facade is
one of the more ambitious rococo compositions as far as scale is
concerned, although it is not his most felicitous work. It has obvious
Italian precedents. The articulation: a tall central element and two
smaller side pavilions, connected by recessed link-pieces, recall
Andrea Pozzo's competition facade for St. John Lateran.[25] The large
concave niche of the central element is divided in two, the lower half
being a convex pavilion, inserted into it. This is a favorite Borrominesque device.[26] With all that, and with all the wrinkling of the
surface of the building with bunched pilasters and columns, the
building uses straight lines only where it is strictly inevitable. Even
the roof lines have undulating ridges, raised at the wall to sculptured

Projet de Sculpture en argent d'un grand Surtout de Table, et les deux Terrines qui ont été executée pour le Millord Duc de Kinston en 1735.
A Paris chez Huquier rue S.'Jacque au coin de celle des Matharins CPR.

Table centerpiece for a noble Polish household. The use of simulated natural shapes aims at making some of the shapes appear almost to be casts, while the whole composition is of an "invented" nature.

finials, like those of a pagoda, to endow the whole outline of the building with movement.

Although it is deliberately "new" and radical, the orders are still used and the thematic Italian material deployed, albeit conventionalized into triviality. The great themes which served Borromini's elaborate microcosmic symbolism[27] have been reduced to counters in the game of providing the church with a novel abstract, picturesque resolution of its form into lines of rhythmical pulsation. The Corinthian order is correctly imposed on the Tuscan—but against the rules; the superior Corinthian is smaller than the supposedly squat Tuscan over which it stands. This design may be taken as a useful point of no return. Even the German architects, who some time later thought nothing of substituting *rocaille* for the proper ornament of the capital of an order, never achieved quite this liquid movement in their facades,[28] in which all is subsumed to the movement and articulation of surface. In these buildings, as in the interiors implied by Meissonier's facades, the "reading" of the building is almost a by-product of its volumetric complexity.

Regular shapes are avoided on plan as far as possible. The square and the circle are replaced by the ellipse and the triangle as generating forms. Simple processions of piers in a nave are tied to elaborate vaulting schemes, so as to suggest that the rectangular envelope of the outside in fact contains a series of interlocking ellipses.[29] Again, this Borrominian invention, so brilliantly manipulated by Guarini is diffused through his reading of it: the Dietzenhofers in Bohemia, Zimmermann, the Asams, Neumann in Germany, Prandtauer, and

*The church of St. Sulpice, Paris, Meissonier's project
for the new facade, elevation and plan.*

Hildebrandt—to a lesser extent Fischer von Erlach in Austria, Vittone in Savoy, all reinterpret this device by elaborating it and loading it with a form of decoration which echoes the movement of the structure in miniature. How essential this form of *rocaille* is to the buildings becomes evident in Balthasar Neumann's last building, the Abbey of Neresheim, begun in 1749 but not consecrated until 1792 [30] whose ornamental structure is coolly "correct," although the articulation of the plan retains the earlier elaboration; here a breaking point was reached. But Meissonier's facade had already shown that, for France at any rate, an extreme position had been taken, and there would be no simple return to the old norms.

Although Meissonier's taste still had quite long innings, on the scale of the church facade that much *licence,* a word which would assume a great importance later,[31] was not acceptable; perhaps the *vicaire,* already disappointed by Oppenordt's fiasco, had set his

J.-A. Meissonier, design for a new high altar for the church of St. Sulpice in Paris.

heart against such decorative excesses. At any rate, a competition was declared for the facade and was won by another Italian-born Frenchman, Giovanni-Niccolo Servandoni.[32] Servandoni had made his reputation in France as a scene painter at the Opéra, where he had succeeded the younger Berain in 1728; he left the position vacant for Boucher in 1744. Throughout his later career, he was to build a certain amount, although many projects remained unexecuted.[33] To his contemporaries, he seemed an almost miracle-working stage designer, as well as the deviser of large-scale fetes and above all, of firework displays throughout Europe:[34] it is difficult now to see this kind of activity as the staple of a famous architect's career. As I will show further, it was perfectly normal in the eighteenth century. Even the austere Blondel, after all, had written a handbook to fireworks.[35]

Although as a scene painter Servandoni owed much to the Bibbienas, his canvases are very like those of his master, Giovanni Paolo Panini, the first of the great painters whose work is almost entirely devoted to the exaltation of ruins: as a painter, he stands

J. N. Servandoni's project of 1732 for the facade of St. Sulpice, winning design of the competition. Foto Electa.

somewhere between Panini and Hubert Robert; but as an architect, his fame rests on the facade of St. Sulpice in Paris, which has been taken by many critics and historians as the first monument of neo-classicism in France, marking the restoration of the "true taste of the ancients."[36]

That is why St. Sulpice is worth examining in some detail. It was a porch enclosed by two corner towers, which were divided into three stories, each corresponding to one of the three Greek orders and crowned with lanterns. The porch proper corresponded to the two lower orders and projected forward; on the Ionic floor it had the conventional three-quarter attached columns, but on the lower floor the wall was pushed back, leaving the Doric columns fully detached, to make a portico, which was two columns deep: Perrault's coupled columns turned sideways, as it were.[37]

The superimposition of solid over void in two orders was conse-crated by Palladio in the Palazzo Chiericati in Vicenza; but it was very unusual at this time. The three central bays carried a pedi-ment. Apart from the freeing and doubling of the four central Doric columns, the treatment of the orders was quite conventional Colosseum-fashion. They were three-quarter attached columns, coupled at the corners of the towers. The Corinthian order was treated in a "modern" way; the outer columns of the couple were replaced by a grotesque console (like the strange supporters in Palladio's Palazzo Valmarana), the pediments were broken by clocks, and the whole thing crowned by a campanile.

The two towers and the pedimented double portico had no exact precedent. Wren's St. Paul's may well have provided the genesis of the motifs, in spite of the many differences.[38] But in any case, the facade itself had subsequently almost as complex a building history as the church proper. Work began on the original scheme in 1733, but long before it was finished, Servandoni had altered the project and engraved the new version. This was in 1742. The pediment now covered the five bays of the facade, the inner coupled columns of the tower becoming the outer columns of the temple front in a kind of *enjambement*. The wall of the central element is also pushed back, so that the portico is free-standing, proud of the wall on both floors. The two towers are also "regularized." There are coupled columns, and the central turret is crowned by a hemispherical dome. The difficulty (a similar problem to that experienced in the central portion of the Louvre facade) was that the pediment was now gigantic.

The facade was raised to the height of the Ionic cornice in 1745, when Servandoni left Paris. Another architect (Oudot de Maclaurin) was engaged to complete the building, beginning with the towers, which he altered, raising them somewhat. Meanwhile a committee

Elevation du nouveau Portail de St. Sulpice?

Servandoni's final project for St. Sulpice and the surrounding square, of 1752, on his return from England. After J.-F. Blondel.

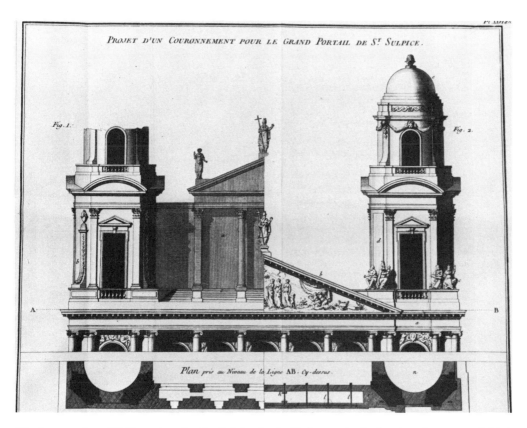

The intermediate (1745) project for St. Sulpice by J. N. Servandoni, showing the recessed third Corinthian-order story and the two gigantic pediments. After Pierre Patte.

appointed by the academy decided that the new pediment would be too heavy to be carried by the colonnade. A compromise suggestion was made: the Ionic order would carry a balustrade, and the Corinthian order of the towers would be carried over the back wall of the portico and crowned with a small pediment, as of the first scheme.[39] It was this facade which was struck by lightning in 1770, fortunately for the architects—Oudot de Maclaurin (with Pierre Patte) charged with the building again when Servandoni died in 1766. Maclaurin finally took charge in 1768, but the final form of the church was fixed by J.-F. T. Chalgrin, a pupil of Jacques-François Blondel, and best known as the architect of the triumphal Arch at the top of the Champs Elysées.

Although St. Sulpice as it now stands owes its outline to the asymmetrical towers and particularly to Maclaurin and Chalgrin, the balustrade between them is bare because at the French Revolution the statues over each order of columns were knocked down. And yet the portico, half a century later, still drew enthusiasm from Jacques-François Blondel. Servandoni alone, Blondel writes with reference to St. Sulpice, managed to sustain the Greek style in all his works, while in his time Paris gave birth to little more than

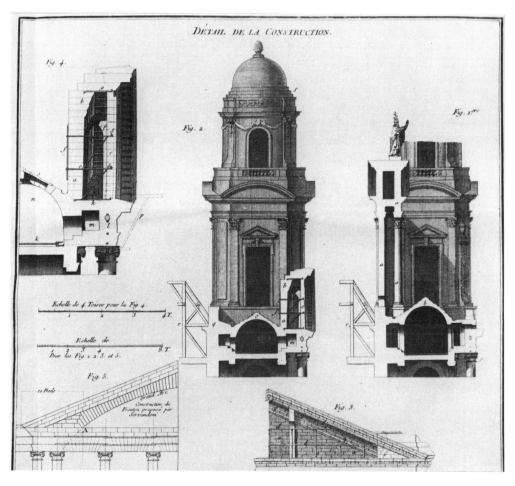

Constructional details for preceding illustration. After Pierre Patte.

monsters.[40] The Greek style of his orders, however, is Perrault's, as is the coupling of the columns.

St. Sulpice was conceived in the shadow of the Mansart *agence:* Oppenordt, Meissonier, and Le Pautre before they became dependents of the masterful architect to Louis XIV's old age. But the spirit to which Servandoni appealed was Perrault's.

It is tempting at this point to name Perrault as the revolutionary who changed French architecture single-handedly. But this is not what I wish to claim: the effects of his influence at St. Sulpice are dual. Meissonier (whose scheme Perrault would certainly have condemned outright) owes him the freedom of believing that ornament, the surface, is where the imagination may have free play, while the positive beauties, which belong to the quality of materials, to workmanship, to the general massing, take care of themselves. Where he differed from Perrault is that he did not think it necessary to govern his imagination by the rule of authority. The pleasures supplied by nature, the power of his invention would, with the help of nature, draw on that fountain of invention which had never before run dry.[41]

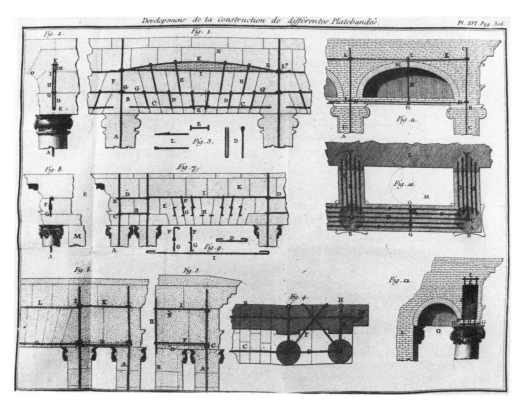

Constructional details of the Ionic order, showing the vault behind the cornice and the reinforcement. After Pierre Patte.

But Meissonier, with his contemporaries and his successors, clearly thought that if ornament was the thing which Perrault described it as, then not only the shackles of metaphor and rhetorical consistency could be broken but also those of the authority of convention; and they could be broken by appealing directly to the observation of natural forms, such as had inspired the makers of the humid and shadowy homes of the nymphs: it is this nature which they brought out into the light of day.

Servandoni is much more directly the successor of Perrault. The use of the orders from Perrault's book, the exaltation of the coupled columns supporting their straight entablature, the appeal to a conventionalized, a schematized and an unspecific antiquity is Perrault's heritage.

Both solutions are therefore made in the wake of the *Ordonnance* and the edition of *Vitruvius*; more so perhaps than in the wake of Perrault's buildings. The Greek style of which Blondel had spoken was not the Greek style which the antiquarian and archeologists would soon identify and the designers emulate and copy. It was the ''style'' of correctly applying the three Greek orders, of using the column as an essential constructional element.

The battles of neoclassicism as a movement would be fought out around these matters: the status of the column, the nature of the

Elevations of the north and south transepts of St. Sulpice, by G.-M. Oppenordt. After J.-F. Blondel.

appeal to the antique, the freshness of inspiration, the conflict of veracity and convention. In all of them the formulations of Perrault would echo. Not so much because they are particularly brilliant—they are often trite, and even more often question-begging—but because the persuasive scholar and administrator could transmit a simplified version of the Cartesian analytic method and its attendant incipient associationist aesthetic ideas to several generations of architectural theorists, his importance is overwhelming. In his theory he established another point which was to have an enormous influence: since the positive beauties of architecture require no particular skill to be appreciated but lie in the domain of common sense, their presence in a building is not due so much to the architect's particular skill but to the proper disposition of the structure, the ability of the workmen, and the quality of the materials themselves. The skill of the architect is in the operation of imagination, which deals with arbitrary beauty: it is in the realm of the irrational, in the realm of taste. The architect, therefore, in so far as he has skill, is the man of taste.

Perrault's work stands at a point when architecture as a profession was formulated; and the notion that the architect is a man of taste would both be taken as a mark of approval and as an irksome stigma which its practitioners would constantly try to expunge or conceal.

And Perrault also bequeathed his successors a taste—a taste for a vision of antiquity. This antiquity was calm and stereometric. An antiquity of orthogonals, of columns supporting long, firm architraves, sparsely broken by the modulations of the plan or by the rising tympani, trophies, and statues. An antiquity whose authenticity was guaranteed by millennia of deposit in terms of custom, so that origins and sources, the actual first and most authentic instances, need not be sought.

It was a vast heritage. Later writers, as I shall show, returned repeatedly to Perrault's ideas as well as to his work, sometimes to traduce it by extrapolating from it ideas and projects which would have been abhorrent to him (as did the rococo designers) but also to find in it a standard against which the new discoveries and inventions could be measured. Seen from our vantage point, however, his work, which seemed one of consolidation, was also dangerously reductionist if not actually destructive: it took the proper work of the architect, his particular skill, out of the realm of reason and secured it in that of taste and fancy. In the reaction which followed, Perrault's example was as often followed as his ideas were inverted or even neglected. Theorists turned their ideas away from the whole business of the orders; but ultimately, what was to strike at the center of Perrault's theory was not anything in architectural theory, but propositions derived from a Lockeian anthropology and Newton's *Opticks*: his Jansenist distrust of human nature, his anatomical theory of vision both suffered in the eclipse of rationalism. The notion of the two beauties, so clearly formulated in the *Ordonnance*, was deformed by many of Perrault's readers, as it was by Christopher Wren, to serve the old and obvious distinction between structure and surface, however that was understood. The imposition of a court style (which Perrault had theorized and justified) was politically irrelevant in the France of the *Régence* and of Louis XV. The intellectual fashions had followed the consolidation of a new British dominance.

1. See F. Piel (1960).

2. See chapter 5.

3. W. Dietterlin (1593–1598). Several plates of ornamental "inventions" appeared in small batches in Nuremburg in 1615, but the contribution of a Nuremburg contemporary, Wendel Jamnitzer, was considered carefully by E. Kris (1926), p. 150 ff.

4. The word appeared in the French Academy dictionary of 1741, as did the description of the craftsmen who produced it as *rocailleur;* Zedler's *Universal-Lexicon* (Leipzig and Halle, 1742) calls it *Grotten-arbeit*, that is, the decoration of underground chambers with pebbles, shells, rocks, snakes; and it may also be associated with fountains, etc. The great *Encyclopedia* of Diderot and d'Alembert also classifies it under *architecture hydraulique* but extends it to mean a kind of rustic architecture which imitates natural rock, by means of pierced stones and other petrifications, shells, etc.

5. Rococo must have been devised before the break of the century about 1820. Stendahl thinks it a *"nom un peu vulgaire"* by which that bad taste whose father was Bernini goes in the studios. With time the romantic poets use it to mean old-fashioned, fuddy-duddy (Théophile Gauthier, Victor Hugo, Arsène Houssaye). But about the middle of the century Jakob Burckhardt was using it to mean something much more like Baroque, a "late, florid, decadent stage of every style" (R. Wellek, 1963, p. 70).

6. St. Simon, who was an involved spectator, gives a highly colored account of the process. It may be taken in a more refined form from Marmontel (1805), pp. 61 ff.

7. Fleury died at the end of January 1743; the duchesse de Châteauroux died in November 1744. The king knew of Mme. d'Etioles before that but did not really meet her until that winter. G. P. Gooch (1956), pp. 139 f. Hence the description of Mme. de Pompadour in Germany as *Rocococotte* is wholly inappropriate. For her patronage and her association with her brother, the Marquis de Marigny, see below.

8. On the two terms, rather cursorily, see A. Blunt (1973).

9. R. Wellek (1963), p. 71.

10. F. Kimball (1943), p. 26.

11. The best account of this quarrel recently is in Bernard Teyssèdre (1964), pp. 152 ff.

12. Watteau painted two versions of this picture. The Academy one is in the Louvre. A larger and more *nuancé* version in the Kaiser Friedrich Museum in Berlin was painted for the connoisseur de Julienne. It was engraved at the time by Nicolas Tardieu.

13. C.-P. J. de Crébillon (Crébillon *fils*) (1736).

14. On Choderlos de Laclos and his literary aims, see *Oeuvres* (1959), pp. xvi ff.

15. See Mme. d'Abrantés (1837), I, pp. 3 ff. On the *salon's* political influence during the Regency, F. L. Ford (1962), pp. 204 ff.

16. E. Dilke (1888), pp. 189 ff., 242 ff. J. Niclausse (1948), passim.

17. S. Roche and P. Devinoy (1957), pp. 9 ff.

18. E. Dilke (1888), pp. 205 ff.; (1901), pp. 144 ff.

19. For the view of Rembrandt at this time, see B. Teyssèdre (1964), pp. 145 ff. No study of the architecture in the paintings of Watteau and his followers

has been done. It is clearly derived from the architecture of such paintings as Rubens' *Garden of Love* in the Prado and is therefore explicitly archaic.

20. F. Kimball (1943), pp. 152 f.

21. Cologne (Amsterdam?), 1721, revised 1754. It went through many editions and had many successors, but also such antecedents as J.-P. Marana's *L'Espion du Grand Seigneur* (1684), Dufresny's *Amusements* (1699), or J. Bonnet's *Lettre écrite à Musala* (1716).

22. "Rubens is too bold and S-like in his contours." William Hogarth (1752), p. ix.

23. Sub v. Meissonier, J.-A., in T-B; also D. Guilmard (1880), pp. 155 ff.; and F. Kimball (1943), p. 154.

24. Fr. Languet de Gergy. On Oppenordt's unfortunate dealings with this enterprise, and his failure which presumably led to the competition, cf. F. Kimball (1943), pp. 144 ff.

25. A. E. Brinckmann (1922), I, p. 138; II, p. 282. Cf. L. Hautecoeur (1948), III, pp. 261 ff.

26. As on the façade of the Oratory or at San Carlino.

27. See Borromini's own comment on the Oratory façade in his *Opus Architectonicum*.

28. As for instance at Zwiefalten (1738–1762) or his Osterhofen (1726–1731); Domenikus Zimmermann's Steinhausen (1727–1733) or the Wies (1745–1754). It is curious how the elaborately molded pulpits and side-altars turn into pagodas. Sometimes the saints (as the St. Jerome at Wies) look positively like mandarins!

29. The most conspicuous example perhaps is Balthasar Neumann's Vierzehnheiligen (1743–1772). See on this point, A. E. Brinckmann (1922).

30. H. R. Hitchcock (1968), pp. 220 ff.

31. See chapter 10.

32. His father, one Servan, was the coachman of a *diligence* traveling between Lyons and Florence. His mother was Florentine. He was born in Florence in 1695 and died in 1766. There is a full biography of Servandoni in Quatremère de Quincy (1830), II, pp. 286–296. A summary of his life and account of his buildings in L. Hautecoeur (1948), III, pp. 267 ff.

33. Notably, the square before St. Sulpice; M. Gallet (1972), p. 81; L. Hautecoeur (1952), IV, pp. 394, 406.

34. He was called to London for the celebrations of the Peace of Aix-la-Chapelle in the autumn of 1748. Servandoni loved traveling and seemed almost temperamentally short of money: "Ce Servandoni," writes Diderot (1765) "est un homme qui tout l'or du Pérou . . ."

35. F. Blondel (1698). So did A. F. Frézier (1706).

36. J.-F. Blondel (1771), IIII, p. 351. F. Milizia (1781), II, pp. 342 f.; and A. C. Quatremère de Quincy (1830), II, p. 290. See also E. Dilke (1900), pp. 16 f.

37. L. Hautecoeur (1948), III, pp. 359 ff. Cf. R. D. Middleton (1962, and 1963). A much closer example, in terms of the two-dimensional arrangement however, seems Giacomo della Porta's St. Atanasio in Rome.

38. Laugier (1765), p. 175, criticized Servandoni for this very feature and wanted columns coupled on the main porch, while Patte thought it both formally and statically superior (1769), pp. 293 ff.

39. See *P.V.* VIII, pp. 8 f.; and P. Patte (1769), pp. 342 ff.

40. "Il a su soutenir le style Grec dans toutes ses productions, tandis que Paris, à son temps, n'enfantoit guère que des Chimères." J.-F. Blondel (1771–1777), III, p. 351.

41. "Il genio dell'Architetto (deve) esser libero, e per quanto bene possano aver pensato gli preandanti valenti Architetti, no, non v'ha ragione . . . che migliorare in qualche modo non si possano i loro pensieri; no, non e credibile che il fonte dell'invenzione chiuso trovasi per gli uomini moderni e loro posteri. B. Vittone, *Istruzioni Diverse*, 1766.

6

Initiates to Amateurs

The profession of architect was isolated in Italy about 1450,[1] in France a century later, and in Britain almost a century after France. Inigo Jones was probably the first Briton to use the word in the sense in which it was coming to be used in the rest of Europe. His achievement was due to a cosmopolitan ambition operating in an insular situation. It is a measure of his insularity that he considered himself a direct disciple of Palladio. He was, in fact, some thirty years younger than Palladio's disciple, Vincenzo Scamozzi, whom he had met during his second Italian visit in 1614.[2] Palladio had died in 1580; Jones could be counted with the generation of Bernini and Borromini, being only ten years their junior, while François Mansart and Jacques le Mercier were Jones' French contemporaries. Baldassare Longhena, however, is the closest in time, and the furthest stylistically: two years younger than Jones, he also worked from the datum of Scamozzi's reinterpretation of Palladio.[3] This bookish and hermetic interpretation required a building industry in which the execution of architect's drawings in terms of classical detail was wholly taken for granted. Longhena had such an industry at hand in the Veneto, while Jones had to devote much of his energy to creating it. Hence craft matters assume such a disproportionate importance in the history of seventeenth- and early eighteenth-century British architecture.

The community of artists-architects had been formed in Italy from a heterogeneous amalgam of trained craftsmen who had already been used to supervise building activities: goldsmiths, painters, joiners, and literary men with a devotion to the antique. They became a loosely organized group of operators who used the title *architetto* to cover work ranging from stage design to fortification. Membership in a masons' guild was not the rule among them.[4]

When the new learning first affected French taste and French building, things proceeded differently. In France there were Italian architects to set an example, often imported by royal patrons who were sometimes Italian or half-Italian and of whom Catherine de' Medici was the most conspicuous. A decisive change occurred as the result of the patronage of a single king, Francis I. It crystallized in the School of Fontainebleau, named after the only palace which Francis called "my home";[5] and it had an even more powerful centralizing effect on the French than Versailles, an indelible mark which an expansive Italianizing court left on French art and to which the French building tradition took half a century to accommodate itself. The accommodation was mediated by a series of publications, particularly by excellent translations of Italian and Latin classics: the dream of Polyphilus, then Vitruvius and Alberti. Serlio, Palladio, and Vignola followed, the last perhaps the most influential in France.[6]

From France, the new fashion spread to the Low Countries and to Germany, to mingle with direct imports from Italy. The first "order" engravings appeared in Germany during the fifteen-forties.[7] Serlio published the fourth of his books on architecture, the one which sets out his account of the orders first, in Venice in 1537. It appeared in Flemish, German, and French within a few years.[8] In 1568 the first architectural treatise to be composed independently in France, that of Philibert de l'Orme, was published in Lyons.[9] All this activity led to a transformation of northern European architecture which did not cross the Channel very quickly. Torrigiani did come to London to make the tomb of Henry VII at Westminster[10] and Henry VIII attempted to emulate Francis I in interior decoration (as he did in other matters),[11] but while affected by fashion, was naturally enough hostile to Italianizers; Nonsuch was no Fontainebleau, and his two daughters had other things to spend their money on than building. At that time Flemish taste dominated Britain. The new nobility which had risen from the middle classes by buying monastic lands (with proceeds of such things as sea trade) and royal favor asserted its power by signposting the country with tall, "lantern" houses. Hardwick in Derbyshire and Wollaton in Nottinghamshire display their designers' passion for pattern-books; it is indulged within a castellated and ciphered manner, *Faerie Queen*'s aura made visible. Spenser's poem was its basic text, and the dressy chivalry of tourneys and festivals its environment. The builders of the lantern-houses, whether newly jumped-up or left over from the old families, had an avid interest in chivalric romance. For these, the new houses with their large glass windows, unstained and untraceried but leaded into elaborate frets and knots, were a perfect setting.[12] They may have been drafty, as Bacon was to observe later ("You shall sometimes see fair houses, so full of glass that one cannot tell where to become to be out of the Sunne or Cold" [13]), but they were conceived as the monument of a legendary past which could be grafted onto more recent historical antecedents. Hence the quasi-medieval forms decked out with archaic Arthurian timeless classical garnish, gathered from pattern-books, mostly Flemish, and even executed by Flemish craftsmen. Many of the craftsmen were native: the lack of royal or church patronage released them for this work; while Antwerp, the great center of guilds, and printing as well, was the theater of some of the worst Spanish repression in the Low Countries. Liberal craftsmen from Walloon lands tended to take refuge in Protestant Britain as French Huguenot craftsmen would in the seventeenth century.

The Flemings brought the new European fashions—which was exactly what English builders, with their veneration of antiquity and their obsession with emblems and devices, wanted.[14] Even if Bacon assured them that things abroad were not quite so marvelous, that vast and famous palaces such as the Vatican or the Escorial had "scarcely a very fair room in them," [15] yet their desire for the new antique was insatiable: magnates demanded new architectural and pattern-books from envoys; soon this was not enough. The Duke of Northumberland, who was to lose his head for Lady Jane Grey, sent a member of the Painters' and Stainers' Company, John Shute, to

Italy. All that survives of this trip is a short book, *The First and Chief Ground of Architecture*, which appeared in the year of Shute's death, 1563.[16] Although its form owes something to Serlio, it is heavily influenced by Flemish order-books.[17] Shute's precepts were followed only very sporadically;[18] they could only reach a very small public.

Contemporary with Shute's mandarin publication is a more thorough if less well-known attempt to introduce the classical "thing" by the great Welsh polymath and magus, Dr. John Dee. Its most evident memento is the preface to the first English translation of Euclid's *Elements*, which contains a strong plea to include architecture "among the *Artes Mathematicall. The Architect*," argues Dee, "procureth, enformeth & directeth the Mechanician to hand-worke & the building actuall . . . and is chief Iudge of the same: yet with himselfe (as chief *Master* and *Architect*) remaineth the Demonstrative reason and cause . . . If this be soe: then, may you thinke, that *Architecture* hath good and due allowance in this honest company of *Artes Mathematicall* Derivative." [19]

Dee's architect has a quite distinct way of operating from the mechanics, from the craftsmen, however exalted: that is probably

John Shute, the Doric order.

John Shute, the Ionic order.

how Shute saw himself working, like many continental contemporaries. But in Britain things were not quite so clear. At Longleat, for instance, it seems that it was John Thynne, the dilettante courtier and virtuoso who did "procure, inform and direct the Mechanician"; he, not the master-mason, Robert Smythson, remained "the demonstrative reason and cause" of the building. Smythson, however, went on to greater things at Wollaton; he lies buried in the parish church there, under a stone which describes him as "Gent Architector and Surveyor unto the most worthy house of Wollaton." [20]

The surface of such newer Elizabethan houses was scored with the essential marks of the new learning and fashion: superimposed orders. The chief exemplars for this treatment were the Colosseum and the Theater of Marcellus in Rome, whose vast size and relatively good state of preservation gave them enormous prestige among architects and patrons. It is not entirely surprising therefore that this superimposition was also demonstrated in theaters, with great insistence on classical precedent. No permanent theater had been built in Britain since antiquity, when James Burbage built The Theatre in Shoreditch in 1576.[21] The whole structure of The Thea-

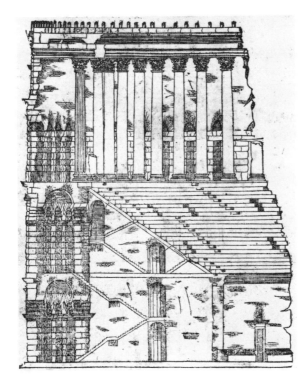

*The ancient theater, as reconstructed from Vitruvius'
description. After Daniele Barbaro's edition.*

The Globe and the Bear Pit. After W. Hollar's view of London.

tre was later dismantled, and reerected on Bankside in 1599 as The Globe, Richard Burbage's and Shakespeare's most famous playhouse. The relationship between Dee, the Burbages, and Shakespeare, seems indirect. Yet is very likely that The Theatre, the Globe, and most other London theaters which followed them were consciously based on classical precept out of Vitruvius but modified by theater examples proposed in books on the art of memory, and that they were conceived as moral emblems.[22]

Dee was familiar with various editions of Vitruvius, as well as with more recent architectural literature. In his Euclid preface, he takes up a passage in which Daniele Barbaro (the most learned Vitruvius editor of the time and a friend of Palladio) incorporates the pagan author into Christian chronology—although Dee gives it an additional hermetic twist: "*Vitruvius* did write ten books of (Architecture) to the Emperor *Augustus* in whose daies our Heauenly Archemaster was borne." In Dee's terms Archemaster was not a vague hyperbole. Archmasterie is the supreme mathematical science in his list; "which name is not so new as this Arte is rare." [23] Directly below archmastery, Dee lists thaumaturgicke, navigation, and architecture. The coupling of navigation (with all its astronomical and astrological implications) with architecture is not really surprising: but thaumaturgicke—literally, "miracle or wonder-working"— looks odd on the list. Dee describes it rationally enough as "that art Mathematicall, which giveth certain order to make straunge workes, of the senses to be perceived, and of men to be greatly wondered at." [24] This art was practiced by Hiero of Alexandria but also by the saintly Albertus Magnus and was closely allied to "natural magick." In his account of natural magic, Dee is heavily influenced by Cornelius Agrippa, whose *Occulta Philosophia* he often quotes.[25]

Cornelius Agrippa, and after him other very influential authors, notably Giambattista della Porta and Francesco Giorgio, held a modified form of the old Neoplatonic teaching. There is a heavenly music, as there is an earthly one; both are governed by number and therefore reveal the whole mechanism of nature.[26] By the operation of number, spirits may be conjured, essential musical and linear harmonies devised, new engines—including illusionistic ones—invented, navigation facilitated, and the humblest crafts properly regulated.[27]

The operator of number had great power over the physical world therefore, but also over persons. In such a scheme, the architect, when he worked in harmony with the universal law of number, was the inevitable, the natural master of all those working in the building trades. Dee knew well that things were out of joint in this realm; he writes: "we may not, of auncient Artes, make new and imperfect definitions in our daies: for scarcitie of artificers," but this did not alter his view of how things were to be ordered, nor of the high calling of architecture among the mathematical arts, close to the Archmastery: "Now then it is euident . . . how aptly and worthely I have preferred *Architecture* to be bred and fostered up in the dominion of the Perless *Princesse*, *Mathematica*.[28]

This is very much the view Inigo Jones had of his calling, and in

that sense, at least, he was John Dee's heir. Like many other architects of his time, he had some training in the building trade, as a
joiner's apprentice.[29] He also traveled extensively; a long tour in
Italy, perhaps also in France and Germany, is often associated with
the travels of Roger Manners (later Earl of Rutland).[30] Jones seems
to have visited Denmark also, at the time of Rutland's embassy there
which brought the Garter to the young king, Christian IV, in 1603.
The year after, he was in the service of the queen of England (she
was Christian IV's sister) as a masque designer.[31] The first mask on
which he worked, the Masque of Blacknesse, with a text by Ben
Jonson, was produced in 1605.[32]

Ben Jonson had already collaborated on a court pageant: on the
festivities for the entry of James I and Anne of Denmark to London
in 1603.[33] The designer on that occasion was Stephen Harrison,
"Joyner and Architect," of whom nothing else is known.[34] The sequence of pageants was marked by a succession of orders: the whole
thing had a Flemish-enough look.

Jones works in a different style from the outset. Both costumes
and settings show his familiarity with Italian models. As the masques
develop, he becomes more eclectic, allowing himself reference
to French models; but he also uses the more elaborate costume-
books, such as Vecellius's and Boissard's, and even more learned
works:[35] Reference to engraved models does not exclude a certain
scholarship. When James I commissioned him to survey and examine Stonehenge,[36] he did so because he respected Jones' knowledge.
In the book on Stonehenge, which he identified as a Tuscan temple
dedicated to the archaic deity Coelus or Uranus, Jones drew on his
extensive, bookish learning: Geoffrey of Monmouth; Matthew of
Westminster; Giraldus Cambrensis for the chronicles; as well as the
more learned mythographers, Natalis Comes and Piero Valeriano.
Odder still are quotations from John Leland's (or Leyland's) antiquarian journeys, which must have been taken from a manuscript.[37] It would have been difficult to find reading of this nature in
the Britain of Jones' time outside—perhaps—John Dee's library.[38]
This alone does not establish the connection between the two Welsh
notables. But although there is no direct evidence about his acquaintance with Dee, he certainly knew another magus—also a
Welshman—Robert Fludd, as the notes on the blank leaves of his
annotated Palladio show;[39] these refer to medical advice about
Jones' complaints, yet the tone of familiar conversation they imply
suggests that they had other contacts.

Apart from his book on Stonehenge, Jones left no systematic
writings, although he may well have intended to do so.[40] The only
publication which, in his lifetime, advanced an English theory of
architecture was Henry Wotton's *Elements of Architecture*, a curious book for a seasoned diplomat to open a literary career late in
life.[41] It was written and published, quickly, to establish Wotton's
claim to the vacant provostship of Eton against formidable rivals.[42]
Il volpone vecchio (the old fox), as an Italian spy called him,[43] was
looking to his retirement and curiously chose architecture as his

topic, although he was familiar enough with science and theology, as well as court and state matters. A contemporary comment retails the rumor that Wotton "is finishing a work he is setting out of mathematics, or perhaps castles in the air." [44] And castles in the air is what the sort of architecture Wotton was commending may have seemed to his readers, since he sets out to show how to adapt Italian High Renaissance building to the British climate, and to the building of a country house in particular. The book is addressed to the British gentry. There is hardly a word about church building. The only building in the country to incarnate this manner of design was the Banqueting House in Whitehall, but Wotton refers to no building in Britain,[45] even if there are passages in the *Elements* which read like a direct reference to Inigo Jones, who would certainly have found the book sympathetic, if schematic.

On such mundane matters as the selection of building materials, however, Jones may not have been entirely in agreement: "the Speculative part of such knowledge may be liberal," wrote Wotton, although he wanted the gentleman-architect free from any "mechanical" taint. He therefore reminds the reader that Vitruvius made the supervision of materials the duty of an *officinator* and not of the architect, "whose glory doth more consist in the designment and Idea of the whole Work . . . to make the Form, which is the nobler part (as it were) triumph over the matter." [46]

The continuity of "mechanical" and "ideal" aspects of architecture is broken hieratically. Wotton's Vitruvian Neoplatonism is quite different from the socially integrative drive which informed Jones, as it did Dee. And there is an interesting parallel: as Jones's style, so Wotton's language[47] echoes that of Scamozzi (whom Wotton never mentions), even when he claims to be formulating his own observations: "I had noted, that all Art was then in truest Perfection when it might be reduced to some natural Principle; for what are the most judicious artisans but the Mimicks of Nature? This led me to contemplate the Fabrick of our own Bodies, wherein the *High Architect* of the World had displayed such skill, as did stupify all humane Reason . . . (and) it plainly appeareth as a Maxim drawn from divine Light, that the Place of every Part is determined by its Use." [48]

Anyone familiar with modern masonic terminology will instantly recognize Wotton's "High Architect" as a pre-echo of the title High Architect of the Universe, by which the Deity is always referred to in masonic documents and rituals. This term was unknown to the old masonic guilds, even in the seventeenth century, nor is there any such expression used in scripture. The Authorized Version of the Bible knows of builders, even master-builders, but the very word *architect* is not mentioned anywhere in it. On the other hand, it is an image which Marsilio Ficino used in his commentary on Plato,[49] and which occupied much of the vast commentary on the book of Ezekiel published by the two Spanish Jesuits, Juan Bautista Villalpanda and Jeronimo Prado, and which I mentioned earlier.[50] There is much about the image of God as the architect of the universe, and of the human body as the primal model of its design. There is, too, a discussion of the relation between David and Solomon as architects of the temple and palace with their *officinator* (Villalpanda uses the Spanish term *apparejador*), against which the function of the architect was defined.[51]

Inigo Jones, on the other hand, never defined his particular position against surveyors or master-masons. His closest associate was the poet Ben Jonson. For some fifteen years, they were the joint authors of the major court entertainments. Curiously, both had a craft training, Jonson as a bricklayer,[52] Jones as a joiner. Throughout his career, first as a theatrical decorator, then as an independent designer of buildings,[53] later as surveyor to Prince Henry, and finally as surveyor to the king's works (the high point which he reached in 1615), he remained familiar with the world of tradesmen, however much he was the connoisseur and the traveler;[54] he presided over the drawing up of the elaborate Jacobean building regulations[55] and acted as arbitrator in demarcation disputes between guilds.[56] Inevitably, he was involved in training craftsmen for both masques and his building enterprises. He had a finicky perfectionism in the matter of materials and finishes. The infinite trouble he took over the cutting of the stone for St. Paul's is told by Webb, and the polychrome effect of the Banqueting House, dependent on Jones' choice of building stone, was evident until its refacing by Sir John Soane.[57] The implications of all were resolved when the partnership with Jonson finally and acrimoniously broke in 1631. From that time on, Jonson took him to task constantly for his arrogance, for his assumption of a directing role, but also for his parade of learning, and—paradoxically—for his familiarity with inferior workmen. Already in 1626, in *Neptune's Triumph or the Return of Albion*, a cook disputes with a poet. When the poet states his business as the presentation of masques, the cook answers: "Sir, this is my room and region too, the Banqueting House," which identified the cook as Jones for the audience. There follows a great deal of ribbing on the

Whitehall Palace, dominated by the Banqueting Hall: the river front, by W. Hollar.

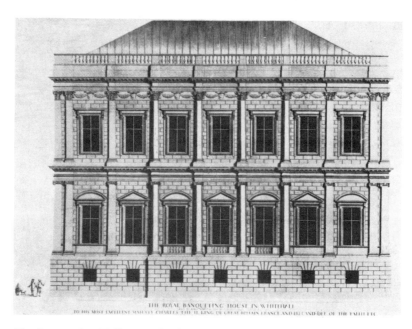

The Banqueting Hall toward Whitehall. Engraving by W. Shittman, which indicates the polychrome character of the original facing and shows Jones' casement windows.

cook's assumption of universal wisdom, who describes himself as ". . . the man of men/for a Professor . . . who/Makes citadels of curious fowl and fish." [58] After the quarrel over the title page of a later masque[59] there is a stream of jibes against Jones; for example, the frontal attack in a poem called *The Expostulation*,[60] the mean characterizations; as In-and-In Medlay in *The Tale of a Tub*,[61] as Coronell Vitruvius, or even more explicitly Iniquo Vitruvius, Jones[62] is presented as the crony of low fellows, chiefly craftsmen; in *Love's Welcome to Bolsover*,[63] the surveyor, Coronell Vitruvius, cries to the carver, freemason, and joiner: "Well done, my Musicall, Arithmeticall, Geometricall Ganesters! It is carried in number, weight and measure as if the Aires were all in harmonie, and the figures in well-timed Proportion." This affable taskmaster of the craftsmen seems quite a different person from the Inigo Jones described elsewhere as haughty, overbearing, and pretentious.[64] But then Jones' self-imposed task would have put him at odds with potential patrons, whose views Jonson may well have been voicing.

Whatever the direct connection (or lack of it) between Jones and Dee, there is little doubt that he breathed the mental climate formed by Dee and his disciples. The Neoplatonic beliefs which the two men shared they attempted to forge into a total mastery of the productive process, the means to endow the everyday with harmony—a harmony which would reconcile political and religious divisions. What the Elizabethan builders saw as a top dressing on an underlying unchanged procedure, that of medieval masons, Dee and Jones wanted to transform into an integrated process. The knots and emblems, the orders even, were not adjuncts; they were to be the regulators of building, the rule by which all the trades were to carry out their separate tasks. Jones' insistence on fraternizing with his craftsmen, to imbue them with the ideology which Jonson (like Wotton) thought fitter stuff for the court and for literati inevitably, set them at odds.

As the King's Surveyor, however, Jones was the most powerful employer of building labor in the country, and he seems to have devoted a great deal of time to guild affairs. We have no knowledge—beyond the negative evidence provided by Jonson and the buildings themselves, where they survive—how the craftsmen responded.[65] Whatever he achieved at the Office of Works was in any case obliterated by the Commonwealth, when his team of men was broken up and the whole of the Platonic policy of the court undermined, devalued.

At this very same time, there is a curious development in England: two gentlemen, both of considerable social standing, one a convinced and lifelong Laudian royalist (but also an alchemist and astrologer), Elias Ashmole, the other a Commonwealth officer, Henry Mainwaring, appear as members of a masons' lodge. Ashmole's record is laconic but helpful: "I was made a freemason at Warrington in Lancashire," he writes in his diary of 16 October 1646.[66] The lodge at Warrington is known from other records:[67] besides the royalist and the parliamentary officer, it included recusant Catholics,[68] which is its symptomatic and evidently irenic feature. Ashmole's initiation is the more celebrated by masonic historians, but another initiation of a gentleman-mason took place a few years earlier on English soil.

Robert Moray was admitted to a special military lodge, delegated from Edinburgh, at Newcastle on 5 May 1641.[69] Ashmole and Moray shared political, religious, and scientific attitudes; both were founder-members of the Royal Society after the restoration of Charles II, of which more later. Ashmole for his part was almost obsessionally concerned with matters of heraldry and ceremony, which was recognized by his connection, again after the Restoration, with the Order of the Garter.

The political, the power structure of the Order of the Garter, and of most of the orders of chivalry, was radically modified in the seventeenth century. But the political character of pageantry: chivalry, masque, procession, festival, is only too easy to underestimate from a twentieth-century vantage. The Order of the Garter, for instance, was in James I's reign, to have been the nucleus of a British academy: Inigo Jones, Sir Henry Wotton, Ben Jonson were all to be members; so was Sir Dudley Digges, one of Dee's best-known disciples. Although the "Senate of Honour" had James' approval, Charles I dropped the scheme after his accession.[70] Another academy was projected at Prince Henry's court when he was heir-apparent; it expired with his death.[71] Academies were an important part of the apparatus of display; they were assemblies of the noble and the learned; they patronized experiment and research, but they also reconciled strife (particularly religious strife) through reasoned debate. There is little doubt that Europe had need of such institutions in the period of religious wars. The Thirty Years' War in Europe and the Civil War in Britain would lead to a decisive change in ideas which Francis Bacon called the Great Instauration.[72]

It was to come about by the extension of learning, its surfacing into public knowledge through printing and through the multiplication of academies, which coincided providentially with the opening of an enlarged area to navigation, great mechanical improvements, and finally the reform and liberalizing of religion. It was to be a change even more world-shaking than anything Dee had foreseen. The extension of natural philosophy would have a consequence quite different from any development of moral philosophy. Natural philosophy was nearest to that kind of knowledge which Adam had of things before his fall; the new knowledge of nature would lead back to the prelapsarian unity of thought and action.[73] The hope was put most eloquently by the young John Milton: "when universal learning has once completed its cycle, the spirit of man . . . will reach out far and wide 'till it fills the whole world and the space far beyond with the expansion of its divine greatness." [74] The old Milton would not echo such rhapsodies, but the attitude he expressed as a young university scholar was shared by many intellectuals, scientists particularly. It contaminated the millenniary, apocalyptic atmosphere of much religious thinking, particularly that of "mechanics." The expectancy and optimism of those involved in scientific experiment and invention, as well as in the visual arts, was in harsh, violent contrast to the conditions of Europe between the outbreak of the Thirty Years' War in 1618 and the relative settlement of the Commonwealth regime in Britain in the middle 1640s.

Francis Bacon provided the most popular model of an institution which was to bring about the new state of affairs—and the ideal society which would go with it; he described in a utopian fragment, which proved to be very popular, the *New Atlantis*,[75] an unknown land governed by a body, a kind of academy he called the Solomonic College. This was not unlike the Senate of Honour I spoke of earlier,[76] being both a supreme scientific body, a promoter of experiment, and a keeper of antiquities. When we look at Bacon through the screen which Lord Macaulay provides, we tend to see him only as the prophet of progress based on empiric inquiry.[77] But Bacon believed, as did many of his contemporaries, that in a remote antiquity things were done better, more was known, even navigation was more extensive than in his own day, and society was certainly much better ordered.[78] New Atlantis was a fragment surviving from that golden age. Nor was that age firmly situated in any particular period. It may well be that Ashmole and Moray, independently, both believed that by joining a masonic lodge they would learn things hidden from their contemporaries and transmitted—from remote antiquity—in the rituals and lore of the craft which was the noblest of all the mechanical skills and which claimed to have been organized and regulated round the holiest and most mysterious of all the works of human hands: King Solomon's Temple in Jerusalem.

The making of the temple is one of the recurring symbols of hermetic operation, as well as the source-legend of masonry.[79]

Neither Ashmole nor Moray, nor any other "speculative" mason of the time, has left reliable evidence for his motives in joining the craft.[80] The first to do so explicitly, much later, was another antiquarian-scientist, also a fellow of the Royal Society, William Stukeley, who confessed that "his curiosity led him to be initiated into the mysterys of Masonry, suspecting it to be the remains of the ancients." [81] This was in 1720; by then the Grand Lodge—of which more later[82]—had been founded and the modern organization of masonry, with "speculative" masons coming to outnumber the "operatives." When Ashmole and Moray joined the craft, however, their decision to do so must have been purposeful as well as maverick.

I have already referred to the belief, among men of goodwill, that forms of communal practice of the inner life would help to override theological differences and attendant savage intolerance. This belief animated a number of academies[83] as well as trade associations, particularly certain guilds: the new trade of printing and the ancient one of building. The first dealt with the stuff of both controversy and conciliation and was the diffuser of all ancient wisdom; the second, by fostering a belief in the continuing presence of a pythagorean-solomonic mystery, offered legitimacy and ceremonial support for the inner life which the external strife of religious controversy obscured. Inevitably, those who were drawn to it were also interested in the mysteries of alchemy and astrology. But there seems also to have been a connection with the Family of Love, a group whose piety went back, before the Reformation, to the *Devotio Nova* and the Brethren of the Free Spirit and who had adherents throughout Europe, radiating from the Low Countries.[84] The London *Domus Charitatis* was one of their centers, and they had many contacts among the learned. Dee certainly met them, although we do not know on what terms.[85] The Family of Love was secretive, however, and their contacts often deliberately obscured, but to many of its members, as to the more pacific Protestant theologians and to many Catholics, the Church of England, especially under the leadership of William Laud, seemed a focus for a united church, whose practice was sacramental but whose government was liberal and decentralized. The great jurist, Grotius, proposed such a program, with Laud as "president" of a united Protestant, even a united Christian church.[86] Laud was prepared to entertain it, as he was the offer of a cardinal's hat,[87] but nothing came of either proposal.

There were other contacts. Lord Herbert of Cherbury sent the first available copy of his book *De Veritate*, the statement of an undogmatic minimal religion (later regarded as the foundation tract of deism) to Grotius for approval, although its *imprimatur* was given by Laud.[88] It was also read and approved by Pope Urban VIII. Marin Mersenne, whom I mentioned earlier as a theoretician of music, translated it into French and sent two copies to Descartes.[89]

It was much commended by the great Bohemian pansophist Amos Commenius.[90] *De Veritate* was certainly not conceived in a deist spirit; it had an explicit Christian apologetic intention: a reinterpretation of the supposed ancient astral religion was offered to justify the assumption that the notion of the divine was innate in man, implanted by the deity, and that in a variety of climates and circumstances, it led to man's different ways of coming to terms with his divine burden. It was an interpretation of ancient religion which was reconcilable with much official church thinking—even if it touched themes which dangerously had occupied Campanella and Bacon.

A century after his death, the autobiography became the most famous of Herbert's writings;[91] it may seem difficult to reconcile the religious philosopher and irenic apologist with the braggart knight of the *Life*. Herbert had been made a Knight of the Bath when young; he took this dubbing rather like Don Quixote his errantry and issued challenges on what now seem less than trivial pretexts, even if the duels were rarely fought.[92] As he grew older, he also took an important part in the ceremonial playing-out of conflict—in jousts and tourneys and the duels of champions which were sometimes the surrogates of battles in war.[93]

Herbert regarded his knighthood as an initiation into a mystery.[94] So did Ashmole, presumably, his entry into a masonic lodge. A link between chivalry and the crafts, masonry in particular, is not nowadays regarded as self-evident, but in the seventeenth century both were still understood as secret societies, with roots in hoary traditions. It is often forgotten that medieval society was made up of a continuous tissue of these, ranging from the pious associations of agricultural laborers to the grandest orders of chivalry which were often stranded in unfamiliar situations.[95] In the seventeenth century, however, the link between chivalry and masonry still seemed easy enough to establish. Elias Ashmole makes it in his description of "the elegant and beauteous structure" [96] of St. George's Chapel at Windsor, which was the home of the Order of the Garter.

The place of "supervisor or surveyor" had been granted to William de Wyckeham (who attained the dignity of bishop of Winchester and was the second Prelate of the Garter).[97] This powerful churchman, and most important officer of the oldest and noblest order of chivalry in Britain, had, according to Ashmole—and masonic tradition following him—been an admitted master-mason.[98] Ashmole had written a history of the Garter, but he intended also to write a history of masonry. A brief one already existed, set down for the Royal Society by Sir Robert Moray. Ashmole's was never written and Moray's is lost.[99] When Moray and Ashmole became masons, the distinction between their "theoretical" or "speculative" membership and that of working, or "operative," masons could not be made clearly.[100] Another foundation member of the Royal Society was Dr. (later Sir) Christopher Wren. At the time of the Restoration, he still had not built anything. He was born in 1632, shortly before his father, another Christopher Wren, was made dean of Windsor in succession to his brother Matthew, who had been advanced to the see of Hereford.[101] The older Christopher was the chief protector of the monuments and records of the Order of the Garter, as Ashmole amply acknowledges.[102]

Wren is now remembered mostly as the architect of St. Paul's, less popularly as a brilliant experimenter and mathematician. It is not often noticed that, like many of his contemporaries, he also had an interest in occult literature, particularly in alchemy and "natural magic."[103] The older Ashmole and Moray were both close to their junior Wren, and it is hardly surprising that their interests overlapped. Of the other fellows of the Royal Society, we know that most of them invested in experimental method, that they had mathematical interests and often hermetic ones as well.[104] There was, however, a complex of other ideas in which they were interested: the possibility of a universal (and rational) language;[105] and forms of cipher and shorthand writing.[106] This pattern of ideas links them both to Dee and to Bacon; the theme which runs through all this is the familiar one of the Great Instauration. Wren was very much part of the movement and is even known to have been a pupil, at Oxford, of a strange person who made the link explicit: the "Rosicrucian" Peter Stahl, who established the first teaching laboratory at Oxford.[107]

There were so many crosscurrents between the "Rosicrucian" alchemists and the early "speculative" masons that almost inevitably connections were suggested and inferred.[108] Both groups shared, moreover, an Old Testament patron, King Solomon, whose "key" affected the alchemical transmutation and who was also the builder of the temple in Jerusalem.[109] The temple had a uniquely binding force: unlike Noah's Ark or the desert tabernacle, it was the only human work done on God's direct and explicit command, whose traces could still be seen on earth.[110] In biblical commentary generally, and in hermetic thinking more particularly, it was the image of production as the path to salvation.[111] There can be little doubt that many masons in the seventeenth and eighteenth centuries saw certain tasks as aspects of the masonic "work." The restoration of the king during the Commonwealth, perhaps the return of James II and the Old Pretender later, were spoken of in such terms. But perhaps above all, the Great Instauration, in all its different forms lent itself to this interpretation.

For the masons the archetype was developed into a legendary lore about their origins in the organization set up for the building of the Solomonic temple, which many held to be the oldest of all permanent buildings.[112] The moral and spiritual interpretation of their particular trade, although one of the great commonplaces of medieval society, was taught to apprentices as a form of discipline, much as is still done in some "underdeveloped" countries.[113] The special place of the masons in the "hierarchy" of medieval trades was related to this notion of the building of the temple of Jerusalem; Solomon, therefore, and the two Hirams were the ancestors of all divinely inspired workers,[114] much as in antiquity the same place was occupied by the building of the maze and Daedalus was regarded as the archetype of all craftsmen.[115]

St. Paul's Cathedral, London, as refaced by Inigo Jones, facade and portico. After Dugdale.

The lodge mysteries, or trade secrets, were a repertory of rules-of-thumb coordinated with a systematic technique of geometrical proportioning.[116] They also taught the spiritual meaning, the analogy of the mason's craft and the symbolic interpretation of his instruments: the compass, the level, the plumb line, and the chisel.[117] These "mysteries" were so much the commonplace that alchemy was quite generally regarded as a special case of craft work.[118]

Victor Hugo has taught that printing killed architecture.[119] Whatever the future will reveal about this prophecy, which seems to have reached fulfillment, printing certainly affected the craft guilds critically. The manuscript trade manual was kept in the control of the guild; a printed manual became common property. The trade manual provided the apprentice with what seemed like a "teach-yourself" short-cut, but a threat was present for masons in a revolution in taste and the abandonment of the old masonic procedures based on geometrical working in favor of new arithmetical harmonic schemes developed with the arrival of Arabic numerals, such as the ones to be proposed by Leone Battista Alberti and in Germany by Dürer.[120] The masons' answer, as far as central Europe was concerned, was to close ranks at their congress at Ratisbon in 1459. The craft was reorganized around four regional capitals, and supreme authority was placed in that of Strasbourg, a primacy which was only ended by an imperial decree many decades after Strasbourg had been annexed by France.[121]

But while in France the strength of the guilds was generally undermined by the encroachment of royal power throughout the seventeenth century—to be abolished "finally" by the French Rev-

*St. Paul's, London, the north face of the building after refacing by Inigo
Jones. After W. Hollar.*

olution, the situation in Britain was more confused. The building
trades had suffered a decline not comparable with the French situation during the sixteenth century. Nor, until the days of Dee and
Digges, were craftsmen concerned to absorb new learning. In
building it was something which was externally applied, out of
books, by virtuosi or "architects." Jones' achievement is often neglected: he was the agent through whom the old craft-mysteries were
translated into the new Scamozzan and Neoplatonic terms which he
shared with Wotton and with Dee's heirs. It is at this time that
speculative masonry appeared in the lodges. At any rate, speculative
and operative masons mixed freely. There are records of what seem
to be speculative lodges at the Masons' Hall in London, which still
acted as a trade union in the eighteenth century;[122] and, there is also
the record of a speculative mason involved with an operative lodge
in Flanders.[123]

The monument in which some of these ideas and events were
summed up was Inigo Jones' heroic refacing of old St. Paul's,
which made it a worthy metropolitan church of the Laudian establishment and a fitting "augustan" counterpoise to the projected
royal palace, of which the Banqueting Hall was the first installment,
and to which Covent Garden was, as it were, a *tertium quid* in the
transformation of Charles I's capital. Building was as much an act of
policy as it was for Louis XIV. For St. Paul's, he commissioned
Jones to design a free-standing Corinthian portico. The columns
were 56 feet high, making it the largest such portico in the Western
world since antiquity, rivaled only by Michelangelo's 110 foot portico for St. Peter's, which was conceived as a rival to the antique one
of the Pantheon; however, by the time Jones' columns were begun,
Michelangelo's mighty portico had been reduced to the articulation
of Maderna's facade for the enlarged basilica.[124] It is notable that the

The Grand Lodge at Strasbourg, spiral staircase designed and executed before 1580, by Thomas Uhlberger.

portico fronted the medieval church, which was adapted, the Norman walls becoming an astylar Tuscan; Ionic columns framed the transept doors, Doric the nave ones. It may be that the Composite would have been used in the choir, but even without that, the rusticoed and porticoed cathedral was the perfect Laudian microcosm and a school for the new masons.[125]

In spite of the high-minded and conciliatory thinking of both sides in the civil war, Charles I's "Platonic" policy was destroyed: with some who were otherwise favorable to it—like Herbert of Cherbury—taking the Commonwealth side, however unwillingly.[126] It is hardly surprising that St. Paul's was one of the main targets of Commonwealth soldiery: horses were stabled in the nave, shops were set up in the portico (as they were in that of the Roman Pantheon), and Inigo Jones' perfect columns drilled to take beams and joists.[127] There was not enough time between the Restoration of Charles II in 1660 and the Great Fire of London in 1666 to return the building to its former state. In spite of the achievement, it was only seen in its perfection for less than a decade.

In terms of built achievement, the Commonwealth period, into which Jones survived inactive, was a backwater. Roger Pratt was the only architect of stature to emerge in the next generation: his most important work, Clarendon House in Piccadilly, was built after the Restoration and pulled down fifteen years later.[128] But the beliefs which were fostered among the successors of Dee, both in the Baconian and the more hermetic strain, were to have a rapid and diversified growth during the time. There can be little doubt that Jones wanted to transform London into an augustan city in which the architecture would be more than a mere setting for royal policy, but would condition and help its implementation. It was a great time for ideal cities: Campanella's *City of the Sun*[129] appeared in 1623, and Andreae's *Christianopolis* in 1619.[130] But while Jones incorporated this idea through the rebuilding of London, others saw the revival of antiquity and the extending of navigation, the diffusion of knowledge (particularly secret scientific knowledge) through printing, the spiritualizing of mechanical processes, the reform of education, and the adoption of a universal language as the means of healing religious disputes, leading to a spiritual renewal which would bring all men nearer to the state of Adam before the Fall. During (perhaps because of) the Thirty Years' War, it required a sound faith in the apocalyptic signs of the age to believe that its accomplishment was near. It certainly was the motive that prompted Herbert of Cherbury to publish *De Veritate* as the manifesto of a basic, innate religion on which all men of goodwill might agree:[131] the irenic spirit in religion was stimulated by the enthusiasm about extending the boundaries of human knowledge. In that spirit, Herbert's Parisian friend, Marin Mersenne, although theologically orthodox and a faithful member of the Minim friars (who were one of the very strictest mendicant orders) became the correspondent of Protestant, even chiliast leaders like Commenius[132] and Samuel Hartlib,[133] and even of more entrenched religious thinkers.[134]

The place of alchemy in all this activity was, as I suggested earlier, natural enough. It had a great revival just before the Great Chain of Being snapped under the strain of mechanistic teaching. Alchemy then split into an empirical and skeptical discipline (still called chemistry) and into theosophical speculation, whose main prophet was the cobbler-poet Jakob Böhme and whose obverse was the seedy speculation already lampooned in *The Alchemist* by Ben Jonson. But before the split became irremediable, the syndrome of ideas was the mainspring in the founding of such august bodies as the French Academy of Sciences and the Royal Society of London.

The Royal Society was compounded of other less formal bodies, such as Robert Boyle's Invisible Club, all dedicated to speculative experiment and the hope of a new world.[135] Among these, Christopher Wren was distinguished by the fame of an infant prodigy at a

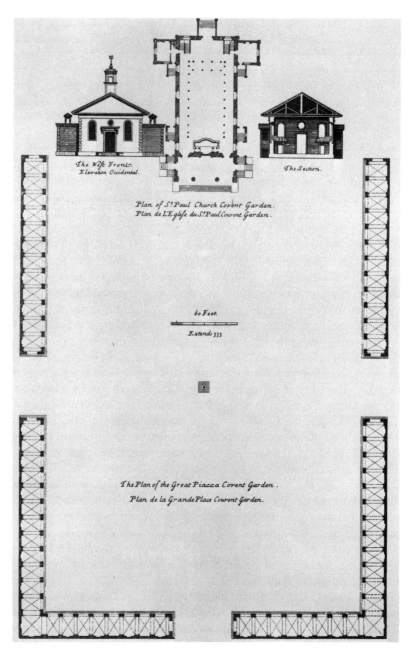

The West Front.
Elevation Occidental.

The Section.

Plan of St Paul Church Covent Garden.
Plan de L'Eglise du St Paul Cowent Garden.

60 Feet.

Extends 333

The Plan of the Great Piazza Covent Garden.

Plan de la Grande Place Cowent Garden.

Here and on facing page: the Covent Garden Piazza and St. Paul's Church, by Inigo Jones. After Vitruvius Britannicus.

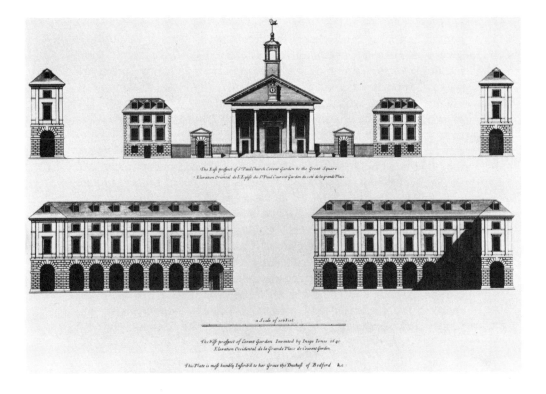

time when intellectual development was much more usually precocious and by a lineage tenaciously loyal to the king.[136] He became a
fellow of All Souls on receiving his master of arts degree in 1653; in
1657, at the age of twenty-four, he was a professor of astronomy at
Gresham College,[137] and Savilian professor of astronomy at Oxford
in 1661, a position which he was forced to resign when his architectural practice had been his main preoccupation for some time.[138]

Wren was not a great innovative mathematician but still brilliantly
exploring; his acumen was backed by an unusual faculty, a great
manual dexterity.[139] He devised many mathematical and astronomical models, navigational and scientific instruments, but he was also
in demand as an anatomical draftsman and is thought to have been
the pioneer of intravenous injection. His discussion of the convoluted
cone seems to foreshadow certain nineteenth- and twentieth-century
ideas about the occurrence of the logarithmic spiral in nature.[140] In
view of all I have said, it is not perhaps entirely surprising that this
brilliant mathematician, astronomer, physician, should also, and
finally exclusively, apply himself to architecture and to regard it as a
proper field for his intellectual ambition. It would not have been
conceivable but for the work of Dee, of Wotton, and of Jones.

Wren's fame and loyalty led to his being offered the reversion of
the surveyorship if he became the surveyor-fortifier of Tangiers,
which Charles II had received as part of his dowry.[141] Wren excused
himself and was appointed deputy to the amiable but incapable Sir

John Denham.[142] Within a matter of months, his uncle Matthew
invited him to design a chapel for Pembroke College in Cambridge.
This is a modest Corinthian four-pilastered hall, its temple front
framing a large window on a Palladian parapet, a formal expedient
which Wren was to go on using frequently.[143] About the same time,
Gilbert Sheldon, who was the acting primate of the Church of England (he was to become archbishop of Canterbury in 1663) asked him
to work on a "theater" to house the rather rowdy university ceremonies away from Great St. Mary's, the university church, where
they had been held since the Middle Ages.[144] Its conception recalls
the preoccupation of the late Elizabethan and early Stuart builders
with antique theater. By then, however, a number of permanent or
semipermanent theatrical halls were being built, mostly for princely
Italian courts but also for the French royal one.[145] In England the
nearest thing had been Inigo Jones' Cockpit theater for the court at
Whitehall and his anatomical theater for the Barber-Surgeons.[146]

It is not certain who decided on the D-shaped plan; the resulting
curved exterior was something of an innovation. So was the treatment: a tall rusticated and arcaded basement, supporting an extended attic, crowned by a heavy cornice.[147] The back (or southern

*Pembroke College, Cambridge, detail of print by D.
Loggan, showing the new chapel by Christopher
Wren.*

front) with the ceremonial entrance was an inverted *frons-scenae;* the architecture which the authorities described as being on the inner stage wall was put on the outside one, where it became the stage-drop for the university processions. The two-tiered front, Composite over Corinthian, contrasted oddly with the curving sur- round walls in a playful allusion to a basilica; the *frons* in classical theaters was usually taken to represent a royal palace. This may well have been the innovation which Wren presented to his fellows at the Royal Society meeting in April 1663 when he showed them the model of the theater.[148] He certainly did describe the extremely in- genious roof structure he had devised, and which, though much admired, was hidden from view by a flat ceiling, corded and painted in imitation of an ancient *velarium.*[149]

The interior, with its high-podiumed, wooden, marbled columns and high gallery, recalled Elizabethan theaters and only through them ancient precedent. The festivities at its opening (as they are recorded by Evelyn) seemed to be designed to display its acoustic properties.[150]

These early architectural efforts of Wren's, in spite of stylistic differences—his greater dependence on Netherlandish and French examples rather than directly on Italian ones—are clearly of the same order of ideas as those of Inigo Jones, to whom he always deferred with admiration.[151] The early achievements were tokens of a passion which was to take fire literally in 1666 and to lead to his two major enterprises, the building of the city churches and of St. Paul's.

But before that came his one visit abroad, to central France. The reason for it is obscure: he may have gone on behalf of the Royal Society to inspect the general state of the trades, make contact with scientists and artists, perhaps proceed to Italy.[152] The dominant ar- chitect in the Paris of that season was Bernini; their brief meeting over the Louvre designs and Wren's disappointment have often been told.[153] On the other hand, he seems to have been familiar and fascinated with the way the masons working on the Louvre were organized. He did drawings of many buildings he admired and bought many engravings, both topographic and ornamental. Al- though the domed churches he saw were the first constructions of the kind he could experience directly, the largest portico he could have seen, Lemercier's 30-foot-high one on the transept of the Sor- bonne church, would have seemed puny to him compared with In- igo Jones' at St. Paul's: that "intire and excellent piece."[154] But he confessed to his travel companion, the physician Edward Browne (who reported it to his father, the great writer, hermetic philosopher, and physician, Sir Thomas) that "the greatest worke about Paris" was "the Quay or Key upon the riuerside . . . built with so vast expense and such great quantity of materials that it exceeds all man- ner of ways the building of the two great Pyramids in Egypt.[155]

We do not know whether Wren made this observation inde- pendently, or if it was suggested to him. Certainly, it was an idea which people in Paris entertained. Wren was not to see any ancient buildings on his journey; while Browne went on to Italy and Germany, Wren turned back early in 1666; and when the Great Fire broke out on 2 September 1666, he was in London. The fire burned for five days. On September 7, the ashes were still smouldering.[156] Four days later Wren had presented his plan for the rebuilding of the city to the king. John Evelyn presented an alternative on September 13, and a few days later, a third was proposed by Richard Hooker.[157]

The city had, before the fire, lost a large proportion of its population in the plague; in the fire, some 13,200 houses, 87 churches, and a number of public and semipublic buildings (exchange, livery halls) were destroyed.[158] The splendor of the proposed plans reflects the intellectual ambitions of the Royal Society, its conception of itself as an estate of the realm. The failure to impose any general plan on the depopulated and flattened city in spite of the desire of the monarchy and the ambitions of the planners—one of whom was the city's own surveyor, Robert Hooke—is a symptom of the economic but also of the political situation in Britain.[159]

The two important plans were Wren's and Evelyn's. Both were based on the fusion of a concentric-radial plan with an orthogonal one. In Wren's, the new cathedral of St. Paul's is shown as a porticoed dome, a Pantheon type of building for which there was no precedent in Britain, and hardly any in the rest of Europe.[160]

It was very much a part of Wren's reconstruction plan, and he was to return to the Pantheon theme in later projects;[161] but it was a rare instance in Britain of a single building which predicated a city plan on itself. The commentators on this point have made too much of the French influence on him, particularly the influence of the garden plans of Le Nôtre.[162] Though he admired Vaux, Versailles, and the Tuileries, Wren—like the other planners—was restoring a fortified city.[163] And within its fortifications, he was proposing to devise a scheme which would reconcile an orthogonal street pattern to a polygonal fortified outline. He did this—as did Evelyn—by devising a compromise between a concentric-radial and a checkerboard layout. Other planners preferred strict orthogonality.[164] Wren's and Evelyn's plans deferred to the planning tradition which was transmitted in an increasingly popular literature of manuals on fortifications, within which town plans were laid out according to such a scheme. These plans were rarely accompanied by texts explaining the sometimes magnificent engravings. Their most powerful disciple was to be Vauban.[165] In Britain the possibility of such planning was addled in the haste with which the stricken city of London had to be rebuilt.

The literature of town planning at the time was more a subdepartment of fortification on the one hand, and economics and husbandry on the other,[166] although both of these were strongly influenced by Utopian writings—by More, of course, but also by Campanella and Andreae, whom I mentioned earlier.[167] Although the plans conceived after 1666 were not carried out, their publication became influential, over the next century, and they were reprinted several times. In the meanwhile, a number of royal proclamations were issued to discourage timber building, regulate street widths, and so on, while the merits of the different schemes were discussed.[168] Wren and Hugh May[169] were appointed commissioners for the rebuilding of the city, with Sir Roger Pratt;[170] John Evelyn continued as unofficial adviser in matters of rebuilding; later, the original committee was enlarged[171] by coopting three other members, one of whom was Robert Hooke.[172]

The enormous increase in building work which reconstruction threatened required the relaxation of the old restrictions on "foreign" labor within the city.[173] The demand, and the easing of the regulations, made London a magnet for all categories of builder and caused a concentration of workmen under various patrons: the city itself, the diocese of London, the corporations, and the king.[174] But this concentration was only geographical; it never had the effect of the centralizing moves on the Continent, in France particularly. Patronage was not hierarchically organized, nor taste imposed by any agency. In so far as an example could be set, it was not the building of uniform street facades which would achieve it, nor the grouping of civic institutions round a royal exchange, such as Wren had planned, but the rebuilding of the city churches which became the leavening lesson. Although he did not design all of them, Wren was certainly the controller of the operation, both in terms of taste and invention. Moreover the most bulky and prestigious of them, St. Paul's, was to be his own achievement.

Before Inigo Jones' rebuilding, the cathedral had already been damaged by fire. In fact, Jones' rebuilding was never completed, and since the Restoration, Wren had been working on St. Paul's. After 1666, the fire damage was extensive; the portico was badly flaked.[175] Still the commissioners were reluctant to pull the fabric down. The portico, as I have already suggested, was regarded as especially remarkable, if very new; with the Banqueting House, it was regarded as the chief exemplar of the New Augustan style.[176] In his plan, Evelyn shows it unaltered. Wren's first proposal, before the fire, was to replace the decayed steeple with a dome; "a noble cupola, a form of church-building not as yet known in England, but of wonderful grace."[177]

In fact, Wren's first projects for a new cathedral are an interpretation of the sketched outline in the city plan: the western part of the church with a portico, based on Palladio's very popular restoration of the Temple of Peace in Rome crowned at the east end with a Pantheon-shaped dome. After some further negotiation, Wren arrived at what is usually called the Great or Favourite design: a Greek cross surmounted by a dome over the crossing, and in the final version preceded by a shallow domed vestibule. The great Corinthian portico (roughly over the site of Jones') carries a pediment which engages with the attic of the church rather after the manner of Lemercier's portico at the Sorbonne. There followed the episode of the Warrant design—it was in 1675, and no work had yet started— which was a version of Jones' recasing of the old cathedral, crowned by an incongruous dome topped by a lantern-spire. At this time, build-

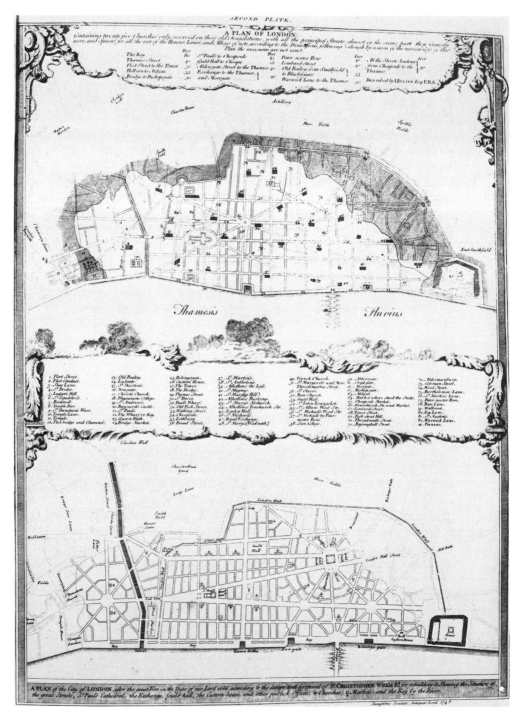

Plans for the rebuilding of London submitted by Christopher Wren and John Evelyn. After Vertue.

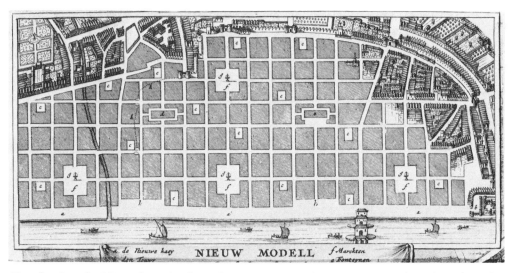

Plan for the rebuilding of London by Robert Hooke (?). After Merian Workshop plan of London (1670). Courtesy of Guildhall Library.

ing began seriously and continued as the final design took shape; the foundation stone was laid on 11 June 1677, but the design of the dome and the portico was not finalized until after 1700. The last episode, Wren's dismissal and the placing of the balustrade around the great cornice, must be told later.[178]

While Wren was supervising St. Paul's and transforming its design, he built Hampton Court and designed Whitehall and Greenwich—and the city churches. He had formed a group of men round him at the Office of Works—where he had succeeded Sir John Denham in 1669—both architect-designers and craftsmen: from artists of the merit of Tijou and Gibbons to simple workhands. In that he was the true heir of Jones; but his architectural formation and his taste were rather different.

The absolute domination of Rome and Venice over European culture had been displaced by the rise of Paris as an artistic center. Jones had taken his knowledge of antiquity from the monuments themselves, mediated by his acquaintance with Palladio. Wren, who had never seen an antique building—not even the Pont du Gard or the theater in Orange, much less the Maison Carrée—had access to the surveys of Antoine Desgodetz from 1682, and Perrault's edition of Vitruvius in 1674;[179] he almost certainly saw the *Ordonnance des Cinq Espèces de Colonnes* of 1683, which John James published in English in 1708. Wren was clearly impressed with the Le Vau-Perrault eastern facade of the Louvre, for which he may have seen a preliminary drawing in Paris;[180] it is difficult to understand how Perrault could not have been on his visiting list, although so far no definite evidence of this has come to light.[181] By 1700, Wren would have read Perrault's defense of coupled columns (he had used them in the Louvre), and he would have seen them—if nowhere else—on the frontispiece to Perrault's Vitruvius.[182]

The complex genesis of the final design for St. Paul's is related to Wren's absorption of the new French style: plain but solemn; while admiring more even the equally solemn, if more grandiloquent, more allusive classicism of Bernini. What was true of Wren's style is equally true of his theory. He never published any book, or even paper on the subject, but at the end of *Parentalia*, Stephen Wren included a number of tracts, headed "From some rough Draughts, imperfect." The very first one approaches a familiar problem. Having established that "Architecture aims at Eternity; and therefore the only Thing uncapable of modes and fashions in its Principals, the *Orders* . . . [which] are not only Roman and Greek, but Phoenician, Hebrew and Assyrian . . . promoted by the . . . Skill of the greatest Artists and Geometricians . . . experiments in this kind being greatly expenceful and Errors incorrigible, is the Reason that the Principles of Architecture are now rather the Study of Antiquity than Fancy. . . . Beauty, Firmness and Convenience are the Principles." [183]

The reader will have noted that the *principals* of architecture are the orders—those who govern and order architecture—and its *principles*, its original postulates, its primordial substance (as Dr. Johnson has it) are the old Hellenistic triad, with delight being changed for beauty. Wren has none of the subtlety or the radical thrust of Perrault. And of his principles, he says: the two first—beauty and firmness—"depend upon geometrical reasons of *Opticks* and *Staticks*; the third only makes use of variety." Wren further makes clear that "opticks" do not govern beauty alone, nor "staticks" firmness. The two first categories are equally determined by both considerations. He goes on to echo, and contradict in part, Perrault's argument: "There are two causes of Beauty, natural and Customary. Natural is from *Geometry*, consisting in Uniformity (that is Equality) and Proportion. Customary Beauty is begotten by the Use of our Senses to those objects which are usually pleasing to us for other causes, as Familiarity or particular Inclination breeds Love to Things not in themselves lovely: Here lies the great occasion of Errors: but always the true Test is natural or Geometrical Beauty."

Perrault had confined the use of geometry to arbitrary beauty:[184] Wren, in common with most of his predecessors and contemporaries, equates geometry with the law of nature. Much of what he says may be paralleled out of Scamozzi's first book;[185] although Scamozzi, in proper Neoplatonic fashion, preferred the circle to all other figures, whereas Wren asserts the logical—and therefore artistic—priority of the straight line. The whole passage seems to rely not on ideas of human nature and of perception but on primary and secondary qualities, as Wren might have found them defined by Locke.[186] In the same way, Wren prefers the perpendicular and the horizontal to the oblique as guarantors of stability: "this from Nature, consequently Necessity," although he adds, "Cones and multiangular prisms want neither Beauty or Firmness, but are not ancient." [187] In the same paragraph, he disapproves of Gothic buttresses as ill-favored;[188] and in another tract, having discussed the orders, he exemplifies what the geometrical method means when applied to firmness and praises the antiseismic provision of the Pantheon and the apparent stability of the Bramantean scheme for St. Peter's, preferable (by implication) to the chain-reinforced Michelangelo dome.[189] And he goes on: "The Free-Masons (by which he signifies medieval builders generally) were not very solicitous about this, because they used Buttresses on the Outside of the Wall which they extended as far as they guessed would be sufficient," and a little further he considers the different forms of vaulting, "either as they were used by the ancients, or the Moderns, whether Free-Masons or Saracens" and explains that he found the medieval method of vaulting the most economic and that he followed it at St. Paul's.[190] It is well known that Perrault did not disapprove of medieval building either but admired the airiness and stability of the great medieval churches.[191]

Wren admits the importance of a "customary" beauty, which he defines almost by translating Perrault verbatim. Yet he is clearly—if the number of words is anything to go by—more interested in the binding force of geometry.[192] This is not only an invocation of the archaic Neoplatonic doctrine of harmony but is the doctrine restated in terms of primary qualities on which ideas of natural beauty depend, while secondary qualities relate to customary beauty. This is a very different doctrine from the subtle thinking of Perrault.

Wren's acceptance of the overwhelming importance of geometry is not dependent necessarily on microcosmic speculations. Even Hobbes maintained that geometry was "the onely Science that it hath pleased God hitherto to bestow on mankind." [193] The *Parentalia* tracts are not the elaboration of a complete architectural doctrine but more justifications of Wren's practice; the more generalized speculation is rather an allusion to the presuppositions which underlie the more particular injunctions: on domes as the only proper roofline apart from the flat roof; on the proper ordering of entrance porticoes; in favor of coupled columns (again, heavily indebted to Perrault); in favor of the structural ingenuity of medieval masons but against their ornament (what John Evelyn called crinkle-crankle).[194] Wren's Gothic is usually very plain and dictated by circumstance—Tom Tower in Oxford, St.-Dunstan-in-the-East in the city, and the restoration of Westminster Abbey are the most prominent.[195]

Wren is now remembered as much as the architect of St. Paul's as the deviser of the enormously varied steeples of the city churches. With one isolated exception, Wren did not attempt to unite steeple with a detached portico.[196] Yet steeple and portico became the mark of the full Anglican establishment. When a Tory Parliament passed an act in 1711 for the building of fifty churches in dissenting districts as a missionary endeavor, stone (for preference) churches were specified, with steeples and proper Laudian railed-off chancels.[197] The commission for their supervision included Wren and his son Christopher, John Vanbrugh, and Thomas Archer; Nicholas Hawksmoor and William Dickinson were appointed surveyors to the commission.[198] Dickinson was succeeded by James Gibbs in 1713.[199] After the accession of George I, the new administration dismissed all the commissioners and appointed a nonarchitectural team which put John James in Gibbs' place but retained Hawksmoor's services.

The original commission united practically all the important architects practicing in Britain at the time—or at any rate in London—but it also continued the tendency established by Wren in the City churches, while giving them a more stately character, emphasized by the island setting.[200]

Although Wren himself had built only relatively few "civil" buildings, he had projected the vast palace at Whitehall and a number of other university structures. The poverty of royal patronage was demonstrated by the sad failure of the royal palace at Winchester, which Charles II wanted to be a monument to his dynastic stability, of the monarchy's interest in the navy, as well as a base for the political centralizing of royal power.

When the church commissioners began sitting, Vanbrugh and Hawksmoor, Wren's junior colleagues at the Office of Works, were engaged on building houses of royal splendor for somewhat independent magnates: Castle Howard and Blenheim, for the earl of Carlisle and the duke of Marlborough. Hawksmoor had come into the Office of Works a year or two before 1680, and remained in

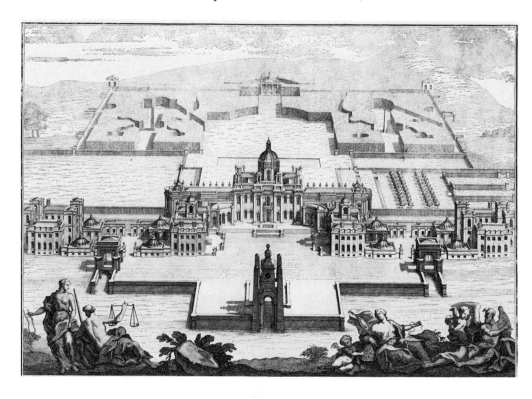

Castle Howard, Yorkshire, by John Vanbrugh and Nicholas Hawksmoor, projection of main front, showing unexecuted monumental gateway. The topiary garden was removed in the seventeen-fifties. After Vitruvius Britannicus.

constant touch with Wren there and also personally until the latter's death. In 1699 he entered into some kind of partnership or association with John Vanbrugh over the design and building of Castle Howard, an association which lasted through various projects until Vanbrugh's death in 1726.[201] In 1702, Vanbrugh was appointed comptroller to the Office of Works; and from that time until Wren's dismissal, it became a triple partnership[202] as well as a kind of unofficial academy of architecture. Naturally enough, the Office of Works took a leading part in the move to provide the fifty churches, though the actual execution was largely Hawksmoor's. In the abortive enterprise—only twelve of the fifty churches were built and three chapels refurbished—Hawksmoor built six by himself and a further two with John James, the translator of Perrault.[203] James built St. George's, Hanover Square, himself; Archer, two churches; and Gibbs, one—St. Mary-le-Strand.

Although Wren had built over fifty belfries for the City churches, most of them were on the site of medieval church towers; however, he had never (with one possible and unexecuted exception) attempted to marry belfry and portico. The commissioners imposed this novel formal problem on the new churches, and both Gibbs and Hawksmoor provided a number of variations on the theme. Hawksmoor himself never attempted a direct union of belfry with a pedimented portico. The nearest he came to it was at Christchurch, Spitalfields, where a brutal, aggressive Tuscan portico, its middle intercolumniation broken into an arch, is surmounted by a wall articulated into an astylar triumphal arch which carries an "antique" pyramidon-crowned steeple. In a later attempt to combine these elements at St. George's, Bloomsbury, he rejected the succession portico–double wall–nave–box chancel which he, Gibbs, and James developed by moving the campanile to the long side of the church; the portico which is on the short side, however, does not answer the chancel axially. The chancel is an apse opposite the belfry on the long side, so that the monumental stairway up to the portico leads into a vestibule-aisle which looks across to a symmetrical element, while the central plan of the church is made explicit by a square clerestory. The belfry, which provides a secondary entrance on the axis, is a curious transformation of the mausoleum of Halicarnassus, topped by a statue of George I.[204]

Archer managed these transitions more easily, using a circular

St. Martin-in-the-Fields, section of first scheme. After Gibbs.

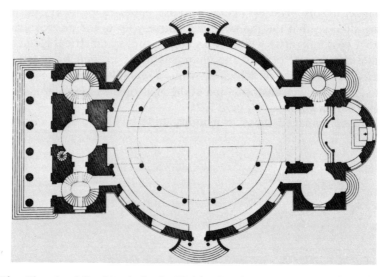

The Church of St. Martin-in-the-Fields, London. First project by James Gibbs for a domed circular church with a portico and a spire. After Gibbs.

St. Martin-in-the-Fields. Courtauld Institute of Art.

steeple, as at St. Paul's, Deptford, or eliding the problem (St. George, Smith Square; St. Philip, Birmingham); Hawksmoor both asserted it (all his churches have a prominent belfry) and varied it by resorting to a classicized Gothic (as at St. Anne's, Limehouse), using obtrusive "antique" finials, or even proposing more radical solutions, such as the Ionic column (St. John, Horseydown) and the fluted obelisk (St. Luke, Old Street) on the churches he designed with James.[205] James and Gibbs (who had finished the steeple of St. Clement Dane's for Wren) went back to a much more Wren-like manner, much less "terrible" than Hawksmoor's way of dealing with this feature.[206]

But in spite of Hawksmoor's *terribilità* in the combining of antique features, sometimes reminiscent of his exact contemporary Fischer von Erlach[207] (if without Fischer's elaborate iconographic complexities), he nevertheless dealt equally brilliantly and more idiosyncratically than his master Wren with Gothic architecture, which he considered as being endowed with its own rules, independent of the "antique" architecture of the orders.[208]

There is little doubt, however, that classical antiquity claimed his primary loyalty. "What I have sent to you," he writes to Lord Carlisle, defending his design for the mausoleum at Castle Howard, "is authentic and what is according to the practice of the Ancients and what is Historicall and good Architecture: Convenient, Lasting, Decent and Beautiful." [209]

Wren's and Hawksmoor's style, which may fairly be called the High Tory Gothic-baroque, was offensive to the taste of a new generation of connoisseurs. Nor was it simply a party matter: the third member of the Office of Works triumvirate, John Vanbrugh, was a Whig, a member of the Kit-Cat club; he was knighted at the first levée held by George I.[210] It was not just a matter of a generation gap either. The main opposition to the Office of Works taste was formulated, it was true, by a great Whig magnate, Anthony Ashley Cooper, third earl of Shaftesbury, when he was a sick, dying man (though only a few years younger than Vanbrugh or Hawksmoor). He spent the last year or so of his life in Naples, bed-ridden, and from there wrote to a close friend, Lord Somers, one-time Whig Lord Chancellor and Lord President of the Council, "in a kind of spirit of prophecy . . . of the rising Genius of our Nation [when] *united* BRITAIN [shall have become] the principal seat of the Arts." Music and painting were already improving, Shaftesbury thought; as for architecture:

> The Genius of our Nation has hitherto been so little
> turned this way, that thro' several reigns we have pa-
> tiently seen the noblest buildings perish (if I may say
> so) under the hand of a single Court-Architect . . . Our
> *State* may in this respect prove perhaps more fortunate
> than our *Church*, in having waited till the national taste
> was form'd . . . but the Zeal of the Nation cou'd not, it
> seems admit so long a delay in Ecclesiastical struc-
> tures, particularly in their *Metropolitan*. And since

> Zeal of this sort has been newly kindled amongst us,
> 'tis like we shall see from afar the many spires arising
> in our great City, with such hasty and such sudden
> growth, as may be the occasion perhaps that our im-
> mediate Relish shall be hereafter censur'd as retaining
> much of what Artists call the Gothick kind.[211]

Both Shaftesbury and Somers were generous patrons of letters and of the visual arts. Somers bought a large collection of prints and a few paintings;[212] Shaftesbury was a programmatic patron of certain artists—of John Closterman and Simon Gribelin in London,[213] of Paolo de Mattei in Naples—in his last years. His taste was not too advanced: Poussin was the one recent artist for whom he expressed unbounded admiration.[214] Although he liked to use analogies with architecture and building, he never advanced any opinion on a contemporary structure apart from this one condemnation;[215] nor does he theorize about architecture. But on the subject of beauty in general, he says a great deal. Wren would have found much that he says unacceptable. In this matter, and in many others, Shaftesbury categorically parted from his mentor and teacher, John Locke. He is much more an "ancient" even than any of the Office of Works trio; he uses the term *gothick* only for condemnation and abuse,[216] and he hopefully sees the freedom-loving British surpass the French in the arts, if only the monarchy had been enlightened enough to found an academy for their study.[217]

Such an academy did not obtain its royal charter and state support until 1768, in spite of several earlier attempts.[218] This is only a parenthesis, however, on Shaftesbury's enormous influence on thinking in Britain and on public life more generally. His influence spread to France and to Italy and made another, greater impact in Germany almost a century after his death.[219] Through him, certain ideas of a group of Neoplatonic theologians and philosophers centered in Cambridge filtered into the mainstream of European thinking in modified form.[220]

But the group also had a more powerful and more faithful disciple: Isaac Newton. Newton was born near Grantham in Lincolnshire, as was one of the most important, perhaps the most important philosopher of the group, Henry More, who was teaching at Christ's College in Cambridge when Newton was studying at Trinity. More was during Commonwealth times a follower—and a correspondent—of Descartes.[221] But the strict separation of spirit and matter which is the cardinal assumption of Cartesian physics came to seem increasingly unsatisfactory to him, suggesting and even implying a certain moral subjectivism, a laxity which might lead to irreligion. More saw the answer in the introduction of a vital principle in all things animate and inanimate: "a substance incorporeal . . . pervading the whole matter of the Universe and exercising a plasticall power therein," [222] an idea echoed by another great Cambridge mathematician, Isaac Barrow, who attributed it to the hermetic philosophers.[223]

Apart from the majestic argument about indefinite and infinite space, Newton took from More, Cudworth, and Barrow the criticism both of Cartesian space and of Cartesian theosophy. The Cambridge philosophers, and Newton with them, opposed a *Deus artifex* to the impersonal *Dieu Fainéant* of Cartesian creation.[224]

Shaftesbury's criticism of Descartes also owed something to More and Cudworth, whom he revered; yet the matrix of his thinking was sociopolitical, that of the Cambridge philosophers epistemological and theological. The Cambridge philosophers—and Shaftesbury with them—could not contemplate a theory of art in which custom was the ultimate rule of taste, nor imagine the practice of it which was based on fixed rules. Locke had influenced many of Shaftesbury's ideas, as he did those of Newton; Newton's mathematical discoveries he could not criticize. Newton, who in his youth had held a form of Cartesian mechanism, moved slowly to a conception of a harmonious universe. In the *Opticks* he had already established a strict correspondence between color intervals and the seven notes of the musical octave.[225] The *Opticks* were the main vehicle of his ideas. The *Principia*, written in Latin and inherently less tractable, became known much more slowly, although their influence was immeasurably more profound.

This remathematization of secondary phenomena was very much what the Cambridge thinkers hoped for. More believed that the sympathetic vibration of tuned springs would affect the growth of vines and even wine pressed from them.[226] There were many in the Royal Society (which was, after all, dedicated implicitly to the argument from design)[227] to whom this way of thinking was profoundly welcome. The God of the argument was very much the *Deus artifex* of Newton's beliefs, whose work was seen in the absolute relation between mass and gravity. But his work, emulated and made known through scientific discovery, could also be experienced scientifically by direct operation in the alchemical process. More, and Newton after him, attached enormous importance to alchemical "work." Shaftesbury could afford to be sceptical about such "mechanical" procedures. He did after all write—as has been said—"with his coronet upon his head" [228]; "Alchemy required more the labour of Hands than Brains," and Shaftesbury could not stomach it: "we have a strange Fancy to be Creators, a violent Desire at least to know the knack or Secret by which Nature does all." [229]

But Shaftesbury's most brilliant contemporaries saw the matter differently: even the Skeptical Chymist himself, Robert Boyle, was an avid alchemical experimenter, and Newton devoted much energy and time to such speculation.[230] Although it did not have any immediate implication for a theory of art, the hermetic literature with which he was familiar had insistently taught the importance of the Solomonic temple as an epitome of Divine Wisdom. The Bible which Newton currently used was the polyglot edition which contained an essay on the temple by the French Hebraist, Louis Cappel. It provided a summary of the views of two Spanish Jesuits, Juan Bautista Villalpanda and Jeronimo Prado, whose three-volume folio commentary on the Book of Ezekiel set up the dominant image of the temple in the seventeenth and even the eighteenth century.[231] A huge model of the temple was made by Johann Jakob Erasmus of Hamburg in 1694 and based fairly closely on Villalpanda's reconstruction; it was exhibited in various European capitals and sometime before 1720 came to London,[232] where it was much discussed. In 1721, William Stukeley showed Newton his drawings for the temple.[233] Sometime later, they returned to the subject, and Newton showed Stukeley his reconstruction.[234] By this time, Stukeley had been admitted a master-mason, as I have already said.[235]

It was a time when freemasonry underwent a curious transformation. Before 1717 the majority were actively involved in the building trades—with a separate association of masons whom we might call speculative or accepted or even geometrical. On the whole the religious atmosphere of their meetings or lodges was pious, trinitarian, sacramental—at least by implication. They maintained themselves free of religious strife by agreeing on the minimal faith proper to a decent man: the kind of minimal faith which Edward Herbert of Cherbury had outlined in *De Veritate*, the sort of belief which Shaftesbury may have combined with his low-church practice and which is associated with Noah, to whom, after all humanity after Adam owes its survival, if not its being.[236]

I have already had occasion to mention Newton's interest in religious speculation. Toward the end of his life he returned to one of his great passions, the exposition of the millenary passages in the Book of Daniel and the Apocalypse. He was concerned with producing a revised world chronology, to which he gave urgent authority by establishing the absolute dates of the Argonauts' expedition on a retrospective astronomical calculation, which also related the Greek legend to the absolute chronology of Scripture.[237] Accordingly, the Solomonic temple was also the world's earliest permanent building. Having reworked the mensuration of the royal cubit as they are set out in the Bible, Newton proposed the temple as an absolute model and the original, divine exemplar for all building.[238]

This assertion of priority echoed that made by Villalpanda and other writers on the temple, however much they differed on the interpretation of the text and consequent reconstruction. But Villalpanda's remained the most exciting visually, and confirmed the vision of an idealized temple in an idealized Jerusalem which haunted the history of the next two centuries, in spite of the increasing discredit which his reconstruction received.[239]

However, many of Newton's contemporaries were prepared either to entertain the strange and exciting—if discredited—vision of the temple or to modify it according to their interpretation of the text or to their taste. William Stukeley did just that, and transformed the temple building into a rather eccentric version of Christchurch, Spitalfields.[240] But he has another claim to my attention. As an antiquarian, he was the first to provide a reliable survey both of Stonehenge and of Avebury. He did not regard these as mere antiquarian diversions; they were part of his major apologetic enterprise (in which he had become interested before he became a mason) to interpret the

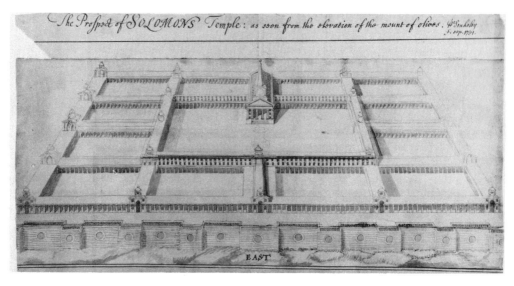

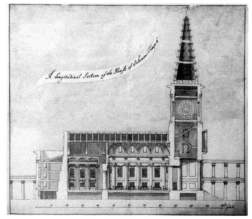

William Stukeley, reconstruction of King Solomon's Temple. Bodleian Library, Oxford.

megalithic monuments of Britain as Druidic remains, to show that the Druids were not only the heirs and transmitters to the original inhabitants of Britain (if they were not the original inhabitants themselves) of the religion of Abraham, as well as Noah, but a pythagorean and trinitarian, benevolent clerisy.[241] It was a form of apologetics which was popular enough in France, though less familiar in Britain and rare enough among Protestants: Pierre la Ramée, the great logician, was its most distinguished advocate. Stukeley took the field against the deist pamphleteer John Toland, whose *Critical History of the Celtic Religion and Learning containing an Account of the Druids* presented them as an evil and oppressive oligarchy whom the Romans were right to suppress, since "their pretended magic and authority, incompatible with the power of the magistrate, were things not to be endured by so wise a state as the Romans." [242]

Although modern scholars' view of the Druids is more like Toland's than like Stukeley's, Stukeley's more benevolent version was preferred by his contemporaries: a college not unlike the Pythagoreans, the Orphics, the Indian Gymnosophists or Brahmins, and even the Chinese priesthood, the carriers and transmitters of an ancient theology which Stukeley himself had hoped to find in another way, in a divinely inspired wisdom carried in the "mystery" of a craft founded by direct divine revelation.

The legend of the temple building and the origin of masonic guilds was, of course, an essential part of masonic lore.[243] It was reinforced by such building mythologizing as Stukeley's, which was superimposed on earlier speculations,[244] but also by the separate legend of the Saracenic origin of cathedral architecture which came to be associated later with the Knights Templar and their mysterious knowledge.[245]

However, not all masons were either as grandiloquent or as exalted as Stukeley; his great friend and patron, the earthy duke of Montague, was the first noble Grand Master of British masonry, elected in 1720, of whose installation the *Constitutions* say that "all express'd great Joy at the happy Prospect of being again patronized by *Noble Grand Masters*, as in the prosperous Times of *Free Masonry*." [246] Montague, like several distinguished masons of the time, did not share Stukeley's theology but had a more skeptical view of mythology as well. Still, prosperous times were to come for the masons. In fact, the custom which appears in history with Ashmole and his fellows at Warrington seems to have spread in the seventeenth century—nor was there any reason why the Stuart monarchs should not favor it. The sacramental conventions, the reconciliatory policies made it monarchic by tendency and also by tradition.[247] There may even have been a lodge at court in the reign of James II. At any rate, there seems to have been a military lodge in Dillon's regiment of Irish guards since 1688.[248] All seems to have gone on quite quietly and uncontroversially until the first years of George I's reign. There are nonmasonic reports of masonic doings; masonic ceremonies take place in public at the laying of foundation—or capstones,[249] but otherwise they occupy little public attention. This all changed in 1717. After some negotiation, the four main lodges in London are united into a Grand Lodge which has authority over all masons.[250] It is difficult to know exactly who the main actors were in this matter, and for what reason. The first grand master to be elected was Anthony Sayer, a Berkshire gentleman, who had long been a mason, but was otherwise undistinguished, indeed poor enough later to receive charity from his lodge.[251] His successor was George Payne (1718–1719 and 1720–1721).[252] Between his two terms, the grand mastership went to the Reverend John Theophilus Désaguliers, F.R.S., who seems a much more interesting and influential character. The son of a refugee of the Revocation, he became a clergyman of the Church of England in 1710 (his father had been reordained by the bishop of London, and was minister of the French Chapel in Swallow Street) and held various livings. He was chaplain to the duke of Chandos at Stanmore, and later to Frederick Prince of Wales, the first royal mason. But he is best known as one of Newton's latter disciples and a popularizer of his ideas through public lectures and demonstrations as well as through various publications. At Newton's invitation he repeated the experiments proving the refrangibility of light which had been questioned, with such disastrous psychological effect on Newton by the French physicist, the Abbé Edmé Mariotte. This he did with complete success in 1714/15 and repeated them, with new variations in 1728. Whatever his minor troubles with Newton, his preoccupation with his master's ideas was total, and in 1725 he published a verse pamphlet on "The Newtonian System of the World, the best model for Government."[253]

All too little is known about his masonic activities.[254] Sometime before 1715, he met Dr. James Anderson when the Scottish Presbyterian congregation (of which Anderson was minister) took over his father's chapel. How Anderson became a mason is not clear.[255] Nor is there any information about Désaguliers' first connection with the craft. There are no minutes before 1723, and the only source for the earliest days of organized Grand Lodge masonry is the admittedly unreliable one of Dr. Anderson's *Constitutions*. It seems, however, that of the four lodges which came together to make the Grand Lodge, only one had more than two or three esquires among its members;[256] and this makes the sudden social eminence of masonry puzzling and requires explanation. Any appeal to the conspiracy theory of history is both seductive and suspicious: in this case destruction of evidence, sudden change, secrecy, dissension make an appeal to conspiracy unavoidable.

And in these doings, the crucial figure was Philip, first duke of Wharton, the fifth Grand Master. Wharton was irregularly installed: "lately made a Brother, tho' not the *Master* of a *Lodge*, being ambitious of the Chair, got a number of others to meet him at Stationers-Hall" where the oldest mason present "without the usual decent ceremonials" proclaimed Wharton as Grand Master. Many masons apparently rejected his authority, but a breach was averted when the duke of Montague summoned a grand lodge and proclaiming Wharton, got him to appoint Désaguliers as deputy. Wharton had been created duke by George I in 1718 in the hope of reconciling a heavy Whig heritage.[257]

Wayward Wharton had already, however, invested rather heavily in Stuart sympathies, as well as the South Sea Company. Ambitious as well as inconstant and profligate, he had made himself a bad name as president of an early Hell-Fire Club,[258] but was very active in the House of Lords until he left Britain finally in 1725. The Old Pretender made him duke of Newcastle: he was outlawed in 1729.[259] Wharton's election to the grand mastership was seen by some as a Jacobite attempt to maintain their hold over a club, a secret society which had for over half a century maintained loyalty to the restored monarchy.[260] After his exile, he seems to have retained a strong interest in the craft. There is a persistent masonic tradition that he founded Spanish masonry and that he was the first Grand Master of the French lodges.[261]

The Hanoverian party showed an instant interest in masonic

lodges. There seems little doubt that many working for the Hanoverian interests wanted to use the masonic secret for a political, and perhaps also for a religious end. The most obvious witness to this is the important lodge—important enough to receive a special mention in James Anderson's *Constitutions*[262] at which Francis of Lorraine (who was about to abandon his duchy to Stanisław Leszczyński, exiled king of Poland and father-in-law of Louis XV, in exchange for the grand duchy of Tuscany and the hand of Maria Theresa of Austria) was made a mason. He was then the obvious candidate for the succession to Charles VI as roman emperor, and the lodge, for which Désaguliers traveled specially to The Hague was held there at the British Embassy, where Lord Chesterfield (of the *Letters to his Son*) was ambassador. Francis was made master-mason some months later, at Robert Walpole's residence, Houghton Hall, while on a visit to Britain, and apparently he maintained his masonic contacts as well as receiving a pension from the British government. At any rate, the Hague lodge opens a period of close alliance between Britain and the Roman Empire.

However, London was full of clubs and secret societies at the time.[263] Even the ritual aspects of masonry were imitated by—or at any rate were common to—a number of them. The Kit-Cat, which I mentioned earlier, seems exclusively political in its makeup; there were several political societies, but also professional, religious, and convivial ones. The masons became the most influential of all such associations; a number of heresies and schisms appeared as soon as the masonic lodges were centralized, and their disputes were an important aspect of the intellectual life of the eighteenth century. They have not been really explored, in spite of the vast literature about the period.

The connection of masonry with architecture is self-evident. The ascendancy which the powerful club, derived from the old "accepted" masonry had over European and American thinking and politics for a century and a half cannot be explained by this connection. Clearly, at the beginning of the organization, at the setting up of the Grand Lodge, ambiguous political motives were at play. It may have been a Hanoverian attempt to win over an organization which in spite of its conciliating aims maintained faith with the exiled Stuarts; it may have been, too, an attempt to create a channel of confidential communication and perhaps accommodation with the exiles. But whatever the political aim, the motives of its perpetrators were certainly mixed. Both Désaguliers and Anderson were convinced Newtonians: Désaguliers became an experimental assistant at the Royal Society soon after his graduation and repeatedly later gave proof of devotion to the master,[264] while Anderson emulated Newton's other obsession in his concern with chronology and genealogy.[265]

Whatever may be said against Newton, no one could have repeated of him the accusation which Boileau had made against Descartes: that he "cut the throat of poesy."[266] On the contrary, as I have already suggested, the *Opticks* gave mathematical backing to the revival of the ancient notion of a concord of the senses. This was a by-product of the way in which Newton concerned himself with what had been generally considered secondary qualities by philosophers. The phenomena of color, of color harmony within the spectrum in particular, which were general and ascertainable (*in vitro*, as they used to say then) corresponded to numerical harmonic divisions, and these in turn to the notes of the tonic scale. From this argument, the step back to a faith in universal harmony (and to the Pythagorean parallel between what is heard and what is seen) is a short one. The psychologism of Epicurean Cartesians, such as Perrault, is eclipsed by the physical Platonism of Newton's disciples, of Désaguliers or William Whiston.[267] There is a great crowd of Newtonians of various magnitudes, from which later Voltaire and Montesquieu stand out. Voltaire in particular devoted a chapter to the parallel between the spectrum colors and the octave notes, with what must have been a deliberately "pythagorean" reference. At the end of the chapter he describes briefly the *clavecin oculaire*, the clavichord for the eyes, devised by a Jesuit scientist-philosopher, Louis-Bertrand Castel, which was so popular that the novelist Abbé Prévost could ask in his magazine *Le Pour et le Contre*, quite rhetorically: Is there anyone who has not heard of the *clavecin oculaire?*

Castel was not a thoroughgoing Newtonian; and like Newton, he claimed to be taking Athanasius Kircher's *Ars Magna* and the notion that sound is the monkey of light as his starting point. Though Voltaire was to speak lightly of this *clavecin* in later years, the idea of the correspondence between color and tone became crucial in a restoration of some validity to proportion.[268]

As the old rationalism was replaced by Lockeian empiricism, the mechanics of the perceptual accord as it had been restated by Newton seemed to give a new validity to the old cosmogonic ideas of a world harmony. In such a context, much of Shaftesbury's thinking seemed also to take on a new interest. His disciples attempted to extend, even to systematize, the ideas of that great enemy of all systems.[269] Francis Hutcheson actually formulated a quasi-mathematical law according to which "where the uniformity of bodies is equal, the beauty is as the variety."[270] This kind of "calculus of the beautiful" was taken up by certain architectural writers.[271] Berkeley's relentless teleology transformed Shaftesbury's belief in the underlying benevolence of nature into a relativism in which beauty is known by the mind, but it is not quite the abstract, universally applicable canon. On the contrary, it is dependent on the character of the thing, on the purpose for which it is made by man or deity. The increasing acceptance of such a relativism was a counterpoise to the search for the handbook formula that was a staple of architectural writing in the middle half of the eighteenth century.[272]

The explosion of architectural publication happened in the second and third decade of the century, however, and coincided with the inception of Grand Lodge masonry. One of the main actors in the constitution of the Grand Lodge was a prosperous architectural publisher, John Senex;[273] according to Anderson's *Constitutions*, he became Grand Warden at the contentious lodge at which Lord Dalkeith succeeded the duke of Wharton as grand master—putting an end to the Jacobite attempt at a takeover. Senex was the publisher of Anderson's *Constitutions*, as well as of the *Royal Genealogies*; and among architectural books, the most important to carry his imprint was John James' translation of Perrault's *Ordonnances*. Senex was one of several personalities linking the origins of masonry and the feverish activity of architectural and building literature in these two decades. The flood began a little earlier. Of Wren and Hawksmoor, there were only scattered prints and "philosophical transactions" in their lifetimes. Even Vanbrugh, prolific enough in other ways, never published anything on architecture. Before the turn of the century the translation of Perrault's epitome of Vitruvius and Evelyn's version of Fréart de Chambray were the most influential books, although pattern-books, such as Hans Blume's order-book, Pierre Le Muet's *Manière*, or even Scamozzi's sixth book were part of that mass of heterogeneous literature, most of it pirated from a number of sources and carelessly re-engraved, which were the bulk of English-language architectural literature in the seventeenth century.[274] The turn is marked by a rather splendid English-language reissue of Andrea Pozzo's *Perspectiva Pictorum* of 1707, prepared by John James; Pozzo's treatise first appeared in 1694 and was enlarged in 1702. Meanwhile, a Latin-English version appeared in Rome in 1700;[275] and on this James based the London version. Pozzo's extremely illusionistic *barochetto* was in contrast to the sobriety and even "correctness" of his architectural devices by eighteenth-century standards.

James was at that point working at Greenwich, and Pozzo's book was just the kind that would have been approved by painters like Thornhill (apart from the three surveyors), who used it in his decoration at St. Paul's and more evidently at Greenwich. James' other two publications of this period are again translations: in 1708 the Senex reengraving of Perrault's *Ordonnances*, and in 1712 the epitome of Le Nôtre's formal kind of garden, in Dézallier d'Argenville's anonymously published *Théorie et Pratique du Jardinage*.[276] These were not harbingers of a new manner but provided theoretical backing for the grand style as it was practiced in the King's Works, and by painters of the period, Thornhill and his Italian contemporaries working in Britain: Verrio and Laguerre, and less evidently by Sebastiano Ricci.

There was a more radical change on its way. Its principal architect, both literally and metaphorically was Richard Boyle, third earl of Burlington. A kinsman of the Skeptical Chymist, he inherited titles and estates when he was two years old, in 1697, and with them also a Whig commitment less binding than that of Philip Wharton, his junior by three years.[277] They went on their respective grand tours about the same time; Wharton turned his, which was designed as a Whig and Protestant exercise, into a political cartwheel, while Burlington, sober and conventional, followed the correct itinerary, buying works of art lavishly but with some discrimination. On his return, he set about enlarging Burlington House in Piccadilly which Sir John Denham had built for his father. The one architect practicing in England at the time who had a professional Italian training was James Gibbs, and he was an obvious enough choice.[278]

Gibbs had returned to England in 1708. In Rome he had studied for the priesthood and having changed his mind, once wavered between painting and architecture.[279] By the time he returned, he was finally committed to architecture, and he sought the patronage of the Tory and Jacobite earl of Mar, who recommended Gibbs to Robert Harley, the powerful earl of Oxford.[280] Gibbs also befriended Wren and seems to have been involved in Godfrey Kneller's "academy." In 1713–1714, he became, as I have already reported, one of the surveyors to the Fifty Churches Commission, though his patrons lost power almost immediately; Mar had escaped into exile, having commanded the Pretender's forces in the 1715 uprising. Oxford, in disgrace on the Hanoverian succession, was in the Tower of London from 1715 to 1717. Gibbs managed to weather this change of fortune, even though it was not only his political friends who lost power since Wren was forced into retirement. The Commission for the Fifty Churches was dismissed on the change of ministry on George I's arrival. Neither Wren nor Gibbs were to work for it again, although Gibbs' one church done for the commissioners, St. Mary-le-Strand, was continued and completed to his design.[281] Gibbs attributed his dismissal to the machinations of a countryman, Colen Campbell.[282]

Campbell also ousted him in Lord Burlington's favor. The personal conflict between those two Scotsmen brings the sharp change of taste into focus. At the official level, this change was operated by subsidiary characters. Wren's retirement, for instance, was hastened by petty harassment. He had already passed his charge at Greenwich to Hawksmoor.[283] The weird planting of the balustrade over the great cornice of St. Paul's in the name of a new taste was in fact an attempt by the new surveyor to deprive Wren of his fees.[284] This new surveyor, William Benson[285] a trifling Whig pamphleteer, only lasted eighteen months at the Office of Works, although when he was dismissed for incompetence, he was replaced by another Whig placeman, Sir Thomas Hewett.[286] There was to be no surveyor of distinction until William Chambers' appointment in 1782, while the obvious Whig candidate for the post, John Vanbrugh, was left without an official position. Still he did not lack work.[287]

Colen Campbell had much to do with Benson's surveyorship, though it is not quite clear who was "using" whom. At the dynastic change of ministry, Campbell must have been collecting material for his major enterprise, *Vitruvius Britannicus*, for some time. The engraved title page of the first volume is followed by a most elaborately flourished dedication to the new king, worded in strangely Stuart style:[288] in spite of the intrusive persona, George I was a successor of Charles I through Elizabeth of Bohemia, the Winter Queen.

Campbell's book had little text: a page of introduction, and seven to explain the plates—not a treatise in the accepted sense. Moreover, Campbell had built nothing in his own name at that time, and he filled *Vitruvius* with his designs, mostly for palatial residences, by way of advertising his skill, so far unemployed; however, at least one of these designs was the product of an actual commission, Wanstead House, which after many vicissitudes and alterations, was built for Richard Child, who was made Lord Castlemaine in 1718.[289]

The first volume starts with plates of Wren's St. Paul's and of St. Peter's in Rome: a demonstration to challenge the superiority of Rome and establish the independence of native British genius, although Campbell spoils his case a little by following these with his own scheme for a church in Lincoln's Inn Fields to unite the virtues of both, while avoiding the faults of each of the other great designs.[290] There are a few other ecclesiastical and public buildings, such as Archer's St. Philip's at Birmingham and Jones' Banqueting House. The bulk of the plates are of houses: Jones' Somerset House and Gunnersbury show the pride of British Palladianism. The advocacy considered, Campbell's balance of plates gives a relatively fair picture of British building at the time. The lion's share goes to Vanbrugh and Hawksmoor, with Talman not far behind, and even Gibbs is given a mention.[291] Plates 51 and 52 show William Benson's Wil-

Colen Campbell, projected church for Lincoln's Inn Fields. After Vitruvius Britannicus.

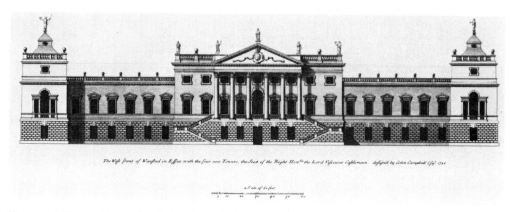

Wanstead House, Essex, by Colen Campbell. After Vitruvius Britannicus.

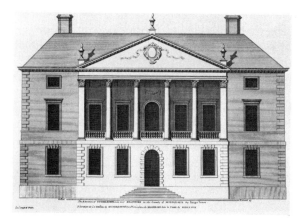

Gunnersbury House, Middlesex, by Inigo Jones (?)
and John Webb. After Vitruvius Britannicus.

bury House which Campbell attributes to its owner:[292] apart from
some advice about fountains which he is alleged to have given
George I at Herrenhausen, when George was still only elector, Wilbury was Benson's only real claim to proficiency in building, as well
as an exercise in a revival of the style of Inigo Jones, being based on
John Webb's Amesbury,[293] and so indicating the intention to bypass
the generations in between. It is not clear what part Campbell had in
its conception, but there was some form of alliance. On displacing
Wren, Benson appointed Campbell in Hawksmoor's place as Clerk
Engrosser to the Works. In spite of subsequent quarrels and strong
animus, the two later volumes of *Vitruvius* which Campbell edited
and which completed his version of the native British style—the
version which became popular with Anglophiles all over Europe—
maintained the proportions allotted to the various architects in the
first volume. Even in the third, Castle Howard is shown on the most
impressively engraved plate of the whole collection.[294]

But the change in officeholders did correspond to a shift of official
patronage, promoted by Burlington. The case of James Leoni, a

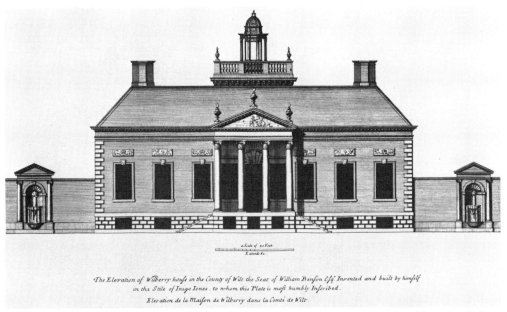

Wilbury House, Wiltshire, by William Benson and Colen Campbell (?). After Vitruvius Britannicus.

Venetian architect who issued a translation of Palladio as grandiose as Campbell's book, shows how this operated: since, like Campbell's, Leoni's book was an advertisement for patronage. Like Campbell's, too, it took some time to prepare. Leoni arrived in London in 1713; with Nicolas Dubois,[295] he produced both a French and an English version of the text, and he commissioned his countryman, Sebastiano Ricci, to engrave a pompous frontispiece as well as a new portrait of Palladio, allegedly after Veronese.[296] As for the original woodcut illustrations in Palladio, he had them re-engraved on copper from his own redrawings, which "corrected," as he thought, Palladio's rather rough and archaic style. This turned out to be a very bad miscalculation.

As a publishing enterprise, however, Leoni's book had a good measure of success. There were many subscribers, and it sold well. Yet in spite of the open flattery of the preface and dedication, Burlington never patronized Leoni.[297] The tampering with Palladio's originals was never forgiven, and Burlington set the record straight later by commissioning an alternative translation, also published as a folio, from his protégé Isaac Ware.[298] Naturally Gibbs' full-blown Roman *barochetto* manner did not appeal to him either, and his patronage was soon transferred to the native Campbell, the self-proclaimed disciple of Jones. With him, Burlington redesigned Burlington House. Campbell incautiously brought on the earl's full emancipation by urging him to revisit Italy, and particularly Palladio's buildings. During this second tour, Burlington met his most important protégé, William Kent.[299] He returned to London with Kent, but also with a number of musicians, including Giovanni Maria Bononcini, and the poet-librettist Pietro Rolli. At that time,

*York Gate and Stairs, Charing Cross, London, by
Balthazar Gerbier, but attributed to Inigo Jones. After*
Vitruvius Britannicus.

Handel, who would be Bononcini's most serious musical rival, was
already a resident of Burlington House.[300] Other musicians and artists, already resident in Picadilly or added to the group later, gave it
all the air of an "academy," which Burlington was determined to
promote, mindful of Shaftesbury's enlightened vision.[301] Between
his original grand tour and his second return with Kent, Burlington
had assumed the position of an official *arbiter elegantiarum* which
his power to press court patronage through official appointments
sustained, until he withdrew from court on his quarrel with Walpole
in 1733.[302] Still, for the twenty years between his resignation and his
death, he went on dispensing and promoting patronage unofficially,
sometimes even beyond his very ample means.[303]

The partnership between Burlington and Kent proved decisive for
British art. Without Kent, Burlington's influence would never have
been quite so pervasive.[304] On the other hand, Burlington's breath-
less patronage instantaneously propelled Kent from a rather hand-
to-mouth existence in Rome into a position which his talent could
not sustain:[305] that of the great British genius of the plastic arts, not
only the national genius like the Hanoverian Handel, but wholly
native.

The tandem partnership between the supercilious, remote, ambitious Burlington and an ingratiating, self-indulgent, unprincipled
Kent worked all too well. Kent made the beginning of the enterprise
credible, in spite of the presence in Britain of the Riccis, uncle and
nephew, of Laguerre, and of the very native Thornhill, who above
the others represented "that damn'd gusto that's been for this sixty
years past" [306] and which Kent was to replace.

And indeed the first episode in his rise was the undercutting of the

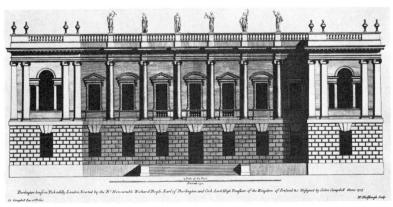

Burlington House, Piccadilly, London, by Colen Campbell (and Lord Burlington?). After Vitruvius Britannicus.

Burlington House, Piccadilly, London, main gate, by Colen Campbell. After Vitruvius Britannicus.

price Thornhill had bid for the decorations of Kensington Palace.[307] It soon became apparent to all, except for Lord Burlington's connection, that Kent was very much Thornhill's inferior. Hogarth took up cudgels on Thornhill's (his father-in-law) behalf: three satirical prints, which provoked Kent's vengeance at court. Nevertheless, Kent joined the Academy in St. Martin's Lane, which had been Thornhill's.[308] It was one of a succession of establishments which assumed the name, in imitation of the Italian and French institutions; but none of them, until much later, were more than art schools, offering some tuition and opportunities to draw figures from the model.

Thornhill did intend to make his academy a much more ambitious establishment with the help of Lord Halifax—help which, however, he did not obtain.[309] State support for an academy had to wait another half-century: under the first two philistine Georges,[310] the arts were effectively thrown on the patronage of those lords who were sufficiently independent, ambitious, and informed to create a focus in their private houses, and of these, Burlington was, in his cold way, the most enterprising and involved.

When he returned from Italy in December 1719, Burlington had

William Hogarth, Masquerades and Operas, *first state of 1723/4. The gate of Burlington House is in the center, labeled "Academy of Arts" and surmounted by a statue of Kent at whom Michaelangelo and Raphael are gazing admiringly.*

brought with him the essential and missing member of his artistic entourage, of his academy. Campbell was his architect and Guelfi,[311] still in favor, his sculptor. Both were at Burlington House. But Burlington had no painter, and with the arrival of Kent, this essential deficiency seemed supplied. In the meanwhile, with Campbell's help, he developed the estate on which his house stood, and that very successfully; Burlington, Cork, Clifford Street, as well as Savile Row still bear his and his wife's family names, although practically none of the houses remain from the original development,[312] with the exception of Queensberry House, designed for the duke and duchess of that title by James Leoni, the only work on his own land. Kent also engaged in some book illustrations during the first decade of his London activity, when Burlington still had faith that Kent would live up to his patron's expectations. Of these the most popular was his cycle of illustrations for Thomson's *The Seasons*: four sub-Claudian landscapes with clumsy Bolognese-style figures, which suited the literary taste of the time exactly and were often reprinted, perhaps because on this one occasion the engraving was a professional job which rescued Kent's banalities from the fate of some of his later work.[313] He never really assumed the role of great history painter, although he retained Burlington's favor until his death.[314]

His work changed in nature and scale. In the mid-twenties, he was increasingly involved in decorating interiors. His appointment as master carpenter at the Office of Works in 1725 gave this work official status. Kensington Palace was followed by the interiors of Wanstead House and Houghton (begun by Campbell and finished by Gibbs) for Sir Robert Walpole.[315] At the same time, he edited the designs of Inigo Jones, which were engraved from Henry Flitcroft's copies.[316] Flitcroft was at this time also working on the designs for the villa at Chiswick which was to become a model for a number of other "Palladian" imitations, although it is much closer to Scamozzi's Rocca Pisani villa at Lonigo than to Palladio's Rotonda, to which it is usually referred.[317] The part which Kent had in the design of the villa is impossible to ascertain, but he certainly dominated the decoration and furnishing of the interiors.

At the same time he became involved with Burlington in the design of the most impressive country house of the period, Holkham Hall for Thomas Coke, later earl of Leicester. The main state block is surrounded by four pavilions; this main block is itself further articulated by a depressed centerpiece which takes the form of a pedimented pavilion on the entrance side, a giant Corinthian portico towards the garden. There are flanking towers with "Venetian" windows at the *piano nobile*.[318] The planes of the building are broken into projecting and receding vertical sections, which in some preliminary designs—drawn in Kent's hand—are further complicated by variant rustications.[319] The rhythmic vertical divisions of a building into disparate elements, their articulation in profile by means of distinct and varied roofs (pyramids, hips, gables, saucer domes) were a mark which the Burlington-Kent partnership would leave on British architecture, and which has little to do with Palladio[320] but shows how the Palladian heritage was mediated for them

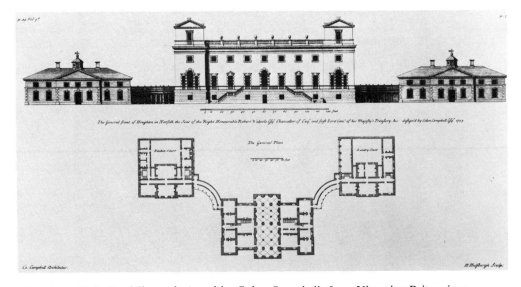

Houghton Hall, Norfolk, as designed by Colen Campbell, from Vitruvius Britannicus.

Holkham Hall, Norfolk, by William Kent. National Monuments Record.

Holkham Hall, Norfolk, by William Kent, the Marble Hall and the main stair. National Monuments Record.

by that very "damn'd gusto" of the Hawksmoor-Vanbrugh generation which they had ousted.

Half a century later, Chambers found that its "excessive variety might exhaust the eye in a perpetual dance,"[321] but it was much admired and emulated for all that, and many nineteenth-century architects made knowing use of it. The varied roofline and the breaking of horizontal surface, implied the internal disposition of rooms in elaborate sequences of a kind which may have been (though was only rarely) learnt from Palladio.[322] In practice, for all the elaboration, the planning turned out to be remarkably inept occasionally.[323]

Still, the grouping with a "depressed" center feature, variegated rustication, and flanking pavilions incorporating "Venetian" windows spanned by a relieving arch was used first by Colen Campbell at Burlington House, at Wanstead, and at Houghton. Burlington and Kent used it in almost all their buildings, most elaborately in Kent's later ones—the Horse Guards and the Treasury.

It was inevitable, perhaps, that the new assurance combined with older injunctions (Shaftesbury's in particular) would lead both Burlington and Kent to consider the two principal public buildings to which new form had not been given: the Royal Palace and the Parliament.[324]

Hampton Court, Winchester, Richmond, even Greenwich were at various times thought of as the British Versailles. But there was no British Louvre. Whitehall was a ramshackle collection of royal, monastic, and legal buildings, part of which had become a palace and part a Parliament. There had been a disastrous fire in 1698; a grand rebuilding scheme by Wren was shelved; there had been the earlier prestigious Jones-Webb scheme, which was engraved and regarded in some ways as the highpoint of British architecture.[325] Kent's one known attempt at a scheme remains in the form of a pearwood model.[326] In spite of influential advocacy, no alternative from the Burlington circle is known to exist.[327] However, there are several versions, and those in some detail, of a vast palace for Parliament which Kent did during the seventeen-thirties.[328] Nothing came of this very ambitious scheme: its pre-echoes of the Adam brothers are perhaps the most remarkable things about it. Instead of a palace, Kent had to be content with the royal stables on the site of what is now the National Gallery.[329] For Parliament, Kent did some renovations in the House of Lords and two courts for the Chancery and King's Bench on the dais of Westminster Hall in a rather fanciful, rococo Gothic style.[330] It was very much the manner which Kent thought "ideally" medieval. There are a number of further essays in it from his hand, ranging from an inkstand for the queen, through a grotto ("Merlin's cave") in the gardens at Kew[331] or the "mill" at Rousham,[332] to earnest endeavors like the Westminster Hall fittings or the choir screen at Gloucester Cathedral. Rather theatrical backgrounds for the scenes in Spenser's *Faerie Queen* (one of Kent's less happy essays in book illustration) are also very much in the same style.[333] This Kentian Gothic had various sources; it was codified

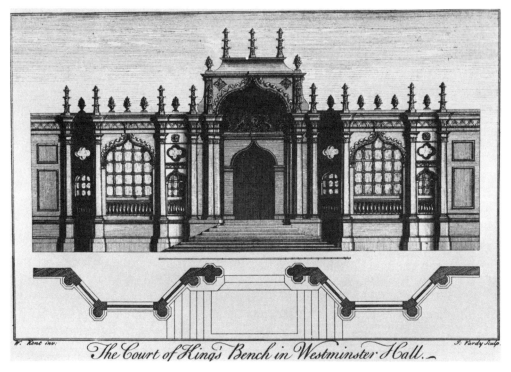

Westminster Hall, London, William Kent's interior construction of a court of the King's Bench inside the hall, after Kent and Vardy.

into a system by Batty Langley, one of the most prolific writers on architecture ever.

Langley's *Ancient Architecture Restored* first appeared in 1742,[334] two or three years after Kent's work at Westminster was completed, and just before he started on the most monumental of his Gothic commissions, the screen for Gloucester Cathedral.[335] Kent's Gothic was hardly authentic: the screen at Gloucester was an arcade whose coupled columns supported short entablatures as imposts for ogee arches. It is almost a "Gothic" caricature of what he might have done, using classical detail in such a context.

Langley claimed to offer a more serious approach than his predecessors. His book was dedicated to two grandees, the dukes of Montague and Richmond, in their masonic roles.[336] Horace Walpole is listed as one of the subscribers to the first edition,[337] although he was to express contempt for Langley's gimcrack and untutored approach, so careless of antiquarian detail, to which his own archeological-rococo fancy seemed enormously superior in refinement and accuracy: for Walpole, only literal quotation could be a guarantee of authenticity. By contrast, Langley offered only two examples of "measured" medieval building (the "orders" of the nave and the choir at Westminster Abbey), the other sixty-two plates being a recreation of Gothic architecture according to geometrical rules, very much in the vein in which certain pattern-books reshaped or modified the orders.[338]

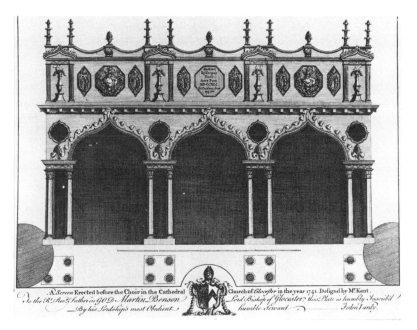

William Kent, choir screen for Gloucester Cathedral. From Kent and Vardy.

Walpole cared little for such general rules: his Gothic was an assembly of unscaled quotation, without any concern for congruities of period or context. In his one masterpiece, Strawberry Hill, which he built for himself, the play on incongruity is compounded by the long period of construction and the many hands which were his amanuenses in the design.[339] It was all exaggerated by changes of mind and rhythm of building over thirty years.[340] At the outset, Walpole confessed that he was "almost as fond of Sharawaggi, or Chinese want of symmetry, in buildings as in grounds and gardens." [341] Certainly, the gallimaufry of stained-glass bits from wrecked churches, tombs used for fireplaces, tiles ripped up to make way for Kent's work at Gloucester, all that was inevitably irregular on the interior, and deliberately so on the exterior: none of it was organized symmetrically like the many collections of classical antiquities, fused into trophylike compositions, which decorated so many Italian palaces, though like the compilers of the antique compositions, Walpole was primarily concerned with the effect of detail within the whole scheme. However, the fragmentation, the half-dark, the glitter alluded to a middle age of mystery and terror, a foretaste of the "gloomth" which Beckford was to require of his architect as the salient quality of his abbey at Fonthill, though Walpole's "gloomth" was on a dinky and harmless scale, without any of Beckford's tragic pretentions.[342]

Excursus on Gardens
Walpole was perhaps the first to move the notion of *sharawaggi* from the garden to the house, and he was quite aware of the impor-

tant step he was taking. Strawberry Hill became a showpiece within a few years after Walpole began the transformation.[343] The word *sharawaggi* had been coined by Sir William Temple in his *Essay on the Gardens of Epicurus* quite by the way;[344] he coined it to describe the harmony in apparent disorder of Chinese and Japanese gardens, although he did not think that such garden design could be commended to his contemporaries. André Le Nôtre undisputably dominated garden design at the time. But there were dissenting voices. Wotton had already written, fifty years before Temple: "as Fabriques should be *regular,* so Gardens should be *irregular,* or at least cast into a very *wilde Regularitie.*"[345] Wotton's *irregularitie* is a great deal more constrained than Temple's *sharawaggi.* He was writing at the high point of the excessively rigid knotted and squared Elizabethan-Jacobean garden and was advocating gardens like the new varied ones which he had seen in the Veneto: even at his own villa at Novento Padovano, some ten miles from Palladio's Malcontenta.[346] He certainly was not thinking of the elaborate clipped gardens of the Lazio or of Tuscany. Temple for his part was writing at the height of the French *parterre* planning, which was highly appreciated in England at the time, a manner which three generations of French gardeners developed from the Roman-Tuscan gardens of the *cinquecento.* They may have been little to his taste in any case. Although a loyal servant of his king (both Charles II and James II), he was a consistent enemy of Francophile policy. He was reputed to have laxist, even Epicurean opinions, but they were formed in the school of Ralph Cudworth and of his Cambridge associates,[347] and like many formed in a Neoplatonic school, he had a veneration for things Chinese.

In this he was like Pierre-Daniel Huet, bishop of Avranches, a prolific apologist for the Ancient Theology, who laid out a Chinese garden in his home abbey at Aulnay in Normandy, perhaps the first Chinese garden in Europe, excepting only the Pavillon de Porcelaine at Versailles,[348] which can hardly be said to have a garden in a congruent style. Huet was not only a prolific brilliant controversialist but a leading man of letters and a courtier, having been Bossuet's associate as the Dauphin's tutor.[349] His garden was unfortunately swept away after his death.

As for Wotton, his observations on the pleasures of irregularity were presumably the product of his own practice as a gardener and a wine grower. It suggests his disquiet with certain current ways of doing things.[350] Bacon dismissed knots and devices ("they be but toyes"), yet the garden which he described as ideal was a square of shorn grass and clipped hedges, although it included a "heath," "framed as much as may be to a natural Wilderness" and filled with fruit and flowering plants. It had to be tidy and trimmed: "kept with cutting, that they grow not out of course." [351] All this is very much of a piece with Bacon's thinking, of his forthright and inquisitive attitude to natural phenomena; in this, too, he was a lawyer. It was a time when the judicial process favored the use of torture for obtaining evidence. It is therefore hardly surprising that Bacon insisted that the scientific inquirer "put nature on the rack." [352] Such an attitude was quite unacceptable to the Cambridge thinkers. In this, as in so many things, Shaftesbury was their faithful disciple. Nature was not to be twisted into extreme situations to yield up her secrets. The order of nature could be scried without the use of force. And, as in inquiry, so in his management of nature, the true order of "things natural" will only be spoiled by the art and caprice of man; "even the rude rocks, the mossy caverns, the irregular unwrought grottoes and broken falls of water, with all their horrid graces of wilderness itself, in representing nature more, will be the more engaging and appear with a magnificence beyond the mockery of princely gardens." [353]

Shaftesbury's enthusiasm for the paintings of Gaspard Poussin and Salvator Rosa is therefore hardly surprising: though the step to be taken from Shaftesbury's refusal to "iron out" natural irregularities to the later contriving of irregularity by design is enormous. There is little evidence that in the later seventeenth century—or early in the eighteenth—patrons consciously sought to imitate paintings when they designed effects which a later generation was to call picturesque.[354] Such patrons, and the designers who often accompanied them, were becoming familiar in their travels with the landscape of Lazio and the Roman Campagna through which they inevitably passed in the course of the grand tour. They could inspect the exact location of the great moments of history and legend, familiar from Vergil, Ovid, or Livy; some had been celebrated in the pastoral paintings of Claude, his imitators and followers. These were landscapes which seemed as relaxed and untrammelled as the shepherds and warriors who peopled them.[355]

The warriors were shepherds by turns, and plowmen, too. The landscape of the Campagna was rustic: much of it wilderness and pasturage. Where cultivated, the vineyards and vegetable patches looked very much more episodic than the hedged fields of England; with farmhouses and classical ruins making cypress-shaded markings on the undulating plains or among the hills, and the vineyards following the contours. The formal gardens were too sparse incidents to count as part of the landscape impression.

The English landscape, partitioned by hedges, was quite different, being much more intensively cultivated. Gardens and woods had, moreover, become quite as much the master's as the peasant's business. John Evelyn's *Sylva* (with its title echoing Bacon's[356]) shows this quite explicitly. The Great Instauration, which presupposed a return to the paradisal state, exalted the figure of Adam, the trimmer and planter of Eden.[357] The "lantskip" of the latter seventeenth century was very much horticultural-arboricultural; this working landscape, rather than the formal garden of *parterres* and clipped hedges, was "improved" in the eighteenth century into the sentimental-picturesque garden.[358]

In spite of royal patronage, the revulsion against the Frenchified *parterres*, with their swags of dwarf box and their colored pebble patterns, had a religious and economic, even a military background.

Tree planting was effectively promoted on a large scale by Evelyn's
Sylva. It was the industrial basis for British naval power, which was
the strongest guarantor of religious liberty (as John Dee had maintained a century earlier), besides providing incidental commercial
advantages to an expanding economy. In any case, the garden of
apocalyptic instauration, as well as the landscape beyond it, had to
look quite different from the explicit, hierarchized panorama which
the grand style might offer to its masters.

Since the restoration of Charles II, England had—in gardening—
become something of a French province. The King certainly wanted
it so.[359] But while Hampton Court, Windsor, St. James' were laid
out on French models, the botanic gardens, an emblematic and
paradisal plan, had its admirers in England and on the Continent: the
Botanic Garden at Oxford and John Tradescant's garden in Lambeth
were still appreciated.[360] The garden as a hieroglyph of classification
and as a mirror of the passage of the seasons continued to reappear
in literature, of which Sir William Temple's description of his favorite garden at Moor Park is important evidence.[361]

This was the "philosophical garden." The sentimental garden, the
garden of retreat which may not be cultivated by its inhabitants
(indeed may not be cultivated at all), also makes its appearance in
European literature early in the seventeenth century. The popularity
of Sannazzaro's *Arcadia*, of Tasso's *Aminta* is reinforced by an
arcadian genre, of which Honoré d'Urfé's *L'Astrée* was the prime
example.[362] The schematic naiveté of relationships, noble and etiolated, is played against the background of a quasi-nature. "High and
spacious trees which nature brings forth in the horrid mountains may
please a spectator more than cultivated plants trimmed in ornate
gardens by knowing hands." So Sannazzaro opens his account of
Arcadia, which was to give its name to the academy Queen Christina
of Sweden posthumously mothered in Rome, and which was to
dominate Italian poetry in the first half of the eighteenth century. On
the slopes of the Janicolo, this academy built and planted the Parra-
sian wood with a fountain shaded by cypress trees and an open-air
theater, all designed by Francesco de' Sanctis, better known as the
architect of the Spanish Steps.[363]

Moreover, another French novelist had codified the garden of
sentiment into a map. Madame de Scudéry's *Clélie* contains a
strange map, in which the course of emotional life, with its fortunes
and misfortunes, is represented as a landscape.[364]

The ingredients of a transformation at the end of the century are
complex therefore. A mythological fantasy derived from art is imposed on the husbanded and paradisal garden of the puritans. This
very fantasy allows the liberation of the layout from the strait-
jacket which the past imposed on it. But there is another ingredient,
which was to become more important with time: the exotic one. The
gardens of the Chinese had been described in numerous travel
books.[365] The philosophy of the Chinese, their language and writing,
their religion were interminably fascinating towards the end of
the seventeenth century. The ideographic nature of Chinese writing

inevitably suggested a parallel to Egyptian hieroglyphs, and other similarities between Egypt and China were exploited by many mythographers.[366] Some even hazarded the opinion that the ancient Egyptians were collateral ancestors of the modern Chinese. Others went further still and maintained that Chinese thought, religion, and constitution were so remarkable that they could only be explained as the surviving fragment of a golden age.[367] Chinese veneration of nature was often admired in this context, and the gentle asymmetrical order of their garden was seen as an ideal figure of hoary antiquity. The superficial exoticism of Versailles yielded to erudite inquiry; and the description of asymmetrical gardens of imitated wil-

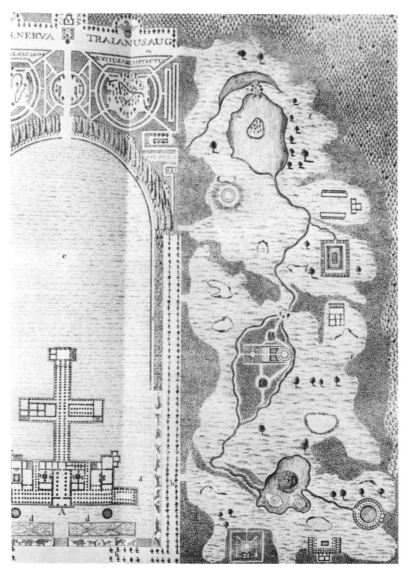

Irregular garden in Pliny's Villa Tusculana. After Robert Castell.

The maze garden in the Yuan Ming Yuan, laid out by European (practically all Jesuits) artists and scientists for the Ch'ien Lung Emperor. The maze was called Tuo Huang Hua Teng, or the garden of the many lanterns with yellow flowers. Engraved by an anonymous Chinese artist.

derness were read into classical texts, such as Pliny the Younger's descriptions of his villas.[368]

The transference of the asymmetry from the garden (where it mirrored the proper respect of a benevolent nature) to the house, the transference which Walpole suggested, was not generally affected until much later. On the contrary, the first masters of the irregular garden were the very proponents of the strictest adherence to the canons of imitated antiquity in their buildings. Kent may well have allowed himself Gothic follies, and even the occasional piece of *chinoiserie*,[369] but his more serious buildings were exercised in that "new gusto" which he and Burlington introduced. The detached portico set against a great screen of rusticated stone, the monumental staircases leading to complex and stately internal arrangements, all that broke at the edge of the house. In the early layouts, such as the one at Burlington's own villa at Chiswick, the main lines of the garden are still obliquely related to the interior of the house: they still have something of the formal park seen from a *mirador*. Kent's later gardens, at Rousham or at Stowe, broke the rigid order of the house at the edge of a lawn.

The whole thing had begun (as Walpole would have us believe) with the devising of the invisible fence, the Ha!Ha! of eighteenth century landscape treatises.[370] Once it had been adopted, the garden of irregular tree planting and shorn lawns, superior even to the contrived irregularity of the Chinese because seeming virtually uncultivated, became the ideal: "a man might make a pretty landskip of his own possessions" as Addison put it.[371] Addison was the perfect

literary-antiquarian voyager, the viewer of nature through Claude
and Virgil. His polemics in favor of the natural garden were inspired,
at close remove, by Shaftesbury.[372] Yet the elements of the new
garden derived, as had the "new gusto," from the very artists which
it claimed to set aside.

The notion of the garden as a framed picture is clearly implicit at
Versailles, being reflected in that vast mirror wall, the greatest ex-
panse of mirror in the world at that time—and a triumph of French
technology. However formal and grandiose the reflected garden of
parterres de broderie, and however spacious, it was only the
greatest of princes who could afford to dominate all that was in their
sight. But all gardeners would have agreed with Henry Wotton that
the view from the house is "the Royaltie of Sight"; for "the Eye [is] a
raunging, imperious and usurping Sence [and] can endure no narrow
circumspection." [373] Lesser beings therefore supplemented the taste
for the *Royaltie* by subterfuge, of which the most common by far
were the views painted on garden walls to be seen from the house, or
down an enclosed walk. Since they were painted directly on external
walls, they had to be refreshed often, or fade into oblivion; which
they mostly did, leaving their traces only in the literature of the
period.[374]

The popularity of the formal garden well into the eighteenth
century—in England as well as in France—is the context of Kent's
gardening achievement, which did not reach the generality until the
half-century, and this in spite of the books. The most influential
rococo theorist of gardening put it: "art must give place to nature,
the garden must be so disposed that it might seem planted by the
Author of nature Himself." [375] We tend to interpret this as an appeal
for the *jardin à l'anglaise*, or even the *jardin anglo-chinois*, as it
came to be called later. At the time it was written, however, the
sentiment referred to a garden which seemed so orderly that it had
the semblance of paradise; not unkempt, but not overtrimmed.
Order in a low key was imposed on what nature provided.

There was, however, one other aspect of the matter which is often
neglected: the obverse of the garden. The garden was a space of
light and of the evident; but "light unto *Pluto* is darkness unto
Jupiter." [376] The hieroglyph of this notion was the nymphaeum or
grotto such as the extraordinary one at Versailles.[377] Most gardens
since antiquity had had one, larger or smaller.[378] A whole style was
evolved in the sixteenth century around them. The *style rustique*
was the visual correlative of *boscarescha* literature, and both received a new lease in the eighteenth century.[379]

Pope had set the fashion at Twickenham, and it soon became a
subject of imitation and of literary rhapsody.[380] But far more important were Kent's two little buildings for Queen Caroline: the hermitage and the Cave of Merlin in Richmond Park. It is odd that these
two garden follies were used by Caroline of Anspach, in spite of her
husband's jibes, to assert a policy of alliance with the Whig administration which did not always accord with George II's wishes.
These structures were built in a primitive and ruined version of the

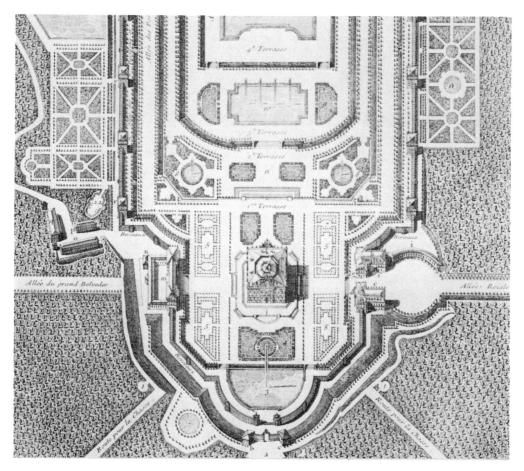

Marly-le-Roi, detail of the plan of the château. The perspective pavilion, marked m, *is directly opposite the circular entrance court. After Mariette.*

more pompous and finished style which Kent had adopted at Westminster and in Gloucester Cathedral. Of course, he also did plain rustic follies, and even classical garden buildings, like the famous series at Stowe. In these, too, he assumed an archaic manner, which—again—owed much to both Vanbrugh and to Hawksmoor. It was at Stowe, whose garden Kent remodeled, at Rousham, rather than at Holkham, which was his principal contribution to the architecture of the English country house, that the new landscape garden was achieved; while in Kensington Gardens and Hyde Park, Queen Caroline is said to have laid out the Serpentine herself,[381] a decisive manifesto of her taste—at any rate in gardening.

However much the gardens laid out later in the century still followed the advice of books which recommended a formal layout (Dézallier d'Argenville—in John James' translation—or Stephen Switzer, or Batty Langley), yet there was a decisive change during William Kent's lifetime, even if the part he played in it has been overstated by Horace Walpole. Kent had no sympathy for the earnest intentions of the seventeenth-century gardeners: a sentiment

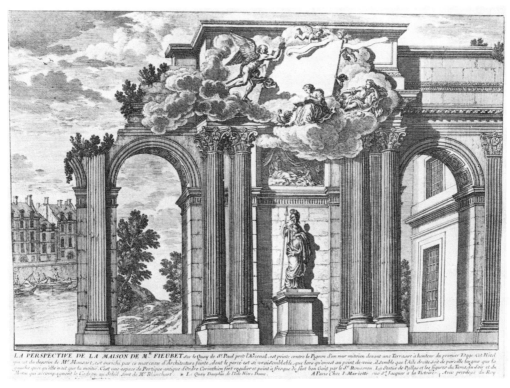

Hôtel Fieubert, garden perspective, by Rousseau and Blanchard. After Pérelle.

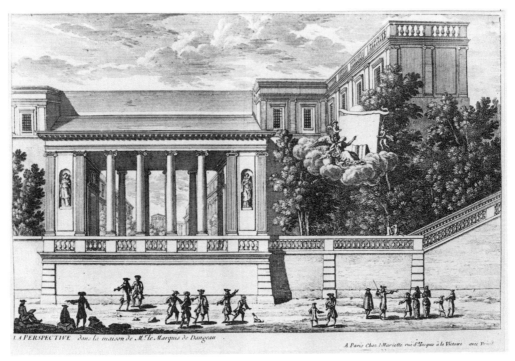

Paris, Hôtel Dangeau; garden perspective. After Mariette.

The Section of MERLIN'S CAVE in the Royal Gardens at Richmond.

Merlin's Cave, Royal Park, Richmond, by William Kent. After Kent and Vardy.

which John Evelyn described in a long letter to Thomas Browne. "Caves, grottoes, mounts and irregular ornaments of gardens contribute to contemplative and philosophicall enthusiasme . . . (they) signifie *rem sacram et divinam.*" [382] Through the changes of taste, English gardeners maintained the notion of the garden as a complex emblem. The great avenues of "modern" French layout inevitably lost any sense of it.[383]

The master himself tended the garden often, since he was taught by the poets and theologians that the trimming and watering of plants was the work of Adam before the Fall.[384] The dignity of the gardener as *Paradisii Cultor* (Evelyn's phrase, again) was not forgotten by the makers of the landscapes which were to be thought of as peopled by Virgilian and Ovidian, even Homeric figures. At Stowe and Rousham, in Henry Hoare's own garden at Stourhead, the complex interplay of prospect and emblematic garden pavilion was intended to provide a chain of responses which were linked into a narrative. The idea is fully realized earlier, however. Vanbrugh, in his remarkable letter to the duchess of Marlborough, pleads for the preservation of the ruins of the old manor house of Woodstock as part of the new Blenheim Park, because the aged, historic ruin awakes associations in the visitor's mind, while its archaic appearance provides a contrast with "modern" building and with the plantations.[385]

At Castle Howard, Vanbrugh and Hawksmoor devised a succession of views linked into a narrative of the kind I described, but

which could also be seen in terms of Claudian landscape. It was
later painted and described in those very Claudian, heroic terms at
which its designers aimed.[386]

At Castle Howard, the monuments: pyramid, mausoleum, and
"temple," as later at Stourhead, stood directly as they would have
done in a painted landscape on the green lawn, without any intermediary garden layout of paths, beds, *parterres*, as had been usual.
They were crystalline incidents in a continuous, quasi-natural landscape.[387]

At least one British painter, Richard Wilson,[388] built his fortune on
commemorating the houses and gardens which had been designed in
the first age of landscape planting and, at the time of his return to
England from the Campagna, where his vision was formed, were
fully mature. Still, the increasing scale of the garden, its extension
over the whole of the grounds of a house—and beyond, at least as far
as the eye could reach—meant dispensing the master of the house
from even a token "mechanic" participation.[389] The very grandeur
of the vision which inspired it rendered the diminutive scale of its
later practitioners liable to justified ridicule.[390] Yet the new country
houses, built in the generation after Burlington's, with their windows coming down to the ground, often opening directly onto a
lawn, had a powerful charm. Through the windows, the visitor
would inspect the clumps of trees which could even form themselves, in the distance, into an old avenue. Disposed among the
trees, he would see sheep and cows whose access to lawns and
house was barred by a fence invisible from the windows. It would be
a landscape at once inviting reflection on the amenities of untram-
meled nature and an appreciation of its productive capacities. The
scene did not demand his active participation. The notion of the
paradisal promise to the Original Gardener had been dispersed in
the very scale to which the image had grown.

The landscape garden, then, which was not conceived between
Chiswick and Twickenham, between Burlington's villa, which his
contemporaries found so truly Venetian, and Pope's Grove, but in
the upper London reach of the Thames, seems to play a quite inordi-
nately important part in the architectural debates of the time. John
James dedicated his translation of Dézallier d'Argenville's gardening
book to "Secretary" Johnston, a moderate Whig politician, who
resided in Twickenham;[391] within two or three years of its publication Burlington designed his *bagno*, the first of his remodeling exercises at Chiswick.[392] Pope moved to Twickenham in 1719; the
Burlington-Kent villa was begun soon after.[393] Kent's work for the
queen at Richmond also belongs to this decade. And during the
seventeen-twenties, Pope with Charles Bridgeman laid out the garden, while the earl of Pembroke with Roger Morris designed the
house for the countess of Suffolk, who as Mrs. Howard had been
George II's official mistress.[394]

Marble Hill is a remarkable exercise in the new Palladian manner.
There is more. In 1728, young Batty Langley, the son of a Twickenham architect, issued his book on gardening, the first of his vast

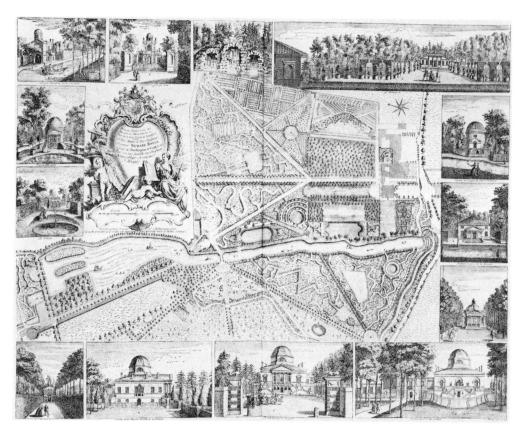

Chiswick House, Chiswick, London, villa and park, by Burlington and Kent. Note that the main avenue and the "trident" in the upper part of the engraving center on the "Bagno" designed by Lord Burlington before his travels (top row of views, second from the left) and not on the main villa, which looks out on a lawn formally bordered by trees, and closed by a sculpture group. After Rocque.

series of publications, while in the same year, another local, Robert Morris, a kinsman of Roger, issued a rather different publication, his *Essay in Defence of Ancient Architecture*, in which the facade and plan of Marble Hill house are offered as examples of the true ancient manner;[395] ten years later Morris offered his ideas in the form of a systematic account of building design based on harmonic proportion, which was as much a geometricized reworking of the Kent-Burlington manner as Batty Langley's had been of the kind of Gothic taste which they shared with Kent, although Morris, unlike Batty Langley, was not interested in the programmatic possibilities of a new style.[396]

The two families, the Morrises and Langleys, must have known each other.[397] They represented two tendencies which are sufficiently contrasted to be worth examining together. The Langley brothers, Batty particularly, were frenetic publishers.[398] Their books and periodical articles were largely directed at practitioners in the building trades. Some were only collections of plates with summary

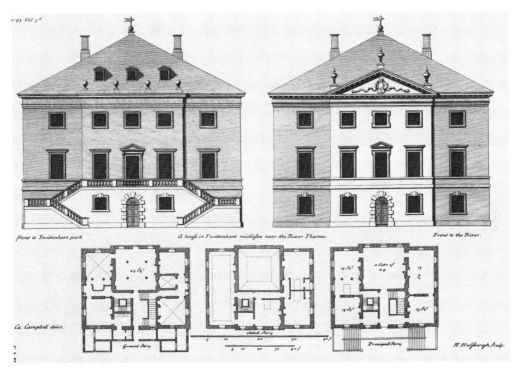

*Marble Hill House, Twickenham, by Colen Campbell (with Lord Pembroke and Roger Morris).
The monumental staircase was omitted and a giant order of pilasters added to the central portion
of the park elevation. After* Vitruvius Britannicus.

introductions, but their tendency is always the same, towards
familiarizing craftsmen, surveyors, gardeners, joiners, plasterers,
glaziers, bricklayers, with the rudiments of design. Running through
their work is the effort at simplifying the proportions of the orders,
reducing them to "aliquot fractions" as Perrault—whose work they
knew well—had suggested, although without any of Perrault's ambitious theorizing.[399] For Langley, it is a simplified presentation for
the craftsman's benefit. The formation of craftsmen fully familiar
with the rationale and the detailed working of classical architecture,
and able to transform Gothic detail according to the same rules, is an
aim which echoes the grand design of John Dee and Inigo Jones.
Langley wanted his disciples familiar with the latest ornamental
fashions from France and Italy: *rocaille* as well as *grand goût*, so as
to be able to rival any foreign workman.[400] But he also had a firm
architectural loyalty: his hero was Nicholas Hawksmoor, whose
cause he defended against the new-fangled *signiors*, the followers of
the Kent-Burlington camp. The bulkiest of Langley's books, one of
the largest architectural books ever published in Britain, was a collection of plates which he dedicated to the most important noblemen
who were also freemasons; the list was headed by Francis of Lorraine
and called *Ancient Masonry*. It may be that the term *ancient mason*
was sufficiently common that no particular significance can be attached to the fact that Langley's title[401] was also used by the most

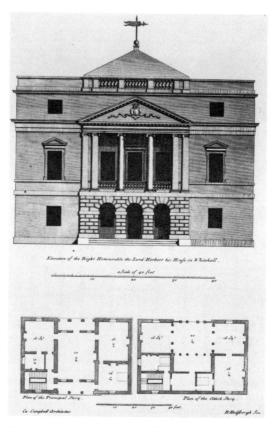

*Pembroke House, Whitehall, London, by Colen
Campbell (with Lord Pembroke?).*

important body of schismatic masons, whose Grand Lodge was
founded in the year of Langley's death, not far from his house.[402] It
was a group in which building workers, many—if not most—of Irish
origin, seem to have been the dominant party, though in masonry, as
in all associations, schism was endemic, and there seem always to
have been lodges which remained independent of the Grand Lodge.
One quasi-schismatic movement, perhaps the one associated with
the duke of Wharton, had William Hogarth as an active advocate.[403]
Hogarth and Langley had much in common. Both were aligned
against the Burlington House party. Both defended the rights of
British artists against foreign importations and incompetent imposi-
tions, and both taught through organizations which were almost
guilds, in that they acted as training bodies as well as protective
unions for artists against stingy patrons and sharp connoisseurs.
Whether Langley ever met Hogarth, we do not know, but they both
knew James Gibbs. Hogarth painted his portrait and was his fellow-
governor at St. Bartholomew's, responsible for some of its decoration.[404] The *Grub Street Journal*, for which Langley also wrote
under the eminently masonic pen name *Hiram*, printed controversy
about these paintings.[405] This draws up the lines clearly enough.
Langley saw himself as the heir of the manner established by the

great trio at the Office of Works, the true British manner which could be strengthened by the disinterring of Gothic architecture in the proper fashion of Wren and Hawksmoor. Gothic architecture, the style of the ancient Anglo-Saxons, could be shown to obey the same geometric rules as the architecture of the Greeks and Romans, but had the great advantage, as an exemplar, of being the manner of building not of the outlandish and barbarous Goths, but of the true native English-speakers: lovers of freedom, devisers of parliamentary government, and champions of the rule of law against absolute monarchy.[406] Langley's attempt at "ordering" Gothic architecture was much more earnest than Walpole allowed; he despised Langley's plebeian taste and would not—or could not—understand his aim, which was to bring the knowledge of Gothic principles within the reach of every building worker.

Against the mass of Langley's repeated, confused pattern-books, Robert Morris' may seem the work of a fastidious theorist. His very first publication appeared in the same year as Langley's *Essay on Gardens*.[407] The book is overtly polemical. Antiquity is to be the only model for the architect. Moreover Greek antiquity is quite sufficient: Roman additions (the Tuscan and Composite orders) are to be discarded.[408] The three Greek orders had been handed over uncorrupted to the Romans, and their authentic syntax and grammar were reformulated by Palladio. True, Bramante before and Scamozzi after him were worthy men, but the Palladian torch passed directly to Inigo Jones and from him—with a bow to Christopher Wren—to the men extolled in the preface, Lords Burlington and Pembroke and Sir Andrew Fountaine. Fountaine, a well-known collector, had succeeded Newton as Master of the Mint;[409] both he and Pembroke appeared in the dedication of Langley's *Ancient Masonry* as prominent freemasons. But this link between the two writers is tenuous. In fact, Morris proposes as the proper model to follow, the pattern on which to explain his compositional principles, a small country house. He names neither architect nor owner. But in fact, although the project was still confidentially treated at the time of publication, it was soon to be known as Marble Hill, the house the earl of Pembroke designed with Roger Morris for Lady Suffolk, which I mentioned earlier.[410] Marble Hill is the only surviving house associated with Lord Pembroke: his own house at Whitehall, the White Lodge at Richmond, and Wimbledon Park, built for the aged duchess of Marlborough, are either destroyed or altered out of recognition.[411] Of all their joint ventures, the one which had the most direct and diffuse influence was the small "Palladian" bridge which they built at Wilton, by Lord Pembroke's famous Inigo Jones house.[412] Pembroke and Morris were more consistent, more harmonious—and worked on a smaller scale than the Burlington-Kent duo. They had their part in the conflict with what Kent had called "that damn'd gusto" when they displaced Hawksmoor's proposal for a historiated column memorial at Blenheim (based on the two Roman ones) with a Doric column on a plain plinth.[413] But such minor triumphs hardly signify when compared with the lasting

influence Robert Morris had to exercise. While Langley, attached to
the old ways, saw himself as a mediator between ideology, fashion,
and the building workman, Robert Morris addressed the new class of
craftsmen who aspired to a change of status. It is not certain when
Roger Morris started to call himself "architect," but it was probably
about 1730. He was one of many contractor-craftsmen who were
advancing themselves in this way.[414] In his earlier buildings, he
worked closely with Lord Pembroke. It is difficult to decide, perhaps
even more than in the case of the Burlington-Kent partnership,
how responsibility is to be apportioned between the two men. Herbert of Pembroke was an even less skillful draftsman than Burlington; practically nothing in his hand survives.[415] It was through the collaboration with well-traveled, cultivated, and fastidious Pembroke,
as irascible as he was kind, that Roger Morris passed from the status
of "carpinter" to that of "architect." [416] Robert Morris, on the other
hand, did not assume the style "architect," although architecture,
as he put it, "was the favourite branch of (his) study." [417] And a few
years after he had written the *Defence*, he gave some lectures on this
"favourite branch" to an obscure society "establish'd for the Improvement of Arts and Sciences." No record survives of such a
society. It is just possible that, like Batty Langley's building school,
it may have been a masonic lodge.[418]

   In the lectures Morris sets out his teaching, which he found
backed up by a strange publication, Hermanszon Ten Kate's little
essay on *Le Beau Idéal,* which was published with the French
translation of Jonathan Richardson's treatise on painting.[419] It is a
dry little work, in which Ten Kate summarizes previous theorists,
summarizes and grossly simplifies. The "Je ne sais quoi" which
Pascal saw as the cause of all passion and of the great upheavals in
world history was reduced by Ten Kate to "harmonic" propriety.
Harmonic propriety differs in common and in ideal beauty, common
beauty being found in the imitation of particulars, as in portraits,
whereas ideal beauty is concerned with general properties, such as
proportion. Morris, of course, was concerned with the ideal, but in
architecture.[420] Ten Kate proposed three measures of the human
body, which are the essence of proportion, and which Morris found
to correspond to three orders, or as he preferred to call them,
modes. Within these Ten Kate found the seven essential harmonies
of the diapason to be the key to all proportional relationships; the
human body, on which they operate, being divided into nine modules.[421] Morris adapted this relatively simple recipe to architecture.
The basic unit of composition is the cube, which provides the module of the building.[422] The main horizontal subdivisions are a basement (rusticated where possible) and two upper stories, usually
united by a "giant" order. The order is chosen among the three
available according to the situation and purpose of the building.
Planning principles are equally dogmatic. The rooms must follow the
specified proportions (for which extensive tables are given, listing
preferred dimensions), as must windows, doors, chimney breasts.
And in the second part of the book, he applies the doctrine to a

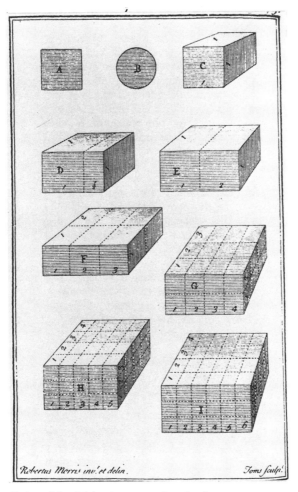

Robert Morris' basic proportional scheme.

number of specimen houses, each with its appropriate decoration. This is limited to orders, simple moldings and a few garlands in the engraving, though in the text Morris does mention rooms decorated "in the modern taste." Like most Burlingtonians, he was not averse to a little latter-day *rocaille*. Even Kent himself had provided *grottesche* (sanctioned after all by Raphael) and the occasional shell ornament.[423] The bulk of his work was heavily antique in contrast to his foreign contemporaries. Morris' admission that *rocaille* is licit reveals an important alteration in ways of understanding environment, rather than in taste. It seemed to Morris, who advocated the most austere antique treatment of the exterior, that interior decoration could be conceived according to a different principle. The stylistic link between interior and exterior might be as arbitrary or at any rate contrasting as between house and garden. There was no contradiction in such contrast. *Rocaille* could be given a home in the most correct of porticoed houses.[424] And perhaps he may have sus-

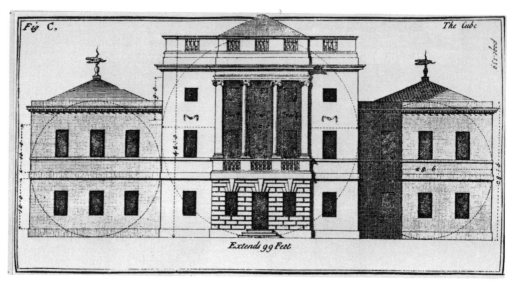

Application of the basic grid to a country house facade. After Robert Morris.

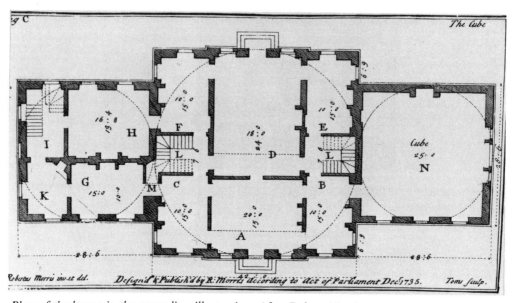

Plan of the house in the preceding illustration. After Robert Morris.

pected, with many contemporaries, with many orthodox Burlingtonians, that if not *rocaille*, then at any rate the "Chinese taste" was, in spite of its apparent frivolity, as venerable as the orders themselves. By such tokens, the unrelenting solemnity of the exterior even sanctioned the indulgence of the joiner's and plasterer's fancy in the interior.

The modern taste was in a later instance to be justified by Hogarth's line of beauty: a formula as elementary as Morris'. But Morris' own emphasis on a numerical justification for all dimensions

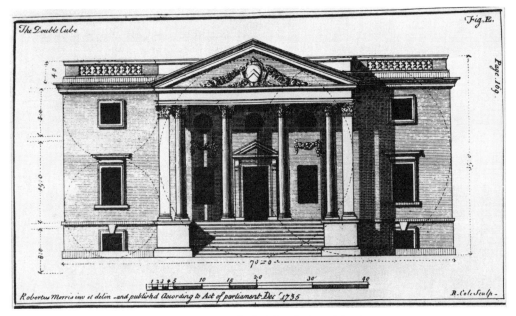

Double Cube house in the Corinthian "mode." After Robert Morris.

in the building, his rhapsodies, his dwelling on the beauties of un-
trammeled nature, even his justificatory quotation of Shaftesbury,
brings to mind that he was a junior contemporary of Hutcheson. It is
therefore hardly surprising that he offers the natural short-cut to a
rule of taste in terms of the modulation of the basic cube unit, done
in terms of preferred dimensions which can be simply read off his
tables to achieve arithmetical or harmonic proportion. The parallel
between what Morris calls Ideal Beauty, in whose achievement he
instructs all those who "make Architecture or the Polite Arts their
Study" is very like what Hutcheson describes as "Original and Absolute Beauty": in which the element of imitation is wholly absent.[425] Yet Hutcheson explicitly, Morris by implication, recognize
their difference from earlier Neoplatonic thinking.[426] The beauty,
even the harmony, is not something which is a property of the object: it is an idea in the mind, an idea which relates to the primary
qualities in the object, as of heat or cold. It is a construction which
Hutcheson owed to Locke more than to Shaftesbury.[427] In the particular extension of it which inspired Morris, he depends on the echo
of another and more revolutionary conception, that could be validated by Newton's parallel between the colors of the spectrum and
the notes of the octave.[428]

Morris is, of course, familiar with the old doctrines about unity
and variety. The desire for variety—so he tells his auditors—allows
for the enormous differences between Greek and Chinese architecture; yet both have an internal uniformity of harmonic relation and
this uniformity is valid for all nations and all periods. Only the Mid-

William Hogarth, The Analysis of Beauty, *plate 1.*

William Hogarth, The Procession of Gogmorgons.

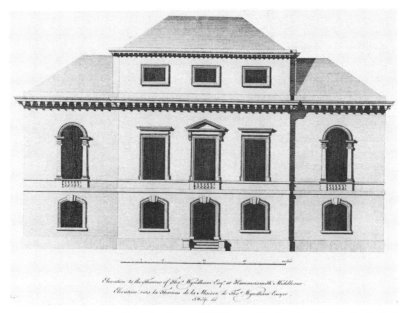

Brandenburgh House, Twickenham, Middlesex. By the time it was included in Vitruvius Britannicus *(from which this and the following plate are taken), Bubb Dodington had died and the house had passed into the property of Thomas Wyndham. The architect was Roger Morris.*

dle Ages are excepted from this instinctual drive to harmony. Gothic architecture is condemned and Westminster Abbey selected for special opprobrium.[429] Even irregularity may be allowed a degree of beauty, but only if it appears in products of nature. In human works irregularity must seem mere deformity.[430] Morris' taste is explicitly derived from Burlington, though it may owe more to Colen Campbell. To Wren as the national genius, he pays conventional homage. Vanbrugh and Hawksmoor, unmentioned, are the victims of his attack.[431] Only Gibbs, though outside the favored circle, is allowed favorable mention.[432]

In his most Campbellesque manner, Roger Morris refaced Brandenburgh house for Bubb Dodington—who had inherited the unfinished Eastbury by Vanbrugh, continued the building, and decorated it lavishly.[433] Dodington, in spite of his rather absurd appearance ("the swollen bullfrog with lascivious face"),[434] his taste in interiors as well as in clothes, his assiduous place-hunting and changing loyalties, had extensive diplomatic connections. He was friendly with Philip Stosch, of whom more below, and even closer with Cardinal Alessandro Albani, Winckelmann's employer. Albani supplied Dodington with statues for his gallery,[435] but before it was installed on the *piano nobile* of Dodington's Twickenham villa, Morris died; either for that reason, or for another, Dodington decided to employ Jean-Nicolas Servandoni, who had not begun working on St. Sulpice but was at the time the most celebrated European designer of festivals and fireworks and had come to London in 1749 to

J. N. Servandoni, the sculpture gallery of Brandenburgh House.

construct the fireworks celebrating the peace at Aix-la-Chapelle in Green Park.[436] He stayed for about a year, in the course of which Dodington's gallery became a showpiece of heavy but sober and exemplary classicism.[437]

Robert Morris' two strictly theoretical books were popular enough; he also published two pattern-books on his own, and others in collaboration where his style may have been diluted, but he remained faithful to cubic forms and their derivatives. The influence of these books was quite out of proportion to their apparent claims. Morris was certainly well known in the United States: Thomas Jefferson's use of Morris' *Select Architecture* has been well documented.[438] Still, while the pattern-books are almost an incidental aspect of Robert Morris' activity, they are the core of the Langleys' work. They addressed themselves, as I pointed out, to a humbler stratum of those concerned with building. The by-product of their work is not the gentleman-builders' or the aspiring architects' ambition, but rather the work of the innumerable craftsmen who produce pattern-books from that time onwards. Thomas Chippendale's *The Gentleman and Cabinet-Maker's Director* boasts an eclectic taste in its very title (household furniture in the Gothic, Chinese, and Modern taste) which might have seemed even a little excessive to Batty Langley.

In a sense the Langleys were the victors. They sponsored a generation of visually informed builders, avid consumers of pattern-books. In this they were vindicating the old idea of independent craftsmen, bound by guild rules but also protected by their fellows against the excessive claims of patrons. It is hardly surprising that Hawksmoor was their hero.

In spite of all differences, in spite of their perplexities before the awesome and ancient problem of the harmony of the senses, all architects and theorists had in common a unitary view of the past. There were different ways of building in different parts of the world:

Chinese, Persian, Egyptian, Greek. At different times different manners prevailed. Some were better, others less good, and some may even have been downright bad. But through all the vagaries, the persistence of certain constants could be recognized. The most important was an instinctive, and perhaps not adequately explicable preference for geometries which could be stated in terms of harmonic proportion. A belief, too, that epochs of the past had vast spans, within which differentiation was unimportant. Medieval English architecture was not divided as between Gothic and Norman until the late eighteenth century; the term *Romanesque* was not coined until about 1815 in France, when English Gothic architecture was also distinguished into its conventional three phases.[439]

In the continuity Antiquity had a privileged position: the Egyptians had handed their secrets to the Greeks; the Greeks devised the orders and passed the secret on to the Romans. The barbarians had wrecked the heritage, but it was rediscovered in the fifteenth century and given its definite form by Palladio. Inigo Jones was Palladio's true heir. That is how the argument looked from Britain in the middle of the eighteenth century. There were skeptics, but most people involved in building would have said that however broken, a direct line could be traced from the pyramids to the Banqueting House. Some even believed that the art of building of all times and of all places could be shown to display obedience, whether instinctive or explicit, to the same universal rule. The conception of world history on which this optimistic vision depended, however, was being put to the question in a context quite different from that of architecture and building.

1. At the outset of the period, in the first "modern" treatise on architecture, L. B. Alberti provides a systematic definition of the new profession in the preface to Book I of *De Re Aedificatoria* (1955), pp. ix ff.

2. For an account of the visit, see J. A. Gotch (1928), pp. 76 ff.; J. Summerson (1966), p. 36; and J. Harris, S. Orgel, and R. Strong (1973), pp. 55 f.

3. On Longhena, see C. Semenzato (1954, 1962), and on his relation to Scamozzi, pp. 3 ff.; and G. Cristinelli (1972), pp. 15 f.

4. The literature of the matter is still vexed and scanty. On the use of the term *architect*, see N. Pevsner (1940). To take an obvious instance, Filippo Brunelleschi belonged to the Arte della Seta as well as to that of the Orafi (having been trained as a goldsmith). The two guilds were in any case interdependent. But Brunelleschi refused to be "immatriculated" in that of the Maestri di Pietra e di Legname, presumably to save money, which led to a long demarcation dispute. See E. Stalley (1906), pp. 226 f., 342; F. Baldinucci (ed. D. Moreni, 1812), pp. 274 ff. More recently, and in a different context, F. D. Prager and G. Scaglia (1970), pp. 114 ff., and E. Battisti (1977), p. 335.

Most Florentine artists belonged either (like Brunelleschi) to the Arte della Seta or to that of the *Speziali*, although most building workers were also members of the masons' and woodworkers' guild. The overlapping of guilds and fraternities is one of the main sources of confusion in this matter; and the Florentine situation is very like that of other European towns, where to belong to two or even more guilds—even practicing more than one trade—was a common enough matter: see W. C. Hazlitt (1892), p. 32.

5. *"Chez Moi"*; see D. Seward (1974), p. 155.

6. The most prolific translator was Jean Martin, of whom little is known; a friend of Ronsard, he was the secretary of the Cardinal de Lennacourt. Having translated Ariosto, Sannazaro and Bembo, he published his version of *Hypnerotomachia Polyphili* with Kerver in Paris in 1546. His version of Vitruvius, illustrated by and after Jean Goujon, appeared with Barbé in 1547. It was the first full translation outside Italy; previously there had only been a Spanish digest translated from Diego del Sagredo's *Medidas del Romano* (1539), although there may have been an even earlier French edition; the Spanish original was of 1542. Alberti was published by Kerver (1553) again and prefaced by a long obituary elegy on Martin by Ronsard.

7. See E. Forsmann (1956), pp. 51 ff. While painters such as Hans Holbein, Jr., and Albrecht Altdorfer used classicizing detail and even issued engravings of pseudoclassical detail (H. Voss, 1910, pl. 45) in the 1520s, a "correct" rendering had to wait for the single-sheet prints of Beham and Hofer in the 1540s.

8. The bibliography and dating of the various editions of Serlio's separate books are discussed by J. Schlosser (1956), pp. 406 ff., 418; the Flemish edition appeared in 1539, German in 1542, French in 1545, all in Antwerp.

9. Although Jacques Androuet du Cerceau's *De Architectura* had appeared in Latin in 1559 (in French later), it was, like the other *Livres* (of which the third is a reissue of the second *Livre*, by a curious bibliographical convention) much more a pattern-book than a treatise. Philibert de l'Orme's *Premier Livre* appeared in Paris in 1568; the *Nouvelles Inventions* followed in 1576. The promised work on proportion does not exist; not even manuscript fragments seem to survive. However, du Cerceau's book had a more immediate impact on English taste than Philibert's.

10. On Torrigiani, see Vasari (1878–1906) IV, pp. 255 ff. On the episode of the breaking of Michelangelo's nose, Vasari (1878–1906), p. 259. An alternative version given by Torrigiani to Cellini is in *Memoirs of Benvenuto Cellini* (ed. Roscoe), I. pp. 36 ff. On his activities in England, Vasari (1878–1906), pp. 260 f.; and H. Walpole, *Anecdotes*, 1876, I, pp. 85 ff., 171 ff.

On the aftereffects of Torrigiani's visit on English architecture, see J. Summerson (1970), pp. 30 ff.

11. On Nonsuch and its place in English architecture, see J. Summerson (1970), pp. 33 ff., and E. Mercer (1962), pp. 39 f.

Horace Walpole (1876) in his *Anecdotes*, I, pp. 99 f., thought that "in his interview with Francis I in the Vale of the Cloth of Gold, he (Henry VIII) revived the pageantry of the Days of Amadis." *Amadis of Gaul* was perhaps the best known of chivalric romances. It was one of Don Quijote's favorite books. Of uncertain authorship, it first appeared in Spain in 1508 (there may have been an earlier printing in 1492). Don Quijote was a fictitious contemporary of Henry VIII.

See most recently, J. Dent (1962), pp. 36 ff.

12. The vast windows were a reinterpretation of the medieval painted glass walls, ironed out. The figured areas of colored and glittering glass, and shimmering changes of color which so charmed the Neoplatonic writers of early medieval France were now changed for the leaded knots, which cast their shadow over floors, transforming them into moving knotted patterns. The leading and even framing followed models provided in a number of printed pattern-books. W. Gidde (1615) claims that "it is not impertinent for Plasterers and Gardiners besides sundry other professions." Gidde's patterns are based on the knotting commonly used by gardeners and almost always based on a square. A vast variety of these patterns would sometimes be assembled in a single garden, as for instance at Saint Maur, where there are forty-two variations on two patterns. But almost every garden plan reproduced in du Cerceau provides examples of the treatment. The first English book to teach the method was Thomas Hill's (1577). The knot was a most important emblem of Neoplatonic thinking and was the subject of much speculation. "Amor nodus perpetuus et copula mundi" wrote M. Ficino in *De Amore*, III, iii, quoted in E. Wind (1958), p. 41. The knot was much loved by emblem writers; the lover's knot is too common an emblem to need particular reference. Leonardo's famous knot (*Accademia*) and the interlacing of branches on the vault of the Sala delle Asse in the Milan Castle is the most exalted instance of this figure (E. Müntz, 1898, I, pp. 205, 225 f.); L. Heydenreich, 1954, pp. 61, 195). The knotting patterns were used by cooks in setting out banqueting dishes as well as by gardeners, decorative painters, glaziers, and so on. But the most common was the dwarf box-hedge pattern of the Italian and French gardeners. A later handbook to this practice is *The Expert Gardener*, London, 1640. But in the middle of the sixteenth century, the knotted patterns were already seen by some as a sign of luxury, or at least sophistication (George Cavendish against Wolsey, quoted in F. Jenkins, 1961, p. 4).

On the medieval origin of the garden knots, see F. Crisp (1924), pp. 58 ff.

13. F. Bacon (1852), p. 160 (essay on building).

14. Sir Thomas Tresham is usually cited as an extreme instance of that inclination: so Summerson (1970), pp. 78 ff. See, however, E. Mercer, (1962), pp. 58 f. on Tresham's apparent lack of interest in architecture and his relation to his mason. The surviving buildings are sufficiently far from

the normal practice of the time to imply a rather more active interest on Tresham's part than Mercer would allow. The most recent and illuminating discussion of the whole problem in M. Girouard (1966).

15. F. Bacon (1852), p. 157.

16. Reprinted with a preface by L. Weaver (1912). Most recently on Shute, see M. Girouard (1966), pp. 28 ff.; and John Summerson (1970), pp. 46 f., 54 f. Northumberland had been dead for some time, and Shute dedicated the book to the queen.

17. Shute himself quotes Guillaume Philander's commentary on Vitruvius (a iii r°) and Serlio (a iii r° and b ii v°) as his sources. He was more "antique," indeed Italianate than some of his European contemporaries. The nearest in style and accuracy (although he adds a highly inventive Germanizing, almost Ditterlinian appendix) was Hans Blume whose *Quinque Columnarum Exacta Descriptio* continued to be immensely popular. There were German editions from 1554 to 1668; English ones from 1608 to 1678; Dutch from 1598 to 1642; French 1562 and 1623; even French/Dutch (Amsterdam 1634 and 1647). See Schlosser (1956), pp. 412, 421; E. Forssman (1956), pp. 75 ff. Blume is again based almost exclusively on Serlio.

18. Shute was said to have built himself a house in the City, which was described in 1550 as the "newe house of John Shute the painter"; always assuming it was the John Shute of the order-book, as is most likely (Shute, 1912, p. 7). But although his epitaph speaks of his "knowledge meet for those that buildings doe erect," no trace of actual buildings survive. IS as a monogram is attached to certain surviving architectural drawings. His influence has not been chronicled; even if the grotesque in the center pilasters of the courtyard at Kirby Hall (after 1570) seems to be based on Shute's title page, the flanking Ionic columns seem to go back to Vredeman or Hans Blume.

19. *The Elements of Geometrie . . . of Euclide of Megara . . . translated into the English Toung by H. Billingsley . . . with a very Fruitfull Preface made by M. J. Dee Specifying the Chief Mathematicall Sciences, What They are, and Whereunto Commodious,* London, John Daye, 1570. On the elaborate table of sciences, Dee dates the book February 2. The tenor of his thinking is underlined at the very beginning of the preface, in his aside (a i) "Herein I would gladly shake of the earthy name of Geometrie." The passage quoted is on p.d. iii v°. Billingsley was to become lord mayor of London (1597) and member of parliament for the city (1604); he died in 1606. The translation became enormously influential through its use at Gresham College. Billingsley was also a well-known antiquarian; see Christopher Hill (1972), pp. 18 ff., 173 ff.

20. On his tomb in Wollaton parish church; in M. S. Briggs (1927), fig. 36 (p. 245); cf. M. Girouard (1966), pp. 30 f., 175, and pl. 190.

The problematic use of the title *architect* by Shute and Smythson comes at a point when the office to which the word corresponds in its present accepted sense was covered by the term *surveyor* for the Elizabethans; and even for the Jacobeans, *architect* had implications of *virtuoso*, not unlike the eighteenth-century use of *dilettante*.

21. See most recently F. Yates (1969), pp. 92 ff. (with bibliography).

22. See E. K. Chambers (1951), II, pp. 390 ff. L. Magagnato (1956), pp. 51 ff. In fact, the Colosseum had four orders, the theater of Marcellus only two. The two buildings were often confused. The very influential edition of Ter-

ence's Comedies by Simon de Leure (1497) has a theater frontispiece inscribed COLISEUS SI/VE THEATRUM showing a theater interior with an auditorium surrounded by an order; antiquarians in the sixteenth century did not distinguish the kind of spectacle shown in an amphitheater from those in a theater.

The use of superimposed orders as a symbol of wholeness was not unusual at this time. The five orders were a symbol of the five ages of man. This emblem could only make an impact when the orders were truly "canonized." At any rate, the triple superimposition appears first in the cortile of the Palazzo Farnese. Various editions of Vitruvius show it on theater exteriors (Cesariano, Barbaro), while Alberti (bk. VIII, cap. 5) suggests a tower of superimposed orders. Philibert de l'Orme uses it at Anet. Solomon de Brosse applies it to the facade of the St. Gervais church in Paris (1616). Some years later, François Mansart uses it both for the Orléans wing at Blois and for the Château de Maisons. In England it appears surprisingly early; the three orders at Longleat, Wollaton, and Burleigh. In Oxford, the five orders are applied as a frontispiece to the Gothic tower of the Old Schools in 1613.

23. Euclid (1570), A i v° and r°. This passage has parallels to the description of natural magic by Cornelius Agrippa. He refers to Archmasterie as *Scientia Experimentalis*, and after a hermetic aside, goes on "but the chief science of the Archmaster (in the world as yet known) is another as it were OPTICAL science."

24. Of Dee's own practice of Thaumaturgicke, it is known that in the summer of 1547 Dee devised the first elaborate stage machine to be used in this country, for a performance of Aristophanes' *Pax*, which had both an aerostatic device and a moving statue. It was much admired but also led to accusations of sorcery, see F. Yates (1969), pp. 31 ff.

25. H. C. A. von Nettelsheim (1531). Dee had come across the book when a student in Leyden and quoted it often. Agrippa's interest in magic as a revelation of natural secrets, combined with experimental methods, necromancy with a form of psychology and a ready application to everyday matters (particularly political ones), and the indirect wielding of power had a great deal in common with Dee's general approach.

26. This essential Neoplatonic teaching passed by Boethius and Augustine through the Victorine monks and the School of Chartres and had a great revival in the fifteenth century and was much developed by Marsilio Ficino and Pico della Mirandola (the Earle of Mirandule, as Thomas More called him). It was taken into more suspect spheres by Cornelius Agrippa and Paracelsus as well as Johannes Trithemius, Abbot of Spannheim, Giordano Bruno, Jerome Cardan, and Giambattista della Porta.

On its medical implications, see most recently, A. G. Debus (1965), pp. 18 ff.

27. Dee had a constant political and professional interest in the navy and in navigation. At Louvain, he had befriended the great geographer and mapmaker Gerard Mercator, with whom he kept up some correspondence. See R. Deacon (1968), pp. 82 ff., 215 ff. On Dee and Frobisher's voyage to find the northwest passage to Cathay, see E. G. R. Taylor (1956), pp. 207 f. On his earlier involvements in naval matters, E. G. R. Taylor (1956), pp. 195 ff.

28. Dee here (Euclid, 1570, d iii r°) presumably refers to the two passages in the *Statesman* (ed. Marsilio Ficino, Lyons, 1590, p. 171) and perhaps *Philebus* (p. 90).

To judge by the catalog of his library, Dee was not very interested in the pattern-books I mentioned earlier; he had a considerable collection of architectural books, perhaps the best in Britain at the time: a number of editions of Vitruvius, including the most splendid Latin one up to date, Daniele Barbaro's 1567 edition, and Jean Martin's French translation, as well as Philander's, and some others. Although he does not seem to have had Palladio's *Quattro Libri* at the time his catalogue was compiled, he had other books of architectural controversy. And he inevitably possessed Luca Pacioli's *De Divina Proportione* with its splendid illustrations after Leonardo and three volumes of Francesco Giorgio's *De Harmonia Mundi Totius*. Of Dürer, he seems to have known the *Unterweysung der Messung* and the *Vier Bücher*. There were many editions of both books; Dee quotes the Latin title of the *Vier Bücher: De Symmetria Humani Corporis* (in Euclid, 1570, c iii r°). Dee's was probably the most important scientific and philosophical library in Britain, more important for recent publications than those of the universities. There is little doubt that Dee wanted it to become a center for a research and teaching institute, at any rate before its partial destruction by an angry crowd in 1583 (F. Yates, 1969, pp. 15 ff.). The catalog of his printed books has so far remained in manuscript (F. Yates, 1969, p. 1). But his manuscript catalog was printed in the nineteenth century and studied by M. R. James: "Lists of the Manuscripts formerly owned by Dr. John Dee." (London, the Bibliographical Society, supplement issue of the *Library*, 2nd ser. vol. I, 1920–1921.)

29. H. Walpole (1828), II, p. 331. J. Summerson (1966), p. 15.

30. J. Summerson (1966), pp. 16 ff. J. Harris, S. Orgel, and R. Strong (1973), pp. 17 f.

31. J. Summerson (1966), pp. 21 ff. J. Harris, S. Orgel, and R. Strong (1973), pp. 35 ff. S. Orgel and R. Strong (1973), pp. 89 ff.

32. S. Orgel and R. Strong (1973), pp. 90 ff. Like many others, it was produced for a Twelfth Night entertainment. The ladies were painted black (to their discomfort) so as to be whitened by the light of Albion.

33. The decorations were engraved and published in March 1603, and graven by William Kip. For Harrison, see D. N. B. and Esdale, s.v.; also H. Walpole (1822), II, pp. 75 ff. Because of the plague, the entry was in fact postponed until February 1604. Ben Jonson's *Entertainment* was published separately: *B. Jon. His Part of King James, his Royal & Magnificent Entertainment through his Honourable City of London Thursday the 15 of March 1603*, London, 1604. In B. Jonson, *Works*, VII, Oxford, 1941, see also J. A. Gotch (1914), pp. 154 f.

34. A "life" is provided by E. B. Chancellor (1909), pp. 50 ff.

35. The most common book on iconology, C. Ripa's *Iconologia* and many subsequent editions was not listed among Jones' books, but there are plenty of explicit derivations from it among his drawings. He also used C. Vecelli's *Habiti Antichi*. As for J.-J. Boissard, Jones almost certainly knew his *Habitus Variarum Orbis Gentium* and most probably *De Divinatione et Magicis Praestigiis*, both with engravings by Theodore de Bry of the great publishing-engraving family. Boissard was an antiquarian and a man of letters (b. 1528, d. 1602), who spent much time in Rome but was a convert to Protestantism. He was at Louvain at the same time as Dee. Onaphrius Panvinus, an Augustinian friar in the household of Alessandro Farnese, was a well-known scholar and antiquarian. His *De Ludis Circensibus et de Triumphis* was first published in Venice in 1602 and reprinted several times.

36. See chapter 1.

37. John Leland or Leyland died in 1552. He was insane for the last two years of his life. His *Journey* was not published until 1710 and the *Collectanea* in 1715. Many of his manuscripts were bought by Dee. See M. R. James (1920–1921), p. 13. The list is fragmentary.

38. Even later in the seventeenth century, the manuscripts were still hard to come by; William Dugdale writes to Dr Thomas Browne (17 November 1658): "let me know where in Leland you finde that expression concerning such buriall of the Saxons, as you mention in your former discourse" ("Miscellany Tracts," in *Works*, III, p. 85), and recalls his fruitless search in Leland's manuscripts in the Bodleian, from which he has had copies made. Browne answers: "As for *Lelandus*, his workes are so rare . . . that quotation of mine was at second hand. You may find it in Mr Inigo Jones' description of Stonehenge, p. 27." Browne further opines that it is taken from Leland's *De Assertione Arturii*.

39. The circumstantial evidence has been examined by F. Yates (1969), pp. 80 ff. Jones certainly seems to have consulted Fludd about his health in later life, whatever their earlier contacts. On the back flyleaf of his much annotated copy of Palladio (reproduced with unreliable transcription, Newcastle-on-Tyne, 1970), there is a series of medical comments and various prescriptions. In the margin (probably noted 1638): "Doc Flud discommendes glisters for weakening the guttes." William Harvey and Robert Fludd were the most distinguished Paracelsans in Britain. Fludd formed, before Harvey's final demonstration of it, a microcosmic theory of blood circulation and later defended Harvey against Gassendi's attack. Inevitably, he recommended chemical treatment in preference to the old Galenic remedy. See A. G. Debus (1965), pp. 101, 115 ff. Jones would also have found Paracelsan medicine sympathetic.

40. The only evidence is in the remaining drawings by Jones, particularly those in the collection of Worcester College, Oxford, which may well have been prepared to illustrate a treatise: see C. Rowe (1947); and R. Wittkower (1974), p. 60.

41. First published in London, 1624; reprinted in the *Reliquiae Wottonianae*, 1651 (four editions) and in John Evelyn's edition of Fréart de Chambray's *Parallèle*. It was printed in Latin in Jan de Laet's Elzevir edition of *Vitruvius*, Amsterdam, 1649.

42. Sir Dudley Carleton (later Lord Dorchester, and Wotton's successor in Venice) and Francis Bacon (already disgraced and Viscount St. Albans). The detailed negotiations are told by L. Pearsall-Smith (1907), I, pp. 199 ff.

43. Daniele da Massa, in the service of the Republic of Lucca (on 9 June 1601); L. Pearsall-Smith (1907), I, p. 15.

44. John Chamberlain, writing to Sir Dudley Carleton in Venice. The letters were published in *The Court and Times of Charles I*, London, 1848 (letter 72); cf. L. Pearsall-Smith (1907), I, pp. 194 ff. Both Chamberlain and Carleton disliked Wotton and referred to him as *Fabritio* (title-tattle, a gossip). So L. Pearsall-Smith (1907), I, p. 118. Chamberlain later made amends for this slur: "I have not had leisure to read it (*The Elements*) but hear it highly commended."

45. Although he mentions Henry Fanshaw's gardens at Ware, Herts., in which he seems to have lent a hand. L. Pearsall-Smith (1907) I, p. 131.

46. Wotton certainly knew the passage in Plato's *Politicus* (Ficino, 1590, p. 171), which is used much in the same sense by Scamozzi (1615), I, p. 11.

47. Although there is little evidence about Jones and Wotton meeting, they

presumably did so either in the entourage of Essex, in Venice, or later at Whitehall. At any rate, in the annotated Palladio, Jones in his late handwriting makes four references to drawings by (or attributed to) Palladio in Wotton's collection.

48. *Elements* (in J. Evelyn, 1723), p. ii. This almost Paracelsan view of the microcosm is probably based partly on Scamozzi and also directly on Ficino's commentary on Plato (In *Timaeum*, cap cli, *Iterum de Homine Quantum ad Animam Spectat et Corpus*; 1590, p. 827 A) and Wotton quotes in this connection the Paracelsan physician, Johannes Huermius.

An analogous idea is expressed by Jones in a sketchbook note dated Rome, 19 January 1615: "As in dessigne, first on studies the parts of the boddy of man. . . . So in Architecture on must studdy the Parts"; in R. Wittkower (1974).

49. This notion is common to much Neoplatonic thinking. Wotton, however, presumably knew Ficino's commentary on Plato, particularly the Symposium: see *Oratio Quinta*, Cap. iv, *Pulchritudo est Aliquid Corpoream.*

50. See chapter 1.

51. J. B. Villalpanda and J. Prado (1596–1608), I, pp. 465 ff.; II, pp. 461 ff., in which the relation between architect and the *apparajedor* or *officinator* is discussed, as well as their relation to the other workmen on a site; a distinction is drawn between masons and mere untrained manuals. The *officinator* of the temple is taken to be the person whom Hiram, the king of Tyre, called "Hiram my Father" (Hiram Abi in Hebrew, which led to the corruption Hiram Abiff), who was to become such an important figure in masonic lore, particularly in the French *Compagnonnage* legends. There is a rhapsodic passage on the temple as a microcosm and its relation to the human body in J. Prado and J. B. Villalpanda, II, pp. 465 f.

52. Nathaniel Brent writes to Dudley Carleton (about *Pleasure Reconciled to Virtue*; S. Orgel and R. Strong (1973), I, p. 277): "Divers thinke fit he (Ben Jonson) should retourne to his ould trade of bricke laying againe." In 1598 Philip Henslow gave an account of Jonson's fatal bout with Gabriel Spencer to Edward Alleyn: "I have lost one of my company that hurteth me greatlie . . . for he is slayn . . . by the hands of Benjamin Jonson, bricklayer." Jonson was saved from execution by benefit of clergy. J. A. Gotch (1928), p. 97.

53. J. Summerson (1966), pp. 25 ff.; J. Harris, S. Orgel and R. Strong (1973), pp. 30 f. There appears to be no evidence for any building activity before 1608.

54. "One Mr Jones, a great traveller" is what the anonymous author in an appendix to Leland's *Collectanea* still calls him; cf. Walpole (1876), p. 331, n. 2; and R. Wittkower, 1974, pp. 67 ff.

55. J. A. Gotch (1928), pp. 115 ff., 192 ff. J. Summerson (1966), pp 39 ff. J. Harris, S. Orgel, and R. Strong (1973), pp. 112 ff.

56. He reports on specimens of glass submitted by Robert Mansfield (with Thomas Baldwyn, comptroller of works) in 1620; J. A. Gotch (1928), p. 125; named commissioner for building, 30 May 1625, pp. 138 ff.; arbitrates dispute between masons and plasterers about repairing stonework, pp. 189 f.; corrects abuses of brickmakers in 1638, pp. 197 f.; consulted on price of lime and sand, and building wages generally, 1639, p. 201.

57. In 1829. J. Summerson (1966), pp. 55 f.; P. Palme (1957), pp. 46 ff. (on the building), pp. 288 (on the facade), pp. 91 f. (on the Soane refacing).

58. J. Harris, S. Orgel and R. Strong (1973), I, p. 365. The performance was in fact canceled.

In *The Fortunate Isles*, next year's Twelfth Night masque, there may well be the first recorded uses of the term *Rosy Cross*, "Rosicrucian" in English. "What mean the brethren of the Rosy Cross so to desert their votary!" cries Merryfool (lines 26–27). See S. Orgel and R. Strong (1973), I, pp. 371 ff. The two essential Rosicrucian manifestos were *Allgemeine und General Reformation der Gantzen Weiten Welt, Beneben der Fama Fraternitatis*, Cassel, 1614; and *Secretioris Philosophiae Consideratio . . . Una cum Confessione Fraternitatis*, R.C., Cassel, 1615. They were first published in English much later, translated by Thomas Vaughan (brother of Henry) in 1652. For bibliography, see F. Yates (1972), pp. 235 ff.

The other fundamental Rosicrucian work, Andreae's *Chymische Hochzeit* appeared in 1616. It may well be that long before their printing, they circulated in English (or for that matter Scots) translation in manuscript; in any case, the originals were certainly imported. In view of Jonson's constant sniping at Jones, it would not be surprising if these were not, once more, jibing references to him: it is difficult to see to whom else the passage in "Neptune's Triumph" could refer at court. Jones' other links with Dee and Fludd are again circumstantially reinforced. Dee's relation to European Rosicrucianism is discussed by F. Yates (1972), pp. 30 ff. For a different and—to my mind—less convincing view, see K. R. H. Frick, (1975), II, pt. 1, pp. 272 ff.

59. *Love's Triumph through Callipolis*. J. A. Gotch (1928), pp. 149 ff. The implications of the quarrel were discussed by D. J. Gordon (1949) in "Poet and Architect: the Intellectual Setting of the Quarrel between Ben Jonson and Inigo Jones"; and again by F. Yates (1969), pp. 86 ff. For the text, see *Works*, 1941, VII, pp. 807 ff.

60. See *Works*, 1925–1952, I, p. 98; II, pp. 146, 356.

61. The original version of *The Tale of a Tub* was only licensed by the Lord Chamberlain on condition that an important character, called Vitruvius Hoop be removed from the text, "exception being taken against it by Inigo Jones, Surveyor of the King's Workes, as a personal injury to him." It is difficult to imagine what insults were removed, reading In-and-In Medlay's self-presentation (Act IV, sc. ii; and Act V, sc. iii). This is not only a very accurate caricature of Jones' general attitudes but adds the pinning details: his father was a clothworker, and it is notable that practically all the known copies of the classics from his possession are in Italian translation (J. A. Gotch, 1928, p. 7, 247 ff.). Even the Vitruvius was in Barbaro's translation of 1567; an alternative Latin printing of the same edition of the same year was also available.

62. In *Love's Welcome to Bolsover*, in *Works*, 1941, VII, pp. 807 ff.

63. Bolsover has a particular place in English architecture as one of the earlier instances of a self-consciously "medieval" castle; see M. Girouard (1966), pp. 159 ff.; and S. Lang (1966) in "The Principles of the Gothic Revival in England."

Charles I found the continuous quarrel very tedious and Jonson's venom excessive, and he intimated that he must modify his tone. But even in the final text, the spectators certainly recognized Coronell Vitruvius, who described himself as "surveyour."

64. Jones left his own account of the quarrel in a long poem, "To his false friend, Mr Ben Jonson," which survives in Thomas Crosse's Ms. Verse Collection and is reprinted in J. A. Gotch (1928), pp. 254 f.

65. Jones was also very concerned with what would now be called planning regulations. J. Summerson, "The Surveyorship of Inigo Jones," in Colvin (1975), III, pp. 129 ff.

66. C. H. Josten, (1966), II, p. 395.

67. A manuscript copy of the Old Charges dated to that day and signed Eduard Sankey (whose father, Richard, was a member of the Warrington lodge) is now in the British Museum (Ms. Sloane 3848) and has been published by W. G. Speth (1891), III, sect. iii.

68. Notably its warden, Richard Penket.

69. See David Murray Lyon (1873), pp. 96 ff. On Robert Moray, see A. Robertson (1922); and D. C. Martin, "Sir Robert Moray," in Hartley (1960), pp. 239 ff. Very little is known further about Moray's activities as a mason, beyond his writing a history of masonry for the Royal Society, of which more later.

70. On Bolton's tripartite Senate of Honour, see *D. N. B.*, s.v. Bolton. Bolton was a close friend of Jones' as is evident from the inscribed dedication in a copy of *De Rebus Praeclare Gestis a Sixto V Pont. Max.*, Rome, 1588. Dudley Digges was a pupil of Leonard Digges, one of Dee's associates, and author of the *Prognostication* (1553 onwards, many editions), which became one of the most popular navigational manuals.

71. On Bolton's and Prince Henry's academies, see C. Hill (1972), pp. 215 ff., esp. p. 216, n. 8. Bolton's strong antiquarian bias is lacking in the scheme which Buckingham advocated and which may have originated with Prince Henry himself.

Another attempt to set up a Royal Academy, proposed by Thomas Allen of Oxford, was rejected by Charles I on his accession as being "too good for the times." R. T. Petersson (1956), p. 37, and n. 22.

72. *Instauratio Magna* was the title of a collection of Bacon's philosophic writings which first appeared in London in 1620. The most celebrated part of it, *New Atlantis*, appeared separately as an appendix to *Sylva Sylvarum* in 1627.

73. Allusions to such ideas may be found throughout Bacon's writings. Explicitly formulated in English: *Filium Labyrinthii* S 7, *Works*, 1859–1870, III, pp. 499 f., 592 f. See Christopher Hill (1972), pp. 87 ff. Hill draws attention to Bacon's aloof style, on which his contemporaries also commented. William Harvey (of blood circulation) "had been physician to the Lord Chancellor Bacon, whom he esteemed much for his wit and style, but would not allow him to be a great philosopher. He writes philosophy like a Lord Chancelor, said he to me, speaking in derision"; J. Aubrey (1949), pp. 229 f. Bacon's style and writings raised the status of "natural philosophy" from the sphere of magi/alchemists and Gresham-mechanics to that of academic discourse, however.

The notion of a Great Instauration brought about by a perfecting of the knowledge of nature, the innocent science, different from the moral inquiry associated with the Fall has its roots in certain cabalistic speculations. See G. G. Scholem, (1965), pp. 68 ff. And it is summed up eloquently at the end of Bacon's *Novum Organum*: "For Man by the fall lost at once his state of Innocence, and his Empire over Creation, both of which can be partially recovered even in this life, the first by Religion and Faith, the second by Arts and Sciences. For Creation did not become entirely and utterly rebellious by the Curse, but in Consequence of the Divine Decree, In the sweat of

the brow shalt thou eat bread, she is compelled by our labours (not as-
suredly by our disputes or magical ceremonies) at length, to afford mankind
in some degree his bread, that is to say, to supply man's daily wants" (p. 322
f.), *Works*, 1901, IV, p. 248 f.

This debt to cabalism is not contradicted by Bacon's explicit opposition to
all occultism, and to the speculative-magical aspect of Neoplatonic thinking
in his day. See P. Rossi (1974), pp. 24, 94 ff. He was aware of most of the
latter cabalistic speculation and had certainly read Joannes Reuchlin; and
his drawing on it would have been consonant with his method.

74. Prolusion VII, *Prose Works*, ed. Wolfe, I, p. 296; and C. Webster
(1975), pp. 1, 144. Webster's book has the most extensive recent commentary on the implications of Milton's rhapsody.

75. F. Bacon (1857–1870), III, pp. 119 ff.

76. See note 71, this chapter. On the enormous importance of private
academies and scientific societies in promoting experimental science, see C.
Webster (1975), pp. 144 ff.; on their organization, see L. Thorndike (1958),
VII, pp. 222 f., 232 ff.; and VIII, pp. 232 ff.

Bacon (1857–1870) tells how the college, founded by King Solomon, came
to be called Solomon's, III, p. 144. This is an indication about his use of
names as near-hieroglyphs here, and in his other works. See H. B. White
(1968), pp. 144 f.; 152 ff., and C. Webster (1975), pp. 328 f. The alternative
title of the institution, the College of Six Days, indicates its encyclopedic
scope in considering creation, but, of course, puts speculation about the
creator of the final cause outside its concerns. Bacon's account of its
equipment shows it to have had scientific apparatus and machinery beyond
the means of any monarch of that—or indeed of a much later—time. The
account of its working, and of the visitation of one of its "fathers" is given
(Bacon 1857–1870, III, pp. 157 ff.) in terms which evoke the dress and
manner of an enlightened Elizabethan bishop. A somewhat different interpretation, with a rather complex account of the color symbolism involved, is
given by H. B. White (1968), pp. 196 ff.

77. T. B. Macaulay (1883), pp. 389 ff.

78. F. Bacon (1857–1870), III, p. 141. Many references to such matters
will be found not only in Bacon's works but in those of his contemporaries.
These views were compounded of the familiar admiration for the unsur-
passed achievements of the ancients, the classical myth of the Golden Age,
and notions about the earthly paradise and an idealized picture of kingly and
prophetic Jerusalem. See on this, C. Webster (1975), pp. 15 ff. (esp. p. 16, n.
32). The motto of this thinking was a verse in the Book of Daniel (xii, 4):
"But Thou, O Daniel, shut up the words and seal the book even to the time
of the end." It was not limited to Puritans, as Webster seems to imply.
Cornelius a Lapide, in what was the most popular Catholic Bible commentary of the time, in a gloss on this verse invokes the Egyptian sphinx, placed
or painted outside temples to signify that dogmas were, like oracles and
mysteries, hidden and abstruse things (1621, p. 149). Bacon had a parallel
interest in the sphinx as an image of hidden wisdom, and Oedipus as the
type of the investigator, an image he strangely shared with the alchemist
Michael Maier (C. W. Lemmi, 1933, pp. 141 ff.; and P. Rossi, 1974, pp. 167
ff.). But Bacon also played much with the notion that the ancients, being our
predecessors, belong to the youth of creation, while we are its old age. Yet
in many ways, we are the inferiors of the ancients, and the whole notion of
the New Atlantis rests on the supposition of an ancient perfection, so H. B.

White (1968), pp. 104 ff. Something will have to be said later (below, this chapter) about Newton's passionate involvement with the interpretation of the Book of Daniel.

79. It is difficult to know how ancient the association of King Solomon's Temple with masonic lore may be. Certainly the existence of initiatory societies of craftsmen is very ancient. In Rome, they were said to have been set up, like so many religious institutions, by King Numa (Plutarch, Vita Numae 17). Though the tradition is mythical, it is interesting that Plutarch already suggests that Numa's purpose, apart from the primary one of a religious organization of trades, was the second one of pacifying the warring tribes of the city by organizing a division which would cut across tribal boundaries. The feast of the *collegia*, or at least some of them, was Minerva's day, March 19 (which also had other religious festivals of no relevance here). It is called *Artificiorum dies* in the Praenestine Calendar (W. Ward-Fowler, 1933 pp. 57 f.) and commented on at length, with much about certain collegia in Ovid III Fasti, 809 ff. "Mille Dea est operum," Ovid says, and identifies himself with the craftsmen: "certe Dea carminis illa est"; see G. Dumézil (1969), p. 592. These *collegia* continued well into the Christian era. On their fate in Rome itself, see F. Gregorovius (1926), pp. 524 f.; and their continuity, J. B. Ward-Perkins (1971). On Germanic guilds, see T. Arundell (1869), pp. 14 ff.

On Byzantine and Italian corporations, see G. Pepe (1963), pp. 249 ff; on the laws of King Rotari of the Lombards (P. Villari, 1901, pp. 309 ff; G. Pepe, 1963, pp. 250 f.) mention Magistri Comacini in 643; a century later a Magister Comacinus named Rupertu worked in Tuscanella; the curious conflation of Dark-Age Latin and the geographical factor: the presence of excellent building stone, and therefore the masons who worked it in North Italy, has been a factor in the creation of a legend about the origin of masonry in Como; as, for instance, Leader Scott (1899), passim, but see also G. T. Rivoira (1908), pp. 128 ff. On the Oriental influence on such guilds, see J. Strzygowski (1923), pp. 82 ff. E. Hutton (1950) did not find it necessary to mention the legend in relation to the Cosmati.

On the organization of work in the general context of early medieval society, and the relative part of barbarian innovation and Roman heritage, see the classic statement in M. Bloch (1949), II, pp. 244 ff. On the guilds in the context of the early northern towns, see E. Ennen (1975), pp. 46 f. M. Mauss (1969), II, pp. 642 ff., comments sharply on the difference between ancient *collegia* and Roman guilds. Nevertheless, as there were attempts to preserve continuity and craft and style, so there were certain carry-overs, inevitably parallel in craft organization. See R. Krautheimer (1969), pp. 181 ff., 203 ff. The cosmopolitan nature of the trade and craft and guilds throughout the Western world is underlined by H. Pirenne (1956), pp. 84 f., 133 f. Moreover, from early times, there is evidence that the work of artists, particularly those involved in church building, was regarded as a sacral activity, see J. von Schlosser (1896), p. 70 (life of Chrodegang), p. 309 (Libri Carolini III, 22): while Solomon was regarded as the exemplary builder and prince. Justinian's exclamation ("Solomon, I have outdone you!") on entering the finished St. Sophia is almost the type; as for the west, the anonymous Monk of St. Gall writes in his life of Charlemagne, of the "edificiis, quae . . . imperator Karolus apud Aquisgrani iuxta sapientissimi Salemonis exemplum Deo vel sibi vel (aliis) . . . mirifica construxit." (I, 27).

When the scriptural story of the building of the temple and its prototypes, the Ark and the Tabernacle, were made part of guild lore, it is impossible to say. All the evidence seems to indicate that they were already highly organized bodies all over Europe by the beginning of the twelfth century. P. du Colombier (1953), pp. 33 ff., and more summary, C. Enlart (1902), I, pp. 62 ff. By the time the first written documents appear, Solomon is cited as one of the prime masters of the art. See D. Knoop, G. P. Jones, and D. Hamer (1938), pp. 170 ff., also on the masonic belief of their dependence on a French organization.

80. Presumably we would have known about them had Ashmole's or Moray's histories of masonry survived (Josten, 1956, I, p. 35, n. 1; A. Robertson, 1922, pp. 162 ff.).

On Moray's choice—apparently related to his cabalistic interests—of the pentacle as his mason's mark, see his letter to Lord Kincardine in H. Hartley (1960), p. 245. The pentacle as a mason's mark is not altogether uncommon. In Scotland, it is found at Killwinning Abbey; see D. M. Lyon's (1873) facsimile, p. 66.

While Ashmole's was to have been an independent book, Moray's was to have been one of the trade histories, analogous to Evelyn's *Chalcographia* commissioned by the Royal Society.

81. W. Stukeley (1882), p. 53. He goes on "when with difficulty a number sufficient was to be found in all London." This presumably refers to his admission as a master; the problem would not have arisen with the lower degrees (D. Knoop and G. P. Jones, 1947, pp. 190 ff.). The lodge was at the Salutation Tavern, Tavistock Street on 6 January 1721. Stukeley was at this time friendly with several early luminaries of masonry: its theologian, Désaguliers, Anderson of the *Constitutions*, and the Duke of Montagu, who was Stukeley's patron as well as his friend. Although a beneficed, active clergyman, Stukeley had a considerable reputation as an anatomist and antiquarian: elected F.R.S. in 1717–1718, he was a cofounder of the renewed Society of Antiquaries. He had also constituted other societies and clubs: See S. Piggott (1950), pp. 40f., 142 ff. His consuming passion for the Druids led him to explore Stonehenge, and his survey became the most reliable one for many years (1740). Martin Folkes, of whom more later, had a mahogany model of Stonehenge made according to these measurements: W. Stukeley (1882), pp. 321, 470; on Stukeley and Newton, see below.

82. See below, this chapter.

83. On academies in general, see chapter 1. On the academies as centers of spiritual life, see F. Yates (1947), pp. 17 f., 199 ff.; and (1972), pp. 72 ff., 216; more generally L. Thorndike (1923–1958), VIII, pp. 232 ff., and A. Wolf (1962), pp. 54 ff.

84. The Family of Love was founded about 1540 in Emden by Hendrik Niclaes, whose initials were also deciphered Homo Novus. For a bibliography of recent material, see J. A. van Dorsten (1970), p. 27, n. 1.

85. He was an acquaintance of Arnold Brinckmann, a member of the Family of Love, one of the Flemings established in London as printer-booksellers. His well-known links with the French logician-theologian Peter Ramus (de la Ramée) and the Italian logician-inventor Jacopo Acconcio suggest, together with his Flemish contacts, that Dee would have come into contact with the Family of Love.

86. On Laud and Grotius, see H. R. Trevor-Roper (1963), pp. 269 f.

87. However mistaken, the offers were made more than once. H. R. Trevor-Roper (1963), p. 307.

88. *De Veritate, Prout Distinguitur a Revelatione a Verisimili, a Possibili, a Falso*, Paris, 1624 (London, 1645). The French translation appeared in Paris

in 1639, J. Aubrey (1949), p. 39. Herbert recounts the story of his sending a copy to Grotius as well as the "vision" he was granted to give divine approval for his publication (1809), p. 277. Urban VIII's interested approval was communicated by Elias Deodati of Geneva to Pierre Gassendi; the book was nevertheless placed on the index in 1634. At the time he wrote it, Herbert was himself British ambassador in Paris (1619–1621; 1622–1624). On the reception of *De Veritate* and Herbert's theological position, see D. P. Walker (1972), pp. 164 ff.

89. Descartes had received a copy of the Latin *De Veritate* from Samuel Hartlib in 1638 (Walker, 1972, p. 168); Marin Mersenne sent him two copies of his French translation on its appearance, which Descartes acknowledges on 27 August 1639; a reasoned criticism followed on 16 October 1639 (*Oeuvres*, 1953, pp. 1055, 1058 ff.). Herbert, who was a friend of both Hobbes and Bacon (and brother of the poet George) attempted, but did not finish or publish, an English translation of the *Discours de la Méthode* (Walker, 1972, p. 170).

90. Commenius corresponded with Herbert. See M. Rossi (1947), II, p. 528.

91. It was first published by Horace Walpole privately in 1764 and publicly in 1770 and 1809. Critical editions: Sydney Lee (1886), and J. Shuttleworth (1977).

92. "Shortly after (King James' coming to London) I was made Knight of the Bath, with the usual ceremonies belonging to that ancient Order." Herbert goes on to tell of Lord Shrewsbury putting on his spur, his wearing the habit of a religious order, and his ceremonial bath, the probationary knot, and other mysteries in (1809), pp. 84 ff. The frustrated duel about an eleven-year-old girl's ribbon, pp. 93 ff., is told with other challenges "that it may appear how strictly I held myself to my oath of knighthood" (p. 99).

93. The duel with Blagny at the siege of Julier (1809), pp. 120 ff. The challenge at the siege of Rees in Cleves, pp. 160 ff.

94. The word *mystery* has a double etymology: from the Latin *minister*, *ministerium*, through the French *mestier*, meaning a "trade or craft," see R. Latouche (1970), p. 241; and the Greek-derived Latin *mysterium*, to do with hidden knowledge, with initiation and so on.

There is no doubt that in the Middle Ages, the two words were confused: in France and Germany, with the help of miracle-plays, usually presented by guilds, in English as simple homonymy. But whatever the distinction in the Middle Ages, seventeenth-century writers played on the confusion. "All the Arts and Trades in the world are *Mysteries*," writes John Sparrow, the lawyer-translator of Jakob Boehme's *Of Christ's Testament*, 1652 (B2v/3r; in C. Webster, 1975, p. 284). Some years later (1681), the gardener John Woolridge called his book: *Systema Agriculturae, being The Mystery of Husbandry discovered and laid open*.

95. There were many guilds of knights: one of the oldest recorded in England is the Cniighten Gild of London, which received land from King Edgar (958–968). A guild of rectors existed to "protect" the beneficed clergy from their poorer brethren and so on. Most of them practiced a system of grading and admitted by some form of initiation, as is still done not only by respectable associations such as the Freemasons, but also in criminal societies, such as the Mafia or the Camorra.

96. E. Ashmole (1672), p. 136. Ashmole was appointed Windsor herald by Charles II on the Restoration (C. H. Josten, 1966, I, pp. 130 f.; II, pp. 780

ff.) when he began to collect material for the history of the Order of the Garter.

97. E. Ashmole (1672), p. 128.

98. The standard work setting out masonic traditions which was used in the eighteenth century was *The New Book of Constitutions* by J. Anderson (1723, heavily revised 1738), pp. 70, 72. This has not been taken seriously by later more critical historians of masonry; see R. F. Gould (1951), pp. 151, 169.

99. On Ashmole's lost "history," see H. C. Josten (1966), IV, p. 1840, n. i. On More's, A. Robertson (1922).

100. In Scotland where the most explicit masonic records seem to survive, for St. Mary's Chapel, Edinburgh (No. 1), the family St. Clair of Roslin are named as hereditary protectors of the Edinburgh masons; but this may be no more than the affiliation of a noble protector to guilds all over Europe. The first "Nonoperative" masons, on the other hand, seem to have been accepted in St. Mary's in 1634 (D. M. Lyon, 1873, pp. 57 ff.; 79 ff.). On the various terms used to signify "nonoperative" masons, see D. M. Lyon (1873), p. 82. On the presence of "accepted" masons in the Worshipful Company of Masons in the City of London, see E. Conder (1894), pp. 140 f., 170 ff. But Conder's account seems to be based on rather shaky evidence. It was, however, a common practice of all trade guilds to admit nonpractitioners to their freedom. The evidence for London is set out by W. Carew Hazlitt (1892), pp. 76 f. However, none seem to have had the implications of the masons' guild at any point.

It does not seem certain whether the distinction between the two kinds of masons was made in the terms *speculative* and *operative*. It is borrowed, apparently, from Francis Bacon who spoke of the speculative worker "searching into the bowels of nature," while the other was "shaping nature as on an anvil." F. Bacon, IV, p. 343, in L. Jardine (1974), p. 99, but see also pp. 116, 133.

101. And then to Norwich (1635) and Ely (1638). He spent most of the Commonwealth in the Tower of London. On the young Christopher Wren's interceding with Cromwell for the release of his uncle and the old man's refusal of the pardon, see C. Wren, *Parentalia*, 1750. The references are to the "heirloom" interleaved copy in the possession of the Royal Institute of British Architects, reprinted 1965; pp. 33 f.

102. E. Ashmole (1672), pp. 201, 250 f.

103. Unfortunately, the libraries of Sir Christopher and his son, also a Christopher, were sold together. Presumably all the books published after 1723 and much of the numismatical material belonged to the son. The published sale catalog (ed. D. J. Watkin, 1972) indicates the range of the interest: Giovanni Battista Porta, Athanasius Kircher, Herwarth, Jean-Louis Vives, Jerome Cardan. Cardan's book may have been a link between Wren's interest in mathematical proportion and his hermetism. An infuriatingly obscure item is "Cabala & 3 eng."

104. On the general hermetic atmosphere of the Royal Society in its early years, not much is written. Even its more skeptical members such as John Evelyn (1955), who regarded his colleague Kenelm Digby as "an arrant mountebank"—diary of 7 September 1650—and "a teller of strange things"—diary of 18 June 1670—took astrological calculation as a matter of course. His friendship with Ashmole and Moray was close, although he did

not think highly of Ashmole's astrology ("to which study he is addicted, though I believe not learned, but very industrious"—diary, 23 July 1678). There is little about all this in the history of itself which the Royal Society commissioned from Bishop Sprat. See Thomas Sprat (1722).

105. The best account is P. Rossi (1960), pp. 201 ff. The Royal Society's patronage produced J. Wilkins' *Essay* (1668).

106. For Dee's interest in the matter, see R. Deacon (1968), pp. 55 ff. The texts which all subsequent writers on the subject used were the *Steganographia and Polygraphia* of Johann von Trittenheim (Tritheimius), both composed in the first decade of the sixteenth century. *Steganographia* remained in manuscript until 1606, but *Polygraphia* was printed in Bâle in 1518 and republished several times; there was a French translation by Gabriel de Collange, published by Krever in 1561. It had two reprints. See Klaus Arnold (1971), pp. 190 ff., 246 f. On Tritheimius' connection of cryptography to demonic magic, see D. P. Walker (1958), pp. 86 ff.

107. See Wren (1750), p. 213; quoting Anthony à Wood (1730), p. 559. Elsewhere Anthony à Wood gives further details, including comments on John Locke's frivolous behavior at Stahl's seminars.

108. For an extreme view of the identity between early freemasonry and the Rosicrucians, see F. de P. Castells (1931), pp. 24 ff. And more recently and more allusively, G. Serbanesco (1964), I, pp. 245 ff. See, however, R. F. Gould (1951). A much more sober, if not altogether conclusive view, is taken by Paul Arnold (1955), pp. 229 ff.; (1970), pp. 225 ff.

109. There is no general account of the legend of Solomon in hermetic lore, but the sources of it in Scripture, the Koran, and apocryphal writings are obvious; also the accounts of Solomon and the temple in Josephus Flavius and Philon of Alexandria. Solomon inevitably plays an important part in the Cabalah, and also in masonry (Matthew Coke Ms. of the Old Charges, ll. 568 ff.). Just before that, the Charge says "the Kyngis sone of Tyr was his master mason" (ll. 561–563). This brief reference is enlarged in later charges and occupies six pages in James Anderson (1738), pp. 11 ff.

The corruption Hiram Abbif, used by Anderson in the *Constitutions* (for the Hiram Abi or Avi of the Hebrew text), appears in the printed version of the Old Charges: *The Beginning and the first Foundation of the Most Worthy Craft of Masonry, By a Deceas'd Brother* . . . London, 1739. It is based on the passage 2 Chron ii, 13, and its corruption in the earlier English printings of the Bible. The sudden death of Huram relates to the tradition of the murder of Hiram (perhaps with Solomon's complicity) among the French *Compagnons,* see E. Coornaert (1966), pp. 341 ff., and R. F. Gould (1951), I, p. 125, who discounts the story as a more recent legend on the suggestion of Armand Perdiguer. But this personage is extremely important in craft lore and is identified with various figures by a process of occult transposition: Aymon, Naymon the Greek, Maître Jacques, and so on. The relation Solomon-Hiram is often taken as a type of employer-craftsman or even architect-mason. As Adoniram, he also appears in variants of the legend of Solomon and the Queen of Sheba. Gérard de Nerval (1862), claims to report an Islamic retelling of it (II, pp. 226 ff., 356 ff.); cf. André Lebois (1972), in which Adoniram, another avatar of Hiram Abbif, is the true lover of the Queen of Sheba and murdered by three journeymen with their instruments (hammer, square, and compasses) at Solomon's instigation. The story was the subject of an opera by Gounod, whose libretto Lebois attributes to Nerval.

110. The Dominical words about the building and destruction of the temple in three days are taken as a guarantee of this archetype.

111. See n. 232, this chapter.

112. A. Horne (1972), passim.

113. On secret societies generally, see H. Schurtz (1902) and H. Webster (1908). The most recent account of the seventeenth century phenomena is in J. M. Roberts (1972). Particular problems are discussed by H. Jeanmaire (1949), pp. 147 ff.; some information in M. Mauss (1967), pp. 148 ff., and A. van Gennep (1960), pp. 82 ff. On the guarding of work-secrets in agricultural societies, see M. J. Hereskovits (1955), pp. 487 ff. An important sociological treatment of the subject is G. Simmel's (1950, pp. 345 ff). An important conflict of secret societies was the involvement of the Compagnie du Saint-Sacrement in the prosecution of the Compagnons, which was instigated by Henri Buch or Buche; see R. Allier (1902), pp. 193 f., 198 ff., who discusses the economic aspect of the prosecution. No investigation exists of other secret societies, whose main activity became a form of friendly insurance, such as the Order of Foresters (W. Potter and R. Oliver, 1967) who claim to go back to the New Forest charter of 1217, but in fact seem to have no records earlier than 1790.

114. E. Coornaert (1966), passim. The grand master's throne of the British grand lodge is still referred to as the Solomonic Throne or Chair, while that of his deputy is called Hiram Abbif's chair.

115. On Daedalus as the type of all inventors, see A. Brelich (1958), pp. 166 ff., who compares him to the other divine and heroic originators of skills. See also K. Kerenyi (1959), pp. 231 ff. There appears to be no study of the relation between the Hiram and the Daedalus legends. In the sixteenth century, the legend was "moralized" playing on Daedalus' lending himself to Pasiphae's turpitudes, and to his other characteristic, that of the archetypal exile. See C. W. Lemmi (1933), pp. 109 ff.

116. This is explicit in the "revelations" of Mattheus Roriczer of Ratisbon and of Hans Schuttmayer. See P. Frankl (1945), pp. 46 ff., which is still very valuable in spite of its rather reductionist approach. There is a summary treatment of these and other masonic "publications" in P. Frankl (1960), pp. 145 ff. The Roriczer-Schuttmayer documents are set in the context of drawing and proportioning techniques by P. Booz (1956).

117. This remains at the heart of masonic ritual, as in the gradual revelation of the points of the compass at admission to the three degrees. It is characteristic that in the legend of Hiram/Adoniram these instruments become murder weapons, the final blow being given by the compass points; a variant, in inverse order, of weapon/instruments in G. Serbanesco (1964), I, pp. 231 ff.

On the literacy of masons and the teaching of the lodge, see P. Frankl (1960), pp. 132 ff.

118. C. G. Jung (1968), pp. 354 f., 476 ff. George Herbert's poem, *The Elixir*, much used as a hymn in the English-speaking world (*English Hymnal* no. 485) is an excellent illustration of this proposition; although most of the people who sing it give a purely moral interpretation and ignore the alchemical terminology.

119. *Notre Dame de Paris*, Bk. V, ch. 2. In Hugo's apocalyptic vision, the mass of printed matter shall become the new Tower of Babel.

120. P. Frankl (1960), pp. 257 ff., 316 ff.

121. The Ratisbon meeting seems to have been the product of some years of negotiation. It organized the masons' craft in German-speaking lands around four lodges: Cologne, Vienna, Berne, and Strasbourg, the last being the *Mutterkollegium*, as it were a Grand Lodge. The lodges of Saxony adhered to the Ratisbon agreement—with reservations—in 1462. The relative documents, and the differences between the various formularies, are discussed by P. Frankl (1960), pp. 127 ff.

By the Peace of Ryswijk of 1697, Strasbourg, which had anyway been annexed by the French in 1681, was formally ceded to the French crown. But the cathedral lodge retained its authority over imperial lodges. The Reichstag abrogated this authority, forbade imperial lodges any communication with Strasbourg, and appointed civil magistrates as arbiters of masonic disputes (Ratisbon, 16 March 1707; F. Janner, 1876, pp. 83 ff.). However, Michael Erlacher, master at Strasbourg (1713–1760) seems to have continued exercising authority. With the general abeyance of the crafts and of craft discipline, the authority of the lodge was eroded but not enough; Erlacher's mastership is discussed by F. Pariset (1929), pp. 176 ff.; 200 f.; cf. F. Janner (1876), pp. 86 f. On 13 May 1717, the Reichstag issued a new *Dictatum* and Charles VI issued a more far-reaching ordonnance in which the apprentices carrying letters of introduction (*Brief-Maurer*) are made equal with those presenting themselves with the mason-word (*Grussmaurer*) and the masonic oath dissolved. F. Janner (1876), pp. 89 ff.; and J. G. Findel (1869), pp. 71 ff., 659 ff.

122. E. Conder, Jr. (1894), pp. 204 f. H. Josten (1966), IV, p. 1700. This is Ashmole's second record of attendance at a lodge; his diary is so fragmentary, however, that no importance can be attached to this. He registers the matter in a very commonplace way, as a normal occurrence. Of the new masons, admitted at this lodge of 11 April 1682 were William Wilson, a mason-sculptor (1641–1710), who had just been knighted (R. Gunnis, 1968, s.v.; H. Colvin, 1954, s.v.), and Richard Borthwick, who appears nowhere else. The others who were "made masons" in the lodge: William Woodman (who had been a freedman of the masons' company since 1678, and was to become a leading mason in Grand Lodge days), William Grey (renter and upper warden of the masons' company), Samuel Taylour (presumed to be a kinsman of the Thomas Taylour who was matriculated in 1634), and William Wise (to become master of the company in 1703) were members of the London Masters' Company, and presumably working masons; as were all the other members of the lodge present—which means that only Ashmole and probably Richard Borthwick were not working with stone in one capacity or another.

123. "On the 10th March 1659 appeared Sir Robert Moray . . . Privy Councillor of the King of Great Britain in Scotland, and colonel of the Scottish Guards in the service of H. M. King of France . . . presented by Everard, Master of the Craft of Masons. He took the necessary oath under this craft and the right of citizenship was granted him, according to custom." Quoted from a document in the Rijksarchieven van Limburg, Maastricht, in A. Robertson (1922), p. 3, who unfortunately does not give the original text.

124. The competition was held about 1606 and Maderno commissioned in 1607. Work was completed in 1625, ten years before Inigo Jones' portico. No doubt the triumphal arch at Temple Bar would have been another element in this suite. See J. Harris, S. Orgel, and R. Strong (1973), pp. 143 f.

125. On Jones' use of the orders at St. Paul's, see J. Summerson (1966), pp. 98 ff.

126. Although he died before Charles I's execution in 1648. He seems to have attempted neutrality but to have been constrained to take sides c. 1645; in 1647 he went to Spa to take the waters; on his return through Paris, he went to visit Gassendi and perhaps Mersenne again. M. Rossi (1947), III, pp. 26, 263 ff.

127. J. Summerson (1966), p. 106, who quotes, too, Webb's extraordinary encomium in the preface to Inigo Jones' book on Stonehenge: "a Piece of Architecture not to be parallell'd in the last Ages of the World."

128. Pratt's achievement is set out in R. T. Gunter (1928). Clarendon House is discussed on pp. 137 ff. On Pratt, see more recently H. M. Colvin (1954) s.v.; and J. Summerson (1970), pp. 149 ff. Although Coleshill, Pratt's best-known building, which was often attributed to Jones in the past has now been given back to Pratt, he certainly knew Jones and admired him; he did reprove him for thinning, timidly, Scamozzi's specified proportions for moldings (Gunter, 1928, pp. 74, 76), but when discussing rusticatations in his "memoranda," he writes: "Of this work were most of the noble temples and basilicas of the Romans and Greeks, and of this is the Banqueting House and the reparations of St. Paul's by Inigo Jones."

129. So far, eleven manuscripts in Italian have been identified, all of them however vary from the Latin edition of 1623, which is the text that became familiar throughout Europe (*Civitas Solis*, Frankfurt, 1623). The first critical edition is that by Norberto Bobbio (1941); most recently edited by A. Seroni (1962).

130. On Andreae, see F. Yates (1972), *passim*, where Andreae's links with Rosicrucianism are discussed in some detail. More recently a translation was done by F. E. Held (1916). A more detailed study by John Warwick Montgomery is in course of preparation.

131. The main tenets of this religion are five: the absolute supremacy of God; the necessity of worship; virtue and piety as the cardinal parts of worship; absoluteness of moral values and the need for repentance of faults committed; an afterlife of reward and punishment. It has certain obvious analogies to the religion of Noah, to which I shall refer later. Aubrey (1949) tells the story (p. 39) that Archbishop Ussher of Armagh refused Herbert communion on his deathbed: see M. Rossi (1947), III, pp. 284 f. On Urban VIII's attitude and Diodati's mediation, see M. Rossi (1947), II, pp. 496 ff.

132. Commenius was the Latinized form of Komensky (1592–1671). He was the last bishop of the Moravian Brothers. In 1641 he came to Britain, but briefly, since the parliamentary commission on the reform of education would not get started (C. Hill, 1970, pp. 103 ff.). A pamphlet he wrote for private circulation at the time, *Via Lucis*, was thought to be the program of the future Royal Society. Oxenstierna guaranteed Commenius' livelihood through a pension. He returned to his see at Lissa (Leszno) in Poland but was expelled and settled in Amsterdam. Toward the end of his life he devoted most of his attention to the apocalypse and became convinced that the millennium had been foretold for 1672.

133. Samuel Hartlib (?–1671) may well have been a Polish Moravian Brother. He had come to London as a merchant, and had connections by marriage in the city; he moved in parliamentary and puritan circles, but he corresponded with Mersenne and maintained a contact with the Cambridge Platonists. It was his aim to establish an Office of Address, a center for scientific exchange in London based on the idea of Théophraste de Renaudot's office in Paris, though without the emulsifying ambitions of the Frenchman. He never got parliamentary support for this idea, although he

was given much sympathy. Milton dedicated his little *Treatise of Education* (1644) and Sir William Petty wrote him the *Advice* proposing a University in London.

But his disciple, Henry Oldenburg (who was also the son-in-law of John Drury, an irenic Protestant spurned by Laud but befriended by Oxenstierna in his plan for establishing the universal Protestant church) became the secretary of the Royal Society, of which Hartlib never became a fellow, though its *Philosophical Transactions* are very much like what he had proposed as *Communications* of his Office of Address. Hartlib's main publications were on agriculture and husbandry; see C. Hill (1972), pp. 100 f.; 122 ff.

134. On Mersenne's correspondence with Soncinian theologians and his latitudinarian attitudes, see R. Lenoble (1943), pp. 564 ff.

135. On the Invisible College, see C. Hill (1972), pp. 93, 105 ff. On Boyle's intentions in this matter, see in greater detail M. Purver (1967), pp. 195 ff.; and on the distinction between the Invisible College and the group round Gresham College, both of which were to be the nuclei of the Royal Society, and their communications, see M. Boas (1958), pp. 14 ff., 32 f.

136. The various works of "that miracle of youth," as John Evelyn (1955) called him (*Diary*, I, p. 293) are enumerated by most of his biographers. They include a model of the moon, made at the command of Charles II (Wren, *Parentalia*, 1750, pp. 210 ff.). The basic list is the one printed here, pp. 182 ff. On the family's loyalty, see p. 20 and n. 6.

137. On Gresham College, see J. Ward (1740); also S. J. Burgon (1839). More recently, brief but very much to the point, C. Hill (1972), pp. 33 f.

138. This was not until 1673.

139. That is what Robert Hooke referred to when he said "that there had not been his equal since Archimedes."

140. On Injection, see Wren, *Parentalia*, 1750, pp. 228 ff.; his mathematical activities, Wren (1750), p. 242; and "Wren the Mathematician" by D. Whiteside in Hartley (1960), esp. pp. 110 ff.

141. On the Tangiers appointment and Wren's refusal, see Bishop Sprat's letter, Wren, *Parentalia*, 1750, p. 260. A useful recent account in B. Little (1976), pp. 37 ff.

142. On John Denham, see *D.N.B.* s.v.; but for a critical account, S. Johnson in *The Lives of the Most Eminent English Poets* has not been bettered.

143. On Pembroke College Chapel, see V. Fürst (1956), pp. 2 ff. A full account by E. H. Minns and M. Webb (1923), pp. 229 ff., also *Wren Society* V, pp. 27 ff. Its debt to Serlio, see E. Sekler (1956), pp. 42 f.

144. Sheldon (for whom see *D.N.B.*) was restored to his wardenship of All Souls in 1659 (Wren was a fellow) but was created bishop of London on the Restoration. For the theater, see *Wren Society*, V, p. 9; Fürst (1956), pp. 2 ff.; Summerson (1964); and Colvin (1974). John Evelyn (1955) attended the ceremony and described it in detail (I, 390 f., and II, 42 ff.).

145. The most prominent was Palladio's Olympic Theater in Vicenza inside the academy buildings. Wren may well have seen Gaspare Vigarini's *Salle de Machines* in the Tuileries, which was finished in 1662. But the interior is clearly based on the earlier Elizabethan and Jacobean theaters, with some help from engravings in Vitruvius. See L. Hautecoeur (1948), II, i, pp. 234 ff.; J. Summerson (1964), p. 7.

146. J. Harris, S. Orgel and R. Strong (1973), pp. 108 f., 186 f.

147. There was probably an earlier scheme, with a more elaborate columnar treatment on the exterior, but it has not survived.

148. J. Summerson (1964), p. 5.

149. The velarium, which was most impressive to Wren's contemporaries (see its description in R. Plot, 1705); H. M. Colvin (1974), p. 279, suggests that the whole purpose of the ingenious ceiling was to maintain the effect of an "ancient" theater, for which the absence of internal supports of any kind was essential. The structure, based on exercises of Serlio and Philibert, is described in Wren, *Parentalia,* 1750, pp. 335 f. It was replaced by the present structure in 1804, having been deflected by the weight of the unsold books of the Clarendon Press (which used the attic as a warehouse, but had its presses under the seating: an idea which may have been suggested by Domenico Fontana's plan for transforming the Colosseum into a textile-factory). See D. Fontana (1604), pt. ii, fol. 18. The painting of the velarium was the work of Robert Straeter or Streeter, who became sergeant-painter to the king in 1663 and was to do some more work with Wren in the city; Pepys was taken to see the preliminary drawings for it on 1 February 1668.

150. These were corroborative proof of the harmonic justice of the proportions used. Such an interpretation was put on the passage in Vitruvius which discusses theatrical acoustics (V, 1–6). Evelyn's account (above, n. 144) suggests stereophonic effects.

151. As is evident from his desperate attempts to protect the great portico of St. Paul's after the fire, and his terror for the Banqueting House during the Whitehall fire of 1698. See also below n., 175.

152. An account of the visit, on which most subsequent lives are based, is given in Wren, *Parentalia,* 1750, pp. 261 ff.; more material in J. Elmes (1852), pp. 209 ff.; R. Dircks (1923), pp. 195 ff. Also J. Ward (1740), p. 102. *Wren Society*, V, p. 14, for the full text to Ralph Bathurst announcing his departure and XVIII, pp. 177 ("Annexe: Biographical Note") for the itinerary.

153. The best account of Bernini's visit is that given by Fréart de Chantelou, though a different view is presented by Charles Perrault; see chapter 2. Wren's account of the meeting: "Bernini's Design for the Louvre I would have given my skin for, but the reserv'd old Italian gave me but a few minutes view. I only had time to copy it in my Fancy and Memory." This letter to Ralph Bateman was first reproduced by J. Ward (1740), p. 102.

154. Wren, *Parentalia*, 1750, p. 277; from Wren's report to the Rebuilding Commission of 1666: *ex autographo.*

155. These were the newly constructed embankments facing the Louvre by François Blondel and Pierre Bullet. L. Hautecoeur (1943–1957), II, 1, pp. 430 ff.; P. Patte (1769), pp. 215 ff. Edward Browne to his father, Sir Thomas, in Norwich; dated Paris, September 1665. Although Browne never had his father's eminence as a writer, he had a highly successful career as a physician. He was president of the Royal College of Physicians from 1704 until his death in 1708. He had been made an M.D. at Oxford and elected F.R.S. in 1667.

156. W. G. Bell (1920), passim. Evelyn writes on 7 September 1666, of "clambering over heaps of yet smoking Rubbish and frequently mistaking where I was: the ground under my feet so hot that it even burn't the soles of my shoes."

157. The first account in John Evelyn (1938) and although it was fairly widely known, being "written two or three dayes after the Incendium"; read to Wren by Evelyn on September 11 and presented to the king, with plates on September 13. On December 22 he sent a copy to Henry Oldenburg as secretary of the Royal Society; the first printing was in William Maitland (1756, 2nd ed.; the 1st ed. 1739, does not contain it), I, pp. 447 ff., and later editions. Another version appeared in 1920. A critical text by E. S. de Beer (1938) corrects earlier mistakes and provides a complete bibliography. But the story has been retold often.

Not only the court, but also the city thought a wholly new plan not only possible but desirable: T. F. Reddaway (1940), pp. 53 f. Beside Wren's, Hooker's, and Evelyn's, two further plans are known to have existed—by Richard Newcourt and Valentine Knight. For detailed comment, see N. G. Brett-James (1935), pp. 298 ff., 312 ff.

On Valentine Knight's imprisonment in this matter, see N. G. Brett-James (1935), p. 300; another scheme, of a financial nature and not related to any drawn plan, was presented to the Commons by John Birch, who at that time was auditor of excise (Pepys, *Diary*, 1875–1879, 24 February 1667).

158. Figures given by T. F. Reddaway (1940), p. 26.

159. This was certainly the opinion of John Gwynn, who published Wren's plan in 1749, and reprinted in 1766 in *London and Westminster Improved*; a similar view is expressed in Wren, *Parentalia*, 1750, p. 269. See T. F. Reddaway (1940), pp. 31 f., 311 f.

160. Strangely enough, the pedimented columnar portico was very unusual in the sixteenth, even in the seventeenth century. Palladio's Malcontenta and Villa Rotonda, the Chapel at Maser were much admired; but even Scamozzi's Favorita (Villa Pisani at Lonigo) had an atrophied portico, such as Palladio's villas Badoer or Emo. Scamozzi (1615), however, in the sixth book of his *Architettura Universale* displayed his specimen orders in the form of a pedimented portico, unlike those of his predecessors. It was a feature which did not appear in painted architecture either: not until the work of the antiquity-conscious artists of the seventeenth century: such as Pietro da Cortona's Triumph of Bacchus (c. 1625, Rome, Capitoline Museum).

Inigo Jones' use of a pedimented Tuscan portico is therefore a programmatic move—even if he interpreted it out of Scamozzi (1615), II, p. 58. In spite of the modest scale of St. Paul's, Covent Garden, no French or Italian architect would have seen anything so "antique," and certainly nothing of the majestic scale of the portico of St. Paul's.

By the time of the scheme, the most obvious analogy to the portico and dome placed between thoroughfares were Rainaldi's twin churches on the "trident" of the Piazza del Popolo. They had been represented on the foundation model which was struck in 1662 and more impressively in Giovanni Battista Falda's engraving of 1665. See most recently, G. Ciucci (1974), pp. 66 ff.

161. The projects are always based on a combination of dome and portico through all its transformations; in some, as in the "Warrant" design and in the executed project, the dome is set on an octagon. The portico of the Warrant design is clearly based on that of the Pantheon, with the traverse colonnades duplicated.

162. The conventional view of the French influence is put in S. E. Rasmussen (1948), p. 106. Wren was certainly very impressed by the embanking of the Seine (above), and the Thames-side quays were one of the major aims

frustrated in the rebuilding: T. F. Reddaway (1940), pp. 221 ff. The Fleet was embanked, however, and became an important feature of the city until it was tunneled over in 1733 and 1766 (T. F. Reddaway, 1940, pp. 200 ff.).

163. On the fortifications of London during and just after the civil war, see N. G. Brett-James (1935), pp. 268 ff.; on their dismantling, pp. 319, 415. On the panic partial reconstructions in 1715 and 1745, see 279 ff.; 318 f.

164. The most radical was Richard Newcourt, who proposed a layout in a series of squares, each centered on its own church, and the city boundary regularized into a parallelogram. The best known of the orthogonal plans was engraved as part of the "Grundtriss der Statt London . . . sampt dem newen Modell" published in the second edition (c. 1670) of Matthew Merian's *Theatrum Europeum*. It has usually been assumed to be Hooke's. The plans were discussed by Sydney Parks in "London Town-Planning Schemes in 1666," *JRIBA*, 1919, XII, 20, pp. 69 ff. George Vertue engraved Evelyn's and Wren's plans which were published by the Society of Antiquaries in *Londinum Redivivum*, London, 1748. Wren's plan had already been published separately by Hulsberg (London, 1724). Discussion of the plans in N. G. Brett-James (1935), pp. 298 ff.

165. Orthogonal layouts within a polygonal wall were not favored by medieval planners. Leonardo uses this form of layout in his scheme for the replanning of Florence, and rudimentary forms of it were drawn by Francesco di Giorgio and later engraved and published by Pietro Cattaneo (1554) in Venice, pp. 13 v., 14 v., 20 r., 24 r. Many of the planner-engineers such as Bonaiuto Lorini (much liked by Inigo Jones) and Francesco de Marchi attempted it; though the two towns in Daniele Barbaro's Vitruvius—as well as in some other Vitruvian commentaries—did not attempt the reconciliation of outline polygon and orthogonal plan. The most popular of them perhaps was the one published by V. Scamozzi (1615), pp. 166 f. A useful collection of illustrative material in M. Morini (1963), pp. 204 ff.

166. The most important figure was Sir William Petty, F.R.S., a physician and geographer: on his planning activities, see N. G. Scott-James (1935), pp. 315 ff.; and T. F. Reddaway (1940), p. 70. On Petty as a geographer, see Hartley (1960), I. Masson, F.R.S., and A. J. Youngson, "Sir William Petty," in Hartley (1960), pp. 84 ff., on the Down survey. On Boyle and Petty, see John F. Fulton, "The Hon. Robert Boyle, FRS," in Hartley (1960), p. 122.

167. See note 130, this chapter.

168. T. F. Reddaway (1940), pp. 49 ff.

169. Hugh May was paymaster of the Office of Works, and his most important work was the rebuilding of Windsor Castle after 1673; though his one surviving house of eminence, Eltham Lodge, is a very chastened version of van Campen's Mauritshuis in The Hague (1633–1635). The most prominent London building was Berkeley House in Piccadilly which was burnt down in 1733 and which stood next to his fellow commissioner's Pratt's Clarendon House. See J. Summerson (1970), pp. 189 ff., and K. Downes (1966), pp. 16 ff.

170. Roger Pratt's architectural papers were edited by R. T. Gunter (1928). He is the only one of the commissioners to have a direct link to Inigo Jones, to whom Pratt's best-known building, Coleshill in Berkshire (destroyed 1952) has often been attributed; see, however, Gunter (1928), pp. 5 ff. But by far the most important and at the time best-known was again in Pic-

cadilly, Clarendon House, built for the Lord Chancellor, much admired by Evelyn, and—in part—the cause of Clarendon's disgrace, see J. Summerson (1970), pp. 149 ff.

171. Of the six commissioners, three—Wren, May, and Pratt—were appointed by the king to be His Majesty's Commissioners for Re-Building. Robert Hooke, F.R.S.; Edward Jerman; and Peter Mills were appointed "surveyors" on the commission by the city; Jerman died in 1668, Mills in 1670. They were joined by John Oliver in January 1668; T. F. Reddaway (1940), pp. 55 ff., 108 f. Jerman is chiefly known for his design of the Royal Exchange; Peter Mills designed one of the few notable country houses to be built during the Commonwealth, Thorpe Hall, on which see J. Summerson (1970), pp. 165 ff., 203 f. Hooke and Oliver were both very closely associated with Wren.

172. For a concise account of Hooke's distinguished scientific career, see E. B. da C. Andrade, F.R.S., in Hartley (1960), pp. 137 ff. On his architectural activities, *Walpole Society* XXV (1936–1937), pp. 83 ff., and M. I. Batten (1937). Although his taste tended to be rather more Frenchified than Wren's, the two often collaborated. See J. Summerson (1970), pp. 255 f.

173. The term *foreign* did not refer primarily to foreigners, or even non-Londoners, but meant all those who had not been "made free" of a company or guild. See Knoop and Jones (1947), p. 45. The corporative restrictions were removed in the first place by the act of 8 February 1667 (18, 19 Car. II, c. viii) and confirmed for seven years by an act of the Common Council (29 April 1667), to be extended for life under certain circumstances. T. F. Reddaway (1940), pp. 32 f., 115 ff., where the opposition of various companies to the relaxing of the regulations is also discussed. For later developments, see T. F. Reddaway (1940), pp. 304 ff. When the masons' company was reincorporated in 1677, work on St. Paul's and the city churches was specifically excluded from their jurisdiction; see E. Conder, Jr. (1894), pp. 197 f.

174. The city was replanned and rebuilt by a series of decisions, which in spite of the king's passionate interest, were taken partly by the commission, partly by the Fire Court set up to deal with the legal problems of replanning and rebuilding, partly by decisions of the Common Council and so on. On the organization of the Fire Court and its activities, see T. F. Reddaway (1940), pp. 91 ff.; on patronage, Reddaway (1940), pp. 244 ff.

175. J. Evelyn, 7 September 1666; "the godly church, St. Paul's—now a sad ruin, and that beautiful portico (for structure comparable to any in Europe, as not long before repaired by the Late King) now rent in pieces, flakes of large stones split asunder, and nothing remaining entire but the inscription on the architrave showing by whom it was built."
On the commission's procedure, Wren, *Parentalia*, 1750, pp. 271 ff. The attempts to repair the structure are described on p. 278.

176. They were the two buildings Inigo Jones had shown on the side panels of his tomb: J. Harris, S. Orgel, and R. Strong, p. 209.

177. The curious stylistic reference was used by many writers at the time. It recurs in Anderson's *Constitutions,* of which I shall have more to say later.
The portico was a "programmatic" building. J. Webb (1725), p. 48, claims that in the portico Jones had finally resolved the problem set in Vitruvius' passage about *scamilli impares* (unequal increases in height of the stylobate, to achieve optical correction, not discovered until the nineteenth century) whose application "hath as much puzzled all his com-

mentators and Architects as to find out a Remedy for the *Gout* or *Stone* all Physicians,'' but it has ''been according to the very *Text* and *Letter* of *Vitruvius* so directly put in Work by Mr *Jones* in the Portico of the Cathedral of St. *Paul*, as no Architect can, or will understand *Vitruvius* but must ingenuously confess the same true.'' Webb further says that he only hints at it, in case some interloper tries to publish this remarkable discovery as his own.

The best-known work of commentary on this passage was written by Bernardino Baldi of Urbino (1553–1617) and printed as an appendix to Jan Laet's edition (1649) of *Vitruvius* (Elzevier, Amsterdam) which Webb (1725) quoted for preference; pt. II, pp. 145 ff. It was also reprinted by Giovanni Poleni (1739–1740), pp. 217 ff. The problem remained puzzling.

178. See below, this chapter.

179. K. Downes (1959), p. 28, n. 1, suggests that the Office of Works bought a copy of the first edition in 1676—to my mind very probable.

180. Wren, *Parentalia*, 1750, p. 289. It is difficult to know now how much of this ''Answer to Objections'' is based on Wren's own writings; Le Vau's project was ready in 1664. Claude Perrault's final scheme was engraved in various transformations by Prelle, Sebastien Le Clerc, Jean Marot.

181. Wren was in Paris on behalf of the Royal Society; he was a mathematician-astronomer with a strong interest in engineering and anatomy. Perrault, like Wren an architect-mathematician-anatomist-mechanical engineer, was a correspondent of Huygens, with whom Wren also kept up contact.

182. In the 1684 edition, n. 16 on p. 78. Wren's ''Answer'' clearly refers to this passage: Wren, *Parentalia*, 1750, pp. 288 f.

183. Tract I in Wren, *Parentalia*, 1750, pp. 351 f.

184. See Chapter 2. On Wren and Perrault, see W. Herrmann (1973), pp. 155 f., and K. Downes (1959), pp. 25 ff. Wren's ideas were formulated in answer to Perrault and therefore, naturally enough were those of the circle to which he belonged: that of Robert Boyle and Robert Hooke, of Wilkins and Brouncker, and even Ashmole. The underlying attitude is best expressed by the most brilliant member of the circle, Isaac Newton: ''I am inclined to believe some general laws of the Creator prevailed with respect to the agreable or unpleasing affection of all our senses; at least the supposition does not derogate from the wisdom or power of God, and seems highly consonant to the simplicity of the macrocosm in general.'' Quoted in D. Hay (1851), p. 5.

185. V. Scamozzi (1615), I, pp. 32, 40; though Wren seems to have paid more attention to the illustrations than to the text.

186. The crucial passage on the primary and secondary qualities is in Locke (1824) in ''The Essay on Human Understanding,'' in *Works*, bk. II, cap. 8, paras. vii ff. To Locke a distinction is essential ''that so we may not think . . . that (qualities) are exactly the images and resemblances of something inherent in the subject; most of those sensations being in the mind no more the likeness of something existing without us, than the names that stand for them are the likeness of our ideas.'' Primary qualities nevertheless ''are utterly inseparable from the body, in what state whatever it be,'' while secondary ''in truth are nothing in the objects themselves, but powers to produce various sensations in us . . . as colours, sounds, tastes.'' Descartes (1952) in *Principes de la Philosophie* (I, pp. 56 ff.; II, pp. 198 ff.; more particularly, I, p. 70. See Perrault's use of these distinctions, chapter 2.

187. This is added in justification of church spires.

188. Hence the buttresses which play such an important part in the structure of St. Paul's are hidden behind a wall which forms the second story of the lateral facades.

189. Though he did use chains in the structure of St. Paul's.

190. The Gothic genesis of the vaults at St. Paul's is described in Wren, *Parentalia,* 1750, tract II, pp. 357 f.

191. Vitruvius (1683), pp. 78 ff., n. 16 (on p. 80). In the note I quoted above, justifying the wide intercolumniation of the Louvre against François Blondel, Perrault says of his taste that "il tient un peu du Gothique, car nous aimons l'air, le jour et les dégagements" and later on adds in justification: "supposé que le Gothique en général . . . ne fust pas le plus beau genre d'architecture, je ne pensois pas que tout ce qui est dans le Gothique fut à rejetter." The Saracenic or Moorish origin of Gothic Wren takes from the more general condemnations of the barbarous medieval architecture which was a commonplace of architectural theorizing since Alberti.

Nevertheless, the derivation of Gothic architecture from that of the Saracens does occur earlier: in a history of the Hieronymite order by José de Sigüenza, which appeared in Madrid in 1600. Wren is unlikely to have known this, but his curious identification of the moderns as "Free-masons" or "Saracens" recalls certain freemasonic ideas about chivalry and the crusades. This is also taken up in John Evelyn's preface to his translation of Fréart de Chambray, of which more later. The unlikely transmitter of this idea is Fénélon, the great archbishop of Cambray, who toys with it in his *Lettre sur les Occupations de l'Académie Française,* and later in the *Dialogue sur l'Eloquence en Général, et Celle de la Chaire en Particulier,* which first appeared in Paris in 1718 and in which the analogy developed between the excessive use of antitheses and Gothic love of ornament, of pinnacles in particular. The rather structural formulation of these two texts (see P. Frankl, 1960, pp. 370 ff.) suggests that Fénélon might indeed have had some knowledge of Wren's ideas, which however were not published with the rest of the *Parentalia* until 1750. The only possible intermediary, it seems to me, would have been the "Chevalier" Ramsay, who became Fénélon's secretary in 1709–1710. See below and P. Chevallier (1964), pp. 131 ff.

192. Practically the whole of Tract I is devoted to it; Tract II is about the orders and vaulting; Tract III raises again the problem of variations in column proportions of ancient buildings (the differing diameters were measured out of Desgodetz); Tract IV is about a number of ancient monuments: Diana of Ephesus, Mars Ultor in Rome, the Temple of Peace (i.e., the Basilica of Maxentius), and the Mausoleum of Halicarnassus. The Heirloom copy has an extra transcribed tract ("Discourse on Architecture" by S^r. C.W.) which is a brief history of architecture out of Scripture, Josephus, Herodotus, and Pliny, which is of course parallel to what was found in the masonic Old Charges, particularly the insistence on the two Enochian columns of Josephus. It contains a reasoned refutation of Villalpanda's design for the temple of Jerusalem, with its elaborate Corinthian order: "which in that Age was not used by any Nation: for the first Ages used grosser Pillars than Dorick" (p. 7). It includes the temple restoration of Humphrey Prideaux.

193. Hobbes, *Leviathan*, 1904, p. 17.

194. Evelyn compares Henry VII chapel at Westminster, "its sharp angles, Jetties, Narrow Lights, lame Statues, Lace and Cut-Work and Crinkle Crankle" very unfavorably with the Banqueting House or Wren's St.

Paul's. "An Account of Architects and Architecture" in J. Evelyn (1723), p. 10.

195. On Wren's Gothic exercises, see V. Fürst (1956), pp. 51, 193 (St. Mary Aldermanbury), pp. 21, 186 (St. Dunstan), pp. 58, 195 (Westminster Abbey); and more generally, pp. 59, 170 f. On the whole phenomenon of seventeenth-century English Gothic, see K. Downes (1966), pp. 121 ff., although C. L. Eastlake (1872), pp. 7 ff., is still well worth reading.

196. V. Fürst (1956), pp. 51 ff., 130. No such parish as "St. Edmund the King, Bloomsbury" is known, and the attribution of the drawing, related to St. Clement Dane's, is still uncertain; the "loggia" designed but not executed for St. Mary-le-Bow was not a portico in this sense at all.

197. 9 Anne xxii. A general discussion of the provisions in K. Downes (1959), p. 161.

198. Gibbs was to build St. Mary-le-Strand for the commission and St.-Martin's-in-the-Fields, which mark the change in the taste of the period in a most radical fashion. See later in this chapter.

199. On Gibbs' view of his dismissal, operated as he thought on information supplied by a countryman, probably C. Campbell, see later in this chapter.

200. K. Downes (1959), p. 161.

201. On the partnership, see K. Downes (1959), pp. 57 f., 69 ff.; and L. Whistler (1939), pp. 70 ff.

202. An interesting, though slight testimonial to the triple working of the partnership, is the three architects' "approbation" of John James' edition of Andrea Pozzo's book on perspective, put rather in the style of the Venetian censor's *Imprimatur*.

203. H. Colvin (1978), s.v. James, John.

204. On the steeple and the restoration of the Mausoleum of Halicarnassus, see K. Downes (1959), p. 187. Wren's (1750) ideas were set down in Tract IV in *Parentalia*, pp. 367 f., and embroidered in the manuscript "Discourse." The statue provoked a certain amount of merriment: E. Beresford-Chancellor (1920), p. 202. Also J. Dallaway in Walpole (1828), IV, p. 72: "the wits of the Jacobite party indulged themselves in many sarcasms upon this extraordinary elevation of the Hanoverian king." James Ralph (1734) in a programmatic Burlingtonian publication reserved some of his most scathing remarks for St. George's: "This structure is ridiculous and absurd, even to a proverb; that the builders mistook whim for genius, and ornament for taste; and that their execrable conceit of displaying a statue of the king on the top of it excites laughter in the ignorant, and contempt in the judges of architecture."

205. On the steeples of Hawksmoor's churches, see K. Downes (1959), pp. 177 f., 182, 196 ff. Also K. Downes (1966), pp. 103 f.; and J. Summerson (1970), pp. 303 ff.

206. Hawksmoor was conscious of *terribilità* as an aim; it is best expressed, however, in Vanbrugh's advice to the church commissioners: "a Temple . . . should ever have the most solemn Awful Appearance both without and within, that is possible." Quoted in Whistler (1954), p. 248.

207. On Fischer's iconography, see chapter 3.

208. Hawksmoor's practice was extensively Gothic. And he sets out the argument for stylistic tolerance to Bishop Wilcocks, who was also dean of Westminster, about the observations of "Gentlemen-Connoisseurs, Criticks or Workmen advanc'd to the degree of Architects, be that as it will." Of

Gothic architecture he says generally that "this manner of Building Mr Evelyn . . . Wren and other regular Artists believed was brought from ye Saracens (in the holy war) by some of the Curious of that time." Letter 147 (1733–1735) undated in K. Downes (1959), pp. 255 ff.

209. Letter 92 (II) of 10 November 1727. *Walpole Society* XIX (1930–1931), pp. 118 f. This tone returns throughout the extended programmatic discussion of the mausoleum, stimulated to some extent by Lord Burlington's criticism, against which Hawksmoor defended himself in a number of letters, beginning in 1732, which make up a kind of learned tract on architectural theory.

210. The slightly disgraceful story of Vanbrugh as Garter is told by Whistler (1939), pp. 165 ff.; in greater detail by Madeleine Bingham (1974), pp. 124 ff. Having made light of heraldry in his play *Aesop*, Vanbrugh was given the sinecure of Carlisle Herald Extraordinary in 1703 and advanced to Clarencieux in 1704. Although he acted as Garter for several years, he was deprived of the office by George I in 1718. The office of Garter was that of which Ashmole had thought himself unworthy.

211. A. A. Cooper (1732), 5th ed., III, pp. 400 f. This program was echoed by Bishop Berkeley, who was to become one of Shaftesbury's most outspoken opponents (see later in this chapter) in *An Essay Towards Preventing the Ruine of Great Britain*, 1721. He suggests that the recovery of a sense of public spirit would be promoted if a parliament house and courts of justice, as well as a royal palace and other public buildings were put up, and that they should be adorned with paintings and sculptures which influence "the minds and manners of men, filling them with great ideas, and spiriting them up to an emulation of worthy actions." An academy is also part of his plan for a national restoration. Although the program is similar, Shaftesbury would have argued that the fine pictures and sculptures were the product of the taste, the dialectical liberty of people. See A. Luce (1949), p. 82.

Berkeley had by this time also met Burlington, probably through Pope, "a Papist, but a man of excellent wit and learning" (Berkeley to John Percival on 7 March 1712–1713 in B. Rand (1916), p. 110. In a letter to Percival of 12 October 1721, Berkeley speaks of his conversations with Burlington who thought it "below him to solicit" the duke of Grafton any further for Berkeley's preferments, B. Rand (1916), p. 179; although Burlington did intercede on other occasions and granted Berkeley privileges on his Irish estates (A. Luce, 1949, p. 174).

Burlington's friendship for Berkeley was based on his enormous intellectual reputation and his familiarity with many of Burlington's friends and acquaintances—Pope and Gay, Arbuthnot, Swift, Addison (P. Smithers, 1968, passim), and Steele—but also on Berkeley's enthusiastic interest in architecture (see at any rate T. Warton, *Essay on Pope*, 1782, II, p. 200, quoted in A. Luce, 1949, p. 82), which his two journeys through France and Italy (particularly the second one, when he also acted as a buyer of prints and some antiquities) helped to form. In a remarkably "advanced" tone, Berkeley writes to Percival from Rome on 28 July 1718: "there is not any one modern building in Rome that pleases me, except the wings of the Capitol built by Michelangelo and the colonnade of Bernini before St. Peter's . . . I forget the little round (church) in the place where St. Peter was beheaded which is very pretty . . . This gusto of mine is formed on the remains of antiquity that I have met with in my travels, particularly in Sicily, which convince me that the old Romans were inferior to the Greeks, and the moderns fall infinitely short of both" (B. Rand, 1916, p. 172).

212. On Somers' collecting, see W. L. Sachse (1975), pp. 196 ff.; on his patronage of writers, W. L. Sachse (1975), pp. 198 ff.; cf. Peter Smithers (1968), pp. 29 ff., 240 f.

213. On John Closterman (1660–1711), see M. Whinney and O. Millar (1957), pp. 71, n. 4, 189 ff. Shaftesbury's portrait (St. Gile's House) is pl. 55; it is the picture on which Gribelin's engraving was based. For Gribelin, see H. Walpole (1828), V, pp. 238 f.: "his prints at best are neat memorandums." On Shaftesbury's patronage more generally, see E. Wind, "Shaftesbury as a Patron of Art," in *J.W.C.I.*, XIX, 1938, pp. 185 ff.: J. E. Sweetman (1956), pp. 110 ff. This concerns "The Dying Philosopher" by Paolo Mattei. On Shaftesbury in Naples, see B. Croce (1927), pp. 272 ff.

214. Poussin is alluded to frequently. See B. Rand (1914), pp. 124, 130, 146, although he approved of other painters (Guido, the Caracci, even Salvator Rosa) enough to buy them for himself and for others. See R. L. Brett (1951), pp. 52 f. Simon Gribelin engraved the painting of Hercules which Paolo de Mattei did for Shaftesbury in Naples for the Judgment of Hercules in 1713. See Shaftesbury (1732), III, p. 345. This theme is the old one of *Hercules between Vice and Virtue*; on which, as an iconographic trope, see E. Panofsky (1930).

215. Apart from a casual remark: "Remember Montague House, which I was never willing to go see after rebuilt and painted, because the better the master, the more violent the conflict and dissonance harsher" (*Second Characteristics*, 1914, pp. 139 f.). This presumably refers to Verrio's illusionistic paintings in the staircase and the great chambers, which perished in the fire of 1686; see J. Evelyn for 19 January 1686, who thought that "for painting and furniture, there was nothing more glorious in England."

216. Shaftesbury (B. Rand, 1914, p. 104) on pictures in Protestant churches: "as beauteous forms polish (taking politeness with its consequences) so ugly barbarize"; and again: "beautiful forms beautify; polite polish. On the contrary, Gothic gothicize, barbarous barbarise" (p. 123).

217. Shaftesbury (1732), III, pp. 405 ff.

218. See N. Pevsner (1940), pp. 124 ff.; 182 ff.; cf. S. C. Hutcheson (1968), pp. 24 ff.

219. R. L. Brett (1951), pp. 186 ff. S. Grean (1967), pp. 246 ff. E. Cassirer (1955), pp. 312, on Shaftesbury's immediate influence in England; Montesquieu called Shaftesbury "un des quatre grands poètes"; the others being Plato, Montaigne, and Malebranche (*Pensées Diverses*, 1879, VII, p. 171). On Shaftesbury and Winckelmann, see C. Justi (1923), I, pp. 72 f., 173 f., 246 ff. Cf. also L. Mittner (1964), pp. 453 ff. The complete edition of the *Characteristics* in French appeared in Paris in 1769 (though Diderot had separately published "The Enquiry Concerning Virtue" in 1749) and in German in 1776–1779.

220. See B.-J. Dobbs (1975), p. 103, n. 22, for the bibliography. Descartes' answers to More are most easily available in *Oeuvres* (1952), pp. 1312 ff., 1332 ff.

221. Henry More (1659), p. 450. Quoted in B.-J. Dobbs (1975), p. 104.

222. Barrow (1860), IX, p. 101 ("Cartesiana hypothesis de Materia et Motu"): "observant his Philosophi (Hermetices) omne corpus naturale mixtum . . . ex duabus partibus omnino diversis atque distinctis constare; non secus ac hominum ex anime et corpore: nimirum ex spiritu subtili, puro, potentissimi, et corpore opaco, foeculento, impuro atque imbelli: atque haec duo ignis beneficio separari."

223. Alexander Koyré (1972), p. 124, n. 2, referring to the correspondence between Samuel Clarke and Leibniz: *A Collection of papers which passed between the learned Mr Leibnitz and Dr Clarke in . . . 1715 & 16 . . .* London, 1717.

224. On Newton's involvement in the correspondence, see F. E. Manuel (1968), pp. 333 f., 455; and A. Koyré (1972), p. 124, n. 2.

225. Isaac Newton, *Opticks*, first appeared in 1704; the definitive edition in 1730 (reprint 1952), pt. I, 2; prop. VI, problem ii; cf. also pt. I, 1, experiment 16. Newton had already formulated his ideas on color harmony much earlier and set them out in a letter to Robert Hooke. See Henry Gourlac in P. Hughes and D. Williams (1971), pp. 131 ff. On vibration theory, see P. Hughes and D. Williams (1971), p. 144, n. 30. The discovery of color harmony in the spectrum was part of Newton's general conviction that his formulation of universal laws was a rediscovery of ancient wisdom, particularly that of Pythagoras, and set him in the succession of "ancient" theologians, as he intended to show in the "classical" Scholia to his *Principia*, which were never published, though their contents were generally known to his disciples and friends. See J. E. McGuire and P. M. Rattansi (1966).

226. Henry More, quoted in B.-J. Dobbs (1975), p. 104.

227. T. Sprat (1722), pp. 345 ff., for a negative demonstration.

228. Cf. E. Cassirer (1955), p. 313.

229. Shaftesbury (1732), II, pp. 189 f. On his relative indifference to Newton, see S. Grean (1967), p. 12; on his hostility to the "mechanics" of the Royal Society, R. L. Brett (1951), pp. 97 f.

230. On Boyle as an alchemist, see F. E. Manuel (1968), pp. 182 ff.; and M. Boas (1958), pp. 154 ff.; and B.-J. Dobbs (1975), 118 ff., 174 ff., 198 ff.

231. It was diffused through a number of subsidiary publications; it was, for instance, the image provided by Fischer von Erlach in his *Entwurff*, and dogmatized by Leonhard Christoph Sturm in his *Zivilbaukunst*. And, of course, Fréart de Chambray's plate of the order invented by Villalpanda was very widely known and reproduced. See above, chapter 1.

232. J. Rykwert (1972), p. 132. It was finished in 1694. It is now housed in the Museum für Hamburgische Geschichte.

233. I. Newton (1728), cap. 5; cf. F. E. Manuel (1968), pp. 360, 462. Newton is known to have possessed—and worked much with—a copy of Brian Walton's polyglot bible: *Biblia Sacra Polyglota . . . cum Apparatu, Appendicibus, Tabulis etc.*, 1657, 6 vols. (cf. F. E. Manuel, 1968, pp. 372 f.). Volume I contains Louis Cappel's *Trisagion sive Templi Hierosolomitani Triplex Delineatio*. See W. Herrmann in D. Frazer, H. Hibbard, and M. J. Levine (1967), pp. 145 f., 157; Herrmann lists some twenty publications on the temple between 1650 and 1720. Cappel's views, and his respectful criticism of Villalpanda, were fairly widely known. Hugo Grotius speaks of the desirability of Cappel's lectures being printed and published in 1644 (*Annotationes ad Vetus Testamentum*, Paris, 1644). On the Villalpanda reconstruction and its rivals, see Herrmann, in Frazer, Hibbard, and Levine (1967).

234. Stukeley (1882), diary for 11 December 1720: "He [it is not clear whether he means Newton or Lord Pembroke] came to see my drawing of Solomon's Temple" (p. 62). 1 April 1726: "I paid a visit to Sr Isaac Newton . . . We had some discourse about Solomon's temple of which he had

formerly made a plan; he says it is older than any great heathen temples; that Sesostris from hence made his temples in Egypt, one in each Nomus, and that from thence the Greeks made theirs & borrow'd their religion'' (p. 78).

235. Stukeley also originated a lodge at Grantham when he moved there; letter to Samuel Gale from Grantham, 6 February 1726–1727; Stukeley (1882), p. 190.

236. On the lineage of the ''Gentile Theology,'' see D. P. Walker (1972), pp. 18 ff. On the law of Noah and the law of Moses, see I. Newton (1728), pp. 189 ff. See also F. E. Manuel (1963), pp. 112, 161, and pl. 10.

237. I. Newton (1728), pp. 86 f., 92, for the dates of the Argonauts; the controversy about the Argonauts and their alleged astronomer, the Centaur Cheiron, is discussed by F. E. Manuel (1963), pp. 22 f., 74 f., 86 f., 166, 175. The Tyrian Hercules and Gallic Hercules, Newton (1728), pp. 113 f.; the dating of the temple, 114 ff.; Sesostris, Iamblichus, and the origin of geometry, pp. 218 ff.; a description of the temple, pp. 331 ff. The drawings are in the library of the Babson Institute at Wellesley, Mass.

238. On the temple as an essential archetype, particularly in the Apocalypse, see I. Newton (1733), pp. 256 ff.; and F. E. Manuel (1963), p. 170. Newton seems to have speculated, too, on the possible return of the Jews to the Holy Land, and the eventual rebuilding of the temple; F. E. Manuel (1963), p. 295, n. 74.

239. Newton must have known of Benito Aria's dismissal of Villalpanda in his Polyglot Bible (Antwerp, 1572) and which he quotes (Newton, 1728, p. 232). The controversy continued; nevertheless Villapanda's model went on being used as a reference. See below. He certainly knew Perrault's restoration since he was familiar with L. Compiègne de Veil's Latin translation of Maimonides, which Perrault illustrated (F. E. Manuel, 1963, p. 268, n. 12).

240. The rather scrappy surviving drawings were never published. They are in the Bodleian Library, Gough Maps, 41°. See S. Piggott (1950), pp. 130 f. There are further drawings in Bodl. MS. Top.gen.b.52.

241. S. T. Coleridge (1839) provides the first definition of the term *clerisy*, much as Stukeley thought it (Stukeley, 1882, p. 49), and a clerisy is—in part—what his apologetic is about.

242. J. Toland (1814). It appeared in 1726, posthumously (Toland died in 1721), in the form of a series of letters to Lord Molesworth. Toland was a fierce controversialist and was best known as the author of *Christianity not Mysterious* (1696), which is the manifesto of English deism. In 1720 he published *Pantheisticon*, a parody of a liturgical text. His rather disreputable dealings with Shaftesbury, whose disciple he professed to be, and from whom he certainly received a pension, are told by R. L. Brett (1951), pp. 41 f., 48 ff., 55 ff. However, it is difficult to dissent from Diderot's judgment on Toland and his fellows: ''mauvais protestants et misérables écrivains,'' ''Essai sur le Mérite,'' in *Oeuvres*, 1875–1877, I, p. 15. There seems to have been a quasi-masonic secret society around Toland, active about 1710 and after. See J. M. Roberts (1972), p. 18.

William Warburton, later (1759) bishop of Gloucester, popularized the doctrine of a hermetic but exalted clerisy faithful to an ancient monotheistic wisdom, teaching rough lessons to their inferiors in a coarse and animal—or hero-worshipping—form in his *Divine Legation of Moses Demonstrated*, 1742. On its sources and the Stukeley-Toland controversy, see F. E. Manuel (1963), pp. 180 ff.

243. On the building of the temple as the paradigm of any work process, see earlier in this chapter. There is a strong link between craft guilds and the temple legend provided by identifying the last master of the Knights Templar, Jacques Molay, burnt on 18 April 1314, with Maître Jacques, one of the Compagnons' founders. It is not certain when this legendary assimilation was accomplished; Maître Jacques is also assimilated to other figures: the apostle James the Less, the patron of Compostella. It is however true that the Templars were generous patrons of the building trades, both in the Holy Land and in Europe, and used their privileges in favor of craft corporations; the Knights Hospitallers who inherited many of them, retained them when they became the Knights of Malta and had an early connection with masonry, of which below, n. 245 and text.

The Compagnonnage is still a powerful organization; it suffered a short eclipse after the 1945 peace, having been favored by the Vichy government of France. But the Compagnons were reformed after the war: see L. Benoist (1966), pp. 97 ff. One of the main events in the Compagnons' year was the pilgrimage to the Ste. Beaume in Provence associated with St. Mary Magdalene, but also with Maître Jacques (perhaps by assimilation to Compostella). It was patronized by the Benedictines resident at St. Maximin nearby, and then by the Dominicans who followed them; it has lapsed, although it was popular in the earlier nineteenth century (E. Coornaert, 1966, pp. 142, 300; and its revival in 1894, p. 238). After World War II, Edmond Truin attempted to build a pilgrimage youth center at the Ste. Beaume connected with a cave-church. This was frustrated by the French episcopate, which boycotted the appeal. The center was to have been designed by Le Corbusier (1954), pp. 24 ff.

244. Stukeley's view of Stonehenge as the product of benevolent and trinitarian Druids, and his work on megalithic monuments generally followed Aubrey's and Jones' researches, and the discussion which Webb's publication of Jones' book provoked. In the interim, others had taken an interest in Stonehenge and British prehistoric antiquities, particularly Edward Lhwyd and John Anstey.

245. Wren's view of the origins of Gothic in the oriental influence imported by the Crusaders was mentioned in this chapter. The first account of the relation between Templars and Freemasons is in the Chevalier (Andrew Michael) Ramsay's oration, pronounced probably for the first time on 26 December 1736, and repeated in a modified version on 23 April 1737, in Paris. The text is given by P. Chevallier (1964), pp. 149 ff.; and G. Serbanesco (1964), II, pp. 87 ff.; this last is given after its first printing in 1742, while Chevallier's followed ms. sources. The idea is echoed by James Anderson (1738) in the second edition of the *Constitutions*; it does not appear in the first. Ramsay's *Discourse* or *Oration* is usually regarded as the foundation text of higher grade masonry in Europe. It is not known at what point this mysterious person became a mason, though it seems to have been before 1724; at any rate, he was reentered a mason in London at the Horn Lodge in March 1730 (*AQC*, 1934, p. 77). In December of the year before, he had been made an F.R.S. and also an honorary Litt.D. at Oxford, for his advocacy of Fénélon's views.

In this context, it might be worth noting that Wren restored the Temple Church in London (1628–1695) and that it was again restored in 1736–1737. All this was undone in the 1840s (J. Mordaunt-Crook in *Architectural History*, 1965, 8, pp. 39 ff.).

The architecture on the temple site was Islamic at the conquest and was not radically affected by the Latin kings of Jerusalem. It continued therefore to be associated, as was the Anastasis, with what was called Saracenic architecture in the seventeenth century; because of that and a play on the term *temple*, a legendary complex was developed, aided by notions about the great hidden treasures of the templar knights. The order of the Knights Templar was instituted at the Council of Troyes in 1128, although it had been in existence about a decade. St. Bernard was associated with its rule, and hence Templar architects were said to be disciples of the Cistercian ones. The order was suppressed by Philippe le Bel with the help of Pope Clement V after some years of suspicion and defense at the Council of Vienna in 1312 by a series of savage sentences for satanic practices and blasphemous mysteries, and many legends developed. The secret of the Templars was later said to be taken to Scotland by the Master of the Templars for the Auvergne, Philippe d'Omont or Aumont; members of his family were said to have succeeded him after the persecution. Louis Marie-Augustin, duc d'Aumont, his namesake, acted as host to the Bussi-Aumont Lodge in the late seventeen-thirties (P. Chevallier, 1974, I, p. 12). The lists of the master of the Temple are provided by Claude-Antoine Thory (1815), I, pp. 285 ff. For the privileges inherited by the Knights of Malta, see H. de Boullainvilliers (1737), II, pp. 56 ff. The relative orthodoxy of the Templars has been vindicated with new evidence by P. M. Tonnellier (1976).

246. John, second duke of Montague (1688?–1749) came of the same Orange-promoted Whig family as Wharton. He had been made Knight of the Garter in 1719 and grand master of the Bath in 1725. Like Wharton, he was of the Kit-Cat club. His loyalty to Hanover was constant; he remained a committed Whig all his life politically. About his ideology, Stukeley, his friend and protégé, wrote ruefully in his commonplace book, enumerating the reprehensible things about Martin Folkes (1882), p. 100. Folkes made many friendly gestures towards Stukeley; he had a mahogany model made of Stonehenge after Stukeley's measurements (S. Gale to Stukeley, 26 January 1740, 1882, p. 470) and S. Gale to Stukeley, 14 May 1740; Pembroke intended to make a similar one of Avebury (1882), p. 324. Stukeley concludes this entry with an account of Martin Folkes' deplorable death.

In the commonplace book, having given a highly favorable account of the similarities of his own character and that of the duke of Montague, he notes "and had he not been born a nobleman and of heathen upbringing, we shd have had the same love for religion." He goes on, more to my point: "We had exactly the same taste for old family concerns, genealogys, pictures, furniture, coats of arms, the old way of building, gardening and the like; in a general imitation of pure nature, in the Gothic architecture, in painted glass, in the open-hearted, candid, undesigning and free manner of conversation" (1882, pp. 114 f.).

Philip's father, Thomas (Honest Tom), baron Wharton, was created earl in 1706 and marquis in 1715; he was the fifth baron, and is most remembered as the author of the Orange ballad *Lilliburlero* (with its music by Purcell) and the bad character of him given by Swift (*Works*, 1934, p. 501 f.). His more positive and bland character provided by Addison and Steele in the dedication of volume V of the *Spectator* is (deservedly) less familiar. See P. Smithers (1968), pp. 155 ff. On his political activities, see most recently W. L. Sachse (1975), passim. Inevitably, he was a member of the Kit-Cat club.

247. There appears to be no parallel development in France, nor in the empire. In France, the Compagnons had a good deal of trouble after a member of the St. Crispin's Guild (of shoemakers) denounced its practices, particularly its initiation ceremonies. The various companies were investigated by the doctors of the Sorbonne and the customs were condemned by a

sentence of 14 March 1655, for impiety, sacrilege, and superstition. Nicolas Perrault was, at that time, still one of the doctors.

The Compagnons did not—not in the sixteenth century at least—have an ecumenical character; the division between *dévoirants* (Catholic) and *gavots* (Protestant) was radical and often violent. The policies of Colbert made activities for the Compagnons, as they did for other craft organizations, difficult. In the eighteenth century the Compagnons were affected by the rising influence of masonry; they were abolished and repressed by the Le Chapelier law of 14 June 1792, and further forbidden by the Code Napoléon. Nevertheless, they have survived in a modified form. The accusation of the Guild of the Most Holy Sacrament, the denunciations and the sentence, are given in detail by E. Coornaert (1966), pp. 350 ff., 415 ff.; see also R. F. Gould (1951), I, pp. 115 ff. Rather meager material about other guild organization is collected by R. F. Gould (1951), I, pp. 169 ff.

John Evelyn shows himself aware of the nature of trade organizations when he discusses the mystery of charing, or charcoal burning which is, of course, the skill of the *Carbonari*, Evelyn (1729), pp. 232 ff.

248. P. Chevallier (1964), p. 33; sketchily (1974), pp. 4 ff. It is possible that when the young Duke of Wharton visited Mary of Modena (James II's widow) at St. Germain, where he borrowed £2000 to prosecute the Stuart cause, he was made a mason of the St. Germain lodge. On the confused relation between Wharton and early French freemasonry, see J. Baylot (1965), pp. 62 ff. On Wharton and his introduction to the Old Pretender when he was at Parma, by the Chevalier Ramsay, see G. Bord (1908), pp. 66 f. His knowledge of masonic ritual and custom when he was made grand master and to which Gould refers in his comments on the constitution of the United Grand Lodge of 1814 (R. F. Gould, 1951, III, p. 100) seems to have outlasted his reputation for philandery. Cf., however, p. 50, n. 3.

249. Apart from ms. sources, most information at this period comes from nonmasonic sources and is not revealing, such as R. Plot's account in his *Antiquities of Warwickshire*. R. Holme III, Clarencieux king at arms, who drew up the masons' arms at the time of the charter of Charles II (1677), was a mason, however, like his fellow herald, Ashmole (R. F. Gould, 1951, II, p. 110 ff.; surprisingly a one-sheet antimasonic pamphlet appeared in 1698. Its tone is religious, but it is too brief and elliptical to indicate whether the objector is a recusant or a puritan; see D. Knoop and G. P. Jones in *A.Q.C.* (1944), pp. 152 ff. However, in public masons appeared in their full gear only at ceremonies connected with building, for which it seems to have been usual to calculate the auspicious moment astrologically.

There is masonic information about this, if not always contemporary: the *Constitutions* (J. D. D. Anderson, 1738, p. 98), for instance, talk of the laying of the foundation stone at the Banqueting Hall in 1609; but the first Banqueting Hall, erected in 1608 to designs by some unknown architect, perhaps Sir David Conyngham (P. Palme, 1957, pp. 115 f.) was not replaced by Jones' until 1619, while Stone, whom Anderson calls grand warden with Lord Pembroke, did not become the king's master-mason until 1632. The next building mentioned in this way by the *Constitutions* (p. 102) is the Royal Exchange, where the stone was laid on 28 October 1669. Evelyn was unfortunately ill that day; and Pepys had ended his diary 31 May 1669; Ashmole, however, calculated a horoscope for the laying of the foundation-stone—in fact for 23 October 1669. See E. Conder, "King Charles II at the Royal Exchange, London 1667" in *AQC* 11, 1898, pp. 138 ff.; and C. H. Josten (1966), III, p. 1112. For the Sheldonian theater (*Con-*

stitutions, p. 102), the craftsmen no doubt did celebrate the *Cape-stone*, as is still usual all over the world, but the "elegant Oration by Dr. South" is taken from Plot's *Oxfordshire*—see above, n. 149. As for the footstone of St. Paul's, Ashmole records it as having been done on 25 June 1675, "6H.30′ AM" perhaps again according to his horoscope. It was also witnessed by Anthony a Wood (1892), II, p. 317.

The last such event mentioned by Anderson is the raising of the ball and cross over St. Paul's in 1708; Wren's *Parentalia*, 1750, does not mention the foundation, except for the omen of a cornerstone being selected from the rubbish, and found to be part of a tombstone inscribed RESURGAM; but "The Highest or last Stone on the Top of the Lantern was laid by the Hands of the Surveyor's Son, *Christopher Wren*, deputed by his father, in the Presence of that excellent Artificer Mr. *Strong*, his Son, and other *Free and Accepted Masons*, chiefly Employed in the Execution of the Work." This was printed after the *Constitutions*, but apart from the turn of phrase, "Free and Accepted," the ceremonial would have been the normal one at the finishing of a building, with which every builder and contractor is familiar in a residual form.

250. The official version is given in the *Constitutions* (J. D. D. Anderson, 1738, pp. 109 f.). The four lodges were: (1.) Goose and Gridiron Ale-House in St. Paul's Churchyard; (2.) Crown Ale-House in Parker's Lane, near Drury Lane; (3.) Apple-Tree Tavern in Charles-Street, Covent Garden; (4.) Rummer and Grapes Tavern in Charles Row, Westminster. These survived in the Grand Lodge as nos. 1, 2 (old 4), 10 (old 3). The two Drury Lane lodges of 1738 (11, Castle Tavern, and 55, Horseshoe and Rummer) seem to have no connection with it. A list of the 20 lodges "working" in 1723 is given in J.D.D. Anderson, *Constitutions*, 1738, on pp. 81 f.; and of the 106 "working" in 1738 on pp. 184 ff. The Apple-Tree lodge was erased in 1736. Anthony Sayer had been a member of it. The events are discussed in some detail by A. F. Robbins (1909); and more recently by D. Knoop and G. P. Jones (1947), pp. 168 ff.

251. R. F. Gould (1951), pp. 200 f.; he petitioned on 21 November 1724, and 21 April 1730; and perhaps on 17 April 1741. What charges of "irregularity" Sayer had to answer on 28 August and 15 December 1730, we are not told (R. F. Gould, 1951, II, p. 221). He seems to have at that time been a member of Lodge No. 10, which had been No. 3, the Apple-Tree Tavern. His portrait was painted by Highmore and engraved in mezzotint.

252. On Payne, see R. F. Gould (1951), II, pp. 201 f.; and D. Knoop and G. P. Jones (1947), pp. 172 f. At his death (1757), he was chief secretary to the commissioners of taxes, which he had been since 1743. The regulations printed in the *Constitutions* (J. D. D. Anderson, 1738, pp. 152 ff.) are attributed to him.

253. It is dated from Westminster, 1728. For his very copious bibliography, see *D. N. B.*, s.v. Most is concerned with elementary scientific exposition, some with particular experiments. This is the only considerable verse composition. It appeared about a year after Newton's death.

The importance of Mariotte's attack on Newton is discussed in every biography of him. On Désaguliers' repetition of the experiment, see the classic account in J. Priestley (1773), I, pp. 350 ff.; most recently A. R. Hall, 1975, pp. 243 ff. Désaguliers was an extremely popular public lecturer. And although Newton did once rebuke him for neglecting his duties as demonstrator to the Royal Society, his reputation was such that when the Abbé

Nollet wanted to take on public lecturing on experimental physics, he came to London to observe Désaguliers' methods: see M.-R. Labriole, XXXV, pp. 439 f.

254. He was born in La Rochelle in 1685; matriculated at Oxford, B.A., and deacon, 1710; M.A. 1712, chaplain to Duke of Chandos, 1712, lectured before George I, 1717; D.C.L. 1718. A perceptive account of his early career is given by R. Priouret (1953), pp. 8 ff.

255. There is a curious masonic tradition, questioned by most masonic historians but symptomatic of a certain tendency in their thinking, that Anderson was made chaplain to the masons sometime after the retirement from that post of Dr. Henry Compton (bishop of London 1675–1713, with interruptions); an unlikely enough supposition. That at his prompting seven gentlemen, three of whom were Payne, Désaguliers and Sayer, were admitted in December 1714 and that some operatives found themselves turned from a lodge meeting at the Goose and Gridiron in September 1715, while the accepted masons were doing something to which they did not want the operatives to have access. It is, however, more usually thought that Désaguliers, at any rate, was a member of No. 4 at the Rummer and Grapes. The story, reported by C. E. Stratton in *The Freemason*, is quoted sceptically by E. L. Hawkins in his comments on A. F. Robbins (1910), pp. 31 f. Compton was bishop of London during the building of St. Paul's, Wren, *Parentalia*, 1750, p. 293.

256. See n. 80, this chapter. Masonic tradition has it that accepted masons tended to congregate in lodge no. 4.

257. See n. 244, this chapter.

258. This was not the society of monks of Medmenham Abbey which Francis Dashwood founded in 1755 or thereabouts, but an earlier society of rakes. See R. J. Allen (1933), pp. 119 ff.

259. His vigorous opposition to the South Sea Company, in which he nevertheless invested heavily with catastrophic loss to himself (£120,000). See J. H. Plumb (1956), I, pp. 297 ff., 370. For his vigorous defense of Francis Atterbury, bishop of Rochester, who had threatened on the death of Queen Anne to proclaim the Old Pretender king "in his lawn sleeves" (B. Williams, 1962, p. 150, and on the Attainder trial, B. Williams, 1962, pp. 183 f.). Wharton accompanied the expelled bishop to Dover on his way to exile (A. F. Robbins, 1909, p. 76). His debts were by then enormous, and his estates were sold; his collection of pictures went to Sir Robert Walpole. The same year he went to Vienna; he was made duke of Northumberland and knight of the Garter by the Old Pretender, whom he visited in Rome in 1726; but his behavior was apparently found unacceptable and he was ordered back to Spain where he saw some military service (for which he was outlawed as a traitor in Britain) where he died in a convent in 1732. His epitaph was provided by Pope (1760), III, pp. 213 ff.; lines 180–207.

260. The *Constitutions* by J. D. D. Anderson, which are the documentary source for these events say nothing about their political implications. Masonic historians tend to gloss over the political aspect of the dispute between the dukes of Wharton and Montague. So R. F. Gould (1951), II, pp. 189 f., 205 ff., III, p. 100. See, however, A. Mellor (1964), pp. 42 f., 106 ff.; and J. Baylot (1965), pp. 56 ff.

261. Although this is admitted by implication by R. F. Gould (1951), II, p. 219; see also P. Chevallier (1968), pp. 12 ff. Sir Hector MacLeane's 1735 proclamation (*Devoirs Enjoints aux Maçons Libres*) refers to the

"gouvernement de N.T.R.G.M. Philippe Duc de Wharton" since whose time "avoit . . . négligé l'exacte observance des réglemens de la maçonnerie" (P. Chevallier, 1964, p. 214). Wharton seems to have mended his ways during his Paris stay. Lord Sempill, the Old Pretender's agent in Paris, writes to Francis Atterbury in Montpellier about the "D. of Wharton whose extraordinary parts . . . his sobriety since he came to Paris, makes him such lustre, that if he kept company suitable to his genius and quality he would force admiration and respect from all the world." Allowing for partisan enthusiasm, this is a different account of him than is given by his English biographers. The letter is printed by P. Chevallier (1968), p. 13; its date is probably 14 January 1731.

262. Anderson, *Constitutions* (1738), p. 129. The Lodge was probably held on 14 May 1731. A circumstantial comment on this lodge is given by A. Mellor (1964), pp. 110 ff., who comments valuably on the part played by John Strickland, then bishop of Namur. Francis of Lorraine was then a young man; he was born in 1708, and was already engaged to the emperor's daughter, Maria Theresa. At the end of the war of Polish succession (1735) in one of the last great dynastic exchanges, he gave his hereditary duchy of Lorraine, which had been handed to the deposed king of Poland, Stanisław Leszczynski, for the reversion of the grand duchy of Tuscany, since Gian' Gastone de' Medici was childless, and sure to remain so. Gian' Gastone died in 1737; in spite of a flirtation with Charles III (of Naples and Spain), Francis succeeded to the duchy and was elected emperor on Charles VI's death in 1745. His constant interest in alchemy may well have been one of the factors in his seeking initiation.

But Désaguliers was active all over the country: in 1721, when called to Edinburgh by the Provost and magistrates to advise on the introduction of mains drainage, he used the opportunity to be admitted to St. Mary's Lodge, and associate it with the London Grand Lodge and its rituals. So D. M. Lyon (1873), pp. 151 ff. He was also a regular attender of the lodge at Bath, which he visited every year from 1714 to 1743. The lodge was influential since "Beau" Nash had been made a mason in 1724. A. F. Robbins (1909), pp. 17, 21.

263. Many clubs of the late seventeenth and early eighteenth centuries had something in common with masonic lodges. There were ceremonial (more or less) meals, initiations, exposures, the use of passwords, hymns, and so on. A specific and notorious one, the Calve's Head Club, met on January 30 to celebrate the execution of Charles I. It was an extreme Whig society, founded as a riposte to certain Anglican divines who composed and celebrated in secret the liturgy of the feast of the Martyr King on that day. They were lampooned by the virulent Tory satirist, Edward ("Ned") Ward (1703; many editions), see H. W. Troyer (1946), pp. 108 ff.; 265 f. Ward, strangely enough, did not seem to have directed attention to Freemasons, but his *History* (pp. 151, 241 ff.) provides an extraordinary view of augustan society, and culminates in an attack on the Kit-Cat and a rather more respectful one of the Beefsteak. For an account of London Clubs in general, see R. J. Allen (1933), who also discusses the Calve's Head (pp. 57 ff.) and Ward's (pp. 61, 99 f.). It is worth remembering that there were also Tory clubs (R. J. Allen, 1933, pp. 74 ff., 250 ff.) of which the most powerful was the Saturday Club (if it can be called a club in the more generalized sense) and the most influential on literature, the Scribblerius, of which Pope, Arbuthnot, Atterbury, Swift, Lord Oxford, as well as perhaps Addison seem to have been members.

264. J. D. Désaguliers was made an F.R.S. in 1714, the year after he came

to London. He may already have known Anderson then; he was a pallbearer at Anderson's funeral in 1739, and they seemed to have been in constant contact. See n. 249, this chapter.

265. Apart from the *Constitutions*, Anderson's major published work was *Royal Genealogies*, n.d. (*D.N.B.* gives it as 1732). This is a fabulist compilation of Johann Hübner's *Genealogische Tabellen*, Leipzig, 1725–1733. Anderson's literary achievements apart from that are discussed by A. F. Robbins, 1909.

Anderson's relationship to masonry (see n. 250, this chapter) before the formation of the grand lodge is obscure. His father, James Anderson of Aberdeen was a glazier and master of the Aberdeen lodge in 1688 and 1694 (R. F. Gould, 1951, III, pp. 209 ff.). Anderson *fils* became a licensed minister of the Church of Scotland after 1702; he came to London before 1710, when he is known to have moved his congregation to the Old French Chapel in Swallow Street. Its minister at that time was Dr. Désaguliers' father, John Theophilus.

266. See above, chapter 2, n. 76; G. Buchdahl (1961), pp. 11 ff.; and the more detailed M. H. Nicholson (1946).

The original passage on sound being the *simia lucis* in A. Kircher (1650), III, bk. IX. A bibliography of translations for Castel is given by E. von Erhardt-Siebold (1932), p. 579, n. 11. The echoes of the *Clavecin* may be heard in Scriabin's *Prometheus*, and in the ideas of the Suprematists and of Kandinsky, as well as in the Prokoviev-Eisenstein collaboration. But the extension of the idea to other senses—to touch, smell, and taste—had to wait until this century: until the Bauhaus smell-organ, and the Futurist banquets. See F. T. Marinetti e Fillia (1932), pp. 23 ff.; cf. L. Moholy-Nagy (1928), pp. 22 ff., and, in greater detail, A. Wellek in F. Blume (1949–1973), s.vv. *Farbenhören, Farbenmusik*.

267. William Whiston (1667–1752) is best remembered as the translator of Josephus. But he was a well-known mathematician and succeeded Newton as Lucasian professor in Cambridge. He was also a theological controversialist, and his profession of Socinian doctrines led to his exclusion from Cambridge and of course also from the chair. He caused much scandal by his preaching and founded a Socinian "Society for the Restoration of Primitive Christianity" with which Newton refused to associate. See F. E. Manuel (1974), pp. 31 f., 62 f. Whiston maintained that Newton had kept him out of the Royal Society for speaking his mind.

268. Although his criticism of Newton was public, he was elected a Fellow of the Royal Society as a mathematician. His criticism of Newton for the difficulty of Newtonian physical ideas is discussed by G. Bachelard (1969), pp. 226 ff. The *clavecin* seems never to have been consistently demonstrated, nor did Castel ever construct one to his entire satisfaction. A description, reprinted from the *Mémoires de Trevoux* of 1735, is in L.-B. Castel (1763), pp. 278 ff. Georg Philipp Telemann translated the description of the *clavecin* into German. For this, and many later references, see E. von Erhardt-Siebold (1932), pp. 577 ff., and A. Wellek in F. Blume (1949–1973), as in n. 266.

Castel was a great friend, it would seem, of Montesquieu; he certainly knew a number of the other Philosophes. Voltaire, having recommended the instrument in his *Elémens* (1819, XXVIII, pp. 185 ff.), took a more ambiguous attitude, perhaps because of the public dispute between Rameau and Castel, in which he took Rameau's side (1969, LXXXVIII, pp. 505 ff., LXXXIX, p. 121). His note to D'Alembert not to forget it in the Encyclopedia article "Clavecin" I take to be sarcastic, or half so. Diderot took it much more seriously in the "Letter on the Deaf-mutes" (1969, II, pp. 530 f.), where he imagined his deaf mute extrapolating from a performance on Castel's *clavecin* a whole language produced by musical instruments; it is characteristic that Francesco Algarotti imagined the *clavecin* being used to translate a tune by Caffariello into a dress fabric (1778, II, p. 255).

Although Castel had hoped to use a prism at first, he resorted to color areas and later to colored glass with a light behind it. Erasmus Darwin describes it with interest as demonstrating the Newtonian harmony (1789, II, pp. 127 ff.). An allusion to the idea is made by Locke, who reports that a man blinded by smallpox in infancy (probably the famous mathematician Nicolas Saunderson) understood what the color scarlet was by analogy to the sound of a trumpet (J. Locke, 1874, II, p. 38) though he did not mention his "subject's" name.

269. Shaftesbury (1732), I, p. 290: "The most ingenious way of becoming foolish is by a system and the surest method to prevent good sense is to set up something in the room of it." Cf. II, p. 191; III, p. 160.

270. F. Hutcheson (1725), p. 15. This is developed further in pp. 187 ff.; in the second edition of the book, the description of the computation is amplified by formulae. On the background of such a notion, both in neo-Cartesian thinking (Wolff, Weigel, even Leibniz) as well as in Hobbes' deductive reasoning, see L. I. Bredvold in R. F. Jones (1951), pp. 165 ff. A system of "hedonistic calculus" was derived from such notions; W. R. Scott (1900), pp. 106 ff.

271. In "Alciphron" (in *Works,* 1901, II, pp. 133 ff.). It is the third of four Dialogues and advances an extremely "rationalist" view of beauty: "a thing is perfect when it answers the end for which it was made." This rationalism is related by Berkeley to his relentless teleology. "For as much as without thought there can be no end or design, and without an end there can be no use; and without use, there is no aptitude or fitness of proportion, whence beauty springs" (G. Berkeley, 1901, p. 138). This teleological relativism was to become the basis of much later speculation and would inevitably lead to a relativism which was to be more radical than Perrault's form of associationism, since it denies altogether the existence of universal canons of beauty.

272. The emphasis on the intellectual nature of *percipi*: the implications of the idea that sight sensations are tactile is already stated in Berkeley's early book on the theory of vision. The full attack on Lockean ideas of sensation was mounted in the *Theory of Knowledge*, Berkeley's most important philosophical work, which abolished the distinction between primary and secondary qualities. On Berkeley as an apologist, see G. R. Cragg (1964), pp. 98 ff.

Although Berkeley was constantly returning to Newton's notions about color in his notebooks (G. Berkeley, 1964, I, pp. 21, 56, 62, 63), he did not discuss the specific problem of the harmony of the "noble senses." The parallel which interested him most closely was between sight and touch.

Since however he asserted that "the proper objects of vision constitute a universal language of the Author of Nature ("A New Theory of Vision," section 147 in G. Berkeley, 1964, I, p. 231), there would inevitably follow a rationalizing aesthetic. This Berkeley provided in *Alciphron or the Minute Philosopher* which first appeared in February 1732, having been written at Newport, R.I., where Berkeley had moved the site of his projected New World university—which was not to be. The book was very popular, caused some discussion at court, a testy reply from Lord Hervey (*Some Remarks on the Minute Philosopher*) as well as several others. On its reception, see R. Halsband, 1973, pp. 140 f. It was a two-pronged attack on deism (the Minute Philosophy, or Free-Thinking) in the form of a Platonic dialogue, whose villains were Alciphron, the deist; Bernard Mandeville, the Hobbesian cynic (as Lysicles); and Shaftesbury, the high-minded Neoplatonist, who thought virtue preferable to vice as a mere matter of taste (as Cratylus). The reasons for Berkeley's misrepresenting Shaftesbury's position are discussed in G. Berkeley (1964), III, pp. 11 ff. But it is in the third of these dialogues that Euphanor and Crito (who set out Berkeley's views) argue Alciphron into admitting that beauty is of sight, not of the other senses; that it consists in the pleasure taken in proportion and harmony, which however are "not, strictly speaking, perceived by the sense of sight, but only by reason through the means of sight." There follows a digression on architecture with a praise of the Greek orders, of the justness of *gonfiezza* or entasis, and the excellence of antique costume against modern "gothic" dress. All this is adduced to show the necessity of a principle of beauty which is dependent on an intelligent, intentional Providence (G. Berkeley, 1964, III, pp. 124 ff.).

273. For John Senex, see *D.N.B.*, s.v. He is remembered chiefly as being the bookseller-printer with whom Ephraim Chambers served his apprenticeship. See also R. F. Gould (1951), II, pp. 205 ff.

274. For the earlier literature, see R. Wittkower (1974), pp. 93 ff.

275. The difference between the editions (Rome, 1700; London, 1707) has not been specifically studied: though see Schlosser (1956), pp. 620, 626, 731; and Comolli (1791), III, pp. 172 ff., is benevolent. On the other hand, another Memmian, Milizia, condemns Pozzo severely (1781, II, pp. 275 f.). Most recently, see K. Traumann-Steinitz (1962), pp. 238 f.

276. Printed in Paris, 1709, by John James of Greenwich and London, 1712.

277. He was the son of Charles, second earl, who had sat as M.P. 1690–1694, voting with the Tories, though he turned against them in the Lords. He died, aged twenty-nine, in 1704; he was grandson of the first earl, who had sided with the king as earl of Cork and was granted the earldom of Burlington on the Restoration, but he took part in the all-party conspiracy to bring William and Mary over. He died in 1697. In October 1713, Andrew Carleton wrote of the third earl: "a good-natured pretty gentleman, but in Whig hands." *G.E.C.* s.v.

278. For Denham's Burlington House, see earlier in this chapter.

In 1715, Campbell published Denham's Burlington House without other comment (I, pls. 31, 32); in 1725 he gave the new facade, the plan of house and forecourt, the main gate (based on the York Watergate, which he also published in II, pl. 28, as by Inigo Jones; it is now more usually attributed to Sir Balthazar Gerbier, see J. Summerson, 1970, pp. 148 f.), and in the text (III, pp. 7 ff.) claimed the house and forecourt (except for the stable block: "built by another architect before I had the honour of being called to his Lordship's service"), although more recent opinion attributes the colonnade to Gibbs. See *Apollo of the Arts*, 1973, pp. 33 f. This colonnade was much admired by Burlington's contemporaries, who, like Horace Walpole, tended to think of it as the earl's own work. See R. Paulson (1971), I, pp. 119 ff.; and also B. Little (1955), p. 89.

But the gate and the wall through which it opened inspired a great deal of criticism; visually, the best known are Hogarth's "Man of Taste" and

"Masquerades and Operas." The literary material has been collected by B. Sprague-Allen (1937), I, pp. 105 ff.

279. B. Little (1955), pp. 17 ff.; T. F. Friedman (1971).

280. There is little doubt that Gibbs acted as an intermediary between members of the Old Pretender's court at Avignon and certain political figures in Britain. See B. Little (1955), pp. 28, 42 ff.

281. On St. Mary-le-Strand, see B. Little (1955), pp. 33 ff., and J. Burke (1978), pp. 75 f. Very considerable changes were made to the original scheme: the church was to be, according to the commissioners' program, isolated in the Strand with a 250-foot column in a piazza at the west end. It was "replaced" on the Hanoverian succession by the steeple; Gibbs published both his earlier, more ambitious scheme and the executed one in his *Book of Architecture*, 1728, pls. 16–23.

282. See K. Downes (1959); and H. E. Stutchbury (1967), pp. 22 f. Campbell is almost certainly that "countryman of mine" who, according to Gibbs, "misrepresented me as a Papist and a disaffected person, which I can assure you is entirely false and scandalous," as he wrote, not altogether candidly to Bishop Wake of Lincoln (later archbishop of Canterbury), a rather high-church prelate; who may also be remembered as Stukeley's patron in his quest for ordination.

283. Although Vanbrugh was appointed surveyor to the hospital in 1716, the work after 1705 when Wren gave up active interest was substantially Hawksmoor's. See K. Downes (1959), pp. 88 f.

284. J. Elmes (1852), pp. 394 ff.; and also most recently B. Little (1975), pp. 249 f. Pope's line "While Wren with sorrow to the grave descends" (*Dunciad*, bk. III, l. 329) may be taken to refer to this and to Wren's dismissal from the Office of Works. It is astonishing that Newton, at this point one of the commissioners for St. Paul's, did not exercise his influence in Wren's favor. Surprisingly little is known about this episode and who originated the idea. At any rate, in Colen Campbell's print (I, plates 3, 4) it is shown with the crowning statues and without the balustrades and described as "finish'd in 1710." George I's opinion in the matter is reported in a little-known episode of his meeting with Matteo Ripa, head of the Lazarist mission to China, who was returning to his native Italy with some Chinese converts; in 1724, he landed in London and was presented to George I, who asked him his opinion of St. Paul's. Ripa replied that apart from the colonnade, St. Paul's exterior was finer, but the interior very inferior.

"Upon this, the King, who had resided in Rome for some time, turned to some Lords of his court, and supposing that I did not understand, said in French "this is exactly the opinion of all foreigners upon the subject." It is not certain that he included himself in this qualification (M. Ripa, 1846, pp. 159 f.).

285. On Benson, see *D.N.B.*, s.v. More recently T. Webb in W. Benson, *Letters Concerning Poetical Translations*, 1739; reprint, 1973. His struggles with Vanbrugh are described by M. Bingham (1974), pp. 301 ff., 315 ff.

286. As Benson does not rate a mention in most histories of English literature, so Hewett is not dignified with an article in *D.N.B.*; see J. Summerson (1970), pp. 293, 298.

287. Vanbrugh's position was anomalous; he had been the recipient of Stuart royal patronage, even though a declared Whig, with notorious political alliances. See M. Bingham (1974), pp. 295 ff. He had been knighted by

George I on the accession (see earlier in this chapter) but passed over both the Garter Herald's office and the Office of Works; M. Bingham (1974), pp. 301, 296 ff.

288. The subscriptions for *Vitruvius Britannicus* had been collected by the end of March 1715. George I had landed at Dover in September 1714; so that although the collection of the subscriptions may have begun later, it is difficult to believe that the ninety plates of Campbell's first volume had been drawn and engraved between September and March. The work must have begun considerably earlier.

289. H. E. Stutchbury (1967), pp. 10 ff.; see also K. Downes (1959), p. 245. However, the Wilbury design has less merit than any of the designs—such as Amesbury—to which it is usually related and has a curiously Dutch flavor. As for the gardens at Herrenhausen, they were done many years before Benson's arrival there and are attributed to André Le Nôtre, though there is no documentary evidence to support this. See E. de Ganay (1962); except Queen Sophie Charlotte's letter to the Electress Sophia which assumes the electress' familiarity with the great gardener, p. 117.

290. *Vitruvius Britannicus*, I, plates 8, 9. "Done 1712," Campbell says in the text (p. 3). The comparison is evident if from no other circumstance than from its placing in the book.

291. On Wanstead, the three schemes and Campbell's work on it, see H. E. Stutchbury (1967), pp. 27 ff., 76 ff., 107 ff., and passim.

292. See n. 289.

293. Amesbury, a few miles from Wilbury, was built by Webb probably to a design of Inigo Jones. The house was pulled down in 1830. C. Campbell (1725), III, pl. 7.

294. C. Campbell (1725), III, pl. 5. Of the subscribers to volume I, there are a couple of foreign names; about fifteen for the second; about the same for the third; but the part *Vitruvius Britannicus* played in the building of the New Palace at Potsdam has already been told. Many foreign architects had a copy: C. da Seta in R. da Fusco (1973), p. 276.

295. Giacomo Leoni (1686–1746) was born in Venice, traveled to Germany about 1705, where he seems to have collaborated with Count Matteo Alberti on Bensberg Castle and received some appointment from the Elector Palatine. He seems to have been working in Germany with Nicolas Dubois about 1708, when he also wrote a short treatise on the orders which survives in ms. Another ms. of "Compendius Directions to Builders" was dedicated in 1713 to the Duke of Kent whose *bagno*, designed by Thomas Archer was being built at that time, and appeared in volume I of *Vitruvius Britannicus* (pls. 31, 33; Campbell gives the date of the design as 1709). At any rate, Leoni came to Britain before 1713, encouraged, R. Wittkower thinks, by G. A. Pellegrini (1974), pp. 79 ff. His very much modified, *barochetto* version of Palladio appeared in installments, 1716–1720. The first volume was dedicated to the king and carried an elaborate dedicatory composition by Sebastiano Ricci, the best-known Italian painter working in northern Europe at the time (on his visit to Britain, see most recently the catalog, A. Rizzi, 1975), whose nephew and collaborator Marco had worked in London with Pellegrini. Ricci was at that time working for Lord Burlington on the decoration of Burlington House; Burlington had a number of easel pictures by him.

296. R. Wittkower (1974), pp. 83 f. On the specific Ricci-Burlington relationship, see B. Nicolson (1963), pp. 121 ff. As the drawing or painting

which the engraving gave to Veronese, the contemporary and occasional collaborator of Palladio whom Ricci often copied or emulated, has not survived, it is not known whether its publication had the ancillary purpose of authenticating a fake.

297. Leoni had a relatively small practice. J. Summerson (1970), pp. 383 f.; R. Wittkower (1974), pp. 82 ff. The Palladio was reissued in English only in 1721, the year in which Leoni undertook Queensbury House in Burlington Gardens on the Burlington lands newly laid out by Campbell; it was published in French in The Hague in 1726 and in English again with some of Jones' annotations in 1742. Meanwhile a small edition of a rival version of the first of Palladio's four books was published, with his own designs by Campbell in 1728 (R. Wittkower, 1974, pp. 86 f.; H. E. Stutchbury, 1967, p. 71), to be soon copirated with Leoni's version.

298. Issued in 1738.

299. On Kent's stay in Rome, see M. Jourdain (1948), pp. 27 ff. Like several other artists, he was maintained by a group of gentlemen in Britain for whom he acted as a copyist, as well as a dealer in antiques and the fashionable art of the day. He was the pupil of Benedetto Luti (1666–1724), "banal et brillant dans tous les genres," who had been taught by Cirro Ferri but adopted Carlo Maratta's successful Bolognese manner. His studio teaching is discussed by *T.B.*, s.v.

Luti was also an avid collector of drawings; all 14,000 items were bought by Kent according to G. Bottari (1822, VI, p. 165), and a portrait he painted of Kent (cut down?) was left in Kent's will to Burlington.

Kent's chief patron, Massingberd, expected that he would turn out to be "a second Raphael" (letter to Kent of 9 July 1714, in M. Jourdain, 1948, p. 28). With this encouragement, Massingberd also announces the auspicious arrival of a neighbor, Lord Burlington: "you will I hope have his encouragement because he loves pictures mightily." Kent was much occupied at this time with Thomas Coke (later Earl of Leicester), who spent large sums of money through him. Kent, who seems to have met Burlington on this first trip, was in Rome from 1711–1712, until 1718. Burlington was now on his Palladian pilgrimage and on his way home. He arranged to meet Burlington in Paris, which he did in November 1719, and he was settled in Burlington House the next month (M. Jourdain, 1948, p. 36).

In his letters from Rome there is nothing about architecture. Even John Talman, with whom he seems to have been intimate (H. Honour, 1954) was "continually preaching to me yt I may be a great painter" (M. Jourdain, 1948, p. 29). He discusses architecture for the first time from Paris: "Since I have left Rome and Florence, I cannot beare to see anything except tow (*sic;* one of his usual misspellings) fine Pallaces of Vitruvio in Genoa that my Ld. carry'd me to see" (to Massingberd, 15 November 1719, in M. Jourdain, 1948, p. 36). There is no telling which of the great Genoese palaces these might be, nor why Kent thought they were "by Vitruvio."

300. A full-scale biography is promised by M. Wittkower. Material for it is used by R. Wittkower (1974), but see also *D.N.B.*, s.v.; E. Beresford-Chancellor (1909), pp. 217 ff.; and H. M. Colvin (1970), s.v.; also J. Lees-Milne (1962), pp. 103 ff. The Handel-Bononcini dispute and the troubles of the Royal Academy of Music (cf. R. Wittkower, 1974, pp. 179 f.) are one of the most extensively discussed episodes in British music, as its relation to the Academy of Ancient Music.

The final episodes of the operatic rivalries are described with his usual acidity by Lord Hervey: see Lord Ilchester (1950), pp. 17 ff. It was the occasion of Swift's epigram which has added an expression to the English language: "Strange! That all this difference should be 'Twixt tweedle-dum and tweedle-dee!" Swift (1757), VI, p. 131.

301. In the early operas and masquerades, or Burlington Gate of 1724 (R. Paulson, 1976, I, pp. 111 ff.) has Burlington House labeled "The Academy of Art"; of course, later in a swipe at both Burlington and Pope, Hogarth was to label it simply "Taste." On Shaftesbury's advocacy of an academy, see above, n. 211. Hogarth seemed implacably opposed to such an institution, as well as the proposed society for the promotion of arts and manufactures; his memorandum in a letter to an unknown recipient was published by J. Ireland (1798), see supplement, p. 85. T. Cook (n.d.), p. 327, already suggested that Hogarth was urged to produce the print by Sir James Thornhill.

302. Burlington hoped to be appointed master of the horse. He had been made a knight of the Garter in 1730. But Kent continued to rise in the Office of Works, and Burlington had the ear of the "patriots" and, of course, also of the Prince of Wales, their figurehead.

303. The sale of some of his Irish estates, reported both by Swift and by Lord Winchelsea, who writes of it: "besides his own debts . . . he has the incumbrance of a wife, my niece, the wickedest mischievous jade upon earth . . . imposing upon her husband and exposing him only to show her own power." Winchelsea's hard opinion of Lady B. does not seem to be shared by other witnesses.

304. In fact for a long time, much of Burlington's work was attributed to Kent alone. The dispute about the Kent-Burlington authorship was in some measure a dispute about the status of the theorist and the professional at the end of the nineteenth century. See R. Wittkower (1974), pp. 135 ff.

305. There was an episode, which M. Jourdain omits: he painted a ceiling for the church of San Giuliano dei Fiamminghi (Lindsay Stainton, 1974, nos. 40, 79). Kent also made much, as did his patrons, of a prize he was given by the Academy of St. Luke. Kent, as Walpole soberly reports, won the second prize in the second category (1828, IV, p. 224), while the first prize was won, in the same class, by another and quite different architect, Cosmas Damian Asam; Massingberd heard of the medal "which I think is ye second you have won" in a rather inflated form, though he adds, correctly and hopefully: "The French newspaper said it was a German yt won it." Cosmas was four years Kent's junior. They presumably met at the award ceremony. See U. Middledorf (1957).

306. Letter to his most enthusiastic early patron, Burrell Massingberd of 15 November 1719, from Paris, announcing his imminent return in Lord Burlington's train; in M. Jourdain (1948), p. 36.

307. The episode is recounted by R. Wittkower (1974), p. 117, mostly out of Vertue's notes. Also R. Paulson (1975), I, pp. 100 f., 157 ff. The plates, apart from the operas and masquerades, are a very shabby parody of Kent's admittedly very clumsy altarpiece for St. Clement Dane's (J. Ireland, 1798, supplement, p. 18; R. Paulson, I, pp. 158 f., 377) and finally, "The Man of Taste," of which more later. The quarrel is briefly told also by M. Jourdain (1948), p. 39, who shows Kent blocking Queen Caroline's patronage of Hogarth.

308. Kneller opened his academy in 1711 and ran it until 1717 (Lord Killanin, 1948, pp. 34, 46). Thornhill had been an officer of it from the beginning and became governor in 1716. In 1724 he reopened it in Covent Garden. The

dispute over the directorship with Laguerre is explained by R. Paulson (1971), I, pp. 92 f.

Kent joined the academy soon after its reopening so as to take his proper place in the London art world, still considering himself primarily as a painter.

309. The episode is told, briefly, by Walpole (1828, IV, pp. 35 f.) and in greater detail by R. Paulson (1975), II, pp. 130 ff.

310. George II's exclamation: "I hate all painting and poetry too! Neither the one nor the other ever did any good!" (reported by J. Ireland, apropos of Hogarth's *March to Finchley*, 1793, II, p. 132; also by T. Cook, n.d., p. 261) has no first-hand source, but seems appropriate to the king whom Thackeray (1873) summed up as one who "tainted a great society by bad example; who in youth, manhood, old age was gross, low and sensual" (p. 328).

Thackeray's picture of the four Georges was certainly harshly colored. But the first two, whatever their vices, were not extravagant patrons of any of the arts. In this Frederick, Prince of Wales, wanted to distinguish himself from both father and grandfather.

311. On Guelfi, see R. Gunnis (1951), s.v. He had come to England in 1715, a pupil of Camillo Rusconi, who had been the most admired Italian sculptor in a cold *barochetto* version of Bernini's style. Shaftesbury had fancied a Berninesque sculptor of the previous generation, Domenico Guidi, a near-contemporary of Rusconi's: see E. Wind (1938), though in the end decided against buying.

Guelfi also acted as a restorer of the Arundel marbles, which had passed to Lord Pomfret and which he, in turn, presented to the University of Oxford (now in the Ashmolean Museum).

The oddest incident is Guelfi's commission to do the heads of the four British worthies which were to decorate Queen Caroline's Hermitage in Richmond Park, only one of which, of Samuel Clarke the theologian and Latin translator of Newton's *Opticks*, was done by him. The others were to be of Newton, John Locke, and William Wollaston—an "intellectual" moralist like Clarke; Francis Bacon and Robert Boyle were added later; however, the commission then passed to Rysbrack. The details of this matter are obscure. Pope had a head of Newton by Guelfi (which may have been done for the queen, and rejected) and which was specifically bequeathed in his will. In 1734, Guelfi went back to Italy and settled in Bologna. It seems that Burlington was by then fully disillusioned with Guelfi.

312. The work on the Burlington estate is described by J. Summerson (1945), pp. 83 ff. See also, however, R. Wittkower (1974), p. 213, n. 36.

Leoni was commissioned by the Queensberrys in 1721 and, possibly forewarned by criticisms of his Palladio (see above), based his design on Inigo Jones' Lindsay House. For Colen Campbell's work, see H. E. Stutchbury (1967), pp. 67 f., 69 f. But in fact Burlington allowed Hawksmoor even to do a house for Lady Irwin in New Burlington Street (K. Downes, 1959, pp. 266, 284) of which nothing is known, unfortunately.

313. The first illustrations, according to Walpole (1828, IV, pp. 227 f.) were those to Gay's *Poems on Several Occasions* of 1720. Gay seems even to have admired them, and Kent also illustrated some of his *Fables*, 1727. Gay knew him well (they were both Burlington pensionaries) and was sufficiently beguiled to speak of Burlington contemplating Kent's painting (c. 1719) in the first flush of enthusiasm. But in fact the most popular illustrations were

done by Kent for James Thomson's *Seasons*. They were done for the quarto edition, while the contemporary octavo one had four allegorical "season" figures from Versailles, highly competently engraved by Picart's studio. They were never reprinted, while Kent's vapid Maratta-Albani confections became the dominant illustrations for half a century. The strange reason for their success, in the typifying of pervasive sentiment in wholly conventionalized imagery, is persuasively if specially pleaded by R. Cohen (1964), pp. 253, 259 ff. The *Faerie Queene* illustrations of 1751 will be considered later (see n. 333).

314. The whole story has been told several times. By Walpole (1828), IV, pp. 216 ff., who coined that mawkish phrase about Burlington: "Apollo of the arts, found a proper priest in the person of Mr Kent" (p. 223) and more recently by M. Jourdain (1948), pp. 32 ff.; J. Lees-Milne (1962), pp. 122 f.; and most learnedly by R. Wittkower (1974), pp. 115 ff. But in fact after Kensington Palace and Burlington House, major painting commissions were scarce. Already at Wanstead, as at Houghton (both by Colen Campbell), Kent was responsible as much for the plaster relief, some of it highly elaborate, as for the paintings. Horace Walpole maintains that his father "would not permit [Kent] . . . to work in colours, which would have been still more disgraced by the presence of so many capital pictures" (p. 225), although this is not altogether true.

315. The style of decoration was different from that of the architecture, and again from that of the decorative paintings; all were quite different from the gardening style. This scission of different genres is perhaps the most remarkable aspect of Kent's work. The plasterwork and furniture, usually fairly heavy, depends on engraved French and Dutch prototypes. The plasterwork is Italianate, of a baroque pseudoantique kind one might associate with some latter-day admirer of Pietro da Cortona; the painting, formed on Bolognese models ("Guido's softer grace . . .") is confused by the Venetian fashions prevalent in London. And the architecture takes its Palladio through Scamozzi, and through Inigo Jones and Webb. Within each style, the elements are never wholly amalgamated, and the trademark of Kent's plasterwork seems the putti which he could have brought entire (perhaps with other molds) from Rome (the "two boxes of wax boys") (M. Jourdain, 1948, p. 36), and which he used at Burlington House and Wanstead. Gothic and gardens are two separate stylistic problems.

316. Flitcroft (1697–1769) seems to have been a faithful member of the circle and to have prepared the drawings for the Kent-Burlington publications as well as for Burlington's architectural commissions. See H. M. Colvin (1978), s.v., and J. Summerson (1970), pp. 362, 367.

317. The villa, symmetrical about two axes, with a cylindrical hall crowned by a dome at the center, was very fascinating to both Palladian and neo-Palladian designers. In fact, while Campbell designed exactly that at Mereworth in 1722 (J. Summerson, 1970, pp. 329 ff.; H. Stutchbury, 1967, pp. 54 ff.), quoting the Villa Rotonda as his precedent (1725, III, p. 8), Burlington's Chiswick is much closer to Scamozzi's Villa Rocca Pisani at Lonigo, as has been pointed out by R. Wittkower (1974), pp. 120 ff., 166 f. J. Lees-Milne (1962), pp. 150 ff., points out that Burlington possessed a drawing by Scamozzi for the villa. For a discussion of the type in the context of the development of a specific British villa, see J. Summerson (1970), pp. 372 ff.

318. The "Palladian" window within an arch spanning its whole width was devised by Palladio in a number of designs; Burlington had several early

drawings with this feature (L. Puppi, 1973; figs. 288, 294, 295, 297) which Palladio uses with a deliberate reference back to Bramante in the Villa Poiana. The unhappy notion of using the "Palladian" window in the flanking pavilions—on the *piano nobile*—of an unotherwise uninflected facade, as he did at Burlington House he could, of course, have claimed on Jones' authority. But Jones did this only on the vast scale of his Westminster Palace project. Campbell did it again on the larger scale of his third Wanstead scheme, and more clumsily at Houghton. Vanbrugh, affected apparently by current fashion, did the same in his projected but unexecuted garden elevation for Grimsthorpe. Kent had learnt to modify this feature already in his treasury scheme of 1734, and even further, and most happily in the Horse Guards western facade of 1750. But the harm was done.

319. M. Jourdain (1948), pls. 8 f. R. Wittkower (1974), figs. 149, 150, 152. This use of rusticated walling was an element which was mediated by the Wren generation, although it is true that they never quite resorted to the unbroken horizontal rustication which Hawksmoor and Archer used to such effect and which was part of their French inheritance. The block-rustication window and door frames of Palazzo Thiene are imitated by Kent in the preliminary designs for the south front of Holkham (R. Wittkower, figs. 149, 150) and by Campbell at Houghton. See R. Wittkower (1974), pp. 167 ff.

320. See particularly how Burlington himself used the screen wall pierced by unmolded openings at Northwick Park, or Kent at Raynham Hall; Kent emulates Hawksmoor in the "archaic" garden buildings, such as the Rousham Praeneste or the Stowe Temple of British worthies.

321. W. Chambers, quoted in M. Jourdain (1948), p. 45.

322. In spite of his generalized disapproval of Kent, Chambers (1825) had kind words to say about the plan of Holkham: "The distribution deserves much commendation . . . both for state and convenience" (p. 391). It is with the greatest respect that I venture to disagree: the main entrance into the vast hall in the rusticated basement seems a piece of inept bathos rather than of mannered complexity. The hall itself is colonnaded and has a climax in the apse, which also, with a rather awkward theatricality, contains the staircase. This hall was, of course, to be the exhibition room of Thomas Coke's (later to take the title of the earl of Leicester) collection of Roman antiquities. The trouble with this elaboration of a basilican space is that within the columnar apse the visitor sees a small exedra, ineptly scooped out of the apse wall, and containing a large door, which in turn leads into the coved but undramatic salon, which is prefaced towards the garden by the main portico.

323. The grand manner of molding internal volume developed by Hawksmoor and Vanbrugh was not replaced by a new sensitiblity until the following generation, and exploited to the most by the Adam Brothers.

Kent, even at the small scale—such as the Finch house in Berkeley Square—never managed to coalesce classical quotation in volume, ornamental pattern, and planning commodity. His and Burlington's main virtue is their undeniable skill in operating the method of mean ratios, taken over bodily from Palladio and applied to the composition of exceedingly complex and varied facades of which Holkham is an excellent example.

324. As Shaftesbury had so emphatically said; see earlier in this chapter.

325. In fact most of the surviving drawings are in the hand of John Webb, though of course the Banqueting House in Whitehall remains as a memento

of it. See J. Summerson (1966), pp. 127 ff.; and J. Harris, S. Orgel, and R. Strong (1973), pp. 145 f.

326. In the Victoria and Albert Museum. M. Jourdain (1948), pp. 46 ff. and fig. 7.

327. See for instance J. Ralph (1784), pp. 88 f., 161 ff., who was obviously inspired in the right quarters both in his criticism of Hawksmoor and in his hints about the employment of "noble hands" (which everyone took to be Burlington's) for the design of parliament and the new royal palace. Ralph was born in the colony of Pennsylvania, and came to London with Franklin in 1724; his known venality (*D.N.B.*, s.v.) suggests that the tone of his book was directly "inspired." Ralph was later a spokesman for Frederick, Prince of Wales, and an intimate of Bubb Dodington, see G. B. Dodington (1965), passim.

328. There are a great many drawings in three groups; in the R.I.B.A. drawing collection, the Soane Museum, and the Victoria and Albert Museum. For an account and bibliography, see R.I.B.A. drawings G-K (1973), pp. 167 ff. All the drawings seem to have been done between 1733 and 1739. Nothing came of them. The work intended for Kent or rather, if James Ralph is to be believed, for Burlington was carried out as a fragment (the Law Courts towards St. Margaret's Lane) by John Vardy and Edward Course in 1753 for the Court of the King's Bench which had been accommodated in Kent's Gothic fittings in Westminster Hall.

329. It has been suggested that they were in fact designed by Burlington: see R. Wittkower (1974), pp. 126, 213, n. 49. See, however, M. Jourdain (1948), pp. 56 f.

330. M. Jourdain (1948), pl. 28; cf. p. 48. H. Walpole (1825, p. 227) is appropriately scathing, and refers to his style as Chinese rather than rococo Gothic. The scheme was published by J. Vardy (1744, pl. 48); showing the lower story only. On the identification of Chinese and Gothic about this time, see B. Sprague-Allen (1937), II, p. 81.

331. The inkstand (*standish*) was important enough to have been engraved by J. Vardy (1744, pl. 31). It was part of a larger scheme, conceived, it seems, by Queen Caroline as an exposition of her policy and its motivation. J. Colton (1976). Kent was, it appears, the executor of the Queen's program. See later in this chapter.

332. M. Jourdain (1948), p. 81.

333. Ten years before the screen at Gloucester was designed, Kent drew a very similar one in his illustrations to the *Faerie Queene* (M. Jourdain, 1948, fig. 13) where his understanding of this kind of composition is emphasized by the use of an Ionic order with a modillioned, coved molding for a frieze. Otherwise, the style of the two screens is fairly analogous. At Westminster and at Gloucester, Kent used the same "Gothic" order: octagonal columns, with capitals which look like a primitive Corinthian; though Kent could just have known about this order either from Lord Sandwich or from Richard Pococke, there were no published engravings as a source.

On the Gothic character of the "modern" epic and its illustrations, see R. Cohen (1964), pp. 74 f.

The relationship was recognized early: the poet Thomas Grey wrote that Kent introduced "a mix'd style which now goes by the name of Batty Langley manner" (1884, II, p. 253); the letter is about Kent's Chinese-Gothic house at Esher. K. Clark (1964), 241; M. Jourdain (1948), p. 78.

334. The several editions under both titles consist of the same set of plates:

sixteen of the five new orders, thirty-two of details and buildings; plus two measured and "geometrized" drawings of piers in Westminster Abbey (choir and nave) to show how the proportional system was formed. These (numbered "A" and "B") were placed either at the beginning or the end. The text, which was bound in some copies of the first edition, was not reprinted.

335. Put in place 1742 and removed in the early years of the nineteenth century with an organ screen designed by a "Rev. Dr Griffith"; see J. Britton, 1829, p. 60. Perhaps at the same time as the East wall was remodeled by Robert Smirke. Bishop Benson, who commissioned Kent, had been chaplain to the Prince of Wales.

T. Rickman (1835) records its destruction with evident satisfaction: "A modern organ screen has lately been erected in the room of one of barbarous composition erected in the last century" (p. 170).

336. On the duke of Montague, see n. 252, this chapter; the duke of Richmond, second of the fourth creation, was grand master of the masons in 1724. His father, according to a masonic tradition, recorded by J. Anderson (1738 only, p. 107) had been grand master in 1695—though he was almost certainly master of a lodge: see R. F. Gould (1951), II, pp. 120, 222.

337. As were his brother and his uncle. Horace's copy has, on the flyleaf, a drawing for the southeast corner of Strawberry Hill by John Shute of the Vyne. However, Walpole would use "Langley's Gothic" as a term of abuse: in a letter to Richard Bentley, another member of his "committee" dated 5 July 1755. H. Walpole (1937–), XXXV, pp. 233 f.

338. The Langleys themselves had done just that in *Ancient Masonry* and in the *Treasury* which is its reduction to a compendium. But there were many others.

339. Richard Bentley and John Shute of the Vyne have already been mentioned; on its activities, see W. S. Lewis (1969), pp. 55 ff., 102 ff. Walpole, Shute, and Bentley were the original members; for the others, see R. W. Ketton-Cremer (1964), pp. 140 ff.

340. He bought the house in which he had lived since 1747 in 1749. His decision to make it Gothic was gradual and is reflected in his letters. See W. S. Lewis (1969), pp. 102 ff.; and at greater length, R. W. Ketton-Cremer (1964), pp. 134 ff.

341. Horace Walpole to Horace Mann, 25 February 1750 (1937–), XX, p. 127. See J. Summerson (1970), p. 403.

342. The word was coined by Horace Walpole: W. S. Lewis (1969), p. 108. Beckford's dislike of Walpole extended to his works, and chiefly to Strawberry Hill. "The place was a miserable child's box—a species of Gothic mousetrap—a reflection of W's littleness" (L. Melville, 1910, p. 299).

343. On the difficulties of admission to Strawberry Hill, and Walpole's tickets and his guiding people round the house, see W. S. Lewis (1969), pp. 129 ff.

344. On the word and its etymology, see N. Pevsner and S. Lang in N. Pevsner (1968), pp. 102 ff.; also H. Honour (1961), pp. 145 ff. The word was coined by Sir William Temple in his essay on the gardens of Epicurus. The way in which he formed the word is obscure (W. S. Lewis, 1969, p. 102, suggests that it was hoax, improbably). There is very little doubt what the word meant to him, and what he thought of the idea in terms of modern gardening: "The Chinese scorn our way of planting,' he says, and adds

their greatest reach of imagination is employed in contriving
figures, where the beauty shall be great, and strike the eye but
without any order or disposition of parts that shall be commonly or easily observed: and though we have hardly notion
of this sort of beauty, yet they have a particular word to
express it, and where they find it hits their eye at first sight,
they say the *sharawaggi* is fine or is admirable . . . And
whoever observes the work on the best India gowns, or the
painting upon their best screens or purcellans will find their
beauty is all of this kind (that is) without order. But I should
hardly advise any of these attempts in the figure of gardens
among us; they are adventures of too hard achievement for
any common hands; and though there may be more honour if
they succeed well, yet there is more dishonour if they fail,
and it is twenty to one they will; whereas in regular figures, it
is hard to make any great and remarkable faults. (W. Temple,
1814, III, pp. 237 f.)

A brief account of Temple's attitude toward Epicurus is provided by S. H.
Monk in W. Temple (1963), pp. xix ff. It is true that the garden which he
most highly favored was at Lady Bedford's, Moor Park in Hertfordshire,
which was certainly regular. The house was rebuilt by the duke of Monmouth and again, much more thoroughly in the seventeen-twenties by
James Leoni (R. Blomfield (1897), II, pp. 287 f.), or more likely by James
Thornhill (J. Summerson, 1970, p. 322) as a great rectangular building with a
detached portico entrance, flanked by curved colonnades.

345. H. Wotton (1685), p. 64.

346. L. Pearsall-Smith (1966), I, p. 57.

347. W. Temple (1814), I, p. 14.

348. For the Porcelain Pavilion at Versailles, see chapter 3.

349. For the most extensive treatment of Huet, see L. Tolmer (1949). Huet
was an ardent apologist for the Ancient Theology. The author of an elegy on
tea (L. Tolmer, 1949, pp. 545 ff.), he had much more serious interests in
things Chinese, see D. P. Walker (1972), pp. 214 ff., 226 ff.; and J. Baltrusaitis (1967), pp. 217 ff. His exegetical method was tested on Oriental
matters, but on Chinese texts and rituals particularly. See A. Dupront
(1930), esp. pp. 262 ff. It was absolutely in keeping with his loyalties and
interests that he retired in his old age to the parisian Jesuit house, where he
died aged ninety-one in 1721 and to which he left his library.

On his garden, see E. de Ganay (MS), pp. 7 ff.

350. He interpreted this partiality in his entering wittily, but not altogether
aptly, into the battle between the moderns and the ancients on the ancient
side, unequivocally: for which Macaulay castigated him that "he made no
proficiency, either in the old philosophy which still lingered in the schools of
Cambridge or in the new philosophy of which Lord Bacon was the founder.
But to the end of his life, he continued to speak of the former with ignorant
admiration, and of the latter with equally ignorant contempt."

351. F. Bacon (1852), p. 165, and he goes on: "You may see as good sights,
many times, in Tarts"; cf. p. 168. This is not so much a foretaste of the
landscape as a continuation of medieval practice.

352. Bacon's attitude to the judicial use of torture is well documented. He
was prosecuting counsel in the Overbury Trials, and examined the wretched
Edward Peacham for libel on the king; see C. Williams (1951), pp. 233 ff.

On the analogy between torture and the experimental method, see P.
Rossi (1974).

353. Earl of Shaftesbury in *The Moralist, a Rhapsody*, 1732, II, pp. 393 f.

354. On the term *picturesque*, see C. Hussey (1927, 1967) who still provides the most comprehensive discussion of it. As applied to gardens, see N. Pevsner (1968), pp. 79 ff. On the picturesque and the landscape garden, see S. Lang (1974), pp. 3 ff.

355. The view of the garden framed by the window was rarely described in "picturesque" terms until the later eighteenth century. Nevertheless, too little has been made of the intermediate element between the painting and the picturesque garden which was provided by the painted perspective, of which more later (p. 71 and n. 2). The most recent discussion of this point is S. Lang's in N. Pevsner (1974), pp. 3 ff. However, B. Sprague-Allen (1937), II, pp. 147 f., 157 ff., is perhaps more equitable. See, too, C. Hussey (1927), pp. 46 ff.

356. *Sylva*, although only a small part of what Bacon considered natural history, reflects Bacon's *Sylva Sylvarum*. It was the first publication sponsored by the Royal Society.

357. See above, n. 73.

358. The term *improvement* was transformed by this development; while in the seventeenth and early eighteenth century, it referred to manuring and cultivating for profit, after the work of "Capability" Brown, it became almost exclusively associated with the visual "improvement" of landscape.

359. H. Walpole (1828), IV, pp. 256 f., speaks of Le Nôtre's London visit to "plant" Greenwich and St. James'. He has nothing to say about the Mollet brothers, André and Gabriel, whose father Claude had been Le Nôtre's master at the Tuileries. The two brothers were in Charles II's pay in 1661 and onwards. (E. de Ganay, 1962, pp. 104 ff.). A *commis* of Le Nôtre, Claude (?) Grillet seems to have done a great deal of important work in Britain, as at Chatsworth: see D. Green (1956), pp. 20, 36.

For Greenwich, however, Le Nôtre was definitely consulted. A drawing by him for the gardens (E. de Ganay, 1962, p. 137, pl. 156) exists—but this was before the establishment of the Hospital.

The two most important English gardeners of the next generation, George London and Henry Wise were so very much influenced by him that inevitably some of their work has gone under Le Nôtre's name.

360. The great botanist, John Tradescant, was the first keeper of the Botanical Garden which Lord Danby gave to Oxford University in 1633, and whose design, probably by Solomon de Caus, was often attributed to Inigo Jones.

On Tradescant's garden, although much is known about the plants which grew in it, little has been transmitted about the layout (see M. Allan, 1964, pp. 132 ff., 254 ff.). The house, known as the "Ark" in its time, was sold for building material in the eighteen-eighties when the site was "developed," together with the Tradescant tomb.

Bacon's *Essay on Gardens* is an eloquent statement, in the very tedium of the enumeration of the seasonal plants justified with the dictum "I do hold it, in the Royall Ordering of *Gardens*, there ought to be *Gardens*, for all the *Months* in the Year." (1852, p. 162.)

361. W. Temple (1814), III, pp. 232 ff. This was the garden of the famous Lucy, countess of Bedford; it was presumably much altered when the duke of Monmouth rebuilt the house, and again when Benjamin Styles had it reshaped radically after 1715 (above, n. 344). Temple called his own house in Surrey Moor Park after the original one in Hertfordshire; an anony-

mous drawing of this second garden is preserved at Moor Park; see J. D. Hunt and P. Willis (1975), fig. 52.

362. The novel was set in the vicinity of the medieval and now ruined d'Urfé castle (called *Les Cornes d'Urfé* by the local people) in the Auvergne, southeast of Vichy.

363. On Queen Christina's Academy, see G. Masson (1968), pp. 362 ff. She had, of course, planned other academies, the first one being the abortive one for which Descartes had drafted statutes shortly before his death. See M. von Platen (1966), pp. 376 ff. The academy had its headquarters at the Palazzo Riario (later Corsini) in Trastevere. Christina also adopted a group of young literati presided over by Vincenzo Leonio, who wished to simplify and purge Italian literary style. They met an unspecified number of times in the garden of Palazzo Riario before Christina's death in April 1689, and which they called the Bosco Parrhasio. There was no settled meeting place under later owners, but in 1726 the academy acquired a small villa near the Palazzo Riario (F. Fariello, 1967, pp. 126 f.) given them by King John V of Portugal. Their peregrinations and the state of the gardens in 1838 are given by A. Nibby (1841), pt. II, II, pp. 166 ff. For a recent bibliography of Arcadia, see E. Börsch-Supan (1967), p. 354, n. 323. Any literary history will discuss its influence on Italian literature and beyond.

364. Later, the same idea was exploited for an intellectual map, which was not a landscape but a battlefield. This engraved map of the battle between the ancients and the moderns is reproduced in most histories of French literature, but cf. chapter 2, n. 27.

365. For the early travel accounts, see G. F. Hudson (1931). They begin with Marco Polo's *Milione*. For more recent literature, see H. Honour (1961), p. 238.

Until Jean-Baptiste Du Halde published his general description of China in 1735, the most influential single book was probably Jan Nieuhoff's *Gezamtschap* of 1665 which appeared in English in 1669. But see other accounts of seventeenth-century literature before Nieuhoff's book in A. Reichwein (1923), pp. 23 ff.; and R. Dawson (1967), pp. 26 ff.

For the English edition, Nieuhoff's plates were reengraved by Hollar.

366. Besides the accounts of missionaries, authentic translations of Chinese religious texts began to appear in the seventeenth century, while the son-heir of the last Ming empress, born in 1648, was baptized as Constantine. This, before the settlement of the Manchu dynasty, marks the most extreme penetration of China by Christian missionaries. And although the Chinese court continued to protect missionaries, particularly the Jesuits, Clement XI's condemnation of their accommodating attitude to Chinese ritual and theology in the rescript of 1706 (which was confirmed by his Bull of 1715) made relations increasingly difficult; less importantly the Gallican Sorbonne had condemned propositions from French Jesuit missionaries' works in October 1700. Nevertheless, the first Latin version of Confucius by four Jesuits: Prosper Intercotta, Christian Herdtrich, François Rougement, and Philippe Couplet, which appeared in Paris in 1687, had an enormous success and influence and was already very well known throughout Europe by the time of the condemnation. In England, James II was interested enough to ask Bodley's librarian, the Persian scholar Thomas Hyde, whether the library had the Jesuits' version of Confucius on his visit to Oxford. The laconic and ambiguous conversation is reported by Anthony a Wood (in H. Honour, 1961, pp. 232 f.).

On the place of China in the Ancient Theology, see generally D. P. Walker (1974), pp. 194 ff. Though he has not enough to say about the most influential of them, Athanasius Kircher, whose achievement has not really been considered in detail.

367. Most importantly, Philippe Couplet, on the authority of Matteo Ricci in his preface to the Latin Confucius (D. P. Walker, 1972, pp. 200 f.).

It is perhaps hardly surprising that John Webb, Inigo Jones' kinsman and spiritual heir, should have devoted his latter years composing an essay proving that Chinese was the language of mankind before Noah's flood, and therefore before the confusion of Babel (1669). The argument was discussed by Ch'en Shou-yi (1935) who also considered Webb's sources. Robert Hook (1670) made light of Webb's argument in a paper to the Royal Society; nevertheless many members were interested in the possibility of a universal language (P. Rossi, 1960, pp. 208 ff.). Leibniz, too, thought Chinese characters (which Kircher assimilated to Egyptian hieroglyphics) were an ideal vehicle for the philosophic language, while he considered the trigrams of the I Ching as the monuments of a primal wisdom in the form of a system of binary numbers, on which he worked, by correspondence, with the Parisian Jesuit Joachim Bouvet; it was Bouvet who thought that Huet's interpretation based on the Mosaic times as datum did not go far enough, since he assimilated the mythical emperor Fo-Hi to Enoch. It could not have escaped the attention of later speculative writers that Fo-Hi (the Accomplished Sovereign) and his wife are represented by compass and square, so at any rate S'seu Ma Ts'ien (E. Chavannes, 1895–1905, I, pp. 3 ff.).

368. This interpretation of the term *imitatio ruris* (C. Plin. Sec. V, ep. 6) given by Burlington's protégé, Robert Castell (1728, pp. 116 f.) who calls it "a rough manner . . . whose beauty consists in a close imitation of nature; where tho' the parts are disposed with the greatest art, the irregularity is still preserved." He believed, further, that "by the accounts of the present manner of designing in China," they had either invented this manner or else reinvented it. A much later witness to this belief in B. Sprague-Allen (1937), II, p. 17. Castell may well, by then, not only have seen the current literature but had an opportunity to see Matteo Ripa's engravings, of which Burlington had bought a copy in 1724 and even spoken to their author, who had visited London in 1724. Castell sanctions the identification of antique and Chinese, therefore the artfully asymmetrical landscape design, if only as one of the several antique modes of gardening.

Burlington is said to have contributed handsomely to Castell's publication, but he nevertheless died young of smallpox contracted while in the Fleet prison for debt (H. M. Colvin, s.v.; J. T. Smith (1846), II, pp. 94, on his maltreatment there). This sanction was backed by the painters' showing ancient sites: Horace's Sabine farm, Cicero's Tusculum and perhaps most interesting, the source of the River Clitumnus near Spoleto, described by Pliny the Younger (Epist. VIII) and where the main temple had survived as a chapel. It had been drawn and measured by Palladio. In a publication devoted to it by Rodolfino Venuti (1753), the view is drawn by Richard Wilson and engraved by Giuseppe Vasi, while the measured drawing is provided by Paolo Posi, better known for his redesign of the Pantheon Attic and his Feste della Chinea (see chapter 9). The sacred and legendary histories of the Caracci, Domenichino, Claude, and Poussin—all of which more or less referred to the Campagna as their model, as well as Salvator Rosa's meditating philosophers may not have stimulated direct imitation but certainly sanctioned it. There had been an earlier visit: Philippe Couplet, the translator of Confucius, came to England with a Chinese convert, Michel Xin, who was painted by Godfrey Kneller in Chinese costume (Lord Killanin, 1948, p. 30; and H. Honour, 1961, pp. 58, 235).

369. On Kent's Gothic exercises, see H. Walpole (1828), IV, pp. 227 f.; and M. Jourdain (1948), pp. 48 ff., both rather damning. J. Summerson (1970), pp. 396 f., is more tolerant and judicious.

370. H. Walpole (1828, IV, pp. 262 f.) attributes it to Charles Bridgeman, of whom very little is known otherwise: see D. Green (1956), pp. 148 ff.; and N. Pevsner (1968), p. 94; on his portraits, see B. Sprague-Allen (1937), II, p. 139; and R. Paulson (1971), I, p. 519, n. 77.

However, the device appears in Dézallier d'Argenville's treatise (translated by John James, 1712, p. 77) as the *Ah, Ah*. His explanation tallies with that given by Walpole: Robert Walpole was a subscriber to the John James translation.

371. *The Spectator*, 414 (25 June 1712); J. Addison, 1721, III, p. 497. On the notion of landscape, see above. Much confusion is caused by looking back at late seventeenth- and early eighteenth-century layouts—or at any rate descriptions of them—and identifying the term *natural* with any irregular or asymmetrical arrangement. But later in the century, Joshua Reynolds warned students in his discourses that in so far as gardening is an art, it is so by deviating from nature. "For if true taste consists, as many hold, in banishing every appearance of Art . . . [the result] would then no longer be a garden." The most obtrusive asymmetrical device to appear in the early eighteenth century is the meandering path, intended like the false perspective, to extend the apparent size of the garden. It appears in all the garden books of the time: most conspicuously in Batty Langley's perhaps. It also appears in Robert Castell's restoration of Pliny the Younger's gardens, though not in Félibien (see above). Something of the kind had been laid out in the Bosquet de la Princesse at Marly before 1714; long before that, Le Nôtre had laid out in a formally confined space the extraordinary Bosquet des Sources, of which Perelle's engravings unfortunately give no adequate idea. See, however, E. de Ganay (1962), pp. 48 ff. The more notable examples were English. Beadslade's engraving of Hammels in Hertfordshire (of 1722) show one very clearly, as do the early plans of Chiswick. In a small way, that is exactly what Pope did in his Twickenham garden. Unfortunately most such arrangements did not survive the next shift of taste.

372. The dream of the emblematic garden, which was to have a most important influence on later thinking and which is the substance of No. 161 of *The Tatler* (18/20, IV, 1710; J. Addison, 1721, II, pp. 316 ff.) is induced by a reading of a Neoplatonic text, the Tables of Cebes, a favorite resource of allegorists and makers of emblems. The importance of the *Tatler* account, in which Addison relates his experience of the landscape to the moods incarnated in allegorical statues, has eluded many historians. See however R. Paulson (1971), pp. 15 f.; and J. Baltrušaitis (1957), pp. 97 ff. The tables of Cebes were later one of the disputed matters between Diderot and the Comte de Caylus. See J. Seznec (1957), p. 91.

373. H. Wotton (1685), p. 8.

374. Wotton (1685), p. 59, recommends, when discussing the placing of pictures in a house that "*Land-Skips* and *Boscage* and such *wild* works" be displayed on open terraces or in summer houses. He may already be referring to the use of false perspectives to increase the apparent size of the garden. Wotton makes a good prospect over the property from the house a "Royaltie of Sight." But it is not so much a view from the house which was

supplemented that way (though that was also dokne) as the closed corners of the garden.

Though the first perspectives were used to provide false "vedute" inside the house, as the Peruzzi perspectives in the Farnesina-Chigi. All this was an extension of the Albertian notion of the picture as a window on another world, via Bramante's three-dimensional use of perspective; which was taken up by Borromini at the Palazzo Spada and more ambitiously by Bernini in the Vatican Scala Regia.

But the painted perspective landscape, although it appears in such varied contexts as the Camera degli Sposi at Mantua and as the ceiling of Corregio's Camera di San Paolo in Parma has not survived either in theaters, where it is known to have been used, nor in gardens. But the interior perspective, from Egyptian relief to "romantic" wallpaper, has been discussed by E. Börsch-Supan (1967).

Inevitably, the garden perspectives were exposed and perishable. John Evelyn saw one in Richelieu's garden at Rueil, representing the Arch of Constantine "painted on a wall in oil, as large as the real one in Rome . . . The sky and hills which seem to be between the arches are so natural that swallows and other birds, thinking to fly through have dashed themselves against the wall" (27 February 1644). Evelyn saw another one at Liancourt (1 March 1644). Twenty years later (1 June 1664), he praised a similar device in Lincoln's Inn Fields. The terms in which he describes the Rueil perspectives—a convention derived from Pliny's account of Apelles—may have been suggested to Evelyn by a guide. It is important for the history of the notion since the device is the first to which the term *perspective* is applied in English. On the device and its implication, B. Sprague-Allen (1973), I, pp. 137 ff., is still best.

S. Lang dismisses the matter briefly (1974), pp. 23 f., but seems to underrate the essential role of the illusionistic perspective as the mediator between the gardens of landscape painting and the real planted ones. A century after its appearance in France, the painted *trompe-l'oeil* on the garden wall was still popular in Britain, as B. Sprague-Allen (1973) reports. In France it had reached a vast size, as in the Bâtiment de la Perspective, opposite the château entrance at Marly which provided a view of a colonnade with a garden beyond, some 13 x 20 meters, painted by J. Rousseau (1630–1691), a Protestant artist exiled after 1685; it was not renewed and the wall was pierced with windows to light up the new "café" installed by the king as a kind of club. J. Marie and A. Marie (1947), p. 12. In France the vogue passed earlier than in Britain, though rather schematic "perspective" trelisses contined to appear in pattern-books and in gardens.

B. Langley (1728) provides a series of patterns for such perspectives as well as advice about how they should be protected from the weather (pp. 195, 202 and pls. XIX ff.).

375. René Rapin (1932), p. 68. The model described by Milton in his account of Paradise was probably much more influential (Bk. IV, ll. 223 ff.).

376. T. Browne (1927), III, p. 199; Browne is quoting Hippocrates' *De Dieta*. Wotton did not like such dark devices, and suggested that they should be converted into *Crypteria*, or dark daytime observatories of the stars, such as Tycho Brahe had built (1685, p. 66).

377. See chapter 5.

378. For the grotto and nymphaeum in antiquity, see N. Neuerburg (1965).

379. The best discussion of the *style rustique* is still that of E. Kris (1926); he devotes as much space to the rustic of the German jewellers as to that of

the Italian and French gardeners, although his hero is Palissy, and his central concern the use of mineral and animal fragments in jewelry, in pottery and in the grotto. Kris insists on the context of Palissy's work in the ideology of the Pléiade, on his debt to Cardan's ideas on fossils and petrification, as well as his rediscovery in the eighteenth century. On the vexed issue of Bacon's debt to Palissy's inductive method, see P. Rossi (1974), pp. 13 f. The most splendid edition of Palissy's writings is still that issued by François Rouault in 1777. See the Diderot and d'Alembert *Encyclopédie*, s.v. *Chymie*. Marin Mersenne had already appreciated him as a surveyor, and an expert on sources on fountains (R. Lenoble, 1943, p. 498), but a more extended reading had to wait for Fontenelle and Réaumur.

The *fons* of *Boscharesca* literature was, of course, the Neapolitan poet Jacopo Sannazzaro, although its most popular showpiece was Tasso's Aminta. Tassoni had identified all pastoral poetry with the *boschareccio* (T. Tasso, 1655, p. xvii), a third genre, neither comic nor tragic. See also F. de Sanctis (1960), II, pp. 216 ff. Palissy's passion for white glazed faience, perhaps Chinese porcelain, his familiarity with the techniques of the della Robbias' and his obsessional curiosity about peasant earthenware technique seem to echo the concerns of pastoral poets almost too neatly.

The Roman Arcadia was, of course, called that after Sannazaro's poem: as Crescimbeni (1697) explicitly says, p. 97. And it had as its headquarters inevitably the wood and grotto mentioned earlier.

M. L. Gothein (1926), II, pp. 29 ff., had pointed out the limited nature of Palissy's achievement as a gardener: he relied, as did his contemporaries, on the medieval heritage for his principal effects. The new Franco-Italian garden was not really achieved until two generations later.

380. It was Pope who advised Lord Burlington to "Consult the Genius of the Place in all" (*Epistle to Burlington*, 1.57; A. Pope, 1760, III, p. 334, with Warburton's comment on the verse). But he developed his ideas on gardening early, in his contribution to the *Guardian* (IX, 29, 1713). Pope's allusions to his garden are too frequent for mention. From 1719 until his death, he went on working at the garden in Twickenham. Pope believed that "all gardening is landscape painting" so that for him the fusion of the two aspects of landscape had become complete (see J. Spence, 1820, p. 144). Kent had a sporadic, if rather unwilling involvement in the work there, the scale being very small but a drawing of his for Pope survives in the British Museum (M. Jourdain, 1948, pl. 4; cf. p. 41). On the literary echoes of Pope's garden, see J. D. Hunt and P. Willis (1975), pp. 247 ff. The grotto in his garden, in which he was drawn meditating (probably by Lady Burlington) was a Palissy-like object encrusted with geological specimens, on which Pope himself eloquently eulogized (1760, VI, pp. 77 f.).

The grottoes encrusted with shells and minerals ("Unpolish'd Gemms no Ray on Pride bestow/And latent Metals innocently glow," A. Pope (1760), VI, p. 77) became the basis for a systematic emblem-garden, square, and centered on a temple of happiness which Aaron Hill discussed with Lady Walpole in 1734. There were to be many statues and entrances but all leading through various grottoes to dead ends. Only the path between the statues of Reason and Innocence would, through the Grotto of Independence, lead to the cave of content from which you acceded to the Temple through a path tunneled under cornfields and canals (A. Hill, 1753, I, pp. 190 f., 199 ff.; a conjectural restoration of the garden, and the background in D. Watkin (1968), pp. 147 ff. The quarrel between Pope and Hill is set out in their correspondence (A. Pope, 1807, supplement, X, pp. 259 ff.) and summed up by I. D'Israeli (n.d.), pp. 290 f.

381. On Queen Caroline's works at Kensington Gardens and Hyde Park, see H. Walpole (1828), IV, pp. 270 f., 291. Cf. B. Sprague-Allen (1937), II, p. 135.

Kent's pavilions in the gardens were restored in 1977. See *Illustrated London News*. Walpole reported that Kent planted dead trees at Kensington to "give a greater air of truth to the scene." It was apropos Kensington, too, that Walpole quoted the dictum that "nature abhors a straight line" as Kent's "ruling principle."

382. Of 21 January 1659–1660. See T. Browne (1946), pp. 299 ff. Much of the material in the letter is reprinted in *Sylva*. Browne considered similar matters in his *Garden of Cyrus* and in two papers: *Plants in Scripture* and *Of Garlands* which were published in the posthumous *Miscellany of 1684*, 1927, III, pp. 218 ff.

383. There is no definite tradition of the master of the house as his own gardener either in France or in Italy.

384. In England, the mechanical tradition is reiterated on both sides of the politico/religious divide. Milton is a most eloquent witness to the blessed nature of Adam and Eve's "pleasant labours" in Paradise (Paradise Lost, bk. IV, ll. 622 ff.). "Gardens were before Gardiners," T. Browne, 1927, III, p. 148, concluded from the account of creation. This was a common opinion. Adam was given God's direct command to tend the garden He planted. Gardening was therefore the Adamite occupation *par excellence,* an idea which was to have many ramifications in the seventeenth century. That the improvement of agriculture to make the work of the farmer and gardener wholly pleasant would be a mark of the lifting of God's curse on Adam ("In the sweat of thy brow") seemed a promise of Instauration (C. Webster, 1975, pp. 325 f.). Hartlib was almost obsessively interested in husbandry, and much of the natural history of the Interregnum and the early times of the Royal Society was stimulated by him (C. Webster, 1975, pp. 426 ff.) as was John Evelyn's interest in arboriculture.

385. Letter dated 11 June 1709 in J. Vanbrugh (1928), IV, pp. 28 ff.; cf. J. D. Hunt and P. Willis, 1975, pp. 119 ff. Though it is interesting that neither at Stourhead nor for that matter at Castle Howard (if *Vitruvius Britannicus*, 1725, III, pls. 5 and 6, is to be believed) could the garden be truly seen from the house.

386. A specific instance of Hawksmoor-Vanbrugh at Castle Howard transformed into a Claude-like landscape is by Hendrik de Cort and still *in situ*. Cf. J. D. Hunt and P. Willis (1975), p. 229. There is, too, a description of the gardens in verse, probably by Lord Carlisle's daughter, Lady Irwin.

387. On the principles which ruled the construction of such a landscape, see R. Paulson (1971), pp. 19 ff. Unfortunately many of the gardens of this period were "improved" in the next generation, as Lancelot Brown did his master William Kent's at Stowe. Canaletto on his visits to England, which began in 1746, painted a number of pictures (Badminton is the most explicit) which show this development. It is remarkable that *vedutisti* could record the views from which the landscape gardens were designed as well as their derivatives in Britain.

388. Richard Wilson was in Italy from 1749–1750 until 1757. He had moved to London in 1748 to the house of Samuel Scott, Canaletto's most distinguished British disciple. But his style was formed in Rome on the basis of Claude and Dughet-Poussin as well as the Dutch masters whom he learned to love before he left for Italy, particularly Cuyp.

389. "Conceptual" participation, the laying-out of the garden with the aid of a manual, was the later landscape patrons' substitute for the active part which the seventeenth-century garden owners played. The early landscapers, such as Henry Hoare, operated without the benefit of manuals, of course. But the layout of a garden became the exemplary amateur skill, requiring none of the science Bacon had lavished on his essay.

390. The reaction in favor of untramelled nature was early: see J. Warton (1744) in *The Enthusiast* (cf. J. D. Hunt and P. Willis, 1975, pp. 240 ff.), anticipating later agitation. Warton collaborated with Chesterfield and Walpole in editing a periodical *The World*, for the bookseller Robert Dodsley which printed two attacks on landscape gardeners (nos. 6 and 15). Although these attacks still assumed that the landscape belonged to a gentleman, a minor poet, Robert Lloyd (best known as the editor of the *St. James Magazine*) satirized the whole repertory in his *Cit's Country Box* of 1757 (N. Lloyd, 1931, pp. 143 ff.) at another social level. There is no corresponding visual satire: though the gardens of the Hell Fire Club at Medmenham Abbey near High Wycombe (with its monuments to Potiphar's wife and the Ephesian widow (R. Paulson, 1971, II, p. 451, nos. 44 ff.) were presumably intended as a parody of the narrative landscape. They were done in 1751–1753. Hogarth, whom one might expect to provide some comment on the matter either way, says and draws nothing; his friend Henry Fielding has the odd approving comment (J. D. Hunt and P. Willis, 1975, pp. 260 f.). On the other hand. Francis Coventry, who wrote the squib against the Kentian gardeners in *The World* (no. 15) identified Hogarth with the landscape meanders: "I am told, in a piece every day expected, that the line of beauty is an S: I take this to be the unanimous opinion of all our professors of horticulture." Hogarth's *Analysis of Beauty* was published later in 1753, although a subscription had been advertised some eighteen months earlier.

391. Secretary Johnston's home, Orleans House, was redecorated by Gibbs; he added the octagon room to it in 1722, specially for the entertainment of the princess of Wales (i.e., Queen Caroline). See B. Little (1955), pp. 51, 98. Though the exterior is in the conventional form of the Office of Works taste, the interior plaster decorations are not far removed from Kent's work at Burlington House. Little record remains of the garden. Johnston was Gibbs' first important Whig client. He had been secretary of state for Scotland. The original house, by John James, was engraved by Colen Campbell (1715, I, pl. 77).

392. C. Campbell (1725), III, pl. 26. Campbell dates this rather wretched but wholly "Palladian" exercise to 1717. It appears in the background of Jonathan Richardson Sr portrait of Lord Burlington as a young man, now in the National Portrait Gallery.

393. The gardens seem to have been laid out 1725 onwards, the villa planned 1727, and built 1730–1732; M. Jourdain (1948), pp. 66 f.

394. The relation between Mrs. Howard, later countess of Suffolk, the king and queen, and her husband are too complex for this book, and have been amply commented on elsewhere. Swift wrote an extended and malicious dialogue between Richmond Hill and Marble Hill house, with the two houses as speakers. On Marble Hill house, see M. P. G. Draper (1970).

395. R. Morris (1728), plates after p. 84. John Gay, a confidant of Lady Suffolk (and author of the *Beggar's Opera*), saw a scheme—perhaps the drawing now at Wilton (M. P. G. Draper (1970), pl. 6) or in some form the scheme reproduced by C. Campbell (1725, III, pl. 93). The executed design seems a conflation of Morris' and Campbell's engravings. Campbell, who

signs his scheme *delt* seems not to have been the architect, though it is close enough to his style.

396. Robert Morris made much show of opposing anything Gothic (1728, pp. ix, xii, 29), though he is prepared to admire Wren's Gothic at St. Dunstans-in-the-East (1736–1759, pp. 48 ff.). Roger Morris, however, was prepared to build Gothic: Inveraray Castle, for the duke of Argyll (who as Lord Islay had been a trustee of Lady Suffolk) and for whom Colen Campbell seems to have designed a house (1715–1717, I, pls. 53 f.), probably on the site on which Morris-Herbert built Whitton park for him; the house was altered by Gibbs, then by Chambers, whose home it became. On the house, see J. Harris (1970), pl. 198.

397. They were almost exact contemporaries in Twickenham. The direct contact is provided by John Carwitham, who engraved both the frontispiece of Morris' *Defence* and a portrait of Batty Langley holding a garden plan dated 1741. What Secretary Johnston was to James, Thomas Vernon, M.P., was to Langley at this time. He was a connection of Chancellor Aislabee, a patron of Campbell's (H. E. Stutchbury, 1967, pp. 31, 49, 66 f.).

398. For a fragmentary bibliography, see E. Harris (1977).

399. Aliquot parts were the essential novelty in Perrault's treatment of the orders. The Langleys offer their simplification for the convenience and ease of mechanics rather than for Perrault's much more ambitious intention.

400. The first *rocaille* pattern-books appeared before the beginning of the eighteenth century. By the time the Langleys began publishing, French— and Italian—decorative engravings were in copious supply in Britain.

401. Even the grand lodge called itself the "Ancient and Honourable Fraternity of Free and Accepted Masons" (J. D. D. Anderson, 1738, title page; 1723 had a shorter formula). However there seemed to be lodges which called themselves *ancient* in contradistinction to those using the grand lodge ways of working which they called *modern* in contempt in 1739 if not earlier. See R. F. Gould (1951), III, pp. 4 f., quoting a 1784 edition of J. D. D. Anderson (1723 and 1738).

402. Batty Langley died on 3 March 1751, in Meards Court, Soho, his house, from which he and his brother ran their school. The first document of the ancients, their regulations, are dated from the Turk's Head Tavern in Greek Street, Soho, 17 June 1751 (see R. F. Gould, 1951, III, p. 6 ff.). Although it was the most notable of the masonic schisms, it was one of many. The breach was finally healed 25 November 1813. R. F. Gould (1951) IV, pp. 222 ff., lists the main masonic schisms and heresies. In his version of the *Constitutions* which the main animator of the ancients, Laurence Dermott called *Ahiman Rezon*, he mentions an "old custom that gave umbrage to the young architects, i.e. . . . the wearing of aprons which made the gentlemen look like so many mechanics," that may indicate one of the real motives of the schism.

403. Hogarth seems to have been violently opposed to Désaguliers' and Anderson's reforms of masonry and to have taken sides with Wharton's faction against them. At any rate, that seems to be the only interpretation which has been put on an important early print, *The Mystery of Masonry Brought to Light by the Gormagons* of 1724; which illustrates some rather curious newspaper reports of 1723–1724 discussed in R. F. Gould (1951), II, pp. 211, summing up his earlier writings on the matter. Hogarth, who is first recorded as a mason in 1725, seems familiar with the texts, and sets the scene in front of the Rummer and Grapes Tavern, the home of

Lodge No. 4, of which Anderson and Désaguliers were members. However, as neither Gould nor R. Paulson (1971, I, pp. 129 ff.) have a convincing interpretation of texts or of the print, it is not for me to go beyond their findings; yet Hogarth was involved in what seems increasingly to look like a schism from modern grand lodge masonry.

404. These paintings are enclosed in the most elaborate of Hogarth's *rocaille* decorations (R. Paulson, 1971, figs. 140 ff.). They were done in 1735/1736. Gibbs and Hogarth who remained governors for some years, and in charge of the decorations, were, of course, both masons; see R. Paulson, I, pp. 382 ff.

405. They were chiefly a defense of Nicholas Hawksmoor against the attack of Burlington's young American henchman, Ralph (see earlier in this chapter). Hawksmoor had eloquently but briefly defended himself against Ralph privately (e.g., to Lord Carlisle, see K. Downes, 1959, pp. 197, 214 f., 255). Interestingly enough, both Hawksmoor and Langley concentrate on a defense of Gothic, and both exclude Henry VII chapel, which John Evelyn had so despised, from their praise of Gothic. See A. Rowan (1975), and E. Harris (1977). Langley had also called one of his sons Hiram: three of the many others were called Euclid, Vitruvius, and Archimedes. A. Rowan (1975), pp. 199 f., proposes an explanation of the sequence.

406. This argument had already been promoted by the Jacobean Society of Antiquaries: John Selden, Henry Spellman, and Robert Cotton in particular. See R. F. Brinkley (1967), pp. 29 ff., 71 ff. But Kent had used Gothic in an analogous way; that may well have been the association of his Westminster Hall alteration (on the other hand they probably just "fitted in" stylistically), while there can be little doubt that the aggressively Gothic temple of Liberty was intended to enshrine these ideas. That is how it was read by visitors; see Gilbert West's *Stowe* in J. D. Hunt and P. Willis (1975), pp. 224 f.

407. Both authors were relatively young. Langley, whose first book it was, was thirty-two; Robert Morris, who speaks as a disciple of his kinsman Roger (b. 1695) was presumably much younger.

408. The idea was illustrated in the frontispiece. It had already been canvassed by other theorists, notably Fréart de Chambray (J. Evelyn, 1723, pp. 2 f.) and repeatedly taken up. Strangely enough, Batty Langley also makes it his own (*Complete Assistant*, p. 105), particularly in disparaging the Composite order. Nevertheless, he arranges the formulae and plates in the usual sequence (Tuscan-Composite).

409. Fountaine (R. Morris, 1728, pp. xii f.) is quoted with Herbert and Burlington as one of the "practitioners and preservers" of Ancient Architecture, "at so critical a juncture, when its Enemies are invading and undermining its beauties." That, at any rate is how the situation looked to Morris. Fountaine, as well as Herbert, are among the noble master-masons who received the dedication of Langley's *Ancient Masonry*. According to Stukeley (1882–1887, p. 64), he was present at the grand lodge which elected Montague grand master with Herbert and others. His house, Narford Hall (N. Pevsner, 1962, pp. 265) was "absolutely the prettiest trinket" Lord Hervey ever saw—so he wrote to the Prince of Wales in 1731 (Ilchester, 1950, p. 74) from Houghton, where he was staying with Sir Robert Walpole, adding "My Lord Burlington could not make a better ragoust [*sic*] of paintings, statues, gilding and virtu." The letter, which suggests the rivalry between Houghton and Raynham ("Kent, gilding and expense can add nothing to the house"), was the reason for the breach between Sir Robert Walpole

and Lord Townshend and is a fascinating reflection on the place of building in policy-making.

A rather different view of Narford Hall was taken by a better informed visitor, the earl of Oxford (though a very partial one). He was Gibbs' patron and called Colen Campbell "that ignorant rascall." He liked neither Raynham nor Houghton. Of Narford he had an opinion not unlike Hervey's: "A very pretty box," but full of unacceptable details and "all parts are most vilely finished by all workmen"; in J. Lees-Milne (1962), p. 211; cf. p. 129. Fountaine was ridiculed by Pope as Annius (after Annio of Viterbo, a fifteenth-century "emulator" of antique) in the *Dunciad* (bk. IV, ll. 347 ff.).

Herbert, probably with Fountaine's help, seems to have condensed Stukeley's ms. guide to the antiquities of Wilton House into a printed book. William Halfpenny dedicated *The Art of Sound Building* to him, but perhaps the most glorious claim Fountaine has on our attention is that he drew the illustrations for Swift's original *Battle of the Books*.

410. See n. 394 this chapter.

411. On Pembroke's and Morris' buildings, see J. Lees-Milne (1962), pp. 83 f.; Walpole quotes it as one instance of Pembroke's accomplishment (1828, IV, p. 216) with Marble Hill and the Water-House at Houghton. For Wimbledon House, see J. Lees-Milne (1962), pp. 93 ff., and Pembroke House, pp. 69 f.

Richmond Lodge was engraved in Wolfe and Gandon (1767, pls. 1–4; though at that time it had already been added to by Stephen Wright). Wimbledon Park is in Wolfe and Gandon (1771, pls. 20–22). Pembroke House by C. Campbell (III, 1725, pl. 3 or 48). Pembroke House is, in terms of authorship, the most puzzling. Campbell signs the engraving *Architectus*, which he usually reserved for his own designs. There is a variant drawing of the house at Wilton, without the attic story signed by Roger Morris. Unfortunately the house, built in 1724, was enlarged twenty years later and demolished in 1756. It stood round the corner from the Banqueting House (the site is now 7 Whitehall Gardens). The main difficulty is that the style of Pembroke and Morris owes more to Campbell than to anybody else. The problem is briefly stated by J. Lees-Milne (1962), p. 70.

412. The bridge was engraved by Wolfe and Gandon (1725–1771, plates 88, 49), but it was already widely known and copied (at Stowe and Prior Park, etc.) soon after being built. And it became well known outside Britain. It is not based on any known design of Palladio but has the Palladian combination of orders, rustication, coffering, and plain wall. It was very much part of a general refurbishing of the garden, sweeping away the one which Isaac de Caux had laid out, presumably with Inigo Jones' approval, and perhaps collaboration: J. Lees-Milne (1962), pp. 96 ff.

413. J. Lees-Milne (1962), p. 92; K. Downes (1959), pp. 206 ff., 282.

414. J. Lees-Milne (1962), pp. 81 ff., discusses the contractual and financial relation to Herbert. He also worked with Burlington at Kirby Hall, Ouseburn, Yorks (J. Lees-Milne, 1962, pp. 160 f.; the attribution was made by Wolfe and Gandon, 1771, V, pls. 70 f.). On his own, Morris built Brandenburgh House for Bubb Dodington, Combe Bank in Kent and Trafalgar House, then known as Standlynch, Wiltshire.

415. Except some drawings for Westminster Bridge (J. Lees-Milne, 1962, p. 86; at Wilton) and a rather patchy sketch for the waterhouse at Houghton, also at Wilton (M. P. G. Draper, 1970, pl. 9).

416. J. Lees-Milne (1962), p. 86. See M. S. Briggs (1927), pp. 302 ff. F. I.

Jenkins (1961), pp. 49 ff. It is quite clear that Burlington and Herbert operated, consciously or unconsciously, a separation between the man of taste, Shaftesbury's *Virtuoso* and the mechanical executor, whom they saw as an intimately dependent hand to their taste and mind. This is the main reason for the exclusion of Campbell and Gibbs, the ony two independent gentlemen-architects from the center of attention in Britain, as much as any political antipathy. After all, Campbell had an impeccable Whig connection, but he was an illegitimate kinsman of the Duke of Argyll. Argyll and his brother, Lord Islay, subscribed to two copies of each of Campbell's *Vitruvius*. Some fifteen more copies were subscribed by other clansmen. Campbell was a university graduate, too, and wholly unsuitable as a sort of mechanic's hand, a part which Flitcroft or Ware could assume and Kent and Morris took on themselves. Gibbs, too, was highly literate and familiar with the classics, having been given a proper scholastic training in Rome. His sympathies (and clients) were Tory, and he may well have continued all his life a Papist and Jacobite, though he certainly did his best to conceal these leanings in later years. He was patronized first by Burlington (perhaps on Argyll's recommendation) and dedicated his 1728 book of architecture to Argyll. On Gibbs as a messenger between the Pretender's Court and Argyll, see B. Little (1955), p. 43. On the Argyll's position in Scotland and their ambiguous opposition to the Jacobites, see most recently D. Daiches (1973), pp. 194 ff. Gibbs built Sudbrooke for Argyll at Richmond (B. Little, 1955, pp. 98 f.; J. Gibbs, 1728, pl. 40; J. Summerson, 1970, pp. 347 ff.). Whatever the hostility and opposition between Campbell and Gibbs, they were heirs of the position in society which the Office of Works architects had occupied in the preceding two generations, though they had been dispossessed from official patronage by the Burlington and Herbert placemen.

It is significant that at this very time, Lord Chesterfield warns his son against being too expert at architecture like Lord Burlington; and Vertue commends Lord Herbert whose familiarity with the rules of architecture has done almost too much honor to the art.

Although Colen Campbell received no official honors, all Gibbs could boast was a fellowship of the Royal Society, to which he was elected in 1729. In the next generation, Robert Taylor and William Chambers would both be knighted.

417. R. Morris (1759). He was called "surveyor" on the title page of the *Modern Builders' Assistant*, which he did with the Halfpenny brothers and Thomas Lightoler in 1747.

418. Certainly, the only probable source for the antiquarian fabulation about Semiramis and the two pillars which opens his brief history of architecture is Anderson's *Constitutions*, cf. (1723) pp. 8, 12, which he seems to conflate; since Anderson, following Josephus, *Antiquities*, I, ii, attributes the columns, which Morris says were built by Noah's sons, to Seth or Enoch, the sons of Adam. For Semiramis, Anderson, p. 20. This is not conclusive proof: as Anderson's *Constitutions*, it seems very much the same use of it in a quasi-technical publication as Batty Langley (1741) had made in his *Companion*.

419. J. Richardson and J. Richardson, 1728, III, pp. iii ff. Although Ten Kate quotes Rubens (letter to Francis Junius) and G. B. Armenini as epigraphs, the burden of his theory is derived from the preface to Bellori's lives of modern painters and architects, which he had read as an oration to the Academy of St. Luke in Rome in 1664. Bellori's *Vite (Lives)* had appeared in 1667 but had been reprinted in 1728 (1976, pp. 13 ff.), although,

of course, Bellori is much more allusive as well as literate than Ten Kate. Cf. his summary elogium of the Ideal in ancient architecture (1976, pp. 23 ff.) with Morris' dry recipe.

420. Morris' rules are derived from a conflation of Bellori's ideology, transmitted by Ten Kate, with Fréart de Chambray's equation of the three Greek orders with two extremes and their mean.

421. R. Morris (1759), pp. 67 ff.

422. R. Morris (1759), pp. 135 ff. The second part is dedicated to Roger Morris, whom he addresses as his master "both in theory and in practice."

423. The most notable use of the decorative shell was the vast velvet one which was the bedhead of the state bed at Houghton, M. Jourdain (1948), figs. 97, 144, but he used the shell a great deal in furniture. Most of his painted ceiling decoration consisted of *grottesche*.

424. Isaac Ware, the most solemn of Burlingtonians, though he provided patterns for *rocaille* ceilings at Chesterfield House at Lord Chesterfield's insistence, but justified them theoretically (1768, pp. 523 ff.) in a very prim fashion.

425. F. Hutcheson (1738), pp. 16 ff.; a brief distinction between the two beauties is drawn on p. 14.

426. Hutcheson (1738) insists, throughout his discussion of original/absolute beauty, on the importance of the subject: "for *Beauty* . . . properly denotes the *Perception* of some mind" (p. 14). Equally important to his argument is the notion of design as the overriding criterion for the judgment of relative/comparative beauty (1738, pp. 44 f.).

R. Morris (1728), pp. 69 f., admits the possibility of beautiful dissonance which Hutcheson (1738) also mooted (p. 28), and he also discusses the "mysterious effects of *Discord*."

Hutcheson derives his conceptual structure of intelligible beauty from Neoplatonic thinking—Plotinus particularly—through Shaftesbury. Like Shaftesbury, he assumes that beauty is the *alphabet of truth,* through which the Creator's law may be read by the humble spectator; but Hutcheson is concerned with the spectator—as against the maker, the artist—even more than his master, and takes Shaftesbury's platonism even nearer to a reductionist psychologism. He does, of course, come to terms with associationist psychology (pp. 72 ff.), but ultimately all differences between individual tastes are reconciled in the bounty of the Great Architect (p. 100).

The doctrine of purpose and proportion, reconciled by a *je ne sais quoi,* is stated most explicitly by Berkeley (1969, III, pp. 123 ff.) in his Platonic dialogue *Alciphron or the Minute Philosopher.* Although the idea of beauty and the discussion of architecture on which it centers are incidental to the main argument, Berkeley makes his Palladian allegiance very explicit.

427. F. Hutcheson (1738), pp. xiv ff.

428. See earlier in this chapter; F. Hutcheson (1738), pp. 3 f., 28 f.

429. R. Morris (1750), p. 49.

430. See R. Morris (1728), p. 70.

431. Unmentioned by name, that is. The plate opposite p. 68 resembles Vanbrugh's work at Grimsthorpe, or perhaps Hawksmoor's at Greenwich; the house which is being damned opposite p. 88 (R. Morris, 1728) has very Vanbrugh-like proportions. However in the *Defence*, 1728, p. 25, he suggests that there is a direct line of descent from Inigo Jones to Wren, whom he calls "that Great Genius" in the *Lectures* (1759, p. 46).

432. (1759), pp. 50 f.

433. Eastbury was published in *Vitruvius* (1715–1717, II, pls. 52 f., for the first scheme; the executed one in 1725–1771, III, pls. 15 ff.). It was commissioned by Bubb's cousin. Thomas Dodington, who died in 1720, and finished by George Bubb in great style. On the house and its building, see L. Whistler (1939), pp. 203 ff., 229 f. It was one of Vanbrugh's largest houses. The strange and brutal massing of the house, the vast Doric hexastyle with blocked columns and the arches of the attic story may have provided Ledoux with a model for the Maison du Directeur at the Salines de Chaux. Of its interiors, Horace Walpole provided the expected, scathing account.

434. Charles Churchill.

435. An account of the Albani-Dodington transactions is given by L. Lewis (1961), pp. 155 ff. Dodington bought the house in 1748 (it had a crossed, interesting history) and had it remodeled by Roger Morris, as well as called La Trappe. This affected name was presumably given in the spirit of Dashwood's Hell-Fire Club. Morris, however, does not figure among Dodington's familiars, while Jean-Jacques Servandoni was forever coming to dinner after their first meeting mentioned in the diary (22 May 1750). He designed not only the gallery with its splendid stone floors but also a number of ceilings. Dodington introduced his protégé to the Prince of Wales, for whom there seems to have been a Kew Garden layout, of which nothing is known. Dodington is now remembered mostly for the fact that his trousers tore loose of their supports as he bent to kiss the queen's hand. He was nevertheless a brilliant diplomat, whose negotiations in Madrid on behalf of the new dynasty were responsible for much of its stability. S. Harcourt-Smith (1943), pp. 115 ff. He may also, about 1734–1735, have organized the surveillance of the Stuart court in Rome, as well as made many antiquarian acquaintances. See L. Lewis (1961), pp. 94 ff.

436. The fireworks display was on 17 April 1749, though the peace had been signed in October-November 1748. Servandoni seems to have been called to England about the time of the peace, and the fireworks machine been built since his arrival. The actual occasion was a crossed one. There had been trouble with Handel about the scoring (the king wanted wind instruments only, Handel strings also). There was a great deal of rain on the day; some of the fireworks did not go off, and one wing of Servandoni's *macchina* caught fire, whereupon he threatened the pyrotechnician with his sword, and so on. Nevertheless, Servandoni collected enough commissions to stay in Britain for some two years after the fiasco.

437. It seems to have been physically as well as stylistically heavy. Horace Mann had the pavement made up, presumably from Servandoni's designs, in three-color marbles in Florence. It is hardly surprising that when Dodington told a visiting wit that people thought the gallery ought to be on the ground floor, the visitor told him it soon would be. See L. Lewis (1961), pp. 158 f. See also J. Walters (1972), p. 75, and S. F. Kimball (1943), who considered Servandoni's design conventional in England, but revolutionary in France.

438. By S. F. Kimball (1916), pp. 22 f., 34 f., 97. It is clear that his early compositional method, as exemplified by Monticello, owes everything to Morris' *Select Architecture*, of which he had a copy, and perhaps also to the *Lectures*, though his later buildings are also influenced by his extensive travel around the grand tour sites and his contact with Clérisseau, who had published the best documentation of the Maison Carrée of Nimes (see

chapter 8, n. 22), which was to be the model for the Richmond Capitol. Jefferson's precocious use of squared paper for his composition is an indication of his continued allegiance to this early technique. Cf. J. Summerson (1970), pp. 546 ff. Also F. D. Nichols (1960).

439. Until the nineteenth century, historians of architecture would not discriminate too carefully among the stages of postclassical architecture: witness Seroux d'Agincourt's very rough treatment of the subject (1811–1823, pls. 35 ff.). This book went through several editions in English, Italian, and French in the first half of the nineteenth century. The term *Romanesque* was coined by M. de Gerville in 1818.

In Britain, since James Bentham (1771), the architecture of the Saxons and Normans was treated as distinct from that of the "Goths," though it was foreshadowed in Thomas Warton's (1762) *Observations*. Their views were popularized in their essays, but the system propagated by Thomas Rickman (1819) was adopted in the English-speaking world. The background of this literature is discussed by E. J. Wilson in A. Pugin (1821), pp. xii ff.; and more extensively in C. Eastlake (1872). Rickman's work is discussed on pp. 124 ff.

7

Pleasure and Precision

The Benedictine congregation of St. Maur was founded in the 1620s. Its aim was yet another reform of the monastic life according to the rule of St. Benedict and a return to its original austerity. Early on the powerful Parisian royal abbey of St.-Germain-des-Prés joined them. A tradition of scholarship, patristic scholarship particularly, was established there. One of its monks, Jean Mabillon (1632–1707), produced a vast volume of publications. His masterpiece, *De Re Diplomatica*,[1] established the criteria by which medieval manuscripts, medieval charters, in particular, could be examined and the authentic distinguished from the fake—of whatever date. In the next generation another monk of the abbey, Bernard de Montfaucon (1653–1741), performed an equivalent service for Greek scholarship with his *Palaeographia Greca*.[2] But his major work—in bulk at least—was the set of ten folio volumes of the *Antiquité Expliquée et Représentée en Figures*.[3] This enormously popular collection was undertaken as a result of his earlier research on the editions of the Greek fathers of the church.[4]

The two monks had established the science of paleography, which involved the accurate, stylistic study of manuscripts. They systematized methods of discerning different styles of handwriting as closely as literary style had been judged. The writing materials, the illuminations, all were to be taken into consideration. The book was to be considered not only as a vehicle for the words but almost as a stylistic ensemble.

Montfaucon's book achieved more than this. Starting with the need to provide adequate background information for the writings of the early eastern theologians, he edited a vast pictorial encyclopedia which was to become a source book not only for scholars but also for many artists. It was arranged, like many earlier compendia, not mechanically (alphabetically for instance) but conceptually. The religious systems of the ancients were considered first. The first volume was devoted to gods of the first, second, and third class—according to the order of time; then come heroes, the religious customs among the Greeks and Romans (though by then it was necessary to include material on the Egyptians, the "Chaldeans," Phoenicians, the Germans and Gauls—and the Chinese), domestic custom, funerary rites, and so on. Each volume is illustrated with hundreds of engravings which Montfaucon collected over more than twenty years (1693–1716)—as he himself observes.

In the course of his labors, Montfaucon attempted to do for all antiquities what he had done for Greek manuscripts and inscriptions: to assess their authenticity, to appeal to the most reliable witnesses, to examine all the evidence. Naturally he worked with fallible documents. To take a relevant instance: the plate in which he showed temples dedicated to the Olympian pair, Jupiter and Juno,[5] has at the center engraved a fragment from the ancient marble map of Rome, which was displayed, during the imperial period, in the

Forum of the Temple of Peace. Several fragments of this map, the *Forma Urbis Romae*, were found in the sixteenth century, and with time excavators added several others. Montfaucon had taken his engraving from Giovanni Pietro Bellori's[6] first publication of the *Forma*; on the same plate he shows a building of a curious Poussinesque-baroque style, a reconstruction taken from a recent guide to Orvieto.[7] There is also an image on a coin. The next plate but one[8] illustrates temples dedicated to other gods, including Minerva. Here Montfaucon relies almost entirely on coins, eleven of them. Number twelve, the only other figure, is a curious stilted perspective of the Parthenon, labeled Spon (Montfaucon always quotes his sources conscientiously).

Jacob Spon, mentioned previously as the author of the little book on the *Usage du Caphé, du Thé, et du Chocolat*,[9] was a Lyons physician of German, Protestant origin, a third generation settler, and had taken his medical doctorate at the Sorbonne in 1667. Like his father, he was a scientist and a polymath, chiefly a theologian and a classical scholar. In 1674 he set out to accompany one of his mentors, the antiquarian Vaillant, on an Adriatic trip. Fortunately for Spon, they were separated; threatened by Barbary corsairs, Vaillant had to swallow the medals he had bought in Provence (which he could recover only after taking a violent purge!), but Spon went on to Rome, where, the following year, he met a *gentilhomme*

The Parthenon, on the Athens Acropolis, as seen by J. Spon.

Bernard de Montfaucon's version of Spon's Parthenon, and numismatic evidence about the appearance of various antique temples.

anglais, George Wheler or Wheeler.[10] They traveled around Greece, collected, measured, noted. Spon's main interest was in medals and inscriptions ("c'est mon feu, c'est ma passion, les inscriptions antiques"),[11] but he also observed and even measured some of the architectural monuments. Wheeler was primarily a botanist and a natural historian. They had therefore their binding interests in natural science and in antiquity as well as their common religious beliefs (both were ardent Protestants, but with a sacramental bias). They were much impressed by the Orthodox patriarch,[12] on whom they called, and with several Greek prelates.

On their separate returns, Spon published first, in Lyons, an account of Athens by a Jesuit missionary.[13] The frontispiece of that

J. Babin's view of the Acropolis (Citadelle) *and the Parthenon* (La Grande Mosquée) *seen from the Olympeion* (Restes du Palais d'Hadrian).

little book, which concentrates on contemporary affairs viewed with a jaundiced eye, shows the city dominated by the Acropolis (Citadella). The great building in the middle, the Parthenon, with its minaret, is not only labeled *La Grande Mosquée* but is shown as an arcaded building. Four years later, Spon published his three-volume account of his own and Wheeler's journey,[14] illustrated with a number of engravings. Among them, in Volume 2, was the picture of the Parthenon, which Montfaucon had reproduced. It was not very accurate. Blurred, it showed the columns coarsely, with an enormous intercolumniation at the center and a squiggle in the exaggerated pediment. This very rough representation became the model which not only Montfaucon but the much more exacting Fischer von Erlach copied;[15] it remained the accepted picture of the most famous Doric temple until the publication of Julien-David Le Roy's *Ruines des Plus Beaux Monuments de la Grèce* in 1758.[16]

On reading Spon's book—and learning that it was to be translated into English, George Wheeler published his own account in two volumes,[17] supplementing Spon's with his botanical notes and with material he had collected after they separated. The two books were both translated and became the best-known guides to Greece for a long time. Wheeler, who was knighted by Charles II and then took orders, continued to write. The only other book which interests us immediately is *An Account of the Churches and Places of Assembly of the Primitive Christians . . . Described by Eusebius and Ocular Observation of Several Very Ancient Edifices of Churches Yet Extant in Those Parts, with a Seasonable Application.*[18] This *Account*

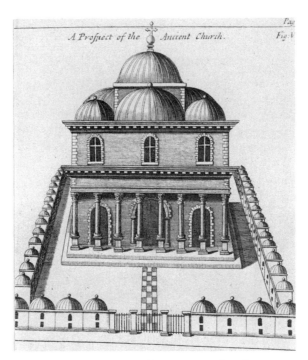

George Wheeler's view of a primitive church.

"reads" the texts of Eusebius, of Zonaras, and of several church fathers into a modern Orthodox church, which Wheeler proposes as a remedy for schism and dissent, naively perhaps but with the greatest irenic goodwill. In this little book, he is all the "formal and particular" man whom Evelyn knew, who would not see why Quakers would not submit to his ministrations in a primitively ordered church which could so easily be adapted to the ways of the Church of England.[19] The apparent primitivism of Eastern Christianity was to exercise a permanent fascination on Western churchmen: the very use of the Greek language, the language of the New Testament, was a direct link to the primitive gospel and to a sacred antiquity which obsessed ecclesiastics as well as church builders in the seventeenth and eighteenth centuries without respecting distinction of nationality or denomination. It was, moreover, a link to a remoter, sacred antiquity, whose documents were almost all known in their Greek form, and in which Plato and Zoroaster could figure as foreshadows of Christ.[20]

Accounts of the Orthodox church and of its ceremonies in the later seventeenth century were much more accurate than those of classical antiquities. And there, too, the philologists were much more precise and exacting than the antiquarians. In view of all this research, it is really extraordinary that such a rough representation of the Parthenon as Spon's could pass muster in the first half of the eighteenth century. There is the excuse, of course, that genuine Greek architecture was somewhat inaccessible physically. In the

Middle Ages, when Athens was the fief of various "Frankish" monarchs and of Venice, the ancient buildings were not much regarded. When the last Christian duke, Francesco Acciajoli, surrendered to the army of Mehmet II in 1456, the city became a fief of the Black Eunuch of the Porte's harem. The Parthenon, which had been the church of the Holy Wisdom since the time of Justinian, was transformed into a mosque in 1459, and the Propylaea housed a powder magazine.[21] The Eastern emperors, who admired the antiquities of Athens, had removed many of them nearer home, to Constantinople.

During the Middle Ages descriptions of Athens were made, but no contemporary visual record exists. It was only in the sixteenth century that Giuliano da Sangallo records in his sketchbook a rather curious blocked building with a straight roofline surrounded by a Doric cornice and prefaced by an octastyle Ionic colonnade which he describes as a temple of Apollo, the drawing for which had been given him by a Greek of Ancona.[22] It is now assumed that the "Greek" was the antiquarian and merchant, Ciriaco d'Ancona, who had indeed kept a notebook of the ancient buildings he had seen in Greece, but these were only fragmentarily published.[23] Ciriaco's

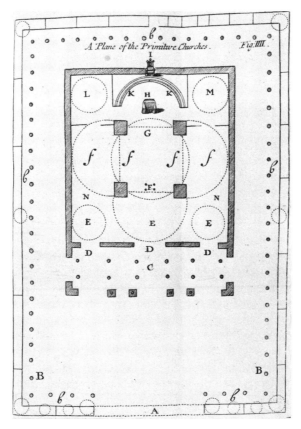

Plan of preceding illustration.

The bombing of the Athens Acropolis in 1687. After F. Fanelli, Athene Attica.

records of inscriptions, however, appeared twice, in the seventeenth and in the eighteenth centuries.[24]

Notice of the antiquities of Athens appeared occasionally in literature, particularly in learned correspondence. This was mostly approximate, sometimes very ill-informed, or even completely invented. Spon himself attacks several such publications.[25] But representations of Athens in Western painting were common enough. Not only in scenes from Greek history and legend but also in illustrations of the Acts of the Apostles (St. Paul preaching on the Areopagus) or in pictures of the legend of St. Denys, his disciple, and the first—if legendary—bishop of Athens. But these scenes, even when handled by a scholar-artist like Poussin, were always given a "classical" background, and that always meant a Roman one.

The problem is more radical, however: Greece and Asia Minor were in the hands of the Moslems, and the way there obstructed by corsairs. But what about Magna Graecia, which, since the early Middle Ages, had become coextensive, on and off, with the Two Sicilies? There were Doric temples at Paestum, a mere seven posts from Naples, better preserved[26] than any considerable ruin in Athens. And yet, until the middle of the eighteenth century, hardly a word is heard about them. The roads, it is true—though posted— were very bad. For another hundred years or more, brigandage was to be common on the Lucanian coast;[27] the voyage by sea was

Jacques Carré, The Marquis de Nointel visits Athens. *Foto Electa.*

awkward, since the winds were often unpropitious. Paestum-Posidonia had been abandoned as a result of malaria and of Saracen incursions. The great Doric temples, though overgrown, were—so eighteenth-century travelers maintained—a sailor's landmark. What had hidden this great complex of Doric temples were "the shadows of the age of ignorance,"[28] although Robert Guiscard used Paestan columns in the building of his cathedral at Salerno.

It is not clear who "rediscovered" the temples. Local historians did occasionally refer to them: but most travelers and geographers describe them as deserted. The first "scientific" description of them was given by Baron Giuseppe Antonini in his account of Lucania, however inaccurately.[29] Soon after this, Count Gazzola, a Neapolitan amateur, had measured drawings made of the main ruins which he showed to Nicolas Cochin and Germain Soufflot (Marigny's companions) when they visited Naples.[30] After 1750 the trip to Paestum became obligatory, in spite of the difficulties. The Greek temples of Sicily emerged somewhat later.

The first book to give some information about them in graphic form, however inaccurate, was a book about the *Antichità Siciliane* by another Jesuit, Paolo Pancrazi, which appeared in 1751, only two volumes of a much longer planned work. Pancrazi's book became—*faute de mieux*—a standard work of reference. As late as 1766, Winckelmann could still maintain that nothing of Greek building was left in Sicily except for the temples of Akargas, then called Girgenti.[31] Johann Joachim Winckelmann was the founder of modern art history as well as of scientific archeology. His hold over antiquarian scholarship, as well as his authority over the new, the "true" revived antique style, was unrivaled. And when he reached the apogee of his career as papal antiquary, he could pronounce with all the weight associated with his employer.

William Sandby, Paestum, *watercolor. London, Tate Gallery.*

The ruins of Syracuse were left unvisited. And yet the remains of the temple of Athena, whose doors, covered with gold and ivory, had been coveted by Verres and celebrated by Cicero,[32] were incorporated into the fabric of the cathedral. Twenty-four columns, as well as the wall of the cella, were presumably exposed by the earthquakes of 1542 and 1693. (The Norman facade of the building fell in the second of the earthquakes and was rebuilt between 1728 and 1754 in a romanizing baroque manner, perhaps by Andrea Palma, of whom little is known.[33]) Yet the columns at Syracuse, like those at Segesta, remained unreported by architectural historians and antiquarians until the early nineteenth century.

There were many reasons for this: banditry, appalling roads (the road journey from Trapani to Messina—some 300 miles—was said to take as much as three weeks about 1730). But there is also the relative lack of curiosity of the antiquarians to consider. Even Winckelmann only managed to deal with the ancient Greek buildings gradually and in a fragmentary manner. Writing about Paestum in his great history of ancient art, Winckelmann sets its monuments beside the temples of Agrigentum and the Roman Pantheon as the best preserved ancient buildings, although he considers the Paestum buildings—rightly—to be the oldest.[34]

Winckelmann thought the temples were Greek; not all antiquarians agreed. Father Paoli, who had published (anonymously) a work on the ruins of Paestum in 1784, maintained that these buildings were too squat to have been the work of the "ingenious

Side wall of Syracuse Cathedral, incorporating the Doric columns in the church wall.

Greeks'' and that their columns were also squatter than the canon set down by Vitruvius allowed.[35] But since the publication of Le Roy's bulky folio on the antiquities of Greece in 1754, any attempt to disqualify the Greek provenance of the southern Italian buildings had also to take account of the more archaic Greek temples, particularly the ones in Corinth.[36]

These Greek buildings, Paoli maintained, must be "Oriental," that is, Etruscan, and quite alien to the cultured and ingenious ways of the Greeks. The temple at Corinth, and the Theseum, which Le Roy had measured and described as having "offensively" squat proportions, Paoli maintained had to be considered as late imitations, deliberately archaizing of Etruscan work, and not authentic Greek examples.

But by the time this correspondence took place, Le Roy's was not the only book which had published measured drawings of the Greek monuments. James Stuart and Nicholas Revett had been in Athens from 1751 to 1755 (as many years as Le Roy had been months, Winckelmann observed), financed by a club of British admirers of the antique, the Society of Dilettanti. They met in Rome, where Revett had been living since 1742 and had been the pupil of Marco

Benefial, a minor follower of the Bolognese School.[37] Malicious people even suggested that Le Roy's visit to Greece was prompted by his being shown the subscription sheets of the Society of Dilettanti for the forthcoming project. At any rate, it seems to have been his express purpose to get in first and in that he succeeded. His book appeared in 1754,[38] while Stuart and Revett were still struggling with climate, disturbances, and Turkish officialdom.

Stuart and Revett worked slowly on their return, and their first volume, which appeared in 1762, contained only minor buildings— the Propylaea, the Tower of the Winds, and so on; the main buildings of the Acropolis were published in the second volume, in 1788–1789, by which time Winckelmann had already died and the neo-Greek movement was in full swing.[39] Stuart and Revett's third volume appeared in 1794; the fourth and last had to wait until 1814.[40] In the meanwhile, the Society of Dilettanti sponsored a companion venture, the Antiquities of Ionia, compiled by Revett without Stuart, but helped by Dr. Chandler, a classical scholar, and the painter William Pars, who also worked on the latter parts of the *Antiquities of Athens*.

Until Stuart and Revett's second volume appeared, the one which contained the drawings of the Parthenon, Le Roy's book succeeded Spon's as cultured Europe's guide to Greek antiquities.[41] Soon, however, other books, chiefly travel books, swelled the bibliography of Hellenica. The travelers visited the sites, struggled with incomprehending and sometimes hostile agas, and measured the monuments. In spite of the publications the act of measuring became one of the essential pastimes of the seventeenth and eighteenth century traveler. The plumb line suspended from the moldings of the column capital in so many engravings became an essential piece of their equipment. William Lithgow, who traveled round the Levant in the 1620s, measured the ruins of Alexandrian Troas, thinking he was at the very site of Ilium. Spon measured both the Erechtheum and the Parthenon. I take the example of those two literary travelers, since neither was interested in publishing the result of their efforts in measured drawings.[42]

The measuring and the noting had become part of the visiting of ruins, since Brunelleschi and Donatello had first done so on their trip to Rome in 1405.[43] Although several travelers did publish measured drawings, particularly for the use of architects and archeologists, the vast majority of those who measured did so for their own edification. Often the drawings, like Carrey's drawings of the Parthenon sculptures, became treasured possessions and were valued as much for what they represented as for their proper quality. They were eagerly examined by antiquarians, as were Count Gazzola's drawings of Paestum by Soufflot and Cochin.[44]

The striking of a pose, the improvising of an ode, the contemplation of past glories, all these were motives for the traveler's visits to the great sites of antiquity. And, of course, the desire to identify the sites familiar from ancient literature. But the taking possession of them: either literally, by carrying away fragments, or metaphorically, by conserving records, which with time had to be increasingly precise, were to come to a climax in the generation of Stuart and Revett, which includes Robert Wood (who visited Baalbeck and Palmyra), Piranesi's account of Paestum, and Robert Adam's visit to Split in Dalmatia. It is worth noting that none of these visitors were what we would call archeologists; if they excavated, it was to reach the bottom of a column or wall. If they brought something back, it was by way of curiosity; William Lithgow was shown some columns in Tyre which the "Moors" said had been pulled down by Samson. As Scripture says this happened in Azath, Lithgow remained sceptical. "Yet, howsoer it was, I brought home a pound weight of it and presented the half of it to King James of Blessed Memory."[45]

Relics, bits of statues (heads, limbs, or even just noses), the odd base, inscriptions, all these were regarded as collectors' curios. The museum was still a new institution, but such patrons as Elias Ashmole or the great spiritual and temporal lords extended their

Lorenzo Lotto, A Cleric in His Study, *pen and ink drawing, 1526–1527, detail showing Lotto's collection of ancient vases. London, British Museum.*

libraries and collections of works of art to include antique and
natural curiosities. Among the antique curiosities, coins, medals,
and inscriptions were particularly valued. To these were soon joined
small pieces of painted ceramic or sculptured bronzes. Destructive
treasure hunting developed into a minor industry: it was the first
archeology.

Around Naples, painted pottery was extremely common. Sir William Hamilton, the British ambassador to the Two Sicilies, collected
many such pots, as well as other antiquities. He had been appointed
to the Neapolitan embassy in 1762. By 1766 his collection was
sufficiently impressive to be published in color, in four volumes
folio.[46] Hamilton, always short of cash, sold it to the newly founded
British Museum in 1772 but immediately started to form another
collection; much of it, unfortunately, still lies at the bottom of the
sea, off the Scilly Isles.[47]

Vases were Hamilton's passion; and he excavated for them and
bought them wherever he could, often from illegal sources.[48] But
the collection had its nucleus in an older one, also based on vases,
that of the Counts Porcinari. Nor was theirs the oldest. In 1720 the
princely House of Valletta, having fallen on bad days, sold 45
vases—with the family library—to the Oratorians, and another 150
or so vases to Cardinal Vualtieri.[49] When Bottari went to Naples in
1734, he found so many vases that he did not have the heart to start
recording them in drawings.[50] They appeared in all polite houses, on
consoles an on *étagères,* over doors and mantelpieces, with porcelain and Bohemian crystal. Even fakes were becoming common.
Pietro Fondi, a Venetian, had become quite well known in this line
of business; the poet and antiquarian Apostolo Zeno had used some
of Fondi's fakes to instruct his pupils in the difference between
antique and modern pieces.[51] But even if they could tell fake from
genuine, the antiquarians were not at all agreed on the origin of the
vases. The Tuscan writers and collectors, Gori, Buonarotti, Passeri,
and the ''Tuscified'' Scotsman, Thomas Dempster, were all convinced the vases were Etruscan. Most of them had, after all, come
from Etruscan tombs. To some extent national, even local pride was
involved: the Neapolitans would not have this. The vases were
identified as Campanian, Siculan, or even Greco-Siculan, though
an increasing number of antiquarians thought them Greek.
Winckelmann changed his mind: they were Greek; they were
Campano-Greek; they were Etruscan copies of Greek sculptures
and paintings. He speculated on the possible relation between the
early Etruscan vase painters and their Greek masters.[52] But for
many Europeans who learned about the vases through Gori or
Passeri, or even the catalog of Sir William Hamilton's collection, the
vases were Etruscan. And so it was in a Staffordshire village re-
named Etruria that Josiah Wedgwood first manufactured his black
ware with its imitated Greek figures and the porcelain cameos which
were to make him famous.

Let us return to the Campagna, where the sporadic and illegal treasure-snatching was being replaced by legal and equally damaging digging, to be quite overshadowed by the discovery of Pompeii and Herculaneum. The extinction of the Farnese dynasty of Parma and the Medici of Tuscany coincided with a vast dynastic swap-round which was the climax of the *ancien régime*. In the course of it, the Spanish Infante Don Carlos, the oldest son of Elizabeth Farnese and Philip V, became first, in 1731, duke of Parma and adopted son of Gian Gastone, the last Medici, and three years later conquered the Two Sicilies from the Austrians in a virtually bloodless campaign. The Two Sicilies, after years of Spanish and Austrian domination, became an independent kingdom. Charles III had brought with him the Farnese treasures from Parma and installed them in a new palace he had built partly for that, partly to serve as a grandiose hunting lodge, at Capodimonte.[53] The remaining Farnese collections, which were housed in the Palazzo Farnese in Rome, were moved by Charles' son, Ferdinand, later in the century.

That was all an internal matter, however. The discoveries at Herculaneum and Pompeii had an enormous international effect on the art and the scholarship of succeeding generations; although, as with Paestum, the revelation came slowly and haltingly.

The histories of the two towns were in any case different. Herculaneum stood in the way of the flow of lava during the great Vesuvius explosion of 79 A.D., which destroyed both towns, and was buried under 15–25 meters of solidified volcanic matter; Pompeii was covered by a fall of ash which was both shallower and more pervious. Pompeii, which had therefore already been looted in antiquity, projected in places above the level of the volcanic matter; some material had been carried away and used for building, and stone used for lime. The actual site was even known as Cività before the excavations ever started. But although the suspicion was current that the modern Torre di Greco was identical with ancient Herculaneum,[54] when Domenico Fontana ran an underground water channel from the nearby river Sarno to Torre Annunziata, he tunneled through the remains of some ancient buildings. No attempt was made at the time to excavate. The first definite attempts were made after 1709; some workmen digging for a cistern came upon an antique statue. The prince d'Elbeuf, a Frenchman who had obtained a cavalry command in the imperial service and was stationed in Naples, was interested, and promoted excavations into the lava. It was the old-fashioned, treasure-hunt kind of excavation: d'Elbeuf kept much of the material at Portici, but some of the prize pieces were sent to Vienna. The excavations were difficult and went on fitfully between 1709 and 1719. D'Elbeuf had left some time before the Austrian retreat, and his house with its collection was sold to the Falletti family.[55]

Charles III had liked Portici. In spite of de Brosse's sneer, it had plenty of fish and some game.[56] Site, climate, game, all suited the king. Furthermore, its archeological associations appealed to Charles and to his queen, Maria Amalia of Saxony, whose brother,

Frederick Christian, was one of Winckelmann's early patrons.[57] Winckelmann was to use this connection in dealing with the obstructionist intrigues of the jealous Neapolitan antiquarians.

In 1738, while the Reggia was still being built and Capodimonte had just been started, Portici was selected for the out-of-town palace. Ground was partly confiscated, partly bought, and a design prepared by Charles' first architect, Gian Antonio Medrano, and his assistant, Antonio Canevari, in the *barochetto* manner then current in Naples. The palace grounds included the original d'Elbeuf well, and the king's master of works, the engineer-colonel, Don Rocco Jaime Alcubierre, urged the king to reopen the excavations. This was done, but unsystematically again. Wells were sunk and tunnels cut. The heavy cover of lava meant that the physical aspect of the city was never really apparent.[58]

In 1748, Alcubierre inspected the channel cut by Fontana, which he believed to cut through the ruins of Stabiae, although they are in fact on the other side of the bay, at Castellamare. This led to the decision that the site should be dug, and the king gave Alcubierre thirty galley-slaves. The dig, it must be remembered, was for treasures to adorn Portici. After the first successes there was a fallow period and Alcubierre moved to Castellamare. In 1750 the house of an epicurean "philosopher" was found at Herculaneum; the building contained a large library of papyri[59] as well as a great many sculptures and paintings. Some years later, in 1754, workmen digging a road near Città came upon a row of tombs. The excavations were started again, and in 1765 the second site was correctly identified as Pompeii through an inscription in the house of T. Suedius Clemens. By this time the bulk of the antiquities which furnish the palace at Portici had been excavated. Charles and Maria Amalia were disillusioned with the palace, although they continued to use it regularly. A volcanic earthquake in August 1742, followed a few hours later by a threatening visit of a British squadron under Commodore Martin, may finally have decided the king, who was at Portici at the time with the whole court, to find another out-of-town residence.[60] This was to become his most splendid architectural enterprise: the palace at Caserta, out of reach of both Vesuvius and hostile naval guns. Luigi Vanvitelli, the most prominent Roman architect of the time (though born in Naples), was commissioned to design Caserta, and another *barochetto* master, Ferdinando Fuga, was summoned by the pious monarch to design a hospice for the poor which was to rival his palace in scale.[61]

Caserta was the last great building which could be labeled baroque in Italy, perhaps in the world; and the largest eighteenth-century building in the peninsula. It was incomparably more magniloquent than the gently modeled, curved Portici. Caserta had the full-blown manner of a Romanizing successor to Versailles. Portici, though both Vanvitelli and Fuga tinkered with it, was full of *rocaille*. In particular, the queen's boudoir was a remarkable *tour de force*: the walls were an assembly of porcelain plaques in the Chinese style made at Capodimonte in the late 1750s. Although the ceiling is deco-

Francesco Piranesi, The Temple of Isis in Pompeii. *London, British Museum.*

rated gesso, even the furniture of this remarkable room was of porcelain in the Chinese taste.[62]

It was in these *barochetto* and *rococo* interiors that the fruits of the excavations of Herculaneum and of Pompeii were displayed, as were the antiquities found elsewhere in Italy, in Tuscany, or in Rome. Even the greatest, the most discriminating collector of the time, Cardinal Alessandro Albani, when he built his magnificent villa on the Via Salaria (the villa where Winckelmann acted as his adviser, and his favorite artist, Anton Raphael Mengs, painted his *Parnassus* on the ceiling of the great salon[63]), had it built in a soberly florid manner by a successful *barochetto* architect of the day, Carlo Marchionni. But it was peopled by statues arranged into elaborate iconographic schemes: quite different from the cheerful piling-up of antique fragments which was usual over the walls of Roman palaces of the day.[64] If the setting was a little heavy and old-fashioned, the idea of turning the antiquities into an allegory did not have any real precedent.

Nevertheless, the fact remains that all the great excavations were given a *rococo* or *barochetto* setting. In any case, until the discovery of Herculaneum and Pompeii, the Roman art which was familiar to the most learned antiquarian was public art, and this was particularly true of architecture. Temples, triumphal arches, circuses,

Villa Albani, Rome, by Carlo Marchionni (and others?), garden layout originally by Giambattista Nolli. Foto Alinari.

The Chinese porcelain room from the Royal Palace at Portici. Capodimonte Museum. Foto Alinari.

theaters, baths were the staple of architectural literature. The private house and its decoration were known by inference only.[65]

In this sense the discovery of Pompeii and Herculaneum may be said to have stimulated the neoclassical movement. The settings in which the *admiranda* of antiquity were displayed were seen to be inadequate, trivial, inferior. The private art of the ancients—the frescoes and the mosaic decorations of the private houses—were a revelation. Their planning and layout suddenly lit up the obscure passages in certain ancient writers.

But there was another aspect to the Pompeii excavations. As the ash and mud were stripped off the ruins, so the outlines of a complete city, with its private and public buildings and all the spaces related in a way which was unfamiliar to the men of the eighteenth century lay revealed.

The result of these excavations did not become known quickly throughout Europe. Charles III was very jealous of his possessions and all travelers, well into the nineteenth century, faced obstructions of all kinds. Drawing of as yet unpublished objects and monuments was always forbidden. And publication went forward very slowly indeed. As the extent and interest of the finds became increasingly clear, the king appointed an antiquarian, Monsignor Baiardi (a cousin of the then prime minister) when his learned curator, the Tuscan Marchese Marcello Venuti, who had arrived with the Farnese treasures, left his service.

Baiardi was learned too, but in the worst pedantic manner. Instead of a catalog of the finds, he produced a near-interminable (2,500 pages) speculation about the mythical origins of Herculaneum. Finally the king, who had posted sentinels before statues and had unlicensed descriptions of the antiquities banned, grew impatient, and demanded the catalog proper. This appeared in 1755, well produced, but nearly useless. Baiardi thereupon retired to Rome, and the Neapolitan minister of justice, a learned and efficient Tuscan, the Marchese Tanucci, had a committee appointed, which, as the Reale Accademia Herculanense, saw to the publication of the finds in a series of nine splendid folios which appeared between 1757 and 1792.[66]

Europe was becoming increasingly avid for a sight of these since the rumors of the excavations had begun to spread and more or less accurate copies of the odd fresco or bronze to appear in travel books or anthologies of antiquities. The king, however, would not have the great volumes of the academy put on sale; he reserved them as personal presents to sovereigns or other distinguished visitors, and sometimes to collectors and antiquarians.[67] The jostling for this useful mark of the king's favor was not—as may be expected—a pretty spectacle.

The copies and replicas soon abounded. The first volumes dealt with the paintings, the subsequent ones with the bronzes. As volume followed volume, the courts of Europe and the more important patrons sought for facsimiles and for illicit exports. Forgeries soon became a problem; the preface to the second volume denounces those perpetrated by the Venetian painter, Giuseppe Guerra, on the basis of the first volume. But the real popularity of the Herculanean paintings was witnessed by two commercial publications: the one-volume edition of the paintings published in London by Thomas Martyn and James Lettice,[68] and Tommaso Piroli's six-volume version of the complete work without the text.[69] In the case of Pompeii, there was no general description of the finds until Sir William Hamilton's quarto of 1774. Nevertheless, drawings and engravings of single objects, of paintings, and of certain of the buildings, had become familiar to all cultivated collectors by this time.

In this archeological flurry, this antiquarian indigestion, it is easy to overlook another Neapolitan figure whose effect on European thought was neither immediate nor direct, and yet without whom the theory of neoclassicism would certainly have been formulated quite differently: Giambattista Vico. He was born humbly in Naples in 1668. In 1694, he was appointed professor of rhetoric at the university. Despite his attempts, he never obtained a more lucrative academic post. But Charles III appointed him historiographer-royal in 1734. He died ten years later.

His literary output was vast: speeches, set rhetorical pieces, history, philosophy. It is his philosophical writings which have remained important. At first, he worked out a moderate Cartesian approach, but this was modified through his interest in physical sciences into a Baconian empiricism.[70] It led him to a reevaluation of the place of history in any theory of knowledge. His view that the constitution of society was incarnate in language and law came to be in the end the focus of his epistemology.

Vico's explicit rejection of the Cartesian *cogito* came, typically, in a book entitled *Most Ancient Wisdom of the Italians*, in which he announced a diametrically opposite principle: *verum ipsum factum*,[71] the rule of truth is to have made it; the *cogito*, the thought of your own thinking, exists not at the level of distinct knowledge, but at that of unreflecting consciousness. Even when you strip down to that, what you build up may be clear and distinct. While clarity may be a criterion of geometrical proposition, and geometry is a science in which the mind builds up its own entities, yet these entities do not have reality in the same sense in which the objects of natural science are realities. The entities of mathematics are man-made fictions. We do indeed know them by the Vican proof. But the realities of physics or biology we can only know by having "made" them in another sense: we know them by experiment.

The geometrical method of proof on this showing does not have the universal application which Descartes sought to give it. It is only God, who made all things, *deus naturae artifex*, who can also know them clearly and distinctly as we know the truths of geometry. Later, Vico even recast the Baconian idea that when we "recreate" nature in experiment, so as to know it, our recreation has a different nature from the original, since it remains outside us; we cannot know it to be true, as a *scienza*. It is only *certum:* not a true science, but a knowledge, a *coscienza*.[72] The originals of mathematical construction are fictions: the originals which our mental constructs re-build for us are out there, in the existential order.[73]

Vico's deduction from this was quite original and had the pro-foundest effect. If the objects of our knowledge, as far as the natural sciences are concerned, exist as part of divine creation, the objects of our historical knowledge are more "knowable," since they are made by man in the first place. History must therefore be a more proper object of scientific investigation than physical nature. These principles were set out in a work with the programmatic title *Princi-ples of a New Science Concerning the Common Nature of the Na-tions*, which first appeared in 1725; the third edition, published in 1744 (the year of Vico's death), is so much enlarged and rewritten as to be another book.

The material of historical study—Vico proposes in the *New Science*—is the whole *detritus* of past civilizations: poems, art, the development of society and of law. They are interdependent, and taken together they will show us man's way with his fellows during the course of humanity. The course began with Adam. Adam fell from grace to a nature which to seventeenth-century philosophers seemed to be so hostile as to render men bestial inevitably. Vico's first men fell from grace to bestiality by degrees. Terror then led men to live in community. The origin of language and the origin of build-ing, as they were described by Lucretius and by Vitruvius, are ex-panded by Vico.[74]

But the society which was so constituted soon developed internal tensions: this was the state of families, which Vico equated with the ancient Egyptian notion of an "age of the gods," or a "golden age," as the Greeks had called it. Each age achieved its apogee only at the expense of developing its internal tensions and so bringing about its own transformation through decay and reconstitution. This is the Vican theory of *recorsi*.[75] Each period belonged to a structural unity with what followed and what went before.

Inevitably, in giving this short account of Vico's ideas, I have to abbreviate to the point of caricature. Yet I must emphasize that Vico was not a determinist; he did not think that one can "situate" one-self in a point in time and see how the cycles will "inevitably" develop. On the contrary, he saw the basic structure of the cyclic development of nations, tribes, and individuals constantly buffeted and modified by accident so as to produce an infinitely varied ac-count of history.[76]

Vico blamed the philosophers and the rhetoricians for having overschematized, overintellectualized human development. It was fear and need which drove men into their first habitations and com-munities, not a conceptual apparatus of legal practices, as the philosophers of natural law tended to think. In the early ages of man, imagination and feeling were the primary ways of mental activity, and ratiocination was subject to these more powerful functions. Primitive law, primitive religion and mythology, therefore also poetry and art, were the product of a logic of the imagination.

All this passed into the eighteenth century, in so far as it did so, through Vico's disciples, who in Naples formed a school of legal and economic thinkers. Their importance is now obscured. No doubt he had his impact on the French Enlightenment through the comparative method of Montesquieu, whose ''Spirit of Laws'' bears the mark of Vico's influence. But Montesquieu was much more impressed by a Neapolitan contemporary of Vico's (as were Voltaire and Diderot), Pietro Giannone,[77] another jurist whose history of the kingdom of Naples and his opinions earned him excommunication and a prison death in Piedmont. But Vico seems to have been apolitical, and to have lived on very good terms with the Neapolitan ecclesiastical censor, who indeed suggested interpolations to him, to mask his more outrageous views.[78]

But though apolitical, Vico was acutely self-conscious. One's own autobiography, in one's own terms, is what is most knowable. In Venice, among a group of admirers, the suggestion arose that Vico should write his autobiography as a series of autobiographies of the great men of his day.[79] It actually appeared in Father Calogiera's *Raccolta*. The most important member of the group was the eccentric Venetian Franciscan friar, Carlo Lodoli, who also attempted to have the second edition of the *New Science* printed in Venice; his intervention was frustrated by a quarrel between the author and the printer. But this link points to the way in which Vico's ideas, not fully appreciated throughout Europe until half a century after his death, passed, through Lodoli's teaching, into architectural theory. Although this theory was only a tributary to the mainstream of eighteenth-century thinking, yet because of this unfamiliar connection, it was a stream which affected the main current.

Notes to Chapter 7

1. J. Mabillon (1681; supplements in 1704 and 1709). The theological and mystical background of the congregation, and the place of study in the life of prayer are discussed by H. Brémond (1922), VI, pp. 80 ff. On the "marriage articles" between Dom Claude Martin (who inspired this ethos) and the Holy Wisdom, pp. 95 ff.

2. Montfaucon (1708). It coined the word.

3. Montfaucon (1719–1724). An English edition appeared 1721–1725.

4. The most important being that of St. Athanasius (1690) and of St. John Chrysostom (1718–1738).

5. Montfaucon (1708), II, plate 12 (p. 70); II, pl. 14 (p. 80).

6. G. P. Bellori, *De Fragmenta Vestigii*, 1673. On Bellori see above, chapter 3, and chapter 6, n. 419.

7. A reconstruction based on F. Lauro (1635).

8. Vol. II, plate xiv.

9. See chapter 3.

10. Robert W. Ramsey, "Sir George Wheeler and his Travels in Greece, 1650–1724"; in *Transactions of the Royal Society of Literature of the United Kingdom*, n.s., XIX (1942), pp. 1–38. John Evelyn described Wheeler as "a very worthy person, a little formal and particular, but exceedingly devout." John Evelyn, *Diary*, 1955.

11. J. Spon (1676), p. 136.

12. It was Dionysius IV known as "the Moslem."

13. *Relation de l'Etat présent de la Ville d'Athènes, Ancienne Capitale de la Grèce, Bâtie Depuis 3,400 ans . . . à Lyon*, 1674. The missionary was Jacques-Paul Babin, a Jesuit.

14. Spon, *Voyage d'Italie*, 1678.

15. Cf. Fischer von Erlach, *Entwurff*, 1737, pl. 19c; he introduced a few modifications; but he used Spon and Wheeler's texts extensively, cf. G. Kunoth (1956), pp. 40 f., 55 ff., 79 ff., 85, 189.

16. Although by 1743 a more accurate picture had at last been provided by Richard Pococke.

17. G. Wheeler (1682).

18. G. Wheeler (1689).

19. G. Wheeler (1689), pp. 103 ff. A similar approach will be adopted, allowing for some differences, by French theorists such as Cordemoy and Le Roy in France in the course of the eighteenth century, although they would not equate French churches, such as the temple of Charenton, with the primitive order, as Wheeler does, pp. 118 f.

20. See chapter 9.

21. The powder magazine was hit during Francesco Morosini's disastrous siege of 1687 on September 26. His further attempt to remove two of the figures from the pediment, when the tackle broke and the figures smashed on the ground, completed the worst deed of destruction on the building since its transformation into a church more than a millennium earlier.

22. C. Huelsen, *Il Libro di Giuliano da Sangallo* (Cod. Vat. Barb. Lat. 4424), 1910, Codices Vaticani Selecti, XI, pp. 39–45, fols. 28, 29.

23. C. Mitchell and E. W. Bodnar (1976). Cf. E. Bodnar (1960). The first "publications" were in manuscript only, though the best of these, the so-called Codex Hamiltonianus, has a relatively "correct" drawing, although

the cornice is without triglyphs and the columns extremely slender. Serlio (IV, 6) and Palladio (I, 15) both refer to fairly accurate Doric orders, while Guarini (1737), pp. 95 ff., discusses the literature, concluding that the order does look better with a base. But the whole question was raised much more expertly by Fréart de Chambray (1650), plates 1–17. See S. Lang and N. Pevsner in N. Pevsner (1968), pp. 197 ff.

24. Cyriacus of Ancona (1645 and 1745), 1749.

25. Spon (1678), II, pp. 149 ff. He attacks several authors by name. For instance, Simon Kabasilas and Theodore Zygomalas, correspondents of Martin Kraus or Crusius. Kraus had been appointed professor of Greek at Tübingen in 1555 and had been put in touch with Byzantine hierarchs through the imperial ambassador, David von Ungnad, and his Protestant chaplain, Stephen Gerlach. Zygomalas was at the time pronotary of the Great Church, and one of the main Western contacts in Constantinople. Crusius' book, to which Spon takes exception, *Turco-Graecia*, appeared in Bâle in 1584, to be followed next year by a smaller book, *Germano Graecia*. These were the principal source for the knowledge of Greece in the West until the appearance of the Spon-Wheeler memoirs. For Crusius' activities see S. Runciman (1968), pp. 247 f.; also 208 f., 254 ff.

The other author, Georges Guillet, purported to publish the travels of a mythical brother, de la Guilletière. He almost certainly never visited Athens and relied on Crusius and other printed sources as well as information received from French Capucine missionaries. But he was more interesting than this curious imposture allows him to appear; the author of a life of Mohammed II, he was appointed historiographer of the Academy of Painting in 1682, and remained in the post—he had been recommended to it by Colbert—until his death in 1706. His portrait was painted by Jacques Carrey, who had drawn the Parthenon sculptures for Ollier de Nointel in 1674. Cf. Comte de Laborde (1854), pp. 15 ff., 85–109; also W. M. Leake (1841), I, pp. 94 f.

26. In J. J. Winckelmann (1784), III, p. 10. He had, however, more accurate details and measurements than those published by Panozzi. These were given him by the Scots architect Robert Mylne who was to become famous as the designer of Blackfriars bridge. *Storia*, III, p. 108. There is no mention of this in the only modern monograph on Mylne by A. E. Richardson (1955).

27. For this and the succeeding material, see L. Hautecoeur (1912), pp. 93 ff.

28. Though the temple of Ceres had acted as the cathedral of the place during the short existence of a bishopric (c. 500–650) which was then moved, like the administration, inland and uphill to Capacchio, which the great German antiquarian-geographer Philip Cluver (Cluverius) visited about 1610. He does not seem to have seen the ruins, which he describes as *cultoribus plane vacuae,* although he records the dialect name, *Piesti* (P. Cluverius, 1624, pp. 1254 ff.). Leandro Alberti (1550) remarks casually that there are some ruins to be seen thereabouts ("in qualche parte"). On the local historians, see P. Laveglia (1971), pp. 18 ff. The character of the buildings at the beginning of the eighteenth century seemed obscure: they were described as theaters, one of them as a "gymnasium." In July 1740, Ferdinando Sanfelice, involved in the subsidiary buildings of Capodimonte, proposes to use columns from the Paestum site as an economy measure: some writers thought that they were of marble; presumably on the analogy of those which Guiscard had brought to Salerno. But in the end, the ruins were considered too low-grade for the trouble of transport. P. Laveglia (1971), pp. 40 f.

29. Giuseppe Antonini (1745), pp. 213–279.

30. Gazzola had complained to the Abbé Barthélémy that Soufflot had made "unscrupulous" use of the drawings. So Barthélémy writing to Caylus on 20 December 1750; see P. Laveglia (1971), p. 33. The letter in D. Wiebenson (1969), pp. 120 f.

On Gazzola's drawings, see P. Paoli in J. J. Winckelmann (1783), pp. 131 ff., and below.

31. Now Agrigentum. J. J. Winckelmann (1783), III, pp. 107 ff.

32. Cicero in *Verrem* IV, but Verres' spoliation had led Cicero to extol the beauties of Syracuse in detail.

33. See A. Blunt (1968), pp. 148, 151.

34. J. J. Winckelmann (1783), pp. 4, n. D, pp. 138 ff.

35. In a letter to Abbe Carlo Fea, a well-known antiquarian and the editor of the second, much enlarged Italian edition of Winckelmann's *History of Art*, 1784, and reprinted there in III, pp. 130 f.

36. J. D. Le Roy (1758), p. 2, p. 5 f.

37. On Benefial, see the obituary letter of 22 July 1764, by G. B. Ponfredi to Count Nicola Soderini in G. Bottari and S. Ticozzi (1822), V, pp. 5–39.

38. A second edition appeared four years later, in 1758.

39. In his *History of the Arts of Design,* J. J. Winckelmann complained that he could not find either an adequate description, or the dedication of the temple to which belonged the caryatid portico, which he knew from ancient authors such as Vitruvius and Atheneus, as well as from coins and the account of a modern traveler. This is the now famous caryatid portico of the Erechtheum. *Storia delle Arti del Disegno*, 1783, III, p. 95.

40. The various proposals are reported in full by D. Wiebenson (1969), pp. 75 ff.

41. Cochin, who is not a wholly reliable witness, writes in his *Memoirs,* 1880, pp. 78 f., that Le Roy's drawings were so *informes* that Caylus had them redrawn by Le Lorrain—who had never been to Greece—and then engraved by J.-P. Le Bas (some plates were engraved by Neufforge). See D. Wiebenson (1969), pp. 33 ff.; Cochin is considering here chiefly Le Bas' greed and Caylus' meanness.

Julien-David Le Roy (whom the *P.V.* calls Julien David-Leroy) is a somewhat obscure figure. He seems to have called on family finances for his trip. His father was a successful clockmaker. At the academy, he takes an active part against the director, Natoire, about the business of confession certificates (H. Lapauze, 1924, I, pp. 287 f., 295 ff.). His book, patronized by Caylus, was very successful (reactions reported by D. Wiebenson, 1969, pp. 97, 102 ff.). It was "reviewed" to the Academy of Architecture by J.-F. Blondel (*P.V.,* VI, pp. 334 ff.) on 1 October 1758, whereupon Le Roy was elected to it, and was extremely active, becoming its historiographer on the same occasion on which Blondel was finally named its professor, 15 November 1762 (VII, pp. 120 f.). A second edition, with additional plates by Patte, appeared in 1770. His projected history was severely criticized (as being a mere appendix to Blondel's *Architecture Française*) by J.-F. Desmaisons (*P.V.*, VII, pp. 113 ff.), Jacques-Louis David's uncle. It was with David that Le Roy was to be found, towards the end of his life, the Revolutionary Institute which succeeded the academy: *P.V.*, IX, pp. 339 f., 349 f.; A. Boime (1971), pp. 5 ff.; L. Hautecoeur (1943), V. Besides being a practitioner and an academic politician, Le Roy was a prolific antiquarian and something of a literary lion; there is an entertaining account of his meeting the Thrales, Dr. Johnson, and Giuseppe Baretti in Paris, at Madame de Bocage's (on her, see chapter 9, n. 27) in 1775. See M. Tyson and H. Guppy (1932), pp. 99 f., 148 f., 170. Mrs. Thrale thought in 1775 that Le Roy had something of the status of "Athenian" Stewart in Britain.

42. But see an account of the pre-Stuart and Revett travelers in J. M. Crook (1972), pp. 1–6. For a more cosmopolitan view, D. Wiebenson (1969), pp. 19 ff.

43. G. Vasari, *Vite*, II, pp. 337 f. F. Baldinucci (1948), pp. 183, 305 f.

44. These were variously said to be done in 1734–1740 or 1755. The later date seems the more probable; they were the basis of the much later publication of Paoli (see above). Count Felice Gazzola was an artillery officer in the service of Charles III, who followed the king to Spain. Whether Caylus had, at Barthélémy's request, sabotaged the Cochin-Soufflot-Dumont publication is not known. At any rate, it did not appear until 1764. The scholarly publication was Thomas Major's of 1768; though they were all put in the shade by Piranesi (1778); see chapter 9.

45. Quoted in R. Macaulay (1953), p. 51.

46. By (D'Harcanville) Pierre François Hugues, 1766–1767. Even in the text which prefaces these plates, Hamilton shows his intention to make his collection a teaching exercise, an instrument for improving taste. His contempt for antiquarians was shown by his training a monkey to examine an object through a magnifying glass; as in Chardin's caricature, on which see below.

In this sense, Wedgwood at Etruria was Hamilton's favorite disciple; he was sent early proofs of Hamilton's plates by Lord Cathcart, and opened his factory at the new Etruria by casting—with his partner, Thomas Bentley—six vases in black basalt ware, based on the engravings and inscribed *Artes Etruriae Renascuntur*: this was on 13 June 1769. Hamilton was also responsible, if indirectly, for the Wedgwood copies of the Portland Vase. See B. Fothergill (1969), pp. 68 f., 195 f.

47. The ship carrying it was wrecked in 1798. Hamilton again hoped to sell the collection. What was rescued was bought by Thomas Hope. But still much remains in the sunken ship. B. Fothergill (1969), pp. 402 f.; and D. Watkin (1968), pp. 35 ff.

48. B. Fothergill (1969), pp. 50, 64 ff. The wreck was identified by divers in 1976.

49. L. Hautecoeur (1912), pp. 91 f.

50. Letter to Caylus in C. Justi (1923), III, p. 369.

51. Cf. A. Zeno (1752), III, p. 3; (1765), IV, 209 ff., and VI, 151 ff.

52. Cf. C. Justi (1923), III, pp. 418 ff.

53. Building was decided on in 1737. There were to be two woods, one stocked for hunting "feather," the other "fur." The palace was enlarged when the collections were moved there in the next year.

The first stone was laid on 9 September 1738. The architect was Giovanni Antonio Medrano, who had come to Naples, or at any rate back to Italy, in the Spanish service with Charles III. See A. Venditti (1961), p. 236 f., 300 ff. He also designed the original theater of San Carlo. See later in this chapter. For the conditions in which the collections were kept, see C. des Brosses (1889), II, p. 128.

54. See P. Cluverius (1624), pp. 1154 f. F. Balzano (1688), pp. 56 f. In fact, the site turned out to be nearer Naples, at Resina, near Portici. On the first "unauthorized" guide by Cochin and Bellicard, see below, ch. 10.

55. A. Maiuri (1963), pp. 8 f., and R. Pane (1959).

56. C. de Brosses (1889), II: "tout ce pays étant de longue main dépeuplé par les paysans ou les lazarellis qui chassent en pleine liberté" (p. 151).

57. C. Justi (1923), passim. On his succession, see III, pp. 261 f.

58. T. H. Dyer (1891), pp. 24 ff. The identification of the site was first made in 1756 (G. A. Fiorelli, 1864, I, p. 2), though an inscription found in 1763 settled any doubt.

59. These were carefully unrolled and preserved by a special process and published in 1793.

60. H. Acton (1957), pp. 58 ff.

61. R. Pane (1956), pp. 131 ff. On Caserta, see R. de Fusco and others (1973), pp. 117–129, 131–159, 254–277, catalog pp. 109–114.

62. H. Honour (1961), pp. 118, 123. There was a more elaborate one at Arranjuez done for Charles III and Maria Amalia when they moved to Spain (cf. H. Honour, 1961, pp. 123 ff.).

63. D. Honisch (1965), pp. 65 f., and Chapter 9, on the villa generally.

64. This is pointed out by C. Justi (1923), II, pp. 354 ff.

65. Though, of course, one or two fragments of fresco were known earlier, such as the much described "Aldobrandini" wedding in the Vatican Museum, which was discovered about 1600.

66. *Le Pitture Antiche d'Ercolano e Contorni*, II, Naples, 1759, preface.

67. 1755–1792. Each volume was prefaced by a portrait of the king; the title page was printed in three colors.

68. 1773. It was stopped after the first volume by a diplomatic intervention of the Neapolitan government. *D.N.B.*, s.v. Thomas Martyn.

69. 1789–1807.

70. Y. Belaval, "Vico and Anti-Cartesianism" in G. Tagliacozzo and H. V. White (1969), pp. 77 ff.

71. G. B. Vico (1929), I, p. 136: "veri criterium ac regulam ipsum esse fecisse . . . quia dum se mens cognoscit, non facit; et quia non facit, nescit genus seu modum, quo se cognoscit."

72. I. Berlin, "A Note on Vico's Concept of Knowledge" (pp. 371 ff.) and M. H. Fisch, "Pragmatism" (pp. 401 ff.) in G. Tagliacozzo and H. V. White (1969).

73. B. Croce (1947), pp. 21 ff.

74. W. Stark, "Giambattista Vico's Sociology of Knowledge" in G. Tagliacozzo and H. V. White (1969), pp. 297 ff. But see also J. Rykwert (1972), pp. 61 f., 105 ff.

75. A. R. Caponigri (1968), pp. 130 ff. On Vico's personal position in political and religious matters, see B. Croce, *La Filosofia di G. B. Vico*, 1947, pp. 285 ff.

76. A. R. Caponigri (1968), pp. 109 ff.

77. On the indifference and political antipathy between Vico and Giannone, see D. Faucci, "Vico and Grotius" (p. 61) and D. Piovani (p. 109) in G. Tagliacozzo and H. V. White (1969).

78. B. Croce (1947), pp. 321 ff.

79. On the periautography, see ch. 8.

8

Neoclassical Architecture

Carlo Lodoli may have been idiosyncratic, but he was not a loner. On the contrary, he was very gregarious. He came of the Venetian *petite noblesse,* his father having a connection with shipbuilding at the Arsenal,[1] and the family moved from the parish of St. Luke (where Carlo was born in 1690) nearer to the Arsenal to that of San Francesco della Vigna, a church already important in the development of architectural theory.[2] At sixteen, he ran away from home, and made his profession as an Observant Franciscan—San Francesco della Vigna belonged to that congregation—in Dubrovnik (which was then still the independent republic of Ragusa). He also took his final vows there before proceeding to Rome. In Rome he was noted as a brilliant student, particularly as a dialectician. In 1720 he was sent to teach scholastic philosophy to the Franciscan novices in Verona and stayed there for ten years. Verona's intellectual and social life was then dominated by the Marchese Scipione Maffei, one of the most brilliant Italians of the time, who in later years was to claim to have formed the young friar's tastes as well as his social manner.[3] He certainly introduced him to the pleasures of that salon life through which Lodoli's teaching was to find its proper context.

After his Verona stay, Lodoli returned to Venice. He was already forty and famous as a teacher of philosophy, a scientific polymath, and a formidably caustic wit. He settled at San Francesco, dealt with awkward family problems (from which he is reputed to have fled), and accepted minor public office. He acted for some time as censor of books to the republic, and later as the Franciscan commissary for the Holy Land. More powerful positions he did not want; he seems to have refused any offer of a bishopric.[4] But perhaps the most important of his activities was semiprivate: a school, or rather a peripatetic seminar for the sons of the nobility.[5] His teaching turned on the nature of society and the meaning of authority and paid particular attention to the duties of patricians. He relied much on the great lawyers, from Cicero to Puffendorf, but he also wanted his pupils to apply the critical method which he taught them to Venetian state documents, and there he came into conflict with the state Inquisition.[6] On the whole, however, it was those of his elders who smarted from his wit who interfered with his activities, rather than the authorities.

Of his own writings nothing seems to have been published in his lifetime. His editing of one of those learned periodicals, so fashionable at the time, the *Biblioteca Volante*, was stopped by illness which afflicted him during the first four years after his return home. The series was taken over by Angelo Calogiera, who was to publish Giambattista Vico's autobiography.[7] Of Lodoli's projected history of the Franciscan order, nothing remains despite the time and money spent in reordering the library and archives of San Francesco in preparation for this work.[8] Although he did not publish, he seems to have written a great deal. Some letters, notably an exchange with

Giambattista Vico, were published soon after his death.[9] The bulk of his writings, however, which may well have included an illustrated treatise on architecture, were dispersed. Some he may have taken with him when he left Venice for the last time for Padua, where he died in 1761.[10] Much remained in his rooms and was sequestrated by the state Inquisition after his death. All his papers were put "for safety" under a leaking roof in the Piombe prisons, where they rotted until they could be destroyed as illegible.[11]

Another, much underestimated relic of Lodoli's was lost after his death: his unique collection of works of art. Unique because he was perhaps the earliest connoisseur, perhaps the very earliest, to collect medieval—or at any rate "pre-Raphaelite"—works of art at this time. Although other collectors (his friend Maffei for instance)[12] did buy the occasional *trecento* picture, and English collectors had begun to collect medieval paintings (Ignatius Henry Hugford, 1703–1778, formed the first of such collections in Florence),[13] at the time Lodoli began to buy, his taste was more or less unique. Memmo, writing long after Lodoli's death, still thought it necessary to apologize for his unusual tastes: "Poor friar that he was, he could not have undertaken to buy paintings by the more famous artists . . . he thought therefore to form (a collection) quite different from the ones you usually see, but perhaps more useful, since he imagined that it would show the progress of the *arte del disegno* from its renewal in Italy until the Titians, the Raphaels."[14]

There is little doubt that he found his own collection delightful as well as useful. Memmo gives a summary account of Lodoli's pictures: beginning with Greek art (that is, Byzantine icons, not necessarily very early); there were pictures attributed to Cimabue and Giotto, of course, to Squarcione, to Gentile da Fabriano and Jacobello dal Fiore, the Vivarinis, and so on, to the Bellinis, and the later masters. Pictures were hung on the walls but also stood against them and against the furniture. The collection overflowed into the gardens, which he filled with architectural "examples," both good and bad; and yet it was systematic, arranged according to "schools,"[15] as it were the system of Vasari's *Lives* translated into a gallery. Algarotti was to give this notion currency: in his program for the completion of the Dresden galleries for Augustus III of Saxony and Poland, Algarotti proposed something on the lines of Lodoli's ordering as the guiding principle for the Saxon collections; and his proposals have become the model for most art galleries in the West ever since.[16]

Lodoli, as I shall have reason to remind the reader, was interested in medieval architecture as well as painting and sculpture. Hugford, too, when showing British visitors the wonders of Florence, seemed concerned to show the medieval buildings as well as classical antiquities or Renaissance (and later) paintings.[17] But in his own circle it was his method rather than his taste which was emulated. Algarotti, for instance, in spite of his advocacy of Italian, and particularly Venetian, artists abroad, had rather cosmopolitan and conventionalized Anglo-Parisian tastes;[18] Angelo Quirini, politically the

Villa Algarotti at Carpenedo di Mestre, by Francesco and Bonomo Algarotti (?).

most radical of the Lodoli pupils, built himself a villa which was a marvel of iconographic subtleties and engraved learning (maps in the living rooms, Piranesi's antiquities in the bathrooms, genteel erotica in the study), altars, and portrait heads.[19] The antiquities were varied: Etruscan and Egyptian as well as classical, but definitely a minor sector of Quirini's "visuals." Of the moderns, he had the bronze busts of Voltaire and Rousseau by Houdon and other portraits by Canova, as well as a Hercules by Algardi.

More important as both patron and collector was Filippo Farsetti, a nephew of Clement XIII Rezzonico.[20] Clement XIII allowed Farsetti to export forty-two antique Doric columns from the temple of Concordia on the Roman Forum; these were incorporated into the wings of the vast villa which Farsetti built for himself at Sta. Maria di Sala, on his family's estate. Although this villa was described as "antique" in its splendor, the building has a rococo, almost Viennese look, with its *bombé* front.[21] The gardens, however, were designed by Charles-Louis Clérisseau (most familiar as Robert Adam's companion to Spalato and the inspiration for Jefferson's Charlottesville capitol), perhaps with help—or at least encouragement—from J. J. Winckelmann.[22] These gardens were certainly intended to emulate those of a great Roman villa, even of an imperial one. This scheme seems to have been begun soon after Clement XIII's accession (in 1758). When Clérisseau left Rome on his travels in 1767, he was sent a detailed survey of the Farsetti grounds, and apparently continued to supply Farsetti with details of the gardens.[23]

Both at the villa and at the Farsetti palace at the Rialto there was a vast collection of plaster casts and copies of ancient as well as some

Villa Farsetti, garden front, showing side wings.

modern painting and sculpture, which was intended as a basis for an academy of fine arts.[24] The villa also included a botanic garden which was well known as a scientific curiosity. This is perhaps the most direct evidence of the link between Lodoli's circle and the epicenter of neoclassical theory in Rome.

The Farsetti houses became the unofficial Venetian academy of painting: Canova, the only great Venetian artist of his day, received his training there. It had been Farsetti's intention to produce a generation of Canovas. But Venetian painting as well as Venetian architecture did not have a great future, and the influence of the circle has to be assessed at a cosmopolitan scale.

The master of the group, to return to Lodoli himself, was very much a Venetian. In spite of his fluency in French, his familiarity with English writing, he rarely moved out of the republic and was thoroughly involved in its social life. Farsetti was very particularly devoted to Lodoli and commissioned his portrait in stone (from a plaster he had had modeled at the time of his death). The plaster head was known to Memmo.[25] Two other portraits of Lodoli were done, one by Bartolomeo Lazari, the other by Alessandro Longhi. This portraiture agrees with Memmo's description of his master: ''the friar's habit . . . contributed to make his appearance too unconventional to appear gallant. If you consider the blood clotted on his face, the unkempt hair, the piebald, stubbly chin and those sparkling fiery eyes, it could almost frighten the more delicate souls: certainly they did not find the bawdy words with which he sometimes peppered his talk agreeable.''[26] The blood clots were due to a chronic skin disease of Lodoli's, which Memmo calls a rare form of nonin-

Villa Farsetti at Sta. Maria di Sala, by Paolo Posi, garden front.

Villa Farsetti, detail of central portion, showing antique column shafts incorporated in the wall.

Paolo Posi, project for a villa, probably the Villa Farsetti. Cooper-Hewitt Museum, New York.

Villa Farsetti, side galleries showing use of antique column shafts.

Villa Farsetti, garden front from distance.

fectious leprosy, and this led him increasingly to give up his duties
after 1750; for some thirty years he practiced the so-called Pythagorean diet of milk, vegetables, fruit, and water, sometimes taking a
little bread with fennel or aniseed—and yet he was always invited
out, and as Memmo said, "everywhere his milk and his biscuit was
readily set for him."[27] On the label of Alessandro Longhi's portrait
of the friar[28] he is described as *forse* ("perhaps") *il Socrate Architetto*. This description was a comment on the Vitruvian tag inscribed on the oval surround, an opening through which the friar
looks. *Devonsi unire e fabrica e ragione,* the inscription says
("Building must be united with reason"), *e sia funzion la rapresentazione* ("and let function be the representation").[29] Above the oval,
the emblematic instruments of the geometer and surveyor; below,
those of the architect-draftsman. On either side of the portrait, tab-
lets with words from Jeremiah's prophecy: "to root out and to destroy" on one side, "to build and to plant" on the other.[30] In sum, a
perfect image of the illuminist thinker, the "Socrates": even the
"new Diogenes" whose caustic reasoning would uproot false belief
and stale custom and recreate society, revive it.[31] But strangely
enough, Lodoli chose to restrict his main polemical activity to architecture.

It may seem strange now, that this brilliant polymath, the teacher
of the most promising youth of Venice, should have chosen architecture as his principal interest. Other reasons apart, the great
days of Venetian building were over. Lodoli himself was only marginally active as a working architect: his primary interests were
theoretical. Perhaps architecture provided him with a perfect ground
to exercise his intensely activist and practical talents and invited his
extreme rationalizing inclinations, which could not be applied with
the same ruthlessness to other areas of public life in that slowly
declining but dazzling Venice that we know from the descriptions of
Casanova or Cardinal Bernis, from the paintings of Longhi, Guardi,
or the younger Tiepolo. A Venice which was frittering away a millennium's riches in half a century of almost continuous carnival.[32]

Important monuments were still to be built in Venice during the first half of the eighteenth century. The Gesuati and the Pietà, San Nicola da Tolentino, and San Simone Piccolo were the most important churches and included early instances of the free-standing temple-front.

St. Mark's Square was to be given its final form with the paving designed by Tirali in 1723;[33] the Fenice was built, and rebuilt. Meanwhile, Venetian statesmanship declined. The great foreign embassies were no longer received with that pomp which the city used to mount to welcome them, nor did the Venetian ambassadors possess their old influence in foreign courts. Lodoli's most faithful disciple, Andrea Memmo, experienced and described all this when he was the *Savio* (the senate officer) in charge of ceremonies, as the Venetian governor of Padua, as Balia (commissioner or minister) in Istanbul, and later Ambassador in Rome, before he returned to the *Dominante* (as the Venetians called their home city) as a procurator of San Marco.[34] As the *Savio ai Cerimoniali,* Memmo was asked to report on the protocol which governed the reception of every foreign potentate. In the three-part report he submitted in 1768–1769, he points out how the weakened economic position of Venice has made the charge to a particular nobleman, to receive some foreign prince, once considered an honor, a ruinous imposition. The princes who used to come to Venice for important political motives now—so Memmo argues—come "attracted by the admiration which the sound repute of the ancient and ever-high virtues of its citizens inspires, as well as the singular nature of the *Dominante,* the magnificence of its shows and the variety of other diversions." Let Venice herself, he goes on, its daily life, be the spectacle for the reception of visiting princes. The great official ceremonies should be discontinued as ruinous to those who organized them and of dubious value to the Most Serene Republic. This realistic document was the first internal recognition by the Venetian government that the city was no longer a great economic and political power, but that it was becoming that cultural and tourist center which Austrian domination and the rapid growth of the port of Trieste would make it.[35]

It has an ancillary interest, since it provides official recognition also for an aspect of everyday life in Venice, the aspect which was celebrated by Goldoni in his plays; in 1761, Giovanni Battista Pasquali, a publisher who was a close friend of Lodoli,[36] issued a new edition of Goldoni's plays, richly illustrated with engravings after Pier Antonio Novelli (1728–1804). As Goldoni himself said, prefacing the second volume of this edition, he was tired of all those muses, Apollos, masks, satyrs, and apes of convention, and "from that love of novelty which has always been my aim," he proposes that the frontispiece to each volume should show a scene from his own life.[37] The plays were moreover illustrated with the same sharply observed genre scenes. This mode already had some vogue in Venice: Pietro Longhi commonly, and Giambattista Piazzetta more grandly, had done some genre paintings which proved very popular. But Novelli's illustrations were something of a novelty, as Goldoni wanted them. And although Novelli himself was to do some rather chilly neoclassical paintings, these illustrations mark a change of attitude, a new interest in the intense experience of the everyday, which Memmo's report celebrated a few years later.[38]

Memmo's report is written entirely in the rationalizing and radical spirit of Lodoli, the dead master Memmo would revere and recall throughout his career. Most of our information about Lodoli does in fact come from a treatise on architecture—if a book as discursive as his can be called a treatise—which Memmo published when he was living in Rome as Venetian ambassador.[39] It was only the first part of a larger work, however. The bulk of the manuscript was published after Memmo's death in 1833/1834 in Zara (now Zadar, in Yugoslavia) in two volumes.

At the very beginning of the book, Memmo makes clear his reason for compiling it. His master's teaching had been current in Europe for some time, circulating in part by word of mouth. But there had also been a published source for the book, whose *raison d'être* Memmo felt bound to set out. Many years earlier, he says, seeing that Lodoli himself was unlikely to write down his ideas, one of his pupils in that seminar which I mentioned earlier, Francesco Foscari, "then a most charming youth, now a weighty senator,"[40] was invited to prepare such a text, but he was too distracted, first by bad health and later by public office, so that the second choice fell on Francesco Algarotti. Algarotti, who had attended Lodoli's "school" from his early days, agreed to do the work on condition that neither Lodoli nor Memmo (who seems to have organized the whole affair) would see the text before publication.[41] It appeared in 1753 and was received with some acclaim.

Algarotti was already a well-known European littérateur and courtier when he prepared the Lodoli text. The son of a very rich merchant, he went to Paris after his schooling; there, aged twenty-one, he wrote what was to be his best-known book, *Il Newtonismo spiegato alle Dame (Newtonianism Explained to the Ladies)*.[42] His agreeable presence and courtly manner in the salons earned him the sobriquet "the Swan of Padua" (which has been attributed to Voltaire[43]), although the great astronomer and geographer Maupertuis, who was to deal with him for many years in Berlin, saw a different side to his character: "if his dress would get tangled up with yours" he writes to a friend, "he will cut a piece from yours to free himself."[44]

Algarotti was to travel much. For a while he lived in London. In Italy, later, he acted as an agent for Augustus III of Saxony and Poland in buying pictures (mostly for the Dresden galleries). And he cultivated a long and sentimental friendship with Frederick the Great, who summoned him to Berlin on his accession, and gave him his title.[45] His delicate health—he died of consumption—forced him to retire from Germany, first to Venice, when he wrote the essay on architecture, and finally to Pisa, where he died.[46]

Memmo's estimate of Algarotti seems to coincide with that of Maupertuis. The brilliant courtier overstated aspects of Lodoli's teaching in some ways: rather French ones, rather chic ones, without actually committing himself to them.[47] Algarotti's essay does not quote Lodoli by name but refers to a "philosopher" (he uses the word in the generalized, eighteenth-century sense) from whom the "Vitruvian Institutes" have much to fear, since his imagination pours out images and he has a particular way of arguing; he is tough yet has the common touch, as well as great dexterity in managing the Socratic weapons.[48] The "Vitruvian Institutes" here take on the appearance of the kind of authority which Lodoli's generation put to question generally.

Lodoli and his friends should have realized, however, that the universally ingratiating, the wholly charming Algarotti was not the right vehicle for the friar's abrasive ideas: what Algarotti extracted from Lodoli's teaching turned out to be both more "advanced," that is, fashionable, and therefore more acceptable than what the friar had said. In fact Algarotti's tone in presenting Lodoli's teaching is definitely ironic. The essential maxim he discusses is the Vitruvian one, that nothing should appear in a building which was not in some way a working part.[49] The maxim was unobjectionable and had been bandied about by various *trattatisti* since Alberti. But Algarotti's "philosopher" wanted it applied in a thoroughgoing fashion. The basis of classical architecture, of the orders in particular, is wooden construction: there is no reason why this architecture should be translated into stone. Ornament should correspond to the characteristics of the material of which it is made. Thus the whole ornamental vocabulary of the ancients could be discarded, and with it that developed by the moderns: the "philosopher" tried to reach a kind of empirical, atomic understanding of the nature of building based on statics and the study of material, and to a lesser extent on function, as the term is now understood.[50] The nature of the argument he attributes to Lodoli obviously seems rather dubious to Algarotti; timber, he says, has always been the basic building material, and the most varied and graceful moldings and ornaments originate in timber construction. If in adapting these to stone the architect were lying, well then, the lie may be more beautiful than the truth.[51]

Ending on a conciliatory note, however, Algarotti suggests that the difficulties raised by the "philosopher" (i.e., Lodoli) would lead to improved structural methods and the avoidance of such expedients as chains, clamps, and other devices used to keep basically ill-constructed buildings in one piece. So that, he concludes, even if the "philosopher," like Socrates of old, will not be able to found a new republic, yet his arguments may lead to the reformation of old and faulty laws.[52]

The detached and patronizing irony, even more than the fundamental misunderstanding of the master's teaching, provoked some indignation in Lodoli's immediate circle. By the time the essay was written, any publication of Algarotti's was guaranteed a European circulation, while Lodoli's true doctrine would be confined to his immediate circle. Various moves were made to correct the impression Algarotti had created, but none were very energetic. Lodoli himself commented on the matter with one of his usual oblique parables.[53]

Although Algarotti's essay was first printed in Venice in 1759, its dedication is dated 1756.[54] Lodoli made it quite clear that Algarotti was more or less commissioned by him and other friends in 1753, who were irritated by the anonymous publication in Paris that same year of the *Essai sur l'Architecture*. It immediately attracted as much attention as (if not more than) Algarotti's *saggio* and was destined to have a much more direct impact on architectural theory and even practice. Two years later, in 1755, the second enlarged and illustrated edition of the *Essai* carried the author's name: Father Laugier of the Society of Jesus.

Lodoli and Laugier have been associated as advocating similar views.[55] But in fact their opinions diverge on important matters, as I propose to show later. It may well be that they were (or were to become) familiar with one another's opinions. Laugier, much the younger of the two men, may have visited Venice early in the 1750s, during the embassy of Cardinal (then still the Abbé) Bernis.[56] Although Bernis was a declared enemy of the Jesuits, Laugier and he seemed to have had a bond: they may well both have been freemasons.[57]

Certainly, Laugier visited Venice before the publication of his history of the Venetian republic, whose first volume appeared in 1759, with a fulsome dedication to Bernis.[58] Whether or not Laugier was a mason, is virtually impossible to say, although he could certainly have been initiated either in Paris, where masonic lodges existed since the 1720s; or in Lyons, where he was exiled after his rather outspoken sermons. It was in Lyons, which boasted three lodges by 1750, that Casanova had been first admitted as a mason.[59]

But the masonic connection has other interesting implications: Casanova was, in the late forties and early fifties—until his arrest by the state Inquisition in the summer of 1755—very close to the Memmo brothers. It was said (and Casanova certainly believed it) that his chief accuser to the Inquisition had been Lucia Pisani Memmo, Andrea's mother, who maintained that her sons were being led astray by an adventurer,[60] although Casanova seemed to think that Donna Pisani Memmo's three sons "were highly spirited and more apt to seduce than to be seduced." Concerning what one of the spies of the Inquisition called "Picureanism," Casanova is himself sufficient witness. But in fact his own masonic allegiance is not documented, and nothing is known of Andrea Memmo's. On the other hand, Bernardo Memmo, who was very close to his brother, is known to have been a mason; and many of Lodoli's disciples joined the Craft.[61] And the attraction of masonry for the group may explain something which I still find puzzling: the extraordinary emphasis which architecture assumes in the activities of polymaths such as Lodoli or Memmo, or even Laugier. True, this was the great age of taste, as I have said earlier. Every gentleman or burgher, even if he could not design his own house, at least could breathe knowingly down his architect's neck. Royalty and eminence felt obliged to subscribe for several copies of any architectural book of importance. It was the latest phase of an old passion: princes and citizens, since the beginning of history, had regarded building as an index of their achievement.

But the men of whom I have been writing here were neither potentates nor oligarchs. They were, on the contrary, bent on the reform of their society. Their energies were invested in building, which they did not regard as the physiognomy of established powers, but as a kind of paradigm, almost as a sympathetic-magical model of society. They lived "in an age of repression, which was fearful, even when it was practised by enlightened despots." The reform of architecture gave them a field of practical activity in which rationality, the desire for a harmony of thought (of rational thought in particular) with action was possible, without fear of prosecution. The aim of such reforming activity was a better, a more consequent, a purer architecture: and society, some of them hoped, would somehow follow the model which had been operated in building. Such ideas certainly inspired some of Lodoli's followers.

Even a generation earlier, they had been foreshadowed by that strange figure, Leone Pascoli: he was a hydraulic engineer, a traveler, a connoisseur, an economist, a planner.[62] The wretched fiscal condition of the papal states exercised him throughout his life. His great scheme for making the Tiber navigable up to Todi, and even further, to his home town, Perugia, was published in 1740, just after the election of Benedict XIV;[63] during the sixth month of the unusually long conclave, the pope had read a previous publication of Pascoli,[64] which had been written for the benefit of the previous conclave, although not published until 1733, in which he set out his ideas about the need which the state had of building. It is to the glory of the prince, he said, it is to the advantage of merchants and of the nation; and—most important—it stimulates the economy, without putting any burden on the exchange. In the vast replanning of Rome which he proposed, a stock exchange on the Capitol had an important part. In another, earlier book, a collection of artists' lives, he had provided a rhapsody on the uses of architecture in the preface. Architecture, he says:

> introduced social organization, united its magistrates and formed republics. . . . It is the first of the arts, being the most ancient, the most noble, the most useful, the most necessary. . . . It is in some way an extension of the divine creative process . . . It turns a sterile and desolate terrain into a fertile and pleasant one. It underlies all human activity, from navigation to war, and has established so stupendous and profitable a commerce throughout its vast domain that it would help to establish it, even with heaven, through church building.[65]

Here is a very different attitude from that of the preceding generations, or even of Pascoli's contemporaries, who could still indulge a
passion for the elaborate symphonies of metaphor and quotation
which consumed so many architects of the seventeenth and early
eighteenth century, which I have attempted to show exemplified,
and perhaps exasperated in Fischer von Erlach's treatment of the
Karlskirche.[66]

In Florence, too, Sir Horace Mann, the British resident, and
Baron Philip von Stosch, Winckelmann's friend, operated as collectors, connoisseurs, and agents; they were both freemasons.[67] In
Venice, the British resident, John Murray, confessed to Casanova in
rather louche circumstances that he was a mason;[68] but it is not
known whether his brother-in-law, Consul Smith, the patron of
Canaletto as well as Pasqualini, may have been one as well. Algarotti was an intimate of Frederick the Great, who had early become a freemason, and who constituted a "royal lodge" at Potsdam
early in his reign.[69] No doubt any intimate, particularly such a
"philosophical" and sentimental intimate of the king, would have
been invited and even urged to join; and Algarotti must already have
been familiar with freemasonry among his London friends.[70]

When Algarotti had come to Paris originally, he had come fresh
from the Lodoli "school" and he had been well received in various
salons. Over a generation, the delicate, handsome, wily Venetian
operated throughout Europe as an intellectual politician—or as an
operator of the intellectual life. He had the backing of Frederick the
Great, as well as of the Saxon court; he had the benevolence of
Voltaire.[71] All this was to his advantage. It may well be that there
was occasion between the Abbé Laugier's move to Paris in 1744 and
the first publication of the *Essai* for the two to have met, or at any
rate to have heard of each other, but there is no record of it.

Nor is there any evidence that Laugier met Lodoli on his Venetian
visits, of which we know so little. But it is easy to assume that at
some point he visited the house of Consul Joseph Smith, if only
because so few Venetian houses were open to the visiting
foreigner.[72]

Smith's house would have been useful to him in many ways. The
consul supplemented the poor income of his office by acting as a
dealer and impresario: he patronized Canaletto, the Riccis, Visentini, Rosalba Carriera; he was also a publisher, working with a Venetian, Giovanni Battista Pasquali, whom I have already introduced
as the publisher of the fine edition of Goldoni's plays.[73] Smith and
Pasquali (particularly Pasquali[74]) were close friends of Lodoli (a
friendship which must have assumed a special character when
Lodoli was Revisore), of Memmo, and of Algarotti. By the time of
Laugier's probable visits, Smith would already have been quite old:
he was seventy-five by 1750. By 1756 he felt remote from social life
and gave up his box at the theater of St. John Chrysostom—he had
been a habitual theatergoer[75]—and although he lived until he was
ninety, he virtually (except for some odd spells) withdrew from the
public and intellectual life of the city.[76]

Palazzetto Smith on the Grand Canal, Venice, now the Argentinian consulate, by Antonio Visentini. The top floor was added by Gianantonio Selva.

Memmo had been an intimate of Smith in his youth, until an emotional complication broke in on the friendship, although in later years he remembered the consul with old esteem.[77]

There was an informal salon in the Smith house: a salon to which any foreigner would tend to gravitate to meet Venetian notables with a certain freedom. The society at Consul Smith's house was congenial:

> Whoever comes to your house [writes Goldoni in his dedicatory letter to Smith of "The English Philosopher"], finds the perfect union of all the arts and all the sciences; you sit among them not as an admirer who enjoys their surface appeal, but as one who really knows them, who is involved in their advancement. The choice library you have proves this. . . . Painting, architecture, sculpture compete for the dominion of your walls.[78]

The house described by Goldoni was the palazzetto on the Grand Canal, just past the Rialto. It was given a new facade towards the

Engraving to show the evils of cutting out parts of moldings to impose cartouches, vases, etc. After Visentini.

L'esempio presente fà vedere quanto sconci il tagliar le Cornici, e Freggio per poner sopra l'Architrave alcuna cosa, sià Cartelle, Scudi, Vasi ò altro, secondo il bizaro capricio di chi inventa tali cose.

Teofilo Gallacini's drawing to illustrate the evils of cutting moldings, from the manuscript of his book. British Museum, London.

canal, in an advanced, chaste neo-Palladian manner, by one of Consul Smith's clients, the *veduttista* Antonio Visentini. Visentini, long-lived like his patron (1688–1782), was also the architect of the country villa which Smith bought at Mogliano. The Palazzetto Smith (later Mangli-Valmarana, now the Argentine consulate) was enlarged by Visentini's pupil Gianantonio Selva (Canova's friend and favorite architect) by the addition of a top story in 1779. Visentini's activity as architect seems limited to his work for Smith and the other palazzo on the Grand Canal, the Colletti-Giusti, in 1766; he may have had a hand in the Villa Valmarana ai Nani in Vicenza. But his most important influence was exercised through his *vedute* and engravings and through his one published treatise.

This was a rather strange book; a manuscript called "On the Errors of Architects," by the seventeenth-century anatomist and mathematician Teofilo Gallacini, had been bought by Smith, who had the manuscript published by Pasquali and annotated by Visen-

The central niche of the Pantheon in Rome, attic story, designed by Paolo Posi.

tini.[79] At the sale of his library to George III it passed into the British Museum where it still is.

The original book had been composed in 1625 and dedicated to Giulio Mancini, Urban VIII's physician and a perceptive connoisseur.[80] It was a protest against the "excesses" of late mannerism and early baroque, as those kinds of architecture were practiced in Rome and Tuscany under the eyes of this "reactionary" observer. It was the only work of Gallacini to reach print; however, a manuscript collection of Roman inscriptions passed through the hands of Baron Philip von Stosch, Winckelmann's friend.[81]

Pantheon, detail of the triglyph at the keystone of the niche arch.

Some years later, Visentini published an up-to-date supplement.[82] In it Gallacini had inveighed against Michaelangelo by name and even criticized the occasional antique example. Visentini directed his attack mostly against contemporaries and near-contemporaries. He damned Bernardo Vittone at length, was dismissive of Paolo Posi's work on the Pantheon, and devoted much attention to the Jesuit church in Venice. This church had a facade designed by Giovanni Battista Fattoretto with Domenico Rossi, and the interior was done by Rossi with the help of Giuseppe Pozzo between 1714 and 1729.[83] Giuseppe Pozzo's brother, Andrea (a Jesuit lay brother), was the author of the most elaborate treatise on painted architecture; in a translated version, it came to be known in England as "the Jesuit's Perspective." The interior of the Gesuiti was encrusted with colored marbles to look like figured damask hanging over and between the pilasters and even draped round the pulpit. Like much of the work of the Pozzo brothers, it epitomized what the enlightened spirits of the next generation would fight and despise. Ironically, the Gesuiti is often confused with the church of the Gesuati on the Zattere, which was one of the centers of Venetian Enlightenment.

Antonio Visentini, proposal for the "improvement" of the Pantheon niche.

The Gesuati, or Poor Jesuates, were a defunct order, whose monastery had been handed over to the Dominicans on its dissolution in 1668. The most famous member of this Dominican community, Daniele Concina (1686–1756) was an acquaintance of Lodoli's and one of the most prolific and influential Italian theologians, a confidant of Benedict XIV, and a popular, virulent preacher. He was the great enemy of Jesuit casuistry.[84] The two disputes which engaged his attention particularly were firstly the popularity of theaters—a matter in which he came into conflict with Lodoli's old friend Scipione Maffei, whom Concina threatened with excommunication and hell-fire; fortunately his views on the matter were more extreme than the Pope's.[85] The second issue was more important, perhaps: the justification of lending capital at interest. Again Maffei was his main adversary, and again the Pope intervened, though more ambiguously.[86] Concina's most interesting publication, however, is his *History of Probabilism and Rigorism.*[87]

Probabilism, the doctrine maintained by the Jesuit school of moralists, was opposed to rigorism, which was also sometimes called purism. The central position in this conflict was taken by St. Alphonso Liguori (1696–1787), whose doctrine of equiprobabilism put the decision firmly into the hands of spiritual advisors and reinforced the spiritual power of the clergy.[88]

Sta. Maria Assunta (The Jesuit Church) Venice, interior, by Domenico Rossi and others. All the apparent cloth decoration is marble intarsia.

Sta. Maria del Rosario (Gesuati Church), Venice, by Giorgio Massari.

The terms *rigorism* and *purism,* which first appear in this context, were to pass from theological to philosophical discourse. Kant considered himself a rigorist in matters of ethics, as did Fichte. The word had an entry in Bayle's great dictionary of human errors. It is interesting therefore that it became a term of abuse in architectural circles and applied to Lodoli's followers,[89] as well as those of Laugier in France. Purism, on the other hand, is a term which in the middle of the eighteenth century applied principally to linguistic pedants, although it was to become important in architectural polemics with the Purist manifesto of Ozenfant and Le Corbusier of 1920. But in spite of being applied by historians as a blanket term to eighteenth-century controversialists, it did not come into common use then.

Rigorism appeared in the first half of the eighteenth century as a moral heresy, tainted with Jansenism. But curiously enough the

Sta. Maria del Rosario, Venice, interior, by Giorgio Massari.

Gesuati Dominicans were building a church during Concina's time which was hardly rigorist—in architectural terms. The church was dedicated to the Madonna del Rosario, designed by Giorgio Massari, decorated by Tiepolo for the most part, and consecrated in 1734.

It faced across the Giudecca the splendid challenge of Palladio's facade of the Redentore; San Giorgio Maggiore and the church of the Zitelle are also visible from it. Its giant order reproduces the proportions of another of Palladio's facades, that at San Francesco della Vigna (Lodoli's home) as the friary which was to be built up around it was to have definite analogies to the nearby Carità convent, also designed by Palladio. But Massari was not an out-and-out Palladian.

The major Palladian of Venice at the time, the learned, even pedantic Tommaso Temanza, did not care for him or for his work.[90]

And the structure of the facade is really anti-Palladian: the four giant columns are three-quarters attached to the facade screen; the solid aedicule of the door has an independent order, which stands a little lower than the main columns; the cornice of the central aedicule is echoed by an ornamental band in the side panels, which divide them into shallow-niched compartments, the lower set rather high in the wall; at either end, the columns are echoed in a sequence of pilasters and oblique end walls, which make the whole facade into a three-dimensional object, which is yet detached from the body of the building. Yet its ornamental structure has not the coherence of a "built" thing, as does for instance that of Massari's professional grandfather, Baldassare Longhena, in the Madonna della Salute. The church was moreover regarded with embarrassment by some of the fathers. It was luxurious in finish (even by Venetian standards) and visitors were assured that funds had come from public subscription.[91]

However, there was none of the tricky opulence of the Jesuit church about the Madonna del Rosario interior.

The Dalmatian sandstone molding contrasted with white stucco wall in the proper Palladian manner, but Massari varied the Palladian themes by inverting them. The cornices join the capitals which support them, the plinth, the column bases: they are of stone. The wall surface and the column shaft are made continuous by being finished in white stucco. And the wall surface is negated, since much of it is occupied by large stone reliefs, so that the column and entablature skeleton of Palladian buildings is quite lost. Even the cornice is split by the white stucco band of the frieze. All this breaks the continuity of ornamental structure, which even in Longhena's buildings retains its classic consistency.

Although there is no record of Lodoli's observations on the Gesuati church, Memmo reports that he had words with Massari about another building: the Church of Sta. Maria della Visitazione, which was also the chapel of the girls' foundling hospital, the Pietà.[92] The plan of the church is oval, the decoration is based on a rather chaste (if paneled) order of flat Corinthian pilasters: hardly rococo, in spite of the few gilt carvings, and the occasional flourish, which gives it that touch of rocaille. Though here, too, there is an inversion: the recessed panels of the pilasters seem to weaken them, the coupled pilasters of the interior seem to contradict the attached columns of the facade.

Massari was the most successful architect of his generation in Venice. Besides the churches I have already mentioned, his best-known designs are the Palazzo Grassi on the Grand Canal, some villas on the mainland, and churches there and in Venice. The showiest are his additions (the top floor and the decorations) to Longhena's Palazzo Rezzonico. In spite of his success, he seems to have been rather unassuming. And that is how Memmo shows him—even if he is made to sound a little exasperated—in the discus-

Sta. Maria della Pietà, Venice, by Giorgio Massari.

sion which he reports in the Preface of his book.[93] One of the coun-
cillors of the Pietà hospital, Memmo says, insisted on having
Lodoli's opinion of the scheme; the friar therefore went to see the
model at Massari's house. The general criticism was summed up in
an improvised (unrhymed) distich.[94] This Massari was prepared to
consider, but when Lodoli got down to detail, Massari protested: he
could not be expected to be "a perfect architect in every hole and
every corner." But Lodoli insisted, so that Massari, ill at ease,
retired to a line of defense that has since become common among
successful professional men.

> You, my dear father, who don't have to live by the
> practice of the profession, won't enter into the spirit of
> it. To earn a living we need to get a reputation, and that
> you will never get by having your maths to hand, but
> by imitating the best examples . . . taking care to avoid
> their defects. . . . Should I produce a completely origi-
> nal design, however reasonable it may be, I am sure
> that another architect, who imitated a facade by Pal-
> ladio for instance, or by Vignola, would be preferred to
> me; and who would keep my family the while? Excuse
> me if my needs won't allow me to discard what has
> maintained this family of mine honourably so far; and
> if I can't renounce all I have thought and done to at-
> tend your lectures, so as to be ruined.

Lodoli (who is reported as telling the story by Memmo in the
Elementi), noticing the mirth of the bystanders and realizing he
would get no further, launched his parting shot: "Signor Giorgio,"
he said, "think that you might show me a district given over to

prostitutes in any city, but that women should nevertheless live decently.''

The discussion is worth reporting in detail, not only as showing Lodoli's way in argument, but also as a witness to the shift in the intellectual climate in which an architect such as Massari moved. The contempt for theoretical issues which Massari expresses, would, of course, have seemed shocking to the exemplars he chiefly claims to imitate: Palladio and Vignola. It would have seemed equally so, however, to more recent architects: to the Torinese baroque masters, from Guarini to Vittone, or to the Roman-Neapolitan *barochetto* masters. It certainly shocked his juniors, especially the stricter neo-Palladians. Tommaso Temanza, their chief polemist, despised Massari's sloppiness, even if he held Lodoli's apparently antihistorical radicalism in great distrust.[95] It is doubtful if Massari had ever read Perrault; still it is a bastardized and popular version of Perrault's argument which Massari contrasted to Lodoli's.

Even if allowance is made that Massari is the successful professional man, parrying the attack of a critic-littérateur, this alone has an arresting element of novelty, since Massari presents himself as a man of taste, whose operation requires no rational justification. His designs, he implies, must be conventional to succeed and based on familiar examples. He feels free to vary quite arbitrarily the themes he derives from the great masters (as he did in the Gesuati church) for the sake of effect. The cooling taste he satisfied by the ironed-out sobriety of his exteriors (though he could do the exuberant thing easily enough, as when completing Longhena's Ca'Rezzonico by an upper story); in the interiors, he allowed himself a little more gilded license.

However, it was not Massari's taste that Lodoli rejected. Nor was he an enemy of ornament in general, as Algarotti had suggested. Lodoli objected to the irrational disposition and choice of ornaments, very much on the lines Gallacini's treatise sets out.[96]

Although he had presented Lodoli's ideas, Algarotti remained, as I said earlier, uncommitted. Before undertaking to write the essay he told Memmo one day that ''even if Lodoli had a paradise for the martyrs to his ideas, he [Algarotti] had no desire to end up there.''[97] Writing privately to Tommaso Temanza in the year his essay was published, Algarotti confessed himself unconvinced by Lodoli: ''Those who wish to have no ornament (on buildings) which has not got some wherefore, seem too stingy to you . . . nor do I wish to embrace the system of such rigorists wholeheartedly; to want that everything which is shown [*in rapresentazione*] should also be a working part [*in funzione*] is to want too much. What might the function of the leaves on a Corinthian capital be?''[98]

Even in the first of Memmo's two volumes, the negative one, Lodoli is shown to have a rather permissive attitude to ornament, an attitude which is clarified in the second, the positive volume. Nor was he indifferent to the past; his teaching had a historical bias, and

it would be surprising if he did not extend this to architecture. Like
the philosopher whom he so much admired, Giambattista Vico, and
like their common master, Francis Bacon, he was "ravished with
the Reverence for Antiquity,"[99] which transpires through all the
critical remarks he makes about ancient buildings. There is further
evidence about Lodoli's attitude to ornament in the description of a
building designed by Lodoli himself as well as in buildings directly
commissioned, or even—in one case—designed by Andrea Memmo.

Lodoli's building is the hospice for the Franciscans serving the
Latin Patriarchate of Jerusalem, who belonged to the same congregation as himself and who usually passed through Venice. The hospice was a kind of *dépendance* of the claustral buildings of San
Francesco della Vigna.

Again, Memmo needs to apologize for his master: "It was only a
poor conversion of a friar's hospice," he says, to explain the lack of
"generosity, magnificence, fine planning, comfort and elegance."[100]
But he praises the great resourcefulness of his master in devising
novel ways of cutting doors and windows. Moreover, he saved
money on the brackets required for a balcony-corridor on which two
luggage-carrying porters should be able to pass each other, by in-
clining the wooden wall of the passage "up and outward: since men
being wider at the shoulder than at the foot so that . . . even the
porters, meeting each other, and carrying on their shoulders the
travelling friars' coffers, could easily pass each other."[101] Memmo

Hospice for the Pilgrims of the Holy Land in San Francesco della Vigna,
Venice, by Carlo Lodoli.

reports the disapproval of the *professori* ("professional men") of the time who found it all very irregular. But even more interesting to Memmo is a structural device of Lodoli's. He prefaces his account of the invention by pointing out that 60 percent of stone thresholds, and many beams, have for twenty centuries been made of one piece of stone, because of the general ignorance of the *eternal laws of lithology* [my italics]; these would have shown that the weight, bearing at either end on a threshold (which is also a single piece of stone), would tend to lower either end because they are more heav-

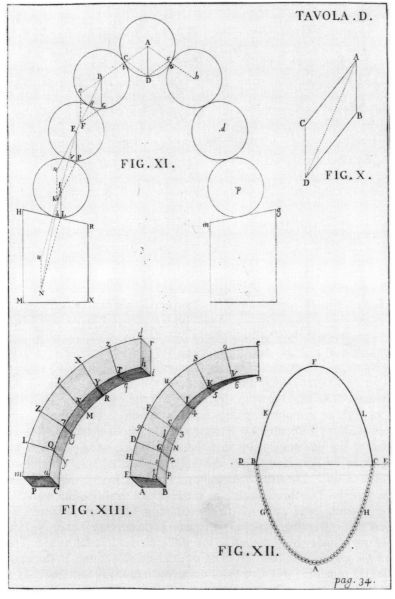

The geometry of catenary curves and its applicaton to the cutting of vous-soirs. After Poleni. London, British Museum.

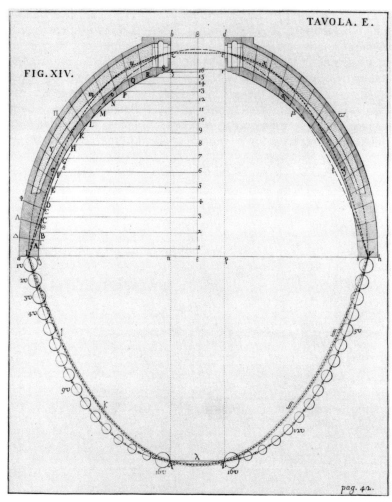

The properties of the catenary curves applied to the dome of St. Peter's. After Poleni. London, British Museum.

ily loaded, so that the stone fractured and the ends sunk, while the center piece remained intact. Some, Palladio among them, surmounted the difficulty by making the threshold a beam of three pieces, but this still meant that the side pieces, weighed down by columns or doorjambs, left the middle piece higher, which was "ugly to see." The lithologue-philosopher (i.e., Lodoli) also divided the threshold in three pieces; he made the central one the width of the opening, and although it carried no weight, he increased its "energy" by giving a catenary curve to its under side, but prevented the unevenness by dovetailing the three pieces to each other. The doorjambs, too, he found broken or cracked sometimes in the middle. He remedied this also by dividing them halfway and inserting a reinforcing piece. which was dovetailed top and bottom; the top of the door frame was also curved and, where appropriate, decorated. The main door of the hospice was all of stone; the top was enlarged almost into a semicircle, and on it Lodoli had a bas-relief done of the holy protector of the Jerusalem friars; but in order that he might be seen to be overlaid *(sopraimposto),* he attached four elaborate sprigs of vine, which sustained him like a frame or a tablet. Memmo adds triumphantly, "if you want an ornament which is appropriate here it is."[102]

Much of the confusion about the application of Lodoli's theory derives from the conviction of most writers on the period that the hospice was destroyed. It was, in fact, much damaged, but enough remains to convince the reader that Memmo's description is accurate enough—and that Lodoli meant what he said. A new form of ornament could be developed from the scientific laws which he and his colleagues were wresting from nature; and that chiefly from the catenary curve.[103]

In 1742, when (according to a commemorative plaque) the hospice was finished, Giovanni Battista Piranesi was twenty-two; he had already been to Rome once, and in the next year was to issue his first set of engravings. It seems fair to say that he was Lodoli's most brilliant and most influential disciple. I will have a great deal more to say about that in the next chapter; but at this point I can best give a reasoned account of the matrix in which his ideas were formed: which of course meant that he would gravitate in Rome to the circle around Cardinal Passionei which was closest to the sort of intellectual atmosphere he knew in Venice as a young man. He was born in the small village of Mogliano Veneto, near Treviso. The family name (sometimes written Piranese) suggests its origin from Pirano (now called Piran) in Yugoslavia, a small harbor town on the northern coast of Istria. His father, a *tagliapietra,* was known to be quirky and hot tempered,[104] a trait that was inherited by the son. Giovanni Battista's brother, Angelo, became a Carthusian; it is from him, so tradition has it, that Giovanni Battista acquired the first elements of his considerable learning.[105]

His professional training began in the studio of his mother's brother, Matteo Lucchesi (1705–1776), about whom too little is known. The bulk of his work depended on his being vice-proto to the Magistrato alle Acque,[106] though he also worked as an independent architect in Venice and the Veneto. His best-known buildings are the Ospedaletto behind SS. Giovanni e Paolo, with a chapel by Longhena in his heaviest manner; San Giovanni Novo (between St. Mark's and Santa Maria Formosa) was—as Lucchesi would confidently claim—"the Redeemer Redeemed"; a facade based on the Redentore, but with Palladio's "mistakes" corrected; however, only the plinth and pedestals were built.[107] On the mainland, there is his vast and now ruined rebuilding of the Polcenigo Castle near Pordenone. But his main work was done for the Magistrato, and it has traditionally been assumed that it is through the hydraulic work of the Magistrato that Piranesi first became familiar with the unadorned construction and the vast, dramatically underlit spaces, which were to mark his work as an engraver.

Lucchesi's collaborator for the Magistrato, the scholar-engineer,

Tommaso Temanza,[108] was in turn the pupil of a maternal uncle,
Giovanni Scalfurotto (c. 1700–1764), who was also one of Piranesi's
early teachers. His best-known work, the church of St. Simeon the
Less, has already been mentioned for its temple-front portico[109] and
was begun in 1718; twelve years earlier, another and even more
impressive temple portico, was built nearby, that of S. Nicola dei
Tolentini, which was designed by Andrea Tirali. Tirali, Lucchesi,
and Temanza, were all employed by the Magistrato.[110] Whether it
was through Poleni and Lucchesi, or through Temanza, or even his
brother, Angelo, Piranesi came into contact with Lodoli. This contact led to a firm friendship and presumably some correspondence.[111] When Memmo came to Rome as ambassador, however, in 1781, Giovanni Battista had already died, but Memmo
maintained a close relationship with his son Francesco, about which
I shall have more to say later.

It was in the Venetian milieu that Piranesi's knowledge of architecture was formed; the building works of the Magistrato were the
most important to be carried out in the Venice of his youth,[112] and
that is presumably where he first came across Fischer von Erlach's
Entwurff, which he seems to have studied with great care.[113] But the

*The church of Sta. Maria Maddalena in Venice, by
Tommaso Temanza.*

connection with Lodoli and his circle has been difficult to establish. Too many authorities accepted Algarotti's account of Lodoli's theory and could not reconcile his apparent condemnation of ornament with Piranesi's immoderate addiction to it. But as I have already suggested, Lodoli did not find ornament damnable at all. He was not concerned with reducing the quantity of ornament but with making it appropriate and coherent. His positive reforming zeal was directed to matters of planning and convenience, as well as to the more exalted sphere which made up the "civil architecture" of his day. The episode of the comfortable chair, designed by Lodoli, illustrates his approach. Memmo gives an account of it in his preface.

The shoulders, Lodoli maintained, should dictate the form of the chair back, and the bottom, that of the seat. He therefore had made the prototype of a novel armchair, based closely on an ancient Roman one, which had not yet become common at the time. Soon after that, a chair not at all unlike, was taken to Paris by "my good friend, the Baly (Ambassador or Commissioner) Giuseppe Tommaso Farsetti, Patrician of Venice."[114] Lodoli's chair, however, not only had a concave back like the French models, but "was curved in the part where you sit, as later became customary in England."

This is an example of what Lodoli meant when he said that "reason must be obeyed—and not only caprice"—in that kind of architecture, for which he was perhaps the first to use the term *organic* and which concerns all kinds of furnishing.[115] He used the chair to extend the argument to buildings proper, and he concluded: "carve then, and varnish, and gild as much as you like to serve your necessary [*sic*] luxury; but do not neglect comfort, or the *resistenza opportuna* ("desirable elasticity")." This lesson of his was obviously taken to heart by Memmo, who became one of the more important patrons of Venetian architecture in the middle of the eighteenth century. The first exercises of it on a large scale were his projects in Padua. He was appointed governor (*provveditore*) of the city in 1775, and almost immediately became immersed in its problems. Although his governorship only lasted from March 1775 to July 1776, he left Padua two of the bulkiest buildings of the century: the new hospital and the Prato della Valle. Both were in fact executed by the Abbé Domenico Cerato (1720–1792), at that time the first professor of architecture at the University,[116] and his assistant Daniele Danieletti (1756–1822). The hospital is a barracklike building. Cerato, although a good Vincentine with a strong Palladian bent, occasionally (as in the communal treasury building of 1772) takes on Memmian themes: the use of rustication for door and window surrounds, even if not following Lodoli's prescription, would have been preferred to many other ornamental patterns. The Prato, however, is Memmo's and Cerato's chief architectural monument. This old common had been a Roman theater (stones from the excavation had been used to build the Ponte del Rialto three centuries earlier[117]), a naumachy, a circus. In the eighteenth century the meadow floodland was used for occasional fairs; it was surrounded by opulent houses, which included the palace of the three Memmo brothers.[118] Andrea

Antonio Canaletto, The Prà della Valle *before Memmo's project.*

Memmo, on taking office, immediately set about organizing the
finances of this project and drawing its outlines. The large open
space was roughly triangular, and Memmo found that an oval figure,
an oval of the shape which the ancients liked for their amphithea-
ters,[119] was more suitable for it. There was an outside ring of planting
and paving; within that a ring of canals, supplied by underground
conduits, and traversed by four bridges. The canals surrounded the
oval island (the Isola Memmiana) on which an oval colonnade for
stalls and shops was erected, which has since disappeared.[120] The
project to raise an amphitheater around the scheme proved abortive.[121] But subscriptions were raised successfully for the eighty-
eight statues of Paduan worthies which stand on either side of the
canal, beginning with Padua's Trojan founder, Antenor. It was part
of Memmo's intention to avoid too much expense by not using the
best stones or the most famous artist: the only statue still of individual interest is that of the mathematician Giovanni Poleni, by the
young Canova.[122] The Piazza and its arrangement caused much
controversy in Padua as well as in Venice, but on balance, the citizens of Padua reckoned it a success. The fairs were moved there,
and even increased. With almost physiocratic fervor Memmo saw to

the raising of the levies on the markets and to the arrangements for disposal of produce. But the Prato was not only a fairground; since antiquity it had been used for spectacles, and a yearly race of riderless horses was run there. The Prato therefore became the nearest thing, in eighteenth-century terms, to an ancient forum. Unfortunately, Cerato's and Danieletti's detailing was as undistinguished as the sculptures. The Prato is more interesting as a practical working-out of Lodoli's ideas about the social function of public building, than as a worthy embodiment of his architectural theories.

Memmo had even more ambitious schemes—connecting Padua with Verona by canal,[123] a vast hemp-factory workhouse.[124] The first was not undertaken, the second was unsuccessful. But it is fair to say that considering how short his stay in Padua was, the achievement of the Prato itself is extraordinary. It was, as Memmo's secretary wrote, transformed into one of the most surprising piazze in Europe.[125] Work was to go on there for several years. In the meanwhile, Memmo moved to Constantinople, having been named Baly to the Sublime Porte, and again decided that his declining position as Venetian representative should be bolstered by the rebuilding of the embassy, procuring the finances and the commission to build against

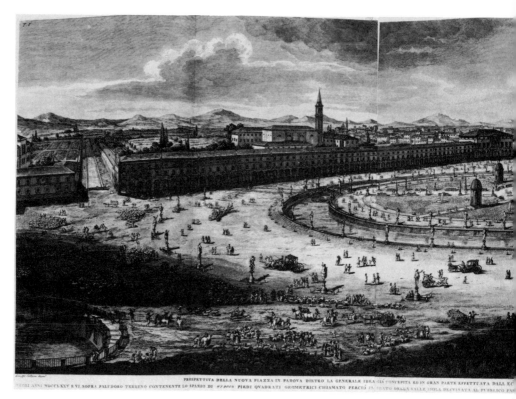

Francesco Piranesi, The Prà della Valle *after Memmo's transformation of it. This view is taken at right angles to Canaletto's, so that the arcades on the left of the Prato replace the garden wall*

home indifference. The building shows Memmo's own view of what his—or Lodoli's—theory implied in practice and is worth looking at in greater detail.

The facade is divided into seven bays by Ionic columns. The three central bays project forward, their columns free-standing, while the side ones appear to be flat pilasters. They carry an entablature with no dentils, as Lodoli would have wished.[126] The columns stand on high pedestals and the stairs wind upwards symmetrically. Balustrades are of the common French type of pierced strap-work. The side windows are square in the basement, double square on the *piano nobile*. All the windows have the three-piece, catenary-curved sill which is described in Lodoli's hospice, although in this building it seems to be used as an ornamental device. The other proportions are relatively simple, apparently based on the relation between the height of the column and the intercolumniation; each bay (except the narrower end ones) is half the height of the column; the curiously discordant arches of the three central bays spring at the height which equals the width of the intercolumniation. They are five modules wide, and the windows are four modules wide; the basement is seven modules high, the *piano nobile* has an order sixteen modules

ALIERE E PROCURATOR DI S. MARCO QVAND ERA PER LA SERENISSIMA REPVBBLICA DI VENEZIA PROVED. ESTRAORD. DI QVELLA CITTÀ
A CHE L' ADORNANO, FIERA DI MERCI E DI ANIMALI PVBLICAZIONE DE SPETTACOLI, BOSCO LAGO, STRADE, FONTI, ED ALTRI MOLTI ORNAMENTI CHE, SI POSSONO RILEVARE SENZA ATTEGGIAZIONE

which runs across the center of the Canaletto etching. The oval space in the center is the Isola
Memmiana. London, British Museum.

and an entablature four modules wide and thirty-six high (to the top
of the urn). The porch, to the top of the cornice, makes a square.
The few ornamental details shown on the drawing (the Ionic capitals, the balustrades) are rather Frenchified, the urns on the ac-
rotoria and on the key stones of the side arches—these last a little
reminiscent of Adam, perhaps accidentally—somewhat inept, as is
the rather pathetic lion of St. Mark in the tympanum.

Such fragmentary knowledge as we have of Lodoli's and
Memmo's building, therefore, confirms what the writings suggest.
Lodoli and his disciples did not look for a Winckelmann, for a revolution of taste, certainly not for a return to an ideal prototype in the
past; nor did they wish to enunciate a priori principles of architectural composition such as Laugier would try to formulate. They
wished to reform the moral climate in which designs were conceived, and the current ornamental organization which was not now
to be based simply on the quotation of precedent but on the principles of xylology and lithology, the scientific laws which govern wood
and stone, the essential building materials.[127]

Lodoli had invoked reason as a master of taste: this was a radical
departure and very much against the majority opinion of his time; it

The Isola Memmiana and the Basilica of Sta. Giustina in the Prà della Valle at Padua.

was equally remote from the establishment of conventionalized
fancy as an unquestionable model, which had been proposed by
Perrault, as from the inversion of this idea practiced by the earlier
eighteenth-century *ornamentistes* and architects. Lodoli's radical
departure was disguised by some rather innocuous proposals; planning, for example, should be based on convenience as a first principle. As for the formal language, it is to be based on the past, as it has
always been; Lodoli did not question this assumption. He not only
approved ornament, he regarded it as an integral part of any architecture. Vitruvius, however, was no canonic source for it; he had
taught the doctrine of the imitation of wooden elements in stone, and
his knowledge of ancient architecture was limited. Architecture did
not originate in the imitation of wooden elements, but the invention
of a true way of building by the Egyptians, which they communicated to the Phoenicians and the Etruscans: the Doric order might
even be called the Egyptian order.[128] Memmo had intended to
document this intuition of Lodoli's by collecting evidence from history and travel books. The publication of Father Paoli's books on
Paestum and on Pozzuoli,[129] as well as his friendly showing to
Memmo the as yet unpublished letter to Carlo Fea (which I mentioned earlier[130]), indicated that the work had already been done; the

greater antiquity, the venerable character of Oriental architecture, from which even the buildings mentioned in Scripture derived, was proved.

But all this had been incorporated and sometimes corrupted in the architecture of the Greeks, and even more (because of the Etruscan influence) of the Romans. By drawing therefore on what the past provided and correcting it by the firm rule of reason, a new formal vocabulary would be created, from which a reformed architecture would arise. In the second volume of his book, Memmo sets out the table of contents which Lodoli had prepared of his architectural treatise, his "ABC of the new art," and which he had given to "his and my Foscari."[131] The treatise was to have been in nine books: the first deals with the proper use of history; the second concerns the technical equipment of the architect and the rational, scientific basis of civil architecture; the third, with simple form and its limitation, as against the range of ornamental form; the fourth book is about the relation of these forms to the nature of materials; the fifth is about proportion and the relation between exterior and interior of various building types; the sixth deals with commodity, planning, economy; the seventh, with ornament, which has arbitrary properties and may be introduced in buildings at will but which must always depend on the "complex mental-mechanical purification of all the matter which regards it"; the eighth is about all those ornamental elements which may be unsuitable for one material but can be used in another, and about all arbitrary elements which may be used in building, provided the rule stated in the seventh book is observed. No indication is given of the possible contents of the ninth and any following book or books.[132]

Although Memmo claimed absolute originality as well as the soundest judgment for his master's teaching, the reader may have recognized, even in this brief summary, the echo of a familiar duality: simple form against ornate form. If one looks at the summary in detail, one will find that the second part of the second book was to deal with the difference between what are "the integral immutable parts of architecture, to be considered primary and possessing elements which may be shown to be eternal by their very nature, and what integral parts are to be considered secondary, and requiring norms which would agree with the inalterable being of the primary integral parts." This is not the familiar theory of the two beauties. But there is a distinction between what is primary and what is secondary, which is echoed by the contrast simple form/ornate form; although ornate form is given the wider range, it remains secondary. It is worth looking at this passage more closely. In the *Corollary* of the alternative account of his treatise sketched by Lodoli on another occasion, the preface to the first book is composed of definitions: of civil architecture; of true function and of representation; of solidity, analogy, commodity, and ornament. And there are further corollaries which illustrate these definitions. True function, true representation are the only two final scientific aims of civil architecture; solidity, analogy, and commodity are the essential properties of representation. Note the apparent paradox: solidity and commodity are not properties of function but of representation; I shall return to this matter. As for ornament, it is not essential but accessory to both function and representation: nevertheless no architectural beauty can be found which does not proceed from truth; if it is treated quite separately, the analogy is broken. Ornament therefore is not just a "top dressing." Lodoli's teaching gives ornament a new dignity. And he continues: "Authority and habit can only produce a borrowed beauty, related to ideas which are too vague, and which are not produced by constant causes, but from causes which may vary from place to place." Lodoli is clearly polemical here, and one may recognize the opponent against whom he has set himself: he is determined to dispute Claude Perrault's division of architectural excellence into positive and arbitrary beauty, and the resulting limitation of arbitrary beauty to the province of habit. Lodoli goes on: "Analogy, commodity and ornament can only be derived from mathematico-physical elements and by rational norms." And he insists on the show, the "display" aspect of his theory in his definition of the crucial term: "*the function of material(s)* . . . is their increased and improved action, when they are used demonstratively, according to their proper nature and the proposed end."

It is therefore essential that the structure of the building should be closely related to the static working of the whole building but that this should be visible to the spectator. This notion is almost the contrary of the "imitation of nature" as it was understood in the theory of art at the time. It must be interpreted in the light of his definition of representation, which is the other term in his essential polarity. "Representation," he says, "is the individual and total expression which results from the way the material is disposed according to geometrical-arithmetic-optical rules to 'achieve' the purpose intended."[133] The very concept of representation links Lodoli's theory with the scientific thinking of his day, but so does his notion of function. It is notable that he nowhere equates it with commodity, the *bienséance* of French theorists, which is so automatic nowadays. Earlier, as the dictionary until the end of the eighteenth century shows, the word *function* had a very definite association with processes: as of the body (digestion, motion, sensation) or the body politic (the fulfillment of an office, or even a public performance—a meaning it has retained in Latin languages). It is never the attribute of an object but always the action or suffering of a process proper to the thing or person of which it is predicated. Towards the end of the seventeenth century it became a technical term of mathematics, both in algebra and in calculus, and refers to the relating of a variable to one or more constants.[134] It is clear therefore that the function Lodoli (and Memmo) speak of has little to do with our understanding of the term but is concerned with how the structure of the building works and the relation of its members to each other by the laws of statics, which may be expressed by the relatively new graphic methods, such as the parallelogram of forces or the lines of loads transmitted. He does not conceive the working relationship between building and inhabitants in such mechanical terms: *bienséance,* even more than the Latin-derived commodity, shows how eighteenth-century (and earlier) theorists considered this relationship in terms of the inhabitants' well-being, not as the capacity of the inanimate object to fulfill the part assigned to it; in a very important sense, this task would have seemed meaningless to an eighteenth-century theorist.

It does nothing to explain Lodoli's theory, therefore, to align Lodoli with the "early functionalists"; there is nothing utilitarian about his concept of function. On the contrary, it is the rational justification of "representation," which not only distinguishes him from later "functionalists" but also from the school of Perrault. In this context, it is worth quoting the last of his definition in this passage: "Analogy," he says, "is that proportionate regular arrangement of parts and the whole, which (in buildings) should result from the combination of stereometric-arithmetical theories with rational norms applied to the shape and measure of the elevations, the members, the openings and the architectural volumes."

This does not imply a full-scale return to speculation on mathematical proportion in the pre-Perrault sense. But there certainly was a revived interest in Italy in the second half of the eighteenth century; Comolli's bibliography, for example, compiled in the seventeen-seventies and eighties, lists a number of books and pamphlets on the subject and (being a subject-bibliography) lists them under the rubric "music."

Unfortunately, for all his garrulity and partisanship, Memmo's discourse is rather insubstantial. In the matter of analogy, Lodoli's attitude remains an allusion. In the matter of ornament, too, he could have been much more explicit. It is clear that, like Lodoli, he took a rather "free" attitude to classical ornament generally. If Lodoli approves of medieval architecture, Memmo adds that he has seen fine columns in Turkey "which needed only to have the turban removed from them, as it were" to be perfectly acceptable.

Medieval architecture is approved with certain qualifications, of course.[135] The practice of the "moderns" is often criticized: Michelangelo, Borromini, Fontana, all are blamed for having departed from classical sobriety, although they are also occasionally praised. On the whole Memmo's Lodoli is a trifle less censorious than Gallacini and Visentini. Even in the embarrassing interview with Massari,[136] Lodoli does not ask his opponent to depart too far from current practice, only to purge it; what he wants to purge is all that is *untrue.* But he does not offer a choice between bare and ornamented architecture. Ornament, as he insists, is essential to any architectural beauty. What must be established is that the overriding criterion for all creation and criticism is truth. What is visible must be "legible" in terms of how it is made and how it works. All details must be controlled by a conception of the material-physical working of the building. The ornamental forms of the past are therefore acceptable, but only after a double scrutiny. First, by the rule of mathematical laws and experimental results, hence, the constant insis-

tence on machinery for the testing of materials, and on details derived from recent speculation and observation, such as the sills with
a catenary curve profile. The second and equally important rule is
that of historical truth. The heritage which the architect of his day
accepted was not that of an idealized Greece, or even an idealized
Rome. Behind the classical ideal, there towered the true stone architecture, invented by the Egyptians and passed by the Etruscans
to the Romans; it was the architecture of the wise ancient Italians.[137]
Historical precision and experimental research unite to provide the
architect with the scientific solidity of Memmo's title and help him to
avoid capricious elegance. Here were truths which could be taught:
the laws which stand outside the accidents of history or the
peculiarities of place could guide the architect into inventions which
might lead him to surpass the achievements of the ancients. This was
a truly Vican ideal.

It would have been fascinating to consider Lodoli's promised
"impartial and philosophical" examination of past styles: Egyptian,
Etruscan, Doric, Ionic, Corinthian, Composite as well as French
and Spanish.[138] These are not "styles" in our sense, of course, but
"orders." Even more interesting perhaps would have been the
promised sixth book of the second summary, which was to cite
instances of many praiseworthy examples of Greek, Roman, Gothic,
German, Moorish, and modern building, as well as the distinction
between interior and exterior ornament.[139]

In the absence of these documents, we must take it that, however
ineptly, Lodoli's intentions were exemplified in his Pilgrims' hostel
and Memmo's Istanbul Embassy.[140] As for Algarotti's essay, it in-
sinuates itself between Lodoli and the more conservative view taken
by Temanza and by his master Giovanni Poleni, an attitude exemplified by a motto devised by another pupil of Poleni, Simone
Stratico: "juxta textum Vitruvii et mentem Newtonii."[141] This could
serve as the motto of much later neoclassical thinking. But Lodoli's
attitude was quite different from this, and his influence more extensive than has been realized. His personal teaching was spread by a
group of worldly, influential diplomats and men of letters, perhaps
the most sophisticated of such groups in the Europe of the time. But
his notes and manuscripts also had a certain amount of currency.
Memmo's text was available and circulating in manuscript before it
was published in Rome in 1786. When it appeared, it was reviewed
with great interest and appreciated.[142] Certainly the second volume
was read and quoted long before the complete book was published in
Zara (Zadar). Moreover, Lodoli could count among his allies, as I
said earlier, one of the greatest artists of his century: Giambattista
Piranesi. Piranesi had, early in his life, left the rather provincial—in
spite of all its sophistication—and smug atmosphere of Venice, a
Paris- and London-oriented milieu, cozy and smart; he left it for the
ruined grandeurs, the somnolent magnificence of an equally cosmopolitan Rome.

1. A. Memmo (1833), I, pp. 41 ff. Memmo's memoir is still the chief source for a life of Lodoli.

2. Cf. R. Wittkower (1952), pp. 90ff., 136 ff; drawing on G. A. Moschini (1815), I, pp. 55 ff.

3. A. Memmo (1833), I, pp. 41 f. Maffei (1735) alludes to this friendship and Lodoli's antiquarian scholarship in *Verona Illustrata*, IV, pp. 35 f. Memmo (1833) gives this reference wrongly on p. 75.

4. *Revisore de'libri da Stamparsi ai Reformatori dello Studio di Padova*, 1736–1739. Comissario di Terra Santa, Venice, 1739–1751. Cf. A. Memmo I, pp. 47 f., 59 ff., 66 ff.

5. A. Memmo (1833), I, pp. 48 ff.

6. G. F. Torcellan (1963), pp. 33 ff.

7. On Lodoli and the *Biblioteca Volante*, see A. Memmo (1833), I, p. 47. The project to publish a series of autobiographies, of which Vico's was in fact the only one to appear, seems to have been conceived by Count Giovanartico di Porzia (whose brother, Leandro di Porzia was Abbot of St. Paul-without-the-Walls and cardinal) in discussion with Lodoli. It was Lodoli who invented the word *periautografia* for the sort of learned and literary autobiography he and di Porzia had in mind. The discussion is reported in the preface to the first volume of Calogiera's *Raccolta*, 1728. The project is reported in full in the same issue on p. 128, and followed (p. 143) by Vico's autobiography.

8. A. Memmo (1833), I. pp. 47 f.

9. The exchange with Vico is published in G. B. Vico, *Opere* (1953), pp. 77 ff.

10. A. Memmo (1833), I, pp. 116 ff.

11. A. Memmo (1833), I, pp. 118 ff.; Memmo writes that a member of the council of ten, the father of one of Lodoli's pupils, knowing that the friar had a number of state documents in his room, saw to it that the council requisitioned the papers before they were placed in the library of San Francesco della Vigna, which was public. The overobsequious friars surrendered Lodoli's papers with the documents. They were placed under the leaking roof and when Memmo, with the help of a highly placed friend who had access to such secret places, discovered them, they were already rotted into unintelligibility. In a letter to Giulio Perini (15 May 1784) Memmo gives further details: the pupil's father retired from the office of inquisitor soon after the incident and the whole matter was either forgotten or obscured. Andrea Quirini (*uno dei ammiratori*), when Inquisitor, finally investigated the matter: but it was too late. Cf. G. Torcellan, 1963, p. 184.

12. G. Previtali (1964), pp. 22 ff.; cf. pp. 79 ff. Maffei was, like Lodoli, a "systematic" as well as a catholic collector.

13. On Hugford's collection, see G. Previtali (1964), pp. 222 ff.; on its fate, p. 245. Although of English parentage, he was born and lived in Florence; his brother Ferdinand was a monk at the Vallombrosa at Forli, where Ignatius did some painting (in the style of his master, A. D. Gabbiani (1652–1726), a dry Marrattian painter). Ferdinand is credited with the invention of *scagliola;* Hugford's most important part in the neoclassical movement was indirect; he introduced Robert Adam to Clérisseau; see J. Fleming (1962), pp. 48, 111, 135.

14. A. Memmo (1833), I, p. 79. Cf. G. Previtali (1964), pp. 218 ff. On the early measures taken by Benedict XIV in his old diocese, Bologna, and the

imperial government in Lombardy to safeguard older paintings, particularly altarpieces, see A. Emiliani (1969), pp. 6 ff.

15. A. Memmo (1833), I, pp. 79 ff.

16. F. Algarotti, *Opere*, 1791–1794, VIII, pp. 351 ff.; cf. F. Haskell (1963), p. 350.

17. James Adam's taste was perhaps that way inclined already; but on Hugford's advice, see J. Fleming (1962), pp. 276 ff.

18. On Algarotti's taste as a collector, see F. Haskell (1963), pp. 355 ff. On his taste and activities in architecture, see later in this chapter.

19. G. A. Moschini (1815), II, pp. 115. Cf. F. Haskell (1963), p. 368.

20. G. A. Moschini (1815), II, pp. 114 f. Cf. F. Haskell (1963), pp. 361 ff.

21. The only extensive description of the villa is given by Emilio de Tipaldo in *Descrizione della Deliziosa Villa di Sala, proprietà del Signor Demetrio Mircovich*, Venice, 1833. Cf. G. Mazzotti (1958), p. 285.

The villa was designed by Paolo Posi of Siena, infamous as the "restorer" of the attic in the Roman Pantheon, more creditably known as the designer of the Festa della Chinea (chapter 9) for its last twenty-five years. On his design, see E. Vio (1967), pp. 26 ff.

22. Winckelmann seems to have met Clérisseau in 1756. See his letter of 29 January 1757, to his friend Berendeis (H. Diepolder and W. Rehm, 1952–1957, I, no. 167, p. 267). He was to meet Farsetti soon after, and writes a letter dated 30 March 1765, about Farsetti's "academy" to another friend, Heyne (H. Diepolder and W. Rehm, III, no. 697, p. 89): "this worthy, rich man, has let his hands fall (in despair) since the Venetians do not allow *Conventicula* in the houses of private persons, and consequently the Academy of Drawing he had projected has fallen into neglect." By 1767 he speaks of him as a familiar (H. Diepolder and W. Rehm, 1952–1957, III, no. 925, p. 345), although they must have met much earlier. Farsetti visited Rome much and often on his antiquarian pursuits, particularly after the election of his cousin to the papacy.

23. On the matter, the letter (no. 925) from Winckelmann to Clérisseau quoted above in H. Diepolder and W. Rehm (1952–1957) and the comment of its original editor in *Lettres Familières de M. Winckelmann* (1781), II, p. 205: "M. l'Abbé Farsetti vouloit que son jardin . . . représentât les débris de l'habitation d'un Empereur Romain dans le style de la Villa Adrienne." There follow circumstantial details of the decoration, most of which has now vanished.

24. This project was a subject for a great deal of speculation in Rome and Paris. On 17 January 1753, Charles Natoire, the new director of the French Academy, gives an account of it to Marigny/Vandières: A. de Montaiglon and J. Guiffrey (1900), X, pp. 434; Marigny's comment of 19 February 1753, p. 438. This may well have been the occasion when Farsetti met the troublesome Clérisseau.

25. A. Memmo (1833), I, pp. 83 f.

26. A. Memmo (1833), I, p. 113.

27. A. Memmo (1833), I, pp. 68 f. This was the—at the time—celebrated diet devised by the Florentine physician-antiquarian, Antonio Cocchi, who was the first Italian grand master of the Florentine masons. Cf. J. B. Baillière et fils (1880).

28. This was published as a frontispiece to the first one-volume edition of Memmo's *Elementi*, e.t. 1833. Cf. below, this chapter.

29. A. Memmo (1833).

30. Jer. 31:28.

31. On Lodoli as an actor in the Italian enlightenment, see F. Venturi (1969), pp. 293 ff.

32. For the economic decline of Venice in the eighteenth century, see A. Fanfani, VI, pp. 27 ff.

33. The Fabbrica Nuova was to come sometime later: it was designed by Giannantonio Antolini (1754–1842) and Giuseppe-Maria Soli da Vignola (1745–1823) on the site of the church of San Gemigniano (which had been rebuilt by Jacopo Sansovino), pulled down on Napoleon's orders. On San Simone and San Nicola, see below, n. 109.

34. Shortly before his death, he was the unsuccessful candidate for the ducate. He was defeated by Lodovico Manin, the weak and rich last doge who was to be shamefully deposed by Napoleon in 1799. G. F. Torcellan (1963), pp. 206 ff.

35. *Archivio Storico Veneziano*: "Ceremoniali, Scritture ed Inserte," 15 f., 111 ff. Quoted in G. Torcellan (1963), pp. 62 ff.

36. On the friendship between Lodoli and Pasquali, see A. Memmo (1833), II.

37. There were seventeen volumes altogether. And the pictures form a visual pendant to Goldoni's autobiography.

38. F. Haskell (1963), pp. 337 ff. Haskell quotes from *Delle Comedie di Carlo Goldoni Avvocato Veneto*, 1762, II, p. 1.

39. *Elementi*, libri due (Vol. I only) in Rome, 1786. *Libri tre. Edizione corretta ed accresciuta dall'Autore*, Zadar and Milan, 1833–1834. It was in fact issued by his daughter, Countess Lucia Mocenigo; G. Torcellan (1963), p. 192, n. 2.; See below, n. 142.

40. A. Memmo (1833), I, p. 24.

41. A. Memmo (1833).

42. First published in Naples in 1737. By this time his more conservative teachers were becoming alarmed at the turn his thinking had taken. "I am here' [in Venice] writes Francesco Maria Zanotti to a colleague in 1739, "with Checco; who as for his intellectual achievements is most enthusiastic for integral calculus and mechanics, but has a touch of Locke'ian fever and a consuming love of some authors which makes him forget that all men are made, and all human things folly."

In fact, Algarotti's *Newtonism*, which gave the ideas implied by the *Optics* almost as much circulation as Voltaire's *Elémens*, and at a more popular level, may have had a much more powerful, if indirect influence on architecture than his *Saggio*.

43. So Domenico Michelesi, Algarotti's biographer in the latter's *Opere*, 1792, I, p. 48. Frederick the Great uses it in a letter, 1792, p. xlviii. L. Valluz (1969), thinks it arose "dans le cercle de Fontenelle" and was not intended to be flattering.

44. J.-H.-S. Formey (1789), I, p. 185. Quoted in L. Valluz (1969), p. 51.

45. Count, in 1740; since Algarotti was childless and likely to remain so, the title was also conferred on his brother Bonomo and his heirs. Algarotti was a member of the Prussian Academy of Sciences and in 1747 was made Court Chamberlain and decorated with the Order of Merit, the highest Prussian decoration.

46. His monument was designed by himself with Mauro Tesi; but it was changed to a more sumptuous one by Frederick the Great. Inscribed: "Algarotto Ovidii Aemulo, Newtoni Discipulo, Fredericus Rex." The last words Algarotti's heir changed into "Fredericus Magnus." F. Haskell (1963), p. 360, pl. 60.

47. A. Memmo (1833), I, pp. 25 ff.

48. F. Algarotti (1792), I, p. 5.

49. F. Algarotti (1823), I, p. 12. Cf. Vitruvius, IV, pp. 2, v.

50. F. Algarotti (1792), pp. 19 ff.; 36.

51. F. Algarotti (1792), p. 37; cf. A. Memmo (1833), II, pp. 41 ff. Algarotti is quoting Horace, *De Arte Poetica*, 151 ff. On the fate of this argument in the following years, see W. Folkierski (1925), pp. 99 ff.; and A. Horst-Oncken (1967), p. 18.

52. F. Algarotti (1792), I, p. 38. His own early taste in architecture is demonstrated by the Algarotti villa at Carpenedo, about a mile from Mestre. This was reputedly designed by Francesco with his father, Rocco; it is a *barochetto* enough little building, with its Tuscan cornices broken by attic windows, flat Tuscan pilasters, and wide pediment—all too robust for the French taste of the time or indeed Francesco's own in a latter day. M. Brusantin (1972), pp. 187 ff.

53. A. Memmo (1833), II, p. 43. On Memmo's "possession" of his charge as procurator of St. Mark, a complementary volume printed, as was usual, by his friends, was an anthology of such fables.

54. In spite of the dating of the dedication, no printed edition of that date seems to exist: it may well be that the book circulated in manuscript before that date, hence the confusion.

55. This suggestion was first made by Andrea Memmo (1833), I, pp. 343 ff. n. 2; according to him, Laugier copied Lodoli without acknowledgment. This suggestion was often repeated, usually on the authority of Comolli's *Bibliography* (s.v. Laugier). It is carried through to E. Kaufmann's *L'Architettura dell'Illuminismo*, Turin, 1966, pp. 162 ff. The distinction is firmly made however in W. Herrmann (1962), pp. 160 ff.; he also points out that Bernis arrived in Venice on 5 October 1752; the Parisian censor had Laugier's manuscript on the same day; it must therefore be assumed that if Laugier had knowledge of Lodoli's ideas before writing his book, the most likely source would have been Algarotti's Parisian title-tattle, though in any case, Memmo quite clearly says that Laugier was in Venice *before* Bernis' arrival on his embassy.

56. Bernis' memoirs and correspondence are still the most reliable account of his activities: F. Masson (1878); this is completed by F. Masson (1884), and an attractive portrait of him "before" and "after" his embassy in E. and J. Goncourt (1906), pp. 204 ff. As the *Mémoires* are a justification of an exiled minister, they say nothing about the side of his activities which Casanova described with such relish.

57. On Bernis as a freemason, see F. Masson (1884), p. 471, n. 3, as well as J. Casanova (1962), VI, p. 110. Casanova is not always a reliable witness—

and the "mysteries" to which he refers may have been erotic rather than
masonic, yet it would have been natural enough for Bernis to have been a
mason. There were many masons in Madame de Pompadour's circle. The
Loge du Roi at Versailles, to which Louis XV may have belonged, was
founded in 1739; and one of Bernis' closest friends, the Abbé Aurillon, was
said to have been initiated in 1739, according to a police report; see P.
Chevallier (1964), pp. 89 f., 176 f. Aurillon was a member of the Custos-
Villeroy lodge, of which the Abbé Filippo Farsetti, the devoted disciple of
Lodoli, was also a member; he had been introduced by the German banker
C. J. Baur (P. Chevallier, 1964, pp. 72 ff.). Later Bernis seems to have
shown masonic interests; he was invited to Cagliostro's recruitment meeting
of his "Egyptian Rite" at the Maltese mission. Those present seem to have
been mostly masons, contacted through the "Amis Sincères" lodge, which
had met in the atelier of Augustin Belle *fils*. Belle was an irregular member
of the French Academy in Rome, the son of a director of the Gobelins
factory, and a kinsman of Nicolas Cochin. In the Cagliostro episode, his
fellow masons as well as he were involved but were allowed to leave Rome
unmolested on the instance of Bernis. F. Masson (1884); E. Patraccone
(1936), pp. 105 ff.; H. Lapauze (1924), I, pp. 422 ff. On Bernis and the
Jesuits, see the *Mémoires* (F. Masson, 1884, II, pp. 102 ff.).

58. M.-A. Laugier, *Histoire de la République de Venise depuis sa Fondation jusqu'à Présent, par M. l'Abbé L . . .* (Paris, 1759–1768). The present
was the year 1750. There is only one witness to Laugier's having been a
freemason: a masonic hymn, which is attributed to M. l'Abbé de Laugier,
Prédicateur du Roi, in a masonic appendix ("Esquisse du Travail d'un Profane au R. F. Marquis de S . . .") to the work of a nonmason, the Abbé
Grandidier (1782). The hymn defies the papal condemnation of masonry
judiciously:

> "Dieu, l'honneur, le secret composent nos liens.
> Rome gronde, il est vrai, nous lance son tonerre . . .
> Que Rome sur les moeurs, sur le dogma s'explique,
> nous connaîtrons les droits du trône apostolique."

Laugier was released from the Society of Jesus through the intercession of
Cardinal Passionei, the great bibliophile and first Roman patron of J. J.
Winckelmann. The circumstances of his release are somewhat obscure but
are outlined by W. Herrmann in his *Laugier* (1962, pp. 9 ff.). The intermediary was the antiquarian and lexicographer Jean-Baptiste de la Curne de
Sainte-Palaye, with whom Laugier remained in contact until the end of his
life. On his death, in fact, Sainte-Palaye claimed back the books and manuscripts he had lent Laugier to prepare the history of the troubadours, which
he was too old or too busy to undertake himself. It was done after Laugier's
death by another abbé, C. F. Millot (1774; cf. I, p. xi): W. Herrmann (1962),
pp. 12, 207 ff. La Curne de Sainte-Palaye, who is best known as the Président de Brosse's companion on his Italian tour, also wrote a history of
chivalry, *Mémoires sur l'Ancienne Chevallerie, Considérée comme un
Etablissement Politique et Militaire* (Paris, 1759). His concern with chivalry
and the troubadours would make him very sympathetic to the masons of his
day. "The masons were the Jesuits of the Enlightenment," says F. Valsecchi (1959), p. 572, and there was an early flirtation between the Society and
the Craft: see J. G. Findel (1869), pp. 209 ff., 253 f. There was a case of a
Jesuit "professed brother" who left the Society and who was also an early
Parisian mason, J.-B.-L. Gresset, who may well have been forced to leave
the society not only because of his rather "libertine" poem, "Vert-Vert,"
but because he gave offense to the Parlement by a political pamphlet; see

L.-N.-J.-J. de Cayrol (1844), I, p. 63. Gresset's sentiments on leaving the Jesuits, some twenty-five years before Laugier, seem to have been very like those of the younger man:

"Qui, même en la brisant, j'ai regretté ma chaîne
Et je ne me suis vu libre qu'en soupirant. . . ."

(J.-B.-L.-Gresset, 1780, Vol. I, p. 63.)

59. Laugier and Casanova were to meet much later, in 1760, when Laugier was, for a short while, chargé d'affaires in Bonn. The rather scandalous doings are described by J. Rives-Childs (1962) II, pp. 29 ff. Cf. W. Herrmann (1962), pp. 15 f.

60. J. Casanova (1962) IV, pp. 191 ff., 251. Since a spy of the Inquisition did borrow his books on magic, the masonic accusation, and the often allied suspicion of occult, even magical practice, must have been connected with the arrest. Casanova speaks of other, quite trivial charges, such as having whistled the comedies of Pietro Chiari which recalls Bernis' account of having a Chiari comedy stopped by the Inquisitors on diplomatic grounds; F. Masson (1878), I, p. 181. Casanova's suspicion about the main charges is confirmed by more recent material published by J. Rives-Childs (1962), pp. 84, ff.

61. G. Torcellan (1963), pp. 44 ff. Also p. 20, n. 1.

62. On Pascoli as a reformer and economist, see F. Venturi (1969), pp. 98 ff.; as a planner, E. Battisti (1962), pp. 327 ff.; as a connoisseur, J. Schlosser (1956), p. 471. On his treatment of specific problems, see E. Battisti (1962), pp. 550 ff.; F. Haskell (1963), p. 324.

63. The title is programmatic: *Il Tevere Navigato e Navigabile in cui si Prova con Autoritá evidenti e non Sospette che ne' Tempi sin da sua Scaturaggine si Navigava che ne' Presenti si puo Almeno da Orte a Pontenuovo e che Alcuni d'Moltissimi Fiumi che vi Sboccano Particolarmente il Chiggio, la Paglia, La Nera ed il Teverone che sono i Quattro Principali Parimente si Navigavano. Con tre Discorsi: due delle Cause di lui Innondazioni, e dei Remedi Loro e l'Altro de'Remedi dell'Innondazione della Chiana con Diversi Nuovi Progetti suoi non Meno che,d'Altri Tratti da i piu Celebri Autori Dedicato alla Santita di Nostro Signore Papa BE-NEDETTO XIV de Lione Pascoli . . . Rome, 1740.* Even the title suggests the antiquarian interests of its reforming author.

64. *Testamento Politico dun Academico Florentino in cui con Nuovi e ben Fondati Principi; si Fanno Vari e Diversi Progetti per Istabilire un ben Regolato Commercio nello Stato della Chiesa . . .* Cologne (Rome?), 1733.

65. *Vite de' Pittori* (1730–1736), II, pp. 11 ff.

66. See chapter 3.

67. On Stosch's political activities, see L. Lewis (1961), p. 38 ff. On Stosch as a mason, pp. 111 ff. On the Stosch collection and Winckelmann's catalog, see C. Justi (1923), II, pp. 263 ff., 289 ff. Recent bibliography in J. Fleming p. 347, but see also A. Mellor (1964), pp. 162 ff. On the other hand, Stosch was threatened with murder in Rome. His Roman eclipse coincided with the heightened morale of the Stuart court, attributed to the visit of Charles Radclyffe, the Parisian grand master, who has even been connected with the murder threats. See L. Lewis (1961), pp. 86 ff.

68. On their meeting see J. Casanova (1960–1962), IV, p. 156. Mary Wortley Montagu corroborates Casanova (1893), II, p. 307.

69. On Frederick's initiation at Korn's Hotel in Brunswick by a Hamburg

lodge in August 1738, see T. Carlyle (1888), pp. 366 ff. Of the various parts played in this matter by the prince von Lippe-Bückeburg and Baron Bielefeld little is certain. Though Carlyle underestimates the interest which Frederick was later to show in masonry. On the foundation of the "Royal Lodge" in Charlottenburg (June 1740), see J. D. E. Preuss (1832), I, pp. 112 ff. This lodge was to continue as the lodge "Aux Trois Globes" of which the king remained grand master; it became the Royal grand lodge of Prussia in 1744. His letter to his nephew Frederick of Brunswick, on presenting the lodge with his portrait, Preuss (1832), p. 442. On his sceptical or indifferent attitude to it in his later years, see Preuss (1832), p. 115; II, p. 121. The Trois Globes lodge, like the other early Berlin lodges "worked" in French.

70. He went to Russia with Lord Baltimore for instance, but also in the company of young Désaguliers, whose father was one of the first and perhaps the most important of the early grand masters of English masonry.

71. Voltaire defended Algarotti's style when Casanova attacked it for its Gallicisms. J. Casanova (1960–1962), VI, pp. 226 f.

72. Patricians were not allowed to have contact with foreigners, particularly foreign representatives; see above, Casanova (1962) gives a rather comical account of Andrea Memmo's casual meeting with Count Rosenberg in the rooms of a courtesan, and his confession of the crime to an Inquisitor of state (IV, pp. 137 f.). In the *Piombe* he meets a fellow-prisoner, confined there for paying a casual gallant compliment to the same ambassador (IV, pp. 251 f.).

73. Above, n. 36.

74. A. Memmo (1833), I, pp. 26, 62 f.

75. F. Haskell (1963), p. 310.

76. G. F. Torcellan (1963), pp. 38 f.

77. On Giustina Wynn and her relation to Memmo and Smith, see G. F. Torcellan (1963), pp. 47 ff. The bulk of her letters to Memmo were published by B. Brunelli (1924).

78. C. Goldoni (1959), p. 261; cf. G. F. Torcellan (1963), p. 39.

79. Venice, 1767. Smith was very interested personally in this book, "impatiently expected by all true lovers of architecture," as he puts it; and he left provision that it should be published with two other books in preparation at the time when he wrote his will in April 1761 (a reprint of Palladio, and a catalog of his collection). Its long seventh paragraph, incidentally, contains interesting details of Smith's financing of the Pasquali publishing house. The will is published by K. T. Parker (1948), p. 59 ff.

80. Most of Mancini's works, like Gallacini's, remained in manuscript. See G. Mancini (1923), p. 8 ff.; and more recently D. Mahon (1971), pp. 32 ff., 277 ff.

81. T. Gallacini (1767), p. vi.

82. *Osservazioni di Antonio Visentini, Architetto Veneto che Servono di Continuazione al Trattato di Teofilo Gallacini sopra gli Errori degli Architetti*, Venice, 1771.

83. E. Bassi (1962), pp. 218 ff.

84. But his opposition was ethical rather than theological: on his dispute with the more theologically minded Paduan Dominican of French origins, Hyacinthe (Giacinto) Serry, who held analogous views, but with a Jansenist, antipapalist cast, see A. Vecchi (1962).

85. D. Concina (1752–1754).

86. Maffei, in his *Dell'Impiego del Denaro,* Verona, n.d. (1744), quotes with approval the work of a Dutch Jansenist theologian, Nicolas Broedesen (1743). In spite of the approval of many Venetian notables (among them Andrea Memmo), the state Inquisition in Verona imposed silence and exile on Maffei, who appealed to the pope. Benedict XIV's noncommittal pronouncement was the encyclical *Vix Pervenit* of November 1745. Concina published a commentary on the encyclical as well as a specific refutation of Maffei's book in 1746. The controversy continued, and was echoed throughout the next decade. Cf F. Venturi (1969), pp. 118 ff., 443 ff.

87. *Della Storia del Probabilismo e Rigorismo, dissertazioni . . . nelle quali si spiegano, e dalle Sottigliezze de'moderni Probabilisti si defendano i Principi fondamentali della Teologia Cristiana . . . ,* Venice, 1743–1748. It is a comment on the adaptation of the exotic drinks, mentioned earlier, that Concina even found himself involved in a controversy about the drinking of chocolate during Lent.

88. Alphonso de'Liguori accused Concina of Pascalism, a form of Jansenism, though Concina's rigorism was much more concerned with the moral issues than with theological speculation. A. Vecchi (1962).

89. Algarotti to Temanza; cf. A. Memmo (1833), II, p. 45. And, of course, G. B. Piranesi (1764), p. 11.

90. E. Bassi (1962), p. 331.

91. F. Haskell (1963), pp. 270 f. In this context it might be worth recollecting that the Gesuati fathers had been accused of making a loan on high percentage (therefore usurious) to the Republic of Genoa during this period.

92. Massari won the competition in 1735; Andrea Tirali also competed, and Giovanni Poleni was one of the two judges. Building did not start until 1744, and the facade, left unfinished, was completed in 1906, following Massari's drawings. The Pietà was probably the best of the musical *ospedali* of Venice. By the time the building was begun, its most famous master of music, Vivaldi, had already died.

93. A. Memmo (1833), I, 7 ff. Cf. E. Bassi (1962), pp. 314 ff.

94. "Non torreggia il sacro tempio/Sopra l'umile spedale." (Let not the holy temple/Dwarf the humble hospital.)

95. "His great enemy, Signor Temanza." A. Memmo (1833), II, p. 100.

96. T. Gallacini (1767), pp. 44 ff.

97. A. Memmo (1833), I, pp. 25.

98. F. Algarotti, *Opere Scelte,* III, 1823, p. 324 (letter dated 14 April 1759). This letter was—apparently—not meant for publication. The words *funzione* and *rapresentazione* appear juxtaposed here for the first time, at any rate in connection with architecture. Since this juxtaposition is essential to Lodoli's theory, it will be discussed later.

99. F. Bacon, "*A Discourse of the Wisdom of the Ancients,*" in *Essays,* London, 1668, p. 224.

100. A. Memmo (1833), II pp. 152 f.

101. A. Memmo (1833), II pp. 154 f.

102. A. Memmo (1833), pp. 156 ff.

103. On the hospice and the theoretical discussion, see J. Rykwert (1976).

The first structural use of the catenary curve, justified by its stability and economy, was at St. Sulpice, when Daniel Gittard took over the work on Le Vau's death. The Academy discusses the vault as being complete on 14 April 1678 (*p.v.*, I, p. 161), but no particular formal value is given to this. In fact, some thirty years later (15 June 1705), La Hire proposes the use of an ellipse to correct the optical distortions produced by semicylindrical barrel-vaults.

104. As he was also cross-eyed he was nicknamed *Orbo cilego,* the "cross-eyed sparrow" in dialect. For this and the information on Piranesi's early life, see H. Focillon (1918), pp. 4 f.; more recent details in the Italian edition of this book, Bologna, 1967.

105. Very little is known about this mysterious personage: not even Moschini attributes any publications to him.

106. G. Rompiasio (1771) pp. 59 ff. Lucchesi was appointed assistant to the experts in 1726; his friend, Tommaso Temanza, a few months later, in April 1727. Lucchesi was raised to the position of vice-proto in 1732, pp. 59 ff. At this time, Giovanni Poleni was an expert independently consulted by the Magistrato, pp. 15, 197. Rompiasio gives an extensive account of organization and financing, as well as the work carried out by the Magistrato.

107. Although these details are given by G. A. Moschini (1804), III, pp. 115 f., Elena Bassi (1962), p. 333, has attributed this church to Massari on the evidence of a contemporary. However, this attribution has been rejected more recently (1972), by M. Brusantin, p. 66.

108. Temanza's ringing phrase about Lodoli "critico insolente ed impostore sfacciato" (*Vite dei piu celebri Architetti e Scultori Veneziani,* Venice, 1778, p. 87, note a; cf. A. Memmo (1833) I, pp. 124 ff.) is accompanied by some words of praise for his talent and learning. Nevertheless, in a curious letter published in Calogiera (1728–1757), V, pp. 175 ff. Temanza rebuts the charge of being "a blind imitator of antiquity," of which the Lodoli party had accused him. Temanza also sets out the three kinds of architecture worthy of attention: Egyptian, of stone alone, the architecture imitated by the Etruscans; Greek, a stone architecture which represents timber construction; and Roman arcuated building, which arises from the two others. This letter is addressed to Lucchesi and is clearly in answer to a rather Lodolian letter sent to Temanza.

109. S. Simone was entirely rebuilt on ninth-century foundations. S. Nicola, a Theatine foundation of 1591, was just given a facade.

110. On Tirali, see E. Bassi (1962), p. 269 ff. On his connection with the Magistrato, G. Rompiasio (1771), pp. 66, 97. Cf. G. A. Moschini (1806), III, pp. 107 ff; IV, p. 131.

111. Memmo is firmly with Piranesi against Le Roy (he cites him together with Stuart and Revett on this issue). A Memmo (1833), I, pp. 160 f., 221; he corrects a mistake of Piranesi as well; but this might be part of the general polemic of the time. He asserts that *Della Magnificenza ed Architettura de'Romani* by the Cavaliere Piranesi, which was published several months before Lodoli died and which was sent to him as a present by the author, who was his friend, is explicit. (A. Memmo (1833), II, p. 139). The friendship must have been of old date since Lodoli hardly left Venice after 1740, and Piranesi did not return there after 1743.

112. A. Hyatt Mayor (1952), pp. 1 f.

113. The Sheet of Studies after the *Entwurff,* now in the Pierpont Morgan collection, is presumably one of several now lost. See H. Thomas (1955).

114. On the choir, see also J. Rykwert (1976). "Bally" Farsetti, Tommaso Giuseppe (c. 1720–1792) was a commander of the Knights of Malta as well as an important literary figure. Casanova makes merry about his rather absurd astrological beliefs (1960–1962), V, pp. 182 ff., as well as his rather far-fetched devotion to Giustina Wynne. He was an early member of the Custos-Villeroy Masonic lodge and was introduced into it by his cousin, the Abbé Filippo Farsetti, probably the first member of the Lodoli circle to become a mason. P. Chevallier (1968), p. 41 f.

115. A. Memmo I, p. 84 f. This may well be the very first incidence of that much-abused term's being applied to architecture.

116. On Cerato, see F. Milizia (1781), II pp. 391 ff.

117. V. Radicchio (1786), pp. 12 f.

118. Président de Brosses, who visited Padua in 1739, thought it "just a fine meadow, which produces the best hay in the world," *Lettres* I, Paris, 1889, p. 196.

119. V. Radicchio (1786), p. 8.

120. V. Radicchio (1786), pp. 46 ff.

121. V. Radicchio (1786), pp. 52 ff.

122. "Since it was enough to make sure of a beautiful view," see F. Milizia (1781), p. 393, for a cynical contemporary comment on this attitude. On the statue of Poleni, see M. Missirini (1824), I, p. 38; on Memmo as a patron, this and the other statues of the Prà della Valle see F. Haskell (1963), p. 367.

123. V. Radicchio (1786), p. 25.

124. V. Radicchio (1786), p. 14; G. F. Torcellan (1963), pp. 117 f.

125. V. Radicchio (1786), p. 3.

126. The drawing is reproduced by G. F. Torcellan (1963), fig. 5. On Lodoli's contempt for dentils, see A. Memmo (1833), II, p. 148.

127. According to Memmo (1833), II, p. 166, Lodoli considered himself a "primitive" of a new architecture.

128. A. Memmo (1833), I, p. 299.

129. *Rovine dell'Antica Città di Pesto detto Ancora Posidonia*. Rome 1784; *Raccolta degli Antichi Monumenti Esistenti nella Città di Pesto*. Rome 1790.

130. See chapter 7, n. 35.

131. A. Memmo (1833), II, p. 50. Statesman and scholar, Francesco Foscari (1704–1794) was Ambassador to the Porte and to Rome, like Memmo. He was responsible for financing, and with Biagio Ugolini, editing the enormous, thirty-four-volume *Thesaurus* (1744–1776). Also a fourteen-volume *Bibliotheca Veterum* (1765–1781) which he edited with the Abbé André Galland. See G. A. Moschini (1806), III, pp. 157 f.

132. A. Memmo (1833), II, pp. 51 ff.; there is a second, and somewhat different summary on pp. 59 ff. which may be an alternative summary of a complete treatise in six books.

133. This concept of *representation* was extremely important for the scientific thinking of the time: "The best method," writes G. Poleni [quoting Fontenelle, 1700, p. 51] "to know the works of Nature would be to imitate them, to give them—as it were—representations [*representanze*] in which the same effects are produced by known causes when they are set in action." G. Poleni (1748), pp. 76, 128. Poleni was referring not only to experi-

mental methods (though he was very interested in these, having made a model of the dome of St. Peter's and tested it to destruction) but also to graphic demonstrations of mechanical and statistical data which were assuming an increasing importance in his day, but see J. Rykwert (1976).

134. On the redefinition of function in the 1690s, see M. Cantor (1898), III, pp, 232 f., 438 ff. On the later fate of the word, see E. Cassirer (1923). Cf. L. W. H. Hull (1959), pp. 226 f.

135. A. Memmo (1833), I, p. 343 ff.; II, pp. 140 f. There are several references to it throughout the book. But classical architecture remains its central concern. The passage about the turbaned columns is in A. Memmo (1833), II, p. 141.

136. See below, nn. 92 ff.

137. A. Memmo (1833), I, pp. 297 ff. Lodoli believed the Doric order, and perhaps the Tuscan as well, to be invented by the Egyptians. In II, pp. 27 ff., Memmo returns to the theme and concludes further that the Phoenicians and the Jews as well as the Etruscans and the Greeks derived their building skills from the Egyptians. This was the opinion of several other scholars at the time: it is argued at length by the Abbé Jacopo Belgrado, an ex-Jesuit, in a book published anonymously in Parma in 1786, the year of Memmo's first publication: *Dell'Architettura Egiziana*. The book was reviewed in the Roman *Memorie per le Belle Arti* in 1787.

138. A. Memmo, (1833), II, p. 51.

139. A. Memmo (1833), II, p. 62.

140. Memmo refers to "a great *palazzo* of my invention which was put up to my designs in a most important city" in which he claims to have used the "Lodolian inventions," though he had softened them; nor was he, as he puts it, "limited by pernickety friarly economy." A. Memmo (1833), II, p. 160.

141. A. Cavallari-Murat (1963), p. 73. On Simone Stratico, see A. Cavallari-Murat (1966).

142. An extended review appeared in *Efemeridi Letterarie di Roma* in May-June 1786, No. 21, p. 161 ff.; No. 22, pp. 169 ff., and in 1787 in the *Memorie per le Belle Arti*, III. Memmo suggests repeatedly that Milizia was familiar with Lodoli's teaching, without specifying how he came to it. But the manuscript clearly circulated, as the unpublished second volume did, long before it was printed. It is quoted, almost literally by G. A. Moschini (1815), I, i, pp. 48 ff.

That Horatio Greenough, to whom we owe the tag that form follows function, became familiar with some of these ideas, probably through the mediation of Milizia, who at the time was the most popular of all Italian *trattatisti*, is almost certain. But Countess Mocenigo did her best to present her father's book to influential people. When the Ruskins were in Venice, Effie Ruskin called on the countess, whom she regarded as one of the leading personalities of Venetian society. The countess, as she records in her diary, gave her a copy of the book, presumably knowing John's interest in architecture. To my knowledge, John Ruskin never referred to it, and that particular copy has not surfaced. See M. Lutyens (1972), pp. 117 ff.

9

Ephemeral Splendors

Pope Clement XII died in 1740. Marco Foscarini, already ambassador to the Roman court, was reaccredited to the conclave, which was to elect the Bolognese Cardinal Lambertini as Benedict XIV. Marco Foscarini[1] was, much later, to become doge for a brief period (1762–1763). He was a man of great learning and the author of a history of Venetian literature.[2] He seems to have been a close acquaintance, even a friend of Memmo's. The draftsman who accompanied him to Rome as part of his suite was the young Giovanni Battista Piranesi.

In Rome, Piranesi lodged in the Palazzo Venezia, with the embassy; he also entered the workshop of Giuseppe Vasi, a Sicilian who was the leading *vedutista* engraver of his day.[3] Although he soon quarreled with Vasi, he stayed in Rome and came into contact with Giovanni Gastone Bottari. Bottari was a Tuscan, like the Corsinis, the family of Clement XII. Presumably through Bottari, Piranesi had access to the vast collection of engravings lodged in the Palazzo Neri-Corsini, the residence of the cardinal-nephew. The collection of Queen Christina of Sweden had passed into the possession of the Corsinis and formed the basis of it. Although Bottari's rise was closely connected with the reign of Papa Corsini, he remained in high favor with Benedict XIV, who appointed him private chaplain and a Vatican librarian under Cardinal Passionei. Like Passionei's, Bottari's theological and ethical sympathies were with the Jansenists; and his villa, l'Archetto, became the home of a Jansenist *salon,* which later was one of the channels for the transmission of English Empirical philosophy to Italy.[4]

When Piranesi arrived in Rome, he already had some proficiency as an artist. He may have acted as a stage painter; at any rate, he had had lessons in perspective from Carlo Zucchi and from the Valeriani brothers. He must have been familiar with the Bibbiena "style": the engravings were popular and widely distributed. Piranesi may even have seen sets designed by Filippo Juvarra, some of whose projects had been engraved by Vasi.[5]

It is often said that Piranesi could not have intended to become an active architect when he chose to stay in Rome.[6] In fact, after his first brief visit, he had gone back to Venice: for a short while he worked with Tiepolo, but he returned to Rome to settle for good in 1744. Of all eighteenth-century artists, he was most crucially involved with the Grand Tour and its attendant anticomania: as an antiquarian, as an artist who celebrated antiquity—and incidentally also modern Rome—as a middleman of ideas, and even as an antique dealer. But in spite of that, he styled himself "architect" all his life, and much of his output of engravings can be judged as a fictitious architecture, more impressive and certainly more influential than his executed work.[7] It is therefore worth examining building activity in the Rome in which he arrived.

In 1703 there had been a competition for the new port of the

Ripetta, won by Alessandro Specchi, and soon completed.[8] In the
twenties, there was another competition, for the Spanish Steps, won
by the Neapolitan Francesco de Sanctis: again building was fairly
rapid.[9] In 1732 there were two important competitions: for the Trevi
fountain, which was won by Nicola Salvi, a Roman sculptor-
architect; and even more important, for the facade and benediction
loggia of St. John Lateran, the pope's cathedral. This was won by
the Florentine Alessandro Galilei. The Galilei building must have
been quite fresh and travertine-beige; it had been finished only a
year or two when Piranesi first saw it.[10] The Trevi fountain was to
retain its scaffolding for several years.[11]

While these competitions accounted for some of the most impor-

Hubert Robert, Trevi fountain, Rome, under construction. Pierpoint-Morgan Library.

tant buildings in Rome, there was much other construction going on. The two most successful Roman architects of the time were Ferdinando Fuga and Luigi Vanvitelli. Both were accomplished professionals, as well as tenacious enemies, and both were to be enticed to Naples within a year of each other, in 1750–1751;[12] Vanvitelli to build the vast palace town at Caserta, and Fuga to build the equally vast work house, the Albergo dei Poveri in Naples, to house 8,000 inmates.

Benedict XIV's reign also began with a spate of building. Fuga, who had already built much on the Quirinal hill—the palace of the Consulta for the papal chanceries and vast extensions to the papal palace—was commissioned to design a small building in the palace gardens which is an epitome of the city's atmosphere at this time. A contemporary, a popular courtier, describes it like this: "work has begun on a closed portico, or the rooms *all'Inglese,* which in that language are called *Caffeaus* [*sic*] with chairs and sofas (*canapé*) all round . . . as H. H. wishes to enjoy the pleasures of the gardens in winter as well."[13] A French visitor is more circumstantial: "Benedict XIV banished etiquette from a small apartment which he had built in the gardens of Monte Cavallo [i.e., the Quirinal Palace]. He went there most days after dinner to take coffee; and there among his most intimate familiars and a few chosen strangers, he banters, jokes and laughs as if he were not the Pope at all."[14]

The Caffeaus consists of an open three-bay portico, recessed, which connects two wings, each containing one room. The wings are one bay wide, and one bay deep. The arcade is triple and is glazed on both sides. The bays are marked by rusticated Doric pilasters and

The Caffeaus of the Quirinal Palace, Rome, by Ferdinando Fuga. After R. Pane.

carry their proper cornice. The attic is a plain parapet wall, as high again as the cornice, and carries busts over each pilaster, and at the center of each bay. The very simple and very shallow modenature is echoed by further shallow profiles; each walled bay is outlined by two sunk bands, and the window is set on a panel. The windows, with their ironed-out Michaelangelesque frames, are the nearest this building has to conventional baroque features. Over the middle bay of the attic, there is a somewhat apologetic central feature: a segmental pediment.

I have considered this little folly in detail as against Fuga's more important and bigger buildings, firstly because its ''chaste'' modenatures and shallow relief are often quoted as being prophetic of a neoclassical approach; but secondly, because a contemporary painter, Giovanni Paolo Panini, provided a most interesting criticism of the building. He altered it considerably when he painted, on commission, the arrival of Charles III of Naples there, to meet Benedict XIV.[15]

Panini, as it happened, painted other buildings by Fuga: the facade of Santa Maria Maggiore; the Palace of the Consulta and the coach house of the Quirinal.[16] These buildings he did not alter at all. But he must have found the coffeehouse an unsatisfactory setting for so splendid an occasion. He destroys its crystalline quality by enclosing the approach with two curved balustrades, each with vases and

Giovanni Paolo Panini, Charles III of Naples visiting Pope Benedict XIV in the Quirinal Caffeaus. *Naples, Museo di Capodimonte. Foto Alinari.*

fountains. The Doric pilasters are reduplicated—except, oddly enough, at the corners—as are the busts on the attic, which becomes a balustrade. The center pediment is pushed back. In front of it, two putti hold up a large papal coat-of-arms. The setting is certainly richer, more *mouvementé*, but it is also trivialized. Panini is only concerned with the building as backdrop. Fuga had provided something which was already too plain, almost alien to a painter like Panini. It does not make much sense to consider Fuga as a proto-neoclassicist.

And yet, in this case, the label "baroque" conceals as much as it reveals. Fuga did use the seventeenth-century formal vocabulary, derived from Michaelangelo through Borromini. But his modenatures are always—here the Caffeaus is typical—shallow, the orders sparingly used. He had a great fondness for the pilaster strip, the kind which had been devised by Roman architects in the sixteenth century; throughout the seventeenth century, they had been used for nonshow elevations (back and sides, as you might say) of buildings. Fuga gives this feature—and its rusticated variant—a new dignity in the Palazzo Neri Corsini. This palace was designed some four or five years before the Caffeaus. The thinning of moldings, the ironing-out of the modenatures, the undemonstrative mastery of the plain wall, the use of the structural network as shallow relief, all these were very attractive to the architects of the succeeding generations, even if they disapproved very much of his "licentious" attitude to ornament.[17]

Fuga and Vanvitelli were busy in papal service, even if they undertook considerable private commissions. This was also the case of another architect, more important for future developments: Giovanni Marchionni of Ancona. He was to collaborate with Vanvitelli on the building of the Lazaretto and of the harbor installations of his home town for the papal administration.[18] He also undertook his most important public commission for it, the sacristy of St. Peter's. The building had a long history; there had been a competition declared by the Academy of St. Luke in 1711; by 1715, there was a project by Juvarra, prepared in uncertain circumstances, and also a closed competition. In 1731, Alessandro Galilei was asked to clear up the matter, but his work, too, was interrupted. Although there had been sporadic attempts to organize the scheme, Marchionni was not finally commissioned until 1775, and the altar was consecrated in 1784. The sacristy[19] was Marchionni's last commission, but his most famous work (and perhaps the most important as well) was the villa for Cardinal Alessandro Albani on the Via Salaria.

Alessandro Albani's dismissive remarks about his villa made to a French traveler have already been quoted.[20] Albani had started to lay out the grounds of his villa in the mid-forties, though building was not begun until after 1750, and went on certainly until 1763, perhaps later.[21] This cardinal had gone into the church from the papal cavalry and had served on various diplomatic missions for his uncle, Clement XI, and had come by his hat *in pectore*. He remained a great figure of the papal court—as was his brother Annibale—and

Pier Leone Ghezzi, Baron Philip von Stosch Holding a Sale of Antiques. *Sitting on the chair, with one of his pet owls perched on its back, he is wearing a monocle. The clerk, the one person not caricatured, is a self-portrait of Ghezzi. Vienna, Albertina.*

acted in various diplomatic capacities, the most important charge being that of protector (a sort of internal ambassador to the papal court) of the Holy Roman Empire from 1746 onwards, and therefore also the *de facto* British representative. In fact, Albani seemed to have acted in the British interest even when it conflicted, as it sometimes did, with his official allegiance to the empire.[22]

In 1715, he had met Filipp von Stosch in Rome and formed a friendship through personal contact at first, which was to continue, mediated by letter, when Stosch was forced to move to Florence: this correspondence continued until Stosch's death in 1757.

Stosch was a paid (if not always fully) British agent, informing the London government on the Stuart court in Rome; he often relied on Albani's letters for useful information. But both men were also passionate collectors of antiquities; Stosch more modestly of the two, of course. Engraved stones, as well as impressions and casts of them, were an important part of Stosch's collection, and it was by Albani's leave, and even with his encouragement, that his librarian-antiquarian, J. J. Winckelmann, was to go to Florence to catalog the Stosch collection of gems.[23]

Both men also acted as dealers; Albani's first collection had been bought by Clement XII in 1734.[24] The Villa Albani was to be the home of the cardinal's second collection, and in it he wanted to emulate the ways of ancient princes, even emperors. That is perhaps why his choice fell on a minor architect, although the evidence of both the architect's and the patron's taste suggests the architect was not complaisant—as far as his style was concerned—and the client not overbearing. Still, even now, it is difficult to decide how much

The Villa Albani in Rome, by Carlo Marchionni. Foto Alinari.

the cardinal dictated the layout and detailed design of the villa, and what, if any, was the part played in the process by Winckelmann, who seemed, at times, to suggest that some credit—if only for details—was due to him.[25]

The vast villa was laid out as two pavilions, separated by a formal garden. The main casino was a two-story complex: a central block of nine bays, with single-story wings on either side, faced a semicircular exedra, as wide as the central part of the casino. It was, as the cardinal had himself said, rather heavy and old-fashioned.[26] The lower order was Ionic, the upper Corinthian. There were two orders in the lower story: the main pilaster order was blocked, the subsidiary extended the arch-imposts into detached columns, making the whole lower story into an arcade which the pilasters interrupted; they carried an unbroken cornice, over which the attic-balustrade of the top story projected and receded. The Corinthian pilasters were plain, but the suborder, framing the window in each panel, was a strange, blocked Doric, the pedimented cornice over each window which it carried marked by a residual triglyph over the pilaster, with a very unorthodox segmental arch spanning its ends, and keystones in the pediment. Over each window, there is a garlanded lunette, blocked except for the three central bays where they provide clerestory light for the main *salon*, but implying a mezzanine attic. The cornice has a console frieze and carries a balustrade crowned by pseudoantique statues.

The exedra echoes the lower Ionic story arcade, but its order is Tuscan; Marchionni avoided the Doric. The organization into three orders was, however, intentional, and seems to have related to the way in which the antique statues of the cardinal's collection were displayed: heroes and emperors in the casino, poets and philosophers in the wings, the Olympian deities in the exedra. It is worth recalling that Winckelmann's "Monumenti Antichi" are ordered into four parts: Gods, "historical mythology," Greek and Roman history, customs and rites.

Albani had his antiquities restored, as was customary at the time, but he did not have them disposed against some neutral background: on the contrary, they were incorporated into elaborate decorative as well as iconographic patterns.

The casino was not furnished—even for seasonal residence. It was intended for daytime occupation, to which a whole court could move out in the morning, and return at night to the town palace. The visitor entered an oval vestibule through a porch: on his right was the chapel, on the left a wide staircase leading to the upper floor; through the vestibule he passed into the arcaded Ionic portico which I described earlier. The end bays of the portico open into back chambers to create "atria," from which the wings are entered. The *piano nobile* opens from the staircase in a large oval antechamber, which spans over the porch and vestibule of the ground floor; it leads into the *Galleria Grande*, the three central bays of the front lit by the oval mezzanine lunettes. Smaller apartments open on either side of the gallery, over the portico, as well as over the back suite of rooms.[27]

The villa is also a museum: even though it was Albani's second, it may well have been the most important private collection of antiquities in his time, which no serious "grand tourist" could afford to miss. The spectacle which they were offered was not of individual pieces, isolated as they would be in a modern or even in a nineteenth-century museum; much of Albani's collection, the bas-reliefs especially, were made incidents in the rich surface decoration devised by Marchionni. Over the door from the gallery, for instance, an ex-voto relief of a Cythara contest victor, an early Hellenistic work (of which several replicas were made), is mounted in a colored marble door frame, surmounted by two gilt sphinxes guarding an animal-footed tripod.[28] The door frame and the label containing the relief are set between the two halves of a Corinthian pilaster and its cornice, whose top molding is continued over the break to crown the whole composition, and on which the sphinxes rest. But there is an earlier drawing by Marchionni for the door. In this, the work is crowned by a conventional, broken segmental pediment with the Albani eagle in the middle. The executed door is not just a *pen-*

Anton Raphael Mengs, Apollo and the Muses ("Parnassus"), *central panel in the salon of the Villa Albani.*

The Villa Albani, the main salon, by Carlo Marchionni, Anton Raphael Mengs, and Antonio Bicchierari.

The Villa Albani, main entrance door of the salon incorporating the votive relief, by Carlo Marchionni.

timento on the part of the architect; in two drawings for the side door and the niche over it, Marchionni tries the sphinx-tripod composition as an alternative to a pointed pediment crowned with a vase, and the Albani eagles, holding garlands as acroteria.[29] The placing of the pediment over the center of the architrave so that the eagles stand plumb over the supporting columns alludes to a feature of the external windows. But the changes from Marchionni's drawings to the executed incrustation is in the same direction, even if motifs are interchanged: the reality is sharper and flatter than the drawing. The vault of this room, after all, carried the Parnassus of Mengs; Winckelmann said of the room: "It outdoes, in my judgment, all that is beautiful in the world . . . and the Parnassus is its chief glory."[30] Writing to Mengs in November 1761, when all the decorations were finished, he assures the painter "that your Parnassus begins to set the whole building in the shade, and all the gold with which it is plastered . . . 'We have only come,' I have heard the Cardinal say several times, 'to see Mengs' Parnassus.' "[31] Allowing for the flattery due to so close an associate and friend, it is interesting to see that not only the aged cardinal, who may well have been a little old-fashioned in his tastes as well as a little hard of seeing, but even Winckelmann, accepted Marchionni's manner to some degree.

There is no doubt that the intellectual climate in which Winckelmann thrived affected the opportunist and somewhat dull Marchionni.[32]

The great gallery was only one of the features of the villa in which Winckelmann was involved. The letter extolling the Parnassus, also mentions the Ionic temple "long finished."[33] The Ionic temple he mentions is sometimes also known as the Temple of Diana from the statue of Ephesian Diana which stood there, "in the niche."[34] It was the end-building of the north wing of the casino; a proto-Corinthian temple, which was used as a billiard room, mirrored it at the southern end. Both garden buildings were much "cooler" than the central parts of the villa. Neither seems based on any known antique building. Only the "ruined temple," a fountain-aviary which lay on the main vista across the gardens from the Via Salaria, was obviously a modified version of the temple at the Fons Clitumni.[35]

In establishing how the responsibilities of Albani, Winckelmann, and the actual architect, Marchionni, for the final result are to be apportioned, there are many unknowns. It is clear that the rather stuffy way in which the villa was designed, its *cinquecento* echoes, were not altogether to Winckelmann's taste. His frequent strictures on modern ways in his *Observations on the Architecture of the Ancients*,[36] particularly on rococo ornament in the last paragraphs, are clear enough. Yet he does not condemn the use of stone and painted garlands, which could be taken to sanction Marchionni's facade decorations. He commends the antiquity of statues and vases on pediments and on acroteria, which might almost apply directly to the two temple-fronts at either end of the long galleries.[37] Strangely enough, he also approves the ancient use of shells in the "archivolts" of niches: a decorative trick used much by Marchionni, but also much liked by Vanvitelli, and practiced to excess by Piranesi: it is, of course, very much a rococo device, though with respectable antique ancestry. Winckelmann had a technical interest in modern as well as in ancient architecture. Again, Cardinal Albani is commended for two technical devices: the use of volcanic clinker as an aggregate for reducing the weight of concrete vaults;[38] also the devising of cavity walls, following the precept of Vitruvius and the example of Hadrian's villa.[39] This commendation occurs in Winckelmann's *Observations*, probably written and certainly published at the time when these details of the Villa Albani were being finished.

The porticoes and the ruined temple are modest efforts at a new revival of antiquity. A few years earlier, in 1758, James "the Athenian" Stuart had built an analogous curiosity: a small Greek Doric temple in the gardens at Hagley for Lord Lyttelton. Lyttelton was a great patron, and Hagley an important house, but Stuart's more "correct" Greek exercise did not have any more immediate effect than the three Albani porticoes.

Winckelmann was well aware of Stuart's activities. He had been awaiting the publication of the *Antiquities of Athens,* and when the first volume finally arrived in Rome more than a year after its publi-

Carlo Marchionni, alternative projects for the main door of the Villa Albani salon. Cooper-Hewitt Museum of Design, New York.

Carlo Marchionni, design for side door of the salon at the Villa Albani. Cooper-Hewitt Museum of Design, New York.

Salon of the Villa Albani, side door, by Carlo Marchionni.

Carlo Marchionni, detail for a door surround in the Villa Albani.

cation in London, Winckelmann was very disappointed. The book
contained only the minor Athenian monuments, although Winckelmann had already seen Stuart's publishing efforts when they met in
Rome and was able to compare the book with the temples of Paestum.[40] Enthusiastic though he was about these primitive buildings,
Winckelmann felt that they did not represent an "exemplary" antiquity. "Architecture" he writes to his friend and patron, Bianconi, "was not formed in imitation of something in nature which
resembled a house; on the other hand, the sculptor had a perfect and
determined archetype offered by nature. We must therefore agree
that the rules of proportion are taken from the human body, and
established by sculptors." In Winckelmann's mind, this justified the
strange discrepancy he noted in Stuart's drawings of the
Parthenon—that the reliefs of the frieze are much more elegant than
the architecture of the building, from which he deduced the paradox
that architecture is more "ideal" than sculpture.[41] He assumes that
the proportions prescribed by Vitruvius are exemplary, and the
contradiction between them and the examples of Greek architecture,
which seemed a little brutal to Winckelmann, justifies his neglect of
Athenian architecture. His taste was formed on late Hellenistic and
Greco-Roman art: the apparent coarseness, the heaviness of the
classic Doric order was not for him. The reverence he felt for the
antiquity of the buildings in Paestum and at Girgenti/Agrigento did
not reconcile him to their proportions.

Winckelmann's taste, then, was not inclined to the purities which
Stuart and before him Le Roy were offering for the edification of
antiquarians and artists. The antiquity which he loved and admired
was that of the Hellenistic reliefs of the Palazzo dei Conservatori or
the Villa Albani—particularly those representing the male nude; he
also much admired the paintings and the bronzes found at Herculaneum. The unadorned classic buildings of Magna Graecia inspired him to wonder and to awe—but not to admiration and love.

Ornament, of course, he admitted as being necessary to architecture, necessary but not essential. The essentials, however, are not
quite the same as they would be for us. They are indicated in the
division of his *Observations,* which I have already quoted. The first
part is divided into materials (brick, stone, lime, and pozzolana—
nothing about wood); then the art of building (foundations, walls);
and the form of buildings, which includes the orders; finally the
internal and external elements. The second part of his *Observations*
is concerned with ornament, which is to be like a dress to the essential building. Monotony is damaging to architecture, as it is to all the
arts; variety is the basis of ornament.

Yet excess in ornament is a bad thing. According to Winckelmann, useless ornament began to be used in Nero's time, while the
earlier Roman work is approved. Winckelmann's rather cursory observations may be compared with Lodoli's outline. Winckelmann's
is a rather chatty anecdotal antiquarian account of antique architecture, which he only incidentally proposes as a model for the prac-

The artificial temple ruin in the garden of the Villa Albani, by Carlo Marchionni (?).

Veduta del Tempio, e Fiume del Clitunno nello stato presente

Giuseppe Vasi after Richard Wilson, The Temple at the Source of the Clitunno, near Spoleto. *After R. Venuti*.

Temple "in the Greek style," a side-wing of the Villa Albani, by Carlo Marchionni.

titioners, although he does complete it with the familiar denunciation of the abuses of Michaelangelo and the stronger ones of his disciple Borromini, such, however, as you would not read in Lodoli. Moreover Winckelmann, though skeptical about Vitruvius' antiquarian method, accepts his proportional teaching almost entirely. If Lodoli's rather exacting categorization is alien to him, Winckelmann seems affected by one idea at least, that the derivation of the details of the Doric order from a timber construction is part of Vitruvius' faulty deduction. His general lack of interest in timber building and in the archetype which the first architects and builders may have imitated, is shared by another antiquarian, Piranesi. Piranesi is even more emphatic in refusing the theory of a timber origin for the Doric order, particularly in his distaste for the triglyph-and-metope frieze which he thinks (at any rate in the *Magnificenza*) an importation from the Jerusalem temple and not a proper part of the order;[42] like Lodoli, he also records his disapproval of the dentil.[43] Winckelmann had quite different reasons for disliking, not the ornament itself, but Vitruvius' account of its origin in timber construction.[44]

Piranesi does not speak of Winckelmann, and Winckelmann for his part makes sparing reference to Piranesi's books but treats him as an engraver of quaint unreliable antiquarian views. It may well be that Piranesi appears on two occasions in Winckelmann's letters as *Maestro Muratore* (a curious sobriquet for someone who insistently called himself *architetto*). Winckelmann may have been mocking his pretensions, as he had built so little.[45] Piranesi was familiar with the

Anton Raphael Mengs in a pseudo-antique style:
Ganymede Handing the Cup to Zeus.

Villa Albani, which he recorded in the last—in order of binding—of
his Roman *Vedute*,[46] but he also engraved a great many of the antiquities it contained, not only in the huge plates of the *Vasi, Candelabri,* which were to be collected by his son, but also as illustrations of his arguments in the much earlier *Magnificenza.* All this
implies a close familiarity with the villa, its patron, but also its
keeper of antiquities, Winckelmann. Their contact may well have
been direct: Winckelmann seems to have had advance notice of
Piranesi's publication plans. They had several common acquaintances. The Abbé Pirmei, for instance, was a member of Piranesi's
household, sometimes named as his "editor"; he seems also to have
been Winckelmann's proofreader and was one of the two minor
beneficiaries in his will (the major one was his patron, Cardinal
Albani), together with the engraver Nicola Mogalli ("well-known to
his Eminence Cardinal Albani"[47]—who forms another link with Piranesi).
  Mogalli had done some engravings for the second edition of the

Raccolta di Varie Vedute which Jean Bouchard published in 1752 (the first edition had appeared in 1747). His own engravings were really rather indifferent, but the glory of the collection were the forty-seven Piranesis (Focillon, nos. 72–119). This collection, much altered, was used as the basis for the illustration of Ridolfino Venuti's guide to Rome, a posthumous publication in two volumes quarto.[48] Of the original edition, twenty engravings by Piranesi remain, and many by French artists. Another twenty are by François-Pierre Duflos,[49] three by Jerome Charles Bellicard,[50] one by Jean Barbault,[51] and most interestingly, four by Jean-Laurent Legeay. These were all pensionaries at the French Academy in Rome under the rule of J. F. de Troy, and contemporaries with Germain Soufflot, C. L. Clérisseau, and Le Roy of the Athenian antiquities during the 1740s. (The exponents of mature French neoclassicism—M. J. Peyre, Charles de Wailly, Victor Louis—were to follow in the next decade.)

Although—perhaps even because—their achievements are meager and disappointing, the first of the two generations is very much the more interesting: most of these artists could not live up to their brilliant Roman promise. But the common cause they had made in Rome, and the ferment, the hope in which they lived there makes their collective impact so much more powerful than the sum of their buildings and publications might reveal. To exemplify: Legeay's was one of the saddest cases. If de Troy was to be believed (and his portraits suggest that he was a fine judge of character), Legeay had great talent, and his drawing show him to have been an artist of "feu et génie."[52] He taught in Paris, and Charles Nicolas Cochin considers the "first period of the return to better taste (to have begun) with the arrival of M. Legeay the architect . . . He was one of the finest geniuses [Cochin goes on] which architecture has had, without any control, and without so to speak any reason . . . However that might have been, Legeay had excellent taste, and he opened many people's eyes . . . the younger architects grasped as much as they could, perhaps more because it seemed new to them, than because of true appreciation of its beauties."[53]

After a relatively short period, his fortunes did not lead to any great accomplishment. The stage sets which he designed in Paris were already thought excessively extravagant.[54] He moved to Mecklenburg-Schwerin, apparently on Jean-Baptiste Oudry's recommendation, and reached the rank of ducal *Baumeister*. His schemes, however, were overambitious, the ducal fortunes declining. While in Schwerin, he seems to have designed the one building which can be properly attributed to him, St. Hedwig's Roman Catholic Cathedral in Berlin. Even here, however, building was suspended for lack of funds soon after his arrival.[55] The cathedral apart, he had also gone to Berlin because Frederick the Great decided to build a huge new palace at Potsdam. Unfortunately, Frederick fancied himself as an architect and was at that time abetted by Francesco Algarotti, who may well have advised Frederick to use Castle Howard as a model for the new palace; this could certainly not have been to Legeay's taste. He left his mark on the Communs building, designed as propylaea to the Neues Palais. There is an account of a dispute between Frederick and Legeay, when Legeay set his hand to his sword. He seems to have done rather badly in Berlin after that.

William Chambers probably saw Legeay's drawings in Paris while he was doing some work for Frederick II, and these contacts may have led to Legeay's visit to London,[56] which probably took place in 1766–1768; his etchings were also published then. From this time onward, his fortunes declined. The last news of him was in 1786, when he wrote from St. Chignan, a village near Narbonne, to the duke of Mecklenburg to ask for a pension which would allow him to spend his last years in Italy.[57]

Though he was a disappointed man, his teaching and his drawings had (as Cochin suggested) an enormous influence,[58] not only on the young postulants he taught during his Paris stay but on the German and English architects with whom he came into contact later. More crucially even, he seems to have influenced his contemporaries in Rome, particularly his colleagues at the French Academy. Whether Legeay was the central figure of the group or simply one of a number of equals is very difficult to establish.

One very important member of this group was Louis-Joseph Le Lorrain. I mentioned him earlier as the "improver" of Le Roy's drawings of Athens before they were engraved.[59] He had been sent to Rome to become a history painter and to copy Raphael's Parnassus in the *Stanze*, part of the great project of the time to provide new cartoons for the Gobelins factory.[60] That enterprise was not to bring him much glory. However, he is also known as the designer of an extraordinary suite of furniture "in the Greek taste" for the collector and amateur Lalive de Jully;[61] another claim to fame is his collaboration with Count de Caylus to "restore" the paintings with which Polygnotus had decorated the *Lesche* at Delphi, and which illustrated episodes from the Iliad.[62] He was to die in St. Petersburg (where he had gone to found a new academy of art) soon after his arrival in 1758. But he has a special claim to my attention here. During his longish stay in Rome (1742–1751), he was commissioned by Don Fabrizio Colonna, the hereditary Constable of Naples, to design the *macchine* (large postiche buildings) which served as a base for firework displays. The constable gave at least two of these yearly, to celebrate the festival of the Chinea.[63]

Rome was a great place for firework displays, which were almost always dispatched from quite large timber, cloth, and plaster buildings, sometimes larger than any surrounding permanent construction, put up at the expense of various ambassadors to further the prestige of the princes they represented; and, of course, temporary constructions, without the embellishment of fireworks, had always had some vogue. In the seventeenth century, the catafalques and ceremonial decorations grew ever more elaborate. The Roman firework *macchine* represent the apogee of a long tendency. They were costly affairs, and although they might not be visible for more than a few days, views of them were quite often engraved, and the engraving given wide circulation. The financing of such fireworks represented a large share of the architectural patronage in early eighteenth century Rome. Certainly designers used these occasions to realize more extravagant or "advanced" schemes than they could in more permanent buildings.

Of the potentates who offered such entertainments in Rome, the kings of Spain and Naples, through their ambassadors, were perhaps the most lavish. Ferdinando Fuga had, for instance, designed such a *macchina* for the Piazza di Spagna to celebrate the wedding of Charles III and Maria Amalia in 1738.[64] Next year he was summoned to Naples to design another, a two-dimensional one, for the square before the Royal Palace, to celebrate the wedding of Philip of Bourbon to Louise-Elizabeth of France. This kind of two-dimensional *macchina* was cheaper than the more ambitious three-dimensional one, but the second kind was also common enough. Every pope went in procession, soon after his election, from the Vatican to St. John Lateran, to take possession of his cathedral. The passage was garnished with triumphal arches and other decorations; a spectacular one would be put up in the Campo Vaccino, the ancient Forum.[65] Fuga, again, had been commissioned to design two of these for Benedict XIV in 1741 and much later for Clement XIII in 1759. Both were engraved by Vasi.[66]

The first of them is worth considering. It is already slightly frenchified: two sets of coupled Corinthian columns, on high pedestals, frame the arch. They carry a cornice with a low attic. Each pair of columns supports a statue. The arch is further surmounted by a label crowned by a recessed segmental pediment; at the center a cartouche is supported by two trumpeting *famae*, a motif much favored by Fuga. The label is linked to the attic by the conventional scrolls. The two sets of coupled columns on either side of the arch are separated by a blank wall. A free-standing statue about half the height of the columns stands on the same podium. Over it the wall is filled by an oval relief medallion.

Since 1722 the Colonna family had commissioned the *macchine* of the Chinea, as well as engravings of them.[67] The first few were done by Alessandro Specchi, the architect of the Ripetta port, who was succeeded in 1728 (Specchi was to die next year) by Gabriele Valvassori, who at that time was also beginning work on the Palazzo Pamphili; several other painters and architects drew and engraved these *macchine*. In 1730 for the first time, the name of Michaelangelo Specchi, a younger kinsman of Alessandro, appears, who was to act as executive architect for several designers. In 1738, the first two foreigners were employed to design the *macchine*: first, the French painter Pierre-Ignace Parrocel,[68] and then the German Marcus Tuscer (or Tuscher).[69] Parrocel was followed by Charles-François Huttin[70] (or Hutin) and Louis-Joseph Le Lorrain, who mostly painted compositions, it seems. Le Lorrain first designed a Chinea fireworks in 1744, when the second *macchina* was produced by the Spanish architect, Francisco Preciado.[71]

J. L. Le Lorrain, The Machine for the Chinea of 1745.

J. L. Le Lorrain, The Machine for the Chinea of 1746.

J. L. Le Lorrain, The Machine for the Chinea of 1747.

In 1745, however, the first *macchina* was a huge construction in the Piazza Farnese, which much overtopped the palace—or so it looked on Vasi's engraving—and was designed by the Roman architect Giuseppe Doria.[72] The second *macchina* that same year, by Le Lorrain, was the first of his really "advanced" projects. It was in the nature of a triumphal arch open on four sides, although oblong in plan. Coupled Ionic columns on high pedestals, decorated with twisted spiral garlands, frame the arches, carrying a projecting cornice. They are backed by a pier. The central arch is set on Tuscan columns whose cornice becomes the impost and peeps out again in the wings, which consist of an opening, flanked by Tuscan columns again. The space between the Tuscan and the Ionic cornice is filled by a relief panel. The terminal piers are divided by a string course which lines up with the Tuscan cornice. The upper part has the usual oval medallion, garlanded, whereas the lower has a statue in a niche, so that the triumphal arch motif appears as a kind of Tuscan "serliana" interrupted by the coupled columns. The upper story of this *macchina* is not the usual attic. There is a dwarf wall over the cornice: the terminal piers support coupled statues, the coupled columns trophies. But the central arch is surmounted by a circular *tempietto,* consisting of a coffered dome supported by piers on the diagonals. The piers are prefaced by two Corinthian columns, over which the cornice projects to carry more trophies. They are also flanked by columns which support the cornice in the "thickness" of the wall. The profile of the dome is curious, almost a scotia, edged with fillets. It was to represent—the Chinea *macchine* always had a more or less elaborate iconography—the return of Charles III to Naples after the fatigues of Velletri.[73]

Even in Paris—more than in the Rome of Benedict XIV—this building, if permanent, would have seemed remarkable: "antique," correct, severe. The use of blank areas of wall, adorned with niches and oval medallions above, go back directly to Perrault as do the coupled columns.[74] The relief panels supported on the "minor" order go back much further—to Bramante, although they again had been adapted to the needs of the Grand Style. The wreathed columns, on the other hand, and the curious profiles of the dome have more precedent in painting, although there were antique wreathed columns which Le Lorrain might easily have known.[75] This wreathed column shaft was to have some success, even in Rome: Fuga used it for the porphyry *baldacchino* columns in Sta. Maria Maggiore some years later.[76] But the remarkable thing is the conjunction of all these motifs in an assembly of an extraordinary syntactic rigor. The alignment of planes, the discrimination between cornice over column and column over wall, the relation of the wall itself to the columns, the very discreet use of pilasters, all this seems almost incredible six years before the publication of Laugier's first essay.

In the same year—a few months earlier—Le Lorrain engraved a very elaborate *macchina* designed for the wedding of the dauphin (the father of Louis XVI) to the Infanta Maria Theresa of Spain, which had been designed by Giovanni Paolo Panini. He had taught perspective at the French Academy, had at one time even been considered a possible director, and generally had a checkered relationship with the Palazzo Mancini.[77]

But as far as the Chinea was concerned, Le Lorrain designed the *macchine* for the next three years. The one for 1746 is altogether more ambitious, more rigorist—for lack of a better word—than its predecessor. In the form of a rectangular building on a high pedestal, it has a portico supported on coupled Ionic columns at either end; these open down shallow flights of stairs. The engraving, by Le Lorrain himself, shows the "side" of the building. In the center there is a hemicycle of six columns, which, with the cornice it carries, makes an open apse. The wall of the building is opened behind it and is replaced by a screen of columns. Between the two colonnades stands a smoking altar and beyond it you glimpse the inner chamber of this temple of Minerva. On either side of the apse, the blank walls of the building are again divided by a string course (though there is only one order in it), the upper part being garnished with a rectangular relief, the lower with a statue in a niche. The porches, apse, and walls are crowned by a continuous cornice and low attic. There is a statue over every column, as well as at the corners of the building, which is crowned by a dome. On the exterior there is a smooth drum encircled by the projecting ring of a sculptured frieze, unframed by any moldings and unsupported by any brackets. The top of the drum inclines to a ring molding and a low cone; it and the statue of Minerva at the top are obscured by smoke which seems to be pouring out of openings in this ring like incense from an incense burner. It is difficult to decide how much of the smoke was painted and how much part of the pyrotechnic effects.[78]

The next year Le Lorrain went even further. The *macchina* stood—apparently—on a vast circular flight of steps, which acted as the podium. The top of the podium extended on either side as two platforms, each with a statue in antique dress, as if pouring libations towards a smoking altar. The center piece is a peripteral, circular Corinthian temple, dedicated to Venus Genetrix, a temple of the kind that may be seen "by the seaside at Baiae" and which is renewed in honor of the birth of a son to Maria Amalia of Saxony.[79] The statue of Venus is visible through a doorway cut in the wall, from floor to cornice, without any visible framing except for flanking detached columns. Again the temple has only one order. Within, there is another circle of the same columns. There is the usual dwarf attic over the cornice, and a statue over each column. And again there is a dome: this one is nearly hemispherical, though deformed by a tall ring frieze. It does not carry any continuous reliefs but is pierced by circular oculi and garlanded. The whole *macchina* is outlined by four obelisks, each raised on a pedestal faced with a shell fountain.

Even the style of engraving is remarkable: the figures are progressively reduced in scale and seem to assume increasingly mannered attitudes. The 1745 engraving is in a rather moderated Frenchified version of the sort of thing that Vasi had been doing. By 1746 the needle had got thinner, the shading more delicate, sharper. A touch of something quite new: had Le Lorrain, like Piranesi been taking lessons from Pollanzani?[80]

In 1747 the city of Paris celebrated the second wedding of the dauphin with a fireworks in front of the Hôtel de Ville. This time they were designed by the leading Parisian teacher and theorist of the time, the author of the architecture articles in the Encyclopedia, Jacques-François Blondel.[81] His project is worth comparing with Le Lorrain's. The actual *macchina* is a tall enough building: some 3 meters of podium and another 16 meters of construction, topped by statues, clouds, and so forth. In the foreground is a quadriga in a pool of water. But the building which dominates the affair is irresolute: an oblong octagon, open in the middle, the oblique sides paneled, open as arches, the end ones so short that they are more like piers than walls, while statues stand against them on podia and the upper part is decorated with conventional rococo garlands. At every corner, columns project, carrying their entablatures. The interior of the building seems subdivided into two sets of hemicycles facing each other, adorned with oval medallions over niches, but packed much more closely and uncomfortably than in the Roman examples. The mass of assorted statuary over the whole thing consorts ill with the conventional statues over the columns.

Blondel had collaborated with Cochin in earlier fireworks, equally lavish and even less remarkable, in my terms, than those of 1747.[82] Although fireworks were well established in France, they were not as frequent as they were in Italy, though more expensive and elaborate when they did happen. Another French architect was to design several of them in Italy and to enter the service of the Bourbon Philip of Parma, and his son Ferdinand—Ennemond Petitot. In 1749, when he was only twenty-two, he designed a vast Chinea *macchina* in the form of an amphitheater of two stories. Like some of its predecessors, it celebrated an event: the discovery of the amphitheater at Herculaneum. It was unusual in that it celebrated an event in archeology, rather than a contemporary achievement or dynastic marriages and births.[83] And the *macchina* itself takes the form of the amphitheater—very, very conjecturally restored as a circular building, with a rusticated lower story pierced by four arches to a side, and an upper story which has a colonnade of three-quarter attached columns, the wall between the order again subdivided in the familiar French way, and triumphal arch motifs at the center. If the structure is not as radical as in Le Lorrain's three *macchine*, it is nevertheless very advanced, very prophetic, very inventive. Two years later Petitot, who was not to design any more for the Chinea, returned to Paris and entered the employ of Caylus. Through Caylus, the Parmesan antiquarian Father Pacciaudi was to hear of Petitot; and there followed the recommendation to du Tillot, first minister of the Infante Philip to whom he had already been separately recommended by the banker Claude Bonnet, who acted as a confidential adviser in Paris to the court of Parma. I will have more to say of his work there, but it was Petitot's only participation in the Chinea.

The last of the French Chinea *macchine* was to follow next year; it was "invented" and engraved by Bellicard and showed the new lighthouse and pier to be built in Naples—a very fancy version of the proposed building, of course—and though not quite as remarkable as its predecessors, clearly the product of the forties at the French Academy.[84]

The second *macchina* for that year was a representation of the explosion of Vesuvius and the death of Pliny the Elder by Francesco Preciado. They were the last two *macchine* done by foreigners. From 1751 onward all were designed by Paolo Posi, the same who designed the Farsetti villa at Sta. Maria di Sala and had been reproved by Visentine for altering the attic of the Pantheon.

Compared with the slow progress of building commissions in the Rome of that time, these brilliant essays must have attracted a great deal of attention.[85] Unfortunately, we have no travelers' de-

scriptions of them. Nevertheless, Giuseppe Vasi had himself published a virtuoso collection of *Macchine da Fuochi*,[86] and at this time
Piranesi applied himself to the genre: in 1746 he drew a projected
macchina (which, of course, may have never been exploded: the
drawing was a kind of get-well card) for the recovery of the sculptor,
Jacques Saly,[87] one of his friends at the French Academy. Piranesi
had established the printing presses he had newly bought opposite
the academy's Palazzo Mancini in the Corso. He had made friends
with a number of the academy's *pensionnaires*. Piranesi's first
French biographer, François Legrand,[88] lists, rather haphazardly,
Joseph Vien, Joseph Vernet, the brothers Challes, Ennemond
Petitot, Laurent Pêcheux, Clérisseau,[89] Augustin Pajou, Gabriel-
François Doyen ''and several others. The painter Subleyras was
also in Rome at the time.''[90]

Saly is not mentioned in this list, and yet he was evidently a close
friend of Piranesi's and had a successful career in Paris first, then in
Denmark, although he returned to Paris shortly before his death.[91]
The other artists who figure on the list were there during de Troy's
directorate. Clérisseau, though a contemporary of Piranesi's, did
not arrive in Rome until 1753 (de Troy had left Rome in 1751).
However, he did not stay at the academy long: headstrong, he came
into conflict with the new director, and in spite of his high reputation, was summarily expelled.[92] On his way back to France, he was
introduced by Ignatius Hugford to Robert Adam whom he was to
accompany to Split; his part, later, in the decoration of the Villa
Albani, at Winckelmann's behest, has already been mentioned.[93]

The list which Legrand sets down casually includes one or two of
the great names of eighteenth-century French art, but Piranesi's
workshop of the academy was a meetingplace. The prints which he
had brought from Venice on his second visit to sell on commission[94]
did very well, and soon he was receiving orders, such as those for
the little views of Rome which I mentioned earlier. But he was not
just an engraver. Antiquarian, theorist, controversialist, Piranesi
seems to have been involved in many archeological exploits as well
as discussions with his French contemporaries. Naturally, the re-
formulation of architectural ideas, under the impact of the violent
impression which the remains of antiquity made on him and his
French colleagues, must have been a constant subject of discussion.

Legrand's list did not include the name of Legeay, nor that of Le
Lorrain among Piranesi's friends. They had both been eclipsed by
the time Legrand's biography was written, and he would not have
thought their acquaintance with his hero of any great interest.
Nevertheless, there is a clear relation between the inventions which
begin to appear in Piranesi's work about this time and the engravings
which Legeay was to publish many years later in Paris.[95] Some of
these features are very similar to ones I have pointed out in Le
Lorrain's Chinea *macchine*. The "suspended" or unmolded narrative frieze is an obvious instance. With its clear dependence on the
engraved fragments so popular in the books of the time, it was very
much in the spirit of the Rome of the seventeen-fifties.

Increasingly, the historiated fragment becomes the representative relic of antiquity, against the more systematic remains: against the orders. For example, at the Villa Albani, as I have tried to point out, the classical orders which govern the building in terms of module and ornamental structure are much less authentic, much less antique than the actual fragments of ancient sculpture, of Greek or allegedly Greek origin which are let into the surface of the wall. Piranesi's view of the Magnificence of the Romans,[96] although concerned primarily with architecture, does not profess to give the reader any normative guidance: on the contrary, from the outset, it concentrates on the particular example, on the eccentric capital, on the extravagant molding. But throughout his work, it is the tangible object, the antiquity-object as against the antiquity-idea, which dominates the author's and the reader's vision.

Piranesi's use of the frieze in the *Osservazioni* compositions, his obsessional concern with bas-relief, again echoes the authenticity of the antique fragment torn from the vast corpse of the past and embedded in an imitatively articulated scaled-down present. By playing on it continuously, he exaggerates the contrast which Winckelmann, too, must have felt sharply in the Villa Albani and to which I have already alluded in describing the setting of the frieze over the door of the central *salone* of the villa.[97] Again, his contemporaries at the French Academy had foreshadowed it: Le Lorrain's use of the free-floating frieze in the Chinea pavilions is a remarkable, prophetic instance. It is perhaps from Le Lorrain that Joseph Vien was to take this particular device and raise it almost to a genre. The much-discussed *Marchande à la Toilette*, which was exhibited in the Paris *salon* of 1763 and is now at Fontainebleau, transformed an uninflected antique wall-painting from Herculaneum which had been engraved and published in the *Pitture* the year before Vien's picture, into a triangular composition with a dominant central figure; Vien also simplified the hair and dress of the figures and turned the generalized, allusive theme into a gross anecdote, which Diderot found so objectionable. Further, Vien flattened out the rather plastic background of the antique prototype, so that the figures as well as the accessories appeared to be modeled on it. The picture has so little "depth" that it was mistaken for an emulation of a relief, although it is true that this very popular subject was also treated later by relief sculptors.[98]

Vien's fame was overshadowed, as he himself realized, by his greater pupil, David, who constantly used the frieze device, a device which had a very respectable past. All artists with interest in great and vanished antiquity used it for this purpose: Giotto in the Arena Chapel, Mantegna, the Tuscan mannerists, Domenicchino, and, above all, Poussin—not only notoriously in the two series of seven sacraments but also in the two versions of *Moses Trampling on Pharaoh's Crown*. In the later of the two, now in the Louvre, Poussin placed the figures (which in the original composition had been outlined against barely articulated walls) against a large hanging cloth suspended between columns—a device he was to use often.[99]

It *implied* an internal volume or extended space, which was then blocked or impeded by a draped background occupying only a part of the picture plane, enough for the figures to be displayed against it in elaborate gestural contraposition. Because of the contrast between the extended space behind and the close action in the foreground, the figures often appeared to be in relief, as if modeled on the immediate background which became a secondary picture plane. This approach had been highly developed by Poussin, not really exploited by his disciples, and entirely dropped in the ruling taste of the next generation, that of Le Brun and Bourdon, inevitably that of Watteau and de Troy. It was to return to favor with the painters of the Rome Academy in the forties. In Italy, too, interest in it revived. Tiepolo, for instance, revamped his *Feast of Cleopatra* at Algarotti's prompting. He did so by flattening the original background, so that the scene takes place against a backdrop of columns and arches, a backdrop which acts in a way similar to Poussin's drapes.[100] Later, in the *Last Supper* which is now in the Louvre, Tiepolo takes up this kind of construction: the scene is deployed against a hanging, suspended between two large Ionic columns. In this picture a volume beyond is not implied since it is backed by a wall.[101] This compositional device, popular with Algarotti, was to be taken up and developed increasingly in France: Greuze's notorious *Septimus Severus and Caracalla* (1765–1768), with which he made his frustrated bid for the coveted place of a history painter, became its *locus classicus*. The earlier sketch of the painting—from which Diderot had hoped so much—showed the figures against a draped screen with an implied volume beyond. The finished *salon* painting

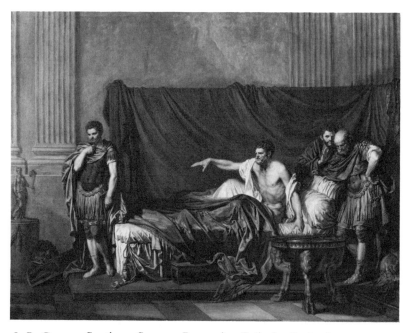

J. B. Greuze, Septimus Severus Reproving Caligula. *Paris, Louvre.*

has the draped screen parallel to the wall behind it, which closes the space. As in some of Poussin's paintings, a giant pilaster order scribed on it rises well outside the picture plane.[102]

The scene parallel to the background wall, with a bed or some other piece of furniture standing next to it and to the picture plane, the figures set in a linear frieze of gesticulating protagonists, became the standard, the cliché compositional device of the second half of the eighteenth century and of the first years of the nineteenth: the reader need only consider how David employed it in his vast *Sacre*.[103]

In Rome, too, the device had great interest. The protoneoclassical Scots painter-antiquarian Gavin Hamilton reinterpreted a number of Homeric scenes in a Poussinesque-antique key. The *Andromache over the Body of Hector* is conceived in this way, with an ample drape almost entirely concealing an arched space beyond. *Priam Begging for the Body of Hector* is similar, as is a non-Homeric "history," *Brutus and the Dying Lucretia*.[104] Even earlier (perhaps before 1758), Hamilton had painted the heroic scene of Dawkins and Wood discovering Palmyra:[105] an event which occurred some years earlier in 1751. The painting was engraved much later in 1773 by John Hall. It shows the two antiquarians, dressed in togas (though booted) and surrounded by equestrian orientals, pointing to the distant ruins, as they are silhouetted in white against the background of a shaded wall.

Hall is best known as the engraver of Bell's edition of Shakespeare and for his work with Benjamin West;[106] for Hamilton he engraved this painting only, though Hamilton was widely known through a series of engravings of his historical paintings,[107] which were mostly executed by a young Italian, Domenico Cunego, whom James Adam had befriended, employed in Verona, and brought to Rome with him.[108] Cunego was to become very well known for his work with Giovanni Volpato and Raffaelo Morghen, his son-in-law, on copies of old masters.[109] He was also to help Giambattista Piranesi, that most jealous and irascible of printmakers, to complete his portrait of Clement XIII.

All these engravings involve the elaborate use of shading. Pure outline engraving was regarded in the eighteenth century as a servile form of rendering, used mostly to record the odd epigraphic transcription or for the utilitarian records of coins and engraved gems. It did not come into its own until the discovery of the "Etruscan" vase. In the early publications of Etruscan antiquities, such as Thomas Dempster's and Francesco Gori's,[110] line reductions were used for the engraving of mirror backs, which are themselves outline incisions on a flat bronze sheet, while the vases are usually shown with a shaded background. There was no escaping the fact that in the presentation of the vase, it was the outline of the vase which was most striking, while the "developed" images of its ornament also directed attention to the outline. Line reduction, however, was not given its full value until the publication of Sir William Hamilton's collection (of which more later), ironically, with the help of hand-applied color.

The emancipation of outline engravings as an "objective" and faithful instrument for the recording of the art of antiquity as well as for presenting the work of modern artists is, curiously enough, contemporary with the perfecting of the mezzotint process,[111] which Prince Rupert of the Rhine had imported into England and which engravers such as J. R. Smith and Valentine Green practiced with a subtlety which reproduced the finest tonalities of oil painting, while the French color-print achieved its greatest sophistication (which even included the faithful reproduction of pastel drawing).[112] It was not until the end of the century that Bénigne Gagneraux would issue the first collection of original outline compositions which finally emancipated the process from its servile state.[113]

The advantage of outline in speed and simplicity is obvious. The utilitarian sort of line presentation is almost as old as engraving itself. Most early woodcuts are outlined with little relief or shading.[114] The first architectural books included great numbers of them; although some of the most important, such as the earliest illustrated editions of Vitruvius, Palladio's *Four Books,* or even Serlio's treatise, enlivened their wood-blocks with perspective relief, shadow, some indication of material texture, occasionally a little vegetation on the ruins. Even in these books, however, the antiquities I mentioned earlier, such as coins and inscriptions, particularly exotic ones, were most often reduced to pure outline.[115] In the representation of buildings, line alone was used primarily to convey dimension and profile; it remained a labor-saving device, a humble expedient. Volume, and the relation of solid and void, were usually rendered by some form of shading. Earlier in the eighteenth century, when interior elevations became a popular form of display, many of the decorators of the period—Meissonier is a prime example—evaded frontality and the linear, indicative nature of their engravings by such devices as showing alternative treatments of a single wall on either side of a center line, making the plate inevitably symmetrical, or by registering the reflections of the wall opposite in the large mirrors in which these rooms abounded—a device which enabled them to introduce elaborate perspective effects within a linear elevation.

Throughout the great quarrel between "Poussinists" and "Rubensists," even the greatest denigrators of color in favor of *disegno* would never have given outline, profile, the status which it was to achieve in the second half of the eighteenth century—and that not only in Winckelmann's theory but earlier. It had already become an important feature of Hogarth's *Analysis of Beauty.*[116] In France the victory of the "Rubensists" marked painting from Watteau to Boucher and even Fragonard, so that such an insistence on the importance of profile and outline would have been out of place. Even a moderate supporter of the ancients, like the Abbé Jean-Baptiste Du Bos (a most influential writer, incidentally), could maintain the superiority of the moderns in the matter of high relief, which, as he rightly insisted, could convey the gradations of atmospheric perspective denied to the flat relief of the ancients.[117]

It is this very argument which Winckelmann reversed. The superiority of ancient relief and ancient contour is what he constantly affirmed, not against Du Bos in particular—he quoted him with approval on other matters[118]—but as a primary article of his critical beliefs.[119] In spite of this insistence, none of the books Winckelmann published contain pure outline engravings, with one rather unimportant exception—the developed decoration of a Greek vase in his late *Monumenti antichi Inediti*.[120] It departed only slightly from the norm of such drawings, which had been provided in earlier antiquarian literature, and had recently been reproposed in the very influential antiquarian anthology of Count Caylus.[121]

When the *Monumenti* were still fresh, there began the publication, in Naples, of the collection of "Etruscan" vases which had been made there by Sir William Hamilton. They were edited and described by a rogue French antiquarian, who styled himself Baron d'Harcanville.[122] Before the first volume of the catalog appeared, sheets of engravings were sent out to privileged subscribers, notables such as Winckelmann—who was genuinely enthusiastic about them—or Wedgwood, who found immediate application for his admiration.[123] Some of the plates represented the vases as three-dimensional objects while others showed their decorations projected or developed on a plane surface, done in line and tinted in color. Only a few were outlines: Hamilton's collection contained many red-figure vases, and his engravers developed an excellent technique for showing the black ground. Hamilton sold this first collection to the British Museum in 1772 but immediately started forming another one,[124] which was most painstakingly engraved, entirely in outline, by Wilhelm Tischbein.[125] Introducing the second volume of the collection, Hamilton writes: "I have confined this new publication to the simple outline of the figures on the vases, and no unnecessary ornaments or colouring have been introduced. By these means the purchase becoming easy, it will be in the power of the lovers of antiquity and artists to reap the desired profit from such excellent models."[126]

The utilitarian justification of the procedure which Tischbein followed for this, as well as for many other reasons, reads like an echo of Immanuel Kant's emphatic and exalted statement of the priority of drawing over coloring.[127] It is hardly surprising that during the second half of the eighteenth century the legend about the invention of drawing, of *disegno*, taken from the elder Pliny,[128] became a common subject for painters and sculptors. The invention involved the tracing of a profile thrown by a shadow, and, of course, that same technique in various transformations also became very popular at the time, receiving its name from the austere, even mean and very short ministry of Etienne de Silhouette, controller of finances for eight months in 1759, and casual practitioner of the art to which he gave his name.[129] This almost obsessional interest in outline and profile was given scientific backing and formulation by Johann Kaspar Lavater in his treatise on physiognomy, which founded a science of "physical" psychology,[130] in which the silhouette was recognized as a most important factor. It is hardly surprising perhaps that some years later Schiller would say forcefully that it is preferable to present the masterpieces of the past in outline, avoiding the ambiguous nuances of color and chiaroscuro. Line is "objective"; it shows the essential feature of a work of art—its outline.[131] Interestingly enough, when Solomon Reinach set out, in the eighteen-nineties, to provide a visual index of all works of art from prehistory until the seventeenth century (excepting the Middle Ages) he was able to issue a number of volumes quickly by making mechanical reproductions of line-engraving collections such as the Hamilton/Tischbein plates and the many engravings Charles Normand had prepared for Count Clarac's *Musée de Sculpture*.[132]

The passion for the objective and scientific representation is allied to the fascination with origins, with primitive things. "Primitive" came to mean Early Christian and medieval art, Byzantine icons, and the art of early Greeks and Etruscans. The association of the two kinds of "primitive," the archaic art of the vases particularly, and that of the ages before Raphael, both seen "scientifically" in terms of outline engraving, completely revolutionized any visual approach to the art of the past. It also affected the work of the artists of the time radically, not least that of architects, in whose thinking primitivism and the "objective" pretensions of linearity operated a total revolution.[133]

The Empire style was accepted throughout Europe very quickly because it was not only transmitted, it was conceived in terms of pure line. The self-conscious creators of the style, Charles Percier and Louis-Philippe Fontaine, often deliberately traduced the tonal values of the executed work for the sake of detailed linear fidelity[134] and emphasized this effect by presenting furniture and even—in some cases—whole buildings in projection rather than in perspective. The tonalities of color engraving achieved a new precision and subtlety.[135] New processes were devised to imitate hand-finishes, such as aquatint, which reproduced color-wash areas and which remained in servile status until Goya raised it to the rank of a major art form.[136] By the end of the century, Aloys Senfelder's invention of lithography gave the artist the possibility of an almost limitless reproduction of his directly drawn pencil line, even if no artist availed himself of it for a couple of decades.[137]

In this dichotomy between the engravers who were eliminating all nuance in the interest of pure outline and those who developed increasingly sophisticated tonalities, and even made their plates carry color, Piranesi had an ambivalent position. If you consider the late antiquarian plates of *Vasi, Candelabri*[138] in particular, the objects are all deeply etched and dramatically shadowed but are shown against a stark white background, relieved only by the elegantly conventional explanatory notes and italic dedication.[139]

The volumes had something commercial about them: some of the antiquities they showed were still for sale. But this does not detract from their gravity, from the violent clinging depiction of their material quality, their weight almost. Of the objects presented, some were single units, others composed, but not into a collage, in which they become subsumed to a higher unity. In the assemblages, each part had its aggressively separate identity. But again, unlike the very popular later exercises in this manner, they are never reduced to planar elements but are given their full surface relief, even when presented frontally. It is all done with obsessional, with almost morbid precision. The morbidity is characteristic, since the whole of Piranesi's overwhelming output is the celebration of his necrophiliac passion for the glory of ancient Rome. This passion had first led him to conceive architectural projects worthy of antique greatness. He did so, quite aware that even the greatest and richest princes on earth would not be able to realize them: the very conception seemed an act of defying all political and economic reality, even any technical resources available to builders. His very first projects seem not even designed as potential stage sets; they are visual invocations of a vanished grandeur achieved by reconstructing the ruins and emulating the vast structures whose remains they are; they are a rebuke to the pettiness of his contemporaries. In the very first collection of engravings he published, this attitude is made perfectly explicit.[140] For the rest of his career, he concentrated on his lifelong "autopsy" of the crumbling remains of ancient greatness, which time and voracious vegetation had spared, and antiquarian research recovered. There was an almost unnatural haste in the passion, a sentiment that antiquity must be recorded before it is destroyed by advancing, engulfing nature. And always, the reproach to the eighteenth century is mordant: even when surveying the superficial charms of contemporary Rome, Piranesi's views almost always show some hieroglyphed obelisk, some giant column, or denuded vault which puts the pretty coaches and the tattered passersby in their place.

One of the earliest of the suites of engravings, the *Grotteschi* ("the Grotesques")[141] are a celebration of the very process of decay, of degradation, and allude to a possible restoration. There are four plates, which were not published until 1750 with his *Opere Varie*, yet they are his most Tiepolesque, his most rococo creations in the repertory of *S*-shapes, of shells and loose drapery, of bat wings and serpents and drooping pines, which is associated with the *Scherzi* and *Capricci*. But while among Tiepolo's adornments, the sage orientals, the soldiers, the maidens are shown occasionally surprised by some sign of mortality—the skull, the burning corpse, the writhing serpents and the bone—as by unexpected portents, all living human figures have been virtually banished from Piranesi's *Grotteschi*. The signs of death and decay are all that remain of human presence—and of ancient grandeur: the great basalt lions, medals, herms, vast unlettered stone panels, and a distant, shadowy architecture. In one of the four etchings, two snakes appear writhing about a stick, as if nature herself made a caduceus, the mark of

G. B. Piranesi, projected apse for St. John Lateran, sectional elevation from the nave.

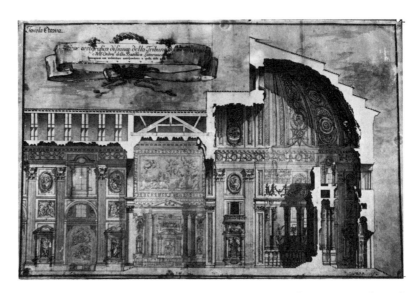

G. B. Piranesi, projected apse for St. John Lateran, long section through center of church. Avery Library, Columbia University.

Hermes, or rather of Mercury, the God-master of occult knowledge. The image may, of course, be incidental. But the whole series can be represented, not as a group of disparate exercises but as a sequence which refers to the four stages of the alchemical process.[142] Shortly before he made these plates, Piranesi had an interesting contact with a contemporary figure who might well have suggested such preoccupations. This was Raimondo di Sangro, prince of Sansevero.

When Piranesi had come to Rome for the second time in 1743, his companion was the much older, and by then cosmopolitan sculptor, Antonio Corradini.[143] Corradini did not stay in Rome long, but went to Naples at the invitation, apparently, of the prince, whose energies were much involved in the construction of a sepulchral chapel for his family, S. Maria di Pietà, known popularly as la Pietatella. Only two statues are ascribed to him directly, of which the most famous is that of *Veiled Modesty*, which is the monument to the prince's mother,[144] although before his death, Corradini also finished the *bozzetto* for the shrouded Christ. The statue, which is the centerpiece of the chapel, was carved by his Neapolitan junior, Giuseppe Sammartino. Almost inevitably, there were rumors that Corradini had been poisoned, since he died in the Sansevero palace,[145] where he lived while working on the chapel.

Raimondo di Sangro was a curious personage: the famous inventor of "miraculous" machinery in the seventeenth-century manner, artillery expert, deist theologian, alchemist, courtier, he is best known perhaps for the chapel and for his not wholly honorable occupancy of the post of Grand Master of the Neapolitan masonic lodge. Like many occultists, he had a rather crossed relation with the church. In 1744 he had in fact received the reluctant authoriza-

G. B. Piranesi, projected apse for St. John Lateran, elevation from the back of the apse looking toward the nave.

Sta. Maria della Pietà, Naples, funerary chapel of the Sangro family. The statues of Pudicizia *by* Corradini *and* Disinganno *by Queirolo are on either side of the main altar. The veiled Christ of Giuseppe Sammartino has now been moved to the center of the nave. Foto Alinari.*

tion from Benedict XIV to read banned books—although it is not known if these were alchemical or deist.[146] His hermetic learning had an obverse: he was familiar with the writings of the English deist controversialists, John Toland and Anthony Collins, even of Lord Shaftesbury.[147] The combination of syncretic hermetism and deism is not unusual at the time: it may, of course, be expected of a leading mason such as di Sangro. But he had another connection which is worth mentioning. Since his childhood, he had known Giambattista Vico who, as was his custom with his friends, wrote two congratulatory sonnets on di Sangro's marriage.[148] If Piranesi had already established some connection with masonry through Lodoli's circle before he left Venice, it may well be that these were confirmed through Corradini and di Sangro. He may also have had personal contact with Vico on this occasion.

Which brings me to the second of his "mysterious" suites of etchings, the *Invenzioni di Carceri*. There are several problems which these etchings set and which are relevant to my theme. Firstly, although they were offered for sale much as Piranesi's other prints, they seem to have provoked even less critical reaction, and this in spite of the fact that they appeared in two distinct editions in Piranesi's lifetime;[149] another problem is their possible relation to scenery, of which so much has been made. Yet another factor is the nature and violence of the architectural forms. Finally, there are the changes which Piranesi operated between the two editions.

He had already included in the *Prima Parte* an essay on a "prison."[150] This is a two-storied chamber, presumably based on the ruined Carcer Tullianum of the Mamertinum at the foot of the capitol (now the crypt of San Giuseppe dei Falegnami) and which led to further chambers out of sight. The Carcer Tullianum was known to consist of many chambers and to have dependencies still unexcavated under the Capitol. In the foreground, an instrument of contemporary torture, the *antenna*, brings both the space and its use into sharpest focus. Among the splendid reconstructions of the vast buildings of antiquity, it is a reminder of the horrors of Roman punitive justice, about which Livy and Tacitus make no secret.[151]

The suite of *Carceri* is to the seven volumes of *Magnificenza* and *Antichità* as the *Carcere Oscuro* is to the splendors of the *Prima Parte*: a meditative obverse. It shows the price the great realm that Piranesi reconstructs and celebrates had to pay for its magnificence. In spite of the horrors implied, few of those actually punished appear in the *Carceri*—or in their first state at least. Only a wretched group of prisoners, victims of some undisplayed torture, are shown on a projecting ledge in plate 10; and a solitary prisoner is chained to the aedicule which frames the title.

The display of the prison as a deterrent, public punishment, is a common theme in antique literature and in eighteenth-century practice. The bridges and the stairs, the ropes and pulleys[152] are not the stage props of the Bibbienas or of Juvarra, but reconstructions of magnificent antiquity in the spirit of the *Prima Parte*. Indeed an architecture of arches and vaults, a substructure of timber struts and scaffolding is a commonplace of the Bibbienaesque prison.[153] But in Piranesi's first *Carceri*, it is developed into two separate architectures: a timber one which follows its own xylological laws, and a stone one following those of lithology.[154] Since the architecture of such prisons was meant to teach not by its ornament but by its tackle and its vast and frightening scale, Piranesi here represented a total Lodolian architecture, stripped of its conventional ornamental apparatus. Almost as if to underline the assemblage character of the piles of masonry, Piranesi defies the laws of perspective, changing vanishing points as he moves up the plate, inserting runs of stairs into nonexisting gaps with the intricacy of some of the impossible objects to which modern experimental psychology is partial.[155]

Between the single *Carcere Oscuro* of the *Prima Parte*, and the first edition of the *Carceri*, there is a breathtaking development of technique. They give countenance to his boast to Clement XIII, made some years after they were done: "It is as easy for me to engrave a plate as it is for Your Holiness to give a benediction."[156] However, he never enlightened his admirers on the meaning of these *capricci*,

Antonio Corradini, La Pudicizia, *Sta. Maria della Pietà, Naples. Foto Alinari.*

not even when he came to re-etch and republish them some fifteen years later. Piranesi added two plates of a rather more complex nature to the suite. When they were finally numbered, they appeared as plates 2 and 5. Moreover, he reworked all of them, darkening and complicating them further; and the last plate, 16, was decorated with a number of inscriptions absent from the first version. The most obvious, on a column in the foreground, is the much-quoted Livian phrase AD TERROREM INCRESCENTIS AUDACIAE.[157] Closer to the picture-plane, on a column-shaft decorated with a relief of prisoners is a stump over which the inscription reads: INFAME SCELUS (arbo) RI INFELICI SUSPE(nde),[158] which refers to another episode in Livy, that of the trial of one of the patriotic Horatii for the murder of his sister. Tullus did not wish to condemn a popular hero to execution; the hero's father proposed a public trial at which the hero would be absolved from the sentence which would "hang a guilty villain on the barren tree." Livy tells of the modified sentence and how guilt is absolved by the ritual of passing his neck under a beam specially set up for the purpose, called the Tigillum Sororis.[159] It is presumably this beam which lies broken in the foreground, a token of the clemency of the early Romans and the

Francesco Queirolo, Il Disinganno, *Sta. Maria della Pietà, Naples. Foto Alinari.*

probity of their laws. The Greek Doric column in the background is a portent of Hellenistic corruption; between the two pieces of the beam stands a large stele, whose inscription is just legible; IM-PIETATI ET MALIS ARTIBUS—for impiety and wicked arts. This is not a classical reference, but more probably a modern one. If it is moved by Piranesi's contemporaries against any one group, it is most commonly moved against the freemasons.[160] I have already alluded to the possibility that Piranesi may well have been a mason. Certainly his son was one, and his activities as Swedish consul and antiquarian agent for Gustav III had a masonic background.[161]

Here I would like to return to plate 2 of the *Carceri,* one of those added in the second edition. The foreground arches of the building are covered in the higher parts with inscribed busts; lower down, a pier supports a block carved with four portrait profiles inscribed with three further names, which I need not enumerate here. All the names are taken from a well-known passage at the end of the Tacitus Annals,[162] which describes Nero's barbarous cruelty to a number of distinguished Romans, all of whom were innocent of their crime but were forced to commit suicide. In the foreground, brought into relief by a screen of eroded and splitting wood, there is a commanding figure, standing on a sculptured column, who seems to be directing the torture of a nude victim stretched on the rack, while groups of agitated figures look on, unable to get access to the action.

In the background, there is an architecture of invented but evidently imperial nature. The Hellenistic injustice and cruelty of the degenerate emperor contrasts with the remote but shining example of primitive Roman justice. This was an argument which fascinated Piranesi at the very time at which he was reetching the *Carceri* plates. In the text of the *Magnificenza,* which was written while the plates were being reengraved, Piranesi turns with some vehemence to the matter of Roman and Greek law.

The argument turns on the legend of the Roman delegation which brought the laws of Solon to Rome, and upon which the laws of the Twelve Tables, the fundamental code of Roman jurisprudence, were based. Vico had already vehemently asserted the independence of Roman law from Greek example and condemned the savage cruelty of the earlier Athenian laws of Dracon.[163] The Romans, says Piranesi, already had a sophisticated and elaborate system of laws when they were apprised of Solon's: he was, according to Piranesi, contemporary with Servius Tullius (Vico had thought Solon contemporary with the end of the monarchy),[164] but it seemed evident to Piranesi that the Roman law was part of a heroic system in which the people had one order only, the knightly one,[165] before it was divided into classes (as Vico also believed). It is this heroic equitable law which plate 16 of the second edition of the *Carceri* celebrates, and to which, presumably, the whole of the first edition was dedicated. Roman architecture was like their laws, as Vico and early Etruscologists had taught. The Tuscan order, separated from the Greek orders by Vitruvius, is accepted by Vico as proof of the great antiquity of the Etruscan nation and their institutions.[166]

Piranesi returns to the charge in plate 37 of the *Magnificenza*; he reproduces a decree inscribed in stone about a wall and a gate to be built for the temple of the Egyptian god Serapis at Pozzuoli, which he then treats as a specification for a wholly "Etruscan" fantasy.[167]

A plain Tuscan portico is the frontispiece to Piranesi's majestic reconstruction in his *Osservazioni,* which were the by-product of a relatively trivial controversy with Philippe Mariette and David Le Roy. This curious and choleric work was occasioned by the appearance of a letter to the editors of the Parisian *Gazette Littéraire* which—in spite of Mariette's later disclaimers—was intended for publication.[168] Piranesi reprints the entire letter with heavy, sarcastic comment in the adjoining column; in the same book there follows the *Parere,* a dialogue between two architectural theorists, and then a suite of plates which display a collection of eclectically but idiosyncratically assembled ornaments. The book ends with a preface to an essay, "The Introduction and the Progress of the Fine Arts in Europe in Ancient Times";[169] finally, there is a suite of three plates of ornaments from Etruscan tombs at Chiusi and Corneto, all inscribed with contentious mottoes and slogans.[170]

G. B. Piranesi, architectural composition from Osservazioni *and* Parere.

The essence of the argument is in the *Parere*. Two characters, Didascalo (the straight talker) and Protopiro (the first firer, the aggressor?) discuss the place of ornament in architecture. Didascalo argues for Piranesi, Protopiro against him. The argument turns on the old issues and on the old hates, although Piranesi finds himself defending James Adam's rather lame project for a new British Parliament (which had been privately exhibited in Rome and criticized in the *Gazette Littéraire*) and its use of an order which the author claimed to be new. James Adam's British order was merely the Corinthian order dressed up in slightly different ornament: lion and unicorn, garter, stars, and so on, while the proportions remained unchanged.[171] This kind of allegorical invention was obviously very congenial to Piranesi, who peppered his works with obscurely allusive vignettes. Indeed, there is a suite of six plates which has never been considered as a sequence, inserted between the Mariette letter and the introduction. It begins with an unadorned Etruscan portico, displaying its constructive features; goes on to two fragmentary wall compositions, elaborately and rhythmically divided into aedicular units: the first of these is ironically inscribed with the much damned quotation from Le Roy, "pour ne pas faire de cet art sublime un vil métier où l'on ne feroit que copier sans choix."[172] That is presumably the reason for the profusion of the ornament. There follow two more inscribed plates, of a rather different character. In them the ornament is much more important than the architectural members. In the first there is an inscription from Ovid's last book of the Metamorphoses;[173] "the great renewer, Nature, makes form from form." This is the introduction to Pythagoras' teaching on transmigration. The next plate has an epigraph from the prologue to Terence's Eunuch: "Wherefore it is but just that you should know this, and make allowance if the moderns do what the ancients used to do." [174] *This* refers to Terence's justification of his cribbing characters from Menander rather than translating him into literary Latin. Again there is an elaborate iconographical scheme which relies on an abrupt play on the scale of intertwining orders. [175]

The next plate shows a whole building, of the same scale roughly as the previous one, but garnished with a much more elaborate repertory of ornament, and inscribed on the attic: "They despise my humble birth [or: my originality] and I their cowardice"—a quotation from Marius' speech to the Senate after he assumed the consulship during the Jugurthine war. Again, in the previous paragraph, Marius had attacked the nobles, *homines preposteri* ("those who put first things last"), who, on taking office, read the acts of their ancestors or Greek manuals on warfare. To such men, Marius opposes himself and his experience: "If the patricians justly despise me, let them also despise their own ancestors, whose nobility like mine had its origin in merit." [176]

This inscription, like all the others and even obliquely the uninscribed plate in the sequence, refers to one idea: slavish copying devalues architecture, even on the evidence of those who seem to advocate it, such as Le Roy. The solution therefore is not to turn to the arbitrary inventions of the first two plates, but to nature, the eternal renewer of forms, and to take courage from the examples of the ancients, inventing a new formal language. And the language of these plates is a hieroglyphic vocabulary of enormous complexity. [177] Its key, perhaps, are the two plaques which adorn the temple of the last plate, although it is too complex to read. The central panel over the pediment shows seven figures, the middle one bearded, all pointing to an altar. Under that knotted serpents with eight bells hung from them are slung over a sphinx between lions' paws. At the bottom of the panel, the horned head of Jupiter Ammon, and on either side of it, a give-away symbol: the winged caduceus over two hands clasped in handshake. That the whole repertory must rely on some hermetic reading of ancient symbolism cannot be put in doubt. [178] The imagery of the latter plates is much more elaborate and enigmatic than the "rococo" earlier ones. Ornament for future buildings Piranesi wanted mysterious and puzzling. Its development is stated in the plates of the *Parere*. If you think that I am overstating my position, look again at the plates and consider the stylistic division between the two parts of the sequence. The continuous frieze, which is the most explicit device, is used once in the earlier ones. But it is not used with the articulate authority of the latter three, nor with their audacity. [179]

Ornament was never to cover and conceal the structure of the building, it was always to be "framed." This essential principle of his, Piranesi repeats in the text of his book on chimneypieces (which followed the letter to Mariette four years later) but also in the one executed building attributed to him with any certainty, the little church of the Maltese Knights' priory on the Aventine. The building was commissioned by Giovanni Battista, Cardinal Rezzonico, the

papal nephew who was also the prior of the Maltese Knights in
Rome—as Piranesi's dedication (*suo Architetto,* he calls himself in
it) of his chimneypiece book importantly declares. It was the same
cardinal who attempted to obtain for Piranesi the commission to
execute the apse of the papal basilica of St. John Lateran. A splendid set of drawings for this aborted scheme has recently been discovered.[180]

The motif which is repeated in the closing plate of the *Lettera* and
in the contemporary facade of the priory church is obvious: the
sheathed swords on the columns on either side of the entrance of the
strange building in the engraving are also used on the pilasters which
flank the entrance of the church.[181] Coupled pilasters on either side
support a shorn two-member cornice, its frieze covered by a heavy
"Greek" fret,[182] while the architrave is used in a twisted pattern to
frame the inner panel and to isolate the doorway. The capitals are of
a rather fancy Ionic, with sphinxes imposed on the volutes flanking a
tower which is the Rezzonico crest. Many other details of the ornament are drawn from various quarterings of the Rezzonico arms.[183]
The pedimented central door has an oculus over it, but its surround
is based on the form of a sarcophagus and flanked by two consoles,
which on inspection turn out to be coiled snakes and are surmounted
in turn by a blank label imposed on the frieze, a device which seems
to set the entry under a tomb. The triple rhythm of the facade is
echoed in the ornamental scheme of the pediment but was taken up
again in the huge square elevation above it which used to crown the
building.[184] The central shield of the pediment is the crowned Rezzonico coat-of-arms with a Maltese cross suspended from it surrounded with an armory of naval weapons. It is framed by a molding
which echoes the projection over the pilasters and which was taken
up in the destroyed superstructure. On each of the pilasters is a label
impaled with a sheathed sword. This figure appears on the columns
of the temple building on the final engraving of the *Parere,* as a
symbol of the guarded entry to a hall of mysteries.

The interior of the chapel appears conventional enough at first
glimpse: a long, barrel-vaulted nave, with four shallow chapels
opening on either side. Three of these are arched and separated by
Ionic pilasters carrying the crowned double eagle from the center of
the Rezzonico arms. Over each chapel is a lunette screened by a
garlanded medallion of an apostle. In the fourth bay, the barrel-vault
is changed into a quadripartite one, pierced by a curious lunette,
whose dome is decorated—conventionally for once—with the dove of
the Holy Spirit, which, however, is only properly visible to the gesso
eyes of St. Basil as he ascends to his glory on the high altar, which I
will describe shortly. This bay has a complex rhythm of pilasters,
half-columns and piers, and introduces an apse slightly narrower than
the nave (and therefore separated from the final bay by an arch)
decorated with coupled half-columns which make it into an ambulatory;[185] it is pierced by three windows and medallions which fill
the complement of apostles. The quarter-dome is coffered and
rosetted, but over this pattern a vast shell is imposed, with a shield

Piazzetta of the Knights of Malta on the Aventine, Rome, end wall with commemorative plaque, by G. B. Piranesi.

Piazzetta of Knights of Malta, wall facing entrance to the property, by G. B. Piranesi.

Detail of wall, above, right.

Sta. Maria in Aventino, Chapel of the Knights of Malta, by G. B. Piranesi.

again carrying the fortress of the Rezzonico arms in a complex con-
fection of trophies and garlands. Silhouetted brutally against the
light from the apse stands the vast bulk of the high altar.[186] The
mensa, with its oculus, echoes the sarcophagus and lunette set over
the entrance door. Behind, the usual *gradine* with a tabernacle, and
over it an octagonal, wreathed frame round a *sacra conversazione,*
and a St. John's lamb crowning the frame. Behind the *gradine* is the
obstacle of a base which echoes the semicircle of the apse but also
crowds it out; on this base stands the strange object, a vast cata-
falque decorated with ships' prows and strangely hollowed out, in
which rests a sphere.[187] Seen from the chapel, the sphere disappears
behind reredos, clouds, putti. From it St. Basil ascends, his eyes on
the dove in the lunette chapel; seen from behind, from the apse, all
the decorations are trivialized by the sheer nudity of the sphere. This
nudity is heightened by the monochrome of the decorations, carried

Sta. Maria in Aventino, detail of pilaster and cornice,
by G. B. Piranesi.

out in a stucco made to a new formula, which Piranesi claimed to
have discovered by analyzing ancient fragments.[188] The reredos
seems the key to the whole thing, its true size hidden from the
visitor to the nave. The strange arc-sarcophagus in which the essential sphere rests, which on entrance appears a rhomboid frame turns
out, on inspection, to be a vast square support for the bulk of the
sphere, which the ascension of the great Neoplatonic theologian
conceals from the profane observer. It is as if the whole ornate
texture of the church was pulled together in an apotheosis, which in
turn masked the essential form at the center of its true and concealed
nature.

Piranesi himself professed a certain contempt for explicit mes-
sages in ornament. In his last writing, the extraordinary essay on
chimneypieces, he answers objections to his arbitrary application of
Egyptian motifs: ''those who require reasons for the many pieces

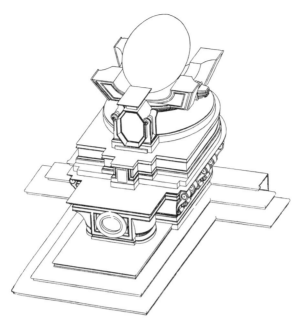

Main altar of Sta. Maria in Aventino. After M. Tafuri.

which I have united together in these Egyptian chimneys, the greatest part of which, if not all, having been used as symbols, do not seem properly applied as to their signification . . . I answer that even the grotesk has its beauty, and gives pleasure . . . Mankind is too fond of variety to be always pleased with the same decorations: we are alternatively pleased with the gay and the serious and even with the pathetic, nay the horror of battle has its beauty, and *out of fear springs pleasure.*"[189]

This passage has often been cited by scholars to support the view of Piranesi as an advocate of a willful protoromanticism; but in much of it, he is echoing the ideas of the Abbé Du Bos, more familiar to his contemporaries than Burke's advanced aesthetic which also depended on Du Bos.[190] It is all part of that post-Longinian passion for the pleasures of terror which interested many eighteenth-century writers on art, and which was articulated in Burke's theory of the sublime, to be reformulated most memorably by Kant.[191]

Returning to the *Cammini,* Piranesi had made it quite clear how far invention could go in making free with ornament. "A Military man will have arms and instruments of war . . . A sea-faring man will have ships . . . An antiquarian will have nothing but ruins of ancient temples . . . Let them have their will, for no curb ought to be put on such caprices of men, but let them be executed according to the rules of art [*sic*] . . . Let the architect be as extravagant as he pleases, so he destroy not architecture, but gives to every member its proper character. . . ."[192] The passage is almost an echo of Lodoli's advice to chair-makers, quoted above, although, of course, Piranesi's words had rather different implications.

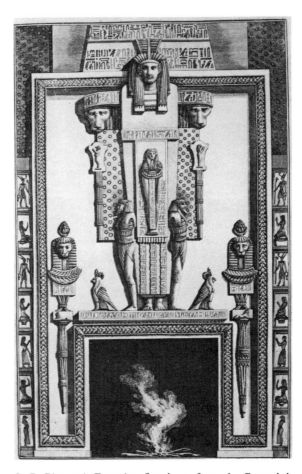

G. B. Piranesi, Egyptian fireplace, from the Cammini.

"Let the architect be as extravagant as he pleases, so he destroy not the rules of art." [193] Piranesi is, of course, much more positive about the caprice than he is about the rule. In fact, he takes this "rule" so much for granted that the reader must assume that it is formulated somewhere in the book. He goes on to affirm that only the contemplation of antiquity will reveal, through constant study, the true manner of applying ornament, which must be somewhat different for "big" architecture than it is for "small." He uses "small" where we would now say interior and "big" for exterior. Palladio, the great master of "big" architecture is in Piranesi's eyes defective in the "small." "There is a sameness in the doors, the windows and chimneys; or there is no correspondance [*sic*] and the thread is broken, as may be seen in the panels of the ceilings, which do not correspond [with] the external design." [194] Rehearsing his old argument against Montesquieu's maxim on excessive ornament with an appeal to Trajan's column, Piranesi goes on to maintain "that chimneys form a particular class in architecture by themselves, which class has its own particular laws." Calling Varro to his aid, he maintains with the ancients that furniture should not only satisfy

necessity but also give pleasure.[195] Chimneypieces, for which, as
Piranesi knew, no ancient precedent had been found, should
have—as his classification implied—quite different ornaments from
doors and windows and be more like pieces of furniture.[196] To those
who seem frightened that he wants everything covered in bas-relief,
he is reassuring; after all, he decorated the English Café in Rome in
the Egyptian taste,[197] as well as the apartment of the Senator Rezzonico in the Greek and Egyptian. These decorations were painted,
as may be many engraved in the book. The essential requirement is
that the ornament should unify the whole apartment.

Virtually nothing was known about Egyptian interiors in the
eighteenth century. Piranesi was well aware of that.[198] But there
were many obelisks around Rome, decorated with rows of hieroglyphs and a good many Egyptian statues. The Romans, wrote Piranesi, did not consider that they were all symbolic, but that many
were just undecipherable ornaments, which reconciled them to the
"enormous and gigantic" in Egyptian architecture.[199]

Surely Egyptian architecture, as well as Etruscan, is too bold and
stiff to adorn modern interiors. Not so, Piranesi maintains, and con-
tradicting himself on one page, goes on to justify the use of elements
once devised as symbols out of their proper context by appealing to

*N. Salvi and Pietro Bracci, detail of the Fontana di
Trevi. Extremes of emulated antiquity and emulated
nature at a point of fusion.*

that doctrine which I have already quoted: *out of fear springs plea-sure*.[200] In further defense of the Egyptian stiffness, Piranesi quotes the opinion of Filippo Buonarotti,[201] that the "stiff and bold" character he spoke of was due to a deliberate archaizing, a strong sentiment of veneration for the antiquity of *sacra:* and this deliberate archaizing is, of course, what Piranesi was emulating.[202]

The Egyptians, in any case, were fine sculptors before the Greeks; and the Romans, who took their manner from the Etruscans, at first knowing no other, later came to mix it with the Greek, not because of any deficiency in their native mode, but simply out of a desire for novelty. Piranesi, like the ancient Romans, proposes a fusion in these chimneypieces, in imitation of the ancients. He turns again to the old argument (which such recent publications as the Caylus and Hamilton collections, as well as the potent polemics of Winckel-mann had revived) on whether antique vases were Greek or Etrus-can, and he claims them definitively for the Etruscans because of their high quality. The range of forms of these vases is, he maintains, imitated from the variety and patterning of shells. This leads him to a consideration of the Ionic capital, which is also derived from a shell.[203] So his argument returns to champion the Oriental origin of the orders and to quote Villalpanda and Lamy[204] as his supporters. He does not follow those two erudite divines literally, but more liberally attributes the spread of the orders from the Orient to Phoenician influence; an opinion which is in some way nearer to twentieth- than to eighteenth- and nineteenth-century archaeological consensus.[205]

Apart from the Ionic shell, the argument is a précis of what Pira-nesi had already maintained in the *Magnificenza* a decade earlier; but in the *Cammini,* he does advance a new notion. The ancients provided a manner and a rule, but also a repertory of elements (of emblems almost) which may be combined into different compo-sitions and help the artist to invent by emulating, not by copying the ancients. The emphasis is on the artist's necessary originality. In all this much is left unsaid: Piranesi himself seems to acknowledge as much in the engraved dedication page of the *Cammini.* It has the form—usual with him—of a relief inscription, and promises "Di-verse maniere di adornare i Cammini ed ogni altre parte degli edifizi desunte dall'architettura Egizia Etrusca, Greca e R . . . The printed title page makes no mention of Roman architecture: it names Egyp-tian, Etruscan, and Greek architecture as the models. In the dedica-tion the first two letters of *Roman*—RO—are recognizable, but the inscription is engraved as if it had been chipped off. Two lines below it seems to have the lettering totally obliterated. Apparently this is another *pentimento.* Piranesi had, of course, already indulged his taste for mystification not only in numerous vignettes but also in the elaborate *Lettere di Giustificazione a Milord Charlemont*, in which the amiable Irish peer is subjected to a flurry of erasure and altera-tion of inscriptions in punishment for his alleged meanness to artists—of a kind the Romans reserved for the worst and cruellest of emperors.

Piranesi must have been conscious of the inchoate, the fragmentary nature of his teaching, of the "occasional" and polemic nature of his writings. Perhaps there was no hermetic intention in the erasure; but as the Charlemont plates show, the device may well have been intentional and expressive.[206]

The juxtaposition of a page entirely devoted to shells with another of motifs drawn from antique art makes the point of the *Cammini* obliquely: the lessons of history must be learned according to nature, and from nature it is variety within the species which we learn.

Variety is ordained by Divine Wisdom. Variety and abundance of ornament do not mean confusion. In all his writings, Piranesi feels obliged to shadow-box with that aphorism of Montesquieu's on the confusion of the eye induced by the excess of ornament. No: ornament, although based on caprice, obeys laws, unstated laws. Its modalities may be indicated here and there by appropriateness to the status and taste of the client; but ornament must take its proper place in the architecture, and that is a subordinate place. It is to be—in interiors, in small architecture—in flat relief or even painted only; it is never to obscure the form of the architectonic object but to emphasize, by framing, its geometry. Trajan's column is quoted by Piranesi as an ideal example; and he was to provide a vast engraving of it about the same time as the *Cammini*.[207]

The primary lesson must always be the study of antiquity. By a sleight which is not easy to appreciate in another time, the lesson is learned by a wilful inversion of scale. In the *Cammini*, the gigantic works of the Egyptians are condensed into paneling and painting: joiners' and upholsterers' work. Piranesi reverses the process in his phantasmagoric reconstruction of the *Campo Marzio*. The suite of engravings was dedicated to Robert Adam, whose style, by another inversion, was still entirely formed by these, and Piranesi's other engravings. However, the *Campo Marzio* was an instance of that titanic imagination operating on what were in fact only too often rather miserable remains: foundations, a few broken columns, an inscription or molding let into the wall of some older building.[208] By a perverse obstinacy, Piranesi chooses the part of ancient Rome which was only settled in late antiquity, and onto which the Roman population withdrew in the Middle Ages as the site of the most grandiose reconstruction.

The *Campo Marzio* contains his last work as a *vedutista*. The perspective *per angolo*, the dramatic lowering of the horizon, the puny figures of his tattered and beggarly contemporaries disappear from his last works, even from his last drawings: his interest concentrates on frontality and on the sort of virtuoso elaboration of a theme which he practiced in the *Parere* and the *Letter to Mariette*. The concentration on this inventive composition drags him into another problem, with which he becomes involved practically: the separation of the method of architecture proper from that of the interior, of what he called small architecture. It is the archetypal rococo problem which he resolves defiantly by a kind of interior architecture of the sublime, quite contrary to the French approach of satisfying *bienséance* in the first place.[209] In this he would be imitated by a succeeding generation of French designers; and in fact, seven years earlier, in 1762, the twenty-six-year-old Claude-Nicolas Ledoux had already done his Café Militaire at the Palais Royal, which was nearer to Piranesi in ornamental invention and in ferocity of attack than to the work of most of his contemporaries.[210]

In 1768, one year before the *Cammini* were published, the young Jean-Charles Delafosse published his *Iconologie Historique*, the most painstaking attempt to establish an *architecture parlante*.[211] Then there was the style which Robert Adam developed out of Piranesi's prophetic asides: it did not seek the sublime in the manner of his master, nor was it *parlant* in any but the most superficial manner, although in his exteriors, as at Keddlestone, there is sometimes an echo, as there is about his rather underestimated buildings for Edinburgh University, of that lithic grandeur which he learned in Rome.

However scaled down in ambition, Adam's output was vast in bulk compared to that of his Roman friend. As an architect, Piranesi was relatively unsuccessful. Besides the Aventine Chapel and its piazza, there are some interiors in Rome and Castel Gandolfo, some furniture and fireplaces in England,[212] perhaps a Roman apartment house,[213] for which there are no drawings and no documents. It is little to set against the thirteen hundred etched plates and the pages of vitriolic writing. They are his memorable achievement, as he foresaw in the *Prima Parte*.[214] Many, among his friends even, made light of his architectural skill. One plate, apparently isolated, is a complex plan for his *Ampio Magnifico Collegio,* which legend records as having been produced spontaneously to answer some of his acquaintances who challenged his right to the title of architect.[215] But even if he had not executed any building at all, he would have established his right to the title by the passion for constructive detail which marked his interpretation of the past, by his attention to the material consistency of every fragment which gives all his archeological reconstructions the precision of working drawings. This precision, and his uncanny perspective skill, have misled even his most passionate admirers about the nature of his phantasmagoric *Prisons,* in which he managed to construct a space of infernally deceptive unreality—construct both in the material and the illusionistic sense. That is the paradox of his art—both hermetic and still of an almost universal appeal. Through his British and French friends, it affected the course of architecture in the next generation quite radically, although neither the later work of the Adam brothers, nor the Empire style are at all what Piranesi had intended.

Notes to Chapter 9

1. On Marco Foscarini as host to Memmo and Poleni, see A. Memmo (1786), pp. 13 f. On Foscarini and Venetian letters, see G. A. Moschini (1806), II, pp. 187 ff. On the circumstances of the embassy, see L. von Pastor (1938–1969), XXXIV, pp. 482 f. and XXXV, pp. 33 f.

2. M. Foscarini (1752), Libri Otto. G. A. Moschini (1806) also mentions his other works.

3. On Giuseppe Vasi, see U. Thieme and F. Becker (1910–1950), S. V.

The celebrated incident when Piranesi attempted to stab Vasi because the older man kept the secret of etching acid from him is maliciously told by Giovanni Lodovico Bianconi in the first published biography of Piranesi: *Elogio Storico del Cav. Gio. Battista Piranesi*, 1769, pp. 34 ff.; reprinted 1802, II.

4. On Bottari's place in the reformist movement, see F. Venturi (1969, 1974), pp. 7 ff.; 21 ff.; 115 f. His work ranged from a republication of Bosio's *Roma Sotterranea* to a new edition of the *Dictionary of the Accademia della Crusca*. No extensive biography of him exists.

5. Juvarra had come, as had Vasi, from Sicily. He worked mostly as a stage designer; as an architect he did one small, if brilliant, chapel interior. The major architectural work was unsuccessful, and he went on to Turin, where he was a very prolific architect to the Sardinian king, though he returned to Rome for a longish period in 1732, hoping to wrest the sacristy project from Galilei. There is an account of this visit in J. Gaus (1967), pp. 80 ff.

6. So, for instance, A. Hyatt Mayor (1952), p. 5. Cf. however, H. Focillon (1967), pp. 42 ff., U. Vogt-Göknill (1958), p. 19. In the dedicatory letter to the *Prima Parte*, dated 1743, Piranesi explains that the decadence of architecture and the overwhelming effect on him "di queste parlante ruine . . . e ch'essendomi venuto in pensiero di farne palesi al mondo alcune di queste: ned essendo sperabile ad un architetto di questi tempi, di poterne . . . essequire alcuna: sia poi colpa"—the fault may be with architecture itself, fallen from its Republican greatness; of the Caesars who followed the republic; or of the patrons; the truth is that buildings like the Forum of Nerva or Nero's palace were impossible in his day. For that reason, he had learned engraving and etching in Rome so as to be able to draw his inventions, and publish them, not being able to build. "Altro partito non veggo restare a me, e a qualsivoglia altro architetto moderno che spiegare con disegni le proprie idee, e sotrarre in questo modo alla Scultura e alla Pittura l'Avvantaggio, che come dicea il grande Juvarra, hanno . . . sopra l'Architettura."

It was not the lack of building in Rome which drove Piranesi to learn etching; it was his passion for the ruins and the pettiness of contemporary building in comparison with these, as well as his intransigent independence.

7. That has been Manfredo Tafuri's reading of all Piranesi's activity, which he has called *Utopia Negativa* in B. Vittone (1972), pp. 265 ff.

8. The competition and the building of the Ripetta port are documented in A. M. Taja (1705).

9. See P. Pecchiai (1941).

10. On the St. John Lateran competition, see R. Wittkower (1958), pp. 250 f. and n. 38; cf. also A. E. Brinckmann (1922), pp. 138 f.

11. A. Schiavo (1956); and C. d'Onofrio (1957). Cf. also R. Wittkower (1958), p. 280, n. 37

12. This may have been due to the death of the two leading Neapolitan

architects, de Sanctis and Sanfelice in 1750; but Charles III may already have been looking for architects of international fame before that. On the hostility between Fuga and Vanvitelli, as seen from the latter's point of view, see F. Strazzulo, "Introduzione all 'Epistolario Vanvitelliano della Biblioteca Palatina de Caserta," in R. de Fusco et al. (1973), pp. 262 ff. Cf. also G. Matthiae, pp. 66 f.

13. On the *Caffeaus*, see R. Pane (1956), pp. 94 ff.; and G. Matthiae (n.d.), pp. 39 ff.; 78. The passage quoted comes from the diary of the papal secretary, Valesio. See V. Golzio (1936), p. 123. On the rise of the *Caffeaus* in Rome, see D. Silvagni (1884), I, pp. 30 ff. The first café was run by a Roman family, the Napoleoni, in Piazza de Sciarra just off the Corso, under the Quirinal. It also had a *canapé*, but straw-filled, round the walls.

14. J. P. Grosley (1764), II, p. 400.

15. On Giovanni Paolo Panini, see U. Thieme and F. Becker (1910–1950), s.v. This painting which is one of several executed for Charles III to commemorate his visit to Benedict XIV after his victory over the Imperial forces at Velletri is discussed there.

16. Panini painted the buildings built in the pontificates of Clement XII and Benedict XIV to decorate the *Caffeaus*. On their dating, see R. Papini (1923–1924), p. 349 f., where their curious dating is discussed.

17. See, for instance, Milizia (1781), II, in his life of Fuga: "Truly he is a glorious architect: he has understood his profession well, in two important parts: solidity and planning; and if in the other parts, which regards beauty, he has not always shown a pure taste (*gusto purgato*), and a polite silhouette (*un profilo gentile*), he has nevertheless managed all his works with a grace which is very rare in Borrominesque buildings" (p. 387).

18. On Vanvitelli's work for the harbour and Lazaretto of Ancona, see R. Pane, "*L'Attività di Luigi Vanvitelli fuori del Regno delle Due Sicilie*," in R. de Fusco et al. (1973), pp. 51 ff. On his enforced collaboration with Carlo Marchionni, see R. di Stefano, "*Luigi Vanvitelli, ingegnere e restauratore*," in R. de Fusco (1973), pp. 178 ff.; also F. Strazzullo in R. de Fusco et al. (1973), pp. 265 ff. See also, however, Joachim Gaus (1967), p. 61, n. 38.

19. See J. Gaus (1967), pp. 85 ff., 77 ff. on the previous designs by Juvarra. F. Milizia (1781), II, pp. 260 f., rounds on it in his usual way in his life of Juvarra. But see, for a more indulgent view, A. Nibby (1838), I, pp. 640 ff.

20. See above, n. 26.

21. It does not appear to have begun when Nolli engraved his plan in 1748, although the ground is already the cardinal's. Nolli, who was to lay out the gardens and who dedicated the small plan of modern Rome with Piranesi's decorations to the cardinal, was presumably well informed of the position. The previous owner's name recorded on the engraving implies that the acquisition would have been later than 1737, a date which is suggested in J. Gaus (1967), pp. 22 ff., where the dating of the rest of the villa is discussed.

The finished villa as it was after the cardinal's death is also described by A. Nibby (1838), II, pp 882 ff.

22. On the cardinal's "intelligence" activities, see L. Lewis (1961). Stosch and Albani are the heroes of the book, which describes their very complex and extended activities.

23. Winckelmann himself writes of Stosch introducing him to Cardinal Albani (H. Diepolder and W. Rehm 1952–1957, I, pp. 268, 276, 444), to Beren-

dis (29 January 1757, p. 167), Francke (9 March 1757, p. 171), and Hagedorn (13 January 1759, p. 262). Winckelmann writes about this repeatedly during his Florentine visit (September 1758–April 1759). On the visit and Winckelmann's relations with Stosch, see C. Justi (1923), II, pp. 263 ff.

24. Albani had already acquired the Cassiano del Pozzo collection through his uncle, Clement XI, and it formed the basis of his holding.

His second collection was bought for George III through the Adam brothers in 1761, apparently to provide a dowry for one of Countess Cheroffini's daughters. J. Fleming (1962), pp. 297 f.; and J. Fleming (1958).

25. On 4 February 1758, Winckelmann writes to Francke that the villa is finished, presumably referring to the main building, and recalls seeing the foundations laid and that the columns of porphyry, granite, and alabaster made the site look like a little forest before they were put in place (H. Diepolder and W. Rehm, 1952 ff., p. 201).

26. He is reported by a French visitor, J. P. Grosley (1764, II, pp. 256 f.) as having remarked, "Cela n'est pas fait pour des yeux accoutumés aux merveilles de l'Art Français. L'idée doit vous paraître extravagante et l'exécution détestable." Allowing for the no doubt heavy irony, the remark must be taken as having the shadow of substance, at least. Cf. C. Justi (1923), II, p. 401.

27. There were a number of contemporary descriptions of the Villa as it was during the cardinal's lifetime. One of the very earliest must be Madame du Boccage's, who indeed claims primacy. *Lettres de Mme. du Boccage, contenant les Voyages en France, en Angleterre, en Hollande, et en Italie Pendant les Années 1756, 1757, et 1758*, Dresden, 1771, pp. 271 ff. The passage is quoted in H. Diepolder and W. Rehm (1952–1957), IV, pp. 403 f. It has been suggested that she may be recording her impressions of a conducted tour by Winckelmann; see H. Diepolder and W. Rehm (1952–1957), IV, pp. 576 f. Winckelmann is constantly talking about the villa in his letters, and although he displays an almost proprietary pride in it often, he is occasionally derogatory (he calls it "a heap of stones" in a letter) though this may refer more to the number of antiquities strewn about the grounds than to the building. Several guides to the Villa and its antiquities were published during the Cardinal's lifetime and just after his death.

28. This remarkable relief (S. Reinach, 1899–1900, II, 151, iii) is described by Winckelmann when still in the restorer's shop: to Bianconi on 25 July 1756, and to Francke, 9 March 1757. (H. Diepolder and W. Rehm (1952–1957) I, nos. 161, 171, pp. 246, 275). There were three of these at the villa, and Winckelmann maintains that the eye of the connoisseur would be able to distinguish the original (the one mounted on this door) from the copies: *Storia delle Arti del Disegno*, 1783, II, p. 104, n. 1; cf. p. 109; there is an engraving of it in this volume, on p. 162. Winckelmann also uses it considerably modified to head the dedication of his *Monumenti* (1767), I, pl. 5; cf. also pl. 9 f.; and II, pl. 67. A fragment of—presumably—a Roman copy of this relief was found in Capri about 1790. See N. Hadrava (1794), p. 28. It was then acquired by Prince Schwarzenberg.

29. This group of drawings is in the Cooper-Hewitt collection; see catalog nos. 31–34 (1973).

Cf. J. Gaus (1967), pp. 56 f. A drawing of the relief is in the collection of Marchionni's drawings of the villa (Gaus, III, p. 186, fol. 92) with other details for these doors.

30. Letter to Leon Usteri (1741–1789), the pretty Swiss minister who met

Winckelmann in Rome while on his grand tour, during which he also met Rousseau; he was to become a prebendary of the Zurich minster. Letter dated 27 November 1762 (H. Diepolder and W. Rehm, 1952–1957, II, no. 524, p. 273). Cf. C. Justi (1923), III, p. 58 ff.

31. Letter to Mengs in Madrid, 10 November 1761; but in the same vein to Bianconi (rough copy, late November 1761; H. Diepolder and W. Rehm, 1952–1957, II, no. 452, p. 190).

32. The exact division of responsibility in the design of the Villa Albani and its outbuildings has never been properly apportioned: writing to a fellow-student, Bernhard Genzmer, by then a minister, and tutor to the ducal house of Mecklenburg-Strelitz (22 December 1746) (H. Diepolder and W. Rehm (1952–1957) no. 688, III, p. 75): "It might seem as if he (Card. Albani) built for me, that he buys statues for me; for nothing is done of which I do not approve." Allowing for quite a lot of boasting, it is clear that Winckelmann did have a lot of say in the villa: Mengs, for instance, and Clérisseau were employed on his recommendation. To Christian Gottlieb Heyne, another old acquaintance, then professor at Göttingen (30 March 1765, H. Diepolder and W. Rehm, III, no. 697, p. 88). On the other hand, he writes of the cardinal and the villa: "He is the only architect of it." By this time, the main buildings of the villa were finished. The chapel by the entrance was consecrated 18 June 1763 (J. Gaus, 1967, p. 27, n. 32) at which point presumably all work on the casino proper was finished. But work went on in the gardens until after Winckelmann's death, and he writes constantly about it to many friends, including Münzell-Stosch, who, of course, knew the place and its owner well.

Of Marchionni, Winckelmann does not say a word, either in his letter or in his published writings. It is almost inconceivable that he did not meet him. The large number of drawings of Marchionni's for the villa testify to the constant contact he had with the work (see n. 29, this chapter). Winckelmann did not claim to design any of the villa himself, he gave credit to the cardinal. And yet Marchionni could hardly have been treated as a menial: he was to become "Principe" of the Accademia di San Luca, though not until 1778; but he held many important posts, both in Rome (*architetto della fabbrica* at St. Peter's since 1752, as well as many papal and private commissions) and in Ancona. Winckelmann was very friendly with Luigi Vanvitelli, on several occasions Marchionni's immediate superior and sometimes his rival, which suggests another obvious, though undocumented link. The account of the Vanvitelli-Marchionni relationship given by J. Gaus (1967), pp. 16 ff., should be corrected by reference to Vanvitelli's newly published correspondence. Cf. F. Strazzullo in R. de Fusco et al. (1973).

33. In the letter to Usteri quoted above, n. 30. Since his correspondent had left Rome at the end of April of that year, when the temple was presumably still being built, this dates the building fairly closely. Other buildings with which Winckelmann had something to do were also completed about this time.

34. H. Diepolder and W. Rehm (1952–1957), II, p. 273, no. 525, of 27 November 1762.

35. This curious little building of late imperial date had been transformed into a church during the Dark Ages; easy of access, between Spoleto and Foligno on the Via Flaminia, it had long been the object of antiquarian curiosity; in the seventeen-thirties, it had been damaged. Shortly before the building of the Albani "ruined temple," Ridolfino Venuti (1763) of Cortona, then papal president of antiquities (an office in which Winckelmann suc-

ceeded him; see the patent of appointment reproduced by H. Diepolder and W. Rehm (1952–1957), IV, pp. 383 ff., doc. 225) published a short dissertation about it. It was republished with three other monographs by Venuti in 1757–1758 or thereabouts. It included an account of the temple as well as of its cult, and the restoration of the building by Palladio. Its main illustration, curiously enough, was a view of the temple by Richard Wilson, engraved by Giuseppe Vasi.

Wilson was to use the temple several times in his landscapes (W. G. Constable, 1953, plate 22a and b, 26b), and there is one straightforward landscape painting of the *Fons Clitumni* (W. G. Constable, 1953, plate 75 b), and although he refers to an engraving by Vasi, it is taken from quite a different view; Constable seems to think it was done from a lost drawing.

36. J. J. Winckelmann (1783), III, pp. 1–106; particularly para. 28, p. 106. Michaelangelo and Borromini are coupled in a familiar fashion by Winckelmann. Though in the previous paragraph, he seems almost to accept the use of *rocaille* ornament for garden *parterres*.

37. Round openings and garlands, II, 17; shell niches, II, 18. On the decoration of temple fronts in archaic times, II, pp. 8 ff; III, pp. 91 ff, 101.

38. I. pp. 16 f. The second manner of reducing the weight of vaults by using hollow pots is described in para. 18, with reference to ancient examples only.

39. Vitruvius, VII, 4. Winckelmann particularly recommends Perrault's illustration of this device (2nd ed., p. 239). Albani used it in his villa at Castel Gandolfo.

40. Winckelmann announces the arrival of volume I on 22 September 1764, to Heinrich Füssli (H. Diepolder and W. Rehm, 1952–1957, III no. 673, p. 57). The comparison between the Athenian (Parthenon) and the Paestan moldings he describes in one of his reports to Bianconi (of mid-July 1758; H. Diepolder and W. Rehm, 1952–1957, I, no. 222, 384 f.). He had been watching out for the appearance of the book, and reports to J. J. Volkmann (27 March 1761, H. Diepolder and W. Rehm, 1952–1957, II, no. 397, p. 131), though prematurely, that it had been published and he quotes one of Stuart's engravers, Robert Strange, as the source of this information.

41. Letter to Bianconi cited above (H. Diepolder and W. Rehm, 1952–1957, III, no. 673).

42. Piranesi, *Della Magnificenza ed Architettura dei Romani*, 1760, p. cxix. Piranesi uses the reconstruction of the temple in Jerusalem made by J. B. Villalpanda in his commentary on Ezekiel: see R. Taylor in D. Frazer, H. Hibbard, and M. J. Levine (1967), pp. 81 ff., and J. Rykwert (1972), pp. 121 ff.

43. Piranesi (1760), pp. clxxi f.

44. J. J. Winckelmann, *Osservazioni* (1783), III, p. 46 f.

45. Winckelmann uses the term *Maestro Muratore* twice: to Bianconi (H. Diepolder and W. Rehm, 1952–1957, II, no. 561, p. 316) on 30 April 1763, and on 3 June 1767 (III, no. 861, pp. 270 f.) to Hans Füssli. To Bianconi, he records a discussion on the statue of an athlete: "In this wavering on the seas of many doubts and conjectures, the Master-builder also wanted to stick his rag into the linen and thought to discover that it was the stopper or top of an *ampullina* [small vase or oil-lamp]." On the same, writing to Pacciaudi, he gives this opinion as his own.

The mention to Füssli is more problematic. "When the Roman *Maestro Muratore* deserves to be translated and able to shed some light on matters here and there, I will be pleased and willing to do it. Much may be said for and against the enterprise. His cobbler's style, the messy way his work is put together, his childish credulity . . . What is useful the whole world knows. It's a book for an Orville.'' Possibly the expression is used for different persons, but it may well have been Winckelmann's nickname for one. Three names have been suggested. Most improbably, Muratori: neither *Roman* nor the faults fit; Vitruvius is the more likely suggestion; it has the advantage that it would explain the reference to the Amsterdam antiquarian, J. P. D'Orville (the author of two folio volumes on Sicily). But it is not wholly convincing; Piranesi would fit both references, and of course, Orville's antiquarian science would be as useful to Piranesi's translator as to Vitruvius'. This explanation has the added attraction of alluding to a discussion between Winckelmann and Piranesi; it has been taken as a reference to Piranesi's known masonic sympathies. See also below, chapter 8, nn. 114, 115.

46. H. Focillon (1967), p. 853.

47. Winckelmann's will, in which Mogalli is left 350 *zecchini*. The will was made by Winckelmann on his deathbed (H. Diepolder and W. Rehm, 1952–1957, IV, pp. 386 ff., doc. 230). Nicola Mogalli (b. 1723) worked often for Winckelmann and is referred to as his *familiare* by the restorer Cavaceppi (in his account of the trip to Germany with Winckelmann given in the preface to his *Raccolta d'Antiche Statue*, II, Rome, 1770) in J. J. Winckelmann (1961), p. 411.

48. Rome, 1763. The Piranesi engravings are nos. 72–119 in the Focillon (1918) catalogue. Venuti was Winckelmann's predecessor as *presidente alle Antichità*, and died as the book was going to print. He was one of the founding members, with his brother Filippo—of the Etruscan Academy of Cortona, as well as its secretary. He was very much the *cicerone,* and Winckelmann somewhat looked down on his predecessor. Writing to Pacciaudi on 30 April 1763 (H. Diepolder and W. Rehm, 1952–1957, no. 559), he reports the printing of the fifth sheet of the book, and Thomas Jenkins' financial interest in the matter—he had lent Venuti 400 *scudi*. Thomas Jenkins was another of the kind of Roman figures that people the period. He was by changes painter, antique dealer, excavator, *cicerone,* spy, banker. He died in 1798, on his return to England from a Napoleonic Rome. As for the book, Winckelmann, for one, was sceptical; he preferred to report the judgment of Contuccio Contucci, the Jesuit censor and antiquarian: "it will be yet another Ancient Rome."

49. Poor Duflos was one of the failures of the French Academy in de Troy's time. In a proposal of regulations which the interim director, Noel Halle addressed to Count d'Angevillers, he speaks of the "example, thirty years ago, of one Duflos, history painter, who was *pensionnaire* for eight years under M. de Troye and returned to France, a mediocre landscape painter." H. Lapauze (1924), I, pp. 342, 345.

50. Bellicard, although he had built very little—the Hôtel de Matharel, some interiors—had worked as *contrôleur* at Compiègne and Fontainebleau; he engraved a good deal: the Chinea of 1749, which he also designed; the illustrations to the guide to Herculaneum, which he wrote with C.-N. Cochin (1754); drawings and designs by Soufflot; and the beautiful vignettes for J.-F. Blondel's *L'Architecture Française,* which are very much at odds with the style of the book.

51. Jean Barbault, although he had come to Rome at his own expense, had a connection with the academy. He received various semiofficial commis-

sions (from Marigny, for instance). He published his own series of Roman views in 1761 and another collection of Italian antiquities in 1770.

52. Correspondance des Directeurs de l'Académie de France à Rome, quoted by J. Harris in D. Frazer, H. Hibbard, and M. J. Levine (1967), p. 190. Cf. also L. Hautecoeur (1943), III, pp. 475 ff.

53. C.-N. Cochin, *Mémoires inédites,* 1880, pp. 141 f.

54. C.-N. Cochin, *Mémoires inédites,* 1880, pp. 141 f.

55. P. du Colombier (1956), I, pp. 60 ff. Cf. also J.-M. Pérouse de Montclos (1969), pp. 40 ff.

56. J. Harris (1970), pp. 148, 246; cf. H. Huth, "Chambers and Potsdam," in D. Frazer, H. Hibbard, and M. J. Levine (1967), pp. 214 ff.

57. See S. Eriksen (1974), p. 200.

58. U. Thieme and F. Becker (1910–1950), s.v.

59. C.-N. Cochin (1880), pp. 78 f.

60. H. Lapauze (1924), I, pp. 219 ff.

61. C.-N. Cochin (1880), pp. 78 f., 143 f.; S. Eriksen (1961), pp. 340 ff. S. Eriksen (1974), pp. 297 f., 321 f.

62. A. C. P. de Caylus (1752). Cf. J. Seznec (1957), pp. 48 ff., on the discussion of this matter between Diderot and Caylus.

63. On the Chinea in general, see G. Ferrari (1919). Cf. also H. Tintelot (1939). The Chinea was a tribute offering of 5,000 gold ducats, which the king of the Two Sicilies paid the Holy See as a token rent for his kingdom. On the feast of St. Peter and Paul or on the Nativity of the Virgin, it usually took place at Santa Maria del Popolo, after which two fireworks displays were given, on successive days, either at the Palazzo Colonna (with the *macchina* or *scena* set up on the retaining wall of the Colonna gardens) or (as in 1745) in the Piazza Farnese. The genre was a familiar one.

64. G. Matthiae, *Ferdinando Fuga,* n.d., pp. 74 f.; R. Pane (1956), pp. 68 ff.

65. There is a description of the *Posessio* of Clement XIII in J. P. Grosley (1764), II, pp. 350 ff.; III, pp. 47 ff.

66. G. Matthiae, *Ferdinando Fuga,* n.d., p. 77; R. Pane (1956), pp. 74 ff.

67. Since the sixteenth century the Colonna family held the hereditary title of grand constable of the Kingdom of Naples, which also made the incumbent constable the Neapolitan representative in Rome. The Chinea representations were engraved every year until 1777.

68. A lesser-known member of the painter's dynasty of that name: he had not won a prize, but was at the academy as a protégé of the duc d'Antin. H. Lapauze (1924), I, pp. 195 ff.; U. Thieme and F. Becker (1910–1950), s.v.

69. Tuscher, who signed the plate—rather portentously in Greek—was to become a successful portrait painter in England and Denmark. The foreign artists employed on the Chinea were practically all French, and connected with the academy. They were well known in Rome for their skill in managing such matters; their carnival masquerades were often notable. H. Lapauze (1924), I, pp. 242 ff.

70. Charles-François Huttin in U. Thieme and F. Becker (1910–1950), s.v.

71. Francisco Preciado (not to be confused with his near-contemporary, Francisco Preciado de la Vega), an abbé, had got the sculpture prize of the Academy of St. Luke in 1739; he was recalled to Spain on the accession of

Ferdinand VI in 1746. W. Stirling Maxwell (1891), pp. 1441 ff. He was to produce an equally conventional, uninspired design two years later.

72. Probably the son of Alessandro Dori (d. 1772), with whom he seems to have worked on the restoration of San Lorenzo alle Grotte in Viterbo.

73. See n. 15.

74. For Perrault's coupled columns, see above, chapter 3.

75. There are very rare precedents: the two columns which flank the climax of the water-theater at the Villa Aldobrandini in Frascati. But they do occasionally occur in *Castra Doloris,* as in the one for the Grand Condé, designed by Jean Bérain. Cf. *Fantastic and Ornamental Drawings,* 1969, no. 63, for a drawing of this engraving. But antique precedent was also available: a Roman Doric column with branches twisting up the shaft was in the Court of the Belvedere in the Vatican—it came from Hadrian's villa. Piranesi shows one in his *Della Magnificenza,* pl. 18 (in Villa Albana extra Portam Salariam).

76. G. Matthiae, *Ferdinando Fuga.* n.d., p. 81.

77. The French *chargé d'affaires,* the abbé de Canillac, seems to have commissioned Panini in a fit of pique against the academy and its director, Nicolas Wleughels. H. Lapauze (1924), I, p. 243.

78. "Tempio di Minerva dell'antica gentilità tenuta per Dea delle Virtú . . . allusione à quelle vere e Regali che si mirano spiccare . . . nel magnanimo petto della Maestà di Carlo Ré delle Due Sicilie." The second *macchina* was again done by Preciado. The incense-burner was a popular enough piece of furniture at the time.

79. "Il Tempio di Venere Genetrice che dell'antica gentilità si osserva anch'oggi da suoi vestigii essere stato eretto vicino al seno del mare che forma il rinommato porto di Baia al nome della . . . tutelare de' parti, si viene pero a rinovare al felicissimo parto della REGINA." The second *macchina* was signed only by its engraver, Michele Sorellò.

80. On Francesco Pollanzani and Piranesi, see H. Focillon (1967), pp. 36 ff.

81. J.-F. Blondel (1747). This plate is inscribed "feu d'artifice qui fut tiré dans la Place de l'Hôtel de Ville de Paris."

82. The structure seems to have been devised by one de Bonneval, whose name is unknown to Hautecoeur.

The plate is inscribed: "décoration élevée sur la terrasse . . . de Versailles pour . . . le feu d'artifice . . . à l'occasion du mariage de Madame Louise-Elisabeth de France avec Don Philippe, le second Infant d'Espagne le XXVI aoust MDCCXXXIX." The plate is still in the Chalcographie Nationale.

83. The building to which it refers is in fact the theater: no amphitheater has so far been found at Herculaneum; it probably did not have one. The perplexities of the excavators about the shape of the ruin and the ideas which were entertained about the building are set out by Cochin and Bellicard in their *Observations* (1754), pp. 12 ff. The inscription this time contains no allegory about royal virtue or dynastic events: "un Idea alludente alla nuova scoperta del Teatro di Erculano, che il perfetto gusto . . . della Maestà del RE . . . e venuto a ravvivarne la memoria . . . E stata . . . ampiamente ricompensata tale spesa, e cura, dalli acquisti d'innumerabili tesori di statue equestri, consulari, busti, colonne . . . e quel che giunge a meraviglia, pitture di ottimo gusto istoriate, serbate intatte dall'ignavia di cosi lunga sepoltura." This was the second *macchina,* the first, again without the name of "inventor" was signed by Michaelangelo Specchi ("ar-

chitetto deputato'') and seems to have been a conventional Fugaesque exercise.

84. "Il molo nuovo, e la nuova strada, fatta fabbricare al porto di Napoli con immensa spesa . . . e maggio ornamento . . . che si rendeva solamente riuscibile all'antica potenza Romana." It is signed by Bellicard on the plate.

85. An English traveler of the twenties, Edward Wright (1730), I, left a description of such a celebration, if not of the Chinea, patronized by the Colonna.

"At the Accession of Innocent XIII, this prince (Colonna) made a musical Entertainment in his garden. The Musick was upon two bridges which lead from the Palace over a publick street to the Garden. The Orange-Trees were hung with Lamps put in the hollow'd Rinds of Oranges, and stuck among the Branches, as growing Fruit. During the Intervals of the Musick, the Fireworks were play'd at each end of the Garden." E. Wright (1730), I (p. 305).

Wright (1730), I, describes another entertainment, given on the same occasion by Cardinal Ottoboni at the Palazzo Cancelleria, which seems to correspond more closely to the sort of celebrations which were involved in the Chinea:

> In the publick Piazza, which is before the Palace, was a Concert of Vocal and Instrumental Musick, of a hundred and fifty Performers: there were two large *Palco's* or Galleries erected, one on each side of the Piazza, for the Performers . . . At a distance, fronting the middle of the Palace, was a Machine, built in very handsome Architecture, rais'd on an arch of Rock-work, with several large Figures, for the Fireworks: the four principal figures representing the four Quarters of the World. These, with others at a further distance, which they call *Girandole,* whirling in a thousand Varieties before the Eye, and so numerous a Chorus of admirable Musick filling the Ear, gave a surprisingly magnificent entertainment to both. The Musick was a sort of *Drama,* wherein the principal *Personae* were the same as were presented on the Machine, i.e., the four Quarters of the World, who, sometimes in alternate Song, sometimes in united Chorus, celebrated the Praises of the new Pope . . . Within the Palace were Entertainments of another sort: a long *Suite* of Rooms finely illuminated, and Tables finely set out with great Variety of Sweetmeats, and all sorts of Fruit represented in Ice (pp. 281 f.).

J. P. Grosley (1764), III, describes the *macchine* for the Chinea of 1758: "Execute sur les dessins de l'Architecte Posi, représentoit un grand Caffé Chinois, distribué sur chacun des deux grandes faces de la Décoration, en neuf pièces, différemment meublées. Du milieu . . . s'élevoit une tour octagone à la Chinoise de neuf étages'' (p. 54).

86. On Giuseppe Vasi, see U. Thieme and H. Becker (1910–1950), s.v.

87. On J.-F. J. Saly and Piranesi, see n. 91. This drawing may well be the one in the collection of the Société des Architectes Diplômés par le Gouvernement, Paris (London, 1978, no. 22).

88. Jacques-Guillaume Legrand (1743–1807) may even have known Piranesi in Rome, although he seems to have drawn most of his information from Piranesi's sons' *notices et pièces,* which may have included some of Giambattista's own notes. See A. Giesecke (1911), pp. 5 ff.; (this is the first part of a doctoral thesis, whose second part appeared separately in the Meister der Graphik series), pp. 5 ff. Legrand's *Notice Historique sur la Vie*

et les Ouvrages de J. B. Piranesi (ms., Paris, B.N., N.A.Fr. 5968) has never been fully published; see however G. Morazzoni (1921).

89. Clérisseau's quarrel with Charles Natoire, the director of the academy, was about the director's right to demand a certificate of Easter confession, which Clérisseau refused to give him. Natoire, with Vandières' agreement (Vandières, who was to become the marquis de Marigny, was Madame de Pompadour's brother: see chapter 10) "made an example" of Clérisseau. A. de Montaiglon and J. Guiffrey (1888), X, pp. 456 ff.; and H. Lapauze (1924), I, pp. 295 ff. The quarrel does not seem to have affected Natoire's very high opinion of Clérisseau, nor a recurrence of the troubles in future years.

90. The list is quoted by Giesecke (1911), I, pp. 12 ff.; and in a different order by H. Focillon (1967), p. 56.

91. On J.-F. J. Saly, see U. Thieme and H. Becker (1910–1950), s.v. When Saly died, his collection was sold at auction. This particular drawing, "Idée d'un Feu d'Artifice pour le recouvrement de la Santé de M. Saly en 1746, beau dessin à la plume et à l'encre de Chine," was bought by the dealer-engraver, Pierre-François Basan, who handled Mariette's succession. This drawing does not appear in the catalogs of Bason's sons, and seems to have disappeared. See C. Blanc (1857–1858), I, p. 316.

92. See n. 89.

93. Above, n. 32. As his part in the planning of the garden of the Farsetti villa at Sta. Maria di Sala. See below, chapter 8, nn. 22, 23.

94. Above, nn. 6, 7.

95. There are four series of etchings, all issued in Paris about the same time: *Vasi,* undated; *Fontane,* 1767; *Tombeaux,* 1768; and *Rovine,* 1768.

The date of the issue of these engravings is not disputed. But there is some discussion about when either the preparatory drawings for them were done or the plates engraved. See J. Harris (1970), pp. 190 ff. Harris' view that either may well have been done during Legeay's Roman stay seems to me to be convincing. See also E. Kaufman (1952).

96. Piranesi (1760). Maria Amalia, curiously enough, commissioned the young Soufflot to design some displays of the Herculaneum antiquities in the palace at Portici when he was there on his trip with Marigny (see chapter 10). Unfortunately his illness prevented their completion. J. Mondain-Monval (1918), p. 106.

97. On this relief, see n. 28.

98. There is a considerable literature about this painting, originally described admiringly by Diderot, who expanded, among other things, on the perfection of accessories: the antique vase on its pedestal ("oh! le joli morceau!"), the incense-burner, the chair ("d'un goût qui frappe"), all more like the furniture of Lalive de Jully. On Diderot, see J. Seznec and J. Adhémar (1957), I, pp. 165 f. For more recent literature, see R. Zeitler (1954), pp. 62 ff.; and R. Rosenblum (1967), pp. 3 ff. The antique painting which Vien used as his model was engraved by Carlo Nolli and published in the *Pitture Antiche d'Ercolano*, III, Naples, 1762, pl. 7. On the reliefs by Clodion and Bosio, see Rosenblum (1967), p. 3, n. 1.

99. A. Blunt (1966), II, pp. 14 f. catalog nos. 15, 16. Poussin sets many scenes in such an architectural background. There are several variations on the theme in the two versions of the Seven Sacraments (Blunt, 1966, Catalog nos. 105–111; 112–118). On Poussin's treatment of the theme, and his debt to the Mannerists as well as to Francis Pourbus the Younger, see Blunt (1966),

I, pp. 28 ff; and on the way it is developed in the Sacrament pictures, pp. 251 ff. Poussin's love of antique relief, and his assiduity in drawing them is too well known to need further reference here. See also chapter 1.

100. Cf. chapter 1, and, on Algarotti as a critic, chapter 8, nn. 16, 46 ff. The sequence of Tiepolo's Marc Anthony and Cleopatra pictures is catalogued by Antonio Morassi (1962), nos. 14, 14a, 15, 15a (Archangel); 368 (Melbourne); 280 (London, Alexander Coll.); 647 (Paris, Cognacq-Jay); 709 (Paris, P. de Rothschild); 1042 and 1043 (Venice, Labia Pal.). Cf. also A. Morassi (1955), pp. 21 ff.

101. A. Morassi (1962), No. 638. It is usually dated 1745–1750. Cf. A. Morassi (1955) where it is grouped with a series of paintings of the Passion. It came from the collection of the comte d'Angevillers, Directeur-Général des Bâtiments from the accession of Louis XVI in 1774.

In this group of pictures is the *Crowning with Thorns,* now in the Hamburg Kunsthalle, which was reputedly painted for Algarotti: see A. Morassi (1955), p. 145.

In both these pictures, a flat ground is both used and partially destroyed: in the Paris *Last Supper,* by the very strong light which floods the picture between the architectural *scenae* and the colonnade; in the *Hamburg Crowning* by introducing the crowd of orientals who assemble round the raised stone platform, itself forward of the stone *scenae,* parallel to the picture plane, in which the central action takes place. But also because, in spite of the directing of the light from a high point to the right of the picture, a secondary source of light is allowed through the central arch over the dramatic action. And although this arch is in turn blocked by the sort of column-and-arch screen which Tiepolo was to use frequently, the sharp light beyond the screen wall, together with the figures crowding into the arch, give the scene a plasticity which contradicts the primary compositional elements.

Tiepolo is, in a sense, the great practitioner of the *scena per angolo* in painting; his use of the squashed, friezelike space is therefore very remarkable. He was always eclectic; in one of his earliest paintings, the *Venus with the Mirror* in the Gerli collection (A. Morassi, 1962, no. 458), Venus is placed on a couch parallel to the picture plane; but the rigid space is contradicted both by the sinuous architectural background, and by the oval mirror in which Venus admires herself. An interesting variant on this kind of space is provided by the Montreal *Alexander and Campaspe in the Studio of Apelles,* where a flat background—the grey studio wall—is contradicted by a large blue canvas hanging on it, while the action is counterpoised to it *per angolo.* (A. Morassi, 1962, no. 503; Cf. A. Morassi, 1955, p. 150). The way in which Tiepolo uses the frieze composition contrasted with a *per angolo* one may be seen in his two *Rinaldo and Araminda* pictures in Munich (A. Morassi, 1962, nos 514 f.). And, of course, he contrasted brightly and ever more airily colored *per angolo* scenes with *grisaille,* or near-*grisaille,* painted to imitate bas-reliefs, as in the two Udine cycles; these are subdued and *rocaille*-inspired in the earlier cycle, in the Patriarcal palace (A. Morassi, 1962, nos. 871–900) while in the later cycle, in the Purità chapel (A. Morassi, 1962, nos. 859–870), the *grisailles* assume a much greater importance; they were executed in fact by Giandomenico.

Although the great fresco cycles (Palazzo Labia in Venice, the Residenz in Würzburg, the Royal Palace in Madrid, etc.) all present problems of great interest which surpass this note, it is fair to say that since his association with Algarotti, Tiepolo developed the frieze scene and gave it much more importance. But he continued to juxtapose it with *per angolo* compositions until the end of his life.

102. The picture was exhibited in the salon of 1769, although the preparatory painting was done a few years earlier. See D. Diderot (1957), IV, pp. 103 ff. On the picture and Diderot's criticism, and the episode in the French Academy on which Diderot comments, see A. Brookner (1972), pp. 67 ff.

103. Now in the Louvre.

104. On Hamilton's Homeric pictures, see E. K. Waterhouse in *Proceedings of the British Academy*, 40 (1954), pp. 57 ff., esp. pp. 69 ff. and (1962) pp. 188 ff. See also David Irwin (1966), pp. 36 ff. Writing to Stosch (H. Diepolder and W. Rehm, 1910–1950, II, no. 380, p. 111, 3 January 1763), Winckelmann compares Hamilton's *Bewailing of Hector* with another picture commissioned by Lord Compton (later Lord Northampton), Pompeo Battoni's *Hector Setting out for his Last Battle*. Winckelmann praises Hamilton's drawing and composition, but finds his color unacceptable. Battoni's color he admired; his drawing he found ignoble.

105. There is a painting by Hamilton of *Hector's Farewell to Andromache* in the Duke of Hamilton's collection at Holyroodhouse (see D. Irwin, 1966, pl. 12), but the picture praised by Winckelmann is only known from Cunego's engraving. The Battoni is unknown. See, however, H. Diepolder and W. Rehm, 1910–1950, II, p. 405. Cf. also C. Justi (1923), II, pp. 378 f. The painting is now at Over Norton Park; it was painted for Henry Dawkins, the brother of one of its heroes.

106. On John Hall (1739–1797), see *D.N.B.*, s.v.

107. G. Hamilton (1773). Beside the masterpieces promised in the title, this volume also included the engravings of the Homeric subjects after Hamilton.

Like several of his Roman contemporaries, Hamilton was an antiquarian, an excavator-archeologist, a dealer as well as a painter. See E. K. Waterhouse, *Proceedings* 40 (1954), pp. 67 ff. On his most important excavations at Hadrian's villa, see D. Irwin (1966), pp. 31 ff. L. Hautecoeur (1912) is however still worth consulting. More recently, see *Il Settecento a Roma* (catalog) Rome, 1959, pp. 127 f.

108. See J. Fleming (1962), pp. 274, 279 f.

109. On Morghen and the Volpatos, see P. Kristeller (1912), pp. 511 ff.; A. Calabi (1931), pp. 35 ff., 58 f. 4. It was published as the dedicatory frontispiece of Piranesi's *Magnificenza*, 1760.

110. For Thomas Dempster and Francesco Gori, see above.

111. On mezzotint, see J. Evelyn, *Sculptura: or the History and Art of Chalcography*, London, 1663; reprinted as *Evelyn's Sculptura*, ed. C. F. Bell, 1906, pp. 145 ff, and part II. P. Kristeller (1912), pp. 456 ff. On Jean-Christophe Le Blon (1670–1740), the German-born pupil of Maratta who developed the method of printing in three instead of seven colors, see Thieme-Becker s.v.

112. On engravings which imitate pastel and crayon, see E. Dilke (1902). pp. 149 ff.; F. Courboin (1923–1938), II, pp. xxiv; on color engraving, see E. Dilke (1902), pp. xxvii f., 199 ff., 209 ff.

113. Even if most of these engravings followed paintings already executed by Gagneraux. See R. Rosenblum (1956), pp. 83 ff.; and his *Transformations*, 1967, pp. 179 f.

114. Though most of them include some kind of elementary shading: even

the *Biblia Pauperum* and other block-books concede some hatching in the background, or in the shading and drapery. Nevertheless, with the development of perspective, greater reliance was placed by the woodcarver on line alone. Many of the blocks in the *Hypernotomachia Polyphili* rely on line alone.

115. Although whenever possible, inscriptions were typeset, to imitate the epigraph very roughly. This is even true of engraved epigraphic reproductions. But while many printers who did antiquarian work were almost bound to have a Greek and a Hebrew type, Syriac or Etruscan or even primitive Latin would be much less readily available and would therefore have to be carved on the block or engraved.

Medals and coins were inevitably often reduced to line alone: even in such works as E. Vico's (1619) and the *Commentarii* (also 1619) in which the copper-engraved coins are shaded, while the woodcut ones are left as line-cuts. But in Vico's book, a distinction is made between the more "common" coins which are set on a squared page (each coin occupying a square, with some squares always left blank) like nests in a collector's drawer, while the more "important" coins are given an elaborate architectural, elaborately modeled setting, into which they fit stylistically. (On Vico, see L. Cicognara, *Scultura,* 1813–1818, V, p. 453). In other early numismatic books, which group coins into framed "collections" such as Fulvio Ursini's *Familiae Romanae in Numismatis*, 1577, all the coins are shown in outline only. This is also true of later books such as Thomas Dempster's (1723) and Bernard Montfaucon's (1719–1724). Separation of color and line is, of course, inherent to block line printing, as is shown by the production of the earliest playing cards. See C. P. Hargrave (1930), pp. 43 ff., 91 ff., 231 ff.; in later packs color block-printing is sometimes replaced with stencil coloring.

116. Hogarth (1753) sets out his attitude to color and line in cha. 9, 10, 15, and 16 of the *Analysis of Beauty*.

On Winckelmann's debt to Hogarth and Burke, see C. Justi (1923), III, pp. 187 ff. On the major issue of the debate between color and *disegno*, see B. Teyssèdre (1964), pp. 44 ff., 152 ff.

117. Du Bos (1715) (1746), I, pp. 484 ff.

118. Although Winckelmann (1783) quotes Du Bos mostly to disagree with him, I, p. 388; II, pp. 55; 285; 1767, I, p. xxi; see also C. Justi (1923), I, p. 322, 431 f.

119. The theme is too insistent in Winckelmann's writings to need cataloging here (from *Reflections,* 1765, pp. 22 ff., to the *Monumenti Antichi Inediti,* 1767, II, pp. 1 ff.).

120. (Winckelmann, 1767), II, pl. 159.

121. Caylus (1752–1767).

122. D'Harcanville (1766–1767). In spite of the issue date, Winckelmann did not receive the first printed and unbound sheets until March/April 1767 (H. Diepolder and W. Rehm, 1952–1957, no. 837, to Usteri, 8 April 1767; to Walther, on the same day (H. Diepolder and W. Rehm, 1952–1957, no. 839), he announces the four-volume work, and says he has had some proof sheets, hand-tinted. He reports a compliment to himself which is to appear in the text; also that all the plates are printed to Usteri (Diepolder and Rehm III, no. 868, p. 277 f.) on 27 June 1767. On 19 December 1767 he writes warmly of his Neapolitan friends to Wiedewelt (Diepolder and Rehm, no. 931, III, p. 342), that he had been to Naples in September/October, where Hamilton and D'Harcanville had feted him, and perhaps helped to smooth

matters with the Marchese Tanucci, who had reason to resent a publication of Winckelmann's *Nachricht*, 1762, which Caylus had had translated into French and published in Paris in 1764.

It had been reported to him by the Abbé Galliani from Paris, and he had also read a favorable notice of it in the *Gazette Littéraire*, 27 August 1764. Hamilton, passing through Paris on his way to Naples to take up his post, undertook to take a copy of the pamphlet for Tanucci with him (H. Diepolder and W. Rehm, IV, pp. 133 ff.). The first volume of the Hamilton collection was not in fact issued until January 1768; and then Winckelmann warns Heyne (Diepolder and Rehm, III, no. 931, p. 357) to buy the book bound, and not in loose sheets, as the plates of the first volume are not numbered. A little later (6 February 1768), Winckelmann writes to Francke that he has a room of his own in Naples, filled with "his very own so-called Etruscan vases." Although he announces that he intends to visit Naples monthly—a plan he did not realize, as he set out for Germany in April that year and was murdered on his return journey in Trieste on June 8. But in the February letter, he is a little less enthusiastic; "einer der gröszten Avanturiers . . . dieser Mann heiszt d'Harcanville." (Diepolder and Rehm, 1952–1957, III, p. 366). Nevertheless, the second volume of the Hamilton collection carries, as a frontispiece, an antique sarcophagus dedicated to the memory of Winckelmann by D'Harcanville, which means that the second volume was issued much later in the year. Several plates in each volume, as well as ornaments, are colored terracotta, and a few heightened with white and with other colors.

On the circumstances of the catalogue, B. Fothergill (1969), pp. 66 ff., 234 f. The book was reissued, in a cheaper version, in Paris in 1787 as *Antiquités Etrusques, Grecques, et Romaines*.

123. In the preface to the first volume: that individual plates might be used as wall decoration but also that they might be used by artists and craftsmen "who would *invent* in the same style, or only *copy* the Monuments which appeared to him worthy of being copied" and who would then have an exact idea of these vases as against the general notion that might be got from the publications of Montfaucon and Caylus.

Hamilton's brother-in-law, Lord Cathcart, who was one of the recipients of the proof sheets, passed them on to Josiah Wedgwood; these seem to have been the immediate inspiration for six black vases decorated in red encaustic with figures drawn from the plates, which were made to celebrate the opening of the Burslem factory in June 1769. See B. Fothergill (1969), p. 69.

124. On the circumstances of Hamilton's two collections, see B. Fothergill, 1969, pp. 117 ff., 144 ff. And more recently, *Sir William Hamilton and the British Museum*, catalog, London 1972.

125. W. Hamilton (1791–1795). Tischbein had met Hamilton on his first visit to Naples with Goethe in February 1787; see Goethe, *Werke*, 1948–1954, XI, pp. 228 ff., 360 ff., 392 ff.; and B. Fothergill, 1969, pp. 231 ff. Besides texts by Hamilton himself, there are some mystagogic comments on individual vases by the Russian ambassador to the Two Sicilies, André d'Italinsky (Andrei Iakovlevim) (1743–1828).

On the circumstances of the publication and on Tischbein's very exacting methods of work, see F. Landsberger (1908), pp. 128 ff.

126. Hamilton in W. Tischbein (1791–1796), II, p. 4.

127. I. Kant, *Critik der Urtheilskraft*, 1790, para. 14.

128. *Natural History*, XXV, 12, xliii. It was certainly the most popular

account of the invention of drawing. In this touching tale, the daughter of Dibutades of Sikyon traces the shadow of her lover (who is about to leave) thrown onto the wall by a lamp. It was frequently drawn and painted in the second half of the eighteenth century and early in the nineteenth. See R. Rosenblum in *Art Bulletin* 39 (1957), pp. 279 ff. Pliny's heroine makes the profile into a relief, not a painting however.

It may be worth emphasizing that Winckelmann was convinced of the temporal priority of sculpture over painting; see *Monumenti Antichi*, 1767, II, pp. xii ff.

129. On Etienne de Silhouette and his policy, see E. Lavisse (1909), VIII, pt. 2, pp. 361 ff., and more personally in E. J. F. Barbier (1844–1856), IV, pp. 308 ff., 330 ff.; also the article on him in the *Biographie Universelle*. He was already an experienced administrator as well as a man of letters (known particularly for his translations from the English); he reached high office in 1757, for eight months only, as the result of the protection of Madame de Pompadour. But the king found his manner boring; and his early successes led to such stringent policies that he became increasingly unpopular, especially with the *Fermiers*. He was made the subject of a satirical campaign: *A la Silhouette* was used to mean meager, of shoddy workmanship, skimped. He was known to favor the cut-out or filled in outline portraits, and even decorated the house at Brie-sur-Marne he retired to after his fall from power with his own productions. The name came to be applied to them soon after his disgrace.

On the silhouette as an art-form, see F. Nevill-Jackson (1938), esp. pp. 2ff., p. 145. The popularity of the medium led to the invention of several pieces of apparatus to systematize outline drawing and cutting, of which the *Physionotrace* devised in the late seventeen-eighties was the most popular; see F. Courboin (1923), pp. 152 f.; and pp. 90, 137 f.; Cf. also F. Nevill-Jackson (1938), pp. 90, 137; and R. Rosenblum (1956), p. 79. The medium combines the ancient art of paper and vellum cutting with the principle of the *camera lucida* or *obscura* which was known since the fifteenth century but was particularly popular with portrait and landscape painters in the late seventeenth and in the eighteenth century; it is usually regarded as the ancestor of the photographic camera. H. Gersheim and A. Gersheim (1955), pp. 25 f.

130. J. K. Lavater, (1775–1778); an enlarged edition *Essai sur la Physiognomie, Destiné à Faire connoître l'Homme et à le Faire Aimer* appeared at The Hague in 1783. The chapters concerned with the silhouette are in ch. 27 f. and ch. 37 of the second edition.

131. Letter to Ludwig Tieck in R. Rosenblum (1967), pp. 179 f. See also W. M. Ivins, Jr. (1953), pp. 88 ff.

132. Chiefly on the comte de Clarac, a reduction of whose *Musée de Sculpture* (in size, not in the number of plates) forms the first of his six-volume *Statuaire Grecque* (1897). Reinach (1897–1924) discusses the rather troubled circumstances of Clarac's publication, I, pp. xv ff. On Reinach's own aim, and the impossibility of producing a photographic *corpus statuorum*, on the propriety of using a poor, cheap medium such as outline, and on his view on the classification called for in the work, 1899–1900, I, pp. iii ff. Reinach's phrasing—even if taken out of context—is symptomatic: "Le point de vue auquel je me suis placé n'est donc celui de l'Esthétique mais de la science." S. Reinach, *Peintures du Moyen Age*, 1905, I, p. ii. Tischbein's corpus is reproduced in the *Vases Peints Grecs*, 1899–1900, II, pp. 277 ff. It is in fact the earliest of such collections which Reinach reprints.

133. The first account of the tendency was given by Louis Hautecoeur (1912), pp. 243 ff. A more extended, and more recent account is Robert Rosenblum's (1956) unpublished doctoral thesis. See esp. pp. 12 ff, 50 ff.

The most important is the series published by Charles-Philippe Landon, called *Annales du Musée et de l'Ecole Moderne des Beaux-Arts*, an illustrated periodical in which the work of current prizewinners in the various competitions was published, together with a selection of masterpieces of all times which had come to public notice: the work published included painting, sculpture, architecture, and some of the ''minor arts'' such as furniture. Sixteen volumes were published 1801–1808; in 1805 Landon began publishing a supplementary series of masterpieces in the Musée Napoléon, which were toned and shaded, and of which five volumes appeared, with two supplementary volumes which were again in outline; from 1808 to 1814, Landon also continued the *Musée* in the form of yearly *Salons*. In addition he published, again beginning in 1805, eight large format fascicules, also illustrated with outline engravings of *Les Vies et les Oeuvres des Peintres les Plus Célèbres*. The bulk of Lenoir's plates, and some of the compositions, such as the frontispieces, were the work of the architect-engraver, Charles Normand, who at this time also engraved most of the plates of J. N. L. Durand's *Précis* (1802–1805; revised 1812 and republished constantly until Durand's resignation from his professorship at the Ecole Polytechnique in 1830) and his *Recueil et Parallèle* (An IX/1800 and often reprinted). These two works are usually known as the *Petit Durand* and the *Grand Durand*. The *Grand Durand* had an introductory text by J. G. Legrand who was to collaborate with Landon on a guide to Paris (1806). Normand also took over the engraving of Charles Percier's and P. L. Fontaine's *Recueil*, 1801, many times reprinted, as well as some of their other works. His own *Guide* was first published in Paris in 1826. Besides these and many other illustrated volumes, he engraved several standard packs of cards: in 1809 after designs of David and Madame Mongez; in 1811 and 1816 the standard French pack. He also provided patterns of bank notes for several banks.

Altogether he is credited with some 17,000 engraved plates of all sizes. His own *Nouveau Parallèle*, 1823, became the basis of most subsequent textbooks on the orders. All this made Normand one of the most active diffusers of the linear style of the 1800s, though he is not usually mentioned in this connection. It may be worth mentioning that Normand became a *pensionnaire* of the Rome Academy on receiving his institute prize in 1792, at the same time as Landon, although both of them had to wait for the settlement of troubles before going to Rome. See on this H. Lapauze (1924), I, pp. 421, 484 f.

Many of the plates of the comte de Clarac's *Musée*, 1826, were also engraved by him. Landon's success encouraged several others: notably Etienne-François Réveil, whose *Museum of Painting* was published bilingually (with descriptive, critical, and historical notes by Duchesne senior) in London and in Paris, beginning in 1829 in twenty-three volumes.

But perhaps the most influential of these works, certainly one of the most interesting and ambitious, was the *Histoire de l'Art* by Séroux d'Agincourt (1823), published posthumously (d'Agincourt had died in 1814), in which the whole history of art from the decline of the Roman Empire until the time of Raphael and Michaelangelo is set out in the captions to 325 outline plates. On Séroux d'Agincourt, see J. Schlosser (1956), pp. 487 f., p. 510; and more recently, U. Kultermann (1966), pp. 152 ff.

134. A conspicuous example is the engraving of the emperor's library at

Malmaison published by C. Percier and P. F. L. Fontaine in their *Recueil,* 1801, pls. 41 f., in which the light-colored but elaborately patterned ceiling appears as rather dark, while the rich mahogany bookcases appear white on the engraving, being rather plain.

135. P. Kristeller (1912), pp. 502 ff; F. Courboin (1923), II, pp. xxiv f., xxvii f.

136. F. Courboin (1923), pp. xxv f.; W. M. Ivins (1953), pp. 83 ff. On the development of half-tone engraving from aquatint, W. M. Ivins (1953), pp. 127 f. On Goya as an aquatint engraver, see pp. 83 and 87.

137. Senfelder's discovery was made in 1797; he first introduced it to Britain. The *Polyautographic Album* containing prints by Benjamin West and Thomas Stothard, the first instance of its use by artists, was published in London in 1803. But these were only mass-produced prints of pencil drawings, as were Andrea Appiani's of 1809. The great artists Goya, Delacroix, Ingres were not attracted to the medium until the mid eighteen-twenties. See W. M. Ivins, 1953, pp. 94 f., 108 ff.

138. Rome, 1778. The two volumes of the collection (Focillon K, 601–718) are made up of plates published separately at various dates; several (apart from the ones signed by him) are by Francesco Piranesi.

139. Of the eighty-five dedicated plates, sixty-two carry English names. They are not particularly distinguished, nor are they partisan. Stuart and Hannoverian sympathizers mix. There are a number of Winckelmann's associates (Reiffenstein, Ermansdorff). Two plates are dedicated to the excavator of Corneto, the Scottish antiquarian James Byres *"mio carissimo Amico"*; it was he who found the friezes reproduced in the three final plates of the *Lettre à Mariette* (the *Introduzione* illustrations). It is clear from this, as well as from other evidence, that Piranesi moved most easily among his British patrons.

140. "Ned apparendo ne' Principi, o ne' Privati disposozione [*sic*] a farneli (il dispendio) vedere; altro partito non veggo restare a me, e a qualsivoglia altro Architetto moderno, che spiegare con disegni le proprie idee, e sottrare in questo modo alla Scultura e alla Pittura l'avvantaggio, che come dicea il grande Iuvara, hanno in questa parte sopra l'Architettura; . . . Per questo fine io ho procurato . . . l'arte di disegnar non solo le mie invenzioni, ma d'intagliarle ancora nel rame." Piranesi, *Prima Parte di Architettura e Prospettive . . . ,* Rome, 1743; Focillon A, 2–13; see however *Giovanni Battista Piranesi,* drawings and etchings at Columbia University, New York, 1972, pp. 69 f.

141. Focillon D, 20–23.

142. This was first suggested by Maurizio Calvesi in the introduction to *Giovanni Battista e Francesco Piranesi,* catalog, Rome, 1967, pp. 24 f.

143. On Corradini, see C. Semenzato (1966), pp. 43 ff., 111.

144. On the Pietatella, see D. Raimondo di Sangro (1767). The statue is described on p. 16 (reprinted, with notes and ed. A. Crocco, 1967).

145. On the relationship between the two statues, see G. Alparone in *Bolletino d'Arte,* 42 (1957), pp. 179 ff. The veiled Christ was to have been placed, according to one interpretation, in the adjoining vault. See the otherwise unconvincing exposition by M. P. Moresca and Vincenzo Vaccaro (1975).

The traditional description of the female statue as Pudicizia does not seem to describe this veiled figure adequately: the veiled woman as hidden virtue is a commonplace in hermetic thinking, and relates to the *nuda veritas;* the statue facing the Pudicizia across the chancel arch of the chapel, and a memorial to the prince's father, is another strange iconographic device: a man liberating himself from a net which envelops, and gazing into the face of an angel who seems to be unveiling a globe; there is an open book in front of the globe, and several strewn behind the main figure, discarded. The analogous situation, function, iconography, and even surround, suggest that the two figures, and perhaps the shrouded Christ form some kind of hermetic emblem. See F. Venturi (1969), p. 540; M. Picone (1959) for a full bibliography. Cf. also L. Cicognara (1813–1818), pp. 235 ff.

146. F. Venturi (1969), pp. 543 ff. The submission to papal authority was purely nominal. Di Sangro was involved in the continued operation of Neapolitan masonry, which was protected by the court and which the Queen enthusiastically supported. See H. Acton (1956).

147. F. Venturi (1969), pp. 540 f.

148. G. B. Vico (1836), VI (Opuscula), p. 442.

149. Focillon E, 24–39, paris numbering 349–364. There is a problem of two editions in relation to four states. It would seem that the plates were first engraved in the forties; they were probably published on their own by the French print seller, Jean Bouchard (whose name is misspelled "Buzard" in the first issue) sometime before 1750 (1745?). For the subsequent history, see J. Adhémar in A. Huxley (1949); and more recently the New York and London catalogs (1972, 1978).

150. Plate 2 of the *Prima Parte* (Focillon, 4). "Carcere Oscura con antenna nel suplizio de'malfatori."

151. Livy, I, 26; the use of the Gemonian stairs for exposing the bodies of malefactors is recorded by Tacitus (*Annals*, III, 14; V, 4; *History*, III, 74, 85). The misreading of a passage in *Velleius Paterculus*, II, led Piranesi to the idea of a bridge in the prisons in the Capitol.
This mistake is sanctioned by Ridolfino Venuti's (1763) guide.

152. The Scala Gemonia was a well-known place of torture and execution, which antiquarians placed in the neighborhood of the prisons. The passages in Tacitus evoke the ropes and pulleys, though, of course, they were also an unavoidable feature of "stage" prisons at the time.

153. On Bibbiena's and Piranesi's prisons, see J. Adhémar in A. Huxley (1949), Calvesi (1967–1968), pp. 11 f. See most recently and extensively S. Gavuzzo Stewart in *L'Arte*, 1973, 15–16, pp. 17 ff., 74; all these sources discuss the prison as a commonplace in late seventeenth- and eighteenth-century theatrical decoration.

154. On Lodoli's xylology and lithology, see above.

155. They have been interpreted in some detail by U. Vogt-Göknill (1958), pp. 26 ff. These effects had remained unnoticed for two centuries, although the plates were often studied.
On "impossible objects," see R. L. Gregory (1966), pp. 224 ff. and R. L. Gregory (1973), pp. 49 ff. The Dutch artist M. C. Escher has specialized in drawing such figures, but he has made no secret of his intentions, and they have always been obvious to those who viewed his engravings.

156. Quoted from the ms. life of Piranesi by J. G. Legrand (Bibliothèque Nationale, Paris) by most of his biographers.

157. The whole phrase runs "Carcer ad terrorem increscentis audaciae media urbe imminens foro aedificatur"; in which he records the building of

the prison by the fourth king of Rome, a just king and the grandson of Numa. Livy, I, 33, viii: To meet this unhappy state of affairs (the increase of crime) and to discourage the further growth of lawlessness, the prison was built in the center of the city.

158. Livy, I, 26, v; Livy's actual words are: "Caput obnube liberatoris urbis huius; arbori infelici suspende" ("Blindfold our liberator's eyes— hang him on a barren tree") No source has been found for the substituted words, nor is there any obvious motive for such a change.

159. There are several such wooden constructions in other *Carceri*; see M. Calvesi (1967–1968), p. 17. Calvesi sees this constant reference to a Tigillum as a symbol of the severe equity and the ultimate clemency of Roman law.

160. Calvesi (1967–1968) suggests that these words are a reference to the Livian account of the Fetials declaration of war, in which the words *iniuste impieque* occur. Besides the very different words of the inscription, there is no reason why the Fetial formula should be quoted here. A more likely source is the Bull "Providas Romanorum Pontificum" of May 1751.

161. On Francesco Piranesi's activities after his father's death, see H. Focillon (1918), pp. 131 ff.

162. Tacitus, *Annals,* XVI passim. The passage was identified some time ago; see Calvesi, 1967–1968, p. 12, n. 24. But its significance was reassessed more recently by S. Gavuzzo Stuart in *L'Arte*, 1973.

163. Piranesi, *Magnificenza*, 1760, pp. vii ff., cf. also clix.

164. "Risposta del Signor Giambattista di Vico nella Quale si sciolgono tre opposizioni fatte da dotto Signore contro il primo Libro 'De Antiquissima Italorum Sapientia." Naples, 1711, in ed. F. Niccolin (*op. cit.*), p. 333 f.

165. Vico reiterated this belief several times in the *Scienza Nuova,* 1953, pp. 467, 523 ff., 762; and reiterated it in the appendix on the 12 Tables, pp. 878, 890. According to him, the division was carried out by Servius Tullius. See ch. 1.

166. See the chronological table in Vico's *Scienza Nuova*, 1953, and the commentary on it.

167. The inscription, in the Palazzo Farnese, had been discussed by William Fleetwood in his *Inscriptionum Antiquarum Sylloge*, 1691, p. 67, n. 1 quoting Janus Gruter.

   Inscriptionum Romanorum Corpus Absolutissimum, Paris, 1603, p. 207; Gruter and Fleetwood record the inscription as being in Naples (in Domo Hadriani Guglielmi ad Sanctum Iohannem Maiorem). Gruter's *Corpus* contains the shorthand system, "Notae Tironis ac Senecae," named after Cicero's freedman and reported stenographer of his Catiline oration.

168. 1765. The kernel of the book, the *Parere* was studied in some detail by R. Wittkower in his "Piranesi's Parere su l'Architettura," *Journal of the Warburg and Courtauld Institutes* II, 2, 1938, pp. 147 ff., reprinted (1975), pp. 235 ff. This essay suggests that there is a radical break in Piranesi's attitude to the relationship between structure and ornament as between the *Magnificenza* of 1760 and the *Parere* of 1765. It does not seem that such a radical break had taken place. Piranesi's tone is always sharply polemical and sarcastic, so much that he sometimes obscures the sense. It seems to me that Wittkower has read him too literally in his interpretation of cap. 62 of the *Magnificenza* (his p. 248, n. 2).

169. No more was heard of this project.

170. Although they are described on the first plate as "découvertes par

Piranesi en Toscane,'' they were presumably drawn on a visit to Corneto with James Byres, to visit the reopened Tomba del Cardinale in 1760 (it had also been opened in 1699 and 1738, and finally in 1780). An account of this visit is given by G. Dennis (1848), I, pp. 314 ff. Piranesi refers to Byres' drawings of the tombs in the *Cammini* (1769), p. 22, where he also suggests that Byres was preparing a book on the subject; in fact, the engravings prepared by Byres were not published until 1842 in London. Byres was a well-known antiquarian, architect, cicerone, dealer, and banker, and is now chiefly remembered for having sold the Portland vase to Sir William Hamilton.

171. This order was devised by James Adam for his projected Parliament building; he was very proud of it, and had it modeled in wax and bronze; it was also included in his portrait by Pompeo Battoni and engraved in the *Works of James and Robert Adam* (1773–1778). See, for the whole episode, J. Fleming (1962), pp. 305 f. Cf. also pp. 317 ff.

172. Also quoted in the text of the *Parere*, 1765, p. 14. Piranesi drew it from Le Roy (1758).

173. Ovid XV, *Met.*, 252/3. "Rerumque novatrix/Ex aliis alias reddit natura figuras.''

174. Ter. Eunuchus, Prologue, v. 41 ff. See the discussion of this and the following quotations in Wittkower (1975), pp. 242 f.

> Denique
> Nullum est jam dictum, quod non dictum sit prius.
> Quare AEQUUM EST VAS (sic! scil. vos) COGNOSCERE ATQUE
> IGNOSCERE
> QUAE VETERES FECITARUNT SI FACIUNT NOVI.

175. The scale is abstract, since only in the last of these engravings is there any—even the most shadowy idea given of the size of a human figure.

176. Salust, *Jugurt.* LXXXV. 14. "Nunc vos existumate facta an dicta pluris sint CONTEMNUNT NOVITATEM MEAM EGO ILLORUM IGNAVIAM: mihi fortuna, illis probra obiectantur.'' On the plate, Piranesi reverses the two first words of the quotation.

177. The difficulty about its decipherment has already been discussed in some detail by Calvesi, while Wittkower (1975) has denied that there had been any intention on Piranesi's part to devise such a "vocabulary" (p. 244). The difficulty is heightened by Piranesi's denial on the one hand that he has any such intention, and his affirmation that it is a matter of course. See *Cammini*, 1769, pp. 9 f., and below, Calvesi's somewhat sanguine remarks on the subject (1967), p. 22.

178. Piranesi's reiteration of this emblem has been discussed by Calvesi (1967), pp. 24 f.; but see also P. Mellis (1975), pp. 90 f.

179. The plates are not arranged in the same order in every copy. I have followed, for convenience, that of the reprint edited by J. Wilton-Ely (1972).

180. The commission was actually granted by Clement XIII in 1764, in the same year in which Giovanni Battista, Cardinal Rezzonico commissioned him to redesign the Maltese priory chapel. Piranesi was inevitably very disappointed by the failure of the commission; in 1767, he presented the finished drawings to the cardinal. These drawings disappeared until very recently; they were rediscovered and are now in the Avery Library at Columbia University, New York. See the Columbia catalog (cit. sup.).

181. These swords are themselves little fantasies on symbols, mostly heral-

dic devices from the Rezzonico arms. Preparatory drawings for one of these swords is in the Pierpont Morgan Library, New York. See A. Hyatt Mayor (1952), pl. 83.

182. In fact, an Etruscan one to Piranesi: it figures in the center of the third plate of the Corneto Friezes, which were published in the *Letter à Mariette*.

183. This capital is based on an example much admired by Piranesi: two identical capitals, of very similar shape, were to be seen in the collections of the Villa Borghese and in the house of Belisauro Amedei in Piazza Navona. It is engraved on pl. 13 of the *Magnificenza*. It has a kind of stylized vegetable torch at the center instead of the Rezzonico tower, and satyrs on the volutes instead of Piranesian *putti*. Piranesi also adds a palmette-leaf moulding below the volutes and sphinxes, which seems modelled on the capitals of San Nicola in Carcere, also engraved in the *Magnificenza*, pl. 20.

By the time Piranesi (1769) had discussed the capital in the *Cammini* (p. 12), Amedei, one of the few Roman antique dealers who dealt in large stones (C. Justi, 1923, II, p. 365), had evidently sold the capital to Robert Adam. Amedei's protesting one of Francesco Casanova's bills of exchange led to the latter's imprisonment (C. Justi, 1923, III, p. 370).

The capital was presumably bought by James Adam, as Robert had left Rome in May 1757.

184. This appears very clearly in Vasi's great view of Rome, as has been pointed out by W. Körte (1933) in *Zeitschrift für Kunstgeschichte* II, pp. 357 f. It was destroyed in the siege of Rome in 1848.

185. The best description of this articulation is given by R. Wittkower (1975), pp. 252 ff.

186. Wittkower (1975) suggests that this is a very Venetian arrangement, but while the changes of level in the floor are unusual, the placing of an altar against sharp light was not extraordinary in Rome, especially where the altar stood between a conventual choir and the chancel, as at Sta. Maria sopra Minerva, San Agostino, San Pietro in Montorio, and so on.

187. The best presentation is the measured drawing produced by the engineering faculty of the University of Rome. See M. Tafuri (1968), p. 41, fig. 5.

188. Legrand (f⁰ 139) quoted in H. Focillon (1967), p. 115.

189. See n. 200, this chapter.

190. On Hume, Burke, and Du Bos, see W. J. Hipple (1957), pp. 48 ff. But see Du Bos (1746) and horror in tragedy, with reference to Aristotle, pp. 27 ff; and the whole problem of the pleasure of pain.

191. In the section on the sublime in the *Critique of Judgment*, paras. 23 ff., see E. F. Carritt (1923), pp. 221 ff. E. Cassirer (1955), pp. 327 ff., though perhaps W. Folkierski (1936), pp. 59 ff., is still the best discussion of the problem.

192. G. B. Piranesi (1769), p. 2. Piranesi is old-fashioned enough to recommend *bienséance*, even in caprice.

193. Piranesi, *Cammini*, 1769, p. 2 f. This, of course, is Piranesi's constant refrain: something like this is meant by the passage in the *Magnificenza*, 1760, p. 175, in which he considers the matter of proportion in the orders; on which he had very definite and rather unorthodox opinions. Having castigated Le Roy many, many times for having said that "the principles which Vitruvius left us about the orders can't suffice," he points to a contradiction. If the proportions suggested by Vitruvius, which are based on his

knowledge of Greek architecture, are inadequate, then whosoever finds them so, by the same token finds Greek architecture such. Whosoever disapproves of them—and they are like nerves holding architecture together—must reject his information on the subject outright; and yet Le Roy—Piranesi so has it—will resort to them as one of the foundations of a new architecture. Having trounced Le Roy on proportion, Piranesi at once goes on to a more serious matter, that of the use of dentils.

But the essential beauties of a building were not even at the time of the *Magnificenza* in any way dependent on the ornament. The defense of the severity of Roman aqueducts and *Cloacae* was, of course, on the grounds of decorum. But Piranesi goes on to defend the general barrenness and poverty of material of Tuscan architecture against the Greek. True, Tuscan (and Roman following them) temples lacked wall-paintings and marble reliefs; "These things, to tell the truth, make a temple rich, but not beautiful. I therefore do not believe," he goes on, "that the temple of Sta. Sophia in Constantinople has lost the beauty proper to its architecture when the Turks deprived it of the ornaments which were added to it." (1760, p. 53.)

The doctrine which Piranesi teaches is of a familiar kind: like the other arts, architecture imitates an original; but this original is not from nature, as it is for painting or sculpture; it is the product of necessity, which is then varied according to the mood of the builder through the law of sequence so insistently quoted by Lodoli (Vitruvius, IV, p. 2). So the Egyptians, who wanted gravity and articulation above all, arrived at one form; the Greeks, seeking a graceful prettiness, at another. Their irregularity may be seen when the different columns in St. Marks in Venice are examined and so on (pp. 95 ff.).

The excesses in the use of curves in architecture is almost exemplified by the Ionic order of the Greeks—so far from the orthogonal sobriety of the virtuous ancients (pp. 115 f.). Not that the curves of arches and domes, curves which follow necessity, come under the same disapproval. They are quite different. And so Piranesi returns to the primacy of Tuscan architecture derived more directly from Chaldean and therefore the sacred original architecture and its immutable primal laws, which invention, guided by divine providence, may enrich and elaborate but never contradict.

194. Piranesi, *Cammini*, 1769, p. 3.

195. Piranesi, *Cammini*, 1769, pp. 6 ff. The passage in Varro is in fact VIII LL 31: "Quod si quis duplicem putat esse summam, ad quas metas naturae sit perveniendum ad usu, utilitas et elegantiae, quod non solum vestiti esse volumus ut vitemus frigus, sed etiam ut videamur vestiti esse honeste, non domum habere ut simus in tecto et tuto solum, quo necessitas contruserit, sed etiam ubi voluptas retineri possit, non solum vasa ad vistum habilia, sed etiam figura bella atque ab artefice (ficta), quod aliud homini, aliud humanitati satis est."

The distinction between *homo* and *humanitas* is translated by Piranesi freely and perhaps a little anachronistically. But the sense of the whole passage is quoted fairly, and it occurs in a passage on style in which Varro suggests that distinctions of manner are appropriate for different features of the house.

196. It is perhaps worth recording here that James Byres (for whom see n. 170) designed some fireplaces of the kind condemned by Piranesi; two of them were reproduced in Carlo Antonini's (1772) edition of Vignola, This was Antonini's first major publishing enterprise. But even disciples of Piranesi, such as the Adams, did not adopt his ideas on chimneypieces and

continued to design them the way in which they had been popularized in Britain by William Kent, as a cornice over two pilasters, columns, or herms.

Piranesi's insistence on making the fireplace part of the general decoration of the room—more like a cupboard or a *burrò* than a door or a window—is more consonant with the practice of the French decorating pattern-books. Cf. Giesecke (1911), p. 38.

197. This was in the Piazza di Spagna, at the issue of the via Due Macelli. The panels represent three-bay architectural frames "decorated with hieroglyphic symbols and other things which allude to the Religion and the politics of the Ancient Egyptians"; through this frame may be seen "fertile fields, the Nile, immense pyramids," and so on.

These decorations were destroyed within Piranesi's lifetime. But he seems to have attached enough importance to them, since the inventory of his house showed that he had kept copies of them. See Piranesi, *Il Campo Marzio dell'Antica Roma* 1958, p. 19. The plates are Focillon nos. 906 and 907; they are numbered 45 and 46 in the *Cammini*, 1769.

198. Piranesi, *Cammini,* 1769, pp. 9 f.

199. Piranesi, *Cammini*, 1769, p. 11.

200. Piranesi, *Cammini*, 1769, p. 10. This has often been considered a reference to Burke's ideas on the same subject, elaborated in his *Philosophical Enquiry* (1757; reprinted 1759 and 1792), pp. 90 ff. The idea, however, was already common to all writers who theorized on the beauty of Tragedy; and Piranesi may much more readily have found it either in Du Bos (1715) in his *Réflections*, I, pp. 28 ff., or in Vincenzo Gravina (1731), pp. 9 f.

201. Piranesi *Cammini*, 1769, p. 13.

202. Piranesi, *Cammini*, 1769, p. 13.

203. On the importance of the shell as a basic ornamental device, see above, n. 37. Piranesi is perhaps the first decorative artist to provide a repertory of shell forms in his first plate in the *Cammini*, pl. I, p. 21.

204. Piranesi, *Cammini* (1769), p. 28.

205. But more important here, it goes back to that very powerful tradition that classical architecture had its origin in the Middle East and that it can be attributed to divine inspiration. Piranesi refers several times to the most important work through which this tradition was transmitted, by which it was in a sense formed: Juan Bautista Villalpanda's and Jeronimo Prado's commentary on Ezekiel, with its complex vision of the temple of Jerusalem to which I have referred earlier (see ch. 1). Piranesi quotes in his support in the *Magnificenza*, 1760, pp. 103, 111 f., and in the *Cammini,* 1769, p. 28. Villalpanda is quoted in fact against Goguet (1758), one of the most popular historians writing at that time.

206. As the whole sequence of the Charlemont plates was designed to justify the removal and change of the dedicatory inscriptions, a procedure for which Piranesi quoted the horrid precedent provided by Caracalla when he had the line with the name of his brother Geta, whom he had murdered, removed from the central inscription on the triumphal arch of his father, Septimus Severus: *Lettere di Giustificazione*, 1757, pp. 15 f. Piranesi's intention had been to pillory the Irish peer by the publication and avenge an affront. And indeed one of the main inscriptions on a rostral column is dedicated to Mars the Avenger instead of Lord Charlemont, on whom see the *D.N.B.* s.v. Caulfield, James. He has an important—and most

honorable—place in the history of architecture as the patron of William Chambers at Marino.

207. Piranesi's great love for the column is shown by the survey of it in his possession after his death; the inventory lists sixty-eight whole plaster casts of sections of the column, and eighteen broken ones, on the walls of his hall and staircase, against which no estimate of value is set (*a prezzo d'affezione*): Inventory in Piranesi, *Campo Marzo*, 1958.

208. He was very conscious of this contrast. See Piranesi, *Campo Marzo*, Focillon 437, 1958, showing the remains of antiquity on the Campo Marzo stripped of any later buildings.

209. On *bienséance* and its synonyms, *convenance, aspect,* see, for instance, J.-F. Blondel (1737), pp. 3 ff., and articles in the *Encyclopédie*.

210. The paneling is now in the Musée Carnavalet.

211. For Delafosse, see below, n. 181. The "invention" of an appropriate ornament for the building, of which Piranesi spoke in the *Cammini*, 1769, p. 2. He had in fact reproduced ancient capitals, Corinthian ones, of the kind which he describes a little dismissively in the *Magnificenza*, pls. 14, 17, 19. The capital on pl. 14 is also discussed, as it happens, by Pier Leone Ghezzi in his drawn catalog of the Ottoboni antiquities, now in the Vatican library, where this and another capital now in the Libighaus in Frankfurt are recorded, one with a long caption written by Ghezzi on his discussions with Jerome Odam on the ignorance of the moderns in inventing suitable ornament. See L. Guerrini (1971).

This was, of course, echoed by Winckelmann's essay on allegory, which first appeared in German in 1766; curiously enough, Winckelmann dwells on the rudder as a symbol of the pure life, which Piranesi very much favored. Nevertheless, Piranesi remained opposed to any "reading" of his ornament by some allegorical/iconographic key, as I have pointed out, and seemed bent on the creation of irreducible "hieroglyphs" even if not quite in the way in which Diderot was to use the term. See chapter 10.

It is worth noting that the actual term *architecture parlante* does not occur in eighteenth-century literature as far as I know.

212. J. Wilton-Ely in G. B. Piranesi (1972), pp viii ff; W. Rieder (1975), and D. Stillman (1977).

213. W. Körte (1933), pp. 381 ff.

214. G. B. Piranesi (1743).

215. These were assumed to be some of his French friends; it is presumably the plan to which Chambers (1825) refers, as having seen it being drawn by a "celebrated Italian artist," pp. 91 f. The most recent and highly embroidered interpretation by P. Mellis (1975).

10

Truth Stripped Naked by Philosophy

While the young Parisians in Rome were scurrying around the ruins and taking sides in antiquarian disputes, a vast work was being prepared in France whose conception and reception was to dwarf other debates and act as a watershed of ideas. It was to influence building practice as it did all the thinking and work of its time. This was the *Great Encyclopedia,* which is usually credited to Diderot and d'Alembert. Its chronology and organization are complex, bedeviled by imprisonment, censorship, swindles, and legal wrangles. Before estimating its involvement with building, I shall set down its outline.

The enterprise may be said to have begun in 1746 when André Lebreton, then the king's printer, commissioned the Abbé Guya de Malves,[1] after some rather disgraceful scuffles, to revise and enlarge the translation of Ephraim Chambers' *Encyclopedia.*[2] Guya immediately invoked the help of scientific and literary friends in the enterprise: Condillac, Diderot, and d'Alembert were the best known of them. Sensitive and shy, Guya de Malves found Lebreton as disagreeable to deal with as did his predecessors and retired to the Collège de France where he taught mathematics. Lebreton then gave the job to Diderot, who—although only thirty-five at the time—had a considerable reputation as a popularizer and efficient literary journalist.[3] The prospectus inviting subscriptions appeared in November 1750; meanwhile Diderot had had his first spell in prison, in the Château of Vincennes (August-November 1749) for his *Lettre sur les Aveugles*: he continued work on the Encyclopedia in prison.

The first volume appeared in July 1751, the second in January 1752, and led to the suppression of the enterprise, in spite of the benevolence and protection of the censor of books, Malesherbes.[4]

The cause of the Encyclopedia was taken up by the powerful alliance of the censor with Madame de Pompadour and the duc de Choiseul.[5] After the appearance of the seventh volume in 1758, d'Alembert retired, weary of the troubles, leaving management and editorship to Diderot.[6] More troubles were to follow. There was a condemnation by the Parlement in January–February 1759, and a rescue by some powerful friends' witty intercession with the king.[7] Troubles went on after the final publication: Lebreton spent some days in the Bastille in 1766, although he had taken the precaution of pruning many of the more philosophical articles of any risky matter, and that without the authors' consent or even knowledge.[8] By then, the climax of the enterprise had been reached: the seventeen volumes of text (eight had been projected) and four volumes of illustrations (there were to be eleven finally) had been issued by 1765.[9]

Meanwhile another enterprise had got going: the Academy of Sciences had begun to publish the Description of the Arts and Crafts *Faites ou Approuvées par Messieurs de l'Académie.* The first volume appeared in 1761, and by the time the Academy of Science was disbanded in the French Revolution, it had reached seventy-six volumes.[10] Both the academy's vast project and the more modest one of the Encyclopedia emulated the proposal of the London Royal Society to establish a "history of the manufacturing arts."[11] Diderot threw himself into the project with unflagging enthusiasm: he visited craftsmen in their workshops, had the processes demonstrated and explained to him, took their instruments to pieces, recorded everything.[12] Yet neither he, nor his contributors, nor even the gentlemen of the academy had any notion of the autonomy of the manufacturing process. Both the Encyclopedists and members of the academy proceeded by analyzing every piece of equipment into components: these were often near-identical for many trades, and inevitably both accounts had a lot of duplication. The notion of analyzing the stages of a process and linking them variously to a source of power which would make the manufacturing process continuous was not conceivable. The idea of housing such continuous pieces of machinery in building-workshops of the kind we now call factories seemed remote, although James Hargreave's spinning jenny was patented in 1770 and Richard Arkwright's water frame in 1769.[13]

The primitives of industrialism were not known in France, and the optimism of the Encyclopedists was fed by improvements in craft methods, which were very noticeable between the seventeenth and eighteenth centuries. Both precision and speed of manufacture had increased. Scientific instruments, complex pieces of furniture, figured woven fabrics—and perhaps most explicitly—elaborate automata, witness to the tonic effect, bordering on euphoria, these improvements produced in their makers and users alike.[14]

The Encyclopedia offered a view of the productive community so clearly detailed, so rationally described, that it should have been possible to construct workshops of any current trade from its plates and explanations. Such a view of their calling had never before been available to workmen; craftsmen received information about their trade almost exclusively through the lengthy process of apprenticeship and initiation into a guild. Now information about skill and apparatus was available in a literate and rationalized form: the process of organizing production by placing it under central government control, which Colbert had initiated with his antiguild legislation (and the foundation of academies), may be said to have been completed by the plates of the Encyclopedia. It would be very difficult to estimate their social and economic impact; it has certainly never been done.[15] But the effect on intellectual life, the way in which the Encyclopedia acted as a focus for conflicting views, and how it became a kind of bulldozer which pushed through the detritus of prejudice and superstition have often been described. In particular, the attention paid by the Encyclopedia to the arts and to the problem of beauty has been seen as central,[16] partly because of the important position these had in eighteenth-century thought generally, but also because Diderot himself had a commitment to it which bordered on obsession. His own entry, "Beau," in the second volume became an account of previous theories and an attempt to restate the problem.[17] In this context, it is worth recalling that he had first made his literary mark with an annotated translation of Shaftesbury's *Inquiry Concerning Virtue and Merit,* in which he departed significantly from the text.[18] To Shaftesbury he owes the argument about the consonance of the good, the beautiful, and the true.[19] This notion he carries over (in spite of his pleas of his own inconsistency) to much of his other writing, the article "Beau" included.[20] From Shaftesbury's more general principle of economy, Diderot also derived a more empirical notion of utility to govern the relationship we perceive as beautiful.[21] Moreover, argues Diderot, Beauty is dependent on our perception of relationships, and this is equally valid as a statement about our recognition of truth. Since such perceptions are mental operations, they are acquired. To learn discrimination between what is beautiful and what is not is what we call taste.[22]

The very use of the word relationship to describe our perception of beauty and the rationalizing of taste implies the whole apparatus of "ancient" precepts: Diderot suggests that everyone who performs the act of appreciating what is beautiful repeats Zeuxis' selection of the most beautiful parts of the maidens of Croton[23] by matching the best we have learned from nature with what we see in art. He devotes little attention to architecture; the subject was left to the expert engaged to look after it from the outset, Jacques-François Blondel, who had his prime article, "Architecture," in the very first volume.

The choice of Blondel seems inevitable—by hindsight perhaps.[24] Of the major architects of the time, the most successful, Jacques-Ange Gabriel, was not given to literary effusions, although he was president of the academy;[25] Soufflot was still untried, and Servandoni averse to speculation, Briseux too old. Blondel, on the other hand, though young for an architect (he was only forty-four in 1749) had published an influential book and established an art school which taught principally architecture, and whose program he had defended in a vigorous pamphlet.[26] His later lectures at the academy, when he had been appointed professor, developed from his private teaching; published after his death, they became the most impressive corpus of architectural theory produced in the eighteenth century. Although a prolific practitioner, Blondel is now chiefly remembered as a teacher and a polemist: he even indulged, rather belatedly, in the genre of sentimental letter-novels, even if only on the subject of taste.[27] At the time of the Encyclopedia negotiations, he would already have been known to be generous, if not extravagant, a trait which was to lead to his penurious death, his modest fortune exhausted by the preparation of the nine-volume *Cours.*[28]

Blondel's eclectic teaching, which made the method of *distribution* the essence of all compositional procedures, the key almost to architectural beauty, seems to have been a doctrine which suited the Encyclopedists exactly. While working on the Encyclopedia, Blon-

G. J. Bellicard, Egyptian architecture, vignette from J.-F. Blondel. London, British Museum.

del also published the most comprehensive work of architectural
criticism to date: the four-volume folio of *Architecture Françoise*,
some five hundred plates issued between 1752 and 1756.[29]

As the *Cours* was the book of his lecture and studio teaching, the
Architecture Françoise commemorated his novel practice of regular
visits to Parisian buildings and building sites with his students: he
was an indefatigable teacher. But these sober volumes, the survey of
current building in which Blondel first developed his views on the
justness of the middle way in architecture, tending neither to rococo
excess nor to "antique" severity, also contained two vignettes by
Jérôme Charles Bellicard, one of the artists who had accompanied
to Italy Abel Poisson (Madame de Pompadour's brother, who is best
known as the marquis de Marigny[30]), to whom all of the *Architecture
Françoise* is dedicated. In spite of their tiny scale, the vignettes were
in that grandiloquent, archaic style learned from Piranesi and
Legeay.[31] Bellicard had, in fact, collaborated with both of them,[32]
and the two engravings are an early link between Blondel and the
impatient young men of the Palazzo Mancini.[33]

Of the two engravings, one is all Hathor capitàls, pyramids, and
obelisks; Egyptian therefore. The other is altogether Doric. They
are, perhaps, pieces for emulation, like the tiny Egyptian and Greek
schools of architecture which Piranesi had engraved in the same
year.[34] It is not quite sure when Blondel met Bellicard, who had gone
to Italy on winning the academy's first prize in 1747. At any rate,
when Marigny, still called M. de Vandières, come back to France in
September 1751,[35] Bellicard had become a protégé of his. Abel had
been promised, through his sister, the office of controller of buildings, which she had obtained for another, more ambiguous relation,

G. J. Bellicard, "Doric" architecture, vignette from J.-F. Blondel. London, British Museum.

M. Le Normant de Tournehem.[36] Tournehem died in November 1751, and Abel Poisson succeeded him. Tournehem may not have been a man of taste, but he had certainly been an able and businesslike administrator and left his office in good working order, as well as in credit. In the meanwhile, Abel Poisson, already interested in matters of art and architecture, had been "formed" by his grand tour, in a company approved of, if not actually chosen, by his sister: the Abbé Le Blanc, connoisseur and antiquarian; Nicolas Cochin *fils*, engraver; and the Lyons architect Germain Soufflot.[37]

Poisson-Vandières-Marigny found friends for life in his companions. Cochin remained in the employment of the state until his death. Le Blanc had been appointed historiographer to the office of building. And Soufflot became the great architect of the Poisson clan, perhaps the leading practitioner-theorist of his generation.[38] Madame de Pompadour had first employed Jean Lassurance, who was an uninspired member of the Hardouin-Mansart/de Cotte school, even though he worked in a more "modern" style.[39] With a mixture of partiality for her family and her sense of public duty, she wanted her brother to acquire—he was only twenty-two at the time of his departure—familiarity with Italian architecture, both ancient and modern, in the company of exalted specialists, so that the office into which she had forcefully eased him (if the two words do not contradict each other) could really become that of the arbiter of taste for France, and not a mere sinecure: he was to prepare himself for his directorship as she had for the position of the king's mistress.[40]

The party made a rather grand progress through Italy, being received in royal and princely (as well as the papal) courts but also

Pier Leone Ghezzi, M. de Vandières, the Abbé
Leblanc, J.-G. Soufflot, and C.-N. Cochin on
Their Visit to Rome, *pen and ink caricature.*
Metropolitan Museum of Art, Rogers Fund,
1972.

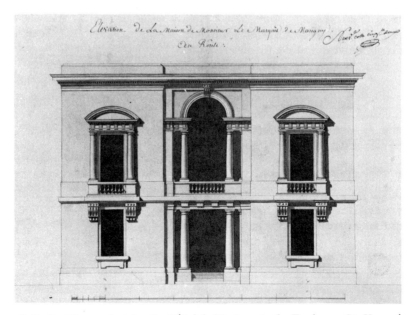

J. G. Soufflot, project for the Hôtel de Marigny in the Faubourg St. Honoré.
Photo Pierrain-Carnavalet.

working hard. In Rome they were lodged at the Palazzo Mancini, and Jean-François de Troy, still director, painted Marigny's portrait.[41] At Rome, Marigny turned back, but others of the party, Soufflot and Cochin, together with Bellicard, went south, to Naples, where they saw something of the new archeological discoveries[42] and further down to Paestum, where Soufflot, with his contemporary from his earlier Roman days, Gabriel Dumont, measured the Greek temples.[43] It is therefore hardly surprising that one of the earliest representations of the Greek Doric order in European art is Cochin's drawing *Lycurgus Showing his Wounds,* which he exhibited in the *salon* of 1764.[44] Madame de Pompadour was certainly successful: Marigny had taken his tour extremely seriously. He had learned a lot, and his companions were to remain not only his friends, but also his advisors for the rest of his tenure of office.[45]

He was determined to work quickly. The attack on the office of the *Intendant* by La Font de Saint-Yenne was the climax of a campaign for the renewal of public works in Paris in which a number of writers had taken part—Voltaire most conspicuously.[46] The campaign was related to a move for the return to the grand style of Louis XIV and Colbert and the manner of the architects they patronized, particularly that of Mansart and Perrault.[47] Tournehem had in fact taken a move in that direction himself. A statue was to be erected to Louis XV—*le bien-aimé*—an equestrian monument to emulate the equestrian state of Louis XIV—*le Grand*—in the Place Vendôme.[48] The work was almost a by-product, a grandchild of Colbert's economic policy, which led to the centralization of the aristocracy on the court but also to the growth and enrichment of provincial cities. Freed from Louis XIV's war taxes by the Regency, they used the excuse of the royal monument to create a series of ordered and quasi-monumental public spaces.[49] The most important was the em-

The Nymphaeum in the Château of Ménars, by J. G. Soufflot. Foto Electa.

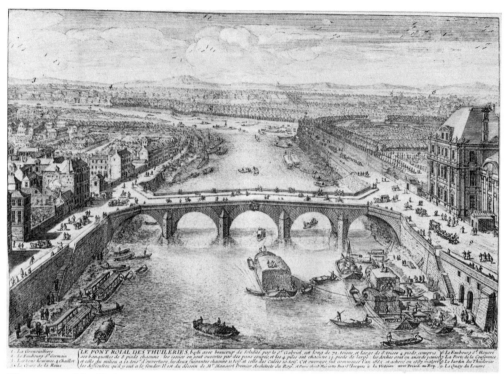

The corner of the Tuileries Palace, the Pont-Royal, the Tuileries garden and the Cours-la-Reine. After Pérelle.

banking of the Garonne and the laying out of the squares in Bordeaux by the two Gabriels (1731 onwards) and the works for Stanisław Leszczyński at Nancy, which were conceived after 1744, although work did not actually begin until 1752.[50] The peace of Aix-la-Chapelle, which was the occasion of Servandoni's fireworks visit to London,[51] and the interruption of his work at St. Sulpice, was also the occasion on which the Prévôt des Marchands and the Echevins of Paris (the mayor and Town Council) commissioned Edmée Bouchardon to cast an equestrian statue of the king.[52] But the placing was undecided and Tournehem turned to the academy for projects, without specifying a site.[53]

More than twenty were presented, and after a good deal of discussion, the king decided the matter by presenting the land between the Champs-Elysées and the Tuileries, where the seventeenth-century city moat joined the river, to make a square. A new competition for that site was declared in January 1753.[54] Marigny did not like it and was impressed by Boffrand's project to replace the Place Dauphine with a colonnaded hemicycle.[55] He corresponded with Boffrand;[56] but the king took matters into his own hands again and asked Gabriel to scramble the existing schemes on the site of the Plateau du Pont-Tournant, now known as the Place de la Concorde.[57] After some further changes and delays, work was begun in 1757, and the king's statue unveiled on 20 June 1763.[58]

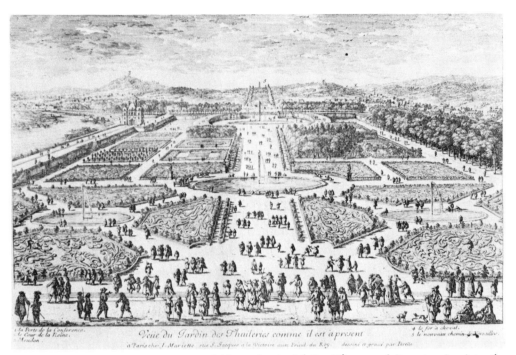

Paris, the garden of the Tuileries as laid out by André Le Nôtre, and its extension into the Champs Elysées. After Pérelle.

Gabriel had decided to articulate the site, too wide in scale for the statue, by isolating it on a rectangular platform in the center, separated from the general street level by sunken gardens, which referred back to the situation of the square over the junction of the city moat with the river.[59] This provided one direction, one axis, if you will, from the river to the Hôtel de Chavilly, on whose site the church of the Madeleine was to be built.[60] The other direction was the view from the center pavilion of the Tuileries, along the middle alley of the palace garden, and further along the Avenue des Tuileries, now called the Avenue des Champs-Elysées, across to the height of Chaillot, which was to be leveled in the seventeen-sixties to improve the view.[61] The king's statue was to stand at the crossing of these two directions, facing the palace; a bridge, at the point which is now the Pont de la Concorde,[62] had been planned by the Echevins since the beginning of the century. In spite of Gabriel's efforts, the statue, once set up, still seemed too small for the square; and he was blamed for exhibiting his model of the square so low that potential critics, seeing the aerial view only, did not appreciate the disproportions of the scale.

Gabriel also added the essential element to the composition—a screen of buildings on the north side of the square—two facades between which a street (still called the Rue Royale) runs north to the Madeleine Church before turning into the Boulevard de la Madeleine.[63] The dome of the church as projected then crowns the

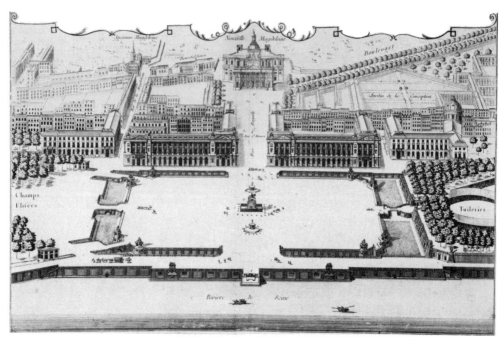

G.-L. Le Rouge, the proposed Place Louis XV and the church of the Madeleine, showing also completed embankments and the place of the proposed bridge, dated 1763. Photo Pierran-Carnavalet.

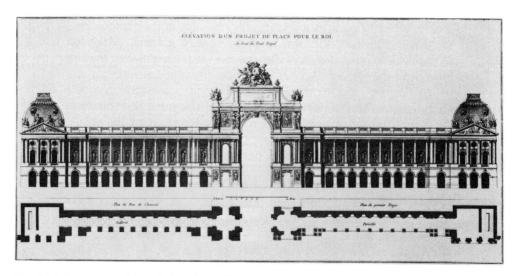

Claude Aubry, competition design for a Place Louis XV opposite the Pont Royal.

J. Hemery after Pierre de Machy, The Setting Up of the Statue of Louis XV in the Place de la Concorde, *detail. Photographic Bulloz.*

pyramidal composition. The two buildings are an interpretation of the facade which Claude Aubry[64] had designed for the south side of the Place Louis XV. In the competition scheme of 1748 he set it to the south of the Pont Royal, on either side of a triumphal arch which connected the Rue du Bac to the new square. Aubry's scheme was clearly an interpretation of Perrault's Louvre facade, in the articulation of the wall, the relation of column to rusticated base, the insertion of a pediment into the balustraded attic, the way in which the projections are managed—all that owes something to Perrault. The Louvre facade was, after all, a quarter of an hour's walk away. It is an explicit homage to the older architect and a clear appeal to revive the glory of Louis XIV's time.[65] Perrault had, however, made a facade which was the frontispiece for the Sun King's palace, to look down the planned avenue eastward, an urban equivalent to the quasi-rural and westward Champs-Elysées, with which it was to be coaxial;[66] Aubry, like Gabriel, was making a veneer facade for any number of buildings whose destination was irrelevant. Theirs were pieces of urban landscape on a larger scale than had been practiced before.[67] Like the landscape of the gardens, the urban scene had been imagined by *Vedutisti*: Claude always had a building in his mythical landscapes and often represented urban complexes, as had Poussin.[68] Of course, in stage sets, the representation of the "classic" town goes back at least to Serlio.[69] And essays had been made in Italy and in France at forms of such urban landscape: the Place Dauphine and the Place des Vosges in the reign of Henry IV and later, on a larger scale, the Place des Victoires and the Place Vendôme.[70] The scale seemed to grow with each executed scheme. Meanwhile, in England, after the isolated instance of Inigo Jones' St. Paul's, Covent Garden, larger in scale than the contemporary French examples—to which it owes something—and more ambitious, there were many eighteenth-century squares in London and in Bath; soon the device spread to other towns and even across the Atlantic.[71]

The Place de la Concorde–Madeleine complex was on a larger scale than any of the pieces of continuous urban landscape that had been conceived so far, and certainly larger than any executed. Certainly none seems to have been so carefully coordinated in dimensions and proportions. From the outset of the project, the facade of the church was considered part of the "decoration of the square."[72] It displayed the same giant Corinthian order as the Gabriel buildings; and Patte, as if to emphasize their identity, sets the church in perspective on his elevation at the same level as the *piano nobile* of the square. The Madeleine departs from Contant's previous, conventional treatment of the church facade in two superimposed orders on the Roman model.[73] There was, a few minutes walk away, the example of St. Roch, a facade designed "in the taste of Mansart" by Robert de Cotte, which had been finished a few years before.[74] And Contant himself had used the scheme to excellent effect in the facade of St. Vaast at Arras, his largest church, which was then building and which has obvious connections with the later design of the Madeleine.[75]

St. Vaast, Arras, showing buttressing.

St. Vaast, Arras, apse, showing flying buttresses.

St. Vaast, Arras, interior, showing a detail of voussoirs, which compose the flat arch in the entablature.

St. Vaast, Arras, interior. Foto Electa.

The Madeleine facade looks like an inversion of the side pavilions of Gabriel's buildings. Both have a quadriportico supporting a pediment: Contant's is a deep porch, with a recessed void on either side, and enclosing it, *in antis,* are two panels framed by pilasters which correspond to side chapels. The columns of Contant's church are the same height as the whole of Gabriel's order, the panels half the width of Gabriel's side features.[76] But there is a larger inversion: Contant has a pedimented portico between panels, Gabriel pedimented panels framing porches. The attic story, which masks the vault of the nave, would have barely concealed from a distance the pedimented drum of the dome, which would therefore have appeared sitting on a double pediment like the Roman Pantheon. The vaulted nave within was the long arm of a Latin-cross plan. But the crossing became an irregular octagon, in which the altar, on a high platform, was surrounded by an ambulatory three-quarters the width of the nave. The small dome appeared to stand on a square of four piers, each as clusters of three columns. Four sacristies, heavily walled domed chambers, act as buttresses in each corner.[77]

The dome therefore became, in its spatial isolation, a *baldacchino* over the high altar; a *baldacchino* which was an integral part of the fabric of the building. In that, as in all details, Contant's practice was

Versailles, the Chapel, interior. Foto Electa.

incarnated academic theory, a theory which was still waiting for its grand formulation in Blondel's *Cours*.[78] The facade recalled to contemporaries the portico-screen of St. Sulpice, also framed by two pilastered pavilions—though otherwise very different.[79] Moreover, it challenged the slightly earlier and potentially grander portico of Ste. Geneviève (now called the Panthéon), which already existed at this time in a full-size lath, canvas, and plaster model, put up as a triumphal arch through which the king and clergy passed during the procession to lay the church's foundation stone on 4 September 1764, by which time the crypt of that church was almost complete.[80]

The Château of Versailles, showing the placing of the chapel in the land-scape. After Félibien.

The Madeleine was offered by the critics and polemists of the time as the model of a Latin-cross church, and Ste. Geneviève was considered the type of the much more uncommon Greek-cross plan.[81] Ste. Geneviève is perhaps the most discussed church building in the second half of the eighteenth century. There had already been a project in the seventeenth century to rebuild the small church dedicated to the patroness of the city by Claude Perrault.[82] It is very difficult to reconstruct Soufflot's precedents. He may have known Perrault's scheme for the extension of the old church; the drawings

Versailles, the Chapel, section, looking toward the high altar, showing the flying buttresses. After J.-F. Blondel.

The Cathedral of the Holy Cross, Orléans. Conway Library.

were not engraved but were housed in the abbey library, where Soufflot might easily have seen them. In any case, it is not so much with the old project for Ste. Geneviève that his church was bracketed, but with the greatest of all exemplars—the Louvre colonnade.[83]

To those who witnessed its building it seemed to be the first token of a new and revived architecture: an architecture which would equal and perhaps even surpass that of the ancients. But it was also to be another kind of enterprise: to explore the great discoveries of medieval builders, whose bad taste may have been deplorable, but whose knowledge of construction was quite different and in some ways superior to that of the ancients.[84] Soufflot's scheme for the new church did not refer back to the Christian antiquity whose anamnesis were the Roman basilicas; and which Perrault revived for Louis XIV, the new Constantine.[85] Soufflot's was a forward-looking architecture, a national architecture—French in its appeal away from anything recent in Italy. Italian architecture was (to French critics

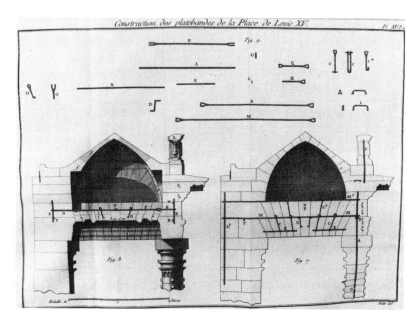

The reinforced construction of the Place Louis XV, by J.-A. Gabriel, section through the colonnade. Note the pointed membrane arches. After Pierre Patte.

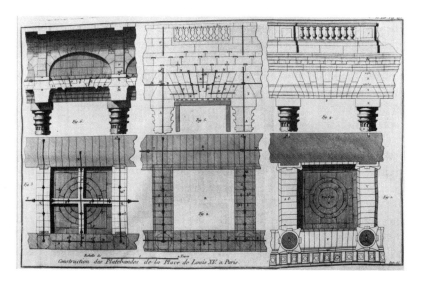

The reinforced construction of the Place Louis XV, long section through one bay and corresponding plans, showing stone joints and reinforcement rods.

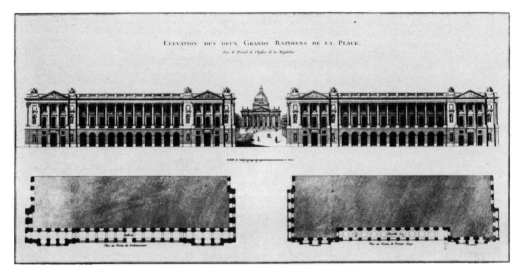

The two facades of the Place de la Concorde (Place Louis XV), by J.-A. Gabriel, and the Church of the Madeleine by Pierre Contant d'Ivry, perspective/elevation, and plan. After Pierre Patte.

and in spite of what I said earlier) still tainted with the taste of Borromini and Guarini, while Contant, Soufflot, and Gabriel were all inspired by Perrault.[86] Cochin indeed clearly stated the relationship. He wrote of a fictional archeologist of the year 2355, who, standing among the ruins of Paris, would without hesitation attribute the church of Ste. Geneviève to the—to him—unknown architect of the Louvre facade. He would be guided in this by recognizing the general inferiority of the eighteenth-century buildings certainly known to him, and the insistent complaints of eighteenth-century architectural critics whose writings he knew.[87]

Cochin knew the mind of Soufflot well enough. He had been to Italy with him on the trip with Marigny, since which time they had shared quarters in the Louvre. The commission for this most important church had gone to Soufflot over all the successful Paris architects.[88] Soufflot had, in fact, gone back to his native Lyons on the return from the Italian trip. He was continuously employed there, executing, among other work, a *baldacchino* in the church of St. Bruno to the designs of Servandoni.[89] But his most important work was, of course, the continuation of the Hôtel-Dieu and a number of large houses, as well as the archiepiscopal palace for the Cardinal de Tencin.[90] He was also in charge of the embanking of the Rhône. But he had already informed himself—and the Lyons Academy, of which he had become a member after his first visit to Italy—about Gothic architecture.[91] And he continued to be interested in it for the rest of his career. At Marigny's insistence, he had taken part, unsuccessfully, in the competition for the Place Louis XV.[92] In 1755, Marigny had his way at last. Soufflot was recalled to Paris, nominated to the first class in the academy by the

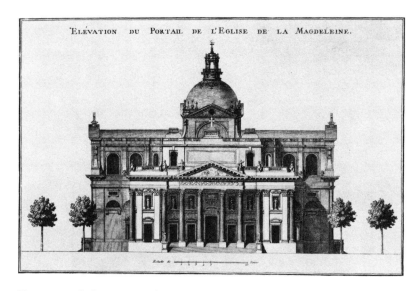

*Elevation of the proposed Madeleine church, by Pierre Contant d'Ivry.
After Pierre Patte.*

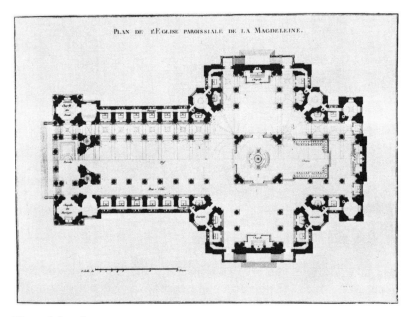

Plan of the above.

The Abbey de Penthémont, Paris, by Pierre Contant d'Ivry. Street façade and dome.

king, and awarded the commission to rebuild the church of Ste. Geneviève, which the king had more or less vowed on his recovery from illness ten years earlier.[93]

The scheme went through many stages, and the final appearance of the building—the blocking of the windows when it was transformed into a Pantheon apart—was rather different from Soufflot's original project.[94] The main conception, however, was already explicit in the beginning, as it is presented in Bellicard's engravings of Soufflot's design, their first presentation to the public. This was the Greek-cross plan, the crossing covered by a double-shelled dome on a drum. The several rival projects for the completing of the church never discarded the type.[95] And for many years, before the

The Abbey de Penthémont, Paris, by Pierre Contant d'Ivry, interior of the dome.

church was actually built in stone, the portico model showed the promise of what was to come.

Soufflot's scheme, in spite of his own familiarity with adventurous building techniques, was no straight proposition for the builders and contractors.[96] But he shared his problem with Gabriel and with Contant. All the main building projects of the decade in Paris—Ste. Geneviève, the Madeleine, the Place de la Concorde facades, the Ecole Militaire—involved the use of long spanning stone beams and required virtuoso stonecutting and ingenious metal reinforcement: the management of such construction became the crucial problem of eighteenth-century French theory and practice. The system of reinforcement had its precedent in Perrault's reinforced stonework in the Louvre.[97] As president of the academy and *premier architecte*, Gabriel was in charge of its completion; though it fell to Soufflot to work out the crowning members of the facade.[98] The unfinished cornices and parapets did not provide sufficient plumb weight to counteract the sideways thrust of the flat vault.[99] Soufflot's part was to complete the crown of the building, but also to strip and restore the *rez-de-chaussée*, which had been concealed and defaced by shacks and workshops.[100] He was to follow the original scheme—perhaps the very drawing which Aubry had presented to the academy.[101]

The Hôtel-Dieu in Lyons, by J. G. Soufflot. Foto Electa.

Perrault had also made both a wooden and a stone model, but there seems to be no trace of them in the eighteenth century.[102]

Soufflot's contemporaries took a certain pride in improving on Perrault by devising a structure of beams upon columns which did not involve their doubling.[103] Of the completed buildings, Gabriel's facades, because of their similarity, were the most obvious parallel to Perrault's. And the vaulting over the coffered ceiling provides an instructive point of comparison: while Perrault had corbeled the stones of the cornice inward over the columns, as he had the crowning stones of the inner wall so as to provide a blind passage over the soffit of the colonnade, which was roofed with huge paving slabs, Gabriel had, behind his cornice and balustrade, a pointed or *ogive* vault running the whole length of the colonnade, with flattened oval arches spanning between the intercolumniation, so that the balustrade really did assume the function of pinnacles on a Gothic buttress.[104] It is perhaps the least familiar piece of Gothic construction in eighteenth-century France and the most explicit adaptation of Contant's *voûte à la Roussillon*.

During this time, Gabriel's most important commission was his vast scheme for the Ecole Militaire, as much Madame de Pompadour's foundation as Chelsea Hospital had been Nell Gwynne's. It had been proposed as an alternative commemoration to the Place Louis XV, as well as an emulation of its vast neighbor, the Invalides.[105] Both of them were part of the urban landscape which the king saw as he drove to Versailles down Cours la Reine from the Tuileries. It is difficult to reconstruct the original scheme for the Ecole Militaire (though it certainly had something of the Place Louis XV *ordonnance*), but as it was built, the central pavilion, called the château, had a tetrastyle Corinthian portico crowned by a pediment front and back, while on either side of the central block

P. de Machy, Laying the Foundation Stone of the New Church of Ste. Geneviève. *Musée Carnavalet, Paris.*

(which contained the main *salon* over the entrance colonnade) were a monumental staircase of Mansart'ian scale, and a duplex chapel whose giant order "justified" that of the portico. The central block was crowned by a slate-covered, four-sided elliptical dome of the kind popularized by Lemercier.[106] In the course of modifying the scheme, Gabriel and his "office" gave the château a rather Italianized elevation towards the Champs de Mars; a *piano nobile* of windows framed by pedimented aedicules, and attic-windows as breaks in the cornice frieze. The *cour d'honneur* elevation was divided into two orders, the lower Doric, extending both into the entrance hall under the central pavilion, and into the colonnades round the courtyard, the higher Ionic. Their rather strange arrangement, as three-quarter detached columns flanking a blank pier, brings Gabriel nearest to Le Vau's fragmented *ordonnance*; yet these subsidiary orders, though in fact merely decorations of the piers which contemporary theorists so much despised, were designed by Gabriel to appear as coupled columns supporting a straight entablature in the approved manner of Perrault.[107]

Gabriel bowed here, as he did elsewhere, to the new fashions. His orders may be of two different scales, like Le Vau's, but he no longer committed the solecism, despised by such theorists as Laugier, of placing their shafts on high pedestals; and in this he broke with the precedent of the seventeenth-century masters. The building of the Ecole Militaire was the most ambitious enterprise of

The Ecole Militaire, the coupled columns of the main entry.

The Ecole Militaire, ground floor arcading. Each coupled column pier is backed by an un-molded arch. The resulting square spaces are roofed by flat quadripartite vaults.

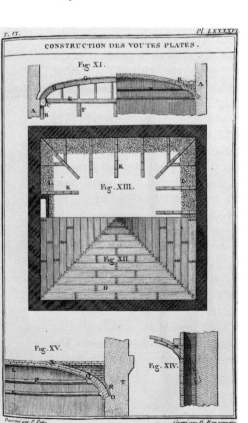

The Ecole Militaire, the construction of the flat quadripartite vaults. After J.-F. Blondel.

The Ecole Militaire in Paris, by J.-A. Gabriel, the Cour d'Honneur.

The Ecole Militaire, the giant order and the coupled column piers.

The Ecole Militaire, the coupled column arcades of the Cour d'Honneur.

Louis XV's reign; although it was not completed until that of his successor and interrupted for most of the Seven Years' War.[108] It fascinated the king, with his passion for architectural projects, and his curious, intimate relation with Gabriel—as intimate almost as Louis XIV's had been with Hardouin-Mansart,[109] though both men seemed to have been much more informed and talented in the matter of building than their great predecessors.

Soufflot's relation to the king was never so close, always mediated through Marigny. As the king relied implicitly on Gabriel and consulted him on every building project, so Marigny drew constantly on his old friends, Cochin and Soufflot. But whereas Gabriel was the executant-organizer, Cochin and Soufflot were the makers of a policy and of a taste by which Gabriel even, as well as the king, were influenced.[110] The amalgam which made up this taste was rather various. The building which enshrined it most successfully, and in which the change may most clearly be seen operating, is Soufflot's second project of 1764 for Ste. Geneviève, whose implications may now be easier to elicit in spite of the various versions which Soufflot prepared in the later years of his working life, perfecting and adjusting his original scheme according to his own changing ideas, and in answer to certain criticisms, although he never again reached the balance of tensions he achieved then.

It is important to realize that the decision to make the church a Greek-cross[111]—against the Latin one at the Madeleine—had church policy implications. As the Ecole Militaire was to be the rallying point of a new army, rising from its disarray at Minden, a monument to a new professional and efficient military power,[112] so the two churches, Ste. Geneviève in particular, were the visible signs of an ecclesiastical policy which occupied France much more energetically than can now be known.[113] At the very time the most interesting of Soufflot's schemes was being published, and the king passing through the painted portico to lay the first stone, the Jesuits had been expelled from France.[114] This crushing defeat of the Ultramontane party had been long prepared. It is absurd to think now that one of its prime movers, Madame de Pompadour, had been in part motivated by a Jesuit confessor's refusal of the sacraments to the king and to herself because of their association, which she maintained was canonically innocent.[115] In fact, the whole Pompadour clan—Bernis, Choiseul-Stanville, Nivernais—were all anti-Jesuit.[116] The king himself, vacillating as usual, had been used to a Jesuit confessor. He was nevertheless apprehensive in his dealing with the Society because of their alleged implication in the attempt on King John of Portugal and the revival of interest in the theological justifications of regicide by Jesuit theologians (Mariana, Suarez) which had even been used a century earlier by English parliamentarians and could be turned against himself, "l'Oint du Seigneur," as he once called himself to Choiseul.[117]

Even in matters of policy, Louis XV had at least something of a religious motive in following the Austrian alliance promoted by Choiseul and Bernis. He saw it as a new alliance of Catholic powers against Prussia in the first place, and England in the second. The king was a sincere conventional believer, if errant in his practice, although he had no profound theological interests. Nor had Marigny. But the Ultramontane loyalty of the Society of Jesus, its behavior as a state within a state, was associated in France with the sovereign's exercise of despotic authority. And it sometimes seemed as if the Society controlled monarchy through the inevitable Jesuit confessor.[118] This made them the inevitable enemies of all *honnêtes gens;* whose citadel was the Parlement.

Now at the time that Louis XV was considering the fulfillment of his vow, in 1754, affairs between the king and the Parlement were somewhat critical.[119] In that year Father Laugier—who was not yet known as the author of the *Essai sur l'Architecture*, published two years earlier—was detailed by the Society of Jesus to preach the Lent sermons, as well as the Easter Sunday one, before the king in the chapel at Versailles.[120] He had already, two years earlier, preached before the king at Fontainebleau; he had preached also at St. Sulpice.[121] But the Versailles sermons were most notorious. Laugier preached not only against the king's levity, political indolence, and indecision, but also urged him to dissolve the Parlement, then already in exile. There was, at this time, a revival of the agitation against the Jansenists, which led the prelates, guided in this matter by Christophe de Beaumont, archbishop of Paris, to demand submission to the anti-Jansenist papal bull, *Unigenitus* (about which there had been so many disputes when Port-Royal was put down), from the dying when they asked for the last rites. This ruling was an abrogation of normal priestly powers to the higher clergy, which linked them with the Ultramontanes and Jesuits against the parish priests and the body of religious.[122]

It was therefore in this atmosphere of open defiance of the higher clergy that Laugier preached his provocative sermon, and his superiors thought it best to recall him to Lyons. What they presumably did not realize was that he had, that same year, set in motion through a parliamentarian, Jean-Baptiste de La Curne de Ste. Palaye and La Curne's friend in Rome, Cardinal Passionei (whom I mentioned earlier as Winckelmann's patron), his transfer from the Jesuits to the Benedictines. It was the standard process for leaving a religious order while remaining a priest.[123]

Laugier had obtained his education in Lyons and Avignon;[124] he presumably knew what passed in the Lyons Academy, of which Soufflot was such a distinguished member, since the Jesuits were, in the first half of the century, the dominant force in the intellectual life of the town.[125] Soufflot therefore, at the time of his first visit to Rome and of his communications about proportion and Gothic architecture

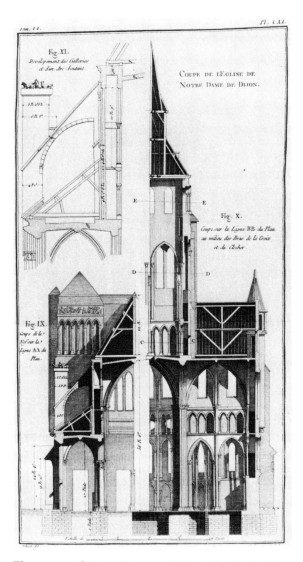

*The survey of Notre Dame at Dijon. After J.-F. Blon-
del.*

to the academy, would inevitably have been in contact with members of the Jesuit community in Lyons.

Both before and after the publication of the *Essai,* Laugier on his
visits to Lyons could not fail to be aware of Soufflot's work there at
the Hôtel-Dieu and the Archiepiscopal Palace for Cardinal Tencin.
There is no knowing how much Laugier had learned of Soufflot's
ideas when he formulated the *Essai*: certainly, they were in the air.
Malesherbes, the censor whom I have already mentioned as Diderot's protector, approved of it highly, and because of its forthright
language, wanted to discuss it with its author—who was unknown to
him—before publication.[126]

Ste. Geneviève, the west front, engraved by Pierre Patte. After Piganiol de la Force.

Soufflot's lecture was one of several contemporary attempts at revaluing Gothic architecute; this revaluation was one of two factors in the creation of a national French style, the attempted renewal of French architecture as a national art. The other was the doctrine of the absolute superiority of the detached "antique" column over all other building elements. Both ideas were discussed in the Lyons Academy during the seventeen-forties;[127] it is difficult to know how they arose and who taught them first. Soufflot certainly took part in their formulation, and his hospital was in a way, its chapel perhaps most notably, the obvious result of these theoretical interests.[128]

Without being factious, it might be worth mentioning that Lyons was, at that time, the center of French masonry, and at least three lodges were already "working."[129] Laugier may well have joined the craft there. At any rate, he made his application to leave the Society of Jesus not only through a parliamentarian, but a mason. It may seem surprising to find a Jesuit consorting intimately with such people, and publishing—if the censor of books is to be believed—a book without his superiors' knowledge and permission;[130] it may well be therefore that when the inflammatory sermon was preached at Versailles, Laugier was performing some kind of bluff-call. At any rate, whether he was already acting as *agent-provocateur,* or whether his mind was made up by his superiors' disloyalty to his extreme advocacy of their position, it was the Pompadour faction which was to look after him from this point on; his living as an independent abbé was in the hands of the Duc de Choiseul.[131]

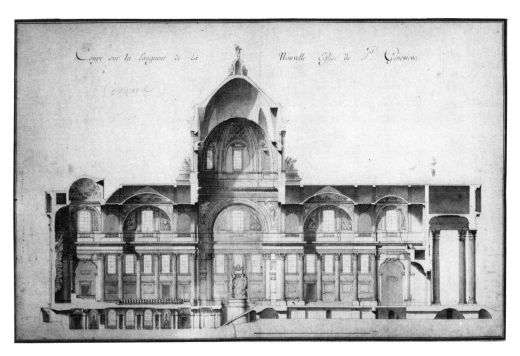

*Ste. Geneviève. Long section of the 1764 scheme. Presentation drawing from Soufflot's office.
Bibliothèque de Ste. Geneviève, Paris.*

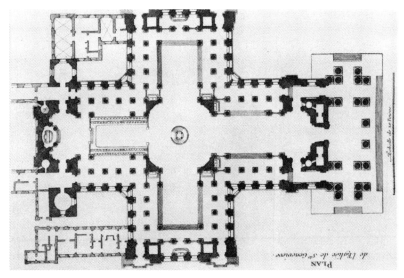

*The Church of Ste. Geneviève in Paris, by J. G. Soufflot, plan in 1764.
engraved by Pierre Patte. After Piganiol de la Force.*

The Numidian tomb known as the Medracen, near Cyrta, engraved by G. J. Bellicard. After Caylus.

It would be foolish to attribute any profound theological views to that circle—to Marigny or to the king. As I have already said, there were enough men in their entourage to work out the implications—obvious to a well-informed Jesuit or ex-Jesuit such as Laugier—of the two dedications, one to the Madeleine, who was reputed to have died at St. Baume near St. Maximin,[132] and whose relics were venerated there (and who therefore formed a direct link between the French church and Our Lord's immediate disciples), and one to Ste. Geneviève, patroness of Paris from its early days. These dedi-

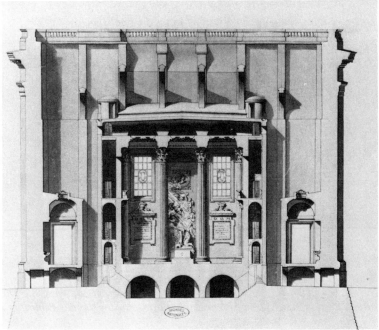

Ste. Geneviève. Long and cross sections through the aisles, showing construction of roof and buttresses and their relation to the screen wall. Archives Nationales, Photographies Bulloz.

C. N. Cochin, Lycurgus Showing his Wounds to the People. *Louvre, Paris.*

Ste. Geneviève, section of the high altar and the crypt, showing the Doric order. Bibliothèque de Ste. Geneviève, Paris. Photographies Bulloz.

cations, at this time, enshrined the antiquity and the pride, if not the independence of the Gallican church. In this matter, the rejection of the *baldacchino* as an extraneous and Ultramontane building element takes on particular importance. The constant use of the retro-choir, which might indicate a connection with Italian precedent, must also be interpreted as a consequence of placing a high altar or shrine under the dome of the church, at the crossing.[133]

The church of Ste. Geneviève was the more radical and the more "advanced" programatically and formally of the two royal churches. The very use of the Greek-cross plan with an "antique" portico indicated the intention, whether it was of the architects, or of the Messieurs de Ste. Geneviève (the Genovefans), or yet of the Intendance—most probably of all three acting in concert. Should the implications be missed, the four piers buttressing the dome carried eight statues of church fathers: four eastern, four western.[134] As the design progressed, a number of interesting features were added to the original conception. What remained unchanged was the Greek-cross plan prefaced by a pedimented hexastyle Corinthian porch; its corner columns doubled to make subsidiary side porticoes.

The high external walls are crowned by a Corinthian cornice continuing that of the portico and an attic balustrade which virtually conceals the roof, giving the bulk of the building the flat outline which current thinking demanded. The wall and cornice are articulated, not by the rejected pilasters, but by astylar pylons, which mark off the internal divisions of the plan, while each bay is pierced by three round-headed windows. The external Corinthian order is related as two to three to the internal one, reproducing the proportion of external to internal Doric order which Soufflot had measured in the temple of Poseidon at Paestum.[135] It is one more instance of the allusive submission to antique precedent.[136] The height from the floor to the key of the saucer dome is twice the height of the order, and the intercolumniation is of two and one-half diameters (a modified eustyle, in Vitruvian terms), so that the shape of the intercolumniation is one to four. These simple ratios, and the ironing out of the orders (architrave as one-fourth of the order; the height of the order one to ten) is almost exactly as Perrault suggested in the *Ordonnance*.[137]

The interior is dominated by five domes—four saucer ones over each arm of the Cross, and a big central one on a drum over the crossing. The saucer domes are roofed in like vaults—as they are at St. Paul's in London. The central dome and its buttresses was the feature which went through the most radical transformations in the different projects. The others were the wall at the west end and the high altar.[138]

The fivefold partition of the plan echoes the Byzantine order: the churches of the Holy Apostles in Constantinople, of St. Mark's in Venice, and—inevitably—of St. Front at Périgueux are quoted as precedent.[139] But at Ste. Geneviève, the vault is built up on light, slender Corinthian columns; only the four central groups of three columns, each supporting the dome, are filled in to form a triangular pier. The ratio of the domes, smaller to bigger, is similar to that of the orders, two to three. Each minor bay is framed by four equal arches, in turn carrying the saucer dome. On either side there is a recessed colonnade. Thus, the rhythm of the elements seen from the entrance—or from any one end—is defined by the coupled columns carrying the framing arches, on which the saucer dome rests: coupled columns, a space—in which you see the recessed colonnade, with a uniform intercolumniation; another bay of coupled columns, the open space of the dome. The flat faces of the pier under the dome disappear, since they act as reredoses for altars.[140] Only the oblique face of the pier, which supports the pendentive, is actually appreciable as wall, and then the same scheme of arch, recess with saucer dome, arch, and final vestibule, or altar space finishes the sequence. In the most completely elaborated scheme, that of 1764, the high altar is detailed, or at any rate, suggested on the section as a *gloria* surrounded by rays. It is lit from a hidden window let into a dome over the sanctuary. For this device, it is difficult to find an equally "theatrical" analogy in the architecture of the two preceding generations. Even as extreme an example as the high altar of Weltenburg Abbey, with its very elaborate light effects, has the source of light—though concealed—facing the spectator. Guarini and Juvarra, Fischer von Erlach, and the Asams attempted their effects with lanterns and domes and side-windows; sometimes they used also concealed windows facing the spectator.[141]

In the designs before 1764, Soufflot had already sought extravagant, but fairly orthodox light effects; but in this scheme, he introduces the new feature whose nearest contemporary is Narciso Tomé's *Transparente* in Toledo Cathedral, done some thirty years earlier but hardly known outside Spain.[142] It is curious to consider the implications of this device in a building which claims a high, antique seriousness. The 1764 revision—which had, incidentally been engraved by Pierre Patte[143]—has other peculiarities; the roof, as in the earlier projects, seems not to be of timber, but, like Contant's, made up of shallow brick vaults which cut the vault in an acute arch over the saucer domes. Of the five arches which relieve the back of the pediment, the central one is again a Gothic ogive. Such Gothic devices are invisible, while the structure of the church, the whole conception of it, is a direct incorporation, an incarnation of Soufflot's express theoretical purpose: to unite the lightness and transparency of Gothic architecture, its structural adventurousness, with the correct and just taste of the ancients, which is the only true guarantee of good architecture.[144]

To return to the arrangements of 1764, the most radical alteration, as I have already suggested, was in the form of the dome. The original structure was a double shell, shallow on the interior—not unlike that of Contant's Madeleine—and on the exterior hemispherical over a drum, octagonal rather than circular in plan, each face divided by groups of attached columns; the panels between the columns were

P. de Machy, The Laying of the Foundation Stone of Ste. Geneviève, *detail of the group in which Marigny shows the plans to the king in the presence of Pingret and Soufflot. The portico "model" is in the background. Musée Carnavalet, Paris.*

subdivided into a framed window with a circular lunette over it. In 1764 this became a tall circular drum lined with evenly spaced half-columns, broken at the corners—over the pendentives—into pedimented aedicules.[145] Windows in the aedicules and the central intercolumniations correspond to eight pedimented windows in the inner shell, and the space between the two domes is lit by lunettes over the windows; over each lunette the shell is reinforced by being broken into an acute arch. The exterior of the dome is not a curve but a step pyramid, a figure familiar to antiquarians and associated with the various reconstructions of the Mausoleum familiar from Pliny, and more recently from Caylus' reconstruction of it, communicated to the Académie des Inscriptions. As an appendix, Caylus provided an engraving, again by Bellicard, of the vast tomb in Algeria, now known as Le Tombeau de la Chrétienne, and, although Caylus does not mention it, already called that at the time. Soufflot's debt to this engraving is obvious, and, of course, it makes a fitting crown to the shrine containing the body of Ste. Geneviève.[146]

Another element of the scheme was ready by the time the stone was laid and must have formed part of the original project, that is, the Greek Doric colonnade in the crypt, over which the foundation stone of 1764 was laid. The crypt, which was built sometime between 1760 and 1763, was designed with rather dumpy Greek Doric columns, which were coupled, and which supported the vault under every Corinthian column.[147] This curious Doric order was certainly designed about the same time as James Stuart's folly at Hagley[148] and is perhaps contemporary with Cochin's use of it in his drawing of Lycurgus.[149] This order and the key ornament which edged the crypt vaulting were the first application of "authentic" Greek detail in a public building.[150] The transformations which the scheme was to undergo have obscured Soufflot's original intentions, and such details may now seem nearly meaningless, although the change in the form of the dome, which was obviously influenced by a study of Wren's St. Paul's, does help to make the hidden "Gothic" character of the structure more explicit.[151] The straight lines of the parapet suggest a blocklike interior. The blank walls, now stained with the shadows of the windows which were filled in about 1800, emphasize the block character.[152] The building was, however, extremely light; on the interior each intercolumniation corresponded to a window in the wall. These windows were in fact rather different in shape from those on the exterior. Where the arms of the cross meet, there is an oblique bay, pierced by a window like the others. On the inside the walls butt directly, and the row of windows carries on for the extra bay. The oblique window outside corresponds to two inside, with a triangular light well between. The interior articulation could only be "read" on the exterior very approximately.[153] The high wall above the windows concealed a series of flying buttresses, and obstructed direct sunlight entering the clerestory arches. In fact, the upper part of the wall, decorated with garlands and cornice and crowned with a balustrade, acts—as does a similar wall at St. Paul's in London—as the anchoring weight against the sideways thrust of the vault, the function which the pinnacles perform on a Gothic cathedral.[154]

The building, as I pointed out, was not complete at Soufflot's death in 1780, and even at the time of the French Revolution, after all the doubts and revisions, the church had still not been consecrated. In spite of all the later alterations, I should like to consider the scheme published in 1764 as the high point of the design, when its coherence was quite established in Soufflot's mind and conveyed to his clients, the Messieurs of Ste. Geneviève as well as to the king and to Marigny in an outstanding set of drawings.[155]

From the low crypt with its Doric columns, we have considered the interior arrangements of the plan, with the *chasse* of the saint under the center of the dome, supported by Germain Pilon's four statues of the Virtues[156] (so different from the ones which Bouchardon had modeled for the king's monument). The five-domed plan was, for lack of a better term, Byzantine; it was another reiteration of the archaic and independent character of the Gallican church, of its links with a primitive Christianity which by-passed Rome. The statues of the Greek and Latin doctors on the crowning projections of the piers supporting the dome reassert this oriental connection.[157] The dome itself, the stepped[158] capping and the three-quarter attached *pteron* around the drum, reinforce the archaic character of the building, while in the hidden places of the building, the Gothic features—the ribs and the flying buttresses—ensure the structural solidity of a church disposed to be diaphanous and light as the most transparent of Gothic cathedrals. But this is a Gothic cathedral wholly "corrected" according to the rules of taste learned from the ancients. At the high altar, the visitor was presented with a distant and dramatic vision of the saint's glory illuminated theatrically—miraculously—from a hidden source of light.[159]

The style of the 1764 drawings—of the drawings as distinguished almost from the building—owes much to the friendships which Soufflot had made in Rome. It is a style of drawing somewhere between the *barochetto* manner of a master like Ferdinando Fuga (without any of the *brio* of Vanvitelli) and the more sober but penetrating manner of Piranesi's friends from the Palazzo Mancini. It is cooler, much cooler than Piranesi ever wanted to be, even when he was at his most matter-of-fact. Yet in the same year in which Soufflot redrew and redesigned Ste. Geneviève, Piranesi had recourse to the same dramatic expedient as Soufflot in his project for an apse in St. John Lateran; Piranesi's scheme was not published anywhere at the time, nor was any work initiated to carry it out.[160] Piranesi suggested raising the new apse in two stages, of which the higher was to be a hidden clerestory, pierced by three circular windows, after the manner of Bramante. These were to cast an otherworldly light over the columnar screen framing the new retro-choir altar of the basilica.[161] The commission came from Clement XIII at the height of his troubles with the Jesuits, and while Piranesi began working on the Maltese priory for Clement's nephew, Cardinal Rez-

C. R. G. Poulleau. Interior of Ste. Geneviève according to the project of 1764. Photographies Bulloz.

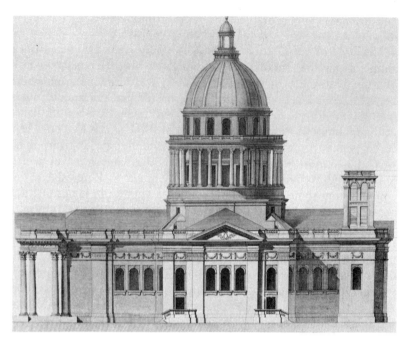

Ste. Geneviève, west and south elevations of the project in 1777, engraved by G. Taraval.

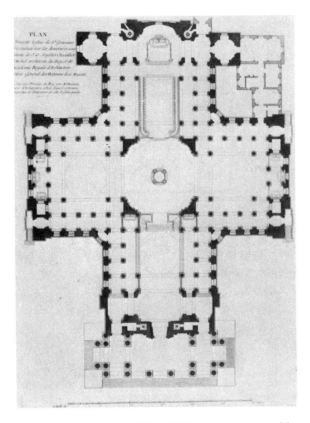

Ste. Geneviève, plan of the 1777 project, engraved by M. Dumont.

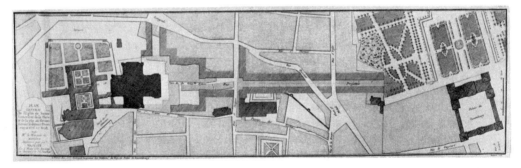

G. J. Bellicard, plan of the new street to connect Ste. Geneviève with the Luxembourg Gardens.

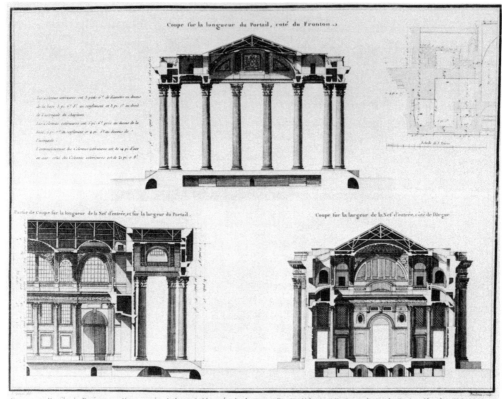

Ste. Geneviève, the west end of the church according to the 1771 scheme.

zonico,[162] the work on St. John Lateran remained a set of splendid variant drawings which he presented to the cardinal a few years later. Presumably without knowledge of each other's projects, and perhaps without either of them being aware of the precedent in Toledo,[163] both had recourse to the same singular arrangement, and in both cases the scheme remained unrealized. It is as if the figure, the rhetorical device of the hidden source of light, had a particular importance for both Soufflot and for Piranesi at this time.

In Tomé's *Transparente,* moreover, the hidden source throws light over a short space onto a towering composition in very high relief, and the function of the light is to provide dramatic chiaroscuro over statues and colonnettes, with the painting and statues continuing into the dormer, hidden only at first sight, after which the viewer is intended to follow the composition up to the window with his eyes, Soufflot—and Piranesi—are not concerned with surface chiaroscuro as much as with the molding of space. In both schemes, few visitors would approach the retro-choir and turn back to see the source of light, and both aim to mold and fill a space observed only from a distance, by means of an unexplained but directed light.

It is perhaps coincidental that all concerned with that laying of the

first stone in 1764, and therefore also with the scheme, were masons:
the king himself; Soufflot; the site architect, Jean-Baptiste Puisieux;
and the canon of Ste. Geneviève who arranged the ceremony, Guy
Pingré.[164] It is right therefore that at Ste. Geneviève, as at the Lateran, the light, incomprehensible to the uninitiated, should bathe the
most sacred part of the buildings: and equally right perhaps, that
neither conception should ever have been executed.

A comment for this is provided by an engraving of the same year,
done in the same milieu, after a drawing of Cochin's, which, although it was printed in the seventh volume, was the frontispiece of
the *Encyclopédie*.[165] In this composition, light radiates from the
figure of Truth, which stands wholly covered by a veil before a
circular Ionic temple (which seems to have an internally coffered
dome) while the figure of Reason attempts to remove the veil;
Metaphysics "tries to divine her presence rather than see her,"
Theology kneels with her back to Truth waiting for an illumination
from above, which descends in a directed ray, and Imagination,
crowned like Reason with a flame, rushes up with a rose-garland.
The rest of this elaborate allegory would be rather tedious to explain, though it enchanted Diderot at the time.[166]

But the reader may remember a possible source for the figure of
Truth, as interpreted by Cochin: this is the figure which stood with
the garland of roses gathered into a fold of her veil over the tomb of
the Duchess of San Severo (mother of Raimondo di Sangro) which,
in the Pietattella chapel in Naples, faced the dramatic release of
another, male figure—this one by Francesco Quierolo, and commemorating the prince's father—from the bonds of error which are
symbolized by a net out of which the figure struggles.[167] The *re-
cherché* character of the iconography, the relative newness and
curiosity of the statues at the time when Soufflot and Cochin were in
Naples, suggests that even if they had not seen them, they certainly
knew about them.[168] There is, I would suggest, a relationship between the two figures which may be more important than any direct
stylistic connection, or even a debt in terms of the *concetto*.[169]

Soufflot and Cochin, the whole entourage of Marigny, which was
as much an "office" as the Office of Works or the Hardouin-Mansart
agence, were involved in a collective enterprise.[170] They were
explicit about their aims and very consequent in their activities.
Through a press campaign, through the manipulation of appointments and the reform of the teaching of art, the taste of France was
to be transformed. In spite of the insistent and nostalgic evocations,
it could no longer be the triumphalist style which Colbert and his
subordinates thought out for the Great Louis. His "well-beloved"
great-grandson required a style not of personal glory, but of national
solidarity. As in Britain, the heritage of the medieval past had been
explored, and the enormous achievements of medieval builders had
to be revalued as an inalienable part of the national heritage.[171] But in
France it was the structural technique (vaulting, in particular) which
aroused admiration, even enthusiasm. In spite of the excesses of
Gothic ornament, the way in which they had been "corrected" by

Ste. Geneviève, the apse.

Ste. Geneviève, the interior and details of the vault.

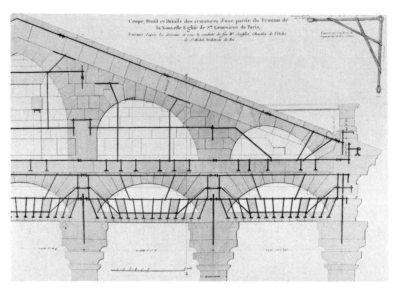

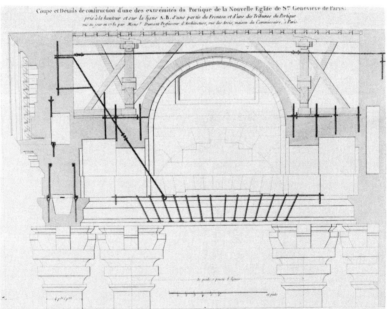

Ste. Geneviève. The construction and reinforcement of the cornice and pediment.

C. N. Cochin, frontispiece of the Encyclopedia.

Antonio Corradini, La Pudicizia, *Sta. Maria della Pietà, Naples. Foto Alinari.*

the mutilation of several medieval buildings, provided a model of
how the fusion between Gothic achievement and antique propriety
could be worked out. Antiquity still provided the canon, but it was
no longer unquestionable. As I have tried to show, the neo-Cartesian
attempt to dismiss the belief of architects in the harmony of the
"noble" senses was at first disregarded, and then with Newton's
powerful help, rejected. It seemed to many of Perrault's successors (as it had seemed to Christopher Wren) that his programmatic
writings could be adapted to avoid the awkward conclusions about
the totally arbitrary nature of beauty when it is related to taste.
Perrault himself was regarded as the prime exemplar of good taste; I
have shown how Gabriel, Soufflot, Contant—all the architects of a
generation—appealed to him constantly.

But the change he had operated, or at any rate influenced radically, was even deeper than the theoretical revolution which he had
not quite achieved. The arbitrary nature of taste came to be recognized as a consequence of the enormous shift in attitudes toward the
past. Antiquity was no longer seen as the ideal wholly out of reach.
In several matters—in technology, in the scale of building operations, in the knowledge of the natural sciences, in warfare—the
achievements of the ancients could not only be equaled, they could

be surpassed. How, in that situation, can a knowledge of the orders be considered as a guarantee, a touchstone of taste?[172]

Since the fifteenth century the past of architecture had been understood as a continuous, if complex, succession. Architecture had been devised by the Egyptians and inherited by the Greeks and the Romans after them. The Chosen People, too, came into the story, but the tissue was always unbroken; the orders of architecture which were transmitted from the remotest times in spite of the intrusion of the barbarous and perhaps even Saracen extravagancies of the "Goths" were the fundamental inheritance of architects, and a study of them would wrest the secrets which the past and nature held and revealed to the diligent inquirer. This belief was retained until the end of the seventeenth century by most architects, but by the turn of the century, it could no longer be held by anyone at all informed. The architecture of the Egyptians was seen as quite different from that of classical antiquity. Suspicions arose that the temple of Jerusalem and the other scriptural buildings which followed the Dominical command were of a quite different "style" or *"ordonnance"* from those of pagan antiquity.[173] Things had been learned, moreover, from the art of exotic peoples—from the Turks to the Chinese—which seemed in some ways admirable; nor could this lesson square with the notion of an absolute primacy of the European tradition.

There were two factors which were perhaps even more important: the closer knowledge of Greek buildings showed that the Greeks and the Romans had quite different architectures and that even within the Roman world there were very considerable distinctions: in Spalato, Palmyra, Nîmes, there were buildings which did not altogether agree with Italian monuments or the normative texts in treatises. The very notion of an absolute and ahistorical norm inherited from the past had broken both by internal fissuring and by external pressure.

It was that break which had led the architects in the early years of the eighteenth century (that and the relaxation of the drive for glory) to turn to the decorators' view of nature and things natural as a guide to taste. Theirs was a light and airy vision of nature, yet of a nature put to the Question, if I may use the term in the legal sense: nature twisted and stretched; nature bound in sheaths and posies; nature picked, gouged clean by sea and wind. That vision was too volatile, too unreflecting. Those who gave it body did not seem to have any understanding of their own aims. They did not even seem ambitious to shape the outer world.[174] The impatience of a rising society, of a society constantly reforming itself, its values changing with a speed which its structures could not absorb, required a more stable and more explicitly justified manner. The epic quality, the grandeur, the stability of the *grand goût* had an enormous appeal for quite different reasons, to the court, and to the *philosophes:* so did the intellectual excellence of its debates. There had been no protagonists to equal the giants of the early days of the Academy of Architecture, Perrault and François Blondel. Laugier's popularity

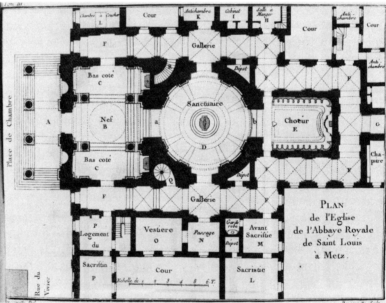

The Abbey of St. Louis at Metz, by J.-F. Blondel, the ultimately articulated church. A pedimented portico leads to a wide but short nave, followed by a vast domed sanctuary and a cubical retro-choir. The orders of the sanctuary and of the portico are the same height. The whole church is four times the column height long, and the sanctuary is three times its height.

lay in having translated their differences—resolved in some way in
Blondel's favor—into the current language of the *philosophes*:[175] it
made him the most popular writer on architecture of the second half
of the eighteenth century. And the dispute was resolved again, and
in another way, in Louis-Etienne Boullée's manuscript treatise.[176]

Boullée and his contemporary, Claude-Nicolas Ledoux, take up
the heritage of Jacques-François Blondel and of Soufflot. The vaults
of Boullée's opera, designed in 1781, the year when he took
Soufflot's place in the first class of academicians, follow the structure of the dome of Ste. Geneviève in the interior, and another composition of Soufflot in the exterior.[177] But it is the strange conflation
of pieces of the past in Ste. Geneviève which now seems its most
rebarbative aspect: the baroque illusionism, the quotation of a late
Hellenistic tomb, the "incorrect" Doric, the Byzantine plan, and the
Perraultian order are an amalgam whose very coherence presents a
problem to which the architects of the next generation would have to
find answers. Two years before that scheme, in 1762, Ledoux had
already provided a miniature of his thinking about it in a paneled
interior of a cafe called the Café Militaire (whose fragments have
been reassembled in the Musée Carnavalet);[178] he articulates the
walls with an order of a sheaf of lances bound together by laurel
leaves and capped by a plumed helmet. The columnar character of
these bundled lances is emphasized by the hanging of the panels
between them with trophies, but more strongly, by setting mirrors in
the corners of the room, at right angles to each other so that the
corners are made to dissolve in reflections. The panels alternate with
mirrors so that each panel, edged by lances, seems a jocular reference, a caricature of Gabriel's curious two-column piers in the Ecole
Militaire.

The power of allegory was invoked by Cochin and Soufflot, but
also by Winckelmann and Mengs.[179] It inspired Cochin's frontispiece for the Encyclopedia, in fact, most of his later work. He was
preparing a vast iconological handbook when he died.[180] Such a
handbook had also appeared for the use of architects: Jean-Charles
Delafosse published his *Nouvelle Iconologie Historique*[181] in 1768. It
was not only intended for the use of architects, but like all such
books, for craftsmen of all kinds—even poets. Like Cochin's ambitious enterprise, that of Delafosse is another symptom of the return to the earnestness of the age of Louis XIV.[182] The kind of
iconology which they proposed was close to the preoccupations of
the *Petite Académie* in the days of Charles Perrault and Jean
Chapelain, but with an inevitable difference: the century which had
elapsed had enlarged the learned public for such devices and the
circle of patrons who had recourse to it. The whole of the middle
class now had an investment of curiosity in such matters. It almost
inevitably follows, therefore, that artists were no longer limited to
the celebration of glorious princes and the unity of the faith (whether
Catholic or Protestant) which the princes professed; the doctrines
they wished to illuminate were often enclosed in cryptograms of
quite explosive ideas that even the artist who devised them wanted

to conceal under figurations legible only to initiates. Yet these cryptograms were often an essential part of the great "machines" of structures which such artists built, metaphorically or literally. Diderot had exalted the irreducible hieroglyph over the explicit allegory.[183] The initiatory light of Soufflot may be taken as an architectural hieroglyph, an indication of the veiled language in which the iconographic themes are couched. The sculptures I have described belong to the commonplaces of church iconography, relatively easy to "read" even for the barely instructed. But the whole form of Ste. Geneviève is more than these allegoric exercises imply. It is perhaps the last architectural hieroglyph, so rarified is "the achieve of, the mastery of the thing," that it had to break: Soufflot himself could not sustain the brilliant amalgam over its many transformations.

The past could never again provide a quarry of detail and of allusion; the division of history into periodic styles separated such forms into specific reference on one hand and conventional surfacing on the other.

Which brings me to what must have been—socially—one of the most insidious changes in the architecture of that time. The argument about the two beauties in architecture had been stated brilliantly and subtly by Perrault. In the mid-eighteenth century, it was restated (for the various reasons I have indicated) in a much grosser manner. It may be found, argued at various levels of sophistication, in any number of publications, from the Encyclopedia to builders' manuals. There is indeed a positive, an a priori beauty in architecture. As Perrault had required, it is a beauty which is evident to everyone. Where Perrault had been at fault, however, was in restricting the realm of common sense too narrowly. The axioms of geometry are axioms only because they are quite evident to common sense.[184] Positive beauty therefore may well be the result of simple ratios in the proportioning of buildings—which even the untutored eye of a "natural" man can appreciate. On this ground, it followed, of course, that Perrault's simplified orders were superior to those offered in surveys of ancient monuments and most "modern" writers who resorted to complex fractions. From such premises, it could be argued further—and was—that the simpler the body, the better the proportion. The sphere and the circle are, by an extension of Perrault's argument (which he would not have sanctioned), proposed as the geometrical bodies which the architect should, for preference, use.[185]

The other side of Perrault's equation is given a different extension: the secondary—or arbitrary—beauty in architecture is produced and appreciated by the irrational faculty of taste, compounded of the most corruptible parts of human nature. Taste had therefore to be formed, on the ground of innate ideas, by habit and association, which had to be guided, because of their corruptibility and waywardness, by the best examples which antiquity, particularly sacred antiquity, could offer.

Since positive and rational beauty was within everybody's reach, it followed—in Perrault's argument—that the architect's training and his mode of operation are primarily concerned with taste. But Perrault's psychology, within which an uncorruptible reason provided a framework that supported the fallen and corruptible faculties of memory and imagination, was unacceptable in the eighteenth century, as were aspects of Perrault's mechanistic physics. Newton had allowed architectural theorists to appeal again to the harmony of the "noble" senses. The anthropology of Rousseau and of the Encyclopedists required that other human faculties, not reason alone, that something in the whole of the personality should be untainted and incorrupt. Taste therefore assumes another and perhaps more crucial role in the architect's practice, which the revival in the absolute value of primary geometries could not dislodge.

The effect of the new extrapolations from Perrault's main argument was in fact a further reduction of the architect's authority over his domain. The criterion by which he was judged was removed a further step from the operations of reason. The way in which he employed the elementary geometry which guaranteed the positive beauty of his buildings was guided by taste: taste alone could ensure the necessary variety in such buildings, and taste was a constant subject of discussion in the Academy of Architecture.[186] The alienation of the architect from his craft and contractual operations, his isolation inside the limits of a disinterested professional status, seemed to involve the rarefying of his works beyond the reach of reason. As the appeal to the past weakened, the criteria by which building operations were to be judged attenuated to snapping point.

Now building is one of the primary human industries. This attenuation seems to me to have been one of the reasons why masonic ideology had such a powerful appeal to architects as well as to their clients. Architects more particularly: they had been removed from the guild to the academy, and they were no longer seen as operators of sacred formulae or the controlling operators of an industry. With the demythifying of sacred history, even their scholarship became a gratuitous pedantry. They therefore gravitated naturally to a secret society which offered their professional activity as a model of the quest for wisdom, as the rationalized form of the spiritual life in terms which implied that the daily details of the building trade were the proper exemplars of social reform.

Throughout the eighteenth century, isolated efforts were made to return to some rational account of the architect's business, mostly by reducing the importance of formal values and giving more weight to mechanical skills. Just after the Revolution, the most influential teacher of architecture in his day, Jacques-Nicolas-Louis Durand (Boullée's favorite pupil), did just that without the mechanical bias, but he did it by sacrificing most of the matters which were the meat of architectural theory before his time; and he resolved the quarrel between Perrault and Blondel to his own satisfaction by declaring what was contended to be a nonproblem.[187]

The Blondel-Perrault discussion looked so trivial to Durand *because* it dealt with unpragmatic ideas, which could only have indirect application. For his part, he was able to formulate, once and for all time, the permanent principles of architecture framed in terms of both structural analysis and geometrical composition. His formulae were widely applied, and his pragmatic teaching methods are at the source of many of our own troubles today.

Seen from the vantage point of the 1970s and 1980s, Durand's positive dismissal of the problems which engaged and worried seventeenth- and eighteenth-century architects does not seem quite final. The nature of our responses to the world of artifacts, the way in which groups and communities appropriate space, occupies sociologists and anthropologists. And we acknowledge these human scientists as important and wholly serious people. Yet their studies are, in the last reduction, almost inevitably about problems of form. This book recalls a time when the architect's business was just that. Perhaps, if there is to be a place for the architect's work within a future social fabric, he will have to learn how to deal with such problems again.

Notes to Chapter 10

1. For the Abbé Jean-Paul Guya (or Gua) de Malves, see *B.U.* He taught both mathematics and philosophy at the Collège de France and died in his home town of Carcassonne in 1783. Lebreton commissioned Guya to do revisions and annotations of the translation of Chambers' *Encyclopedia* which had been done by Johns Mills and Gottfried Sellius. Mills was an Englishman who lived in Paris; Sellius, born in Danzig, had been professor at Göttingen but also settled in Paris. Lebreton seems to have ruined Mills by manipulating the printing privilege. Mills' return to England left Lebreton with unedited but bulky text and some financial investment.

2. Guya suggested that the work should be entirely redone and enlarged. The Mills-Sellius version which was subscribed for—and announced in a four-volume folio (with a fifth volume containing plates and a reference dictionary in several languages) for 1746 was never issued.

3. He had by then written, besides the *Lettre sur les Aveugles* and the Shaftesbury translation, another Shaftesburyan essay, the *Pensées Philosophiques*: mathematical essays; and a giggly, scabrous "novel," *Les Bijoux Indiscrets*; but his reputation for efficiency rested on his editing of the French version of Robert James' *Medicinal Dictionary* (1743–1745; Diderot's *Dictionnaire Universel de Médicine* appeared in Paris 1746–1748).

4. For the chronology of the first edition (1751–1757 for I–VII; 1765 for VIII–XVII; 1762–1772 for the plates), see J. Lough (1968), pp. 463 f. The matter is complicated by the issue of a supplement (1776–1777) and index (1780) by which time six other editions had already appeared (for which, see J. Lough, 1968, pp. 2 ff.), as well as pirated versions.

Chrétien de Lamoignon de Malesherbes (1721–1794) was the controller of the press on behalf of his father, who was appointed chancellor of the Paris *Parlement* in 1750; he made it his business to know the literary world well. His kindness to Diderot and constant sheltering from police prosecution was partly responsible for the continuing work on the Encyclopedia. Malesherbes is remembered most for his return from exile in 1792 to take part in the legal defense of Louis XVI before the convention. He was himself guillotined with his family in 1794. His intervention with Abbé Laugier to prevent alarming notices about the Encyclopedia appearing in the official *Gazette* in W. Herrmann (1962), p. 206 f.

5. As marquis de Stainville, he had been ambassador to Rome and very friendly with Benedict XIV. He became minister for foreign affairs and duc de Choiseul in 1758.

6. On the details, see J. Lough (1968), pp. 243 f.

7. The dukes de Nivernois and de la Vallière were of the *affaire* of which Voltaire gives a graphic account in E. Goncourt and J. Goncourt (1906), pp. 177 ff. The Goncourts also report Madame de Pompadour's constant recommendations of caution to Diderot and requests to the king for a pension for d'Alembert.

8. Diderot noticed this on consulting an article in the finished but not issued volume XV on 12 November 1764. His letter of rage to Lebreton: "A votre ruine et à celle de vos associés . . . se joindra, mais pour vous seul, une infamie dont vous ne vous laverez jamais. Vous serez traîné dans la boue avec votre livre, et l'on vous citera dans l'avenir comme un homme capable d'une infidélité et d'une hardiesse auxquelles on n'en trouvera point à comparer" is a model of invective.

9. Translation, extracts, and attacks had followed already on the publication of the first volume: one volume, for instance, of a projected English

translation appeared in 1752 (sponsored by Sir Joseph Ayloffe, an antiquarian also involved in the Westminster Bridge affair), but was a failure.

10. The system of *brevets d'invention* suggested the need for something like the *Description*, which was promoted by René Ferchault de Réaumur from about 1710 onwards. But the government grant promised to Réaumur in 1721 did not actually come to be paid until 1778, by which time its value had been reduced by inflation. Lavoisier took the matter in hand in 1787. A further effort was made just before the French Revolution by a group of young scientists who called themselves the *Société Philomatique* (R. Hahn, 1971, pp. 66 ff., 123 f., 178 f., 231). Polemical comparisons abounded. Charles Palissot, author of the disagreeable comedy, *Les Philosophes*, compares the academy's halting but serious and "professional efforts" to the hasty amateurishness of the Encyclopedists (in J. Lough, 1968, p. 335). Elie Fréron kept alive the accusation of plagiarism from the unpublished academy material by the Encyclopedists, which was first made by the architect, Pierre Patte, Blondel's disciple and assistant, of whom more later (see J. Lough, 1968, pp. 346 ff., 381 f.). This change was further provoked by the publication of the academy's *Avertissement* of the publication of its plates in 1760.

11. On the Royal Society's endeavors, see above. For the original policy of the Parisian Academy, see R. Hahn (1971), pp. 22 ff.

12. Diderot and d'Alembert (1751–1765), "Discours Préliminaire" and s.v. "Arts." Cf. S. Giedion (1948), pp. 135 f.

13. I have followed the reasoning of G. Simondon (1969), pp. 90 ff., 113 ff.

On the early development of cloth-making machinery, see A. Wolf (1968), II, pp. 458 ff.; and P. Mantoux (1961), pp. 204 ff. Until 1788 water and wind were the only possible sources of power.

14. The elaborate automata of Jacques de Vaucanson were much admired in the eighteenth century, see the enthusiastic description of his duck by d'Alembert in the Encyclopedia, s. v. *Androïde*. Vaucanson was appointed "inspecteur des manufactures de Soie" by Cardinal Fleury in 1741. In 1748 he became a member of the Académie des Sciences, to which he had presented an automatic flautist in 1738. These, and other less perfect ones constructed for instance by the Droz family of Neufchâtel, had a powerful impact on the common-sense mechanistic thinking (for a general survey of such automata, see A. Chapuis and E. Droz, 1949), and was formulated into a quasi-scientific philosophical position by J. de La Mettrie in his *l'Homme Machine*, 1960, pp. 67, 190 f., 246 f. As *inspecteur* of silk-making, he applied the devices which he had used in the automata to devise a mechanical loom for figured silks, which extended out of recognition the older methods of ribbon-weaving. The factory which he set up at Aubenas near Lyons (still a silk-manufacturing center) about 1755 extended the manufacturing process to spinning and provided a type of building in which the whole process could be settled. Vaucanson described it in a communication to the academy ("Sur le Choix de l'Emplacement et sur la Forme qu'il faut donner au Bâtiment d'une Fabrique d'Organsin"), *Histoire* (1702–1797), vol. for 1776, p. 168.

Nevertheless, the guild organization of silk-weavers proved too strong for Vaucanson, and his factory was shut down. The loom, deposited with the academy, passed into the Conservatoire des Arts et Métiers, which was based on the collection of inventions which Vaucanson had made for the academy. See S. Giedion (1948), pp. 34 ff. Vaucanson's loom was reactivated by Jean-Marie Jacquart in 1804 and became the basis of modern weaving machinery.

Modern industrial historians have treated Vaucanson's researches as being only interesting in the light of Jacquart's use of them: P. Mantoux (1961), p. 240. The Encyclopedia, in spite of its enthusiasm for Vaucanson's automata, does not mention his loom or his mill in the article on silk-making.

15. See, however, R. Barthes (1975).

16. On the place of aesthetic speculation in eighteenth-century philosophy, see E. Cassirer (1955), 275 ff., 332 f.

17. Beginning with Plato and St. Augustine, Diderot pays some attention to Christian Wolf but concentrates on Crousaz, André, and Francis Hutcheson. See E. Migliorini (1966), pp. 313; and more recently D. Funt (1968). But W. Folkierski's (1936) treatment, pp. 355 ff. remains valuable.

18. On Diderot's debt to—and treatment of—Shaftesbury, see particularly R. L. Cru (1913), particularly pp. 119 ff., which begins with a consideration of the way in which Diderot treated the *Inquiry*. More recently and in greater detail, this had been discussed by D. Funt (1968), pp. 19 f. On Diderot's debt to Shaftesbury in the matter of the *Kalokagathos,* see W. Folkierski (1936), pp. 388 ff.; and R. L. Cru, pp. 402 f.

19. Although he rejects Shaftesbury's utility as the only criterion of beauty: see above, n. 272, and W. Folkierski, p. 389.

20. His own prime definition is a question as begging as the ones he rejects. "Beautiful is that which contains without reference to myself what will awake in my understanding the notion of relationship; and beautiful with reference to myself everything which awakes this idea."

Diderot uses the Eastern facade of the Louvre to demonstrate his point, to distinguish "forms which are *in* the objects, from any notion I may have of them," since, he points out, its beauty will only be beauty, however you conceive its elements and their composition, for beings composed of body and soul such as we human beings. For other beings, it might be indifferent, or even ugly. From which—surprisingly—he derives an idea of two beauties again: one real, the other perceived, and this while denying the existence of an absolute beauty. Our appreciation of relative quantities (musical or proportional) is usually separate from our appreciation of the object they govern. Our pleasure in appreciating them is separate from any knowledge and is more a matter of feeling than of reason: they belong to perceived beauty therefore. Nevertheless, my understanding neither detracts anything from its objects nor does it add anything to them. Whether I think of the facade of the Louvre or do not do so, its internal relationships are such as they are—and presumably they are such as will awaken in us the notion of relationship.

Having disposed of divine design and of the whole teleological apparatus, Diderot offers a notion of conceptual economy learned in common need and therefore possessing a social pervasiveness. Cf. D. Funt (1968), pp. 121 ff.

21. In fact, the article "Goût" was written by Montesquieu with Voltaire and d'Alembert.

22. For Diderot's view of the matter in the Encyclopedia, see *"Beau,"* p. 618 b. This in spite of his protestations (IV, 616 b) in which he reproaches Shaftesbury's utilitarianism. Consistency in this, as in other matters, was not really expected and inevitably Diderot appealed often to the ultimate criterion of utility: in the formation of taste, for instance, in the course of the

Encyclopedia article, he declares the essential notion of beauty to develop through use (IV 618 b–619 a), or at any rate through the combination, the relation of uses. But he was even more critical of Shaftesbury's supposed utilitarianism in his letters to Sophie Volland (2 September 1762). It is not wholly expected, but nevertheless true, that his aesthetics were translated into the upholding of the ''ancient'' critical criteria against the ''modernity'' of the sculptor Falconnet (D. Diderot, 1969–1973, VI, pp. 381 ff.; VII, pp. 482 ff.). On this discussion, see J. Seznec (1957), pp. 45 ff. He even comes near to defending the harmony of the senses: in D. Funt (1968), pp. 130 f.

23. Diderot quotes with approval a dictum of d'Alembert's from the general introduction to the Encyclopedia that, having made an art of learning music, we should also make an art of listening to it (625 a/b), and something of the same kind appears in 621 b (2nd principle). This is a highly developed echo of Shaftesbury's (1732), I, conclusion: that ''there must be an art of hearing found ere the performing arts can have their true effect'' (p. 235). Cf. D. Funt (1968), pp. 37 f.

The notion of *belle Nature* is always referred to the legend of Zeuxis choosing different parts of several Crotonian girls to assemble the perfect figure of Helen and is told several times in ancient literature (Cicero, *De Inv.*, II,1,i; Pliny HN. XXXV, 64; Dion. Hallicarn. De Prisc.Script. Cens.l.) and reentered the literature of art with Alberti's *Della Pittura*, III. On the popularity of the legend among poets and writers on art, see E Panofsky (1968); pp. 15, 49. But in Diderot's evolutionary view of the model, it is inevitably shaped by the dialectic between the creation of the artist and his public's rediscovery of nature through art. D. Funt (1968), pp. 140 ff.

24. Jacques-François Blondel was one of the original groups of contributors, and signed (P). In the same volume he also signs the articles ''Architecte,'' ''Arabesque,'' ''Arc-Boutant,'' ''Arcade,'' ''Architrave,'' and so on.

25. Jacques-Ange (or Ange-Jacques) was born in 1698. He succeeded his father, Jacques-Jules (1667–1742) as *premier architecte* and president of the Academy, which he remained until his death in 1782, though after Louis XV's death in 1775, he withdrew from court employment, not being in sympathy with the taste of the new monarchs.

He came of a long line of mason-designers; the first notable was Jacques I (Jacques-Jules is sometimes known as Jacques V), who died in 1628 and worked in Argentan and Rouen. Through Jacques IV's wife, Marie Delisle, his grandmother, he was related to the Mansarts as well as to Robert de Cotte—the major architects of the preceding generation and more remotely, to Germain Pilon: this was the dominant family-contractual-office nexus in French building for a century and a half. J.-A. Gabriel never published any writings and was even a notoriously lax correspondent: witness the complaints of Natoire: ''Je seray toujours très sensible au souvenir de M. Gabriel quand il voudra m'honorer d'une lettre.'' (E. Dilke, 1900, p. 23.) Gabriel's early involvement in his father's office prevented even the obligatory visit to Italy; he seems never to have left France in his life.

26. J.-F. Blondel (1747) which he refurbished, setting out his revised course in 1754. In the same year, Pierre Patte, who was to act as the editor of Blondel's *Cours,* published a *Discours* with a similar title. Contemporary reviewers inevitably compared the two, favorably to Blondel (A. Comolli, 1788–1792, I, pp. 8 ff.). Patte, although he worked with Blondel later, was a pupil of Boffrand, as he proudly claims in his *Discours.* Boffrand had died that year.

27. J.-F. Blondel (1774).

28. So A.-N. Dézallier d'Argenville (1787), p. 471. Blondel married, *en deuxième noces*, Manon Baletti (Marie-Magdalène) who was the daughter of the famous Silvia and Mario, the principal actors of the Comédie Italienne; her aunt, known as Flaminia, had been the cause of a jealous dispute between Antonio Conti and Scipione Maffei (on whom, above, chapter 8, nn. 4, 86), and a third *letterato*, Pier-Giacomo Martelli. The Balettis welcomed Casanova to Paris (1960–1962, III, pp. 120 ff.; and V, pp. 14 ff.); his later (1760) liaison with Manon, nearly contemporary with his relation to Memmo's friend, Giustina Wynne, was interrupted by her marriage to Blondel. Her letter breaking the news in the terms which he reports has been found among his correspondence. See J. Casanova (1960–1962, V, pp. 169 ff.; on the break, VI, pp. 28 ff.). On Blondel's extravagance, see A.-N. Dézallier d'Argenville (1787), pp. 471 f.; who praises Manon's "moeurs exemplaires, mille qualités aimables et esprit," as well as the patience and sweetness with which she put up with the aging Blondel's disease and impatience.

29. Blondel's *Architecture Françoise* not only emulates Jean Mariette's *Architecture Françoise* (1727–1738), but he had also contributed several plates as an engraver, see E. Kaufmann (1955). Blondel reused many of Mariette's plates, even quite a number which Mariette had taken over from Jean Marot's older (c. 1670) collection. Marot's plates had been sold to Mariette by one of his grandchildren, and the lettering and numbering reworked. Jombert, Blondel's publisher, who succeeded Perrault's Coignard as the principal architectural publisher in Paris, in turn bought Mariette's stock of metal plates. There seems little doubt that Blondel's quite independent text was often tied to existing engravings and that new plates were only engraved if considered essential. On Marot's enterprise, see A. Mauban (1944; reprinted 1967); on Mariette's, A. Mauban (1945). On Blondel's borrowing, see A. Mauban (1945), pp. 72 f., 78 f.

30. Abel-François Poisson was born in 1727, six years after his sister, who continued to call him *frérot* in the days of their greatness. Even Louis XV came to call him *petit frère*. He took the title de Vandières from an estate which the king gave to his father, François Poisson in 1747, while the title of de Marigny, by which he is more generally known, was attached to another property which Madame de Pompadour had got for her father, in a somewhat scandalous manner in 1750, and which Abel Poisson inherited, with the title, on his father's death in 1754. But during the first years of his tenure of office, and before that on his entry at court and during his travels, he appears as Monsieur de Vandières (which produced some ribald court puns on M. Avant'Hier: J. Goncourt and E. Goncourt, 1906, pp. 96 ff.). He remained in charge of buildings after his sister's death in 1764, although he renounced it after friction with the du Barry entourage in 1773, a year before the king's death. Besides his direction of building, he was a commander of the Order of St. Louis in 1756 and was made governor of the Orléanais in 1764. He was also a counsellor of state and governor of the Château of Blois, near which he had another property, Ménars, whose name he took as his title towards the end of his life. He died in 1781.

31. See above, chapter 8; chapter 9, particularly nn. 52 ff.

32. On engraving the views of Rome for Bouchard, see chapter 9, n. 50.

33. Their character is quite contrary to that of Blondel's whole book, and more severe than anything which appears in the posthumous *Cours*.

34. Focillon 128. "Scuola antica architetta alla Egiziana e Greca." In the

Opere Varie for which Bellicard may have engraved a vignette by Le Lorrain (H. Focillon, 1918, II, n. 1206). It may well be that Marigny, to whom the book was dedicated, suggested their insertion. Bellicard was later to conceive an ambitious work, *Architectonographie, ou Cours Complet de l'Architecture,* which his poverty—the result of gaming debts—did not allow him to finish. *Académie de France à Rome,* pp. 52 ff.

35. Madame de Pompadour was determined that her brother should have high office and fixed on the reversion of the office of *directeur-général des bâtiments* from Monsieur de Tournehem (on whom see n. 36) in 1746, when Marigny was eighteen.

36. Charles-François Le Normant de Tournehem (16?–1751) became the literal (as well as, presumably, the metaphorical) protector of Madame Poisson, Madame de Pompadour's mother, while the disgraced François Poisson went into hasty exile in 1725. Tournehem was a *fermier-général* and a director of the Compagnie des Indes. His nephew, Charles-Guillaume Le Normant d'Etioles married Jeanne-Antoinette Poisson on his uncle's urging, and with a promise of a large dowry and an inheritance. He seems to have fallen in love with her after the marriage. Madame de Pompadour obtained the office of director of buildings for her uncle-in-law on the resignation of Philibert Orry, comte de Vignory, Tournehem seems to have been more interested in the affairs of the Academy of Painting than those of the Academy of Architecture, although he administered matters equably, looking after payments to members (*P.V.,* VI, pp. 129 ff.) and giving the academy collections of engravings (Zabaglia and Fontana; *P.V.,* VI, pp. 165 ff.). He also initiated the competition for the Place Louis XV in 1748 (*P.V.,* VI, pp. 105 ff).

37. This celebrated and influential journey has been documented (E. Goncourt and J. Goncourt, 1906, p. 100, who published some of the correspondence between the brother and sister). In the most interesting perhaps, written in January 1751, she suggests that he should be in no hurry to accede to his office. As it was, Tournehem died in November of that year. The route and the method of the sightseers are recorded in some detail in Cochin's *Voyage d'Italie,* which includes some rather surprising opinions for the modern reader. At S. Vitale in Ravenna, built as Cochin rightly observes, in the reign of Justinian, there is, according to him, nothing very arresting for taste, if it were not for some mosaics of that remote period which are very bad, though the church itself is curious and "may have been the model for San Lorenzo in Milan." They also visited the tomb of Galla Placidia without noticing any mosaics (perhaps it was too dark). What does arrest Cochin's attention is a rather badly conserved painting by Frederico Barocci (1773) in the sacristy, to which he devotes half a page.

On Cochin, see. S. Rocheblave (1927), though the account by E. Goncourt and J. Goncourt (1895–1896), II, pp. 333 ff., remains unrivaled. On the Abbé Le Blanc, H. Monod-Cassidy (1941) and S. Eriksen (1973), pp. 198 f. On Germain Soufflot, see J. Mondain-Monval (1918), i, ii, and M. Petzet (1961); also L. Hautecoeur (1943–1957), III and IV passim.

It is easy enough to see how Cochin came to be selected: he had an early entry into the circle of Madame de Pompadour. He was also in relation with the comte de Caylus, with whom he was to quarrel later (C.-N. Cochin, 1880, pp. 30 ff.,). Le Blanc, too, was a friend and (published) correspondent of Caylus, to whom he extolled Inigo Jones and Burlington, and deprecated Vanbrugh and Wren. He was appointed salaried historiographer of the *bâti-*

ments du roi in November 1749 at the outset of the journey. Being the oldest and the most articulate, he was perhaps the ideologue of the group.

As for Soufflot, he too was articulate, as well as talented. He is known to have written some verse (including an epitaph for himself); little is known about his training. He was presented to the director of the French Academy, Nicolas Wleughels, by the count de St. Aignan, French ambassador in Rome (where Soufflot had gone to study on his own initiative), on the orders of the duc d'Antin in 1734. He stayed in the academy until 1738. Soufflot's presentation by d'Antin was not an isolated instance. François Franque was similarly presented in 1733 (H. Lapauze, 1924, I, p. 195). Soufflot had already made some contacts in Lyons on his way to Italy and sent the Carthusians there, who were proposing to build the project for a dome—which he later said was his best work—and there built the Servandoni *baldacchino* in 1742. But he had secured the commission for the Hôtel-Dieu in 1740 and its first stone was laid in 1741; the design was published by Blondel in *L'Architecture Françoise,* and Soufflot had been presented to the academy on 17 November 1749 (*P.V.,* VI, pp. 129 f.) irregularly and elected into the second class before his departure with Marigny. But little is known about his first contacts with the Poisson circle.

38. Gabriel was more successful as a practitioner, and Jacques-François Blondel much more prolific as a theorist.

39. Jean Cailleteau (1695–1755) was known variously as de l'Assurance or as Lassurance, like his father, the architect Pierre (1655–1724). He did most of Madame de Pompadour's day-to-day work at Crécy, Compiègne, and Versailles, as well as the alterations at the Hôtel de l'Elysée (now the Palace, her main Paris home). See L. Hautecoeur (1950), III, pp. 549 ff.

40. On Madame de Pompadour's preparation and high notion of her calling, all biographers agree. Her family nickname (the Poisson family rather went in for them), Reinette, was only half a joke, and Madame de Pompadour pensioned the fortune-teller who foretold that she would "rule the heart of a king."

41. Marigny/Vandières made a considerable contribution, anonymously, to the *pensionnaires'* expenses. He was received officially as the heir to an office, of which the academy was a charge. H. Lapauze (1924), I, pp. 194 f.; on the papal reception, the sceptical letter of Madame de Pompadour, see E. Goncourt and J. Goncourt (1906), pp. 104 f.

42. The little book which Bellicard and Cochin wrote about this subsidiary was also dedicated to their patron, already under the title Marigny, and published in 1754. Although the title only mentions Herculaneum, it was in fact an account of all the antiquities around Naples, and one of the first accounts of the excavations to be printed. See above, chapter 9, n. 50.

43. On Gabriel-Pierre-Martin Dumont (c. 1715–after 1790), see S. Eriksen (1973), p. 174; and M. Gallet (1972), pp. 53, 159. The joint work on Paestum did not appear until 1764.

44. On that drawing, illustrating a text of Plutarch inscribed under it, see S. Rocheblave (1927), p. 80. It was a "retrospective" *morceau de reception.* Diderot in his *salon* for that year is critical but highly respectful (1957, I, pp. 105 ff., 138 f.).

45. See n. 88.

46. The attack on the royal office of works centered on the incomplete fabric of Perrault's Louvre, still partly scaffolded, and what was thought

even worse, the building of some temporary structures in the square court:
these are visible on the "Turgot" plan: which, being taken from the west,
does not, of course, show the facade. La Font de Saint-Yenne (1752) indeed
quotes Voltaire's verses as an appendix to his attack (pp. 177 f):

>   "Faut-il . . . que les nations qui veulent nous braver
>   . . . soient en droit de nous dire
>   Que nous commençons tout pour ne rien achever.
>   Mais ô nouvel affront: quelle coupable audace!"
>   (Here La Font footnotes the buildings in the square court I
>   mentioned.)
>   "Veut encore avillir ce chef d'oeuvre divin? . . .
>   Louvre, palais pompeux dont la France s'honore
>   Sois digne de Louis ton maître et ton appui:
>   Sors d'état honteux ou l'univers t'abhore
>   Et dans tout ton éclat montre-toi comme lui."

By the time the Abbé Laugier (1765) criticized the proportions of the lower
story of the facade (pp. 94 f.), the scaffolding and the obscuring buildings
had been removed.

There is a curious aspect of La Font's text which has perhaps not been
stressed sufficiently: his almost interchangeable use of *patriot* and *citoyen*
or rather *bon citoyen*. It is as an exemplar of the national style that the
supremacy of Perrault's facade is extolled: in particular, over the Italian
exemplars. Perrault's victory over Bernini is set up as a token of his true
superiority. The replacing of the statues of conquered slaves or abstract
virtues on the statue of the *bien-aimé* are another symptom of this tendency,
which Diderot found ridiculous.

47. Blondel's veneration of Perrault and Mansart has already been mentioned. Mansart particularly, Blondel's "dieu de l'architecture" is constantly deferred to. But this harping back to the two heroes was a commonplace of mid-eighteenth-century architectural polemics.

48. On the Place Vendôme, see L. Hautecoeur, 1948, II, pp. 607 ff., where
the scheme to construct a street joining it to the Place des Victoires is also
mooted. Hautecoeur's fig. 477 (p. 609) shows Mansart's debt to Perrault in
his *"ordonnance"* very clearly. The northern vista was closed by François
d'Orbay's convent church of the Capuchine nuns which was destroyed in
1790. See also A. Laprade (1960), pp. 220 ff.

49. The whole episode is the subject of P. Patte (1765).

50. On the work at Bordeaux, see E. Frisch, *Conte de Fels*, 1924, pp. 20 ff.
On the Nancy undertaking, a contemporary account was given in great
detail by Héré de Corny (1753, 1756) and in the *Compte Général de la Dépense*, 1761. A recent bibliography in P. Simonin and R. Clement (1966).

51. On Servandoni's visit to London and the work at St. Sulpice, see
chapter 5; and L. Hautecoeur (1950), III, pp. 477; and P. Lavedan (1959),
III, pp. 301 ff.

52. An account of the public and festive casting of the statue was given by
M. Mariette (1768). See E. Dilke (1900), pp. 77 ff., 89 f. The statue was not
placed on its site until 1763. Like the statues of Louis XIV in the Place des
Victoires and the Place Vendôme, it was pulled down in August 1792. There
is a drawing of the statue in the Place des Victoires being pulled down by
Jean-Louis Prieur in the Musée Carnavalet. The statue of the king on horse-
back, with a Virtue at each corner of the pedestal, provoked the epigram,
attributed to Voltaire: "Grotesque monument, infâme pedestal/Les Vertus
sont à pied, le Vice est à cheval."

53. The whole issue has its own monument in Pierre Patte's monograph on the subject which appeared in 1765, in which most of the schemes submitted are well illustrated. The competition was announced by Tournehem to the academy on 27 June 1748, in a special session, and the conditions were agreed on 1 July 1748 (*P.V.*, VI, pp. 105 f). The treaty was not actually signed until the October of that year, but even the agreement of the pre-liminaries moved the City Council of Paris to vote funds for a monument and a square. S. Granet (1963).

54. Session of 18 January 1753, when Marigny (M. de Vandières) announced the royal decision to make the Pont-Tournant between the Tuileries and the Champs-Elysées the site. *P.V.*, VI, p. 191.

55. L. Hautecoeur (1950), III, pp. 503 ff. Boffrand's project is shown in Patte's collection (1765; project C, with the king's statue on a tall column).

56. L. Hautecoeur (1950).

57. L. Hautecoeur (1950), III, pp. 139, 504.

Patte was Germain Boffrand's pupil; and although Boffrand was then an old man, he was really regarded as the most accomplished designer of his time by such critics as Blondel (1771), V, p. 21.

58. The setting of the statue in place was painted by Pierre de Machy and engraved for M. Mariette's book by Jacques Deny. On the unveiling, see S. Granet (1963).

59. S. Granet (1963).

By the time the Turgot plan was engraved in 1734, there was no sign of the defenses round the edge of the river beyond the stretch of landscaped moat which acted as a kind of ha-ha between the pont-Tournant and the Champs-Elysées. The defenses had been slowly dismantled from the middle of the seventeenth century, and on 7 June 1671, the first planting out and leveling of the foundations into a *cours*, later to be called *boulevard*, was ordered. Only the Bastille de St. Antoine remained of the defenses of Charles V. L. Hautecoeur (1948), II, pp. 438 ff.

60. A church existed on the site since the reign of Charles VII, which was rebuilt twice in the seventeenth century. The decree establishing the new building and providing funds was issued by the king on 21 June 1757 on the plea—Hautecoeur suggests (1950, III, pp. 592 f.)—of Madame de Pompadour, who was a parishioner at the Elysée. A further requisition of land was made on 6 February 1763; the king laid the first stone himself on 3 April 1764. In September of the same year, he was to do the same at St. Geneviève.

61. The vista from the Tuileries was planted by Le Nôtre (see E. de Ganay, 1962, pp. 14 f.; E. Lazare and L. Lazare (1855), pp. 260 ff. He also planned an oblique avenue to Roule symmetrical with the Cours-la-Reine in 1670. L. Hautecoeur (1948), II, pp. 441.

62. The bridge was designed and built by Jean-Rodolphe Perronet (1787–1792), although his design was done in 1771. Funds for the bridge were first voted by the city of Paris in 1722.

63. Both Gabriel and Soufflot, but particularly Soufflot, had an alternative scheme for continuing the Rue Royale northward, towards Clichy. See J. Mondain-Monval (1918), i, pp. 256 ff.

But in fact, the Rue Royale—the Rue de la Paix—was (since even the entry into the Tuileries was through the Rue and Porte St. Honoré) the main entry into Paris from the southwest.

64. Very little is known about Claude Guillot-Aubry (1703–1771), still often taken for his namesake, François Debias-Aubry, although they simultaneously double-barreled their names to avoid this confusion. He certainly taught (*P.V.* VI, p. 64; VII, pp. 44, 267) and was often an arbiter on schemes presented to the academy. He was a commissioner when Tommaso Temanza (whom I mentioned earlier as an adversary of Lodoli's and Lucchesi's: chapter 8) was proposed as a corresponding member of the academy.

On 15 April 1756, Aubry offered to the academy a portfolio of drawings—including (*P.V.*, VI, pp. 256 f.) details of the metal reinforcement for the facade of the Louvre. H. Lemmonier (*P.V.*, VI, pp. 256 f., notes) suggests that these drawings were used by Pierre Patte as a basis for his engravings (1769, pls. 13, 17 ff.) and that they were among the drawings burnt in the Tuileries fire of 1871. In Patte's (1765) book of monuments, Aubry's project is marked L. It is a large square on the south of the river, its northern side formed by a quay, and centered on the Pont-Royal, and the Rue du Bac enters it through a vast triumphal arch. The massing is clearly a precedent for Gabriel's facades on the other side of the river, with a basement of arcades and a column over every pier and a pedimented pavilion at either end, although Gabriel simplified the massing, rusticated the basement, and refined the detail into the finely adjusted double facade.

65. Gabriel was, of course, quite conscious of this debt of his: see E. F. de Fels (1924), pp. 77 f.

66. This avenue was to lead from the center of the eastern side of the Louvre, and was implicit, even in the state entry of Louis XIV and Maria Theresa into Paris in 1661. It was the sine qua non of Bernini's plan and inevitably also of Perrault's. The matter was raised at regular intervals; the last complete scheme was prepared by Charles Percier and Louis Fontaine: it extended from the Rue de Rivoli to the Palais Royal and included a new opera opposite the Palais, as well as a monumental chapel for the Louvre; it also provided for a semicircular *place* before it, with an eastward road, arranged in arcaded blocks like the Rue de Rivoli to link the palace with the Barrière du Trône. The possibility of the link was killed by Napoleon III's extension of the Rue de Rivoli into the Faubourg St. Antoine.

67. While the site of the eastern block belonged to the crown in part, and in part to the heirs of the financier John Law, which implied fairly speedy proceedings, the western part was divided among several proprietors, and the facade was for some years supported with buttressing walls with no accommodation at the back. See Y. Metman (1954) and S. Granet (1963).

68. Though Poussin set most of the scenes in the country, with some urban background—and even his Rome and Jerusalem are unfinished, scaffolded towns. Claude also saw his buildings in a landscape, or towns in a distance. And this is also true of their Italian contemporaries. Even stage settings before 1700 are a disappointing source for such visions. It is remarkable, too, how much scaffolding obtruded in seventeenth-century urban landscapes.

69. The classic scene is famous (as are the comedy and satire). And there are several other instances: the intarsias of Fra Giovanni da Verona, the "tragedy" scene panels of the Casa Strozzi in Florence, the Peruzzi scene in sanguine (on which Serlio's may in fact be based) and the inevitable "Piero" panels of Urbino and Baltimore. But such representations are not on the increase in the mid-seventeenth century.

70. The quoined brick wall of the Places des Vosges and Dauphine were in a sense adopted by the *gens de robe* as their iconographic architectural expression, against the ashlar stone of the old aristocracy. For the Place des Victoires and Vendôme, see above.

71. Inigo Jones' buildings at Covent Garden owed as much to Italian precedent as to French. Of the great plans for the rebuilding of London, not much came in architectural actuality. The great noble townhouses did not contribute much to the creation of an urban landscape in the Strand and in Piccadilly. This was first done by developers who hit on the notion of facing a terrace of two-up and two-down houses with a country-mansion facade. The first may well have been the east side of Grosvenor Square; its north side was also shaped as a unit but unsuccessfully; J. Summerson (1945), pp. 86 f. Much of this was done before 1730. In Bath, the north side of Queens Square was begun in 1728 (W. Ison, 1948, p. 127), although it was the beginning of a large urban landscape which has been discussed elsewhere.

72. The general approach is stated in Blondel's *Cours,* 1771, II, pp. 308 f. See also P. Lavedan (1959), III, p. 312; P. Patte (1769), p. 192. The "high" critics did not find it altogether satisfactory; the Abbé Laugier (1765) disavowed the plan as very inferior to the Panthéon (p. 185), although he was very enthusiastic about its position in the urban landscape which he considered probably superior to any in Europe (Laugier, 1765, p. 106).

73. Or more correctly, the Sta. Maria Novella-Gesù model, which was the most common church facade model and which Contant varied for the most important of his works, the abbey of St. Vaast (now the cathedral) at Arras, as well as his earliest Parisian work, the facade for St. Eustache, although the executed one is by Jean Mansart de Jouy, the less talented of Hardouin's two sons, about which Laugier (1765) was so rude, pp. 149 f., but which La Font de Saint-Yenne (1754) had liked, p. 3. It also involves the superimposition of two orders. The decision to have a single portico at the Madeleine was regarded as a great innovation, although not as grandiose as the hexastyle of Ste. Geneviève, as is made plain by any number of critics. Laugier has already been quoted; see also D. Le Roy (1764), pp. 87 f.

74. It was in fact executed by Robert's son, Jules-Robert (1683–1767). The first stone was laid in 1736. A Corinthian over a Doric order, of nearly the same size, and the rather easy rhythm of the arrangement, led to accusations of frivolity: J. G. Legrand and C. P. Landon (1818), I, pp. 118 ff., but see L. Hautecoeur (1950), III, pp. 112 ff., 353 ff.

75. The interior of this cruciform church was perhaps the largest instance of a whole church vaulted over flat cornices supported on columns; as in the Madeleine, the vault was ribbed, each rib falling over a column, although in the Madeleine, the cornice is made to project over the columns, with a vase over each of them. The vaulting was to be covered by lightweight countervaults *(voûtes à la Roussillon)* which Patte (1769) favored as a method of fireproofing (p. 53); and J.-F. Blondel (1771), VI, pp. 85 ff.; although Frézier attacked them as adding unduly to the thrust (see L. Hautecoeur, 1950, III, pp. 182 f.). R. Bloomfield (1921), II, p. 143, n. 1, describes the details of this construction revealed by bombing during the 1914–1918 war.

At St. Vaast, Contant employed very heavy flying buttresses, or rather flying buttresses with heavy pinnacles, but he already devised a way of supporting the crossing dome on three columns rather than a pier. At the Madeleine the vaulting was clearly intended to be much lighter, and the buttresses are the walls separating the side-chapels. Patte's (1769) doubts

are put in the *Mémoires,* pp. 192, 200 f., about the prudence of the construction, as well as the details of the existing foundations. On the place of
these constructional forms in the growth of the "greco-gothic" church, see
R. Middleton (1963), pp. 92 ff.

76. The porch did not satisfy the "rigorist" critics, as I observed earlier, but
was considered too abrupt and harsh by the admirers of Gabriel; note the
shocked description by R. Blomfield (1921), II, pp. 144 f. Presumably, one
was meant to see the whole facade, with the attic story behind the pediment,
from a distance, crowned by the dome. The cross of the lantern on the dome
is cut off from view by the cross on the attic masking the clerestory at a
point about the length of the nave outside the porch. It is a little unfortunate
that the details of the scheme on Patte's engraving of the Gabriel facades,
which has the church between them, do not entirely correspond to his
detailed presentation of the church on three separate plates.

77. This was a much more "advanced" structural solution than Contant's
previous domes. It was admired for its subtlety but was also an attempt to
solve a problem which had come to interest church designers: that the dome
should be of itself the canopy or *baldacchino* over the high altar of the
church. It was something of an Italianate importation; many older French
churches still had the Sacrament reserved in a suspended ciborium on a
pulley. This followed a decree of the Second Council of Tours (in 566–577,
the third canon). St. Paulinus of Nola (who was the subject of Charles
Perrault's epic poem—see above—also commented on the matter in one of
his Epistles to Sulpicius Severus). The notion that the ciborium of ancient
churches (including St. Sophia) was the dome over the high altar meant that
the *baldacchino* (of which Bernini's in St. Peter's was regarded as the prime
example, emulated in Paris at the Val-de-Grâce and the Invalides) was
regarded as a theatrical and Ultramontane innovation. It was clearly and
explicitly stated by Cordemoy (1714), with learned quotations from patristic
sources (pp. 149 ff., 212 ff.) and conciliar decrees. In a sense therefore the
plan of the Madeleine may be taken to be an almost literal interpretation of
Cordemoy's Gallican teaching.
    The second (1714) edition of Cordemoy's book was published shortly
before the infamous bull *Unigenitus,* at the height of the Gallican unease;
the Sieur de Moléon or de Mauléon was traveling around France, looking
for liturgical antiquities for his *Voyage Liturgique,* with its listing of and
praise of the *Suspens,* the suspended tabernacle-pyx, whose origins had
already been investigated by J. B. Thiers (1688). See a summary in E.
Viollet-le-Duc (1867), s.v. *Autel;* and L. Hautecoeur (1950), III, pp. 407 ff.

78. The theory, as I have shown above, has come down from Cordemoy,
but the full import is retained sixty years later when Patte publishes the
Cours, 1771, II, pp. 369 f. And, as might be expected, Blondel is equally
insistent on the importance of a fine forecourt.

79. If there is a similarity, it is the Doric ground order of Servandoni's first
design of 1733, which is articulated into central tetrastyle portico, recessed
bay and side pavilions flanked by coupled columns (where Contant has
column and pilaster), although Servandoni's scheme had been so radically
changed in 1742 that the resemblance is not easy to find.

80. M. Petzet (1961), pp. 24 f., 46 ff. De Machy, who painted the portico,
also did a painting of the scene which was exhibited in the *salon* of 1765. J.
Seznec and J. Adhémar (1957), II, p. 130.
    The very act, of course, challenged comparison with the building of the
triumphal arch to Perrault's designs at the Barrière du Trône a century

earlier: it had been taken down at the Regent's orders (above). The King had been slow to start the building, but once it was begun, he importuned Soufflot about its progress. The facade was a sop to the king, and Soufflot justified the expense in that he used scaffolding only to mount the painted facade (letter to Marigny in Petzet, 1961, p. 24).

On the criticism of the crypt (more like a prison than like a church), see M. Petzet, 1961, pp. 48 f. But on the significance of the Doric order and its place in the scheme, see later in this chapter.

81. The Greek-cross plan really was uncommon: of centralized plans, the polygon, as François Mansart's unexecuted but prestigious Valois tombs for St. Denis, was a model which Hardouin Mansart emulated in the Invalides. There were one or two others: in Paris the little rotunda of the Filles de Ste. Marie (now a Protestant chapel) in the Faubourg St. Antoine and the circular and porticoed dome of the Assumptionist nuns by the Louvre which was built by Charles Errard, although the designs were sent from Rome (see chapter 4). Presumably it is the church which Frémin mocks as the temple of Chastity and the House of the Vestals, in Frémin (1702), pp. 59 ff. Even Contant's Penthemont church was a centralized, domed nave, with a vast retro-choir.

But as for the Greek cross proper, it was quite exceptional and had no real precedent, particularly as far as the treatment of the exterior was concerned. In view of the enthusiasm with which Cochin (1773) I, p. 24, writes about the Superga in Turin, it would be interesting to have had his travel notes about Pietro da Cortona's S. Martino e Luca, and Rainaldi's Sta. Maria in Campitelli, which provide the nearest visual architectural precedent, except for Piranesi's engravings.

82. M. Petzet (1957).

I make the assumption that the drawings passed from the Abbey into the Bibliothèque Ste. Geneviève. If Petzet is correct in his dating and attribution, they are among the very few Perrault drawings to have survived.

83. The status of the Louvre colonnade has already been sufficiently discussed above, and it is referred to in the short report on the church which is quoted by Petzet.

84. This is already implicit in the teaching of Frémin and of Cordemoy. See Frémin's (1702) praise of Notre Dame and the Ste. Chapelle against St. Sulpice and St. Eustache, pp. 27 ff. And Cordemoy (1714) argues it more explicitly (pp. 110 ff. and passim). The argument goes back, of course, to Perrault.

85. Constantine was a standard mythical progenitor of Christian princes, and Louis XIV appealed to the antecedent several times. See above, chapter 3.

86. Borromini and Guarini are often coupled as the two corruptors of architecture; in Cochin's *Voyage*, his periodical publications and earlier. Le Blanc and Caylus often also use them as negative examples. It is to their evil influence that all the excesses of rococo are ascribed.

87. I paraphrase N. Cochin (1757), pp. 76 f. Gabriel de St. Aubin translated this text into a charming drawing reproduced by E. Dacier (1929), no. 416. Cf. M. Petzet (1961), pp. 78 f.

88. Since their return from Italy, Marigny had advanced his companions energetically and successfully. Cochin became his most trusted adviser; already *dessinateur et graveur* to the office of *Menus-Plaisirs* when they departed, he became a full member of the academy on his return (he had

already become *agrée* in 1741); the next year he was *garde des desseins* (curator of drawings) to the king and in 1755, secretary and historiographer to the academy (both the last posts were salaried). He was also made a knight of the Order of St. Michel, with lodgings in the Louvre, and ennobled. Cochin and Soufflot would still stay with Marigny at Ménars after he had resigned his office.

Soufflot had, it is true, returned to Lyons. But although he had much work there Marigny tried to prefer him on a number of occasions. Soufflot certainly competed for the *place:* his was one of the schemes redrawn by J.-F. Blondel in the portfolio which was once in St. Petersburg (L. Hautecoeur, 1950, III, p. 504, n. 1) and he had, of course, offered a scheme for the original competition (P. Patte, 1765, 'A'), and one of the most ambitious, since it covered the bed of the river and joined the Ile St. Louis to that of the Cité.

At this time he seems to have stayed in the Louvre with Cochin, who was to have an apartment there until the end of his life. He came again in 1753, at the time of the second competition, although Marigny, who favored Boffrand's scheme, openly disliked his friend's solution; and Soufflot, for his part, confessed that he disliked the problem and the destruction of the harmony between the Tuileries and the Champs Elysées—and told Marigny about his doubts when presenting the plan (J. Mondain-Monval, 1918, pp 124 ff.). As a consolation he was offered the rebuilding of the cathedral at Rennes; there, however, the money ran out and although some work was carried out by Nicolas-Marie Potain (1738–1791), the building, a larger version of the St. Philippe-du-Roule type basilica was not completed until after the Restoration (L. Hautecoeur, 1955, VI, pp. 144, n. 2, 215 f.).

Soufflot had come to Paris in February 1755 (M. Petzet, 1961, p. 21, n. 62). The king had been somewhat remiss about his vow of 1744, but when he went to a tenth anniversary service at the rather dilapidated church, he was persuaded to act. The Arrêt du Conseil is dated 6 January 1755. The plan was approved by the king on 2 March 1755. This plan involved the reconstruction of the tract of the city between the new church and the Luxembourg.

89. L. Hautecoeur (1950), III, pp. 409, 412, 416, 596, for which he had supplied the design of a dome when he was in Rome (see n. 37). Laugier (1765) criticizes it for the wide spacing of the columns, leaving large tracts of entablature virtually cantilevered: "c'est la faute la plus insoutenable qu'on puisse commettre" (p. 108). Presumably the pun is intentional. See J. Mondain-Monval (1918), pp. 86 ff.

90. A summer residence: J. Mondain-Monval (1918), pp. 110 ff. He had already rebuilt the town palace (J. Mondain-Monval, pp. 91 f.). His other work in Lyons is discussed in detail by Monval, including a theater, an exchange, some *hôtels particuliers,* as well as speculative housing.

91. Reproduced by M. Petzet (1961), pp. 135 ff. Soufflot represented it to the Paris Academy of Architecture (*P.V.*, VII, pp. 85 f). He associated it with the presentation to the academy of measured drawings of Notre Dame de Dijon by Charles Michel Le Jolivet, which were later engraved for Blondel's *Cours,* 1771, V, pp. 206 ff. See later in this chapter.

92. Above, n. 63. Discussed at length by J. Mondain-Monval (1918), pp. 124 ff.

93. For the King's illness and recovery see G. P. Gooch (1956), p. 108; incidentally, also on the place of Louis XV's *maîtresse-en-titre* in court life at the time. The building was to be financed by a tax on lotteries, a common

enough way of raising funds for church buildings at that time. Though the tax on the 1755 lottery was not without its problems for the clergy of Ste. Geneviève. M. Petzet (1961), pp. 20 f.

94. For the transformation of the scheme and Soufflot's reactions to criticism, see M. Petzet, 1961, passim. Radical alterations appear in the engraving of 1764; the dome is heightened and the portico straightened out about 1770, and there are further changes, the definitive ones shortly before Soufflot's death.

The changes from church into national Panthéon, decided after Mirabeau's death on 4 April 1791, were carried out by Quatremère de Quincy; they involved the blocking of all windows below the clerestory, the removal of the two eastern belfries, and the restructuring of the apse as well as the removal of all religious symbols. Napoleon returned the building to the church authorities. This was confirmed by the restored monarchy and the church was finally consecrated on 2 January 1822, only to be returned to its secular use by Louis Philippe in 1830. Quatremère had in the meanwhile been replaced by Soufflot's nephew, Soufflot-le-Romain, who in turn was succeeded by the great engineer-architect; Jean-Baptiste Rondelet; he had been Soufflot's assistant, and he may have been mostly responsible for the system of reinforcement, perhaps even the use (which would be the first recorded) of reinforced concrete. But see L. Hautecoeur (1952), IV, pp. 195 f.

95. A scheme like the new church attracted criticism and counterproposals from the beginning. They are discussed by M. Petzet (1961), pp. 58 ff. When Pierre Patte called for a competition (1755), the decision to exclude the obvious candidate—Jacques-Ange Gabriel—and to grant the commission directly to Soufflot had probably already been made. In 1753, however, Laurent Destouches independently offered the Canons of Ste. Geneviève a project which was not engraved until after his death in 1770. While certain details (the Greek-cross plan, the semicircular clerestory windows over a cornice, and so forth) are like those of Soufflot's scheme, others are more literal quotations of Wren's St. Paul's (dome over octagon-squinches, the two towers, the relation between inner and outer dome colonnade) as well as the older arrangements with double columns supporting the porch cornice. As in the case of Perrault's project, Soufflot probably knew it, but the difference between Soufflot's assured and masterly treatment and Destouches' rather overemphatic and gross project suggests that Marigny made the right choice, whatever the reason.

Laurent Desboeufs' rather blush-making attempt to supplant Soufflot would hardly be worth mentioning—he was sufficiently punished for it at the time by being suspended from the academy's register on 19 August 1765 (*P.V.*, VII, p. 223: the academy refers to his *brochure* as being "indécente, peu réfléchie et remplie de faussetés" and shows its disapproval of his *procédé malhonnête* by suspending him in perpetuity, although he does turn up later—see M. Gallet, 1972, p. 156). But he has the merit of having pointed out Soufflot's debt to Piranesi (the *"Vestibolo dell'Antico Tempio"* in the *Opere Varie*, Focillon, no. 12) and does discuss Soufflot's "misunderstanding" of it (in M. Petzet 1961, pp. 65 f.). As for Laugier, there seem to have been two separate projects, one for a circular church, sent to Marigny anonymously from Lyons, without a date in 1755–1756 and offering "suggestions" to Soufflot for whom the author professes great admiration; he leaves the name of a Monsieur Chenet de l'Académie as his *poste restante*. The drawings accompanying this letter were lost; the scheme is reconstructed by M. Petzet (1961), fig. 45. But then, of course, in his *Essai*,

Laugier provided a description of a new kind of Christian church which is not different from Soufflot's Ste. Geneviève in essentials: the two sizes of order (Soufflot had two superimposed orders in the interior), the barrel vault (against Soufflot's saucer domes), and so on. It is all set in the *Essai*, pp. 178 ff. His condemnation of the dome over the crossing (pp. 190 f.) is the most explicit point of difference between himself and Soufflot: although in fact he does consider a "calotte en forme de thiare ou de figure parabolique," which echoes the ideas of the dome as a *baldacchino* launched by Cordemoy, but also suggests that this dome might have the light work of a Gothic rose window. Since Laugier (1755) quotes Bernini's designs for the unexecuted belfries at St. Peter's and the tower of Strasbourg Cathedral as his ideals for church belfries (pp. 200 ff.), the reader is licensed to wonder if, after all, he did not have something on the lines of Vittone's—or even Guarini's—ribbed domes in mind.

It is conceivable that the dome of Soufflot's 1764 project was an attempt to meet Laugier's ideas. At any rate, returning to the charge in his *Observations*, he explains the idea of the rose-window in the dome and asserts that Soufflot's Ste. Geneviève—and to a lesser extent Contant's Madeleine fulfills his condition for the new church building (1765, pp. 285 f., 297).

96. There is an account of the difficulties in M. Petzet (1961), pp. 23 ff.; 51 ff. The great quarrel between Pierre Patte (1765) and Soufflot was largely about this. Although he was highly critical of the way Contant had operated at the Madeleine (pp. 192), he is merely detailed and descriptive of Soufflot's precautions on the very difficult terrain (pp. 176 ff). A fuller account in J. Mondain-Monval (1918), pp. 449 ff.

The dome on the three-column piers seems to have caused most discussion. Patte (1770), passim, wanted the dome to be single-shell. He did not care for the profile of the 1764 scheme. Cf. M. Petzet (1961), pp. 67 f., and the details of the discussion in M. Matthieu (1940), pp. 181 ff., with bibliography, pp. 387 ff. On the contrary, Emiliand Gauthey, a follower of Soufflot's, thought the piers adequate, in fact excessive, and he suggested that the three solid pylons might be emptied, leaving the attached columns detached and holding the dome without the help of the piers. Soufflot called in outside technical opinion, particularly Perronet. J. Mondain-Monval (1918) reprints an edited version of Perronet's report, pp. 453 ff., but see also pp. 510 ff.

Léonard La Planche's project for underpinning the dome, also of 1771, seems largely included for the sake of completeness; it has little interest. M. Petzet (1961), pp. 70 f.

97. The frontispiece of La Font de Saint-Yenne's little book (1752) provides an image of the building before Soufflot took over.

98. Clarac (1853), pp. 384 ff., on the neglect of the Louvre in the last years of Louis XIV's reign and on Perrault's part in remolding the courtyard and the difficulties of the interior order.

99. In spite of being very heavy. See Patte's (1769) admiring remarks on the skill of Perrault (pp. 262, 266 ff., 329 ff.; and in J.-F. Blondel, 1771, VI, pp. 164 ff.).

100. Edward Wright (1730) who has already been quoted, saw it in 1720 "almost ruinated . . . the front of it is very fine, but seen to disadvantage by reason of the narrowness of the street it stands in." But almost every architectural writer of the time complained of the neglect of the building in tones similar to those of La Font de Saint Yenne. "Le Louvre semble condamné à ne jamais être fini . . . Devant cette superbe colonnade une multitude de petits fripiers étalent en plein-air sur la place . . . grandeur et

misère, côte à côte,'' writes Sebastien Mercier in *Le Tableau de Paris* half a century after Wright (in H. de Noussanne, 1900, p. 73). On how the Louvre was occupied, a summary account in Clarac (1853), pp. 391 ff. There is little doubt that many of the shacks put up as studios—particularly for sculptors and masons' yards—damaged the stonework of the facade, and stones were even drilled to take beams and purlins. Soufflot's struggles to free the Louvre of its accretions and to finish the structure (J. Mondain-Monval, 1918, pp. 165 ff.), even after the inevitable interruption of the Seven Years' War make very depressing reading.

101. H. Lemmonier (*P.V.*, VI, pp. 256 f.) assumes that these were the drawings known to have been destroyed in the Tuileries fire of 1871; it is not known how Aubry came by them. The Procés-Verbal makes it clear that they were technical working drawings, showing all the metal reinforcement and fully dimensioned, and that they also indicated the different qualities of the stone used; presumably Lemmonier is right, and Patte's account of the structure, which I have quoted above, is the only record which remains of the drawings.

102. See above, chapter 4, nn. 14–19.

103. Servandoni was thought to have solved the problem very neatly when he doubled the columns, not on the face but in depth: see chapter 5, nn. 37 f.

104. This is exactly what Laugier (1753) recommended in *Essai*, pp. 178 f., 198 f.; although Soufflot, by having one internal order only, very considerably simplified the recipe given by Laugier, who had modeled his own on St. Peter's. As Fiske Kimball (1931) insisted, *Vitruvius Britannicus* was already available; and Soufflot was a friend of Chambers' who indeed invited him to England (M. Matthieu, 1940, pp. 398 f.), while Patte went to England in 1768 to study dome construction. On Soufflot's interest in this expedition and his use of the information, see M. Matthieu (1940), pp. 183, 398 f. Patte includes a eulogy of Wren in Blondel's *Cours*, 1771, VI, pp. 59 ff., which Blondel might not have wholly endorsed. A generation earlier the Abbé Le Blanc (1747) expressed a common enough view when he dismissed Wren's achievement as an architect, II, pp. 42 f. On Father Ricci's equally superior attitude, see above.

A summary is in M. Petzet (1961), pp. 113 ff.; and R. Middleton (1959), p. 140.

105. Though Madame de Pompadour would not, perhaps, have relished the parallel. It was conceived by Jean-Baptiste de Machault d'Arnouville (who was a senior member of the administration) and Paris-Duvernay suggested the establishment of a Collège Académique as the great prestige enterprise of the reign in 1748, though he found that Gabriel took the prestige side of the project too literally.

See R. Laulan (1950), pp. 15 ff., 115 ff. On the extravagance of Gabriel's plan, there was a lot of comment, apart from the first letter of Paris-Duvernay. See C.-N. Cochin (1880), p. 109.

Paris-Duvernay, the putative father of Madame de Pompadour worked in this matter first with Lenormant de Tournehem, then with Marigny. On Madame de Pompadour's part in it, see R. Laulan (1950), pp. 28 ff.

106. It was covered with slate and edged with zinc or lead: it was first used on the west side of the old Louvre courtyard, as the crowning element of the Pavillon de l'Horloge (c. 1625), although the features had been devised by Solomon de Brosse and Jacques-Antoine du Cerceau, a ''French'' one to contrast with the ''Italianate'' one over the Invalides.

107. They faced the court between two astylar pavilions, making the facade equivalent to the *corps-de-logis*. The courtyard was framed by a continuation of the lower, Doric order. The use of a detached or semidetached giant order, with two suborders (usually different) is characteristic of Louis (not François) Le Vau; Vaux-le-Vicomte, the Collège des Quatre Nations, Raincy—even the Hôtel Lambert. It was a solecism that the architects of Gabriel's generation tended to avoid fairly studiously (though to be fair, Le Vau himself did not use it at Versailles); moreover, there is no arch visible on the facade, each of the two-column piers corresponds to an arch spanning between the pier and the wall; and between each arch, there are flat, groined vaults.

This elevation belonged to the late solution: work on the great scheme had been interrupted because of a shortage of government funds but also because of the building of a rival establishment at La Flèche.

L. Hautecoeur (1950), III, pp. 584 f., writes that Gabriel's use of an order standing directly on the ground, without an intervening basement was affected by Laugier's (1765) criticism of the Place Louis XV (p. 35). Since the criticism was that the *ordonnance* was not masculine enough, it might fairly be thought applicable here.

R. Blomfield, who might be taken as speaking for the Ritz/RAC Louis XV revival, despised the antiquarian critics who reduced French architecture to the pedantries of Soufflot and Ledoux, but he also disliked these colonnades so much that he could not think them designed freely by his idol, Gabriel, and supposed that they had been imposed on him by Marigny or some other impersonation of *force majeure*. But Gabriel used a similar Le Vau-like solution in one of his last schemes for the rebuilding of Fontainebleau (Y. Bottineau, 1962, pl. 35, who dates it 5 November 1773; R. Blomfield, 1921, II, pp. 127 ff.; and, of course, Blomfield may be right in that they were probably drawn, if not designed, by an employee.

108. R. Laulan (1950), pp. 38 ff; who also describes Madame de Pompadour fretting about it. No doubt, she saw herself its protector, not on the model of Nell Gwynne, but much as Madame de Maintenon protected St. Cyr: E. Goncourt and J. Goncourt (1906), pp. 181; at one point, when official money was short, she certainly offered to devote most of her year's revenue to continue building (1755).

109. St. Simon, who loathed and despised Hardouin-Mansart, gave an extended account of the relationship, with suitably bitchy remarks: Louis XIV's continued favors to the architect, such as encouraging him to cover his head in the royal presence (reported by the Abbé Lambert in P. Bourget and G. Cattaui, 1956, p. 20) were intensely resented by the courtiers of birth. The continuous correspondence between Mansart and the king went on even when the king was away at war (he was capable of commenting on details of paneling at Versailles in his dispatches before a battle in his tent). But there is a complete register of proposals and royal comments; see P. Bourget and G. Cattaui (1956), pp. 122 ff. On Louis XV's attitude, see the *Mémoires Inédites* of the Prince de Croÿ (1906), I, pp. 213 ff., a kindly and observant witness, who describes the king discussing projects by "Gabriel and himself" (for the Petit Trianon, at Madame de Pompadour's) and his constant inquiries about building projects, while referring to himself as M. de Croÿ's architect. N. Mitford (1955), p. 148.

110. See above, n. 4. The remarkable instance is in fact the Petit Trianon, and the matter is discussed by Gustave Desjardins (1885), pp. 40 ff., in this connection.

111. Something has already been said about that above. In 1746, David Le Roy makes the appeal quite explicit: the Venetians adopted a Greek construction for St. Mark's based on the primitive, cruciform St. Sophia of Justinian: he tells again the story about Justinian's exclamation on entering St. Sophia—"Solomon, I have outdone you!"—(pp. 15 ff.) and recounts how the use of the dome was "improved" from Brunelleschi to Hardouin-Mansart. Le Roy sets Ste. Geneviève and the Madeleine at the summit of achievement (pp. 86 ff.). In this context, it is interesting to read Cochin's criticism of St. Mark's (1773), III, p. 2, whose fine proportions seemed to him spoiled by having one instead of two orders.

112. The effect of the Battle of Minden (1 August 1759) was perhaps more psychological than its real importance warranted. See P. Muret (1949), pp. 545 f.; construction starts at the Ecole Militaire again, R. Laulan (1950), pp. 43 ff., and the *Encyclopédie*, s.v.

113. The court itself was divided. The king would not take sides. The queen was a fierce partisan of the archbishop of Paris and of the Jesuits, while the Pompadour faction aligned itself against the Jesuits for reasons I explained earlier: though Bernis was, and remained even in his later piety, a confirmed "antienthusiast" on religious grounds. Other members, such as Choiseul, took sides in the matter almost entirely on party political grounds. Much of the discussion centered on the bull *Unigenitus* of Clement XI directed against a moderate book by Paschal Quesnel of the Oratory, *Réflexions Morales sur le Nouveau Testament*. The whole matter is brilliantly, if partially described by Marmontel (1805), II, pp. 217 ff., and the quarrel had assumed a daily character about the middle of the century. The queen, for her devotion to the extreme Ultramontane party, was nicknamed *Unigenita*. But the Gallican party had its charter in the four articles on the independence of princes drafted in 1682 and never explicitly condemned by the papacy. A clear distinction between the Gallican loyalty of the Parlements and the Jansenist loyalties among them is given by J. Egret (1970), pp. 18 ff.

The whole business of written testimonials of explicit assent to the condemnation was first demanded before the death of Louis XIV: without it neither marriages could be celebrated nor the Last Sacraments administered to the dying. Cardinal Fleury had attempted to settle the argument in 1730 with a *lit de justice* and failed. The Jansenist periodical, forbidden reading to the clergy, had wide circulation (*Nouvelles Ecclésiastiques*).

The complicated threefold dispute between the *Parlement* tending to take a Jansenist position, or at any rate ready to defend the Jansenists from the imposition of the crown and the higher clergy on the other side, and both against the *philosophes* (in particular, at this point, against Montesquieu), is set out by F. Diaz (1962), pp. 41. In May 1753 it leads to a constitutional crisis and the exile of the Parlement, which by passive resistance, gains its point in September 1754 (F. Diaz, 1962, p. 64). The archbishop was in turn exiled. The issue was settled in practice between Choiseul and Benedict XIV.

114. It is difficult now to estimate the effect of the rather feeble assassination attempt the wretched Damiens made on Louis XV on Twelfth Night in 1757. The king was only slightly wounded, but as he had a horror of dying like Henry IV; Robert-François Damiens was put to death after tortures which elicited nothing in a reconstruction of the execution of Ravaillac (M. Foucault, 1977, pp. 9 ff.). He had been at one point an employee of the Jesuits, and eighteen months later, an alleged attempt on the life of Joseph I in August 1758 revived suspicion against the Jesuits. Their savage persecu-

tion by Pombal, however, evoked sympathy from the *philosophes;* it united, in Voltaire's aphorism, the maximum of the ridiculous to the maximum of horror. Nevertheless the expulsion from France (by dissolving the order in 1764 to make all Jesuits secular clergy and expelling them in 1767) followed without the king making much of a move. Franco Venturi (1976), II, pp. 31 ff., gives a clear summary of the various responsibilities in the matter, particularly the importance of the article *"Collège"* in the Encyclopedia as an attack on Jesuit education; d'Alembert's pamphlet on the expulsion of the Jesuits puts the parliamentarians and the Jansenists in "their place." Venturi details its European, particularly its Italian reception.

115. E. Goncourt and J. Goncourt (1906), pp. 156 ff.

116. As against the queen's. Stanisław Leszczyński sympathized with his daughter in this matter. He was, in so far as he was king, an elected monarch, his Saxon adversary a hereditary one. Inevitably therefore he had some sympathy with republican, if not regicide, ideas.

117. This, Choiseul noted rather maliciously in his diary—but after his dismissal—would not allow him to be damned as long as he upheld the church in his kingdom, in G. P. Gooch (1956), pp. 111 f.

118. It was particularly in the late years of Louis XIV that the Jesuit confessor became a state institution. The power of Le Tellier over Louis XIV was described bitingly by Marmontel (1805), II, p. 225, though Jesuit confessors had already been customary in the royal family since Louis XIII.

119. Some account of the quarrel has been given above. The king's personal entourage was largely composed of the clerical party called *feuillants* after the *porte-feuille* of church livings (which amounted, in revenues, to nearly half of those of the crown) as against the *théatins*, the party of the archbishops, whose principal spokesman had been a Theatine (their main French house was Ste. Anne-la-Royale by Guarini), Louis Boyer, Bishop of Mirepoix, who held the *porte-feuille* which had passed on his death to cardinal de la Rochefoucauld. Boyer's first appointment, Christophe de Beaumont, was the only archbishop who could be seen to be taking the Ten Commandments seriously. In the last years of the reign of Louis XIV, Bossuet, Massillon, and Fénélon occupied high positions in the church, in which they were replaced by men like the Cardinals Dubois, Tencin, and de la Rochefoucauld. De Bernis himself was archbishop of Albi. The position between the king and Parlement was complicated by its invitation for the peers to assemble and the king to appear at it; the more enlightened peers, such as the prince de Conti, the duke of Orléans, the comte de Clermont failed in their pressure on the king to summon the house of peers (F. Diaz, 1962, pp. 55, 72 f.) and the preecho of the States-General of 1789 died, though not quietly. The most recent account of the religious and constitutional aspects of the dispute is given by J. Egret (1970), pp. 50 ff.

120. This was a high preferment. It was recorded in the court circular; the sermons were heard by two memorialists who commented on them: the comte d'Argenson (1859), VIII, pp. 250, 265 ff., 277 f., 284) and the duc de Luynes (1860), X, p. 26; XIII, pp. 148, 221, 228, 247). D'Argenson was scandalized at Laugier's suggestion that the *Parlement* should be abolished, even at the price of blood, although the suggestion did not seem as improbable then as it does now.
    Cf. W. Herrmann (1962), pp. 6 f., on the conflict between the bloodthirsty sentiments of the sermons and the known character of Laugier, amiable and accommodating.

121. At St. Sulpice on Easter of 1748 and 1749; he also preached at Notre-Dame. At Fontainebleau the Advent and Christmas sermons were given in 1749. W. Herrmann (1962), p. 4.

122. The matter was compounded by the unprecedented proposal, whose deviser was one of Madame de Pompadour's protégés, Jean-Baptiste Machault d'Arnouville, controller of finances at the time, to extend the traditional 10 percent crisis levy on estate into a 5 percent tax, to be continued until the extension of the national debt, but *applied also to the clergy*, whose contributions to the Exchequer had hitherto been voluntary. This tax was acceptable to the Parlement, and much resented by the clergy, particularly by the prelates, including the virtuous archbishop of Paris as an attack on clerical privilege (F. Diaz, 1962, pp. 13 ff.). At the same time the archbishop deprived the director of the Hôpital Général de Paris, which was a kind of central office of charities; the Parlement claimed its authority over that institution.

The 5 percent tax was in the end substituted by an *ex gratia* payment of 16 million livres; the affair of the Hôpital involving the king's withdrawal, dragged on.

But both these matters were involved with the problem of the *billets de confession*, which had made the archbishop and his most zealous follower, the parish priest of St. Etienne-du-Mont, extremely unpopular in Paris. See B. Plongeron (1974), pp. 34 ff. I have already mentioned it in connection with Clérisseau's troubles at the academy in Rome. The king's typical indecision in the matter followed the gift of an abbey to the Vicar while the archbishop was exiled.

Apart from the Dominicans, traditionally anti-Jesuit, and involved against them recently in the struggle over the Chinese rites (see above), the regular clergy on the whole sided with the parliamentarians. Many were quasi-Jansenists. This would certainly be true of the Genovefans.

123. While not allowed to renounce their vows, the religious were relatively free to move from one order to another: at any rate canonically. It was often used as a way for the member of an order to become a secular priest, his passage to another order being a fiction in canon law. But in the case of Laugier, it seems connected with the gift of a living, the Priory of St. Sauveur de Ribauté. Passionei makes the procedure explicit in his correspondence; moreover he obtained the brief for free—in exchange for which he expected Laugier to do some small services for him—perhaps connected with his book collecting. See W. Herrmann (1962), p. 9.

There is no question of Laugier's having lapsed from the church or even abandoned his priestly office. The death certificate describes him as "prêtre des Religieux professés de l'ordre de Saint Benoît": there is nothing particularly anticlerical about any of his writings, not even the *History of Venice*.

It is not known when exactly Laugier made the first move, but it could not have been long after the Easter sermon of 1754; perhaps even before. By the September of that year, the king had in fact surrendered to parliamentary pressure. J. Egret (1970), p. 63. At any rate, things had advanced sufficiently in February 1755 for Passionei to have asked Laugier for what he referred to as *mémoires*. The release did not come finally until March 1756. La Curne, the historian of the Troubadours and of Chivalry, has already been discussed.

124. Avignon was at that time still a papal province, governed by Legates, and was not finally annexed by France until 1791.

125. See M. Garden (1970), pp. 538 ff. The academy was founded in 1700 and two members of the better-known Jesuit College, the Trinity, were members from the outset. But the founder, Brossette, was a lawyer; the majority of the academy were nobles (though inevitably *de robe*), and many members, whatever class they belonged to, had been pupils at the College of the Trinity. The academy was incorporated by a royal charter in 1724; the charter also groups the first academy with a second one, *Le Concert*, which had taken the title of Académie des Beaux-Arts. The two academies were not united until 1758. Their influence, if numbers are to be taken as an index, declines in the older academy after 1740, while it grows in the Academy of Fine Arts. Soufflot probably belonged to the first of these academies: J. Mondain-Monval (1918), p. 19. The ms. archives of the two academies were grouped together at their union in 1758: M. Petzet refers to the papers as read to the Académie des Beaux-Arts. Soufflot's other papers (on the state of Vesuvius in June and November 1750 and on the mineral waters at Viterbo—by which he had himself been treated, as witness his letter to Marigny from there on 23 August 1750) were in fact scientific. He also read a paper on his *Salle de Spectacles* in 1753. Interestingly enough, the Canons of the Cathedral (who were all known as "Count-Canon" and had to prove sixteen quarterings of *Ancienne Noblesse* to be admitted to the chapter; de Bernis was a canon until he obtained his archbishopric) did not produce one member until 1775. Another source of Jesuit influence was the proximity of Trévoux, which beside its own *parlement*, being the capital of the sovereign Principality of Dombes, also had a Jesuit college and printing presses: their influence on the Lyons book trade in M. Garden (1970), pp. 464 f. Laugier was to preach the funeral sermon of the Prince de Dombes, who had protected these Jesuit enterprises, but who died in December 1755. It was his last published sermon as a Jesuit.

126. The report of the censor to Malesherbes is quoted in part by W. Herrmann (1962), p. 205; he finds that while there is no fundamental criticism, it does offend *bienséance* by an occasional excess.

127. For the papers by François Delamonce (so L. Hautecoeur; W. Herrmann calls him Ferdinand), see W. Herrmann (1962), pp. 236, 240. Delamonce, who built the Oratory at Avignon, with a heavy Mansartian portal and an amply buttressed dome oval (L. Hautecoeur, III, pp. 330, 374) and who designed the dome on squinches for the Carthusians (for which Soufflot also sent a design from Rome, L. Hautecoeur, III, p. 380; J. Mondain-Monval, 1918, pp. 19, 84 f.), was a successful practitioner at Lyons, doing some *hôtels particuliers* (L. Hautecoeur, III, p. 220) and a monumental Port de l'Hôpital on the Rhone, based on the Porto della Ripetta in Rome. He also worked on the Hôtel-Dieu presumably in competition with Soufflot and designed the chapel for the Jesuit college of the Trinity. Herrmann (1962) also quotes a paper by the lawyer, André Clapasson, author of a popular guide to Lyons under the pen-name Rivière de Brinais (M. Garden, 1970, p. 4) which went through several editions after 1741. See W. Herrmann (1962), pp. 80 f.

128. The chapel was at the center, under a *dome à la Française*, and visible from the four wards in the arms of the cruciform plan. Unfortunately, the most reliable evidence for Soufflot's intentions are the engravings by J.-F. Blondel sometimes bound in *Architecture Françoise*. See J. Mondain-Monval (1918), p. 21, who maintains, without offering evidence, that it was these engravings which attracted Madame de Pompadour's attention. The first stone was laid on 3 January 1741, and work continued until Soufflot's sec-

ond visit to Italy, during which time he also did minor alterations on buildings which were the property of the Hôtel. He presented the scheme to the Academy of Architecture in Paris on 2 May 1747 (*P.V.*, VI, pp. 72, 118) and—presumably in a revised version—on 28 April 1749. The building is discussed by J. Mondain-Monval (1918), pp. 85 ff., 112 ff., who gives an account of the completion with modifications by Soufflot's assistants, Melchior Munet and Toussaint Loyer.

129. In the second half of the century, Lyons was to become the center of French masonry, particularly of occult masonry; so M. Garden (1970), p. 545. There were certainly lodges there before 1750. G. Bord (1908), I, p. 437) listed three; Kloss (1852), I, p. 35, one before 1740. The duc de Villeroy, whose family had sovereign rights over Lyons (M. Garden, 1970, p. 491), succeeded the masonic "martyr," John Coustos, as master of a lodge to which he had himself entered in 1737. It counted among its members the German banker, Christian Baur, who introduced Filippo Farsetti into the lodge (see chapter 8) and who had also acted as the intermediary between Cardinal Fleury and Stanisław Leszczyński when the latter was besieged in Danzig. Two Polish notables, Prince Stanisław Lubomirski, first cousin to the queen, and Count Czapski were also members. If Louis XV did indeed become a mason, he would have been initiated by Villeroy. At any rate, the *honnête personne* who introduced Casanova to freemasonry (1950, III, pp. 114 f.) was encountered at the house of the Marquis de Rochebaron who, partly at the instigation of Villeroy, was attempting to revive the municipal guards of the town (M. Garden, 1970, pp. 524 ff).

130. See W. Herrmann (1962) on the authority of the MS *Journal de l'Inspecteur d'Hémery* (p. 205).

131. I presume that his editorship of the *Gazette de France*, which must, with his priory, have been his main source of income, was in Choiseul's gift, or at any rate within his influence, and that it must have been the implication of the remarks about Laugier being one of the duke's "oldest protégé's" quoted by W. Herrmann (1962), p. 15 and n. 33.

132. On the cult of St. Mary Magdalene at St. Maximin and the Compagnonnage, see above.
    The facade of the Madeleine was in a sense, with the Gabriel screens, the gate of Paris: the main entry from the west, either along the Cours-la-Reine or the Champs-Elysées being blocked by the *Pont-Tournant* and the Tuileries gardens. As I noted above, see n. 63, there was, in any case, a gate (the Porte St. Honoré) on the street, just where it crossed the present Rue de la Paix.

133. The retro-choir is in fact a typical enough arrangement in Italy, particularly in monastic churches; but, as many liturgical writers point out at the time, it is also "primitive," being the arrangement of the Early Christian basilica. This, again, would have been familiar not only from publications on Roman churches, such as Poleni's *Memoria*, 1746, and Fontana's *Templum Vaticanum*, 1694, but from the republished studies of the patristic church, and the work of the Maurist fathers (see chapter 7). It was also the standard arrangement of Orthodox churches. However, in the eighteenth century, its use is related to the very elaborate hierarchy within cathedral chapters. See B. Plongeron (1974), pp. 120 ff.

134. They were clearly identified at the time: see Piganiol de la Force (1765), as St. Augustine, St. Ambrose, St. Gregory, and St. Jerome for the

West, St. Basil Nzanzien, St. Basil the Great, St. John Chrysostom, and St. Athanasius for the East.

135. The use of two orders of different sizes, one inside, one outside a church was sanctioned by the precedent of Paestum: the internal arrangement of the Parthenon, for instance, was not given by David Le Roy (1758). It is worth pointing out that, as he indicated in his paper on proportions to the Lyons Academy (in M. Petzet, 1961, p. 133), the different sizes require slightly different proportions. The internal columns are 10.76 diameters high, the external ones about 10.57. The diameters are related as eleven to seven, a rather odd proportion, which reappears in other buildings as in the Gabriel Place Louis XV.

136. That is how it was read by his contemporaries: see A. Piganiol de la Force (1765), VI, pp. 101 ff.

137. On Perrault's preference for simple ratios, see chapter 1. His column was in fact twenty-eight "small" modules high, one module shorter than Soufflot's which corresponds exactly to Perrault's composite order however, in height.

The eustyle intercolumniation, as specified by Vitruvius, is in fact two and one-quarter diameters, widening to three diameters at the center. But Perrault's view on the architect's freedom to innovate in this matter has already been discussed.

138. The dome went through a radical transformation after Patte's visit to London and whatever may be said about other influences, that of St. Paul's cannot be denied. There are several versions of the dome, most are catalogued by Petzet; a useful summary of profiles in P. Chevallier and D. Rabreau (1977), p. 49; cf. M. Petzet, (1961), pl. 6 f. It would appear that about 1770, Soufflot raised the ribbed, scaffolded dome over the drum left virtually unaltered from the 1764 scheme. This meant that there were three shells, not two as in the previous schemes—which required a windowed attic over the drum order. In 1776–1777, two further schemes appear, both of which were engraved by François Sellier: in one the attached columns of the drum are transformed into an octagonal detached *pteron* round the circular drum; in the other, perhaps later one, the profile is higher and the continuous colonnade is broken rhythmically into eight alternating bays of six detached and four attached columns, so arranged that the edge columns of the "porch" bay could be read as being "in antis" to the walled bay. The scheme, revised again the same year as the second Sellier engraving, was drawn by an assistant of Soufflot's, Renié (he is otherwise unknown to Hautecoeur and Gallet), showing a continuous circular colonnade with only a difference in the profile of the shell and lantern to distinguish it from the finished scheme.

To derive this project from the circular building in Perrault's *Vitruvius*, as was done by some critics—or even Bramante's *Tempietto*—seems beside the point: these were in any case also well known to Wren; and it would seem strange for Soufflot to have waited until 1777 to absorb Perrault's influence.

139. This is exactly what David Le Roy (1764) does in a pamphlet which was, in a sense, the official apologia of the two churches when he invokes the dependence of St. Mark's on St. Sophia, pp. 16 f. They were sufficiently well known for there to be no need to suppose that the young Soufflot made a journey to the Near East; the evidence for and against in M. Petzet (1961), p. 110, who also suggests the possible alternative sources: San Salvatore in Venice and St. Front in Périgueux—which Soufflot himself may after all

have seen. Certainly Cochin (1773), I, p. 36, visited San Salvatore, but he had a printed guide and as usual in Venice, he only concentrates on the paintings.

I have already mentioned the Christian antiquarian literature by the Maurist fathers which poured out from St. Germain des Près, folio volume by folio volume. In their Abbey church, the Maurists maintained a high standard of what might be called liturgical decorum; they were a bastion of learning, moral rectitude, and regular public devotion in the center of Paris rivaling Notre-Dame. Many of them had more or less explicit Jansenist tendencies (B. Plongeron, 1974, pp. 162 ff.). In a way, the—to my mind— underestimated painting of the Mass of St. Martin which Eustache Le Sueur painted for the Benedictines of Marmoutiers near Tours typified their attitude (Louvre 563).

The Gallican liturgical books were eagerly researched by the Maurists: Father Marthène's *De Antiquis Ecclesia Ritibus* in four volumes folio appeared in 1736–1738. But more important even was the work of a secular priest and orientalist and diplomat, Eusèbe Renaudot (1716) whose *Liturgiarum Orientalium Collectio* remained a standard work of reference in spite of its somewhat controversial purpose. They were, of course, not isolated works: Jean Goar's *Euchologion* had been printed in Paris in 1676 (in 800 pages folio) and the Maurist Le Brun wrote a dogmatic dissertation on liturgies which appeared at the same time as Renaudot's book.

140. Laugier, who makes some rather disobliging remarks about the "heaviness" of the dome as compared with the neighboring Val-de-Grâce, criticisms which may well have touched Soufflot (1765), pp. 26 ff, did not object to the pilasters of these piers. But the uniformity of the intercolumniation and square soffits which resulted from it, as well as the cutting of the vaults, all excited Laugier's admiration.

141. The prime examples are, of course, Bernini's Altar of the Chair, where the source of light is visible; the Cornaro Chapel at Sta. Maria della Vittoria (St. Theresa's ecstasy), and the altar of S. Andrea al Quirinale, where the source is invisible. In the earlier scheme, as is evident from the engraving by François-Philippe Charpentier of 1757 and the unsigned section drawing (M. Petzet, 1961, p. 156, no. 3 d), Soufflot intended the high altar to have a "gloria" whose window faced the spectator, and was not even concealed—as it might easily have been—by any projection.

The one possible contemporary precedent in Paris was the Calvary Chapel at St. Roch by Louis-Etienne Boullée of 1754 (J.-M. Pérouse de Monclos, 1969, p. 55), but it did not please. See the disobliging remarks Diderot made about it to Grimm quoted by Pérouse de Montclos (1969).

142. The two publications were an *Ottava rima* rhapsody to celebrate the "eighth wonder of the world" by F. Rodriguez Galán (1732) and a guide to the liturgical delights of the city by F. J. Castañeda of the same year. It was hardly a work to appeal to the Marigny circle, even though its patron, Archbishop Porto-Carrero was largely responsible for the succession of Philip V to the Spanish throne.

143. M. Petzet (1961), p. 162; t, a, and b; for the 1765 edition of Piganiol de la Force, VI, opp. pp. 101 and 103.

144. That this was possible and even advisable was proved by an inverse process: the "correcting" of the bad taste of otherwise admirable medieval buildings by purging their barbarous and grotesque ornament in favor of some in much better taste. This process of architectural bowdlerization was surprisingly popular in the eighteenth century. Michel-Ange Slodtz had re-

decorated that of St. Méri in 1752; Claude Baccarit that of St. Germain l'Auxerrois (which was the parish church of the Louvre and the chapel of the Academy) with the sculptor Louis-Claude Vassé (his brother-in-law), a protégé of Caylus; Caylus (so Cochin, 1880, pp. 32 ff., would have it) had the Slodtz *modèle* rejected by the intermediacy of Mariette. Laugier (1765) had unkind things to say of the remodel of St. Méri (p. 134): he disapproved of the rounding of the pointed arches and of the facing of Gothic pillars with pilasters carrying fragmentary cornices; all this, he considered, broke the harmony of the building. About St. Germain l'Auxerrois—*pace* Cochin—he was very nice; he liked the Gothic pillars encased in fluted circular columns, the capitals made of "correct" moldings and garlands (a method which he thoroughly recommends to anyone wishing to "correct" a Gothic church, pp. 137 f.). The academy, having delegated a commission to examine the Baccarit-Vassé model (24 May 1756; *P.V.*, VI, p. 264) at Marigny's invitation (Cochin, 1880, gives his sceptical opinion about that procedure, pp. 67 f.), named the two Blondels, Soufflot, Contant, and two others, who chose the project which was actually executed in preference to a more ornate one (by the same architect; which is not known). Both Laugier and Cochin, however, disapproved of the Hardouin-Mansart/de Cotte redoing of the choir of Notre-Dame (P. Bourget and G. Cattaui, 1960, pp. 158 f.), who reproduce Mariette's engraving; although Mansart's marble facing is best known from David's *Sacre de Napoléon*; a more detailed image of the high altar, with its *trompe-l'oeil* painting by Nicolas Coustou imitating a sculpture group by Jean Jouvenet, is in the Louvre (440); it was all swept away in Viollet-le-Duc's restoration). About Notre-Dame, Laugier (1753) was disapproving in the *Essai* (p. 156) and scathing in the *Observations* 1765, pp. 132 f. Cordemoy (1714) had already condemned the arrangement (p. 116) but not on stylistic grounds. However these three examples are only isolated but well-known instances of a well-known practice: see L. Hautecoeur (1950), III, pp. 388 ff. The problem of dealing with Gothic architecture at a time when "holy antiquity" provided the unquestionable model for building has been dealt with by E. Panofsky (1968) and R. Wittkower (1974). The general framework has been established by P. Frankl (1960). For his own time, Cochin wrote what many believed: "C'est un problème difficile à résoudre . . . si ayant une église gothique à décorer, on doit volontairement et sciemment chercher une décoration dans le goust manifestement mauvais de ces architectes goths, ou s'il est plus convenable de négliger les rapports de tout ensemble et de faire de la belle architecture dans la partie qui nous est confiée." No one ever really gave a final and convincing answer to Cochin's question: allowing for the changed times, it is still with us.

145. The dome, as it was presented in 1757, was a double shell—internally fairly low, and pierced by oval lunettes which corresponded to rectangular windows on the outside of the drum. The lunettes over the windows let light into the upper shell; the two shells were connected by a spiral staircase, and the outer dome, which was smooth, was topped by a pedestal carrying a statue of the saint. There was no lantern. The outer shell was presumably to be vaulted; there is no indication of any truss. The triangular piers which support the dome are in this scheme already made to project into buttressing pinnacles topped by sculpture: the cornice which runs continuously around them and the base of the dome makes it appear to be an octagonal drum on a square base. But the relation between drum and dome is unhappy and unarticulated (as Laugier rightly said) and this was the most obvious change in the 1764 scheme. The new dome is circular. The pinnacles of the piers are

made to project beyond the square base of the dome in two steps, their outer corners chamfered. Corresponding to the piers on the drum are the pedimented aedicules, their cornices projecting over detached columns backed by pilasters. The edge columns of the circular section are at the same distance from the pilasters, so that the apparent structure of the drum is four detached (in fact presumably three-quarters attached) columns, two piers fronted by columns supporting the pediment, four detached columns and so on, alternating. The middle intercolumniation of the four-column run has a window with a lunette above; so has the aedicule. The alternating blank walls have oval reliefs at the level of the lunette. Over the cornice there is a sparely molded attic, topped by a balustrade. The new element is the capping of the dome which is not curved, but a stepped cone, rising to a platform on which stands the saint's statue, as in the older schemes. There can be little doubt that the immediate source of this device was the newly "discovered" *Medracen*, a vast cylindrical mausoleum, some 60 meters in diameter surrounded by sixty engaged Doric columns. A sketch of it had been communicated to Caylus by some traveler, who had it engraved by Bellicard and published in his memorandum on the reconstruction of the Mausoleum at Halicarnassus (*Mém. Ac. Insr.* 1759, XXVI, p. 321). It is shown with only twenty-four columns, and if the human figures are to be used as a scale, about half the size of the real monument. Still Caylus does apologize for the sketchy nature of his account. The original monument between Constantine/Cyrta and Lambesis is in all probability a Numidian Royal tomb (though nineteenth-century excavators found nothing), Hellenistic-Punic (c. 250 B.C.), and predating the Roman conquest, perhaps by as much as a century. It is somewhat earlier than the *Tombeau de la Chrétienne*, a larger and more famous monument (K'bor-er-Roumia near Tipaza. See S. Gsell, G. Marçais, and G. Yver, 1929, pp. 14 f.) which although much more accessible than the *Medracen*, does not seem to have been so well known.

The other source, the *Medracen* being Doric, was the *Choragic Monument of Lysicrates*, which David Le Roy (1758) had published in his *Ruines*, and which was commonly known as the Lantern of Demosthenes and was part of the property of the French Capuchins. That within this interesting conflation (which meets Laugier's criticism to some extent), there should have been "Gothic" vaulting seems quite symptomatic of the enterprise. The relationship of the heights remains the same; the dome up to the statue base equals the height of the order with its cornice, up to the top of the statue, of the pediment, taken from the top of the steps. The order used, though more slender than Perrault's, preserves Perrault's relation of cornice as one quarter of the column. The column is also one quarter of the whole width of the building, the projecting walls in the transepts being a capital high. The order of the drum is half the height of the big order of the portico; and this is again true of both schemes. What changes the appearance of the building most radically is the high attic above the cornice, with its balustrade and the shallow slope of the steps. There are further "aliquot measurements." The whole height of the building, up to the apex of the sloping steps, is three times the height of the columns. The intercolumniation is three diameters, the windows are one intercolumniation of the portico high by half wide, which is also equal to the stylobate of the internal columns. The order of the dome is half the height of the portico order. The stepped base to a dome, as in the 1757 project, is a reference to the Roman Pantheon, though Borromini's S. Ivo della Sapienza, which has a stepped capping to its dome, ribbed by six flying buttresses, is an earlier essay in combining "classic" and "Gothic" in a way quite unacceptable—as I have already said—to Soufflot and his friends. This precedent is discussed by A. M. Vogt (1969), pp. 158 ff., and at more length by W. Oechslin (1972), pp. 206 ff.

146. The image of the mausoleum, suitably groomed into its Corinthian guise for the maidenly saint, has replaced the more conventional dome over the saint's relics.

147. M. Petzet (1961), fig. 15; the crypt is only colonnaded under the chancel. The other parts were astylar. It was to be entered by two semicircular stairways around the base of the shrine, like the *confessio* of an early basilica. The Doric order of the basement has the diameter of a module of the internal Corinthian order and is as high as the imposts of the interior. It is a rather peculiar Doric, situated on a circular projection which is not a recognizable base as in a Roman Doric; its "Greek" intentions are clear; it is more a kind of circular stylobate than a base. Since it was finished in 1764, it is clearly part of the original scheme.

148. The Hagley folly (J. Mordaunt-Crook, 1972, pp. 96 f., most recently) was presumably a year later or thereabouts. At this point even "Athenian" Stuart hesitated—or at any rate his builder did—to bring the fluted column directly down onto the step without an intervening base.

149. See fig. 235. If not earlier, this might have been a possible time for Cochin to consider the theme of the hero and the Doric order in its Greek form. See above, n. 44.

150. The "key" ornament had already been used by Serlio, but with a consciously "Hellenizing" intention by Neufforge on the title pages of his collections from 1757 onwards and on many of the buildings in them, although the Doric he uses is mostly Perrault's. The most discussed use of the ornament was on the ebony and ormolu furniture which Louis Le Lorrain designed for the financier, Ange-Laurent Lalive de Jully, who, to return to the same circle of people, had obtained the post of *introducteur des ambassadeurs* (marshal of the diplomatic corps in modern parlance) through the agency of Madame de Pompadour. He collected ebony and brass Boule furniture which, to quote Marigny, was already rising in fashion as being more "noble" than the usual mahogany. It is another instance of the return of the *grand goût* of the previous reign about which I have already written enough. The years between the designing of the crypt and its unveiling were the years in which the *goût grec* assumed the scale of a major fashion mania whose symptoms have been discussed by S. Eriksen (1973), pp. 44 ff.

151. See D. Le Roy (1764), pp. 40 ff., which, although critical, is highly appreciative of St. Paul's. But see R. Middleton and D. Watkin (1977), pp. 28 f.

They are, again, a case of the *voûte à la Roussillon*, to which I referred earlier in connection with Contant's St. Madeleine. See M. Petzet (1961), pp. 95 f., 113 ff., and P. Chevallier and D. Rabreau (1977), pp. 32 f.

152. The blocking of the windows was demanded by Quatremère de Quincy in his report of 1791 in order to give the building the more "serious" character it was to assume as a national monument and was carried out soon after that. P. Chevallier and D. Rabreau (1977), p. 55.

153. Light enters the church indirectly, wherever possible; the windows, so light in the drawing, were presumably not transparent—as they do not correspond with the shape of the exterior openings, even when their placing is roughly the same, inside and outside. It seems that this is in direct con-

tradiction of any "rococo" character the building might seem to have (A. Braham, 1971, p. 585) if the description of the downward force of rococo light given by H. Bauer (1962), pp. 32 ff., has any validity.

154. See chapter 6. In spite of all the accusations against Soufflot and his adviser Perronet, it became clear during the nineteenth-century reconstructions that the damage to the stonework of the piers was due to the quality of the stonework, rather than to engineering miscalculations. See M. Petzet (1961), pp. 58, 67 ff.; cf. J. G. Legrand and C. P. Landon (1818), pp. 110 ff.

155. These were studied by A. Braham (1971).

156. These survive in the Louvre, though without their painting. The *chasse*, which rested on them, was taken to the Hôtel de la Monnaie, the saint's body burned on the Place de la Grève on 21 November 1793, the ashes thrown into the Seine. After the Reign of Terror, the *chasse* was returned to St. Etienne-du-Mont, where it remains, but the Virtues stayed in the Louvre.

Soufflot's Corinthian columns of the interior seem to be twice the height of Pilon's four Virtues; it may well be that they provided Soufflot with a "datum" for his dimensions and proportions.

157. Originally the figures were to be the Four Evangelists. These were transferred to the corner of the shrine under the dome. But this iconography was further extended to the whole sculpture of the church. The entry arm of the Greek cross referred to the Old Testament; the right to the Roman church; the left to the Greek church and the choir to the Gallican church. P. Chevallier and D. Rabreau (1977), p. 40.

158. Caylus commented at length on the *pteron* round the tomb in the text on the Mausoleum which I quoted earlier.

159. See above, nn. 141 f.

160. The group of drawings, now in the Avery Library, New York, was published by A. Placzek and others (1972), pp. 13 ff., and is illustrated on plates 6–10.

161. They faced east-southeast, while the windows in the apse would have faced west, and in any case be blocked from direct sunlight by the existing buildings linking the baptistery with the sacristies. The device of a wide flat arch, pierced by five medallions, was used by Bramante at Sta. Maria presso San Satiro and Sta. Maria delle Grazie in Milan; at Genzano, in his scheme for St. Peter's, Palladio had used it in the Villa Poiano. The complex overloaded character of the drawings conceals the way in which Piranesi takes the existing building as his guide: the most prominent element, the columnar screen, takes up the level of the impost of the arches between Borromini's giant Corinthian order. The rather curious sleeved order which Piranesi invents for his screen is the same height as the bronze columns which Pier Paolo Oliveri put around the altar of the Santissimo in the transept about 1600. And from these, by simple operations, he goes on. The whole screen is twice the height of the order; the subscreen is the same height as the double capitals; the intercolumniation of the screen repeats the dimensions of the oculi, and so on.

162. On Cardinal Rezzonico, for whom Piranesi also did some interiors and to whom he dedicated the *Cammini* (as well as carrying out the work at the Maltese Priory on the Quirinal), see chapter 9.

163. A commission such as the one for St. John Lateran would have been a sufficiently public matter for rumors of it to have come to Paris, particularly

in view of the number of Piranesi's friends there. But the detail I mention is too singular to allow of direct influence. But see above, n. 142.

164. As was the goldsmith, Jacques Roëttiers, who cast the medal for the foundation-laying ceremony. Puisieux and Pingré were not ordinary masons, but both masters of a lodge. Pingré did in fact write an ode on the occasion which includes the "significant" couplet about the tender fatherhood of the king; and rhyming on *père*, continues: "Si, pour fonder un temple il prend en mains l'équerre/Dans son frère un maçon voit le plus grand des rois." Quoted by P. Chevallier (1968), pp. 176 f. On Pingré's ecclesiastical role, see B. Plongeron (1974), p. 166. The Maurists were, more than the Genovefans, important in the higher ranks of masonic dignitaries until their collective but discreet withdrawal in 1783. See B. Plongeron (1968), p. 165.

165. The original drawing in sanguine was exhibited in the *salon* of 1765. J. Seznec (1960), III, pp. 230 f. The engraving is by Benoît-Louis Prévost. In some editions it was inserted into the first volume, which had appeared in 1751 (see above). But it is also bound in with volume I of the plates.

166. See his comment in the *salon* of 1765, quoted above. The explanation of the plate in the Encyclopedia (1765, vol. 1, preliminary leaf) simply enumerates the various figures.

167. See chapter 9, n. 144.

168. Corradini died in the Sansevero Palace in 1752, by which time the statue was finished, as well as the terracotta model for the shrouded Christ which was completed after his death by Giuseppe Sammartini and which is now the central figure in the chapel (see above). There is no evidence on when exactly the chapel was finished; probably about 1770. But until his death Corradini was acting as architect of the chapel as well as its sculptor. It would be reasonable to assume that he had the statue placed on the duchess' tomb before Cochin left Naples. But the first guide to the chapel only appeared in 1767, when the high altar (a bas-relief by Antonio Celebrano) was not yet finished. Cochin does not mention the chapel among the buildings he visited in Naples: since he is much more observant about paintings than he is about sculpture, this is not conclusive.

Marino Vasi (1815), pp. 119 f., who seems to have been transcribing the 1767 guide describes the shrouded Christ being placed *"d'un [sic] côté."* But the itinerary does not read as if it had been written by an eyewitness. Don Raimondo's son, Don Vincenzo, achieved quite a different notoriety (H. Swinburne, 1841, I, pp. 136 f.) by that time.

169. The discrepancy is more violent in the architecture than in the sculpture, which in the *Pietatella* is the most faded conventional *barochetto*, using colored marbles, whereas Cochin sets his figures in an Ionic circular temple, though the order is not very "pure" and the clouds do billow about it in a somewhat old-fashioned way.

170. This is clear from the Marigny-Soufflot correspondence about the Gobelins, of which Soufflot had been appointed director (the correspondence was published by J. Mondain-Monval in 1918), but also from the incidental remarks in Cochin's memoirs (1880). Cochin was the most fluent polemist of the group and involved himself in journalistic controversy. He also produced a number of more considerable pieces and satirical prints. On the Mansart-de Cotte *agence*, which worked under Louis XIV first and with his total backing, and then under the strain of the Regency, see above.

171. In Britain, writing about medieval architecture is concerned largely

with antiquarian collection of detail—the important and honorable exception being Wren. There was little technical interest in stone-cutting as a geometrical problem which rescued French "Gothic revivalism" from antiquarian patination. The revaluation of the *voute à la Roussillon* as a common construction was discussed earlier. The Academy in Paris, not just the one in Lyons, was receiving reports about medieval buildings, some of which needed restoration. In particular, Notre-Dame de Dijon received a great deal of attention from Soufflot, who presented a survey of it, done by Jean-Baptiste Jallier, which had been commissioned by Charles-Jean le Jollivet (himself a pupil of Desgodetz, the surveyor of Roman monuments) to the Academy of Architecture (*P.V.*, VII, pp. xxi f., 84 ff., 127 ff.). It was discussed together with Petitot's survey of San Agostino in Piacenza (on 6 December 1762). Notre-Dame became the model of a Gothic church presented by Patte in Blondel's *Cours*, 1771, VI, pp. 206 ff. But see also the way the academy regarded medieval buildings, for instance, the careful examination of Charles de Wailly's report about the structural restoration of the Romanesque church of Ste. Bénigne in Dijon (*P.V.*, VI, pp. xxvi, 140 ff.).

172. This was already stated clearly by E. Frémin (1702), pp. 22 f. But see above, nn. 176, 187.

173. This had already been suggested in the sixteenth century and learnedly asserted by Perrault. But their reasons were disregarded by most writers on architecture and certainly by most architects. The ideology of freemasonry and the presence of Solomon and the five orders on the frontispiece of Anderson's *Constitutions* in their second edition (1738) perpetuated a popular trust in the legend—if only by association.

174. See above, chapter 5, nn. 18, 22–27, 41 and J. Rykwert (1976), pp. 21 ff.

175. The Blondel-Perrault dispute went on occupying architects into the nineteenth century. Soufflot, in his early paper to the Lyons Academy on proportion (in M. Petzet, 1961, pp. 131; read in 1739) confesses that he had always deferred to Blondel's opinions rather than to those of Perrault and that the measurements he took in Roman churches have confirmed his allegiance. Charles-Etienne Briseux, by then an octogenarian, wrote his *Traité du Beau Essentiel* in 1752 to justify the advocacy of harmonic ratios as the basis of all proportion. The title is borrowed from the Malebrancheian Jesuit André (1843, on whom see above) as is the argument about the arbitrary nature of the orders (Y. M. André, 1843, pp. 16 ff.) and the essential nature of harmonic proportion (André, 1843, pp. 66 ff.). The Academy of Architecture, which had always been almost equally divided on the matter, seems to come down on Blondel's side, when his book 5, chapter 16, was read on 15 July 1765, and the following two sessions; Blondel's argument could not be induced completely satisfactorily in his own presentation, but in the present state of science, the Academicians obviously found it acceptable.

Laugier wonders (ironically) at all the trouble to which the aged Briseux had gone to argue a case which anyone of good sense found acceptable. Perrault (1755)—he goes on to say (pp. 108 f.)—had only fought against the necessity of proportion out of pure contrariety (*esprit de contradiction*); and, Laugier says, realized full well that his paradox was absurd. Pure obstinacy made him hold on to it. Instead of arguing against Perrault, Briseux would have done better (according to Laugier) to set out the rules in a satisfactory manner and admit other than harmonic proportions.

Briseux was, of course, appealing, like André, to the color/note value analogy of Newton. But Laugier rejects this, agreeing here with his critic Frézier, who had poured scorn on the pretended scientific argument about proportion, maintaining that there was no strict analogy between hearing and sight (as Perrault had already firmly announced) and that a visual clavichord (an obvious reference to Père Castel, a fellow Jesuit still living in the Jesuit house in Paris at the time) could only be born out of an imagination abounding in peculiarities, but no friend to what is true and soundly reasoned. In spite of his scathing remarks on Perrault's theory, Laugier, of course, admires his architecture and puts the Louvre facade in his preface as a model of greatness.

Laugier therefore dismissed Perrault's Cartesian arguments as quite inapplicable to architecture. Instead he appealed to a mythical type which had an enormous popularity—that of the noble savage. He assimilated the Vitruvian account of the origin of the orders, which he presents as the proper origin of architecture altogether to his preferred myth; and called for a reform of architecture to conform to its mythical prototype. This appeal was much stronger than the reasonable cynosures of Cordemoy on whose reasoning his argument is based, with acknowledgment. And he offers (beyond the timeless justice of the mythical model) rational relationships—of aliquot parts—as the proper ones for an architect to exploit with the rider that not enough is known about them and that research was to be undertaken into this matter—hence his reproach to Briseux. But Blondel's (1765) traditional argument is hardly mentioned. The whole first section of his *Observations* is devoted to the setting down of the appropriate rules, so that presumably Laugier undertook the research in the intervening decade.

176. L. E. Boullée (ed. J.-M. Pérouse de Montclos, 1969) wrote his *Essai* about 1780. He rejected at the outset Perrault's assertion of the arbitrariety of taste but also Blondel's analogy with music. And he attempted to found his theory on "nature," by which he seems to mean an a priori understanding of the regular bodies. He discusses the Blondel-Perrault quarrel at the outset of his book (1969, pp. 60 ff.) and returns to it in his summary (pp. 154 ff.).

177. J.-M. Pérouse de Montclos. The drawing for a Comédie Française building on the Quai Conti is in the Bibliothèque Nationale (fig. 73) and unsigned.

178. The interior has been reassembled. M. Raval and J.-C. Moreux (1946), p. 20, fig. 1. It was also called (after its proprietor) the Café Godeau and was on the corner of the Rue St. Honoré and the street now called Rue de Valois. At least one contemporary critic (Elie Fréron (1763) in his *Année Littéraire*) praises the concept of the "warriors' rest": "tout y est riche, grand, simple et respire la belle et saine antiquité," which is an excellent specimen of the complimentary adjectives of the time.

179. See above. Winckelmann (1767) devoted much attention to it in his *Monumenti Inediti*, pp. 11, 24, 164, 187, 269, but see R. Assunto (1973), pp. 59 f., 107, and much of his "Observations on Ancient Architecture" in the *History*, 1783, III, p. 86. On Mengs' ideas, see above.

180. This was in fact published by Gravelot (Hubert Bourgignon) as a joint work with Cochin in seventeen volumes: an almanac from 1765 to 1781. Altogether 216 engravings, of which 12 were titles. They were divided into arts, sciences (two parts); metaphysical beings, muses, seasons, months, man, moral beings, virtues, and vices (seven parts). These engravings were reprinted as *Iconologie par Figures* in four volumes without a date, and with different titles and text. For the bibliographical details of both

editions, see H. Cohen (1876), pp. 176 f. It was a very popular work. See also S. Rocheblave (1927), pp. 81 ff.

181. Delafosse's plates were in fact engraved and printed in 1767, and the collection enlarged to include a number of pieces of furniture. Delafosse was not a member of the academy, though a gift of his book was gratefully acknowledged (*P.V.*, VIII, p. 34). He may be the same Delafosse who presented some drawings to the academy in July 1771 (p. 104). On his activities as an architect, see S. Eriksen (1974), p. 170; and M. Gallet (1972), pp. 22, 60 f., 70 f., 117. His book was reprinted in Holland without date and with a Dutch text.

182. On the importance of allegory and its composition, particularly with reference to the origins of the Académie des Inscriptions in the *Petite Académie*, see above.

183. The status of the hieroglyph in Diderot's thinking is discussed by D. Funt (1968), pp. 55 f. Diderot echoes J. J. Rousseau's (1815) eulogy of the hieroglyph in the *Essai sur l'Origine des Langues*, pp. 505 ff. Cf. J. Starobinski (1974), pp. 373 ff.

184. This, as I have suggested, was the assumption made by Boullée; it was shared by Durand and his pupils at the Ecole Polytechnique. But it was, as I pointed out earlier, already the reading of Perrault which Wren had proposed—to himself, in manuscript at any rate, and later, of course, in public with the printing of the *Parentalia* in 1750.

185. See W. Oechslin in *G.B.A.*, April 1971, pp. 201 ff.; and A. Perez-Gomez (1977), pp. 150 ff.

186. It had, of course, been revived by the Encyclopedia article as a controversial matter. The academy started reading the article on 28 July 1777, and continued on 4 August 1777; it was read again, in conjunction with Le Camus de Mézières' *Génie de l'Architecture* on 12 June 1781, and continued with interruptions until 18 July 1781 (*P.V.*, VIII, pp. 309 f.; IX, pp. 22 ff., 50). See also W. Weisbach (1947), pp. 9 ff.

187. J.-N.-L. Durand (1802). He divided all forms into three classes: the approximate ones derived from the nature of materials; the more precise ones derived from custom and history (of which the orders are the most important), and those derived from a priori geometrical principles, which being the simplest to understand, are also the most important (pp. 53 ff.). While this echoes the previous debates, it also reflects the new status of geometry as the overriding ordering procedure. It is a new descriptive geometry which has no room for the subtleties of earlier speculation.

Giovanni Battista Pittoni, Monument to Isaac Newton.

Bibliography

Bibliographical categories include books and articles, classical sources, and periodicals. Works cited in the notes that are not included in the principal bibliography may be found in the bibliographical addenda, immediately following the periodicals listing.

Books and Articles

Abrantés, Laure Permon Junot, Duchesse d', *Les Salons de Paris: Tableux et Portraits du Grand Monde,* Brussels, 1837.

Abravanel, Judah (Leone Ebreo), *Dialoghi d'Amore,* Rome, 1535.

Académie des Inscriptions et Belles-Lettres, *Histoire de l'Académie depuis son Établissement jusqu'à Présent,* Paris, 1717–1843.

Académie de France à Rome. *See* Anatole de Montaiglon.

Accademia Ercolanese di Archeologia, *Antichità di Ercolano,* Naples, 1755–1792.

Acton, Harold, *The Bourbons of Naples* (1734–1825), London, 1956.

Adam, Antoine, *Histoire de la Littérature Française au XVIIe Siècle,* Paris, 1948–1956; new ed., 1962–1968.

Adam, Antoine, *Les Libertins au XVIIe Siècle,* Paris, 1964.

Adam, Robert, and Adam, James, *The Works in Architecture,* London, 1773–1778; third volume, 1822.

Addison, Joseph, *The Works,* London, 1721.

Addleshaw, G. W. O., and Etchells, F., *The Architectural Setting of Anglican Worship,* London, 1948.

Adhémar, Jean, *Influence Antique dans l'Art du Moyen Age Français,* London, 1939.

Agrippa Cornelius (Heinrich von Nettesheim), *De Occulta Philosophia,* Antwerp, 1531.

Agrippa Cornelius (Heinrich von Nettesheim), *Three Books of Occult Philosophy or Magic,* edited by W. F. Whitehead, New York, 1971.

Alberti, Leone Battista, *De Re Aedificatoria,* translated J. Leoni, edited by J. Rykwert, London, 1955.

Alberti, Leone Battista, *On Painting and On Sculpture,* edition with introduction and notes by Cecil Grayson, London, 1972.

Algarotti, Francesco, *Il Newtonismo per le Dame, ovvero, Dialoghi sopra la Luce e i Colori,* Naples, 1737.

Algarotti, Francesco, *Opere del Conte Algarotti, Edizione Novissima* (with the "Memorie intorno alla vita ed agli scritti del Conte F. Algarotti," by D. Michelessi, ed. by F. Aglietti), Venice, 1791–1794.

Algarotti, Francesco, *Opere Scelte,* Milan, 1823.

Allan, C. W., *Jesuits at the Court of Peking,* Shanghai, n.d.

Allan, Mea, *The Tradescants: Their Plants, Gardens, and Museum, 1570–1662,* London, 1964.

Allen, R. J., *The Clubs of Augustan London,* Cambridge, Mass., 1933.

Allier, Raoul, *La Cabale des Dévots: 1627–1666,* Paris, 1902.

Alparone, G., "Note sul Cristo Velato nella Cappella Sansevero a Napoli," in *Bollettino d'Arte*, XLII (1957).

Amelot de la Houssaye, Abraham-Nicolas, *Histoire du Gouvernement de Venise*, Paris, 1676.

Anderson, James, D. D., *The Constitutions of the Free-Masons, Containing the History, Charges, Regulations, etc., of that Most Ancient . . . Fraternity*, London, 1723.

Anderson, James, D. D., *The New Book of Constitutions of the Fraternity of Free and Accepted Masons . . . Collected and Digested by Order of the Grand Lodge, from their Old Records . . . and Lodge-Books . . . by J. A.*, London, 1738.

Anderson, James, D. D., *Royal Genealogies: or the Genealogical Tables of Emperors, Kings, and Princes from Adam to These Times*, London, n.d.

André, J. *Oeuvres Philosophiques du Père A . . .*, edited by Victor Cousin, Paris, 1843.

[Andreae, Johann Valentin], *The Hermetick Romance: or the Chymical Wedding . . .*, translated by E. Foxcroft, London, 1690.

Andreae, Johann Valentin, *Christianopolis* (translated as *Christianopolis, an Ideal State of the Seventeenth Century* by Felix Emil Held), New York, 1916.

Andreae, Johann Valentin, *Les Noces Chymiques de Christian Rosencreutz*, traduit . . . et suivi des commentaires . . . par Augier, Paris, 1928.

Androuet du Cerceau, Jacques, *Les Plus Excellents Bastiments de France*, Paris, 1576–1607.

Anthony, E. W., *Early Florentine Architecture and Decoration*, Cambridge, Mass., 1927.

Antonini, Carlo, *Il Vignola illustrato proposto da G. B. Stampani e C. A.*, Rome, 1770. *See also* Barozzi; Vignola.

Antonini, G., *La Lucania: Discorsi*, Naples, 1795.

Argan, Giulio Claudio, *Studi sul Neoclassicismo*, from *Storia dell'Arte*, VII–VIII, 1970.

Argenson, René Louis de Voyer de Paulmy, Marquis d', *Journal et Mémoires*, Paris, 1859–1867.

(Arnauld, Antoine, and Lancelot, Claude), *Grammaire Générale et Raisonnée*, Paris, 1660.

Arnold, Klaus, *Johannes Tritheimius (1462–1516)*, Würzburg, 1971.

Arnold, Paul, *Histoire des Rose-Croix et les Origines de la Franc-Maçonnerie*, Paris, 1955.

Arnold, Paul, *La Rose-Croix et ses Rapports avec la Franc-Maçonnerie: Essai de Synthèse Historique*, Paris, 1970.

Arnott, James A., and Wilson, John, *Le Petit Trianon, Versailles*, New York, 1929.

Arts Council, *The Age of Neo-Classicism*, catalog of the fourteenth exhibition of the Council of Europe, London, 1972.

Arundell, T., *Historical Reminiscences of the City of London and its Livery Companies*, London, 1869.

Ashmole, Elias, *The Institutions, Laws, and Ceremonies of the Most Noble Order of the Garter*, London, 1672.

Assunto, Rosario, *Stagioni e Ragioni nell'Estetica del Settecento*, Milan, 1967.

Assunto, Rosario, *L'Antichità comme Futuro*, Milan, 1973.

Aubrey, John, *Lives*, edited by A. Powell, London, 1949.

Bacon, Francis, Lord Verulam, "A Discourse of the Wisdom of the Ancients," translated by Sir Arthur Gorges, in *Essays*, London, 1668.

Bacon, Francis, *The Essays, or Counsels Civil and Moral and Wisdom of the Ancients*, by Francis Lord Verulam, edited by B. Montagu, Esq., London, 1852.

Bacon, Francis (Lord Verulam), *Works*, edited by J. Spedding and R. L. Ellis, D. D. Heath, London, 1859–1870.

Bacon, Francis, *Essays, Advancement of Learning, New Atlantis and Other Pieces*, selected and edited by R. Foster-Jones, New York, 1937.

Badolle, Maurice, *L'Abbé Jean-Jacques Barthélemy*, Paris, 1926.

Baillière, J.-B., et fils (editors), *Le Régime de Pythagore d'après le Docteur Cocchi; De la Sobriété . . . par L. Cornaro; Le Vrai Moyen . . . par L. Lessius*, Paris, 1880.

Baldinucci, F., *Vita di Bernini*, Milan, 1948.

Ballantyre, Archibald, *Voltaire's Visit to England, 1726–1729*, London, 1893.

Balteau, J.; Barroux, M.; Prevost, M.; D'Amat, R.; and Limouzin-Lamothe, R., *Dictionnaire de Biographie Française*, Paris, 1933–.

Baltrušaitis, J., *Essai sur la Légende d'un Mythe; La Quête d'Isis: Introduction à l'Egyptomanie*, Paris, 1967.

Baltrušaitis, J., "Un Musée des Miroirs," *MACULA* 2, 1978.

Balzano, F., *L'Antica Ercolano, ovvero la Torre del Greco tolta all'Obblio*, Naples, 1688.

Barbet, L-A., *Les Grandes Eaux de Versailles*, Paris, 1907.

Barbier, E. J. F., *Journal Historique et Anecdotique du Règne de Louis XV*, edited by A. de la Villegille, Paris, 1844–1856.

Barchillon, Jacques, "Les Frères Perrault," *Revue du XVIIe Siècle*, LVI 1962.

Barozzi, Giacomo, called Il Vignola. *See* Vignola; Ziborghi, G.

Barozzi, Giacomo, called Il Vignola, *Regola delli cinque Ordini d'Architettura*, Venice, 1596.

Barrow, I., *The Mathematical Works of I.B. D.D.*, edited for Trinity College by W. Whewell, Cambridge, 1860.

Barthélemy, J. J., *Travels in Italy, by the late Abbé Barthélemy, Author of the Travels of Anacharsis the Younger; in a Series of Letters Written to the Celebrated Count Caylus*, London, 1802.

Barthes, R., *Microcosme*, Paris, 1975.

Bartholmess, Christian, *Huet, Evêque d'Avranches ou le Scepticisme Théologique*, Paris, 1850.

Bassi, E., *Architettura del Sei e Settecento a Venezia*, Naples, 1962.

Batten, M. I., "The Architecture of Dr. Robert Hooke F.R.S." in *Walpole Society*, Vol. XXV, pp. 83 ff, London, 1937.

Battisti, E., *L'Antirinascimento*, Milan, 1962.

Bauer, Hermann, *Rocaille*, Berlin, 1962.

Baylot, Jean, *Dossier Français de la Franc-Maçonnerie Régulière*, avec une introduction par Ernest van Hecke, Paris, 1965.

Belevitch-Stankevitch, H., *Le Goût Chinois en France au Temps de Louis XIV*, Paris, 1910.

[Belgrado, Jacopo], *Dell'Architettura Egiziana, Dissertazione d'un Corrispondente dell'Accademia delle Scienze di Parigi*, Parma, 1786.

Bell, W. G., *The Great Fire of London*, London, 1920.

Bellori, G. P., *Le Vite de' Pittori, Scultori e Architetti Moderni*, edited E. Borea and G. Previtali, Turin, 1976.

Bellori, G. P., *Fragmenta Vestigii Veteris Romae, ex Lapidibus Farnesianis Nunc Primum in Luce Edita*, Rome, 1673.

Benoist, Luc, *Le Compagnonnage et les Métiers*, Paris, 1966.

Benot, Yves, ed., *Diderot et Falconet: Le Pour et le Contre*, Paris, 1958.

Bentham, James, *History of Ely Cathedral*, London, 1771.

Bérard, A., *Histoire de l'Imprimerie Royale au Louvre*, Paris, 1868.

Berengo, Marino, *La Società Veneta alla Fine del Settecento*, Florence, 1956.

Beresford-Chancellor, E., *The Lives of British Architects*, London, 1909.

Berger, Robert W., *Antoine Le Pautre*, New York, 1969.

Bergot, François, *L'Hôtel de Ville de Rennes*, Rennes, 1963.

Berkeley, G., *Works*, edited by A. Campbell-Fraser, Oxford, 1901.

Berkeley, G., *Works*, edited by A. Luce and T. E. Jessep, London, 1964.

Bernard-Maitre, Henri, *Sagesse Chinoise et Philosophie Chrétienne*, Paris, 1935.

[Bernis, François Joachim de Pierre de], *Oeuvres Complètes de M. le C. de B****, nouvelle édition, London (?), 1786.

Bianconi, G. L., *Lettere . . . al Segretario dell'Accademia Clementina di Bologna. Sopra il Libro del Canonico Luigi Crespi . . . Intitolato Felsina Pittrice, Vite de' Pittori Bolognesi*, Roma, 1769; Milan, 1802.

Bibliotheca Veterum Patrum Antiquorumque Scriptorum Ecclesiasticorum, Postrema Lugduniensi Longe Locupletior atque Accuratior, cura et studio Andreae Gallandii, Venice, 1765–1781.

Billingsley, H., *The Elements of Geometrie . . . of Euclide of Megara . . . Translated into the English Toung . . . with a very Fruitfull Preface Made by M. J. Dee Specifying the Chief Mathematicall Sciences, What They Are, and Whereunto Commodious,* London, 1570.

Billy, André, *Les Frères Goncourt,* Paris, 1954.

Bingham, M., *Masks and Façades,* London, 1974.

Birch, Thomas, *The History of the Royal Society of London,* with introduction by A. R. Hall and bibliographical note by Marie Boas Hall, New York and London, 1968.

Blanc, Charles, *Le Trésor de la Curiosité Tiré des Catalogues de Ventes de Tableaux, Desseins, Estampes, Livres, Marbres, Bronzes, Ivoires, Terres Cuites, Vitraux, Médailles, Porcelaines, Meubles, Emaux, Laques et Autres Objets d'Art* . . . , 2 vols. Paris 1857–1858.

Bloch, Marc, *La Société Féodale,* Paris, 1949.

Blomfield, Sir Reginald, *A History of Renaissance Architecture in England,* London, 1897.

Blomfield, Sir Reginald, *A History of French Architecture from the Death of Mazarin till the Death of Louis XV,* London, 1921.

Blondel, F., *Cours d'Architecture Enseigné dans l'Académie royale de l'Architecture,* 2nd ed., Paris and Amsterdam, 1698.

Blondel, J.-F., *De la Distribution des Maisons de Plaisance, et de la Décoration des Edifices en Général,* Paris, 1737; reprint, Farnborough, 1967.

Blondel, J.-F., *Discours sur la Manière d'Étudier l'Architecture et les Arts qui Sont Relatifs à Celui de Bâtir,* prononncé par M. Blondel, architecte à Paris à l'ouverture de son deuxième cours public sur l'architecture le 16 juin 1747.

Blondel, J.-F., *L'Architecture Françoise, ou Recueil des Plans, Élévations, Coupes, et Profils des Eglises, Maisons Royales, Palais . . . de la France,* Paris, 1752–1756.

Blondel, J.-F., *Fête Publique Donnée par la Ville de Paris à l'Occasion du Mariage de Monseigneur le Dauphin,* 13 February 1747.

Blondel, J.-F., *Cours d'Architecture, ou traité de la Décoration, Distribution, et Construction des Bâtiments,* edited by M. Patte, 9 vols., Paris, 1771–1777.

Blondel, J.-F., *L'Homme du Monde Éclairé par les Arts,* Paris, 1774.

Blondel, J.-F., *See* Vignola, Giacomo Barozzi.

Blum, Hans, *Quinque Columnarum Exacta Descriptio atque Delineatio cum Symmetrica earum Distributione Conscripta per I.B.,* Zürich, 1550.

Blunt, Anthony, *François Mansart and the Origins of French Classical Architecture,* London, 1941.

Blunt, Anthony, *Art and Architecture in France, 1500–1700,* Harmondsworth, 1953.

Blunt, Anthony, *Nicolas Poussin,* London, 1966.

Blunt, Anthony, "Naples as Seen by French Travellers, 1630–1780," in F. Haskell et al., *The Artist and the Writer in France,* Oxford, 1974.

Blunt, Anthony, "Some Uses and Misuses of the Terms Baroque and Rococo As Applied to Architecture," *British Academy Proceedings* 158 (1972, 1974).

Boas, M., *Robert Boyle and Seventeenth-Century Chemistry*, Cambridge, 1958.

Bodnar, E. W., SJ, *Cyriacus of Ancona and Athens* (Collection Latomus XLIII), Brussels, 1960.

Boehme, Jakob, *Of Christ's Testaments, viz: Baptisme and the Supper* . . . Translated by J. Sparrow, London, 1652.

Boileau-Despréaux, Nicolas, *Oeuvres,* avec des éclaircissements historiques, nouvelle édition revue, corrigée et augmentée, The Hague, 1722.

Boime, A., *The Academy and French Painting in the Nineteenth Century*, London, 1971.

Boissard, Jean-Jacques, *Habitus Variarum Orbis Gentium*, Oppenheim, 1581.

Boissard, Jean-Jacques, *De Divinatione et Magicis Praestigiis, Quarum Veritas ac Vanitas Exponitur per Descriptionem Deorum Fatidicorum Qui Olim Responsa Dederunt . . . Adjunctis . . . Omnium Effigiebus, ab Ipso Autore e Gemmis . . . Antiquis ad Vivum Delineatis, jam Modo . . . Aeri Incisis per J. J. de B.* Oppenheim, n.d.

Bonnet, Joseph, *Lettre Écrite à Musala, Homme de Loy à Hispaham, sur les Moeurs et la Religion des François et sur la Querelle entre les Jésuites et les Jansénistes*, Paris, 1716.

Booz, Paul, *Der Baumeister der Gotik*, Berlin, 1956.

Bord, Gustave, *La Franc-Maçonnerie en France: Des Origines à 1815*, Paris, 1908.

Borgerhoff, E. B. O., *The Freedom of French Classicism*, Princeton, N.J., 1956.

Borromini, F., *Opera . . . Cavata da suoi Originali; Cioè, la Chiesa e Fabrica della Sapienza di Roma, con le Vedute in Prospettiva e con lo Studio delle Proporzioni Geometriche, Piante, Alzate, Profili e Spaccati*, Rome, 1720.

Borromini, F. *See* Piazzo, M. del.

Börsch-Supan, E., *Garten-, Landschafts- und Paradiesmotive im Innenraum*, Berlin, 1967.

Boscarino, Salvatore, *Juvarra Architetto*, Rome, 1973.

Bosio, Antonio, *Roma Sotterranea. Opera Postuma . . . Compita, Disposta & Accresciuta dal M. R. P. Giovanni Severani da S. Severino . . . Nella quale si tratta de' sacri cimiterii di Roma . . .*, Publicata dal Commendatore Fr. Carlo Aldobrandino, Rome, 1632.

Bottari, G., *Raccolta di Lettere sulla Pittura, Scultura ed Architettura*, Milan 1822–1825.

Bottineau, Yves, *L'Art d'Ange-Jacques Gabriel à Fontainebleau*, Paris, 1962.

[Bouhours, Dominique, SJ], *Doutes sur la Langue Françoise Proposez à*

Messieurs de l'Académie Françoise par un Gentilhomme de Province, Paris, 1674.

[Bouhours, Dominique, SJ], *La Manière de Bien Penser dans les Ouvrages d'Esprit,* Paris, 1709.

[Bouhours, Dominique, SJ], *Pensées Ingénieuses des Anciens et des Modernes,* Paris, 1734.

Boulainvilliers, Henri, Comte de, *Etat de la France,* London, 1737.

Bourget, Pierre, and Cattaui, Georges, *Jules Hardouin-Mansart,* Paris, 1956.

Boyer, Abel, *Le Tour de France d'un Compagnon du Devoir.* Preface by Daniel Halévy, Paris, 1957.

Boyceau, Jacques, *Traité du Jardinage selon les Raisons de la Nature et de l'Art,* Paris, 1638.

Braham, Allan, "The Drawings for Soufflot's Sainte-Geneviève," *Burlington Magazine* CXIII (October 1971), pp. 582 ff.

Braham, Allan, and Smith, Peter, *François Mansart,* London, 1973.

Braham, Allan, "Funeral Decorations in Early Eighteenth Century Rome," *Victoria and Albert Museum Brochure 7,* London, 1975.

Brault, Eliane, *Psychanalyse de l'Initiation Maçonique,* Paris, 1975.

Bray, R., *La Formation de la Doctrine Classique en France,* Paris, 1927.

Brelich, A., *Gli Eroi Greci,* Rome, 1958.

Brémond, Henri, *Histoire Littéraire du Sentiment Religieux en France,* Paris, 1923–1926.

Brett, R. L., *The Third Earl of Shaftesbury,* London, 1951.

Brett-James, N. G., *The Growth of Stuart London,* London, 1935.

Brigante Colonna, G., *Porporati e Artisti nella Roma del Settecento: Albani, Winckelmann, Kaufmann, Goethe,* Rome, n.d.

Briggs, M. S., *The Architect in History,* Oxford, 1927.

Brinckmann, A. E., *Die Baukunst des 17. und 18. Jahrhunderts,* Berlin, 1922.

Brinkley, R. F., *Arthurian Legend in the Seventeenth Century,* London, 1967.

Briseux, C. E., *L'Art de Bâtir des Maisons de Campagne,* Paris, 1756; reprinted Farnborough, 1966.

Britton, J., *Cathedral Antiquities,* London, 1814–1836.

Brody, Jules, *French Classicism: A Critical Miscellany,* Englewood Cliffs, N. J., 1966.

Broedersen, Nicolaus, *De Usuris Licitis et Illicitis,* Utrecht-Delft, 1743.

Brookner, Anita, *Greuze,* London, 1972.

Brosses, Charles de, *Lettres Familières Ecrites d'Italie en 1739 et 1740 par C. de B.,* 3rd ed., Paris, 1889.

Brown, Harcourt, *Scientific Organizations in Seventeenth-Century France,* Baltimore, 1934.

Browne, Sir Thomas, *Works* (edited by G. Keynes), London, 1964.

Brugmans, Henri L., *Le Séjour de Christian Huygens à Paris et ses Relations avec les Milieux Scientifiques Français suivi de son Journal de Voyage à Paris et à Londres,* Paris, 1935.

Brunelli, A., *Un' Amica del Casanova*, Milan and Palermo, 1924.

Brusantin, Manlio, *Illuminismo e Architettura del '700 Veneto,* catalog, Castelfranco Veneto, 1972.

Buchdahl, Gerd, *The Image of Newton and Locke in the Age of Reason,* London, 1961.

Burckhardt, C. J., *Richelieu and his Age,* London, 1971.

Burgon, S. J., *The Life and Times of Sir Thomas Gresham,* London, 1839.

Burke, Edmund, *A Philosophical Enquiry into the Origin of our Ideas of the Sublime and Beautiful,* London, 1757; reprinted 1759.

[Burlington, Lord,] *Apollo of the Arts, Lord Burlington and his Circle,* catalog, John Wilton-Ely, Nottingham, 1973.

Burr, William H., *Ancient and Modern Engineering and the Isthmian Canal,* New York, 1903.

Bury, J. B., *The Idea of Progress,* London, 1932.

Caccia, E., *Carattere e Caratteri nelle Commedie del Goldoni*, Venice 1959.

Cacérés, Benigno, *Le Compagnon Charpentier de Nazareth,* Paris, 1974.

Calabi, A., *La Gravure Italienne au XVIIIe Siècle,* Paris, 1931.

Calvesi, Maurizio, *G. B. Piranesi e Francesco Piranesi*, catalog, Calcografia Nazionale, Rome, 1967–1968.

Calvesi, Maurizio, and Monferini, Augusta. *See* Focillon, Henri.

Camden, William, *Britannia: Sive Florentissimorum Regnorum Angliae, Scotiae, Hiberniae, et Insularum adiacentium ex Intima Antiquitate Chorographica Descriptio,* London, 1586.

Campanella, T., *Civitas Solis,* edited by Norberto Bobbio, Turin, 1941; edited by A. Seroni, Milan, 1962.

Campbell, Colen. *See Vitruvius Britannicus.*

Cange, Charles Du Fresne du, *Glossarium Mediae et Infimae Latinitatis, Conditum a C.D.F. Domino du Cange; Auctum a Monachis Ordinis s. Benedicti, cum Supplementis Integris d.P. Carpenterii, Adelungii, Aliorum, suisque, Digessit G.A.L. Henschel; Sequuntur Glossarium Gallicum, Tabulae, Indices Auctorum et Rerum, Dissertationes. Editio Nova, Aucta Pluribus Verbis Aliorum Scriptorum a Leopold Favre.* Nouveau Tirage, Paris, 1937–1938.

Cantor, Moritz, *Vorlesungen ueber die Geschichte der Mathematik,* Leipzig, 1898.

Caponigri, A. Robert, *Time and Idea: The Theory of History in Giambattista Vico,* Notre Dame, Indiana, 1968.

Caramella, Santino, *Dialoghi d'Amore,* A cura di S.C., Bari, 1929.

Cardano, Girolamo, *Hieronymi Cardani Mediolanensis . . . opera omnia*, edited by Charles Spon, Leyden, 1663.

Carew Hazlitt, W., *The Livery Companies of the City of London*, London and New York, 1892.

Carlyle, Thomas, *History of Frederic II of Prussia*, London, 1888.

Carré, Jacques, *Lord Burlington et son Cercle*, unpublished typescript.

Carritt, E. F., *The Theory of Beauty* (2d edition), London, 1923.

Casanova de Seingalt, J., *Histoire de ma Vie*, Paris and Wiesbaden, 1960–1962.

Cassirer, Ernst, *Substance and Function*, Chicago and London, 1923.

Cassirer, Ernst, *Individuo e Cosmo nella Filosofia del Rinascimento*, Florence, 1935.

Cassirer, Ernst, *The Philosophy of the Enlightenment*, Boston, 1955.

Cassirer, Ernst, *Platonic Renaissance in England*, New York, 1970.

Castell, Robert, *The Villas of the Ancients Illustrated*, London, 1728.

Castells, F. de P., *English Freemasonry in its Period of Transition, A.D. 1600–1700*, London, 1931.

Cataneo, Pietro, *I Quattro Primi Libri di Architettura*, Venice, 1554.

Cavallari-Murat, A., "Alcuni Contributi di Simone Stratico alla Storia del *De Re Aedificatoria* dell'Alberti," *Atti e Rassegna Tecnica della Società degli Ingegneri e degli Architetti in Torino*, N.S., 20, 7 (July 1966).

Cavallari-Murat, Augusto, *Giovanni Poleni nel Bicentenario della Morte*, Padua, 1963.

Caylus, Anne Claude Philippe de Tubières, Comte de, *Tableaux Tirés de l'Iliade, de l'Odyssée d'Homère et de l'Eneide de Virgile; avec des Observations Générales sur le Costume*, Paris, 1752.

Caylus, Anne Claude Philippe de Tubières, Comte de, "Dissertation sur le Tombeau de Mausole," in *Mémoires . . . de l'Académie des Inscriptions*, Vol. 26, Paris, 1752–1754.

Caylus, Anne Claude Philippe de Tubières, Comte de, *Recueil d'Antiquités Egyptiennes, Etrusques, Grecques et Romaines*, Paris, 1752–1767.

Caylus, Anne Claude Philippe de Tubières, Comte de, *Oeuvres Badines et Galantes du Comte de Caylus* (Ed. Radeville et Deschamps), Paris, 1920.

Cayrol, L. N. de, *Essai sur la Vie et les Ouvrages de Gresset*, Amiens and Paris, 1844.

Cecil, Evelyn (Lady Amherst), *A History of Gardening in England*, London, 1910.

Celano, Carlo, *Notizie del Bello, dell'Antico e del Curioso che Contengono le Reali Ville di Portici, Resina . . .*, Naples, 1792.

Cellini, Benvenuto, *Memoirs*, edited by Thomas Roscoe, London, 1823.

Chambers, E. K., *The Elizabethan Stage*, Oxford, 1951.

Chambers, Sir William, *A Treatise on Civil Architecture in which the Principles of that Art Are Laid Down*, London, 1759, third edition, 1791.

Chambers, Sir William, *A Treatise on the Decorative Part of Civil Architecture*, edited by J. Gwilt, London, 1825.

Chapuis, Alfred, and Droz, Edmond, *Les Automates. Figures Artificielles d'Hommes et d'Animaux: Histoire et Technique*, Neuchatel, 1949.

Chassinand-Nogaret, Guy, "Une Elite Insulaire au Service de l'Europe: Les Jacobites au XVIIe Siècle," *Annales*, XXVIII, 5 (1973).

Chavannes, E., *Les Mémoires Historiques de Se-ma Ts'ien*, Paris, 1895–1905.

Cheke, Sir Marcus, *The Cardinal de Bernis*, London, 1958.

Chevallier, Pierre, *Les Ducs sous l'Acacias*, Paris, 1964.

Chevallier, Pierre, *La Première Profanation du Temple Maçonique*, Paris, 1968.

Chevallier, Pierre, *Histoire de la Franc-Maçonnerie Française*, Paris, 1974.

Chevallier, Pierre, and Rabreau, Daniel, *Le Panthéon*, Paris, 1977.

Chinard, G., *L'Exotisme Américain dans la Littérature Française au XVIe Siècle*, Geneva, 1970.

Chippendale, Thomas, *The Gentleman and Cabinet-Maker's Director; Being a Large Collection of the Most Elegant and Useful Designs of Household Furniture in the Gothic, Chinese and Modern Taste Including . . . to Which Is Prefixed a Short Explanation of the Five Orders . . . : With Proper Directions for Executing the Most Difficult Pieces . . .* , London, 1754.

Chippendale, Thomas, *The Gentleman and Cabinet-Maker's Director; Being a Large Collection of the Most Elegant and Useful Designs of Household Furniture, in the Most Fashionable Taste. Including a Great Variety of . . . To Which is Prefixed a Short Explanation of the Five Orders . . .* , third edition, London, 1762.

Choderlos de Laclos, Pierre A. F., *Oeuvres Complètes*, texte établi et annoté par M. Allem, Paris, 1959.

Choisy, François Timoléon, Abbé de, *Mémoires pour Servir à l'Histoire de Louis XIV*, par feu M. l'Abbé de Choisy, Utrecht, 1727.

Christian, A., *Débuts de l'Imprimerie en France*, Paris, 1905.

Cicognara, Leopoldo, *Storia della Scultura dal suo Resorgimento in Italia Fino al Secolo di Napoleone, per Servire di Continuazione alle Opere di Winckelmann e di d'Agincourt*, Venice, 1813–1818.

Cini Foundation Papers, *Civiltà Veneziana del Quattrocento*, Florence, 1957.

Cini Foundation Papers, *Civiltà Veneziana del Rinascimento*, Florence, 1958.

Cini Foundation Papers, *Civiltà Veneziana del Settecento*, Florence, 1960.

Cini Foundation Papers, *Civiltà Veneziana nell'età barocca*, edited by A. Malraux et al., Florence, 1959.

Ciucci, G., *La Piazza del Popolo*, Rome, 1974.

Clarac, Charles Othon Frédéric J.-B., Comte de, *Description Historique et Graphique du Louvre et des Tuileries,* Paris, 1853.

Clarac, Charles Othon Frédéric J.-B., Comte de, *Répertoire de la Statuaire Grecque et Romaine,* Paris, 1897.

Clark, Kenneth, *The Gothic Revival: An Essay in the History of Taste,* Harmondsworth, 1964.

Clément, P., *Lettres, Instructions, et Mémoires de Colbert,* Paris, 1861–1882.

Clérisseau, C., and Legrand, J.-G., *Monuments de Nîmes (Antiquités de la France,* vol. I; no more published), Paris, An XII–1804.

Cluverius, Philippus, *Germaniae Antiquae Libri Tres,* Leyden, 1616.

Cluverius, Philippus, *Italia Antiqua,* Leyden, 1624.

Coats, Peter, *Great Gardens of Britain,* London, 1967.

Cobban, A., *A History of Modern France,* Harmondsworth, 1961–1965.

Cocchi, Antonio, *Del Vitto Pitagorico di Soli Vegetabili per Conservare la Sanità e per la Cura di Alcune Malattie,* Florence, 1743.

Cocchi, Antonio, *Opere,* Milan, 1824.

Cocchiara, Giuseppe, *Storia del Folklore in Europa,* Turin, 1954.

Cochin, C.-N., *Observations sur les Antiquités d'Herculaneum,* Paris, 1754.

Cochin, C.-N., *Voyage d'Italie ou Recueil de Notes sur les Ouvrages de Peinture et de Sculpture qu'on Voit dans les Principales Villes d'Italie,* Lausanne, 1773.

Cochin, C.-N., *Mémoires Inédites,* edited by C. Henry, Paris, 1880.

Cohen, Henry, *Guide de l'Amateur de Livres à Figures,* third edition edited by Charles Mehl, Paris, 1876.

Cohen, Ralph, *The Art of Discrimination,* London, 1964.

Coleridge, S. T., *On the Constitution of Church and State,* London, 1839.

Colmenero de Ledesma, A., *Curioso Tratado de la Naturaleza y Calidad del Chocolate . . . por el Licenciado . . . ,* Madrid, 1631.

Colombier, P. du., *L'Architecture Française en Allemagne au XVIIIe Siècle,* Paris, 1956.

[Colonna, Francesco], *Hypnerotomachia Poliphili,* Venice, 1499.

Colton, Judith, "Merlin's Cave and Queen Caroline," *Eighteenth-Century Studies* X (1976), pp. 1.

Colvin, Howard, *Dictionary of British Architects,* London, 1954.

Colvin, Howard, and Harris, John, eds., *The Country Seat: Studies in the History of the British Country House, presented to Sir John Summerson on his 65th Birthday,* London, 1970.

Colvin, Howard, *The Sheldonian Theatre and the Divinity School,* Oxford, 1974.

Colvin, Howard, ed., *The History of the King's Works,* London, 1975–.

Colvin, H. M., and Craig, M. J., *Architectural Drawings in the Library of Elton Hall*, London, 1964.

Comolli, Angelo, *Bibliografia Storico-Critica dell'Architettura Civile ed Arti Subalterne*, Rome, 1788–1792.

Compte Général de la Dépense des Edifices et Bâtiments que le Roi de Pologne, Duc de Lorraine et de Bar a Fait Construire pour l'Embellissement de la Ville de Nancy, Lunéville, 1761.

Concina, Daniele, *Della Storia del Probabilismo e del Rigorismo, Dissertazioni . . . nelle quali si Spiegano, e dalle Sottigliezze de' Moderni Probabilisti si Difendano i Principi Fondamentali della Teologia Cristiana*, Lucca, 1743–1748.

Concina, Daniele, *De Spectaculis Theatralibus, Christiano cuique tum Laico tum Clerico Vetitis Dissertationes Duae*, Rome, 1752.

Conder, E., *Records of the Hole Crafte and Fellowship of Masons*, London, 1894.

Constable, W. G., *Richard Wilson*, London, 1953.

Conti, Antonio, *Le Quattro Tragedie*, Florence, 1751.

Conti, Antonio, *Versioni Poetiche* (a cura di Giovanna Gronda), Bari, 1966.

Convegno B. Vittone, *Atti del Convegno Bernardo Vittone e la Disputa fra Classicismo e Barocco nel Settecento*, Turin, 1972.

Cook, G. H., *Old St. Paul's Cathedral*, London, 1955.

Cook, T., *Hogarth Restored, Being a Complete Edition of the Works of That Much Admired Artist*, London, n.d.

Cooper, Anthony Ashley, Earl of Shaftesbury, *Characteristics of Men, Manners, Opinions, Times*, 3rd ed., London, 1732.

Cooper-Hewitt Museum of Decorative Arts and Design, designs catalog, London, 1973.

Coornaert, E., *Les Compagnonnages*, Paris, 1966.

Cordemoy, Père J. L. de, *Noveau Traité de Toute l'Architecture ou l'Art de Bastir Utile aux Entrepreneurs et aux Ouvriers*, 2nd ed., Paris, 1714.

Corneille, Pierre, *Théâtre*, with commentaries by F. M. A. de Voltaire, Paris, 1765.

Couperie, Pierre, *Paris through the Ages*, London, 1970.

Courboin, F., *Histoire Illustrée de la Gravure en France*, Paris, 1923–1928.

Cragg, Gerald R., *Reason and Authority in the Eighteenth Century*, Cambridge, 1964.

Crébillon, C.-P.-J. de (*fils*), *Les Egarements du Coeur et de l'Esprit*, Paris, 1736.

Crébillon, Prosper Jolyot, Sieur de Crais-Billon, *dit* Crébillon, *Les Oeuvres*, Paris, 1754.

Crescimbeni, G. M. de', *L'Istoria della Volgar Poesia*, Rome, 1697.

Crisp, Sir Frank, *Mediaeval Gardens*, 2 vols., edited by Catherine Childs Paterson, London, 1924.

Cristinelli, Giuseppe, *Baldassare Longhena, Architetto del '600 a Venezia*, Padua, 1972.

Croce, Benedetto, *Uomini e Cose della Vecchia Italia*, Bari, 1927.

Croce, Benedetto, *La Filosofia di G. B. Vico*, Bari, 1947.

Cronin, V., *The Wise Men from the West*, London, 1955.

Croÿ, Prince de Meurs et de Solre (Emmanuel), *Journal Inédit du Duc de Croÿ* (1718–1784), Paris, 1906.

Cru, R. Loyalty, *Diderot as a Disciple of English Thought*, New York, 1913.

Cust, Lionel, *History of the Society of Dilettanti*, edited by Sidney Colvin, London, 1898.

Cyriacus of Ancona (Anconitanus), *Inscriptiones Antiquae Basilicae Scti Paoli ad Viam Ostensem*, Rome, 1645.

Cyriacus of Ancona, *Epigrammata seu Inscriptiones Antiquae Graeco Partim Idiomate, Partim Latino Exculptae Variis Basibus, Lapidibus ac Marmoribus per Illyricum ad Liburniam Repertae ac Defossae*, Rome, 1749.

Dacier, Emile, and Vauflart, A., *Le Livre de Croquis de Gabriel de Saint-Aubin*, Paris, 1943.

Daiches, David, *Charles Edward Stuart*, London, 1973.

Dandré-Bardon, Michel, *L'Impartialité sur la Musique: Epitre à M. J. J. Rousseau*, Paris, 1754.

Dandré-Bardon, Michel, *Traité de Peinture, suivi d'un Essai sur la Sculpture*, Paris, 1765.

Dandré-Bardon, Michel, *Histoire Universelle, Traitée Relativement aux Arts de Peindre et de Sculpter, ou Tableaux de l'Histoire Enrichis de Connoissances Analogues à ces Talens*, Paris, 1769.

Dandré-Bardon, Michel, *Costume des Anciens Peuples*, Paris, 1772.

Danis, Robert, *La Première Maison Royale de Trianon (1670–1687)*, Paris, n.d.

Dati, Carlo, *Delle Lodi del Commendatore Cassiano dal Pozzo*, Florence, 1664.

Dawson, R., *The Chinese Chameleon*, London, 1967.

Deacon, R., *John Dee*, London, 1968.

Deane, Phyllis, *The First Industrial Revolution*, Cambridge, 1967.

Debus, Allen G., *The English Paracelsans*, London, 1965.

Degueret, Emile, *Histoire Médicale du Grand Roi*, Paris, 1924.

Dehaye, Pierre, *Louis XV: Un Moment de Perfection de l'Art Français*, catalog, Paris, 1974.

D'Elia, Pasquale M., SJ, *Le Origini dell'Arte Cristiana Cinese*, Rome, 1939.

Dempster, T., *De Etruria Regali, Libri VII nunc Primum Editi Curante Thomas Coke*, Florence, 1723–1724.

Dennerlein, Ingrid, "Die Gartenkunst der Régence und des Rokoko in Frankreich," Ph.D. thesis, Bamberg, 1972.

Dennis, George, *Cities and Cemeteries of Etruria,* London, 1848.

Dent, John, *The Quest for Nonsuch,* London, 1962.

Dermott, Laurence, *Ahiman Rezon, or a Help to All That Are or Would Be Free and Accepted Masons,* London, 1756; second edition, 1764.

Derrida, Jacques, *De la Grammatologie,* Paris, 1967.

Désaguliers, John Theophilus, *Lectures on Experimental Philosophy, Wherein the Principles of Mechanicks, Hydrostaticks, and Opticks are Demonstrated and Explained at Large* . . . *by J. T.D. . . . M.A., F.R.S.,* London, 1719.

Désaguliers, John Theophilus, *The Newtonian System of the World, the Best Model of Government: an Allegorical Poem* . . . *to Which is Added Cumbria's Complaint Against the Intercalary Day in the Leap-Year* by J.T.D. LLD, chaplain to His Grace the Duke of Chandos and F.R.S., London, 1728.

Descartes, René, *Oeuvres et Lettres,* edited by A. Bridoux, Paris, 1952.

Desgodetz, Antoine, *Les Edifices Antiques de Rome Déssinés et Mesurés Très Exactement,* Paris, 1683.

Desjardins, Gustave, *Le Petit Trianon,* Versailles, 1885.

Despierres, G., *Les Gabriel,* Paris, 1895.

[Dézallier d'Argenville, Antoine Joseph], *La Théorie et la Pratique du Jardinage. Ou l'On Traite à Fond des Beaux Jardins Appellés Communément les Jardins de Propreté Comme Sont les Parterres, les Bosquets, les Boulingrins etc.* . . . , Paris, 1709.

[Dézallier d'Argenville, Antoine Joseph], *The Theory and Practice of Gardening* . . . *Done from the French Original Printed in Paris Anno 1709 by John James of Greenwich,* London, 1712.

[Dézallier d'Argenville, Antoine Joseph], *Voyage Pittoresque de Paris par M. D.,* *** 3rd ed., Paris, 1757.

[Dézallier d'Argenville, Antoine-Nicolas], *Vie des Fameux Architectes Depuis la Renaissance des Arts, avec la Description de leurs Ouvrages,* par M.D., Paris, 1787.

Diaz, Furio, *Filosofia e Politica nel Settecento Francese,* Turin, 1962.

Diderot, Denis, *See* Benot, Yves.

Diderot, Denis, *Les Salons,* edited by J. Seznec and J. Adhémar, Oxford, 1957–1967; new edition, 1975.

Diderot, Denis, and Alembert, Jean d', *Encyclopédie, ou Dictionnaire Raisonné des Sciences, des Arts, et des Métiers par une Société de Gens de Lettres,* 17 vols., Paris, 1751–1765.

Diderot, Denis, *Lettre sur les Aveugles,* edited by Robert Niklaus, Geneva and Paris, 1963 (second edition).

Diderot, Denis, *Oeuvres Complètes,* ed. Roger Lewinter, Paris, 1969.

Diepolder, H., and Rehm, W., eds., *Johann Joachim Winckelmann, Briefe,* Berlin, 1952–1957.

Dietterlin, W., *Architektura: von Ausstheilung Symmetria und Proportion der fünf Säulen und aller daraus volgender Kunst-Arbeit*, Nuremberg 1593–1598.

Digby, Kenelm, *Journal of a Voyage into the Mediterranean*, edited by John Bruce for the Camden Society, London, 1868.

Digges, Leonard, *A Prognostication Everlasting*, London, 1556.

Dilke, Lady Emilia Frances Strong, *Art in the Modern State*, London, 1888.

Dilke, Lady Emilia Frances Strong, *French Painters in the Eighteenth Century*, London, 1899.

Dilke, Lady Emilia Frances Strong, *French Architects and Sculptors of the Eighteenth Century*, London, 1900.

Dilke, Lady Emilia Frances Strong, *French Decoration and Furniture in the Eighteenth Century*, London, 1901.

Dilke, Lady Emilia Frances Strong, *French Engravers and Draughtsmen in the Eighteenth Century*, London, 1902.

Dinsmoor, William Bell, *The Architecture of Ancient Greece*, London, 1950.

D'Israeli, Isaac, *Calamities and Quarrels of Authors*, London, n.d.

Dobbs, B.-J., *The Foundations of Newton's Alchemy*, Cambridge, Mass., 1975.

Dodington, G. Bubb, *The Political Journal* edited by J. Carswell and L. A. Dralle, Oxford, 1965.

Dorival, Bernard, *Philippe de Champaigne et Port-Royal*, catalog, Musée National des Granges de Port-Royal, 1957.

Dorsten, J. A. van, *The Radical Arts*, Leyden, 1970.

Downes, Kerry, *Nicolas Hawskmoor*, London, 1959.

Downes, Kerry, *English Baroque Architecture*, London, 1966.

Draper, Marie P. G., *Marble Hill House*, London, 1970.

Drayton, M., *Poly-Olbion*, London, 1612.

Du Bos, Abbé Jean-Baptiste, *Réflexions Critiques sur la Poésie et sur la Peinture*, Paris, 1715; fifth corrected edition, 1746.

Duchet, Michèle, *Anthropologie et Histoire au Siècle des Lumières: Buffon, Voltaire, Rosseau, Helvétius, Diderot*, Paris, 1971.

Dufresny, Charles, *Amusements Sérieux et Comiques*, Paris, 1699.

Dumesnil, M. J., *Voyageurs Français en Italie*, Paris, 1865.

Dumézil, Georges, *La Religion Romaine Archaique*, Paris, 1966.

Duplessis, Georges, *Les Ventes de Tableaux, Dessins, Estampes, et Objets d'Art aux XVIIe et XVIIIe Siècles (1611–1800)*, Paris, 1874.

Dupront, A., *P. D. Huet et l'Exegèse Comparatiste au XVIIe Siècle*, Paris, 1930.

Durand, J. N. L., *Recueil et Parallèle des Edifices Anciens et Modernes*, Paris, An IX/1800.

Durand, J. N. L., *Précis des Leçons d'Architecture*, Paris, 1802–1805.

Dürer, A., *Unterweysung der Messung mit dem Zirckel und Richtscheyt, in Linien ebnen und gantzen Corporen*, Nuremberg, 1525.

Dürer, A., *Vier Bücher von Menschlicher Proportion*, Nuremberg, 1528.

Duthoy, Jean-Jacques, *Michel Lequeux: Architecte Lillois du XVIIIe Siècle*, catalog, Lille, 1969.

Dyer, T. H., *Pompeii: The History, Buildings and Antiquities*, London, 1891.

Eastlake, C. L., *A History of the Gothic Revival in England*, London, 1872.

Egret, Jean, *Louis XV et l'Opposition Parlementaire: 1715–1774*, Paris, 1970.

Elling, Christian, *Jardin i Rom*, Copenhagen, 1943.

Elmes, J., *Sir Christopher Wren and his Time*, London, 1852.

Emiliani, A., *La Pinacoteca Nazionale di Bologna*, Bologna, 1969.

Enlart, C., *Manuel d'Archéologie Française*, 2 vols., Paris, 1902.

Ennen, E., *Storia della Città Medievale (Die Europäische Stadt des Mittelalters)*, Bari, 1975.

Erdberg, E. von, *Chinese Influences on European Garden Structures*, Cambridge, Mass., 1936.

Erhardt-Siebold, E. von, "Harmony of the Senses in Romanticism," *Proceedings Modern Language Association*, 1932.

Eriksen, S., "Lalive de Jully's Furniture à la Grecque," *Burlington Magazine*, 1961.

Eriksen, S., *Early Neo-Classicism in France*, London, 1974.

'Espinasse, Margaret, *Robert Hooke*, London, 1956.

Essex, James, *Observations on the Antiquity of Masons and Masonry*, unpublished manuscript, The British Library, London.

Euler, Léonard, *Musique Mathématique*, Paris, 1865.

Evelyn, John, *A Parallel of the Ancient Architecture with the Modern . . . Written in French by Roland Fréart, Sieur de Chambray . . . Made English for the Benefit of Builders . . .* London, 1723.

Evelyn, John, *Silva or a Discourse of Forest-Trees, and the Propagation of Timber in His Majesty's Dominions*, 5th ed., London, 1729.

Evelyn, John, *Evelyn's Sculptura, with the Unpublished Second Part*, edited by C. F. Bell, Oxford, 1906.

Evelyn, John, *London Revived: Considerations for its Rebuilding*, edited by E. S. de Beer, Oxford, 1938.

Evelyn, John, *The Diary of J. E., Now First Printed in Full and Edited E. S. de Beer*, Oxford, 1955.

Falconet, Etienne. *See* Benot, Yves.

Fanfani, A., "Il Mancato Rinovamento Economico in la Storia della Civiltà Veneziana del Settecento," in *Civiltà Veneziana VI*, Fondazione Giorgio Cini.

Fariello, Francesco, *Architettura dei Giardini,* Rome, 1967.

Fasolo, Furio, *Le Chiese di Roma nel '700,* vol. I., Trastevere (all published), Rome, 1949.

Félibien, André, Sieur des Avaux et de Javercy, *Description du Château de Versailles, de ses Peintures et d'Autres Ouvrages, Fait pour le roy,* Paris, 1696.

Félibien, Jean-François, Sieur des Avaux, *Les Plans et les Descriptions de Deux des Plus Belles Maisons de Campagne de Pline le Consul,* Paris, 1699.

Fels, Edmond Frisch, Comte de, *Ange-Jacques Gabriel: Premier Architecte du Roi,* Paris, 1912; 2d ed., 1922.

Fenwick, Hubert, *Architect Royal: The Life and Works of Sir William Bruce, 1630–1710,* Kineton, 1970.

Ferrari, G., *Bellezze Architettoniche per le Feste della Chinea in Roma nei Secoli XVII e XVIII,* Turin, 1919.

Findel, J. G., *History of Freemasonry from its Origin Down to the Present Day,* London, 1869.

Fiorelli, G. A., *Pompeianarum Antiquitatum Historia,* Naples, 1860–1862.

Fischer von Erlach, J. B., *Entwurff einer historischen Architektur,* Vienna, 1721. *A plan of civil and historical architecture in the representation of the most noted buildings of foreign nations, both ancient and modern . . . translated into English . . . with notes by T. Lediard,* Second edition, London, 1737.

Fitzgerald, C. P., *China: A Short Cultural History,* London, 1954.

Fleetwood, William, *Inscriptionum Antiquarum Sylloge,* London, 1691.

Fleming, John, "The Hugfords of Florence," in *The Connoisseur,* November 1955.

Fleming, John, *Robert Adam and his Circle,* London, 1962.

Flottes, Abbé, *Etude sur Daniel Huet, Evêque d'Avranches,* Montpellier and Avignon, 1857.

Focillon, Henri, *Giovanni Battista Piranesi,* Paris, 1918. Italian edition, edited by M. Calvesi and A. Monferini and translated by G. Guglielmi, Bologna, 1967.

Folkierski, W., *Entre le Classicisme et le Romanticisme,* Paris, 1925; second edition, 1936.

Fontana, Domenico, *Della Trasportazione dell'Obelisco Vaticano,* Naples, 1604.

Fontenelle, Bernard le Bovier de, *Histoire de l'Académie Royale,* Paris, 1700-.

Fontenelle, B., le Bovier de, *Entretien sur la Pluralité des Mondes; Digression sur les Anciens et les Modernes,* edited by R. Shackleton, Oxford, 1955.

Ford, Franklin L., *Robe and Sword: the Regrouping of the French Aristocracy after Louis XIV,* Cambridge, Mass., 1962.

Formey, Jean-Henri Samuel, *Souvenir d'un Citoyen,* Berlin, 1789.

Forsmann, Erik, *Säule und Ornament,* Stockholm, 1956.

Foscarini, Marco, *Della Letteratura Veneziana,* Padua, 1752.

Fothergill, Brian, *Sir William Hamilton,* London, 1969.

Foucault, Michel, *Surveiller et Punir,* Paris, 1975.

Fouquier, M., and Duchêne, A., *Des Divers Styles de Jardins,* Paris, 1914.

Fowler, Thomas, *Shaftesbury and Hutcheson,* London, 1882.

Frankl, P., and E. Panofsky, "The Secret of the Medieval Masons," *Art Bulletin,* XXVII (1945).

Frankl, P., *The Gothic,* Princeton, N. J., 1960.

Fraser, D., Hibbard, H., and Levine, M. J., *Essays in the History of Architecture Presented to Rudolf Wittkower,* London, 1967.

Fréart, Paul, Sieur de Chantelou, *Journal du Voyage en France du Cavalier Bernin,* Paris, 1930.

Fréart, Roland, Sieur de Chambray. *See* Evelyn, J.

Fréart, Roland, Sieur de Chambray, *Parallèle de l'Architecture Antique et de la Moderne: avec un Recueil des Dix Principaux Auteurs qui Ont Écrit des Cinq Ordres . . . ,* Paris, 1650.

[Frémin, Michel de], *Mémoires Critiques d'Architecture Contenans l'Idée de la Vraye et de la Fausse Architecture; une Instruction sur Toutes les Tromperies des Ouvriers Infidels Travaillant dans les Bâtiments; une Dissertation sur la Formation des Mineraux, leur Nature et leur Employ et sur l'Abus dans l'Usage du Plâtre; sur la Qualité de la Fumée et des Moyens d'y Remédier et sur des Autres Matières non Encore Eclaircies,* Paris, 1702.

Frézier, A. F. [le Sieur F.], *Traité des Feux d'Artifice . . . ,* Paris, 1715.

Frézier, A. F., *La Théorie et la Pratique de la Coupe des Pierres et des Bois pour la Construction des Voûtes et Autres Parties des Bâtimens Civils et Militaires ou Traité de Stéréométrie à l'Usage de l'Architecte,* Paris, 1737.

Frick, Karl R. H., *Die Erleuchteten,* Graz, 1975.

Friedman, T. F., "James Gibbs, 1682–1754; the formation of his Architectural Style," Ph.D dissertation, University of London, 1971.

Frisch, Teresa G., *Gothic Art 1140-c. 1450,* sources and documents in the History of Art series, edited by J. W. Janson, Englewood Cliffs, N.J., 1971.

Fulcanelli, *Le Mystère des Cathédrales,* 3rd ed. with prefaces by Eugène Canseliet, Paris, 1964.

Funt, David, *Diderot and the Aesthetics of the Enlightenment,* Diderot Studies XI, edited by O. Fellows and Diana Guiragossian, Geneva, 1968.

Fürst, Viktor, *The Architecture of Sir Christopher Wren,* London, 1956.

Fusco, Renato da et al., *Luigi Vanvitelli,* Naples, 1973.

Galilei, Vincenzo, *Dialogo di V. G. Nobile Fiorentino, della Musica Antica e della Moderna,* Florence, 1581.

Gallacini, Teofilo, *Trattato di T. G. sopra gli Errori degli Architetti ora per La prima Volta Publicato,* Venice, 1767.

Galland, André. *See* Bibliotheca Veterum Patrum.

Galland, Antoine, *De l'Origine et du Progrez du Café (Sur un Manuscrit Arabe de la Bibliothèque du Roy)*, Caen and Paris, 1699.

Galland, Antoine, *Les Mille et Une Nuits: Contes Arabes*, edited by Dessains and C. Nodier, Paris, 1822–1825.

Galland, Antoine, *Journal Parisien d'A. G. 1703–1715, Précédé de Son Autobiographie, 1646–1715*, edited by Henri Omont, Paris, 1919.

Gallet, M., "Un Modèle pour la Madeleine d'après le Projet de Contant d'Ivry," *Bulletin Carnavalet XVIII*, no. 1 (1965).

Gallet, Michel, "Le Salon de l'Hôtel d'Uzès," *Bulletin Carnavalet XXII*, no. 2 (1969).

Gallet, Michel, "Un Ensemble Décoratif de Ledoux: Les Lambris du Café Militaire," *Bulletin Carnavalet XXV* (1972).

Gallet, M., *Paris Domestic Architecture of the Eighteenth Century*, London, 1972.

Ganay, Ernest de, *André le Nostre*, Paris, 1962.

Ganay, Ernest de, *Les Origines du Jardin Anglois en France*, unpublished manuscript, Bibliothèque des Arts Décoratifs, Paris.

Garden, Maurice, *Lyon et les Lyonnais au Dix-Huitième Siècle*, Paris, 1970.

Gaume, Maxime, *Les Inscriptions et les Sources de l'Oeuvre d'Honoré d'Urfé*, St. Etienne, 1977.

Gaus, J., *Carlo Marchionni: Ein Beitrag zur Römischen Architektur des Settecento*, Cologne and Graz, 1967.

Gavuzzo-Stewart, Silvia, "Nota sulle Carceri Piranesiane," *l'Arte*, 15–16, pp. 57 ff, 1973.

Gaxotte, Pierre, *Le Siècle de Louis XV*, Paris, 1933.

Gaxotte, Pierre, Silvestre de Sacy, et al., *Le Marais*, Paris, 1964.

Gaxotte, Pierre et al., *Le Faubourg St. Germain*, Paris, 1966.

Gazette Littéraire de l'Europe, Paris, 1764–.

Gennep, A. van, *The Rites of Passage*, London, 1960.

Gersheim, H., and Gersheim, A., *The History of Photography*, London and New York, 1955.

Ghezzi, Pier Leone. *See* Guerrini, Lucia.

Gibbs, James, *A Book of Architecture, Containing Designs of Buildings and Ornaments*, London, 1728.

Gidde, Walter, *Booke of Sundry Draughtes, Principally Serving for Glaziers: and not Impertinent for Plasterers and Gardiners, besides Sundry Other Professions*, London, 1615.

Giedion, Sigfried, *Spätbarocker und Romantischer Klassizismus*, Munich, 1922.

Giedion, Sigfried, *Mechanization Takes Command*, Cambridge, Mass., 1948.

Giesecke, A., *Studien über G. B. Piranesi*, Berlin, 1911.

Gillot, Hubert, *La Bataille des Anciens et des Modernes en France*, Nancy, 1914.

Giorgio, Francesco, *De Harmonia Mundi Totius, Cantica Tria*, Venice, 1525.

Girouard, Mark, *Robert Smythson*, London, 1966.

Giudizio delle Romane Efemeridi su l'iscrizione scoperta in Vercelli ai 18 settembre 1783 e dubbj intorno al medesimo (by G. A. Ranza), Vercelli, 1784?

Goethe, J. W., *Werke* (Gedankausgabe), edited by Ernst Bentler, Zurich, 1948–1954.

[Goguet, Antoine Yves], *De l'Origine des Loix, des Arts et des Sciences, et de Leur Progrès chez les Anciens Peuples*, Paris, 1758.

Goldoni, Carlo, *Tutte le Opere* . . . , a cura di Giuseppe Ortolani, Milan, 1935–1956.

Golzio, V., "Notizie sull'Arte Romana Tratta dal Diario del Valesio," in *Archivi*, 1936.

Gombrich, E. H., *The Ideas of Progress and their Impact on Art*, New York, 1971.

Goncourt, E., and Goncourt, J., *L'Art du XVIIIe Siècle*, Paris, 1895–1896.

Goncourt, E., and Goncourt, J., *Madame de Pompadour*, Paris, 1906.

Gooch, G. P., *Louis XV: The Monarchy in Decline*, London, 1956.

Gordon, D. J., "Poet and Architect: the Intellectual Setting of the Quarrel between Ben Jonson and Inigo Jones," *Journal of the Warburg and Courtauld Institutes* XII (1949).

Gotch, J. Alfred, *Early Renaissance Architecture in England*, London, 1914.

Gothein, Marie-Luise, *Geschichte der Gartenkunst*, Jena, 1926.

Gould, R. F., *History of Freemasonry*, revised by Rev. H. Poole, London, 1951.

Grandidier, Abbé Philippe André, *Essais Historiques et Topographiques sur l'Eglise Cathédrale de Strasbourg*, Strasbourg, 1782.

Granet, Solange, "Images de Paris: La Place de la Concorde," *La Revue Géographique et Industrielle de France*, n.s., no. 26, Paris, 1963.

Gravina, Vincenzo, *Della Tragedia*, Venice, 1721.

Gray, Thomas, *The Works, in Prose and Verse*, edited by Edmund Gosse, London, 1884.

Grean, Stanley, *Shaftesbury's Philosophy of Religion and Ethics: A Study in Enthusiasm*, Columbus, Ohio, 1967.

Green, David, *Gardener to Queen Anne: Henry Wise (1653–1738) and the Formal Garden*, London, 1956.

Green, David, *Grinling Gibbons: His Work as Carver and Statuary (1648–1721)*, London, 1964.

Gregorovius, F., *Geschichte der Stadt Rom im Mittelalter*, Dresden, 1926.

Gregory, R. L., and Gombrich, E. H., eds., *Illusion in Nature and Art*, London, 1973.

Gregory, R. L., *Eye and Brain*, London, 1966.

Gresset, Jean-Baptiste Louis de, *Oeuvres*, London, 1780.

Grimal, Pierre, *Les Jardins Romains à la Fin de la République et aux Deux Premiers Siècles de l'Empire*, Paris, 1943.

Gromort, Georges, *Le Hameau de Trianon*, Paris, 1928.

[Grosley, J. P.], *Observations sur l'Italie et sur les Italiens Données en 1764 sous le Nom de Deux Gentilshommes Suédois*, 2nd ed., London, 1764.

Grote, Andreas, *Der Vollkommen Architectus: Baumeister und Baubetrieb bis zum Anfang der Neuzeit*, Munich, 1959.

Gruterus, Janus, *Inscriptiones Antiquae Totius Orbis Romani, in Corpus Absolutissimum Redactae, Ingenio ac Cura J. G.*, Heidelberg, 1602?

Gsell, S, Marçais, G., and Yver, G., *Histoire d'Algérie*, Paris, 1929.

Guarini, Guarino, e l'Internazionalitá del Barocco: Atti del Convegno Internazionale promosso dall'Accademia delle Scienze di Torino, 30 September-5 October 1968, Turin, 1970.

Guarini, Guarino, *Architettura Civile: Opera Postuma Dedicata a sua Sacra Reale Maestá*, Turin, 1737.

Guénon, René, "Initiation and the Crafts," *Journal of the Indian Society of Oriental Art*, 1938.

Guerrini, Lucia, *Marmi Antichi nei Disegni di Pier Leone Ghezzi, catalog*, Città del Vaticano, Biblioteca apostolica vaticana, 1971.

Guiffrey, J., ed., *Comptes des Bâtiments*, Paris, 1881.

Guilmard, D., *Les Maitres-Ornamentistes*, Paris, 1880.

Gunnis, R. ed., *Dictionary of British Sculptors*, London, 1968.

Gunter, R. T., *The Architecture of Sir Roger Pratt*, Oxford, 1928.

Gusdorf, Georges, *Les Sciences Humaines et la Pensée Occidentale*, Paris, 1966-.

Gutton, Jean-Pierre, *La Société et les Pauvres, L'Exemple de la Généralité de Lyon, 1534-1789*, Bibliothèque de la Faculté des Lettres et Sciences Humaines de Lyon, Paris, 1969.

Hadrawa, Norberto, *Ragguagli di varii Scavi . . . fatte nell'Isola di Capri dal Sig. Hadrawa*, Dresden, 1794.

Hahn, Roger, *The Anatomy of a Scientific Institution: the Paris Academy of Sciences 1666-1803*, Berkeley and Los Angeles, 1971.

Hahnloser, Hans R., *Villard de Honnecourt*, Graz, 1972.

Haley, Sister Marie Philip, *Racine and the Art Poétique of Boileau* (John Hopkins Studies in Romance Literatures, Extra Volume XII), Baltimore, London, and Paris, 1938.

Hall, A. Rupert, *The Scientific Revolution 1500-1800: The Formation of the Modern Scientific Attitude*, 2nd ed., London, 1962.

Hall, A. Rupert, "Newton in France: A New View," in *History of Science*, XIII (1975).

Hallays, A., *Les Perrault*, Paris, 1920.

Halsband, Robert, *Lord Hervey*, Oxford, 1973.

Hamilton, Gavin, *Schola Italica Picturae sive Selectae quaedam Summorum e Schola Italica Pictorum Tabulae Aere Incisae Cura et Impensis G. H. Pictoris*, Rome, 1773.

Hamilton, William, *Collection of Engravings from Ancient Vases Mostly of Pure Greek Workmanship Discovered in Sepulchres in the Kingdom of the Two Sicilies*, Naples, 1791–1795.

Hamilton Collection: a Bicentenary Exhibition (catalog), London, 1972.

D'Harcanville (P.-F. Hugues), *Collection of Etruscan, Greek, and Roman Antiquities from the Cabinet of the Hon. W. Hamilton*, Naples, 1766–1767.

Harcourt-Smith, S., *Alberoni or the Spanish Conspiracy*, London, 1943.

Hargrave, C. P., *A History of Playing Cards*, New York, 1930.

Harris, E., "Batty Langley: A Tutor to Freemasons," *Burlington Magazine*, May 1977.

Harris, J., *William Chambers*, London, 1970.

Harris, J., Orgel, S., and Strong, R., *The King's Arcadia: Inigo Jones and the Stuart Court*, catalog, London, 1973.

Harrison, Stephen, *The Arches of Triumph Erected in Honor of the High and Mighty Prince James, the First of that Name, King of England, and the Sixth of Scotland, at his Majestie's Entrance and Passage through his Honourable City and Chamber of London, upon the 15th day of March 1603*.

Hartley, Sir Harold, *The Royal Society*, London, 1960.

Harvey, John, ed., *English Mediaeval Architects*, London, 1954.

Harvey, John, *The Mediaeval Architect*, London, 1972.

Haskell, Francis, *Patrons and Painters*, London, 1963.

Haskell, Francis; Levi, Anthony, and Shackleton, Robert, *The Artist and the Writer in France: Essays in Honour of Jean Seznec*, Oxford, 1974.

Hautecoeur, L., *Rome et la Renaissance de l'Antiquité à la Fin du XVIIIe Siècle*, Paris, 1912.

Hautecoeur, L., *Histoire de l'Architecture Classique en France*, Paris, 1943–1957.

Hautecoeur, L., *Les Jardins des Dieux et des Hommes*, Paris, 1959.

D'Hauterive, Ernest, *Le Merveilleux au XVIIIe Siècle*, Paris, 1903.

Hay, D., *The Geometric Beauty of the Human Figure Defined*, Edinburgh, 1851.

Hazard, P., *La Crise de la Conscience Européenne (1680–1715)*, Paris, 1935.

Hazlehurst, Franklin Hamilton, *Jacques Boyceau and the French Formal Garden*, Athens, Ga., 1966.

Helyot, Hyppolite, R. F., *Histoire des Ordres Monastiques, Religieux et Militaires et des Congrégations Séculières de l'Un et de l'Autre Sexe*, Paris, 1714–1719.

Hennebo, Dieter, and Hoffmann, Alfred, *Der Architektonische Garten: Renaissance und Barock*, Hamburg, 1965.

Heraeus, Carl Gustav, *Inscriptiones et Symbola Varii Argumenti*, Nuremberg, 1721.

Herbert of Cherbury, E., *De Veritate, Prout Distinguitur a Revelatione, a Verisimili, a Possibili, a Falso*, London, 1645.

Herbert of Cherbury, E., *Autobiography*, edited by Sydney Lee, 1886; edited by J. M. Shuttleworth, 1977.

Herbert, Edward, Lord Cherbury, *De Religione Gentilium Errorumque apud Eos Causis*, Amsterdam, 1701.

Herculaneum (Reale Accademia Herculanense), *Pitture Antiche d'Ercolano*, Naples, 1757–1792.

Héré de Corny, Emanuel, *Plans et Elévations de la Place Royale de Nancy et des Autres Edifices qui l'Environnent*, Paris, 1753.

Heré de Corny, Emanuel, *Recueil des Plans, Elevations et Coupes . . . de Châteaux, Jardins et Dependances que le Roy de Pologne Occupe en Lorraine*, Paris, n.d.

Hereskovits, Melville J., *Cultural Anthropology*, New York, 1955.

Herrmann, Wolfgang, *Laugier and Eighteenth Century French Theory*, London, 1962.

Herrmann, Wolfgang, *The Theory of Claude Perrault*, London, 1973.

Heydenreich, L., *Leonardo*, New York, 1954.

Higounet, Charles et al., *Histoire de Bordeaux*, Bordeaux, 1963–1974.

Hill, Aaron, *Works*, London, 1753.

Hill, Christopher, *Intellectual Origins of the English Revolution*, London, 1972.

Hill, Thomas, *The Gardener's Labyrinth: Containing a Discourse of the Gardener's Life, in the Yearly Travels to be Bestowed on his Plot of Earth, for the Use of a Garden*, London, 1577.

Hipple, W. J. Jr., *The Beautiful, the Sublime, and the Picturesque in Eighteenth-Century British Aesthetic Theory*, Carbondale, 1957.

Hitchcock, H. R., *Rococo Architecture in South Germany*, London, 1968.

Hobbes, T., *Leviathan; or the Matter, Forme and Power of a Commonwealth, Ecclesiasticall and Civill*, edited by A. R. Waller, Cambridge, 1904.

Hofman, J., *Leibniz in Paris (1672–1676)*, Cambridge, 1974.

Hogarth, William, *The Analysis of Beauty: Written with a View of Fixing the Fluctuating Ideas of Taste*, London, 1753; edited, with an introduction by Joseph Burke, Oxford, 1955.

Hohnholz, Jûrgen, *Der Englische Park als Landschaftliche Erscheinung*, Tübingen, 1964.

Honisch, Dieter, *Anton Raphael Mengs und die Bildform des Früh-klassizismus*, Recklinghausen, 1965.

Honour, Hugh, "J. Talman and W. Kent in Italy," *The Connoisseur*, 1954.

Honour, Hugh, *Chinoiserie: The Vision of Cathay*, London, 1961.

Hooke, Robert, *The Diary of R. H.*, edited by Henry W. Robinson and Walter Adams, London, 1935.

Horne, Alex, *King Solomon's Temple in the Masonic Tradition*, Wellingborough, 1972.

Horst-Oncken, A., *Ueber das Schickliche*, Göttingen, 1967.

Hubert, J. (Auguste Cheval, dit), *Rapport sur l'Embellissement du Palais et du Jardin National, du Pont et de la Place de la Révolution*, 20 Floréal, n.d. (1794).

Hudson, G. F., *Europe and China: A Survey of Their Relations from the Earliest Times to 1800*, London, 1931.

Huelsen, Christian, *Il Libro di Giuliano da Sangallo*, Cod. Vat. Barb. Lat. 4424, con introduzione e note di C. H., Codices Vaticani Selecti, XI, Leipzig, 1910.

Huet, Pierre-Daniel, Bishop of Avranches, *de Interpretatione Libri Duo . . . Hic Accessit de Fabularum Romanesium Origine Diatriba*, The Hague, 1683.

Huet, Pierre-Daniel, Bishop of Avranches, *Huetiana*, Paris, n.d.

Hughes, P., and Williams, D., eds., *The Varied Pattern: Studies in the Eighteenth Century*, Toronto, 1971.

Hugo, Victor, *Notre Dame de Paris*, edited by Jacques Seebacher and Yves Gohin, Paris, 1975.

Hull, L. W. H., *History and Philosophy of Science*, London, 1959.

Hunt, J. D., and Willis, P., *The Genius of the Place*, London, 1975.

Hussey, Christopher, *The Picturesque: Studies in a Point of View*, 2nd ed., Hamden, Conn., 1967.

Hutcheson, F., *An Inquiry into the Original Ideas of Virtue*, London, 1725.

Hutchison, S. C., *The History of the Royal Academy 1768–1968*, London, 1968.

Hutin, Serge, *Les Sociétés Secrètes*, Paris, 1960.

Hutt, Allen, *Fournier, the Compleat Typographer*, London, 1972.

Hutton, E., *The Cosmati: the Roman Marble Workers of the Twelfth and Thirteenth Centuries*, London, 1950.

Hyatt Mayor, A., *Giovanni Battista Piranesi*, New York, 1952.

Ilchester, Earl of (Giles Stephen Holland Fox-Strangways), *Lord Hervey and his Friends (1726–38)*, London, 1950.

Il Settecento a Roma (catalog), Rome, 1959.

Ingarden, Roman, *Studia z Estetyki*, 2d ed., Warsaw, 1966.

Ireland, J., *Hogarth Illustrated*, 3 vols., London, 1791–1798.

Irwin, D., *English Neo-Classical Art,* London, 1966.

Ison, W., *The Georgian Buildings of Bath from 1700 to 1830,* London, 1948.

Ivins, William M., Jr., *Prints and Visual Communication,* London, 1953.

Jacob, Heinrich Eduard, *Biografia del Caffè,* translated and edited by Aldo Oberdorfer, Milan, 1936.

Jacob, J. R., "Restoration, Reformation and the Origins of the Royal Society," in *History of Science,* 13 (1975).

Jallier de Savault, J. B. C., *Motion à l'Ouverture de l'Assemblée du Tiers-Etat,* 21 April 1789.

James, John. *See* Dézallier d'Argenville, A. O.

Janner, Ferdinand, *Die Bauhütten des Deutschen Mittelalters,* Leipzig, 1876.

Jardine, L., *Francis Bacon, Discovery and the Art of Discourse,* Cambridge, 1974.

Jarkius, J., *Specimen Historiae Academiarum Eruditarum Italiae,* Leipzig, 1725.

Jeanmaire, H., *Couroi et Courètes,* Lille, 1939.

Jenkins, Frank, *Architect and Patron,* Oxford, 1961.

Jeramec, Jacques, *La Vie de Scarron,* Paris, 1929.

Jones, Inigo, *The Most Notable Antiquity of Great Britain, Vulgarly Called Stone-Heng,* 3rd ed., London, 1725.

Jones, Inigo. *See* Harris, J., Orgel, S., and Strong, R.

Jones, Richard Foster, et al., *The Seventeenth Century,* Stanford, 1951.

Jones, Richard Foster, *Ancients and Moderns: A Study of the Rise of the Scientific Movement in Seventeenth-Century England,* second edition, St. Louis, Missouri, 1961.

Jong, H. M. E. de, *Michael Maier's Atalanta Fugiens: Sources of an Alchemical Book of Emblems,* Janus, supplementary, vol. VIII, Leyden, 1969.

Jonson, Ben, *Works,* edited by C. H. Herford and Percy and Evelyn Simpson, Oxford, 1925–1952.

Josten, C. H., *Elias Ashmole,* Oxford, 1966.

Jourdain, Margaret, *The Work of William Kent,* introduction by Christopher Hussey, London and New York, 1948.

Jung, C. G., *Psychologie und Alchemie,* Zurich, 1944.

Junot, Laure Permon. *See* Abrantés, Duchesse d'.

Justi, C., *Winckelmann und seine Zeitgenossen,* Leipzig, 1923.

Kambartel, Walter, *Symmetrie und Schönheit,* Munich, 1972.

Kant, Immanuel, *Werke,* Herausgeb. Ernst Cassirer, in gemeinschaft mit Cohen, Buchenau, Birek, Görland, Keller, Berlin, 1912–1922.

Kaufman, S., coll., *Fantastic and Ornamental Drawings* (catalog), Portsmouth, 1969.

Kaufmann, Emil, "Three Revolutionary Architects: Boullée, Ledoux and

Lequeu'' in *Transactions of the American Philosophical Society*, n.s., XLII, pt. 3, Philadelphia, 1952.

Kaufmann, Emil, *Architecture in the Age of Reason*, Cambridge, Mass, 1955.

Kerenyi, K., *The Heroes of the Greeks*, London, 1959.

Ketton-Cremer, R. W., *Horace Walpole*, London, 1964.

Killanin, Lord, *Sir Godfrey Kneller and his Times 1646–1723*. London, 1948.

Kimball, S. F., *Thomas Jefferson, Architect*, Boston, 1916.

Kimball, S. F., ''Les Influences Anglaises dans la Formation du Style Louis XVI,'' *Gazette des Beaux-Arts* 1931, 231–55, 9–44.

Kimball, S. F., *The Creation of the Rococo*, Philadelphia, 1943.

Kircher, Athanasius, SJ. See also Nieuhoff, J.

Kircher, Athanasius, SJ, *Musurgia Universalis, sive Ars Magna Consoni et Dissoni in X libros digesta*, Rome, 1650.

Kircher, Athanasius, SJ, *Oedipus Aegyptiacus, Hoc est Universalis Hieroglyphicae Veterum Doctrinae Temporum Iniuria Abolitae Instauratio* . . . Rome, 1652.

Kircher, Athanasius, e Soc. J., *China Monumentis, qua Sacris qua Profanis, nec non Variis Naturae et Artis Spectaculis, Aliarumque Rerum Memorabilium Argumentis Illustrata, Auspiciis Leopoldi Primi R.I.*, Amsterdam, 1667.

Kircher, Athanasius, *A.K. als Musikschriftsteller, Ein Beitrag zur Musikanschauung der Barock*, edited by Ulf Scharlau, Kassel, 1969.

Kircher, Athanasius, *Studia Kircheriana*, edited by P. Conor Reilly, SJ, Wiesbaden and Rome, 1974.

Klibansky, Raymond, *The Continuity of the Platonic Tradition during the Middle Ages: Outlines of a Corpus Platonicum Medii Aevi*, London, 1939.

Kloss, Georg, *Geschichte der Freimaurerei in Frankreich aus ächten Urkunden dargestellt*, Darmstadt, 1852–1853.

Knoop, D., Jones, G. P., and Hamer, D., *The Two Earliest Masonic Manuscripts*, Manchester, 1938.

Knoop, D., and Jones, G. P., *The Genesis of Freemasonry*, Manchester, 1947.

Körte, Werner, ''Giovanni Battista Piranesi als Praktischer Architekt,'' *Zeitschrift für Kunstgeschichte*, II (1933).

Kortum, H., *Charles Perrault und Nicolas Boileau*, Berlin, 1966.

Koyré, Alexander, *Studi Newtoniani*, Turin, 1972.

Krautheimer, R., *Studies in Early Christian, Medieval, and Renaissance Art*, London, 1969.

Kris, Ernst, ''Der Stil Rustique: Die Verwendung des Naturabgusses bei Wenzel Jamnitzer und Bernard Palissy,'' *Jahrbuch der Kunsthistorischen Sammlungen in Wien*, n.f, 1926, pp. 137–208.

Kristeller, Paul, *Der Kupferschnitt und Holzschnitt*, Berlin, 1912.

Kroll, Maria, *Sophie, Electress of Hanover: A Personal Portrait*, London, 1973.

Kröter, Willy, *Charakteristik der Märchen Perraults*, Leipzig, 1915.

Kultermann, U., *Geschichte der Kunstgeschichte*, Vienna, 1966.

Kunoth, G., *Die Historische Architektur Fischers von Erlach*, Düsseldorf, 1956.

Laborde, Comte de, *Documents . . . sur l'Histoire et les Antiquités d'Athènes*, Paris, 1854.

Lacour-Gayet, G., *L'Abbaye de Saint-Germain des Près et son Monastère Bénédictin*, Paris, 1924.

Lacroix, P., ed., *Charles Perrault, Mémoires*, Paris, 1878.

[La Font de Saint-Yenne], *L'Ombre du Grand Colbert, le Louvre et la Ville de Paris, Dialogue, Réflexions sur Quelque Causes de l'État Présent de la Peinture en France avec Quelques Lettres de l'Auteur à ce Sujet*, nouvelle édition corrigée, second edition of first tract, Paris, 1752.

[La Font de Saint-Yenne], *Sentimens sur Quelques Ouvrages de Peinture, Sculpture et Gravure, Ecrits à un Particulier en Province*, Paris, 1754.

La Fontaine, Jean de, *Oeuvres Complètes*, edited by Jean Marmier, Paris, 1965.

Lagarde, A., and Michard, Laurent, *La Littérature Française*, Paris, 1970.

La Mettrie, Julien Offray de, *L'Homme Machine: A Study in the Origin of an Idea*, critical edition with an introductory monograph and notes by Aram Vartanian, Princeton, 1960.

Landon, C.-P., *Annales du Musée et de l'Ecole Moderne des Beaux-Arts*, Paris, 1801–1808.

Landon, C.-P., *Les Vies et les Oeuvres des Peintres les Plus Célèbres*, Paris, 1805.

Landsberger, F., *Wilhelm Tischbein*, Leipzig, 1908.

Lang, S., "Vanbrugh's Theory and Hawksmoor's Buildings," *Journal of the Society of Architectural Historians*, vol. XXIV, no. 2, 1965.

Lang, S., "The Principles of the Gothic Revival in England," *Journal of the Society of Architectural Historians* XXV (1966).

Langley, Batty, *New Principles of Gardening or the Laying Out and Planting of Parterres, Groves, Wildernesses, Labyrinths, Avenues, Parks etc. . . . By B.L. of Twickenham*, London, 1728.

Langley, Batty, *Ancient Masonry, Both in the Theory and Practice, Demonstrating the Useful Rules of Arithmetick, Geometry and Architecture, in the Proportions and Orders of the Most Eminent Masters of All Nations*, London, 1736.

Langley, Batty, *The Builder's Director, or Benchmate: Being a Pocket Treasury of the Grecian, Roman and Gothic Orders of Architecture, Made Easy to the Meanest Capacity*, London, n.d.

Langley, Batty, *City and Country Builder's and Workman's Treasury of Designs or the Art of Drawing and Working the Ornamental Parts of Architecture . . . Proportioned by Aliquot Parts*, London, 1740.

[Langley, Batty], *The Landed Gentleman's Useful Companion: or a Sure and Easy Method of Improving Estates . . . by a Country Gentleman,* London, 1741.

Langley, Batty, *Ancient Architecture, Restored and Improved by a Great Variety of Grand and Useful Designs, Entirely New, in the Gothick Mode for the Ornamenting of Buildings and Gardens,* London, 1742.

Langley, Batty, *Gothic Architecture, Improved by Rules and Proportions* (second edition of *Ancient Architecture*), London, 1742.

Lapauze, H., *Histoire de l'Académie de France à Rome,* Paris, 1924.

Lapide, Cornelius à, SJ, *Commentaria in Danielem Prophetam,* Antwerp, 1621.

Laprade, A., *François d'Orbay,* Paris, 1960.

Laugier, Marc-Antoine, *Essai sur l'Architecture,* Paris, 1753.

Laugier, Marc-Antoine, *Apologie de la Musique Françoise, Contre le Sentiment de M. Rousseau,* Paris, 1754.

Laugier, Marc-Antoine, *Histoire de la République de Venise depuis sa Fondation jusqu'à Présent,* par M. l'Abbé L . . . , Paris, 1759–1768.

Laugier, Marc-Antoine, *Observations sur l'Architecture,* The Hague, 1765.

Laulan, R., *L'Ecole Militaire de Paris,* Paris, 1950.

Lauro, G., *Breve Descrizione . . . di Orvieto,* Rome, 1635.

Lavater, J. K., *Physiognomische Fragmente,* Leipzig, 1775–1778.

Lavater, J. K., *Essai sur la Physiognomie, Destiné à Faire Connoitre l'Homme et à le Faire Aimer,* The Hague, 1783.

Lavedan, Pierre, *Urbanisme et Architecture: Etudes Écrites et Publiées en l'Honneur de Pierre Lavedan,* Paris, 1954.

Lavedan, Pierre, *Histoire de l'Urbanisme: Renaissance et Temps Modernes,* Paris, 1959.

Laveglia, Pietro, *Paestum, dalla Decadenza alla Riscoperta fino al 1860,* Naples, 1971.

Lavisse, E., *Histoire de France,* Paris, 1909.

Lazare, Félix, and Lazare, Louis, *Dictionnaire Administratif et Historique des Rues et Monuments de Paris,* Paris, 1855.

Leader Scott, P., *The Cathedral Builders: The Story of a Great Masonic Guild,* London, 1899.

Leake, W. M., *Topography of Athens with Some Remarks on its Antiquities,* London, 1841.

Le Bihan, Alain, *Francs-Maçons Parisiens du Grand Orient de France,* Paris, 1966.

Le Bihan, Alain, *Francs-Maçons et Ateliers Parisiens de la Grande Loge de France au XVIIIe Siècle,* Paris, 1973.

Le Blanc, Abbé Jean Bernard, *Lettre sur l'Exposition des Ouvrages de Peinture de l'Année 1747; Lettres . . . Concernant le Gouvernement, la Politique et les Moeurs des Anglais et des Français,* Paris, 1747.

Lebois, André, *Fabuleux Nerval*, Paris, 1972.

(Le Brun de Marettes, Jean-Baptiste, Sieur de Moléon), *Voyages Liturgiques de France, ou Recherches Faites en Diverses Villes du Royaume par le Sieur de Moléon Contenant Plusieurs Péculiarités Touchant les Rites et les Usages des Eglises, avec des Découvertes sur l'Antiquité Ecclésiastique et Payenne*, Paris, 1718.

Le Camus de Mézières, *Le Génie de l'Architecture ou l'Analogie de cet Art avec nos Sensations*, Paris, 1780.

Le Clerc, Daniel, *Histoire de la Médecine*, new ed., The Hague, 1729.

Lees-Milne, James, *Earls of Creation: Five Great Patrons of Eighteenth-Century Art*, London, 1962.

Legrand, J-G., and Landon, C-P., *Description de Paris et ses Edifices*, Paris, 1806–1809; second edition, 1818.

Leibnitz, Gottfried, *Novissima Sinica Historiam*, 1697.

Lemmi, Charles, *The Classic Deities in Bacon: A Study in Mythological Symbolism*, Baltimore, 1933.

Lemmonier, H., *Procès-Verbaux de l'Académie Royale d'Architecture, 1671–1793*, Paris, 1926.

Lenoble, Robert, *Mersenne ou la Naissance du Mécanisme*, Paris, 1943.

Le Pautre, Antoine, *Les Oeuvres d'Architecture d'Antoine Le Pautre*, Paris, 1652.

Le Roy, J.D.-, *Les Ruines des Plus Beaux Monuments de la Grèce*, Paris, 1758.

Le Roy, J.D.-, *Histoire de la Disposition et des Formes Différentes que les Chrétiens Ont Données à leurs Temples, depuis le Règne de Constantin le Grand jusqu' à Nous*, Paris, 1764.

Lettres Édifiantes et Curieuses Écrites des Missions Étrangères par Quelques Missionaires de la Compagnie de Jésus, 1707–1773.

Lévy-Valensi, J., *La Médecine et les Médecins Français au XVIIe Siècle*, Paris, 1933.

Lewis, Lesley, *Connoisseurs and Secret Agents in Eighteenth-Century Rome*, London, 1961.

Lewis, Wilmarth Sheldon, *A Catalogue of Horace Walpole's Library*, New Haven and London, 1969.

Libby, Margaret Sherwood, *The Attitude of Voltaire to Magic and the Sciences*, New York, 1935.

Lind, Karl, ed., *Mittheilungen der K.K. Central-Commission zur Erforschung und Erhaltung der Kunst und Historischen Denkmale*, XX Jahrgang, Neue Folge, Vienna, 1894.

Lipking, Lawrence, *The Ordering of the Arts in Eighteenth-Century England*, Princeton, 1970.

Little, B., *The Life and Work of James Gibbs*, London, 1955.

Little, B., *Sir Christopher Wren*, London, 1976.

Lloyd, Nathaniel, *A History of the English House*, London, 1931.

Locke, John, "An Essay Concerning Human Understanding," in *Works*, 12th ed., London, 1824.

Londreix, Georges, *Le Petit Chaperon Rouge*, Paris, 1970.

Lough, John, *Essays on the Encyclopédie of Diderot and d'Alembert*, Oxford, 1968.

Louis, Louis Nicolas, *Réfutation des Nouveaux Développemens du Citoyen Lhote sur la Place de la Paix Projettée pour la Ville de Bordeaux*, Paris, n.d.

Longinus, D. C., *De Sublimitate . . . J. Tollius . . . Emendavit . . . Novamque Versionem Suam Latinam et Gallicam Boilavii . . . Addidit*, Paris, 1694.

Loos, Erich, *Alessandro Tassonis "La Secchia Rapita" und das Problem des heroisch-komische Epos*, Krefeld, 1967.

Lovejoy, A. O., "The Meaning of Romanticism for the Historian of Ideas," *Journal of the History of Ideas*, 1941.

Luce, A. A., *The Life of George Berkeley, Bishop of Cloyne*, London, 1949.

Luschin von Ebengreuth, Arnold, "Das Admonter Hüttenbuch und die Regensburger Steinmetzordnung vom Jahre 1459," in Lind, Karl (1894), pp. 168–171, 227–241.

Lutyens, Mary (editor), *Effie in Venice: Unpublished Letters of Mrs. John Ruskin Written from Venice between 1849–1852*, London, 1972.

Luynes, Charles Philippe d'Albert, Duc de, *Mémoires sur la Cour de Louis XV (1735–58)*, Paris, 1860.

Lyons, Alexander, *Shaftesbury's Ethical Principle of Adaptation to Universal Harmony*, Ph.D. thesis, New York, 1909.

Mabillon, J., *De Re Diplomatica*, Paris, 1681.

Macaulay, Rose, *The Pleasures of Ruins*, London, 1953.

Macaulay, Thomas Babington Lord Macaulay, *Critical and Historical Essays contributed to the Edinburgh Review*, London 1883.

Madonna, M. L., "Septem Mundi Miracula," *Psicon 7*, Florence, 1976.

Maffei, Scipione, *Verona Illustrata*, Verona, 1735.

Magagnato, Licisco, *Teatri Italiani del Cinquecento*, Venice, 1956.

Maginniss, Joseph, *Le Petit Trianon, Being a Reproduction of Plates from a Work by James A. Arnott and John Wilson, Architects of Edinburgh*, year book of the Boston Architectural Club, Boston, 1913.

Mahon, Denis, *Studies in Seicento Art and Theory*, Westport, Conn., 1971.

Maier, Michael. *See* H. M. E. de Jong.

Mair, Esther, *The Discovery of Britain: The English Tourists, 1540–1840*, London, 1964.

Maitland, William, *The History and Survey of London from its Foundation to the Present Time*, London, 1756; new edition by E. S. de Beer, Oxford, 1938.

Maiuri, A., *Pompeii*, Naples, 1964.

Maiuri, A., *Herculaneum*, Naples, 1964.

Malebranche, Nicolas, *Oeuvres Complètes de M.*, 2 vols. Paris, 1837.

Malebranche, Nicolas, *Oeuvres: Texte établi par A. Robinet.* (Bibliothèque des Textes Philosophiques, dirigée par H. Gauthier) Paris, 1962–.

Mancini, Giulio, *Viaggio per Roma,* edited by Ludwig Schudt, Leipzig, 1923.

Mantoux, Paul, *The Industrial Revolution in the Eighteenth Century: An Outline of the Modern Factory System in England,* London, 1961.

Manuel, Frank E., *The Prophets of Paris,* Cambridge, Mass., 1962.

Manuel, Frank E., *Isaac Newton, Historian,* Cambridge, Mass., 1963.

Manuel, Frank E., *A Portrait of Isaac Newton,* Cambridge, Mass., 1968.

Manuel, Frank E., *The Religion of Isaac Newton,* The Freemantle Lectures, 1973, Oxford, 1974.

Marana, G. P., *L'Espion du Grand Seigneur et ses Relations Secrètes Envoyées au Divan de Constantinople; et Découvertes à Paris, Pendant le Règne de Louis le Grand*, Paris, 1684.

Marandon, Bartholomé, *L'Usage du Caphé, du Thé et du Chocolat*, translated by Jacob Spon, Lyons, 1671.

Marie, J., and Marie, A., *Marly,* Paris, 1947.

Mariette, M., *Description des Travaux Qui Ont Précédé, Accompagné et Suivi la Fonte en Bronze d'un Seul Jet de la Statue Equestre de Louis XV, le Bien-Aimé à Paris. Dressée sur les Mémoires de M. Lempereur,* Paris, 1768.

Marin, Louis, *L'Art des Jardins et les Mouvements de l'Esprit Humain: Le Luxembourg, Jardin Classique et Paysager,* Paris, 1971.

Marinetti, Filippo Tommaso, e fillia, *La Cucina Futurista*, Milan, 1932.

Marmontel, J.-F., *Oeuvres Posthumes: Régence du Duc d'Orléans*, Paris, 1805.

Marot, D., *Nouveau Livre de Cheminées à la Hollandoise,* Amsterdam, 1712.

Marot, Pierre, *Emanuel Héré (1705–1763). Biographie du Premier Architecte du Roi Stanislas d'après les Notes de Pierre Boyé,* Nancy, 1954.

Masson, Frédéric, *Le Cardinal de Bernis depuis son Ministère,* Paris, 1884.

Masson, Frédéric, *Mémoires et Lettres de François-Joachim de Pierre, Cardinal de Bernis,* Paris, 1878.

Masson, Georgina, *Queen Christina,* New York, 1968.

Matthews, W. H., *Mazes and Labyrinths,* London, 1922.

Matthiae, Guglielmo, *Ferdinando Fuga e la sua Opera Romana,* Rome, n.d.

Matthieu, M., *Pierre Patte,* Paris, 1940.

Mauban, A., *Jean Marot, Architecte et Graveur Parisien,* Paris, 1944.

Mauban, A., *L'Architecture Française de Jean Mariette,* Paris, 1945.

Maupertuis, P. L. Moreau de, *Degré du Méridien entre Paris et Amiens Determiné par la Mesure de M. Picard,* Paris, 1740.

Mauss, Marcel, *Manuel d'Ethnographie*, Paris, 1967.

Mazzotti, Giuseppe, *Palladian and Other Venetian Villas*, London, 1958.

Médailles sur les Principaux Evénements du Règne de Louis le Grand, avec des Inscriptions et Médailles, Paris, 1702.

Meissonier, Juste-Aurèle, *Oeuvre de J. A. M., Peintre, Sculpteur, Architecte, et Dessinateur de la Chambre et Cabinet du Roy*, Paris, n.d.

Mellis, Paolo, "G. B. Piranesi: Un "Ampio Magnifico Collegio" per l'Architettura: Intenzionalità Iconologica in un Documento storico dell'Illuminismo," *Psicon 4*, Anno II (1975).

Mellor, A., *Our Separated Brethren, the Free-Masons*, London, 1964.

Mellor, A., *La Vie Quotidienne de la Franc-Maçonnerie Française du XVIIIe Siècle à nos Jours*, Paris, 1973.

Melville, Lewis, *The Life and Letters of William Beckford of Fonthill*, London, 1910.

Memmo, A., *Elementi dell'Architettura Lodoliana ossia l'Arte del Fabbricare con Solidità Scientifica e con Eleganza non Capricciosa*, Libri due, Rome, 1786.

Memmo, A., *Elementi d'Architettura Lodoliana*, Zara, 1833.

Menninger, Karl, *Zahlwort und Ziffer*, Göttingen, 1958.

Mercer, Eric, *English Art 1553–1625*, Oxford, 1962.

[Mersenne, Marin], *Questions Harmoniques. Dans Lesquelles Sont Contenues Plusieurs Remarquables pour la Physique, pour la Morale & pour les Autres Sciences*, Paris, 1634.

Metman, Y., "Urbanisme à Paris au XVIIIe Siècle. Les Conventions du 3 Juin 1758 entre la Ville et les Héritiers de Law pour l'Aile Occidentale de la Place de la Concorde, in P. Lavedan (1954).

Middleton, R. D., "The Abbé de Cordemoy and the Graeco-Gothic Ideal: A Prelude to Romantic Classicism," *Journal of the Warburg and Courtauld Institutes*, 1962, 1963.

Middleton, R. D., "Jean-François Blondel and the Cours d'Architecture," *Journal of the Society of Architectural Historians*, Vol. XVIII, n. 4, December 1959.

Middleton, R. D., and Watkin, D., *Architettura Moderna*, Milan, 1977.

Migliorini, Ermanno, *Studi sul Pensiero Estetico del Settecento*, Florence, 1966.

Milizia, Francesco, *Memorie degli Architetti Antichi e Moderni*, 3rd ed., Parma, 1781.

Milizia, Francesco, *Principi di Architettura Civile*, Bassano, 1785.

Milizia, Francesco, *Discorso sul Teatro*, Venice, 1789.

Milizia, Francesco, *Dizionario delle Belle Arti del Disegno, Estratto in Gran Parte dalla Enciclopedia Metodica da F. M., Bassano, 1797.*

Milizia, Francesco, *Dell'arte di Vedere nelle Belle Arti del Disegno. Secondo i Principi di Sulzer e di Mengs*, Venice, 1798.

Milizia, Francesco, *Lettere di Francesco Milizia a Tommaso Temanza,*

Pubblicate per la Prima Volta nelle Nozze Muzani-di Caldogno, Venice, 1823.

Millot, Abbé C. F., *Histoire Littéraire des Troubadours,* Paris, 1774.

Milton, John, *Of Education,* London, 1644.

Milton, John, *Complete Prose Works,* edited by D. M. Wolfe, New Haven, 1953–

Minns, E. H., and Webb, M., *Sir Christopher Wren,* London, 1923.

Missirini, Melchiore, *Della Vita di Antonio Canova,* Milan, 1824.

Mitchell, Charles, and Bodnar, Edward, *Cyriaco de' Pizzicolli of Ancona's Journeys in the Propontis and the Northern Aegean (1444–1445),* Philadelphia, 1976.

Mitford, Nancy, *Madame de Pompadour,* London, 1955.

Mittner, L., *Storia della Letteratura Tedesca,* Turin, 1964.

Moholy-Nagy, Laszlo, *Von Material zu Architektur* (Bauhaus-Bücher 14), Munich, 1928.

Moléon, le Sieur de. *See* Le Brun de Marettes, Jean-Baptiste.

Molière, Jean-Baptiste Poquelin, *Le Bourgeois Gentilhomme* in *Oeuvres Complètes,* ed. by Maurice Rat, Paris, 1956.

Mondain-Monval, Jean, *Soufflot: Sa Vie, son Oeuvre, son Esthétique,* Paris, 1918.

Monk, S. H., ed., *Five Miscellaneous Essays by Sir William Temple,* Ann Arbor, 1963.

Monod-Cassidy, H., *Un Voyageur-Philosophe au Dix-Huitième Siècle: L'Abbé J.-B. Le Blanc,* Cambridge, Mass., 1941.

Montagu, Lady Mary Wortley, *Select Passages from Her Letters,* London, 1892.

Montaiglon, A. de, and Guiffrey, J., eds., *Correspondance des Directeurs de l'Académie de France à Rome,* Paris, 1888.

Montesquieu, C. L. de Secondat, Baron de la Brède et de, *Oeuvres Complètes . . .* Texte présenté et annoté par Roger Caillois, Paris, 1949–1951.

Montfaucon, B. de, *Palaeographia Graeca, Sive de Ortu et Progressu Literarum Graecarum et de Variis Omnium Saeculorum Scriptionis Graecae Generibus: Itemque de Abbreviationibus et de Notis Variarum Artium ac Disciplinarum. Additis Figuris et Schematibus ad Fidem Manuscriptorum Codicum,* Paris, 1708.

Montfaucon, B. de, *L'Antiquité Expliquée et Représentée en Figures,* Paris, 1719–1724.

Montgolfier, Bernard de, "Le Cardinal de Noailles, Archevêque de Paris: un Portrait Inédit," *Bulletin du Musée Carnavalet,* 25 (1972).

Montuori, Mario, "Tre Lettere di Locke a Limborch sull'Unità di Dio," *Atti dell'Accademia Pontana,* n.s., XXIII, Naples, 1974.

Morassi, A., *G. B. Tiepolo,* London, 1955.

Morassi, A., *A Complete Catalogue of the Paintings of G. B. Tiepolo,* London, 1962.

Morazzoni, G., *Giovanni Battista Piranesi, Notizie Biografiche,* Milan, 1921.

Mordaunt-Crook, J., "The Restoration of the Temple Church," *Architectural History,* 8 (1965).

Mordaunt-Crook, J., *The Greek Revival,* London, 1972.

More, H., *The Immortality of the Soul, so Farre Forth as it Is Demonstrable from the Light of Nature and the Light of Reason,* Cambridge, 1659.

More, Thomas, *Complete Works,* edited by Edward Surtz, SJ, and J. H. Hexter, New Haven, 1963–.

Moreni, Domenico, ed., *Vita di Filippo di Ser Brunelleschi . . . scritta da Filippo Baldinucci,* Florence, 1812.

Moresca, M. P., & Vaccaro, V., "Massoneria ed Ermetismo nella Napoli del '700: La Cappella San Severo," *Psicon 4,* Anno II (1975).

Morini, M., *Atlante di Storia dell'Urbanistica,* Milan, 1963.

Morris, Robert, *An Essay in Defence of Ancient Architecture or a Parallel of the Ancient Building with the Modern: Shewing the Beauty and Harmony of the Former and the Irregularity of the Latter* by R. M. of Twickenham, London, 1728.

Morris, Robert, *Lectures on Architecture, Consisting of Rules Founded upon Harmonick and Arithmetical Proportion in Building Design'd as an Agreable Entertainment for Gentlemen . . . Read to a Society Establish'd for the Improvement of Arts and Sciences,* London, 1759.

Morris, Robert, *Rural Architecture,* London, 1750.

Morrison, S., *Letter Forms,* London, 1963.

Moschini, G. A., *Della Letteratura Veneziana del Secolo XVIII fino a' Nostri Giorni,* Venice, 1806.

Moschini, G. A., *Guida per la Città di Venezia all'Amico delle Arti,* Venice, 1815.

Mosser, Monique, "Monsieur de Marigny et les Jardins: Projets Inédits des Fabriques pour Menars," *Bulletin de la Société de l'Histoire de l'Art Français,* 1973, pp. 260 ff.

Müntz, Eugene, *Leonardo da Vinci, Artist, Thinker, and Man of Science,* London, 1898.

Muret, P., *La Prépondérance Anglaise,* Paris, 1949.

Murray Lyon, David, *History of the Lodge of Edinburgh (Mary's Chapel),* no. 1, Edinburgh, 1873.

Mylne, Robert Scott, *The Master Masons to the Crown of Scotland and their Works,* Edinburgh, 1893.

Naudon, Paul, *Les Origines Religieuses et Corporatives de la Franc-Maçonnerie,* Paris, 1953.

Nerval, G. de (Gérard Labrunie), *Voyages en Orient,* Paris, 1862.

Nerval, G. de (Gérard Labrunie), *Oeuvres*, texte établi, annoté, et présenté par Albert Beguin et Jean Richer, Paris, 1952–1956.

Neuerburg, N., *L'Architettura delle Fontane e dei Ninfei nell' Italia Antica*, Naples, 1965.

Nevill-Jackson, F., *Silhouette, Notes and Dictionary*, London, 1938.

Newton, Isaac, *The Chronology of Ancient Kingdoms Amended, to which is Prefix'd a Short Chronicle from the First Memory of Things in Europe to the Conquest of Persia by Alexander the Great*, London, 1728.

Newton, Isaac, *Opticks, or a Treatise on the Reflections, Refractions, Inflections and Colours of Light*, London 1704–1730; reprint with a foreword by A. Einstein, 1952.

Newton, Isaac, *Observations upon the Prophecies of Daniel and the Apocalypse of St. John*, London, 1733.

Newton, Isaac, *A Treatise of the System of the World*, edited by I. Bernard Cohen, London, 1969.

Nibby, A., *Roma nell Anno MDCCCXXXVIII*, Rome, 1838.

Nichols, Frederick D., *Thomas Jefferson's Architectural Drawings*, Boston, 1960.

Nichols, S. G., Jr., ed., *Concepts of Criticism*, New Haven and London, 1963.

Nicholson, M. H., *Newton Demands a Muse*, Princeton, N.J., 1946.

Nicole, P., *An Essay on True and Apparent Beauty in Which from Settled Principles is Rendered the Grounds for Choosing and Rejecting Epigrams*, translated by J. V. Cunningham, California, 1950.

Nicolson, Marjorie, *Science and Imagination*, Ithaca, New York, 1956.

Nicolson, Marjorie, and Rousseau, G. S., *"This Long Disease, My Life"; Alexander Pope and the Sciences*, Princeton, New Jersey, 1968.

Nieuhoff, Jan, *Het Gezamtschap der Nederlandtsche Oost-Indische Compagnie aan den grooten Tartarischen Cham*, Amsterdam, 1665.

Nieuhoff, Jan, *An Embassy from the East India Company to the Grand Tartar Cham, Emperor of China . . . described by J.N. . . . also an appendix . . . taken out of . . . Athanasius Kircher . . .* , translated by John Ogilby, London, 1669.

Nolhac, P. de, *Versailles*, Paris, 1901.

Norberg-Schulz, Christian, *Architettura Barocca*, Milan, 1971.

Norberg-Schulz, Christian, *Architettura Tardobarocca*, Milan, 1971.

Nordick, Agnes, *Der Stil der Märchen Perraults*, Münster, 1934.

Normand, C., *Nouveau Parallèle des Ordres d'Architecture*, Paris, 1823.

Normand, C., *Guide de l'Ornamentiste*, Paris, 1826.

Noussane, Henri de, *Paris sous Louis XVI et Paris Aujoud'hui*, Paris, 1900.

Oechslin, Werner, "Pyramide et Sphère: Notes sur l'Architecture Révolutionnaire du XVIIIe Siècle et ses Sources Italiennes," *Gazette des Beaux-Arts*, 1971.

Oechslin, Werner, *Bildungsgut und Antikenrezeption des frühen Settecento in Rom: Studien zum Römischen Aufenthalt Bernardo Antonio Vittones*, Zurich, 1972.

Onofrio, Cesare d', *Le Fontane di Roma*, Rome, 1957.

de l'Orme, Philibert, *Le Premier Tome de l'Architecture*, Paris, 1568.

de l'Orme, Philibert, *Nouvelles Inventions pour Bien Bastir et à Petits Fraiz*, Paris, 1576.

de l'Orme, Philibert, *Architecture de P. de l'O. Oeuvre Entière Contenant Onze Livres, Augmentée de Deux; et Autres Figures non Encore Veues*, Paris, 1626.

Ostrowski, Jan, *Nurt Egzotyczny w Architekturze Stanisława Leszczyńskiego w Lotaryngii*.

Ostrowski, Jan, *Tschifflik, Maison de Plaisance Stanisława Leszczyńskiego w Zweibrücken*, Biuletyn Historii Sztuki.

Ouvrard, René, *Architecture Harmonique ou Application de la Doctrine des Proportions de la Musique à l'Architecture*, Paris, 1677.

Palissy, Bernard, *Les Oeuvres . . . revues par B. Fillon et Louis Audiat*, Niors, 1888.

Palme, Per, *The Triumph of Peace*, London, 1957.

Pancrazi, P., *Antichità Siciliane Spiegate, Colle Notizie Generali di Questo Regno cui si Comprende la Storia Particolare di Quelle Città, delle Quali se ne Riportano, ed Illustrano Separatamente Gl'antichi Monumenti*, Naples, 1751.

Pane, Roberto, *Ferdinando Fuga*, Naples, 1956.

Pane, Roberto, *Ville Vesuviane del Settecento*, Naples, 1959.

Panofsky, E., *Hercules am Scheidewegen*, Leipzig and Berlin, 1930.

Panofsky, E., *Renaissance and Renascence in Western Art*, Stockholm, 1960.

Panofsky, E., *Idea: A Concept in Art Theory*, translated from the second German edition by J. S. Peake, Columbia, South Carolina, 1968.

Panofsky, E., *Meaning in the Visual Arts*, New York, 1968.

Panvinus, O., *De Ludis Circensibus et de Triumphis*, Venice, 1602.

Paoli, Fr. Paolo Antonio, *Rovine dell'Antica Città di Pesto detto Ancora Posidonia*, Rome, 1784.

Paoli, Fr. Paolo Antonio, *Di San Felice Secondo, Papa e Martire, Dissertazioni Indirizzate ad Illustrare l'Antico suo Epitaffio Nuovamente Scoperto, e a Difendere la sua Santità ed il suo Pontificato*, Rome, 1790.

Papini, R., "Pitture inedite di G.P. Panini," *Bolletino d'Arte*, III, 2nd series, 1923–1924, pp. 349 ff.

Pariset, F., *Etude sur l'Atelier de la Cathédrale de Strasbourg, entre 1681 et 1789*, Paris, 1929.

Parker, K. T., *The Drawings of Antonio Canaletto in the Collection of H. M. the King at Windsor Castle*, London and Oxford, 1948.

Parks, Sydney, "London Town Planning Schemes in 1666," *Journal of the Royal Institute of British Architects*, 1919.

Pascal, Blaise, *Oeuvres Complètes,* edited by Louis Lafuma, Paris, 1963.

Pascoli, Lione, *Vite de' Pittori, Scultori ed Architetti Moderni,* Perugia, 1730–1736.

[Pascoli, Lione], *Testamento Politico d'un Academico Florentino in cui con Nuovi e Ben Fondati Principi; si Fanno Vari e Diversi Progetti per Istabilire un Ben Regolato Commercio nello Stato della Chiesa . . .* Cologne (Rome?), 1733.

Pascoli, Lione, *Il Tevere navigato e navigabile in cui si prova con Autorità Evidenti e non Sospette che ne' Tempi sin da sua Scaturaggine si navigava che ne' presenti si puo almeno da Orte a Pontenuovo e che alcuni de' moltissimi fiumi che vi sboccano particolarmente il Chiggio, La Paglia, la Nera ed il Teverone che sono i quattro principali parimente si Navigavano. Con tre Discorsi: due delle cause di lui Innondazioni, e dei remedi loro e l'altro de' Remedi dell'Innondazione della Chiana con diversi nuovi Progetti suoi non meno che d'altri tratti da i piu celebri Autori dedicato alla Santita di Nostro Signore Papa Benedetto XIV de L.P.* Rome, 1740.

Pastor, L., *History of the Popes,* edited and translated by F. I. Antrobus, R. F. Kerr, E. Graf, and E. F. Peeler, London, 1891–1953.

Pastore, Nicholas, *Selective History of Theories of Visual Perception, 1650–1950,* New York, 1971.

Patraccone, E., *Cagliostro nella Storia e nella Legenda,* Milan, 1936.

Patte, Pierre, *Discours sur l'Architecture, ou l'On Fait Voir Combien il Seroit Important que l'Etude de cet Art Fit Partie de l'Education des Personnes de Nassance* [sic]; *à la Suite du quel On Propose une Manière de l'Enseigner en Peu de Temps,* Paris, 1754.

Patte, Pierre, *Monumens Erigés en France à la Gloire de Louis XV,* Paris, 1765.

Patte, Pierre, *Mémoires sur les Objets les Plus Importants de l'Architecture,* Paris, 1769.

Paulson, Ronald, *Hogarth: His Life, Art, and Times,* New Haven and London, 1971.

Pauthier, G., *Histoire des Relations Politiques de la Chine avec les Puissances Occidentales,* Paris, 1859.

Pearsall-Smith, L., *The Life and Letters of Sir Henry Wotton,* Oxford, 1907.

Pecchiai, P., *Le Scalinate di Piazza di Spagna,* Rome, 1941.

Pepe, G., *Il Medio Evo Barbarico d'Italia,* Turin, 1963.

Pepys, Samuel, *The Diary and Correspondence . . . ,* transcribed and edited by the Rev. Mynors Bright and Lord Braybrooke, London, 1875–1879.

Percier, C., and Fontaine, P.-L., *Recueil de Décorations Intérieures,* Paris, 1801.

Perez-Gomez, Alberto, "The Use of Geometry and Number in Architectural Theory," Ph.D. thesis, University of Essex, 1977.

Pérouse de Montclos, J.-M., *Etienne-Louis Boullée*, Paris, 1969.

Perrault, Charles, *Parallèle des Anciens et des Modernes*, Paris, 1688–1697.

Perrault, Charles, *Mémoires de ma Vie*, with introduction and notes by P. Bonnefon, Paris, 1909.

Perrault, Charles, *Les Contes*, edited by G. Rouger, Paris, 1967.

Perrault, Charles, *Les Contes*, edited by André Lefêvre, Paris, n.d.

Perrault, Claude, *Mémoires pour Servir à l'Histoire Naturelle des Animaux*, Paris, 1671.

Perrault, Claude, *Les Dix Livres d'Architecture de Vitruve, Corrigez et Traduits Nouvellement en François, avec des Notes et des Figures*, Paris, 1673; second edition, 1684.

Perrault, Claude, *Vitruvius Pollio, Abregé des Dix Livres d'Architecture de Vitruve*, Paris, 1674.

Perrault, Claude, ed., Vitruvius Pollio (Marcus), *An Abridgment of the Architecture of Vitruvius . . . Illustrated . . . To which is added . . . the etymology . . . of the terms used in architecture. First done in French by Monsieur Perrault . . . and now Englished, with additions*, London 1692.

Perrault, Claude, *Ordonnance des Cinq Espèces de Colonnes, selon la Méthode des Anciens*, Paris, 1683.

Perrault, Claude, *Recueil de Plusieurs Machines de Nouvelle Invention*, posthumous work, Paris, 1700.

Perrault, Claude, *Oeuvres Diverses de Physique et de Mécanique de MMs C. & P. Perrault*, Leyden, 1721.

Perrault, Claude, *Voyage à Bordeaux*, edited by Paul Bonnefon, Paris, 1909.

Perrault, Pierre, *De la Musique des Anciens, en Oeuvres Diverses de Physique et de Mécanique de MM. Claude et Pierre Perrault*, Leyden, 1721.

Peterson, Charles E., ed., *The Rules of Work of the Carpenters' Company of the City and County of Philadelphia 1786*, Princeton, 1971.

Petersson, R. T., *Sir Kenelm Digby: The Ornament of England, 1603–1665*, London, 1956.

Petzet, Michel, *Soufflots Sainte-Geneviève und der Französische Kirchenbau des 18. Jahrhunderts*, Berlin, 1961.

Pevsner, Nikolaus, *Academies of Art, Past and Present*, Cambridge, 1940.

Pevsner, Nikolaus, et al., *The Buildings of England*, Harmondsworth, 195–

Pevsner, Nikolaus, *Studies in Art, Architecture, and Design*, London, 1968.

Pevsner, Nikolaus, ed., *The Picturesque Garden and its Influence outside the British Isles—Dumbarton Oaks Colloquium on the History of Landscape Architecture*, Washington, 1974.

Piazzo, Marcello del, *Ragguagli Borrominiani, Mostra Documentaria*, catalog, Rome, 1968.

Picard, Roger, *Les Salons Littéraires et la Société Française, 1610–1789*, New York, 1943.

Picone, M., *La Cappella Sansevero*, Naples, 1959.

Piel, Friedrich, *Die Ornament-Grotteske in der italienischen Renaissance*, Berlin, 1960.

Piganiol de la Force, *Description Historique de la Ville de Paris et de ses Environs*, Paris, 1765.

Piggott, S., *William Stukeley*, Oxford, 1950.

Piles, Roger de, *Dissertation sur les Ouvrages des Plus Fameux Peintres Dédiée à Monseigneur le Duc de Richelieu*, Paris, 1681.

Piles, Roger de, *Cours de Peinture par Principes*, Paris, 1708.

Pillement, Georges, *Paris Disparu*, Paris, 1966.

Pinot, Virgile, *Documents Inédits Relatifs à la Connaissance de la Chine*, Paris, 1932.

Pinot, Virgile, *La Chine et la Formation de l'Esprit*, Paris, 1932.

Piranesi, G. B., *Della Introduzione e del Progresso delle Belle Arti in Europa ne' Tempi Antichi, Prefazione*. See Wilton-Ely, J.

Piranesi, G. B., *Prima Parte de Architettura e Prospettive*, Rome, 1743.

Piranesi, G. B., *Lettere di Giustificazione Scritte a Milord Charlemont e a di lui Agenti di Roma dal Sig. Piranesi*, Rome, 1757.

Piranesi, G. B., *Della Magnificenza ed Architettura dei Romani*, Rome, 1760.

Piranesi, G. B., *Osservazioni di G. B. P. sopra la Lettre de M. Mariette aux Auteurs de la Gazette Littéraire de l'Europe Inserita nel Supplemento dell'istessa Gazzetta Stampata Dimanche 4 Novembre MDCCLIV*, Rome, 1765.

Piranesi, G. B., *Diverse Maniere d'Adornare i Cammini ed Ogni Altra Parte Degli Edifizi Desunte dall'Architettura Egizia, Etrusca e Greca*, Rome, 1769.

Piranesi, G. B., *Vasi, Candelabri, Cippi, Sarcophagi, Tripodi, Lucerne ed Ornamenti Antichi Disegnati ed Incisi dal Cav. G. B. Piranesi*, Rome, 1778–1791.

Piranesi, G. B., *Prisons. With the "Carceri" Etchings*, preface by Aldous Huxley and critical study by Jean Adhémar, London, and Paris, 1949.

Piranesi, G. B., *Il Campo Marzo dell'Antica Roma*, edited by Franco Borsi, Rome, 1958.

Giovanni Battista Piranesi; his Predecessors and his Heritage (catalog), British Museum, London, 1968.

Piranesi, G. B., *The Polemical Works*, edited by J. Wilton-Ely, Farnborough, 1972.

G. B. Piranesi, Drawings and Etchings at Columbia University, catalog, Avery Library, New York, 1972.

Piranesi, G. B., and Piranesi F. *See* Calvesi, Maurizio.

G. B. Piranesi, Etchings, catalog, Colnaghi and Co., London, 1973.

Piranesi, G. B., *Piranèse et les Français, 1740–1790*, catalog, Rome, 1976.

Piranesi, G. B, *Catalogue by John Wilton-Ely,* Arts Council, London, 1977.

Pirenne, Henri, *Medieval Cities, Their Origin and the Revival of Trade,* New York, 1956.

Pirro, André, *Descartes et la Musique,* Paris, 1907.

Placzek, Adolf K. See *G. B. Piranesi,* New York, 1972

Platen, Magnus von, ed., *Queen Christina of Sweden: Documents and Studies,* Stockholm, 1966.

Pletscher, Theodor, *Die Märchen Charles Perraults. Eine literarhistorische und literarvergleichende Studie,* Berlin, 1906.

Plongeron, Bernard, *La Vie Quotidienne du Clergé Français au XVIIIe Siècle,* Paris, 1974.

Plot, Robert, *Enquiries to be Propounded to the Most Ingenious of Each County in My Travels through England and Wales,* London, 1670.

Plot, Robert, *The Natural History of Staffordshire,* Oxford, 1686.

Plot, Robert, *The Natural History of Oxfordshire, Being an Essay Towards the Natural History of England,* 2nd ed., London, 1705.

Plot, Robert, *The History and Antiquities of Glastonbury,* edited by Thomas Hearne, Oxford, 1722.

Plumb, J. H., *Sir Robert Walpole,* Cambridge, 1956.

Pococke, Richard, *A Description of the East and Some Other Countries,* London, 1743–1745.

Poleni, G., *Exercitationes Vitruviane,* Padua, 1739.

Poleni, G., *Memorie Istoriche della Gran Cupola del Tempio Vaticano,* Padua, 1748.

Pomeau, René, *La Religion de Voltaire,* Paris, 1956.

Pope, A., *The Works . . . with his Last Corrections, Additions and Improvements . . . together with the Commentary and Notes of Mr. Warburton,* London, 1760; supplement, London 1807.

Port-Royal Grammar. See Arnauld, A., and Lancelot, C.

Poussin, Nicolas, *Lettres,* edited by P. Colombier, Paris, 1929.

Prado, Jeronimo and Villalpanda, Juan Bautista, *In Ezechielem Explanationes,* Rome, 1596–1602.

Prager, F. D., and Scaglia, G., *Brunelleschi: Studies of His Technology and Inventions,* Boston, 1970.

[Preston, William], *Illustrations of Masonry,* London, 1772. Reprinted with biographical notice, by William Watson, London, 1887.

Preuss, J. D. E., *Friedrich der Grosse,* Berlin, 1832.

Previtali, G., *La Fortuna dei Primitivi,* Turin, 1964.

Priestley, Joseph, *The History and Present State of Discoveries Relating to Vision, Light and Colours,* London, 1772.

Priouret, Roger, *La Franc-Maçonnerie sous les Lys,* Preface by Pierre Gaxotte, Paris, 1953.

Pugin, A., *Specimens of Gothic Architecture,* London, 1821.

Purver, Margery, *The Royal Society: Concept and Creation,* Cambridge, Mass., 1967.

Quatremère de Quincy, Antoine Chrysostome, *Histoire de la Vie et des Ouvrages des Plus Célèbres Architectes*, Paris, 1830.

Racine, Jean, *Oeuvres Complètes,* presentation, notes et commentaries par Raymond Picard, Paris, 1951.

Radcliffe, Anthony, "Monti's Allegory of the Risorgimento," in *Victoria and Albert Museum Bulletin,* July 1965.

Radicchio, Don Vincenzo, *Descrizione della . . . Idea Concepita . . . dall' Ec.mo Signore Andrea Memmo . . . sul Materiale del Prato, che Denominavasi della Valle,* Rome, 1786.

Raffron du Trouillet, N., *Recherches sur l'Origine des Ornemens d'Architecture,* Paris, 1794?

Ralph, J., *A Critical Review of the Public Buildings in and about London and Westminster*, London, 1734. Reprinted with additions, 1784.

Ramsay (the Chevalier) Andrew, *The Travels of Cyrus, to Which Is Annex'd a Discourse upon the Theology and Mythology of the Ancients* (second edition), London, 1728.

Ramsey, Robert W., "Sir George Wheeler and his Travels in Greece, 1650–1724," in *Transactions of the Royal Society of Literature of the United Kingdom,* London, 1942.

Rand, Benjamin, ed., *The Life, Unpublished Letters and Philosophical Regimen of Anthony, Earl of Shaftesbury,* London, 1900.

Rand, Benjamin, ed., *Second Characters or the Language of Form by . . . Anthony, Earl of Shaftesbury,* Cambridge, 1914.

Rand, Benjamin, *Berkeley and Percival,* Cambridge, 1916.

Rapin, Renatus, SJ, *Hortorum—Libri IX*, with an English translation by James Gardiner, Worcester, Mass., 1932.

Rau, Julia, Gräfin von der Schulenburg, *Emmanuel Héré,* Berlin, 1973.

Raval, M., and Moreux, J.-C., *Claude-Nicolas Ledoux, 1756–1806,* Paris, 1946.

Réau, Louis, *Etienne-Maurice Falconet,* Paris, 1922.

Recht, Roland, *La Cathédrale de Strasbourg,* Stuttgart, 1971.

Reddaway, T. F., *The Rebuilding of London after the Great Fire,* London, 1940.

Reichwein, Adolf, *China and Europe: Intellectual and Artistic Contacts in the Eighteenth Century,* London, 1925.

Reinach, Salomon, *Répertoire des Vases Peints Grecs et Etrusques,* Paris, 1899–1900.

Reinach, Salomon, *Répertoire de la Statuaire Grecque et Romaine,* Paris, 1897–1924.

Reinach, S., *Répertoire de Peintures du Moyen Age et de la Renaissance,* Paris, 1905.

Réveil, E. F., *Museum of Paintings and Sculpture, or Collection of the Principal Pictures, Statues and Bas-Reliefs, in the Public and Private Galleries of Europe,* London and Paris, 1829–1834.

Rey, Léon, *Le Petit Trianon et le Hameau de Marie-Antoinette,* Paris, 1936.

Richardson, A. E., *Robert Mylne,* London, 1955.

Richardson, Jonathan, *An Essay on the Theory of Painting,* London, 1725.

Richardson, J., and J., *Traité de la Peinture et de la Sculpture,* Amsterdam, 1728.

Rickman, Thomas, *An Attempt to Discriminate the Styles of Architecture in England from the Conquest to the Reformation,* London, 1819; fourth edition, 1835.

Rieder, W., "Piranesi's 'Diverse Maniere,' " in *Burlington Magazine,* LXV (1973).

Rigault, Ange-Hippolyte, *Histoire de la Querelle des Anciens et des Modernes,* Paris, 1856.

Ripa, Cesare, *Iconologia, overo Descrittione d'Imagini delle Virtu, Vitij, Affetti, Passioni humane,* Rome, 1603.

Ripa, Matteo, *Memoirs during Thirteen Years' Residence at the Court of Peking,* selected and translated by Fortunato Prandi, New York, 1846.

Rives-Childs, James, *Casanova: A Biography Based on New Documents,* London, 1961.

Rives-Childs, J., *Casanova Gleanings,* London, 1962.

Rivoira, G. T., *Le Origini della Architettura Lombarda,* Milan, 1908.

Rizzi, A., ed., *Sebastiano Ricci Disegnatore,* Milan, 1975.

Robbins, A. F., *Dr Anderson of the Constitutions,* Transactions of Quatuor Coronati Lodge, vol. 23, London, 1911.

Robbins, A. F., *The Earliest Years of English Organized Freemasonry,* vol. 22, Transactions of Quatuor Coronati Lodge, London, 1911.

Roberts, J. M., *The Mythology of Secret Societies,* London, 1972.

Robertson, Alexander, *The Life of Sir Robert Moray,* London, 1922.

Roche, Serge, and Devinoy, Pierre, *Mirrors,* London, 1957.

Rocheblave, Samuel, *Essai sur le Comte de Caylus,* Paris, 1889.

Rocheblave, Samuel, *C. N. Cochin. Graveur et Dessinateur,* Paris, 1927.

Rodis-Lewis, Geneviève, *Nicolas Malebranche,* collection Les Grands Penseurs, Paris, 1963.

Rompiasio, Giulio, *Metodo in Pratica di Sommario . . . delle Leggi . . . appartenenti . . . (al) Magistrato alle Acque,* Venice, 1771.

Rosenblum, R., "The International Style of 1800: A Study in Linear Abstraction," unpublished doctoral thesis, Institute of Fine Arts, New York University, 1956.

Rosenblum, R., "The Origin of Painting: A Problem in the Iconography of Romantic Classicism," *Art Bulletin* XXXIX (1957).

Rosenblum, R., *Transformations in Eighteenth-Century Art*, Princeton, N.J., 1967.

Rossi, M., *La Vita, le Opere, i Tempi di Eduardo Herbert di Cherbury*, Florence, 1947.

Rossi, P., *Clavis Universalis: Arti Mnemoniche e Logica Combinatoria da Lullo a Leibnitz*, Milan, 1960.

Rossi, Paolo, *I Filosofi e le Macchine (1400–1700)*, Milan, 1971.

Rossi, Paolo, *Francesco Bacone, Dalla Magia alla Scienza*, Turin, 1974.

Rousseau, Jean-Jacques, *Essai sur l'Origine des Langues*, Paris, 1815.

Rowan, A., "Batty Langley's Gothic," in *Studies in Memory of David Talbot Rice*, Edinburgh, 1975.

Rowbotham, A. H., *Missionary and Mandarin*, London, 1942.

Rowe, Colin, "The Drawings of Inigo Jones, Their Source and Scope," M. A. thesis, University of London, 1947.

Runciman, S., *The Great Church in Captivity*, Cambridge, 1968.

Rykwert, J., *On Adam's House in Paradise*, New York, 1972.

Rykwert, J., "Lodoli on Function and Representation," *Architectural Review*, July 1976.

Sachse, W. L., *Lord Somers: A Political Portrait*, Manchester, 1975.

Sagredo, Diego de. *See* also Vitruvius Pollio, M.

Sagredo, Diego de, *Medidas del Romano Agora Nuevamente Impressas y Añadidas de Muchas Pieças y Figuras Muy Necessarias alos Officiales que Quieren Seguir las Formaciones de las Basas, Colunas, Capiteles y Otras Pieças de los Edificios Antiguos*, Lisbon, 1542.

Saintyves, P., *Les Contes de Perrault, et les Récits Parallèles*, Paris, 1923.

Sanctis, F. de, *Storia della Letteratura Italiana*, edited by L. Russo, Milan, 1960.

Sand, Georges, *Compagnon du Tour de France*, Paris, 1928.

Sandys, Sir Edwin, *Europae Speculum or a View or Survey of the State of Religion in the Westerne Parts of the World*, London, 1599.

Sangro, Raimondo di, Principe di Sansevero, *Breve Nota di quel che si Vede in Casa del Principe di Sansevero D. Raimondo di Sangro nella Città di Napoli*, Naples, 1767.

Scamozzi, Vincenzo, *L'Idea dell'Architettura Universale*, Venice, 1615.

Scarron, Paul, *Le Virgile Travesty en vers Burlesques de M.S.*, Paris, 1648.

Scarron, Paul, *Oeuvres de Scarron; Nouvelle Edition Plus Correcte que Toutes les Précédentes*, Paris, 1786.

Schiavo, A., *La Fontana di Trevi e le Altre Opere di Nicola Salvi*, Rome, 1956.

Schlosser, J. von, *Schriftquellen zur Geschichte der Karolingischen Kunst*, Vol. 4, n.f., Vienna, 1896.

Schlosser, J. Magnino, *La Letteratura Artistica*, 2nd ed., translated by Filippo Rossi, Florence, 1956.

Schofield, P. H., *The Theory of Proportion in Architecture*, Cambridge, 1958.

Scholem, G., *On the Kabbalah and Its Symbolism*, London, 1965.

Scholz, Heinrich, *Mathesis Universalis*, edited by Hermes, Kambartel, and Ritter, Basel and Stuttgart, 1961.

Schurtz, H., *Alterklassen und Männerbünde*, Berlin, 1902.

Scott, William Robert, *Francis Hutcheson: His Life, Teaching, and Position in the History of Philosophy*, Cambridge, 1900.

Scully, Vincent, *American Architecture and Urbanism*, London, 1969.

Sedlmayr, Hans, *Johann Bernhard Fischer von Erlach*, Vienna and Munich, 1956.

Sekler, Eduard, *Wren and his Place in European Architecture*, London, 1956.

Semenzato, Camillo, *L'Architettura di Baldassare Longhena*, Padua, 1954.

Semenzato, Camillo, *La Scultura Veneta del Seicento e del Settecento*, Venice, 1966.

Serbanesco, Gérard, *Histoire de la Franc-Maçonnerie Universelle*, Beauronne, 1964.

Séroux d'Agincourt, Camille, *Histoire de l'Art par les Monuments*, Paris, 1823.

Seward, D., *Prince of the Renaissance*, London, 1974.

Seznec, J., and Adhémar, J. *Essais sur Diderot et l'Antiquité*, Oxford, 1957.

Seznec, J., and Adhémar, J. *See* Diderot, Denis.

Shaftesbury, Anthony, Earl of. *See* Rand, Benjamin.

Shaftesbury, Anthony, Earl of, *Characteristics of Men, Manners, Opinions, Times*, London, 1732.

Shenstone, William, *Works*, London, 1764.

Shute, John, *The First and Chief Groundes of Architecture Used in All the Ancient and Famous Monuments*, London, 1563.

Shuttleworth, J. M. *See* Herbert of Cherbury, E.

Sigwalt, Armand, *Une Mystification de Charles Perrault*, Paris, 1948.

Silvagni, D., *La Corte e la Società a Roma*, Rome, 1884.

Simmel, George, *The Sociology of G. S.*, edited by K. H. Wolff, New York and London, 1950.

Simondon, Gilbert, *Du Mode d'Existence des Objets Techniques*, Paris, 1969.

Simonin, Pierre, and Clément, Roland, *L'Ensemble Architectural de Stanislas*, Nancy, 1966.

Simson, O. von, *The Gothic Cathedral*, London, 1956.

Siren, O., *China and the Gardens of Europe*, Stockholm, 1950.

Smith, John Thomas, *An Antiquarian Ramble in the Streets of London*, edited by Charles Mackay, London, 1846.

Smithers, P., *The Life of Joseph Addison*, Oxford, 1968.

Soriano, Marc, *Les Contes de Perrault*, Paris, 1968.

Soriano, Marc, *Le Dossier Perrault*, Paris, 1972.

Soulié de Morant, G., *Histoire de la Chine jusqu'en 1929*, Paris, 1929.

Spence, Joseph, *Observations, Anecdotes and Characters of Books and Men . . .* with notes by E. Malone, London, 1820.

Speth, W. G., ed., *Masonic Reprints*, Margate, 1891.

Spon, Jacob, *See also* Marandon, Bartholomé.

Spon, Jacob, *De l'Usage du Caphé, du Thé, et du Chocolat*, edited by J. Spon, Paris, 1671.

Spon, Jacob, *Recherches des Antiquités et Curiosités de la Ville de Lyon, Ancienne Colonie des Romains et Capitale de la Gaule Celtique*, Lyons, 1676.

Spon, Jacob, *Voyage d'Italie, de Dalmatie, de Grèce et du Levant Fait en Années 1675 et 1676*, Lyon, 1678.

Sprague-Allen, B., *Tides in English Taste (1619–1800): A Background for the Study of Literature*, Cambridge, Mass., 1937.

Sprat, Thomas D. D., *The History of the Royal Society*, 3rd ed., London, 1722.

Stainton, Lindsay, *British Artists in Rome 1700–1800*, catalog, London, 1974.

Stalley, E., *The Guilds of Florence*, London, 1906.

Starobinski, Jean, *Jean-Jacques Rousseau*, Paris, 1974.

Stephen, L., *English Literature and Society in the Eighteenth Century*, London, 1904.

Stillman, Damie, "Chimney-Pieces for the English Market: A Thriving Business in Late Eighteenth-Century Rome," *The Art Bulletin*, vol. 59, no. 1 (1977).

Stirling-Maxwell, W., *Annals of the Artists in Spain*, London, 1891.

Stooke, H.J., and Khandavala, K., *The Laud Ragamala Miniatures: Studies in Indian Painting and Music*, London, 1953.

Stothard, T., and West, Benjamin, *The Polyautographic Album*, London, 1803.

Stratton, C. E., *The Freemasons*, n.p., n.d.

Strzygowski, J., *The Origin of Christian Church Art*, Oxford, 1923.

Stuart, James and Revett, Nicholas, *The Antiquities of Athens Measured and Delineated by J. S. and N. R.*, London, 1762–1816.

Stukeley, W., *Stonehenge: a Temple Restored to the British Druids*, London, 1740.

Stukeley, W., "Abstract of my Life," in the *Family Memoirs of the Rev.*

William Stukeley, M.D., Publications of the Surtees Society, Vol. 23, 1882–1887.

Sturm, Leonhard Christoph, *Die Unentbärliche Regel der Symmetrie oder: des Ebenmaasses. Wie sie zuförderst an dem herrlichsten Exempel des Göttlichen Tempels von Salomone erbauet Wahrzunehmen,* Augsburg, 1720.

Sturm, Leonhard Christoph, *Der ausserlessheste und nach den Regeln der Antiquen Baukunst sowohl als nach dem heutigen Gusto verneuerte Goldmann,* Augsburg, 1721.

Stutchbury, Howard E., *The Architecture of Colen Campbell,* Manchester, 1967.

Sullivan, M. Donovan, *The Arts of China,* revised edition, London, 1973.

Summerson, John, *The Sheldonian in its Time,* Oxford, 1964.

Summerson, John, *Inigo Jones,* Harmondsworth, 1966.

Summerson, John, ed., *Concerning Architecture—Essays on Architectural Writers and Writing presented to Nikolaus Pevsner,* London, 1968.

Summerson, John, *Architecture in Britain 1530–1830,* Harmondsworth, 1970.

Summerson, John, *Georgian London,* new ed., London, 1970.

Sweetman, J. E., "Shaftesbury's Last Commission," *Journal of the Warburg and Courtauld Institutes,* xix, 1956, pp. 110 ff.

Swift, J., *The Works of Jonathan Swift,* Edinburgh, 1761.

Swinburne, Henry, *The Courts of Europe at the Close of the Last Century,* edited by Charles White, Esq., London, 1841.

Tadgell, M.C., "L'Eglise Royale et Paroissiale de Choisy," *Bulletin de la Société de l'Histoire de l'Art Français,* 1973, pp. 171 ff.

Tafuri, Manfredo, *Teorie e Storia dell'Architettura,* Bari, 1968.

Tafuri, Manfredo, "G B Piranesi, l'Architettura come Utopia Negativa," in Convegno B. Vittone *(see above).*

Tagliacozzo, G., and White, Hayden V., *Giambattista Vico: An International Symposium,* Baltimore, 1969.

Taja, A. M., *Lettera e Poetici Componimenti in Ragguaglio, e in Encomio della Nuova Ripa . . . nella Presidenza Edilizia di Monsig. Niccolò Giudice,* Rome, 1705.

Tallmadge, Thomas Eddy, *The Story of Architecture in America,* New York, n.d.

Tasso, T., *Aminta, Farola boscareccia . . . con le Annotationi di Egidio Menagio,* Paris, 1655.

Tassoni, Alessandro, *De' Pensieri diversi di A. T.,* Venice, 1676.

Tatarkiewicz, W., *Estetyka Nowozytna,* Wrocław, 1967.

Taylor, E. G. R., *The Heaven-Finding Art,* London, 1956.

Temanza, Tommaso, *Vite dei Più Celebri Architetti e Scultori Veneziani,* Venice, 1778.

Temple, Sir William, *Works*, 2nd ed., London, 1814.

Tesauro, Emmanuele, *Il Cannocchiale Aristotelico*, Turin, 1655.

Teyssèdre, Bernard, *L'Histoire de l'Art vue du Grand Siècle*, Paris, 1964.

Teyssédre, Bernard, *L'Art Français au Siècle de Louis XIV*, Paris, 1967.

Thackeray, W. M., *Roundabout Papers; the Four Georges; the English Humorists*, London, 1873.

Thieme, Ulrich, and Becker, Felix, *Allgemeines Lexikon der Bildenden Künstler von der Antike bis zur Gegenwart*, Leipzig, 1910–1950.

Thiers, Jean-Baptiste, *Traité de l'Exposition du St. Sacrement de l'Autel*, new ed., Paris, 1677.

Thiers, Jean-Baptiste, *Dissertation sur les Porches des Eglises dans Laquelle On Fait Voir les Divers Usages ausquels ils sont destinez; que ce Sont des Lieux Saints et Dignes de la Vénération des Fidèles; et qu'il n'est pas Permis d'y Vendre Aucunes Marchandises, non pas Mesme Celles qui Peuvent Servir á la Piété*, Orléans, 1679.

Thiers, J. B., *Dissertations Ecclésiastiques sur les Principaux Autels des Eglises*, Paris, 1688.

Thomas, H., *The Drawings of Giovanni Battista Piranesi*, London, 1955.

Thorndike, Lynn, *A History of Magick and Experimental Science*, New York, 1923–1958.

Thory, Claude Antoine, *Acta Latomorum, ou Chronologie de l'Histoire de la Franc-Maçonnerie*, Paris, 1815.

Tintelot, H., *Barocktheater und Barocke Kunst*, Munich, 1939.

Tischbein, Wilhelm, *Collection of Engravings from Ancient Vases*, Naples, 1791–1795.

Toland, John, *Christianity not Mysterious; or a Treataise Shewing That There is Nothing in the Gospel Contrary to Reason, nor above it*, London, 1696.

Toland, John, *Pantheisticon, Sive Formula Celebrandae Sodalitatis Socraticae*, London, 1720.

Toland, John, *A Critical History of the Celtic Religion and Learning Containing an Account of the Druids or the Priests and Judges . . . of the Ancient Gauls, Britons, Irish and Scots, with the History of Abaris the Hyperborean, Priest of the Sun*, edited by R. Huddleston, London, 1814.

Tolmer, Abbé Léon, *Pierre-Daniel Huet*, Bayeux, 1949.

Tonnellier, Chanoine P. M., "Les Graffiti de Domme ou la foi des Templiers," *Archeologia*, 1976.

Tonnellier, Chanoine P. M., "A Domme en Périgord; le Message des Prisonniers," *Archeologia*, 1976.

Torcellan, G. F., *Andrea Memmo*, Venice and Rome, 1963.

Tory, G., *Champ Fleury ou l'Art et Science de la Proportion des Lettres*, Paris, 1529.

Traumann Steinitz, K., "Trattato Studies II," *Raccolta Vinciana*, XIX (1962).

Trevor-Roper, H. R., *William Laud,* Oxford, 1963.

Trittenheim, Johann von (Tritheimius), *Polygraphia,* Basel, 1518.

Trittenheim, Johann von (Tritheimius), *Steganographia,* Basel, 1606.

Troyer, Howard W., *Ned Ward of Grub Street,* Cambridge, Mass., 1946.

Tyson, Moses, and Guppy, Henry, *The French Journals of Mrs. Thrale and Doctor Johnson,* Manchester, 1932.

Ugolino, Blasio, *Thesaurus Antiquitatum Sacrarum Complectens Selectissima . . . Opuscula in Quibus Veterum Hebraeorum Mores, Leges, Instituta, Ritus Sacri et Civiles Illustrantur,* Venice, 1744–1769.

Unwin, George, *The Guilds and Companies of London,* 4th ed., London, 1963.

Updike, D. B., *Printing Types,* London, 1937.

Ursinus, Fulvius, *Familiae Romanae quae Reperiuntur in Antiquis Numismatibus,* Rome, 1577.

Valluz, Léon, *Maupertuis,* Paris, 1969.

Valsecchi, Francesco, *L'Italia nel Settecento, dal 1714 al 1759,* Milan, 1959.

Vardy, J., *Some Designs of Inigo Jones and William Kent,* London, 1744; reprinted Farnborough, 1967.

Vartanian, Aram. *See* La Mettrie, J. O. de.

Vasari, G., *Vite* (ed. G. Milanesi), Florence, 1878–1906.

Vasi, Marino (Marien), *Itinéraire Instructif de Rome à Naples, ou Description Générale . . . de cette Ville Célèbre et des ses Environs,* Rome, 1815.

Vaucanson, Jacques de, "Sur le Choix de l'Emplacement et sur la Forme qu'il Faut Donner aux Bâtimens d'une Fabrique d'Organsin, à l'Usage des Nouveaux Moulins que j'ai Imaginé à cet Effet," 1776; *Mémoires . . . de l'Académie Royale des Sciences,* Paris, 1782.

Vaudoyer, Antoine Laurent Thomas, *Idée d'un Citoyen François sur le Lieu Destiné à la Sépulture des Hommes Illustres de France,* Paris, 1791.

Vecchi, Alberto, "Correnti Religiose nel Settecento Veneto," in *Civiltà Veneziana,* Studi, 15, Venice, 1962.

Vecelli, Cesare, *De gli Habiti Antichi et Moderni in Diverse Parti del Mondo,* Venice, 1590.

Venditti, A., *Architettura Neoclassica a Napoli,* Naples, 1961.

Venturi, Franco, *Settecento Riformatore, da Muratori a Beccaria,* Turin, 1969, 1974; Vol. II, Turin, 1976.

Venuti, Ridolfino, *Osservazioni sopra il Fiume Clitunno, detto Oggi Le Vene . . . Pubblicate dall'Abate R. V. Cortonese,* Rome, 1763.

Venuti, Ridolfino, *Accurata e Succincta Descrizione Topografica delle Antichità di Roma dell'Abate R. V. Cortonese,* Rome, 1763.

Vertue, George, *Notebooks,* published by the Walpole Society, 1929–1950.

Vico, Enea, *Commentarii in Vetera Imperatorum Romanorum Numismata,* Venice and Paris, 1619.

Vico, Enea, *Augustarum Imagines*, Venice and Paris, 1619.

Vico, G. B., *Opere*, a cura di Giovanni Gentile e Fausto Nicolini, Bari, 1911–1940.

Vico, G. B., *La Scienza Nuova*, a cura di Fausto Nicolini, Bari, 1953.

Viel de Saint-Maux, C. F., *De la Solidité des Bâtimens*, Paris, 1806.

Viel de Saint-Maux, C. F., *Des Erreurs Publiées sur la Construction des Piliers du Dôme du Panthéon Français*, Paris, 1806.

Vignola, Giacomo Barozzi, *Livre nouveau; ou Règles de Cinq Ordres d'Architecture . . . Revu, Corrigé et Augmenté par Monsieur Blondel, Architecte du Roy*, Paris, 1767. *See also* Barozzi.

Villari, P., *Le Invasioni barbariche in Italia*, Milan, 1901.

Vio, E. *La Villa Farsetti a S. Maria di Sala*, Venice, 1967.

Viollet-le-Duc, Eugène and Emmanuel, *Dictionnaire Raisonné de l'Architecture Française du XIe au XVIe Siècles*, Paris, 1867.

Visentini, Antonio, *Osservazioni di A. V., Architetto Veneto che servono di Continuazione al Trattato di Teofilo Gallacini sopra gli Errori degli Architetti*, Venice, 1771.

Vitruvius Pollio (Marcus), *Architecture ou Art de Bien Bastir . . . Mis . . . en François par Ian Martin*, Paris, 1547.

Vitruvius Pollio (Marcus), *Vitruvius Teutsch. Des Baumeisters M.V.P. zehen Bucher von der Architectur und Künstlichen Bawen. Alles mit . . . Figuren und . . . Commentarien . . . gezieret . . . Erstmals verteutscht und in Truck verordnet durch G. H. Rivius*, Nuremberg, 1548.

Vitruvius Pollio (Marcus), *I Dieci Libri dell'Architettura di M. Vitruvio Tradutti e Commentati da Monsignor Barbaro eletto Patriarca d'Aquileggia*, Venice, 1556.

Vitruvius Pollio (Marcus), *M. V. P. de Architectura Libri Decem. Cum Notis . . . G. Philandri Integris, D. Barbari Excerptis et C. Salmasii Passim Insertis. Praemittuntur Elementa Architecturae collecta ab H. Wottono equite Anglo. Accedunt lexicon Vitruvianum B. Baldi, et Ejusdem Scamilli Impares Vitruviani. De Pictura Libri Tres L. B. de Albertis. De Sculptura Excerpta ex Dialogo P. Gaurici. L. Demontiosii Commentarius de Sculptura et Pictura. cum Variis Indicibus*, Amsterdam, 1649.

Vitruvius Pollio (Marcus), *Les Dix Livres d'Architecture de Vitruve. See* Perrault.

Vitruvius Pollio (Marcus), *Architectura, Textu ex Recensione codicum emendato cum Exercitationibus notisque . . . Joannis Poleni et Commentariis Variorum Additis nunc Primum Studiis Simonis Stratico*, Udine, 1825–1830.

Vitruvius Britannicus; or the British Architect, Containing the Plans, Elevations and Sections of the Regular Buildings, both Publick and Private in Great Britain . . . by Colen Campbell, London 1715–1717; new edition by P. Breman, D. Addis, 1967.

Vitruvius Britannicus. See Wolfe, J., and Gandon, J.

Vittone, B., *Istruzioni Elementari per Indirizzo de' Giovanni allo Studio dell'Architettura Civile*, Lugano, 1760–1766. *See also* Convegno B. Vittone.

Vogt, Adolf Max, *Boullées Newton-Denkmal: Sakralbau und Kugel-idee,* Basel and Stuttgart, 1969.

Vogt-Göknill, U., *Giovanni Battista Piranesi—"Carceri,"* Zurich, 1958.

Volkmann, Hans, *Giovanni Battista Piranesi, Architekt und Graphiker,* Berlin, 1965.

Voltaire, François Marie Arouet de, *Le Siècle de Louis XIV,* Paris, 1803.

Voss, H., *Albrecht Altdorfer und Wolf Huber,* Leipzig, 1910.

Wade, Ira O., *The Clandestine Organization and Diffusion of Philosophic Ideas in France from 1700 to 1750,* Princeton, N.J., 1938.

Wade, Ira O., *The Intellectual Development of Voltaire,* Princeton, 1969.

Wade, Ira O., *The Intellectual Origins of the French Enlightenment,* Princeton, N.J., 1971.

Walker, D. P., *Spiritual and Demonic Magic from Ficino to Campanella,* London, 1958.

Walker, D. P., *The Ancient Theology,* London, 1972.

Wallis Budge, Sir E. A., *The Monks of Kublai-Khan, Emperor of China,* London, 1928.

Walpole, H., *Anecdotes of Painting in England,* edited by James Dallaway, London, 1828.

Walpole, H., *Anecdotes of Painting in England,* edited by Ralph Wornum, London, 1876.

Walters, H. B., *The English Antiquarians of the Sixteenth, Seventeenth, and Eighteenth Centuries,* London, 1934.

Walters, J., *The Royal Griffin,* London, 1972.

Ward, E., *The Secret History of the Calves-Head Club,* London, 1705.

Ward, J., *Lives of the Professors of Gresham College,* London, 1740.

Ward-Fowler, W., *The Roman Festivals of the Period of the Republic,* London, 1933.

Ward-Jackson, Peter, *English Furniture Designs of the Eighteenth Century,* London, 1958.

Ward-Perkins, J., "Quarries and Stoneworking in the Early Middle Ages," in *Studi XVIII sull' Alto Medioevo,* Spoleto, 1971.

Warton, Thomas, *Observations on the Fairy Queen of Spenser,* London 1762.

Waterhouse, Ellis K., "The British Contribution to Neo-Classical Painting," in *Proceedings of the British Academy XL* (1955).

Waterhouse, Ellis K., *Painting in Britain 1530 to 1790,* Harmondsworth 1962 (2nd ed.).

Watkin, David, *Thomas Hope and the Neoclassical Idea,* London, 1968.

Watkin, D. J., ed., *"Architects" Sale Catalogues of Libraries of Eminent Persons,* London, 1972.

Webb, John, *An Historical Essay Endeavouring a Probability that the Lan-*

guage of the Empire of China is the Primitive Language. By J. W. of Butleigh in the County of Somerset Esq., London, 1669.

Webb, John, *The Vindication of Stone-Heng Restored*, London, 1725.

Webster, C., *The Great Instauration*, London, 1975.

Webster, Hutton, *Primitive Secret Societies. A Study in Early Politics and Religion*, New York, 1908.

Wedgwood, C. V., *Richelieu and the French Monarchy*, Harmondsworth, 1974.

Weigert, Roger-Armand, *Le Panthéon—Nefs et Clochers*, Paris, n.d.

Weisbach, Werner, *Vom Geschmack und seinen Wandlungen*, Basel, 1947.

Wellek R., *Concepts of Criticism*, New Haven and London, 1963.

Wheeler, Sir George, *A Journey into Greece*, London, 1682.

Wheeler, Sir George, *An Account of the Churches and Places of Assembly of the Primitive Christians . . . Described by Eusebius and Ocular Observation of Several Very Ancient Edifices of Churches Yet Extant in those Parts, with a Reasonable Application*, London, 1689.

Whiffen, Marcus, *Stuart and Georgian Churches: The Architecture of the Church of England outside London 1603–1837*, London, 1947–1948.

Whinney, Margaret, and Millar, Oliver, *English Art, 1625–1714*, London, 1957.

Whistler, L., *Sir John Vanbrugh, Architect and Dramatist*, New York, 1939.

Wiebenson, Dora, *Sources of Greek Revival Architecture*, London, 1969.

Wilde, Emil, *Geschichte der Optik*, Berlin, 1838; reprinted 1968.

Wildenstein, Georges, "L'Ordre Français," in *Gazette des Beaux-Arts*, May 1964.

Wilhelm, Jacques, "Le Grand Cabinet Chinois de l'Hôtel de Richelieu, Place Royale," *Bulletin du Musée Carnavalet, 20*, no. 1 (1967).

Wilhelm, Jacques, "Une Miniature Représentant l'Inauguration de la Statue Equestre de Louis XV," *Bulletin du Musée Carnavalet, 18*, no. 2 (1965).

Wilhelm, Richard, *A Short History of Chinese Civilization*, London, 1929.

Wilkins, J., *An Essay towards a Real Character and a Philosophical Language*, London, 1668.

Willard, Nedd, *Le Génie et la Folie au Dix-Huitième Siècle*, Paris, 1963.

Willey, Basil, *The Eighteenth Century Background*, London, 1940.

Williams, Basil, *The Whig Supremacy*, London, 1962.

Williams, C., *James I*, London, 1951.

Wilton-Ely, J. *See* Lord Burlington.

Wilton-Ely, J. *See* Piranesi, Giovanni Battista.

Winckelmann, J. J., *Nachricht von den neuesten Herculanischen Entdeckungen*, Dresden, 1764.

Winckelmann, J. J., *Reflections on the Painting and Sculpture of the Greeks,* translated by Henry Fusseli, A.M., London, 1765.

Winckelmann, J. J., *Monumenti Antichi Inediti Spiegati ed Illustrati,* Rome, 1767.

Winckelmann, J. J., *Storia delle Arti del Disegno,* translated and edited by C. Fea, Rome, 1783.

Winckelmann, J. J., see Barthélemy, J. J., *Travels in Italy . . . With an appendix, containing several pieces . . . by the Abbé W . . . and Other Learned Men,* London 1802.

Winckelmann, J. J., *History of Ancient Art among the Greeks,* translated by G. H. Lodge, London, 1850.

Winckelmann, J. J., *Briefe, See* Diepolder, H., and Rehm, W.

Winckelmann, J. J., ed., *Lettere Italiane,* Milan, 1961.

Winckelmann, J. J., *Geschichte der Kunst des Altertums,* Vienna, 1934.

Wind, Edgar, "Shaftesbury as a Patron of Art," *Journal of the Warburg and Courtauld Institutes,* 1938.

Wind, Edgar, *Pagan Mysteries in the Renaissance,* London, 1958.

Wittkower, Rudolf, *Architectural Principles in the Age of Humanism,* London, 1952.

Wittkower, Rudolf, *Art and Architecture in Italy, 1600–1750,* Harmondsworth, 1958.

Wittkower, Rudolf, *Palladio and English Palladianism,* London, 1974.

Wittkower, Rudolf, "Piranesi's Parere su l'Architettura," in the *Journal of the Warburg and Courtauld Institutes,* II, 2, 1938; reprinted in *Studies in the Italian Baroque,* London, 1975.

Wolf, A., *A History of Science, Technology, and Philosophy in the Seventeenth and Eighteenth Centuries,* London, 1968.

Wolf, Christian, *Gesammelte Werke,* edited by J. E. Hofmann, Hildesheim, 1971.

Wolf, John B., *Louis XIV,* London, 1970.

Wolfe, J., and Gandon, J *See Vitruvius Britannicus.*

Wood, Anthony à, *Athenae Oxonienses 1691–2,* Oxford, 1730.

Wood, J., *Choirgaure, Vulgarly Called Stonehenge on Salisbury Plain,* Oxford, 1747.

Wotton, Sir Henry, *Reliquiae Wottonianae: Or, a Collection of Lives, Letters, Poems; with Characters of Sundry Personages,* London, 1685.

Wotton, Sir Henry. *See* Pearsall-Smith, L.

Wren, Stephen, *Parentalia, or Memoirs of the Family of the Wrens,* London 1750; republished, Farnborough, 1965.

Wright, E., *Some Observations Made in Travelling Through France, Italy etc., in the Years 1720, 1721, and 1722,* London, 1730.

Yates, Frances, *The Theatre of the World,* London, 1969.

Yates, Frances, *Giordano Bruno and the Hermetic Tradition*, New York, 1969.

Yates, Frances, *The Rosicrucian Enlightenment*, London, 1972.

Yates, Frances, *Astraea: the Imperial Theme in the Sixteenth Century*, London, 1975.

Zanotti, Francesco Maria, *Ragionamenti su l'Arte Poetica e Orazioni su l'Arti del Disegno*, Parma, 1829.

Zedler, Johann, *Grosses vollständiges Universal-Lexikon aller Wissenschaften und Künste*, Leipzig and Halle, 1732–1750.

Zeitler, R., *Klassizismus und Utopia*, Stockholm, 1954.

Zeno, Apostolo, *Estratti di Diverse Lettere di A. Z. Ricavati dall' Edizione delle Lettere di lui Fatta in Venezia in tre Volumi nel Corrente Anno 1752*, edited, with remarks by G. M. Rizzardi, Brescia, 1752.

[Ziborghi, Giovanni], *L'Architettura di Jacopo Barozzi da Vignola Ridotta a Facile Metodo per Mezzo di Osservazioni a Profito de'Studenti . . . Aggiuntovi un Trattato di Meccanica . . .* Venice, 1748.

Classical Texts

Aristotle, *The Poetics*, translated by W. H. Fyfe, Loeb Classical Library, London, 1927.

Celsus, Aurelius (Aulus) Cornelius, *De Medicina*, translated by W. G. Spencer, London, 1935–38.

Cicero, Marcus Tullius, *In Verrem: The Verrine Orations with an English Translation* by L. H. G. Greenwood, London and New York, 1928–1935.

Cicero, Marcus Tullius, *De Oratore*, translated, E. W. Sutton, Loeb Classical Library, London, 1942.

Dionysius of Halicarnassus, *De Priscis Scriptoribus Censura*, in *Scripta, quae Extant Omnia*, edited by Frederic Sylburg, vol. II, pp. 68 ff., Leipzig, 1691.

Ennius, Quintus, *Annals*, edited by Ethel Mary Steuart, Cambridge, 1925.

Euclid (of Megara), *The Elements of Geometrie . . . of Euclide of Megara . . . translated into the English Toung by H. Billingsley . . . with a very fruitful Preface made by M. J. Dee*, London 1570.

Gellius, Aulus, *Noctes Atticae*, with an English translation by John C. Rolfe (Loeb Classical Library), London, 1927–1928.

Horatius Flaccus Quintus (Horace), *Satires, Epistles and Ars Poetica*, with an English translation by H. Rushton Fairclough (Loeb Classical Library), London, 1936.

Josephus Flavius, *Works*, translated by H. Thackeray, R. Marcus, A. Widegren, and L. H. Feldman, Loeb Classical Library, London, 1926–.

Livius, Titus (Livy), *Livy*, with an English translation by B. O. Foster (Loeb Classical Library), London, 1939.

Longinus Dionysius, *De Sublimitate*, Paris, 1694.

Ovid (Publius Ovidius Naso), *Metamorphoses,* translated by Garth, Dryden et al., New York, 1976.

Plato, *Divini Platonis Opera Quae Exstant: Marsilio Ficino Interprete . . .,* Lyons, 1590.

Plautus, Titus Maccius, *Plays,* with an English translation by Paul Nixon (Loeb Classical Library), London, 1930–1938.

Pliny the Elder (Gaius Plinius Secundus), *Naturalis Historia,* with an English translation by H. Rackham, London 1938–1963.

Plutarch, *Moralia,* translated by C. W. King and A. R. Shillets, London, 1898.

Plutarch, *Moralia,* edited and translated by F. C. Babbitt, W. C. Helmbold, and H. N. Fowler, London and Cambridge, Mass., 1957–.

Publius Terentius Afer (Terence), *Eunuchus, Prologue*, with an English translation by John Sargeaunt (Loeb Classical Library), London, 1912–1918.

Sallust (Gaius Sallustius Crispus), *The Jugurthine War,* translated with an introduction by S. A. Handford, Harmondsworth, 1963.

Tacitus, Cornelius, *The Histories,* with an English translation by Clifford H. Moore (Loeb Classical Library), London, 1925–1937.

Varro, Marcus Terentius, *De Lingua Latina,* with an English translation by Roland G. Kent (Loeb Classical Library), London, 1938.

Velleius Paterculus, Gaius, *Compendium of Roman History; Res Gestae Divi Augusti,* with an English translation by Frederick W. Shipley (Loeb Classical Library), London, 1924.

Vitruvius: see main bibliography.

Periodicals

Annales, Economies, Sociétés, Civilizations, Paris, 1925–.

Architectural History, Newcastle-upon-Tyne, 1958–.

Architectural Review, London, 1896–.

Archives de l'Art Français, publié sous la direction de Ph. de Chennevières, première série, Paris, 1851–1860.

Archives de l'Art Français, publié sous la direction de M. Anatole de Montaiglon, deuxième série, Paris, 1861–1885.

Archives de l'Art Français, publié sous la direction de M. Marc Furcy-Raynaud, troisième série, Paris, 1884–1907.

Archives de l'Art Français, nouvelle période, Paris, 1907–.

Archivi: Archivi d'Italia e Rassegna Internazionale degli Archivi, Rome, 1949–1961.

Art Bulletin, New York, 1913–.

L'Arte, Rome, 1898–1963.

Bolletino d'Arte, Rome, 1908–.

Bulletin de la Société de l'Histoire de l'Art Français, Paris, 1909–.

Bulletin du Musée Carnavalet (Collections Historiques de la Ville de Paris), Paris, 1947–.

The Burlington Magazine, London, August, 1902–.

Chinese Social and Political Science Review, Peking, 1916–1937(?).

The Connoisseur, London, 1755–1756.

Efemeridi Letterarie di Roma, 1772–1797.

Supplimento all'Efemeridi . . ., 31 December 1775, see Calogiera, A., *Nuova Raccolta d'Opuscoli*, 1755.

Eighteenth-Century Studies, Davis, California, 1967–.

History of Science, Chalfont St. Giles, Bucks, 1962–.

Janus, Revue Internationale de l'Histoire des Sciences, de la Médecine, de la Pharmacie et de la Technique, Leyden, 1896–1941.

Journal of the History of Ideas, New York, 1940–.

Journal of the Indian Society of Oriental Art.

Journal of the Royal Institute of British Architects, new series, May, 1960–.

Journal of the Society of Architectural Historians, Philadelphia, 1941–.

Journal of the Warburg and Courtauld Institutes, London, 1937–.

Macula, Paris, 1977–.

Mémoires de Littérature Tirées des Registres de l'Académie Royale des Inscriptions et Belles-Lettres, Paris, 1717–1809.

Mémoires de la Société de l'Histoire de Paris et de l'Ile de France, XLVI (1919), Paris, 1920.

Memorie per le Belle Arti, Rome, 1785–1788.

Proceedings of the British Academy, Oxford, 1903–.

Proceedings Modern Language Association, New York, 1886–.

PSICON, Florence, 1974–.

Raccolta d'Opuscoli Scientifici e Filologici, Venice, 1728–1757.

Raccolta Vinciana, Milan, 1905–1963.

Transactions of the American Philosophical Society, Philadelphia, 1771.

Transactions of the Royal Society of Literature of the United Kingdom, London, 1853–.

Zeitschrift für Kunstgeschichte, Berlin, 1932.

Bibliographical Addenda

Books and Articles

Algarotti, Francesco, *Opere*, Cremona, 1778–1784.

Algarotti, Francesco, *Saggi*, ed. G. da Pozzo, Bari, 1963.

Bachelard, Gaston, *La Formation de l'Esprit Scientifique*, Paris, 1969.

Blume, Friedrich (ed.), *Die Musik in Geschichte und Gegenwart*, Kassel and Basel, 1949–1973.

Boyer, Carl B., *The Rainbow; from Myth to Mathematics*, London and New York, 1959.

Briseux, C. E., *Traité du Beau Essentiel*, Paris, 1752.

Brumfitt, J. H., "Voltaire and Warburton," in *Studies on Voltaire*, XVIII (1969).

Burke, J., *English Art, 1714–1800*, Oxford, 1976.

Cartwright, Michael T., "Diderot Critique d'Art et le Problème de l'Expression," in *Diderot Studies*, XIII (1969), pp. 1 ff.

Castel, Louis Bertrand, S. J., *Esprit, Saillies et Singularités du Père Castel*, ed. by J. de la Porte?, Amsterdam, 1763.

Cochin, Claude-Nicolas (le Jeune), *Recueil de Quelques Pièces Concernant les Arts, Extraites des Plusieurs Mercures de France*, Paris, 1757–1771.

Condillac, Etienne Bonnot de, *Oeuvres*. Paris, 1798.

Darwin, Erasmus, *The Botanic Garden, a Poem, In Two Parts*, London, 1791, 1789.

Denon, Vivant, *Voyage dans la Basse et la Haute Egypte pendant les Campagnes du Général Bonaparte*, London, 1802.

Doolittle, James, "Hieroglyph and Emblem in Diderot's *Lettre sur les Sourds et Muets*," *Diderot Studies*, II (1952), pp. 148 ff.

Dorival, Bernard, *Philippe de Champaigne*, Paris, 1976.

Drexler, Arthur (ed.), *The Architecture of the Ecole des Beaux-Arts*, New York, 1977.

Fletcher, Dennis J., "The Chevalier de Jaucourt and the English Sources for the Encyclopedic Article *Patriote*," *Diderot Studies*, XVI (1973), pp. 23 ff.

Gotch, J. Alfred, *Inigo Jones*, London, 1928.

Histoire de l'Académie Royale des Sciences (1666–1699), Paris, 1733.

Histoire de l'Académie Royale des Sciences, avec les Mémoires de Mathématique et de Physique Tirés des Registres de Cette Académie (1699–1790), Paris, 1702–1797.

Labriolle, Marie-Rose de, "Le *Pour et Contre* et Son Temps," *Studies on Voltaire*, (i) XXXIV, (ii) XXXV (1965).

Lewis, Wilmarth Sheldon, *Horace Walpole*, London, 1961.

Loehr, George Robert. *Giuseppe Castiglione (1688–1766) Pittore di Corte di Ch'ien Lung, Imperatore de la Cina*, Roma, 1940.

McGuire, J. E. and Rattansi, P. M., 'Newton and the Pipes of Pan' in *Notes & Records of the Royal Society of London*, XXI, 1966, pp. 108 ff.

May, Georges, "Observations on an Allegory: The Frontispiece of the *Encyclopédie*," *Diderot Studies*, XVI, pp. 159 ff.

Petzet, Michel, "Un Projet des Perrault pour l'Englise de Sainte-Geneviève à Paris," *Bulletin Monumental*, CXV (1957), pp. 81 ff.

Potter, Warren, and Oliver, Robert, *Fraternally Yours: A History of the Independant Order of Forresters*, Toronto, 1967.

Quatremère de Quincy, Antoine-Chrysostome, *Dictionnaire Historique d'Architecture*, Paris, 1832.

Vartanian, Aram, "*Fiat Lux* and the Philosophes," in *Diderot Studies*, XVI (1973), pp. 375 ff.

Voltaire, François Marie Arouet de, *Oeuvres Complètes*. Nouvelle Edition, Paris, 1817–1820.

Voltaire, François Marie Arouet de, *Oeuvres Complètes*, ed. T. Besterman et al: *Correspondance* (vols. 85–135), Geneva and Oxford, 1968–1977.

Walpole, Horace, *Correspondence*, ed. W. S. Lewis, London, 1937–.

Warburton, William, Lord Bishop of Gloucester, *The Works*, London, 1787–1789.

Classical Texts

Cicero, Marcus Tullius, *De Inventione Rhetorica*, with an English translation by H. M. Hubbell, Loeb Classical Library, London, 1949.

Plinius Secundus, Caius. *Naturalis Historiae* Libri XXXVII. ed. Jean Hardouin, Paris, 1685.

Periodicals

Diderot Studies, edited by Otis Fellows, Norman L. Torrey and Diana Guiragossian, Geneva, 1951–.

Notes and Records of the Royal Society of London, London, 1935–.

Studies on Voltaire and the Eighteenth Century, edited by Theodore Besterman and others (Publications de l'Institut et Musée Voltaire), Geneva, 1955–.

Voltaire Studies, I: *Travaux sur Voltaire et le Dix-Huitième Siècle*, edited by Theodore Besterman, Geneva 1955; II: *Studies on Voltaire and the Eighteenth Century*, Geneva, Thorpe Mandeville, Oxford, 1956–.

Index